COMMANDANTS
OF THE
MARINE CORPS

COMMANDANTS OF THE MARINE CORPS

EDITED BY

Allan R. Millett

AND

Jack Shulimson

Naval Institute Press
Annapolis, Maryland

Naval Institute Press
291 Wood Road
Annapolis, MD 21402

This book has been brought to publication with the generous assistance of Edward S. and Joyce I. Miller.

Library of Congress Cataloging-in-Publication Data
Commandants of the Marine Corps / edited by Allan R. Millett and Jack Shulimson.
p. cm.
Includes bibliographical references and index.
ISBN 0-87021-012-2 (alk. paper)
1. United States. Marine Corps—Officers—Biography. 2. Generals—United States—Biography.
I. Millett, Allan Reed. II. Shulimson, Jack.
VE24.C65 2004
359.9'6'092273—dc22

2004003858

Printed in the United States of America on acid-free paper ♾
11 10 09 08 07 06 05 04 9 8 7 6 5 4 3 2
First printing

Contents

Preface

Counting the commandants is one exercise, but measuring them is quite another. If one counts Samuel Nicholas, the wartime administrative head of the Continental Marines, thirty-one men have served as the chiefs of the United States Marine Corps. The first Marine officer to bear the title of commandant was William Ward Burrows, who received the title lieutenant colonel commandant from Congress in 1800. Two years earlier, Congress had established a Corps of Marines as distinct from the detachments of ships' guards raised for sea service in the Revolution and again in the 1790s. In accordance with the act of 11 July 1798 (1 Stat. 72), Burrows became the senior officer with the rank of major but had not used the title commandant. Thus for two hundred years the Marine Corps has had a commandant, and that officer serves as the unquestioned head of service and official leader of the Corps.

This collection of original essays traces the history of the United States Marine Corps through the service of its commandants. Each essay describes the personality of each commandant, but the author's primary responsibility was to assess the subject's performance as commandant and assess his historical significance. The latter was not an easy task because, for a variety of reasons, every commandant does not leave a lasting impact of the Marine Corps just as few presidents of the United States assume the ranking of "great" in the minds of professional historians and the public. To a great degree, the question of historical significance cannot be easily answered until decades after the incumbent leaves office. Of course, Marine officers, an opinionated lot, draw quick conclusions about the qualities of their senior leaders, and the commandants are not spared this examination while in office, let alone afterward. Each of the authors of these essays tries to make a balanced case for their subject and to do so in some detail. Therefore, the readers should be able to make their own judgments about the value of the various terms of the commandants.

The history of the terms of the five most recent commandants—Paul X. Kelley, Alfred M. Gray Jr., Carl E. Mundy Jr., Charles C. Krulak, and James L. Jones—are not in this anthology. I had the opportunity to know the first three commandants on an unofficial and personal basis and even participated in a peripheral way in the tours of Generals Kelley and Gray, both of whom I admire for very different reasons.

In the 1991 revision of my history of the Marine Corps, *Semper Fidelis,* I made my own assessment of the Kelley and Gray years, but I know that both of them deserve more dispassionate and document-based study than they would have received if we had included them in this book. In all candor, neither of these commandants has completed their oral histories, and their papers are not organized and in many cases still subject to security classification. In even more candor, I could not recruit any knowledgeable and competent historian (especially a Marine officer) to write about General Kelley, whose tour was tainted by the Beirut bombing of 1983, actually the round of recriminations that followed the bombing. Many marines (unfairly, in my view) think that General Kelley betrayed the Corps to further his own ambition to be chairman of the Joint Chiefs of Staff or director of the Central Intelligence Agency, goals he thought he could advance by unusual cooperativeness with the incumbent president and secretary of defense, both of whom needed willing scapegoats at various times in 1981–89. His critics conveniently forget that General Kelley designed and pushed to fruition the most ambitious equipment modernization program in Marine Corps history and laid the groundwork for more force improvements in the 1990s. He also saw to it that the Marines would play a significant role in any Middle East crisis through his personal identification with the creation and maturation of U.S. Central Command.

In General Gray's case I found too many volunteers who wanted to tell the world how their hero, a pure warrior of such legendary proportions that his name tripped from the lips of the worshipers faster than one could say Smedley Butler or Chesty Puller. Thus, for different reasons, it would have been a challenge to get a balanced assessment of General Gray. Let me assert for the record that I liked Al Gray from the moment I met him when he was a brigadier general, and I always look forward to seeing him in retirement when we attend conferences and meetings about the future of the armed forces. I have never met a more spirited, imaginative, and inquisitive mind in a general officer of any service.

When General Gray succeeded General Kelley as commandant, and General Kelley was not happy about the succession, I was traveling in France and went to the American embassy in Paris to meet a friend, the air attaché. When the Marine sergeant at the security booth checked my military ID card, he smiled and said, "Isn't it great that we now have a *real* marine for commandant?" I nodded, but with some internal turmoil because I knew General Kelley was a real marine, too. If the Marine Corps had elected a commandant, Alfred M. Gray Jr. would have won hands down because for more than twenty-five years he had served almost continuously in the field from the rank of captain to major general. He enlisted in the Marine Corps in the summer of 1950 to fight in Korea and reached the rank of sergeant before he was commissioned; whether he cultivated the legend that he was the ultimate "mustang," the "boot" who became commandant, or whether other marines did such mythmaking for him was beside the point. How could a general who chewed tobacco and spit into a camouflaged canteen cup be anything but a field marine? At the time of his enlistment, however, General Gray had completed three years at Lafayette College, but he thought a war would be more adventurous than classes and baseball. He never lost his interest in studying history, especially the history of warfare. And he could talk about his passion for operations with anyone and make them learn. On the other hand, General Gray's very enthusiasm and dedication to the Marine Corps deepened a personality (some blame it on his prolonged avoidance of marriage) that did not deal well with negotiations, meetings, compromises, and some tactical trimming and prevarication, all essential to success in Washington.

General Gray made marines train to the skills they claimed, and he placed his primary emphasis on internal issues of leadership, the operational art, and the use of the most modern technology for gathering intelligence and target acquisition. He wanted deployed Marine expeditionary units to be "Special Operations Capable," and he invented a training and unit enhancement plan to make it so. The list of his initiatives, many of which have proved their worth, could fill this book. Yet Al Gray never felt very comfortable in Washington, and one might argue that the other services might have stolen a march on the Corps when it came to budgets and end-strengths if Gray had not turned over his office to Carl Mundy, a Washington operator with proven achievements in interservice bargaining. Highly regarded by key congressmen, admired by the senior officers of the other services, and with a welcome change of style from General Gray's in dealing within the rarified bureaucracy of the office of the secretary of defense, General Mundy fought a successful battle to hold Marine Corps manpower numbers close to the demands of the Corp's commitments abroad. He did so with an admirable ability to keep the numbers between 170,000 and 180,000 and the budget on the high side of $9 billion at a time that the other services were taking much larger proportional reductions. He bought time and stability when neither was certain.

A valued protégé of both Gray's and Mundy's, Charles C. Krulak was not the first Marine Corps "junior," a general who is the son of a general, but his pedigree must be the best known. His father, Lt. Gen. Victor H. Krulak, USMC (Retired), became an innovator and policy insider at the tender rank of first lieutenant in the 1930s and remained one of the most influential Marine officers in history until his retirement in 1968. The history of the amphibian tractor, the helicopter, amphibious doctrine, the air-ground task force, counterinsurgency, and staff organization in the Marine Corps has the name Krulak all over it. Upon light occasions, Chuck Krulak called his father "the real General Krulak," which no one believes since there are two Generals Krulak and have been for some time. Although a combat veteran and career infantry officer, Chuck Krulak served as the chief logistics officer for the I Marine Expeditionary Force in the Persian Gulf War, and made the support system work, much to the pleasant surprise of the Marines and the amazement of the U.S. Army, which has always suggested that Marine "mom and pop" logistics had never matured since the Banana Wars. Chuck Krulak also brought to the office a set of personal relationships and experiences closely tied to the U.S. Navy, which started with his graduation from the Naval Academy in 1964. More at ease with the customs and traditions of the Navy than many of his peers, General Krulak pioneered the concept of the maritime power projection (" . . . From the Sea") as a flexible and appropriate military capability for the post–cold war armed forces. The descriptions of these commandants may be obtained from the Reference Branch, History and Museums Division, Headquarters Marine Corps, Washington, D.C. 20380. These skeletal media releases hardly catch the men, but they tell more than one might imagine if one reads between the lines and knows something of Corps history. For the moment these press releases will have to do for the curious.

Like some lost patrol, we must circle back to the question of measuring commandants. These essays deal with each officer's full career from commissioning to retirement, but they stress the time each officer spent as commandant. For some of these officers that time was short since retirement, death, and disgrace took three of them from office in less than three years. On the other hand, longevity in office, which once served as an indicator of greatness, is no longer a factor as commandants since World War II have served fixed four-year terms.

One might start with a general interpretation of the history of the Marine Corps. I divided that history into four epochs in *Semper Fidelis:* the seagoing, ships detachments years that spanned the nineteenth century; the colonial infantry years that started in Panama in 1885 and ended with World War II; the amphibious assault force years when the Corps organized and trained for seizing advanced naval bases in a major war with Japan; and the post–World War II period in which the Corps became a maritime-based force-in-readiness, organized for wartime expansion and adaptable to extended land campaigns. In the first period Archibald Henderson (commandant, 1820–59) preserved the Corps when its importance was not self-evident except to a few good men. George Barnett (1914–20) and John A. Lejeune (1920–29) preserved the best of the colonial infantry years, put the Marine Corps into the American Expeditionary Forces in France, and recreated it after the war into an amphibious assault force, brought to increased size and exceptional operational performance in World War II by Thomas Holcomb (1936–43), a close associate of both Barnett and Lejeune and President Franklin D. Roosevelt. In all four cases, these commandants faced challenging times, periods of opportunity, and moments of institutional crisis, and they all served more than four years in office. Yet their tenure does not exhaust the list of influential commandants if one thinks about the office differently and *pairs* commandants who had personal ties and shared goals that shaped the Corps.

For example, Charles McCawley (1876–91) and Charley Heywood (1891–1903) turned the Marine Corps into a disciplined, trained, experienced, versatile service after the Civil War in their twenty-seven combined years of service as commandant. Heywood then guided the Corps through the war with Spain, the China Expedition, and the Philippine pacification campaign and into the hearts of the State Department and the American people. The qualities that people around the world associate with the Marines are really a creation of McCawley and Heywood, not Madison Avenue advertising executives and enthusiastic recruiters. In another era, Ben H. Fuller and John H. Russell, both Naval Academy graduates, like Barnett and Lejeune, guided the Corps in the crucial years 1930–36, which saw the drafting of the *Tentative Manual for Landing Operations* (1931–34) and the creation of the Fleet Marine Force (1933). They ensured a place for the Marine Corps in American planning for a war with Japan and established its interservice responsibility as the creator of amphibious warfare doctrine, equipment, techniques, and tactics. After World War II, Gen. Clifton B. Cates and Gen. Lemuel C. Shepherd Jr. revived the amphibious assault at Inchon, Korea (15 September 1950), brought the Fleet Marine Force to an effectiveness that surpassed World War II and ensured that the Corps would not lose in Washington what they won in the field with the passage of the Mansfield-Douglas Act in 1952, which guaranteed an FMF of three divisions and three aircraft wings. Their years (1948–55) set the course for the force-in-readiness.

The last of the four paired commandants are Louis H. Wilson and Robert H. Barrow, both Southerners, both respected front-line leaders in three wars (Wilson with a Medal of Honor and Barrow a Navy Cross), and both close associates in saving the Marine Corps from the ravages of the Vietnam War. In their linked tours as commandant (1974–83), Wilson and Barrow wrenched the Corps from the slough of despond created by the youth drug culture, teenage crime, violent racism, sloppiness, and indiscipline. Their relentless programs to eliminate poor recruiting and recruit training and permissiveness in the FMF paid dividends in the 1980s when the mood of the people and Congress shifted to building a quality armed forces, a goal the Corps had never abandoned. On a personal note, my own career intersected with those of Generals Wilson and Barrow from the time I entered the 25th Officers Candidate Class (1959) until my own retirement in 1991—and beyond. Then-colonel Wilson asked me during an inspection at OCC why I did not yet have "military glasses" instead of fraternity-boy horned rims, and I answered that I didn't know. Indeed, I didn't know there were "military glasses," those colorless plastic horrors that still sit in my battered footlocker. Commandant Wilson years later told me at a reception in Quarters One that he liked my current glasses much better; they were the fashionable aviators glasses so favored by chic colonels, of which I fancied myself one. General Barrow once complemented me at a briefing, to the discomfiture of the staff of my MAU commander, especially when he called me by my first name and said how much he liked *Semper Fidelis.* Like Al Gray, Bob Barrow helped me through a long week as a Battalion Landing Team commander, but we had already met through my service at the Command and Staff College and my research on the Marine Corps. Not long ago he called me at home on a Korean War history question and opened the conversation with "This is Bob Barrow." We happened to have guests at the moment, so when I returned to the table, my wife asked, "Who was that?" When I answered, "The commandant," she said, "Which one?" I laughed at our guests' surprise and said, "General Barrow." "Oh yes," my wife said, "I've talked with him when he's called before. What a nice man!" There are some Japanese, North Koreans, Chinese, and Vietnamese who would not agree, but that is their problem. One of my former graduate students, then working as a staff member for the House Armed Services Committee, once asked me whether the Marine Corps had some secret base where it made tall, spare, craggy, Southern generals who oozed truthfulness, heroism, and integrity. I knew exactly which generals he meant.

On a personal basis my favorite commandant is neither Southern nor craggy, but a flinty Vermonter, Wallace M. Greene Jr., one of the military Greenes that always seem to appear out of New England and New York and into American military history since the Revolution. I met General Greene only after his retirement in December 1967, when, heartsick about the Vietnam War and the duplicity and moral cowardice of the Johnson administration, he turned his office over to Leonard F. Chapman Jr., who was certainly in appearance and manner close to the Wilson-Barrow team that would come later. If the Vietnam War had gone differently and if they had not been succeeded by a conspicuous disappointment, Robert H. Cushman Jr., the Greene-Chapman paired commandancy would probably have fared better in the historical sweepstakes. In my research on the 1960s and the Vietnam War in general for *Semper Fidelis,* I found General Greene's papers, precisely annotated and filed, invaluable sources. They were matched only by the papers of General Krulak ("the real one"), who was then serving as commanding general, Fleet Marine Force Pacific and appeared to be Greene's obvious successor. General Greene gave me full access to his papers (as did General Krulak), and I had several opportunities to discuss the 1960s with both of them. I formed a deep impression that these generals (certainly not tall and spare) shared a common dedication to the truth and the Marine Corps, which they did not view as irreconcilable. When this book project started, I volunteered to write General Greene's biography because I knew it would be important on the Marine Corps's entry into the Vietnam War and because I knew General Greene would spare no one (including himself) from careful historical scrutiny. The interest was typical of the man, not his ego or his lust for immortality, but the care and precision with which he handled all his assignments. At no time did he pressure me to put him in a more favorable light.

I am also delighted to have General Krulak write the essay on General Shepherd, with whom he had worked closely since World War II. General Krulak should (in my mind and many others) have been appointed commandant in 1968 with General Chapman next in line since Chapman was only fifty-four when President Johnson made him the commandant. The story of how Johnson chose Chapman is also included in Ronald H. Spector's essay, but I know from my own research that Johnson could not abide the outspoken and aggressive Krulak, whose friends ran from John F. Kennedy and his brother Robert to the Orange County Republicans who rallied their money and political leverage behind Richard Nixon and Ronald Reagan. Whatever his feelings, Secretary of Defense Robert S. McNamara had lost his taste for government, and the reigning members of the Joint Chiefs of Staff feared Krulak's ability at interservice infighting. I reassured General Krulak that General Greene was not a party to denying him the office he so deserved.

The cause of Marine Corps history has no greater champions than Generals Greene and Krulak, so it is a bonus that they would be an important part of this book as subject and author. Both Generals Greene and Krulak are receiving appropriate recognition for their efforts to bring expertise, candor, and a sense of duty to the decision-making process in the Vietnam War, most recently in Maj. H. R. McMaster's *Dereliction of Duty*

(New York: HarperCollins, 1997). Their reputational fall and rise illustrate my earlier point that all the commandants deserve a fair hearing. Only one, Anthony Gale (1819–20), should be drummed from the ranks of history.

The collective portrait of the past commandants (and I am including all thirty-two) reveals no special surprises since their characteristics reflect long-term developments in the officer corps of the Marine Corps. Excluding the first nine commandants, products of a pre-professional military establishment, the twenty-two twentieth century commandants spent their entire adult lives as marines. Their average age at appointment was fifty-six, the youngest Kelley (fifty-two) and the oldest Russell (sixty-two). Although their athletic skills and hobbies varied widely, they were as a group blessed with physical endurance and unusual vigor. Only one commandant (Neville) died in office. Only three died within five years of retirement, and only two more died within ten years of retirement. Of the last eight commandants only two (Cushman and Chapman) have died as of this writing. Health may help explain the problems of two disappointments as commandant (Pate and Cushman); both had serious health problems in office, readily apparent to their closest staff officers. On the other hand, Lejeune and Holcomb won no prizes for good health in office either. Nevertheless, I continue to suspect that commandants (and many other senior officers) often have difficulty in office because they are aging men who have spent a lifetime in an occupation that does not promote good health, no matter how much they jog.

There are no special clues to how certain Marine officers become commandant. First of all, commandants do not name their successors, and sometime they do not even press hard for their preferences—at least obviously. Ultimately, the responsible political officials make a nomination for appointment to Congress, and no officer who is likely to be controversial will survive the confirmation process. Early in the process of selection there is likely to be consultation on the nomination between the secretary of the navy and the secretary of defense with the appropriate congressional leaders, which means the chairs of the committees that do business with the Department of Defense and any congressman and senator who has a personal interest in some candidate. The secretary of the navy receives nominations (usually three) from the incumbent commandant and then will probably discuss the matter with the chief of naval operations since the Navy sometimes has strong preferences about which Marine general with whom it collaborates. For the last forty years the members of the Joint Chiefs of Staff, especially the chairman, may advise the secretary of defense on their preferences, more than likely casting a negative veto, but not making a strong recommendation to appoint since such intervention would suggest that *their* successors should be chosen by another service. Jointness, thankfully, has not progressed that far, but it has advanced to the point where a service chief is just as likely to come from the ranks of the joint commanders (the CinCs) as he is from within the service headquarters, that is, in the case of the Marine Corps, the assistant commandant. The final nomination comes from the president, but the available evidence suggests that the secretary of defense will make the choice and that the president will support the secretary's choice. One exception was the selection of Robert H. Cushman Jr. by Richard M. Nixon in 1971, a decision so unmoored from the Corps's approval that Cushman began his tour already tarnished by his selection.

The source of a commandant's commission eludes easy categorization. There are many routes to the top, although they always pass through a war or two. One-third (seven) of the twentieth century commandants graduated from the Naval Academy, but only one of them (Krulak) in graduating classes since World War II. The two commandants commissioned well before the twentieth century who were not Annapolis graduates came directly from civilian life with an educational level somewhere between high school and some college; social connections and family wealth, however, ensured that no one would confuse William P. Biddle with George Elliott. During the "colonial infantry years," which overlapped with World War I, the educational requirements started to climb, largely because of the Corps' growing popularity. Thomas Holcomb joined the Marine Corps in 1900 with some classes at Georgetown University. Vandegrift left the University of Virginia after three years to win a commission by examination in 1908. The Virginia Military Institute sent Shepherd and Pate into the Corps in 1917 and 1921. Clifton Cates graduated from the University of Tennessee in 1916 and had been admitted to the Tennessee bar. In the interwar period and World War II the future commandants often had participated in Army ROTC and after graduation applied for Marine Corps commissions or did short tours as enlisted men (true only of Barrow) before becoming officers. In the cold war period only Gray enlisted and then received a commission in the field in Korea. The newest variant is commissioning through Navy ROTC, the route taken by Kelley and Mundy.

No marine believes that anyone can become commandant since an officer has to become a general first, and that means he must be one of the 10 percent or less of the favored colonels who become brigadier generals each year. Although about half of the brigadier generals become major generals, they will not be likely candidates for commandant unless they serve somewhere in the rank of lieutenant general and *that* will depend upon the sponsorship of the incumbent commandant and an equally powerful coalition of supporters in the other services for joint commands or staff appointments. Other factors often come into play: the preferences of the secretary of the navy, age, health, family situation, education, and political connections or lack thereof. Thus far, no Marine aviator has ever served as commandant, although that is likely to change through the growing interchangeability of command and staff assignments between ground and air officers. This is not to say that aviator generals might not have been fine commandants; Roy S. Geiger and Keith B. McCutcheon certainly fell in this category, but serious health problems ended their careers. Obviously the perfect commandant would be a revered combat leader dripping with decorations, a highly trained professional manager and innovator, a deft diplomat in handling civilian political leaders, a man comfortable with all the latest technology with military applications, a media charmer, and a charismatic leader of his fellow marines. No one has met all these requirements, and no one will.

Commandants of the Marine Corps function within five broad bands of culture that define their possibilities. The first is the outer band that can be called the international security environment, the nether world of potential or real threats and allies, of military capabilities and the intended policies of others. The second band is the American political world in which the outside world mixes with the domestic politics of the American people, the world in which all the claims upon the lives, wealth, and sacred honor of the nation must be reconciled or accommodated since destruction is seldom an appropriate option. The third band is the policy-making world of Washington, D.C., where another muddy mix occurs between the well-being of the nation and the well-being of elected and appointed officials and the civilian bureaucracy. The fourth ring is the relationship of the American armed forces to the three external rings and with each other, the world of QDRs, POMs, FYDPs, CORMs, and BRACs. The inner ring is the Marine Corps itself, an institution that might be best compared to a perpetual teenager (indeed it is full of virtual and perpetual adolescents in every rank) that is capable of the most amazing feats, most of them for good, some not so good, but all a challenge to an incumbent commandant. I can think of no general officer I met at Headquarters who said he was bored.

The commandant is also at the mercy of his own Headquarters organization, so I have included an essay on the organization of Headquarters Marine Corps that may help the reader find the way through the commandant's organizational environment. One recurrent theme in all the essays is the demands that face every commandant in judging whether his staff is truly adequate for his demands. The tension between "spaces" and "faces" will last as long as the Marine Corps. Compared with the other services, the Corps tends to think that "faces" are more important than "spaces," which means that the quality of the staff officers is more important than the arrangement of their offices by function and mission. The answer, of course, is that both count, so it is the commandant's responsibility to find the proper balance between putting one's most effective officers in the service headquarters or putting them in the field with the Marine units or operational staffs. I hope that the appended essay will guide readers through the labyrinth of Headquarters organization.

However one judges the performance of our commandants, our authors have done their best to provide informed analysis and sound information about their subjects. We are all in their debt for the conscientious way they have portrayed the commandants who have shaped our Corps.

Allan R. Millett

Acknowledgments

If the measure of a book's greatness is its gestation period, then this anthology must rank with the giants of English literature. It doesn't. Some people might suggest that to use the words "Marine Corps" and "literature" in the same sentence is an oxymoron. Although this assertion is ungenerous, it is true that it is sometimes hard to harness marines and historians (and many of the authors of this book are both) to long-term projects, and this book has been no exception. Yet after almost twenty years of toil, and nontoil, I believe the final book is worth the wait since it is the first attempt to tell the story of the Marine Corps through the experiences of all its commandants.

The book is the brainchild of two professors in the history department at the U.S. Naval Academy, William R. Love Jr. and Merrill L. Bartlett. Bob Love and Skip Bartlett, both of whom never met an anthology they didn't like, conceived of a volume of scholarly essays on the commandants in 1979–80. My contract for this book shows that I signed it in June 1981 and that I promised to deliver my essay the next year. The project then foundered when Bob Love turned his interests elsewhere and Skip Bartlett became critically, almost fatally ill with a brain tumor that forced his medical retirement from the Marine Corps at the rank of lieutenant colonel. In the meantime, the prospective publication date slipped from 1982 to 1985, then slipped again into a black abyss of complete uncertainty.

Since twelve of the original prospective authors had in the meantime deserted the project, Bob and Skip in frustration decided to retire as coeditors, but they asked me whether I wanted to replace them as the editor of record and try my hand at reorganizing the book (i.e., dragoon in new authors). Assured by Paul Wilderson of the Naval Institute Press that he and the press would be patient, a promise fulfilled beyond the call of duty, I accepted the challenge with typical Marine Corps confidence that I could quickly turn the project around and make the concept work. I was partially right on both scores, but I was much too optimistic about the pool of prospective authors and the intellectual attractiveness of the subject matter, the latter of some importance since the honoraria in the best Marine Corps tradition would be a "well done" for institutional loyalty but not much income. Nevertheless, as the years passed, the essays straggled in, and enough of them arrived to keep me cautiously optimistic that the book was alive—if breathing raggedly. I had never worked on a book with a sucking chest wound, but here it was.

The team of corpsmen that kept the book alive followed the inspired leadership of Skip Bartlett, who never lost his commitment to the project and proved it by writing five of the essays himself, all of them setting the bar high for scholarship and readability. In medical retirement Skip himself studied Marine Corps history and in the intervening years wrote three books, edited four more, and contributed essays and articles to almost every journal and magazine that served the field of naval and military history. My greatest satisfaction in this project is that Skip Bartlett, who has shown uncommon dedication to the cause of Corps history, will see the completion of *Commandants.* When I became the book's editor in 1986, I would not have bet that Skip would be around for the finish.

I also want to recognize the patience of the original authors who stayed with the project even in its darkest hours: James C. Bradford, the late Brendan P. Ryan, Jack Shulimson, Robert J. Cressman, Donald F. Bittner, John W. Gordon, Paolo Coletta, Howard Jablon, Ronald H. Spector, and David H. White Jr. To this group of survivors of a literary Tarawa, we added some very able replacements: the late Gerald C. Thomas Jr., Joseph H. Alexander, Brian M. Linn, Jon T. Hoffman, Keith V. Fleming, Victor H. Krulak, John G. Miller Jr., and Edwin H. Simmons. With the exception of Professor Linn, the new authors run to a type. They are distinguished retired Marine officers (two of flag rank) whose interest in Marine history had already led them to write books and articles in the field. I count twelve books alone on the Marine Corps from this group, so although they might have been new to *Commandants,* they were not new to the subject. Many of them had worked alongside the real commandants since World War II, and two of them, Generals Krulak and Simmons, had fought in three wars. Only Colonel Hoffman had not fought in Vietnam since he is too young. About the only good thing about this book's long march to completion is that these officers' duties and subsequent retirement from active duty allowed them to become authors in this anthology.

The principal source of original documents for the history of Headquarters Marine Corps is the Headquarters records, especially the correspondence of the commandant and the chief of staff, in the Records of the United States Marine Corps, Record Group 127, National Archives and Records Administration, supplemented by the commandant-secretary of the Navy correspondence in Record Group 80, General Records of the Department of the Navy. I used both sources in writing *Semper Fidelis: The History of the United States Marine Corps* (New York: Macmillan, 1980) and *In Many a Strife: Gerald C. Thomas and the Marine Corps, 1917–1956* (Annapolis: Naval Institute Press, 1991) as did the authors of the chapters in this anthology, especially the chapters on Generals Barnett, Lejeune, Neville, Russell, Holcomb, Cates, Shepherd, Pate, Shoup, Greene, Chapman, Cushman, and Wilson.

An important additional source is the collection of senior officer oral history memoirs, collected by Benis M. Frank, former director of the Marine Corps Oral History Collection, History and Museums Division.

The professional journal of the Marine Corps officers corps, the *Marine Corps Gazette,* carries news of Headquarters on a routine basis. The most useful printed source (outside of the annual reports of the commandants) is Kenneth W. Condit, Maj. John H. Johnstone, and Ella W. Nargele, *A Brief History of Headquarters Marine Corps Staff Organization,* rev. ed. (Washington, D.C.: Historical Division, HQMC, 1971), but one should see also Lt. Col. Merrill L. Bartlett, "The Road to Eight and Eye," Naval Institute *Proceedings* 114 (November 1988): 73–80, and staff of the *Marine Corps Gazette,* "HQMC: A New Look," *Marine Corps Gazette* (January 1974): 30–37. The work of Headquarters in World War II is described in a section of Rear Adm. Julius A. Furer, *Administration of the Navy Department in World War II* (Washington, D.C.: GPO, 1959). In addition, see the subject file "Headquarters Marine Corps" in the Reference Branch, History and Museums Division.

I also profited from a two-year tour as a Reserve colonel with the Special Projects Directorate, Office of the Commandant, and my association with several commandants, chiefs of staff, and deputy chiefs of staff, including the late Wallace M. Greene Jr., P. X. Kelley, Alfred M. Gray, Bernard E. Trainor, the late Louis H. Buehl, C. D. Dean, and Joseph A. Went.

As always, my research on the Marine Corps benefits from the wise counsel of Brig. Gen. Edwin H. Simmons, USMC (Ret.), the director emeritus of the History and Museums Division. General Simmons assured the *Commandants* authors that the archives, research files, oral histories, private papers collections, and books held at the Marine Corps Historical Center, Washington Navy Yard, would be completely available, including emergency processing and declassification when necessary. The members of his staff, many of whom now are retired, could not have been more helpful, even without his prodding: Henry I. Shaw Jr., Benis M. Frank, Joyce Bonnett, G. Michael Miller, Danny Crawford, Robert V. Aquilina, Evelyn A. Englander, Pat Morgan, and the other staff members of the Division who helped our authors.

Over the years various members of the professional and administrative staff of the Mershon Center, The Ohio State University, some paid, some not, contributed to the preparation of this book, most notably Ms. Claudia Riser and Ms. Beth Russell, and a sturdy list of graduate assistants that includes William B. Feis and Mark Jacobson. We all owe a debt of special gratitude to Sean McCarthy, who volunteered to edit many of the essays simply because he was interested in Marine Corps history. Now a law school student, Sean is the son of Lt. Gen. and Mrs. Dennis M. McCarthy, U.S. Marine Corps Reserve, Columbus, Ohio, so we all thank Dennis and Rosemary for Sean as well as their own many years of service to the Marine Corps.

We also want to thank the Marine Corps Historical Foundation for its support of many of the individual essayists, who used grants from the foundation to research the lives of their respective commandants. We are especially delighted that Col. Gerald C. Thomas Jr., one of our fellow authors, became the foundation's principal spokesman for sound scholarship in Marine Corps history. If the current plan to build a Marine Corps Heritage Center at Quantico, Virginia, comes to pass, it will to a large part because Jerry Thomas kept this vision alive even until his death in 2003.

My wife, Martha, has shared my impatience and frustration with this book, so she deserves her share of satisfaction at seeing its completion as well as my thanks for her encouragement and support. She has been an acute and astute student of both the commandants and the authors and wise counselor in dealing with them all.

Commandants of the Marine Corps is the work of many and took years to produce. So, too, is the Marine Corps.

Allan R. Millett

My introduction to this book began in the dimly remembered past. Sometime in the 1980s, aware that I was working on my dissertation about the Marine Corps of the nineteenth century, Lt. Col. "Skip" Bartlett and Professor Bob Love of the Naval Academy asked me to write the essays on Commandants Charles McCawley and Charles Heywood for this anthology. Finally in the early 1990s, after the publication of *The Marine Search for a Mission,* I turned in the final draft on Commandant Heywood to Allan Millett, who by that time had taken over the editorship of the volume. I conveniently then forgot about the book except for occasionally hearing grumbling from Allan about late-arriving manuscripts.

This all changed in 1999 after my retirement from the Marine Corps Historical Center. In April or May of that year at a meeting of the Society for Military History, Allan and Paul Wilderson of the Naval Institute Press asked me to make a final review of the essays. While Paul expressed some concern over the length of the book, I found few of the essays could be pared to any extent. After some smoothing of text, I then turned to the task of checking names, correcting a few errors of fact, comparing text to endnotes, and making some stylistic recommendations, some of which were accepted and some not. Despite the frustrations of computer glitches and the tedium of the above as well as the reading of page proofs, it has been fun and worthwhile. I believe the result is a major contribution to Marine Corps history. I join Allan in thanking all the contributors, especially Lt. Col. "Skip" Bartlett, and the staff of the Naval Institute Press. In addition I again owe everything to my wife Corinne, who does not complain too loudly about being a "book widow" on occasion.

Jack Shulimson

COMMANDANTS OF THE MARINE CORPS

Introduction

Commandant of the Marine Corps and Headquarters Marine Corps

COL. ALLAN R. MILLETT, USMCR (RET.)

Throughout the history of the U.S. Marine Corps, the commandant of the Corps and the Headquarters Marine Corps staff that supports him have played a crucial role in building an effective Marine Corps. The commandant and his staff have one principal function: to ensure that the nation's government, executive and legislative branches alike, understands that the Marine Corps is a separate service within the Department of the Navy, prepared to perform maritime missions but also available for duties ashore in a variety of roles as the president directs. The commandant not only directs the recruitment, organization, equipment, and training of the Marine Corps field forces but also provides the political leadership necessary to win annual appropriations and legislative approval and to protect Marine Corps roles, missions, and administrative freedom. A commandant is largely measured by his success as a spokesman for the Corps to Congress in the budget process, and his staff is judged by how effectively it crafts policies for the wise and frugal use of the resources provided by Congress. Since World War II, the commandant has also functioned as a military adviser to the president and secretary of defense.

From its creation in the act of 11 July 1798, the Marine Corps appeared too small and dispersed to require a central headquarters, but on 12 July 1798, Congress approved the appointment of William Ward Burrows as major and senior Marine officer. Two years later, it specified that Burrows would hold the rank of lieutenant colonel commandant of the Marine Corps, and in another two years it approved an action Burrows had already taken: the appointment of three junior officers to serve as his adjutant, paymaster, and quartermaster. Congress gave him this option in the law of 1798, provided the number of marines serving ashore required administrative support separate from the marines who were ships' guards and thus became members of a ship's company upon embarkation. Burrows planned to establish Marine Corps barracks at every major naval station in order to organize and train the ships' guards; the marines at these barracks would also act as sentries to guard Navy property, a service the Navy welcomed. By 1809, the Marine Corps had established barracks detachments at Brooklyn, Washington, Boston, Philadelphia, New Orleans, and Baltimore. Although all the barracks commanders enjoyed considerable administrative autonomy, the commandant argued (and Congress agreed) that he should supervise them and account for their use of public funds through a central headquarters staff. Additional legislation in 1817 and 1834 increased the ranks of officers, provided them with tenure in their staff positions, and established three permanent staff departments: Adjutant and Inspector (A&I), Paymaster, and Quartermaster.

When the federal government moved from Philadelphia to its permanent site in the District of Columbia, Headquarters Marine Corps moved too, first to a campsite in the district's northwest quadrant (1800), then to a rented office building near the new executive mansion on Pennsylvania Avenue (1800–1804), and finally to the newly built brick Washington Marine Barracks on Eighth and I Streets, SE, near the navy yard on the east branch of the Potomac River (Anacostia Creek). Through much of the century, therefore, the commandant's staff often doubled as the staff of the Washington Marine Barracks. The staff, however, benefited most from its close proximity—physically, politically, and socially—to Congress, which valued the careful accounting of public funds and quick information on constituent problems, especially Corps officers who wanted special consideration in assignments. (Promotions came through seniority, but appointments themselves often involved patronage politics.) After the long and autocratic rule of Col. Cmdt. Archibald Henderson (1820–59), the adjutant and inspector, the paymaster, and the quartermaster exercised considerable freedom of action, due principally from their close working relationships with key congressmen on the naval affairs committees.

The Marine Corps of the nineteenth century did not require an elaborate or large Headquarters staff, for it was a small force that performed missions of no great consequence. With the exception of the limited and temporary increases in strength during the Mexican War and the Civil War, the Marine Corps numbered fewer than one hundred officers and two thousand enlisted men. All three departments carried out their duties in the fields of personnel administration and inspections, the procurement and distribution of ordnance and equipment, the payment of personnel, and the settlement of public accounts in accordance with Navy Department regulations and the internal orders issued by the commandant. The commandants retained officer procurement and enlisted recruiting under their direct control, usually through a personal assistant, and they influenced training either through officers assigned to instructional duties at Washington Barracks or through the A&I's inspections.

The principal role of the commandant, defined by Henderson through his long service in the position, became chief lobbyist for Marine Corps participation in whatever military crises the federal government faced. In the nineteenth century, the Corps fought in three Indian campaigns, captured John Brown and his abolitionist raiders, suppressed urban riots, and provided expeditionary battalions for land campaigns in the Mexican and Civil Wars. In part, the commandants responded to threats to the Corps's existence, especially its status as a separate service (confirmed by law in 1834) with its own central Headquarters. Seven different times between 1829 and 1897, officials of the executive branch, most often Army or Navy officers, proposed to abolish or fundamentally change the Corps. Sensitive to charges that Headquarters had no purpose for a force so small, the commandants kept their staffs austere and inconspicuous.

In the aftermath of the war with Spain (1898), the Marine Corps began a period of dramatic organizational growth and functional change that demanded equally dramatic changes in the duties of the commandant and the responsibilities of Headquarters Marine Corps. His staff did not, however, expand to assist him. As late as 1915, the Adjutant and Inspector Department had six officers, two at Headquarters. The Quartermaster Department numbered seventeen officers, four at Headquarters. Of the six officers in the Paymaster Department, three worked in Washington. Supported by an enlisted and civilian clerk force that could not have been larger than fifty, these staff officers performed duties that had not changed substantially in one hundred years. Even when the commandant requested more staff assistance in 1915, he asked for only five more officers and twenty more enlisted men.

In the first two decades of the twentieth century, the reforms at Headquarters did not keep pace with the expanded missions of the Corps. The central focus of change was to reorganize the traditional departments (Adjutant and Inspector, Quartermaster, and Paymaster), not create a true general staff like the War Department General Staff (1903) or even to establish a limited planning staff like that of the Office of the Chief of Naval Operations (1915). In retrospect, the reluctance to reform came from sources more complicated than sheer traditionalism. The emerging Marine leadership elite of the "imperial years" saw the Corps as a small, personal service that did not require an elaborate staff system. The Corps's missions and size argued otherwise. By 1908, the Marine Corps had tripled in size to 267 officers and 9,100 men; at the height of its mobilization in World War I, it numbered a staggering 2,464 officers and 72,639 men. Symbolic of the turmoil of change, the offices of Headquarters left the Washington Barracks, which required extensive renovation, and moved to three different office buildings in downtown Washington before arriving at permanent quarters in May 1919 at the Main Navy Building, Eighteenth Street and Constitution Avenue, NW.

American colonial expansion into the western Pacific and an era of military activism in the Caribbean created challenging problems for Headquarters Marine Corps. The number of ships with Marine Corps guards and the number of naval bases and stations (some now overseas) increased with the size and reach of the fleet. To these traditional missions came new tasks: the creation of the Advanced Base Force to defend temporary wartime naval bases in the Caribbean and Pacific and the requirement to provide battalions, regiments, and even brigades for expeditionary duty abroad. In 1900, the General Board of the Navy, a group of officers who advised the secretary of the navy, began serious contingency planning and asked for supporting Marine Corps staff estimates. A Marine officer joined the board's secretariat, and the commandant became an ex officio member of the board itself. Advanced Base Force doctrine and contingency planning placed new burdens on the commandant, who tried to influence planning through a handful of junior officer aides. For George F. Elliott (brigadier general commandant, 1903–10), the press of Navy Department business proved too taxing for an officer with no taste for planning duties. Elliott demonstrated his command skills in leading a Marine expedition to Panama in 1903, but he dealt ineptly with a Navy Department plan in 1908–9 to remove Marine Corps guards from American warships, a move calculated to force Elliott to form the Advanced Base Force. This episode, which placed the Corps between the ire of President Theodore Roosevelt and the outrage of his congressional critics, demonstrated among other things that Headquarters needed reforms that would better serve the commandant.

The next two commandants, William P. Biddle (1911–14) and George Barnett (1914–20), recognized that the size of the Marine Corps and the diversity of its peacetime and wartime missions required some reorganization at Headquarters. Between 1911 and 1916, or before entry into World War I halted reform, Biddle and Barnett created and expanded the Office of the Assistant to the Commandant, an ad hoc planning and executive staff headed by a senior line colonel. In 1912, Congress changed the law on assignments to the Adjutant and Inspector's Department, so that line officers with recent field experience could replace the permanent A&I staff officers, who might be incompetent or inexperienced in operational matters. The principle of temporary staff assignments (adopted earlier by the U.S. Army) was extended to the Quartermaster and Paymaster Departments in 1916 for all officers serving in those departments below the rank of colonel. The same legislation limited the Headquarters staff to 8 percent of total Marine officer strength and allocated the staff assignments as one-fifth to the A&I, three-fifths to the quartermaster, and one-fifth to the paymaster. In reality, the technical requirements of staff assignments brought about de facto permanent assignments to these departments, sometimes with short tours outside of Washington, but the concept of absolute staff tenure had been abolished. Staff rotation also meant that the Marine Corps could create a cadre of experienced staff officers available for field service. In 1918, for example, the Marine Corps had four brigades deployed abroad, two in France and two in the Caribbean, all of which required competent staffs.

When John A. Lejeune became commandant in 1920, he brought to the office a keen appreciation that Headquarters reform had not gone far enough. In his nine years in office (1920–29), Lejeune, the most important twentieth-century commandant, changed his staff to reflect his emphasis on preparation for the wartime mission of seizing advanced naval bases in support of the fleet, especially for a war with Japan in the Pacific. By temperament, experience, and personal prestige, Lejeune had the power to push reform forward. A graduate of the Naval Academy, he had broad contacts in the Navy. He had served on expeditionary duty abroad on several occasions before World War I and had attended the Army War College and knew the issues and problems that came with the creation of the War Department General Staff. During World War I, he had commanded the 4th Marine Brigade and the U.S. 2d Division with distinction. More important, he had supervised the Marine Corps mobilization of 1917 as Barnett's assistant and enjoyed wide popularity and confidence among the elite of the federal government. Even though Lejeune did not accomplish all the changes he favored, he established the Corps's agenda for the entire interwar period.

The pattern of Headquarters organization under Lejeune and his successors combined a proliferation of agencies with a complementary centralization as the pace and complexity of their functions increased in the 1930s with the formation of the Fleet Marine Force (FMF). Although the Paymaster and Quartermaster Departments retained much of their autonomy, the A&I Department began to surrender its work to newer agencies, retaining only the major functions of records management and inspection reporting. The first major change at Headquarters came in the reorganization of 1920. In order to give the commandant and his personal staff more help, Lejeune created three sections: Personnel (which handled all matters pertaining to officer recruitment and career management), Recruiting (established as a bureau in 1911 to handle publicity and enlisted procurement), and Education (which managed the Marine Corps Institute and nonmilitary educational program at Marine bases). The greatest change, however, came with the reorganization of the Planning Section (1918) into the Operations and Training Division, headed by a general officer by the 1930s. The Operations and Training Division began with five sections: Training, Intelligence, Operations, Materiel, and Aviation, the last section transferred from the Office of the Director of Naval Aviation. The Operations and Training Division added a sixth section, War Plans, which had started in 1924 directly under the commandant.

The evolution of the Headquarters staff organization created a distinction in theory between long-range organizational policy planning and specialized, routine administration. The Operations and Training Division would handle the former; all other divisions, departments, and sections would be responsible for the latter. No such real difference existed since the Headquarters staff had also changed to reflect the demands of overseas peacetime deployments (most notably to Nicaragua and China) and wartime mobilization planning for the use of the FMF in a war with Japan. Planning and the execution of policy fused and created four centers of power at Headquarters below the commandant and his assistant as well as several new agencies of less influence, but real missions. The first was the Division of Plans and Policies (1939), which had five sections (Personnel, Intelligence, Training, Materiel, and War Plans) by the eve of World War II. The second was the Division of Aviation (1936), headed by a general officer with direct access to the commandant. The third was the Division of Personnel (1937), also headed by a general officer and raised to department status in 1943, which controlled officer and enlisted procurement (including the recruiting service) and established personnel policies and management. The fourth remained the Quartermaster Department, which argued that it should absorb its junior partner, the Paymaster Department. When the Naval Reserve Act of 1925 gave the Marine Corps the firm legal basis to form an organized reserve, Headquarters formed a reserve section the same year and raised it to the Division of Reserve in 1937. In 1933, the Publicity Bureau became a section apart from the recruiting establishment and then became the Public Relations Division in July 1941, when Headquarters recognized that mobilization demanded a greater emphasis on expert advertising and media relations.

Lejeune's immediate successors—Wendell C. Neville (1929–30), Ben H. Fuller (1930–34), John H. Russell (1934–36), and Thomas Holcomb (1936–43)—faced common problems as the Headquarters staff became larger and more complex, but only Holcomb faced the additional challenge of wartime urgency. Once again the physical move of Headquarters dramatized the end of one era and the beginning of another. On 10 November 1941, Holcomb dedicated the Corps's new Headquarters location in the western half of the Navy Department's Arlington Annex, a yellow brick building placed on a rise between Columbia Pike and the southern border of Arlington National Cemetery. In a reclaimed swampland below the Arlington Annex another building neared completion—the Pentagon—first home of the War Department and eventually all the other services and the Office of the Secretary of Defense and other defense agencies. The Marine Corps remained in Arlington Annex, despite deterioration and overcrowding, in part a symbolic statement of its uniqueness and its political and psychological separation from all other elements of the defense establishment.

Although the Marine Corps suffered no special penalties for its Headquarters staff work in World War II, senior Marine officers recognized that the Corps could not function after the war with the same degree of waste, lack of coordination, thoughtless haste, and misdirection of personnel and materiel resources that had characterized the wartime mobilization. The Corps's problems were not unique in the U.S. armed forces and no worse than the other services' difficulties, which came from three basic conditions: the rapid expansion of the armed forces, the flood of new money to spend on the war effort, and the creation of large and complicated field forces to fight a global conflict in every imaginable physical environment. Basically, the Marine Corps fought its Pacific war with a Fleet Marine Force of six divisions and four aircraft wings (with a vast structure of corps troops and a service establishment) and a Headquarters staff that did not change much in formal structure.

General Holcomb did not think wartime an appropriate moment for a major reorganization, and he profited from the services of some exceptional senior staff officers, especially Quartermaster Gen. Seth Williams. By prewar standards, managing the Headquarters personnel, about twenty-four hundred marines and nine hundred civilians, proved challenge enough without changing their functions. The greatest difficulty was in the Division of Plans and Policies, which added special sections to cope with a flood of specialized personnel and equipment issues. The division added new sections (e.g., Gunnery, Communications, Mess Management) or new subsections within the existing sections. Inevitably, the proliferation of sections made it difficult for the director of plans and policies to control his own division and allowed aggressive subordinates to poach on the responsibilities of other Headquarters divisions, including the sacrosanct Aviation Division. The creation of the Administration Division (1943) and

Inspection Division (1945) did not really address the problem of policy coordination and supervision below the commandant himself.

The second of the World War II commandants, Alexander Archer Vandegrift (1944–47), recognized that Headquarters needed more central control and a clearer division of functions, but he did not accept the recommendations of his director of plans and policies, Brig. Gen. Gerald C. Thomas, that Headquarters have a general staff on the Army model (chief of staff, G-1, G-2, G-3, and G-4) that would provide more responsible planning and better supervision of policy execution. Such a system, however, was already being used to good effect in FMF operational organizations. Although Thomas received permission to bring greater order to his own division, where he consolidated or abolished a number of sections and subsections, his Headquarters reorganization proposal met determined opposition from the quartermaster general, director of aviation, and director of personnel. Until 1952, the changes at Headquarters did not fundamentally alter the "federal" nature of staff organization, although they did bring some redistribution of power. The quartermaster general became the head of a merged Quartermaster and Paymaster Department, renamed the Supply Department (1946) as part of a general reorganization of the Department of the Navy. The Division of Plans and Policies continued to expand and contract with the creation and abolition of special purpose sections, and the Division of Reserve reemerged from its wartime union with the Personnel Department, which lost, only temporarily, the recruiting function as well. To enhance his status and recognize his coordinating powers, the assistant to the commandant became the assistant commandant (1946) and gained the additional title of chief of staff (1948). The basic issues, however, remained unaddressed. To what degree should planning and execution be divided or joined? How many subordinate staff directors could the commandant and his assistant directly supervise? How much centralization did Headquarters require to function effectively in the maelstrom of interservice politics in postwar Washington?

The Corps's general staff faction argued that the Corps's internal governance might stagger along under the existing arrangements, but the raging struggle over service roles and missions in a period of fiscal scarcity and strategic uncertainty required deft staff work in organizational long-range planning and programming, something they believed the existing departments did not provide. Expert staff work would bolster the Marine Corps's struggles in Washington to receive clear recognition of its separate service status and its unique function as an amphibious force-in-readiness for contingency missions short of full-scale war. Another related sore point was the imperial tendency of the CNOs to regard the commandant as one of their subordinates, not a coequal under the common supervision of the secretary of the navy. The National Security Act of 1947, as amended in 1949, gave the Marine Corps the formal legislative protection it sought, but it did not place the commandant on the Joint Chiefs of Staff, where he would be better positioned to deal with the secretary of defense or the joint staff and its supporting directorates. (Marine officers, however, as they had in World War II, continued to serve on the CNO's staff and the Joint Staff, but they required expert support from

Headquarters in order to express Marine positions and defend Marine interests.) Impressed by the FMF's Pacific war performance—recognized by elevation of the commandant's rank to full general in 1944—Congress and public opinion tended to favor the Marine Corps, but much of its future depended on its success in the intramural battles for strength levels and budgets within the Department of Defense and the White House in which Congress and a doting media could play only a crisis role. In bureaucratic warfare there was no substitute for fine staff work and dependable internal management.

As commandant of the Marine Corps (1948–52), Clifton B. Cates did not put staff reorganization high among his priorities, largely because he spent his first two years fighting off the erosion of the FMF in the budget process and the second two years mobilizing the Marines to participate in the Korean War. Although he was no stranger to Headquarters, where he had first served as a much-decorated World War I officer and aide to General Barnett, Cates did not have the same experience or interest in Headquarters organization as his successor, Lemuel C. Shepherd Jr. (1952–56), who had served in staff billets up to the level of assistant commandant for Vandegrift. The Division of Plans and Policies remained the hotbed of reform agitation, for it produced a major study (23–49) that urged a general staff system that would give the staff the power to plan and supervise the execution of plans by the other Headquarters departments and divisions. Faced with a host of unhappy senior Headquarters generals who already had their hands full with building a Corps three times larger than its pre–Korean War predecessor, Cates did not approve Study 23–49.

In January 1952, Shepherd replaced Cates as commandant and immediately announced that he would create a Headquarters General Staff with three of the four G-divisions (Personnel, Operations and Training, and Logistics) headed by general officers. Intelligence functions would be conducted by a separate but lesser office with a colonel in charge. Four assistant chiefs of staff (G-1, G-2, G-3, G-4) would work for the assistant commandant/chief of staff, who would have another general as deputy chief of staff to assist him. Shepherd recalled Gerald C. Thomas from command of the 1st Marine Division to head the reformed staff, which he had championed since 1944. Shepherd, however, softened the blow by placing most of the existing departments and divisions outside of the supervisory powers of the G-sections since he wanted the G-sections to concentrate on long-range planning, not policy implementation. In other words, the G-sections simply replaced the Division of Plans and Policies and even had to share some of the planning function with a new Policy Analysis Division, which would focus on issues with joint planning significance. Shepherd and Thomas, however, did weaken the independence of the quartermaster general by transferring his budgeting duties to the new Fiscal Division.

The Headquarters General Staff system of 1952 did not, as Shepherd and Thomas may have hoped, start a movement to centralization and consolidation of power at Headquarters, for the press of business from outside the Marine Corps, generated by the Defense Department and the Joint Chiefs of Staff organization, brought another wave of new agencies. In June 1952, Congress passed PL 416 (82d Congress), which authorized the commandant to sit with the JCS on matters he deemed of concern to the Marine Corps. Since much of the JCS work was done by the "operations deputies," the Marine Corps needed its own "ops dep," a position the chief of staff and the deputy chief filled until 1956. A new commandant, Randolph McCall Pate (1956–60), divided the Office of Deputy Chief of Staff in two, establishing a deputy chief of staff (Plans) who would be the "ops dep," and a deputy chief of staff (Research and Development). The next year Pate split the Office of Assistant Commandant and Chief of Staff between two general officers, one of whom would be the commandant's official stand-in at home and abroad, the other the staff coordinator at Headquarters. Under the press of joint business and the budgeting wizardry that began in 1961 under Secretary of Defense Robert S. McNamara, the deputy chief of staff (Plans) became (Plans and Programs) in 1962 with a general officer deputy to handle each function. In addition, the director of the Division of Aviation advanced to the rank of lieutenant general and became the assistant commandant (Air) in 1952, although he took a "reduction" in title, if not rank and power, ten years later as the deputy chief of staff (Air).

The other additions to the Headquarters staff reflected either the establishment of new positions or the creation of an "official" office to support what had been heretofore personal assistants to the commandant. These offices included those of the legislative assistant to the commandant, the counsel to the commandant, the director of Women Marines, and the offices of the staff medical officer, staff chaplain, and staff dental officer, all assigned by the Navy. In 1960, Cmdt. David M. Shoup (1960–64), who had cut his teeth on Headquarters politics as the G-4, Division of Plans and Policies, and the first independent fiscal director, established a separate Data Processing Division to guide policy on electronic data processing, the ultimate weapon in defense policy making. He also created the Emergency Actions Center (1961) to improve Marine Corps participation in crises, always a challenge in the joint and combined system of the 1960s.

For all their fears about the excessive bureaucratization of Headquarters, the senior Marine generals of the 1960s produced the monster they abhorred, for by 1968, the commandant, through the chief of staff, had twenty-seven principal staff officers to supervise. Granted that not all held responsibilities of equal importance and that General Shoup and his successors, Wallace M. Green Jr. (1964–68) and Leonard F. Chapman Jr. (1968–72), were experienced Headquarters staff officers. Nevertheless, the commandant, even with a brilliant chief of staff, had difficulty controlling the design and execution of policy. The stress of the Vietnam War mobilization and the continuing problems of policy coordination within the Department of Defense (now far more serious than the same function in the Navy Department) forced further expansion of independent staff organizations. Although not dictating the Headquarters response, the result was the creation of a new tier of senior staff officers, the deputy chiefs of staff, who grew from one in 1952 to five by 1967 after Greene created a post for Manpower (1967) and Administration (1965). The assistant chiefs of staff (the four G-sections of 1952) remained, but held less power than the deputy chiefs of staff. Eight different specialist staff assistants advised the commandant on everything from legislative affairs to dental policy. The eight divisions and departments that survived the 1952 reorganization continued to survive; a ninth agency, the Crises Actions Center, became the Marine Corps Command Center in 1963. This tier of agencies increased to ten with the addition of the Data Systems Division, expanded and retitled in 1964.

The number of people at Headquarters predictably increased, but numbers were not the problem. In 1952, 1,041 Marine Corps officers and enlisted personnel served at Headquarters, joined by 1,785 civilians. The numbers were hardly excessive by World War II standards or those of the other services, even when measured by service total strength. The difficulty was the overlapping responsibilities of so many staff divisions; a lesser problem was the crowding of so many authoritative senior officers into a building that had not grown, owned by a Navy that had not surrendered any of its own office spaces. The only significant relief at Headquarters was the movement of the disbursing operation within the Fiscal Division to a new facility in Kansas City, Missouri (1967). The complexity of relations at Headquarters was not simplified by the addition of more general officers to staff assignments; persuaded that the Marine Corps deserved more generals for its total strength in 1967, Congress authorized an increase of generals from sixty to seventy-nine. About half of these new generals came to billets at Headquarters.

Although the proliferation of staff agencies slowed with the waning participation in the Vietnam War and the reduction of the size of the Marine Corps, the process of consolidation and reorganization did not begin until 1973–74. The History and Museums Division (1969) joined the rank of new divisions, but some consolidations brought the total number of separate organizations at Headquarters down to twenty-six by 1974. The senior officers around another commandant, Robert E. Cushman Jr. (1972–75), argued that Headquarters badly needed to cut the number of offices and to join the planning responsibility with the power to execute plans with the establishment of four functional "czars" in the areas of personnel, logistics and materiel, training and operations, and plans and programs.

After five months of study, Cushman ordered the recommended changes in 1973. The changes started with the abolition of the 1952 G-sections and their assistant chiefs of staff, joined in their demise by the deputy chief of staff (Plans and Programs). To manage the major functional areas of Marine Corps business, the commandant (and the chief of staff) would now work with six deputy chiefs of staff, who should head the Manpower Department (M), the Division of Installations and Logistics (L), the Plans and Operations Department (P), the Division of Requirements and Programs (RP), the Division of Research, Development and Studies (RD), and the Aviation Division (AA). The assistant commandant, a full general, would substitute for the commandant; the chief of staff, the senior lieutenant general at Headquarters, would run the staff. The two most dramatic changes came in the establishment of the consolidated Manpower Department, which contained four major divisions (each headed by a general officer) that would give comprehensive direction to Marine Corps manpower planning and management. The Installations and Logistics Division brought similar consolidations, including the disappearance of the gallant old bureaucratic campaigner, the Quartermaster Department. With some modification, most of the pre-1973 divisions remained: History and Museums, Fiscal, Reserve, Inspection, Headquarters Support, Information (Public Affairs), Information Systems Support and Management, Intelligence, Judge Advocate, and Telecommunications. The latter three were new or recently established offices. The commandant also still maintained offices for his legislative director, counsel, staff chaplain, staff dentist, staff medical officer, and director of special projects. In addition, Headquarters continued to maintain special boards and study groups. Nevertheless, the commandant had consolidated planning and execution in the most important functional areas, and the number of agencies at Headquarters had dropped to twenty-three (measured by separate correspondence codes).

The next decade brought modest changes to the 1973 Headquarters organization, for the next three commandants—Louis H. Wilson Jr. (1975–79), Robert H. Barrow (1979–83), and Paul X. Kelley (1983–87)—faced challenges that required high quality staff work but no major reorganization. Wilson and Barrow drove the Corps out of its post-Vietnam despond by stressing quality manpower recruitment and retention (including a war on malcontents and drug users); Kelley exploited the fiscal largesse of the Reagan Defense Department and a compliant Congress to sponsor a program of materiel modernization and firepower improvements unmatched in peacetime Marine Corps history. All three promoted greater readiness in the FMF, including the prepositioning of equipment and supplies on board cargo shipping (three locations) or in Norwegian caves. The 1970s focus on NATO-only deployments shifted to additional regional planning, especially for the Middle East, Korea, and Latin America. Over these three administrations, changes did occur, and they reflected some shifts in priorities. The deputy chiefs of staff for manpower, plans, programs and operations, installations and logistics, and aviation clearly emerged (all in the rank of lieutenant general) as the "Big Four" with Requirements and Programs (the architect of the annual Program Objectives Memorandum or defense budget submission) and Research and Development only a step behind in the pecking order. When Congress decided to stress Reserve forces improvement in the late 1970s, it created the Office of Assistant Secretary of Defense for Reserve Affairs, which sent the services hurrying off to improve their own reserve offices. At Headquarters, the director of the Reserve Division became deputy chief of staff (Reserve Affairs). As the span of responsibility of the deputy chief of staff for plans, policies, and operations expanded in the flurry of joint and combined planning and exercises—complicated by the creation of two new joint commands for the Middle East and the Caribbean—his office surrendered its training mission to a new assistant chief of staff for training (T), whose activities not only overlapped with PP&O, but Manpower as well. The flux of the concentration and dispersion of power and functions continued to influence Headquarters organization, although the separation of planning and execution ceased to be a major issue.

The next wave of change at Headquarters came in 1987 from two coincidental events, the passage of the Defense Reorganization Act (Goldwater-Nichols) of 1986 and the succession of Gen. Alfred M. Gray Jr. to the office of commandant (1987–91). Unlike his predecessors as far back as David M. Shoup, Gray had not served at Headquarters for multiple tours at various stages of his career, and he had served no Headquarters tour as a general officer. He came to Washington, in fact, almost as an "anti-Headquarters" commandant, predisposed to see his staff as a barrier to reshaping the FMF for Third World contingency missions that would range from small-unit special operations to brigade-sized assaults from the sea. One change he made stemmed from the Goldwater-Nichols act, which limited the number of deputy chiefs of staff to five. The Division of Reserve Affairs disappeared, and its chief became an assistant to the deputy chief of staff (Manpower and Reserve Affairs). Two other major changes had the commandant's personal stamp. Convinced that the Marine Corps would function better if it did its serious thinking on force development outside of Washington (but not too far away), Gray changed the Marine Corps Development and Education Command, Quantico, to the Marine Corps Combat Development Command (MCCDC) (1987) and tasked its commanding general to lead the Corps's operational renaissance through the direction of five special centers: Warfighting, Training and Education, Intelligence, Wargaming and Assessment, and Information Technology. While a brigadier general would supervise Quantico's traditional training and educational responsibilities through the new Marine Corps University, the successor of the Marine Corps Schools, the assistant chief of staff for training would move his office to Quantico and become the director of the Training and Education Center, which would direct Corps-wide formal training and education.

The other organizational change stemmed primarily from a Department of Defense high-level study conducted in 1986 that found that materiel management and research and development in the Navy Department needed reform. Gray responded by approving a plan to merge the Acquisition Planning and Project Management Offices in Installations and Logistics with the Office of the Deputy Chief of Staff (Research and Development) and the Development Center into one office, the Marine Corps Research, Development, and Acquisitions Command with its headquarters at Quantico and its offices divided between Quantico and the Washington area and its testing facilities and agencies throughout the Marine Corps base structure. This change also occurred in 1987, driven by Gray's conviction that Marine Corps materiel managers needed to work more quickly, cheaply, and imaginatively, and with greater sensitivity to the reported requirements from the FMF. This reform, along with the establishment of MCCDC, also reduced the number of personnel serving at Headquarters, a blow for better working conditions and diminished stress among harried commuters. Between 1970 and 1989, the number of marines at Headquarters fell from thirty-five hundred to twenty-five hundred.

The organization of Headquarters Marine Corps continued to change in the 1990s, largely because of pressures from outside the Corps. The single largest influence became the effort of the armed forces to adjust to a post–cold war international security environment that has been variously interpreted by Congress and the White House as still threatening or not threatening or both, depending on the part of the world and the nature of the threat one sees. The only sure reduction of military threat is the diminished strategic nuclear threat of Russia and the demise of the Warsaw Pact as a major conventional threat to the members of NATO. Neither of these problems had much concerned the Marine Corps. As Cmdt. Carl E. Mundy Jr. (1991–95) liked to remind Congress, the Corps had been the nation's "911 Force" for more than one hundred years, and the series of small crises that followed the Persian Gulf War of 1991 demonstrated its continuing utility as the "State Department's troops." When crises occurred in Kurdistan, Liberia, Haiti, Somalia, and again in the Persian Gulf, the Marine Corps arrived to put guns behind American diplomacy. Only in Bosnia did Marine ground troops avoid extended service ashore, but Marine aviation remained nearby, as did embarked Marine Expeditionary Units (Special Operations Capable) with the special mission of rescuing downed American aviators.

The organizational dimension of a high operational tempo (a euphemism for too many missions for too few marines) and the refinement of the joint commands abroad (e.g., Central Command, Atlantic Command) has been the reduction of Headquarters staffing (down from twelve hundred in 1991 to 774 in 1998) and the reorganization of the Headquarters staff for greater participation in the Office of the Secretary of Defense, the organization of the Joint Chiefs of Staff and the Joint Staff, and the Offices of the Secretary of the Navy and the Chief of Naval Operations. A complementary move reformed the Marine Corps support structure, both by consolidating existing offices in Washington and by moving other organizations to the Marine Corps Combat Development Command, Quantico, Virginia. The Corps now has two major Headquarters locations, Washington and Quantico. One dramatic demonstration of this policy of greater service integration in Washington occurred in January 1996, when Cmdt. Charles C. Krulak (1995–99) moved his office and that of the assistant commandant of the Marine Corps to the Fourth Floor, E Ring, of the Pentagon. After some fifty years of organizational unity in one physical location, the condemned Navy Annex, Headquarters Marine Corps had redeployed to different locations in the Washington area and on the Marine base at Quantico by the end of 2000. Plans, Policies, and Operations and other key planning staffs (Aviation, Programs and Resources) moved to the Pentagon to allow closer coordination with their counterparts in the other services with the exception of PP&O's current operations rear guard, housed in Henderson Hall. The commandant's special staff officers (the judge advocate, the director of public affairs, and the commandant's personal staff) have also moved to the Pentagon. The personnel managers have moved to Quantico while the logisticians will split their offices between Quantico and new quarters in nearby Crystal City until they can be consolidated in new offices in the Pentagon. Whether electronic "connectivity" will be a satisfactory substitute for face-to-face coordination remains to be proven, but it may reduce the urge to hold long staff meetings.

When Gen. James L. Jones became commandant in 1999, he changed all the deputy chiefs of staff to deputy commandants, a rationalization of title that recognized that the

Marine Corps no longer had a chief of staff but a director, Marine Corps Staff (1993), in the rank of major general. The change of title was reversed in less than a year. The commandant sent a clear message that he would deal directly with his deputies for Aviation, Installations and Logistics, Manpower and Reserve Affairs, Programs and Resources, and Plans, Policies, and Operations. In theory, the assistant commandant and director, Marine Corps Staff directly supervise eight Headquarters agencies, the commandant thirteen as well as the separate commands for Development, Recruiting, and Material Management. Whether this new form of decentralized control works or produces the opposite effect remains in doubt. The new obsession with joint service planning that became legislation with the Goldwater-Nichols act created cascading demands for high-quality staff work. The act itself mandated a quadrennial defense review (QDR) by the secretary of defense for Congress; the first three QDRs in 1989, 1993, and 1997 sent all of the joint and service staffs to the barricades since the purpose of the QDR appeared to be a zero-sum game in which the only winner would be Congress, which would pare down the defense budget. The QDR hardly exhausted the flood of similar joint studies. The Base Force studies of 1989–90 made by the JCS chairman, Gen. Colin Powell, USA, were unsatisfactory to Secretary of Defense Les Aspin, who decreed his own Bottom Up Review (BUR) in 1993, when he took office with the Clinton administration. The BUR did not produce budgetary suicide by the armed forces, so Congress directed a division of effort by creating the Base Realignment and Allocation Commission (a quaint way to say "close that base") and the Commission on Roles and Missions in the Armed Forces (1994) to look for further ways to consolidate support and training functions. The accumulative message of all these investigations could not have been clearer: be ready to defend the efficiency and effectiveness with which you generals and admirals run your services. By 1998, the number of marines assigned to joint staff duty (1,450) almost equaled the number working at Headquarters (1,659).

At Headquarters, the pressure to plan and budget fell to the deputy chiefs of staff (serving in the rank of lieutenant general), some of whom still had staffs whose functions had remained fairly stable since the 1950s: Manpower and Reserve Affairs; Aviation; Plans, Programs, and Operations; Logistics and Installations; and Programs and Resources. In these directorates, two major changes shifted power to new offices established at Quantico, the first the fusion of all officer and enlisted recruiting and entry-level training in a Marine Corps Recruiting Command, headed by a major general. The second was the transfer of PP&O's Training Division to Quantico in order to centralize Corps internal training policies and to put them closer to the Marine Corps University and the doctrine developers. Many of the manpower-personnel staff also relocated to the new James W. Marsh Building at Quantico in 1998–99. In part to align the major staff directorates at Headquarters with the other services, the deputy chief of staff (Requirements and Programs) became a lieutenant general in 1993 and gained a new directorate, Programs and Resources. This organization absorbed the traditional Fiscal Department, thus consolidating in one agency the analysts and accountants who oversee the preparation of budgetary plans and see that they are executed as intended. It thus profited by the enhanced status of the research and development activities at Quantico, renamed the Marine Corps Systems Command in 1992. These changes exhausted the rank requirements for deputy chiefs of staff, so the general officers in charge of the divisions and departments of Control, Communications, Computers, and Intelligence (C4I) had for appointment an assistant chief of staff (C4I) in the rank of brigadier general. The assistant chief of staff C4I supervises the activities of the chief information officer of the Marine Corps (1995), who is a Senior Executive Service (SES) civilian appointee. The intelligence chief remains a Marine brigadier general.

To support Headquarters positions and provide significant ties to Marine Corps test units and to joint development activities, Cmdt. Alfred M. Gray Jr. established the War Gaming and Assessment Center and Marine Corps Intelligence Center at Quantico in 1990, activities that reflected his lively and innovative interest in fusing operational planning and intelligence analysis, especially through the exploitation of tactical electronics and data processing. General Krulak expanded the mandate of the War Gaming and Assessment Center by retitling it the Marine Corps Warfighting Laboratory in 1995 and making it the focal point between doctrinal exploration and field experimentation.

The commandants of the 1990s did much of their internal policy analysis through ad hoc study groups that crossed Headquarters division boundaries and usually brought in representatives from the Quantico agencies. Generals Gray and Krulak especially like the creative chaos (usually creative, always chaotic) of extemporized study groups. This technique, however, did not work well in dealing with the challenges presented by the joint planning system, especially the construction of the annual Joint Strategic Capabilities Plan, the key document used by the JCS to plead its case with the secretary of defense when the defense budget is drafted. In part, representatives of the Headquarters divisions provide staff support, but it proved more important after the Goldwater-Nichols act to place keen and clever Marine officers throughout the Pentagon in joint billets or abroad in the joint staffs of the geographic joint commands. The CinCs (the theater or functional commander in chief) may have almost reached political parity with the service chiefs in access and influence with the secretary of defense and the chairman, Joint Chiefs of Staff. Alive to this reality, successive commandants nominated the most qualified Marine officers for important joint assignments with increased success. The first such appointment was that of then–lieutenant general Kelley as the first commanding general, Rapid Deployment Joint Task Force in 1983, a command that evolved into the Central Command with Middle East missions. By 1998, Marine generals had held three different CinC commands and still held two a year later, Central Command and Southern Command. A lieutenant general served as personal assistant to the secretary of defense and another represented the United States on the NATO military council.

By 1999 the redistribution of key Headquarters directorates and sections and the assignment of senior Marine officers to joint billets continued to reflect the reduction of Marine Corps leadership tied directly to Headquarters. Nineteen Marine Corps generals filled "external" billets in joint and combined headquarters throughout the world while only eighteen general officers held assignments in Headquarters offices at the Pentagon or the Navy Annex. Five major staff departments—Plans, Policies and Operations; Aviation; Programs and Resources; Installations and Logistics; and C4I—remained in the Washington area along with such special staff offices as the deputy naval inspector general for Marine Corps matters, staff judge advocate, the legislative assistant, and the public affairs officer. Fifteen other general officers held posts at the Marine Corps Base, Quantico, and the Marine Corps Combat Development Command. Their major responsibilities included the Marine Corps University, Systems Command, Recruiting Command, Manpower and Reserve Affairs, the Marine Corps Warfighting Laboratory, the Training and Education Division, and the Warfighting Development Integration Division.

Washington insiders have always known that the Marine Corps enjoys a special relationship with Congress. Now it is on the march to take over the Department of Defense while its detractors amuse themselves with Marine jokes that reflect their ignorance of marines' ability to mix candor, conviction, and cleverness. Like the Marine Corps itself, Headquarters will find ways to survive and be useful.

1

Samuel Nicholas

Senior Officer, Continental Marines

JAMES C. BRADFORD

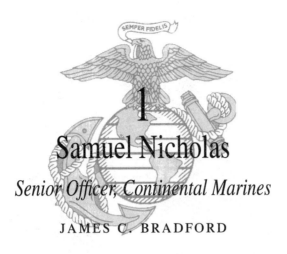

Shortly after noon on 3 March 1776, more than two hundred marines and fifty "landsmen" splashed ashore at Hanover Sound on Providence Island in the Bahamas. In command was Samuel Nicholas, the senior officer in the infant Marine Corps of Britain's rebellious North American colonies. Quickly he formed his men on the beach and marched them westward to take possession of Fort Montagu, which defended the town of New Providence against naval attack from the west. After resting his men overnight (they had been confined to small boats since the day before without opportunity to rest), Nicholas led them into New Providence, where they seized the governor's residence and occupied Fort Nassau without firing a shot. With the Marines in control of both forts and the town secured, it was safe for the Continental squadron to enter the harbor. Thus ended the first amphibious assault by the U.S. Marine Corps on enemy shores. Its complete success demonstrated the wisdom of the Continental Congress in establishing a separate Marine Corps only four months before.

The decision to establish the Marine Corps had, in fact, been a natural one flowing directly from the formation of the Continental Navy in October 1775. Both services were based on British models, and both had antecedents in state and national service in the dawn of the American Revolution. Marines served with George Washington's squadron under the Pine Tree flag during the summer of 1775, and in August of the same year, they were included in the pay table established by Connecticut for its state forces.[1]

In the fall of the year, Congress laid plans for seizing Britain's naval base at Halifax, and on 10 November it resolved that "two Battalions of marines be raised" to effect the capture. The act specified that men be enlisted who were "so acquainted with maritime affairs as to be able to serve to advantage by sea when required." This last phrase and the stipulation that these "American Marines . . . be considered as part of . . . the continental Army before Boston" betrays the fact that these men were not to serve primarily at

Maj. Samuel Nicholas, first commandant.
Created image by Lt. Col. John Joseph Capolino, USMCR (Ret.), n.d. U.S. Marine Corps Photo.

sea or to form a permanent part of the naval establishment.[2] When Washington informed Congress that he could not spare forces for the attack on Nova Scotia, the plan to raise the "American Marines" was abandoned.[3]

In October and November, Congress took the steps necessary to form a national naval service. That a Marine Corps should form a part of that service must have seemed only natural to the members of the Naval Committee. The Rules and Regulations of the Navy of the United Colonies enacted by Congress on 28 November 1775 made no mention of marines when outlining the duties of various officers and crew members but did list them in the pay scale appended to the regulations which provided that the "captain or commander" of a ship receive thirty-two dollars per month and that the "Captain of marines" be the next highest paid officer at twenty-six and two-thirds dollars per month.[4]

On the same day, Samuel Nicholas was commissioned the senior captain in the new Continental Marine Corps. Nicholas's background was something of a mystery but the reasons for his selection are clear enough. He was a lower-middle-class tradesman, born the son of a blacksmith in 1744, and received his education at the Academy and Charitable School in the Province of Pennsylvania. The school was established in 1751, a year before Nicholas began attending, and in 1755 it became the College, Academy, and Charitable School of Philadelphia. Nicholas continued his studies through December 1759, and it was there he became acquainted with children of the city's leading citizens. By 1775, he was a tavern keeper at his mother-in-law's Sign of the Conestogoe Waggon, a middling establishment whose clientele ranked below that of the Indian King but was comparable to the Tun Tavern, which Robert Mullen used as a rendezvous for new Marine recruits.[5]

Nicholas had risen high enough in society to be elected a member of the Schuykill Fishing Company, an exclusive gentlemen's club, and to be a founding member of the Gloucester Fox Hunting Club in 1766. Thus he moved in higher social circles and must have attained the manners of a gentleman, clearly a criteria for a congressional appointment during that era. At the same time, he must have been on good terms with the lower orders of society from which recruits would be drawn. An ability to recruit volunteers was more important than actual military experience, which Nicholas lacked. The other half dozen officers commissioned during the next month also lacked experience, but together they were able to fill the muster rolls of the five Marine companies authorized by Congress.

Recruiting proved to be no problem, but equipping the recruits was more difficult. It was mid-January before Nicholas obtained enough arms. Uniforms were scarce or nonexistent for a year. When Congress designated a Marine uniform in September 1776, it prescribed one very similar to the uniform worn by the Philadelphia militia, an early example of the Corps being forced to adopt and adapt equipment originally designed for another service. What time he could spare from administrative duties, Nicholas devoted to the rudimentary training of his recruits. It is unlikely that very much was accomplished before the embarkation on board Commodore Esek Hopkins's squadron just after the first of the year.

Hopkins's orders were to proceed to the Chesapeake Bay and to clear the area of enemy raiders, then to carry out similar operations along the Carolina coast, after which he was to turn northward and clear Narragansett Bay of the enemy. The Marine detachments varied in size from about five on board the schooner *Wasp* to about sixty each on the *Alfred* and *Columbus*.[6] At the start of the voyage they must have expected to carry out their traditional duties, that is, to assist officers in maintaining discipline and to provide small-arms support during sea battles. When not engaged, they were expected to assist in all ship's work except going aloft. They would assist in manning the capstan or pumps, in hauling on lines, and even in scrubbing and holystoning the decks. Their more military duties included frequent parade and arms drill as well as sentry duty at various places in the ship. During battle they provided sharpshooters to pick off enemy officers and guarded each hatchway to prevent frightened sailors from seeking cover below. Nicholas commanded the marines on the flagship *Alfred,* but officers commanding contingents on board the other vessels reported not to Nicholas but to the captains of their ships.

Once at sea, Commodore Hopkins took advantage of a loophole in his instructions that gave him discretion "to follow such courses as your best judgment shall suggest to you as most useful to the American cause" and ordered his ships to rendezvous at Abaca in the Bahama Islands. There he hatched his plan for a descent on the enemy capital at Nassau. Captain Nicholas was ordered to load the squadron's 234 marines and 50 of its sailors on the *Providence* and two captured enemy sloops. According to Lt. John Paul Jones on board the *Alfred,* "It was determined that they should keep below Deck 'till the sloops were got in Close to the Fort—they were then to land Instantly—take possession before the Island could be alarmed. . . . We then anchored at a small Key 3 leagues to windward of the Town and from thence . . . [the] Commodore dispatched the marines."[7] Meeting negligible opposition, the Marines captured Forts Montagu and Nassau, captured the royal governor, and secured the town. Within two weeks, the munitions captured in the forts were loaded on board the American ships, which set sail for home. En route to New England, the squadron met and was roughly handled by HMS *Glasgow.* During the battle, Nicholas deployed his marines in the barge carried on the *Alfred's* main deck and personally took command of the contingent on the quarterdeck. Two of the marines in the barge and three of the twelve in the quarterdeck were killed.[8] Thus the new Continental Marine Corps received its baptism of fire both afloat and ashore.

As Hopkins's fleet languished in harbor after the raid, detachment after detachment of Marines was transferred to other vessels, and Nicholas found himself with little to do. When his hope for another voyage on board the *Alfred* finally died, he sought permission to go to Philadelphia on personal business. Upon his arrival in the city, he learned that the Continental Congress had recently promoted him to major.[9] Nicholas spent the remainder of the summer and fall in Philadelphia recruiting marines for service on the four frigates under construction there. Recruitment went slowly but Nicholas did have time to establish a rudimentary administrative structure for the Marine Corps. He established a barracks and headquarters, obtained arms and equipment, and drilled the recruits. Each of the four companies was commanded by a lieutenant whose major duties during the summer of 1776 consisted of recruiting. The enlisted men stood guard over the Continental and state navy vessels under construction and docked in the Philadelphia area.[10]

Nicholas was the "senior Marine officer" but did not have administrative control over all Marine Corps units. To facilitate the recruitment of detachments for the nine frigates under construction in cities other than Philadelphia, Congress asked the various agents and naval boards to recommend prospective officers. The committee appointed to direct the construction of the two frigates in Rhode Island decided that a "Captain of Marines shall Inlist forty good men a Lieutenant thirty three, a second Lieutenant Twenty seven before they be intitled to their Commissions."[11] Documentary evidence is fragmentary, but there are indications that Nicholas did have some degree of control. Early in 1777, the captain in charge of recruiting marines in New Hampshire for service on the frigate under construction in Portsmouth answered charges that he was illegally recruiting into the Marines men serving in the state militia. He explained that he was acting under "orders from the Major of Marines."[12]

During the late summer and fall of 1776, British forces captured New York City and pursued George Washington's army across New Jersey. In early December, Nicholas led three Marine companies from Philadelphia to join Washington at Trenton.[13] Their status was unclear to the commander in chief, who wrote to Col. John Cadwalader ordering him to make arrangements for feeding and sheltering the Marines and asking him to let "me know . . . if they came out resolved to act upon Land or meant to confine their Services to the Water only."[14] During the ensuing Trenton-Princeton campaign, they served in Cadwalader's brigade and went into winter quarters first at Morristown and then at Sweets Town, two miles away. There, the number of marines under Nicholas's command dwindled from 131 to 80 as deaths, desertions, and transfers took their toll. Continental Army units suffered even greater losses. By the end of January so many artillerymen had left camp (many men's terms of enlistments were up) that Henry Knox, the commander of the artillery, had more field pieces than he had men to work them. To replace these losses, the three Marine companies were transferred from Nicholas's command to Knox on 1 February 1777. Within six months, three of the four Marine lieutenants had left the service: Isaac Craig had resigned his commission to join a newly formed Pennsylvania artillery regiment, Andrew Porter had transferred to the Continental Army to serve under Knox, and Benjamin Porter had resigned from the Corps when the enlistments of his men ran out in June 1777. Only John Mullin remained in the Marines.

Charles R. Smith, the historian of the *Marine Corps in the Revolution,* concludes that the "incorporation of Nicholas' three companies into the army . . . crushed the idea of an independent corps of Marines, finally reducing them to a series of ship's detachments." The effect on their commander was similar. He "no longer functioned as the head of the Marines but remained essentially a high-ranking officer without assignment."[15] This contrast is basically accurate for the Marine Corps as a whole (though there is little evidence anyone ever contemplated an independent corps of Marines) but implies a much greater change than really took place for Samuel Nicholas. Prior to 1777, Nicholas had fulfilled few of the roles usually ascribed to the commandant. The instance of the commander of the Marine contingent on board the *Raleigh* informing New Hampshire officials that he was acting under "orders from the Major of Marines" took place after, not before, the incorporation of the four Philadelphia companies into the army.

In reality, the fortunes of the Marine Corps were linked, like the service itself, to those of the Continental Navy. Few people realized it at the time, but Hopkins's raid on the Bahamas was to be the Continental Navy's only fleet action. Congress remained determined to build a mighty fleet. On 20 November 1776, it authorized the building of three 74-gun ships-of-the-line, five 36-gun frigates, one 18-gun brig, and a packet-boat, in addition to the thirteen frigates already under contract.[16] Few of these ships would be completed and those which made it to sea did not have long careers.[17]

Plans were proposed for a number of expeditions by squadron forces. John Paul Jones, for example, suggested a cruise along the coast of Africa to attack British trading posts and Robert Morris suggested a five-ship assault on Pensacola in West Florida.[18] Marines would have played important roles in such operations, but none were ever executed. In January 1778, Capt. John Trevett led twenty-six marines in a second capture of New Providence in the Bahamas, but that expedition was planned by Capt. John Peck Rathbun and carried out with only a single ship.[19] Marines also participated in the disastrous 1779 attack on Penobscot, the largest American amphibious operation of the war, but that expedition was largely a Massachusetts enterprise, and militiamen from that state formed the bulk of the forces.[20]

Most marines served on board ships where they had no chance to act independently, sharing in the Continental Navy's few victories and suffering in its many travails. By the end of 1778, the frigates *Hancock, Washington, Effingham, Randolph, Virginia, Raleigh,* and the ships *Alfred* and *Columbus* were all lost with their Marine detachments. Only ten Continental Navy ships remained in operation. Two years later, four detachments were lost at once when their ships surrendered as a part of the capitulation of American forces at Charleston, South Carolina. This left only five Marine detachments assigned to ships, the frigates *Alliance, Deane, Confederacy,* and *Trumbull* and the sloop of war *Saratoga.* The last three were all lost in 1781. In European waters, John Paul Jones made good use of the Marines. In April 1778, he and Lt. Samuel Wallingford led landing parties that raided Whitehaven in England and St. Mary's Isle in Scotland. A day later, Wallingford died in the battle between the *Ranger* and the *Drake.*[21] Marine musketry played an important role in the victory of the *Bonhomme Richard* over HMS *Serapis* and the *Providence* over HMS *Diligent* in 1779 and in the *Alliance*'s defeat of the *Mars* and the *Minerva* in 1781.[22]

In each of these cases, the Marines acted under the direct orders of the naval officers commanding the ship to which they were attached. Samuel Nicholas was, for most of the time, stationed in Philadelphia and did not exercise direct command over the various scattered detachments. That he was in overall command of the companies in the capital is illustrated by the headings used on muster rolls, for example, "A Copy of Return Given in to Major Samuel Nicholas of Men Enlisted by Capt. Robert Mullan. Since Augst 9th 1779 to Jany 1st 1780."[23]

After the Trenton-Princeton campaign, Nicholas served the Continental Congress in a number of capacities. In September 1777, he was sent to Connecticut to obtain arms and lead for the Continental Army. When the British evacuated Philadelphia in June

1778, Nicholas returned to the city and reestablished the Marine Barracks and began recruiting. Most of his time was devoted to administrative work, not all of it directly related to the Marine Corps. In August, for example, he was appointed a signer of Continental currency. He went on a number of special missions for Robert Morris, who at this time was the functional head of both the Continental Treasury and Navy. In 1778, he made a trip to Boston to bring back specie which had arrived from France. In September 1778, he returned to Boston, this time to protect a shipment of army uniforms sent from France. In May 1779, he was also named a signer of Continental bills of credit.[24] Morris and Nicholas had probably known one another before the war, and it was natural that in a time when there was little governmental bureaucracy he should make use of Nicholas in every way possible.

Lines of authority were not clearly drawn between the services at that time, and it was not clear whose responsibility it was to guard the naval prisoners beginning to collect in Philadelphia at the time. Pennsylvania forces had been doing so, but by the summer of 1779 there were simply too many. Congress then ordered the Marine Committee to establish prison ships to hold the prisoners. The committee obtained a ship and asked the Board of War (in effect the Army) to provide guards. When the board refused, Nicholas was ordered to raise "a company of Marines" for such duty. He delegated the task to Capt. Robert Mullan, who began recruiting. It soon became clear that enough men could not be recruited for guard duty and the entire plan was abandoned and the prison ship sold.[25]

Nicholas seems to have chafed under these duties and to have wished for more active service. In developing a table of ranks, the Board of Admiralty had ruled that a major of Marines should serve at sea only on board a ship of the line. Congress had authorized the construction of three such ships, but only one was actually built. It was the *America,* then under construction in Portsmouth, New Hampshire. On 20 November 1779, Nicholas wrote to Congress requesting assignment to the *America* but was denied a transfer from his administrative duties in the capital. In June 1781, Congress appointed John Paul Jones to command the *America* with orders that he complete work on it and put to sea as soon as possible.[26] The appointment of Jones, who was well known for his action, may be what motivated Nicholas to write directly to Congress on 10 August, renewing his request for assignment to the *America.* For some reason, that body referred his letter to the Board of War, not the Board of Admiralty.[27] While the committee deliberated, Robert Morris had more pressing duties for Nicholas. The French frigate *Resolve* had arrived in Boston carrying much needed specie to underwrite the war effort. Someone had to be sent to receive the money and guard that portion of it being returned to Philadelphia. For the latter, Morris thought of Nicholas. "I sent for Major [Nicholas]," he recorded in his diary, "who cheerfully agrees to the Journey and says he can be ready tomorrow."[28] Nicholas left the following day in the company of Tench Francis, who was to arrange the packing and shipping of the specie. The two men successfully completed their mission, and Nicholas arrived back in Philadelphia on 1 November 1781. On the twelfth, he called on Robert Morris who "desired him to make a return to Marine Officers now on Pay," thus indicating that Morris still viewed Nicholas as having administrative responsibilities for the entire Marine Corps. Over the next two weeks Nicholas made requests for payment of "Money on Account of his Pay." The Continental treasury was severely strained at the time, but Morris finally "Ordered 100 Drs. for the Major . . . Which is Absolutely Necessary for [his] Subsistence."[29] Morris found still another way to utilize Nicholas when he appointed him to a court of enquiry to investigate the loss of the frigate *Trumbull.* The three men appointed made their report to Morris, who forwarded it to Congress on 30 November.[30]

Earlier, on 22 November, Congress had finally responded to Nicholas's August request for assignment to the *America* and for recompense for prize money he had been denied the opportunity to earn by being kept in Philadelphia. His letter had been referred to two different committees, one of which recommended that Nicholas "be appointed to command the Marines on board the Ship *America.*" The committees ignored his request for money. In September, Congress accepted most of the committee's proposals, but not the one concerning Nicholas. Congress' reason is not hard to understand. Between August and November, victory had been achieved at Yorktown, and Congress saw little need for a Marine major. (The Navy consisted of only a few small ships in service and the *America,* which was still under construction.) Thus in November, when Congress finally acted on Nicholas's request, it "Resolved, That major [Nicholas's] accounts be settled up to the twenty-fifth day of August 1781, at which time he be considered as retiring from service."[31] This meant that Nicholas was not technically in the Marines during his expedition to Boston.

Thus Nicholas returned to private life. His financial standing in the community was probably helped little by his Revolutionary War service. After "retirement," he engaged in land speculation in the area and probably resumed tavern keeping. Socially he may have risen a few notches. As a former officer he was eligible for membership in the new Society of the Cincinnati. He soon joined and also attended the same Masonic lodge as Benjamin Franklin. In 1782, he stood for election as sheriff of Philadelphia city and county, but the election results are unknown.[32]

Though no longer in the Marines, Nicholas appears to have acted as a spokesman for Marine officers when he wrote to Congress requesting that their pay be adjusted to take into consideration the inflation which was rampant at the time. Nicholas's "memorial" was referred first to the agent of marine and then to the same committee that considered a similar memorial to the secretary at war. That committee reported to Congress on 21 November 1782, suggesting that "Congress make good to the officers of Artillery, Cavalry and Infantry . . . and to the officers of the Marine of the United States . . . the deficiency of their original pay occasioned by the depreciation of Continental bills of credit, in the same manner as it is allowed to the Line of the Army by Act of Congress of the 10th of April 1780." Six months later, Nicholas, describing himself as "late Major of the Marines," joined army officers in another memorial to Congress concerning their pay.[33]

When Nicholas died in 1790, there was no American Marine Corps. There would not be one for almost four years, and there would not be a commandant of the Marine Corps for eight years. Nicholas had not been a commandant in the modern sense of the word. He had been the "senior marine officer." As such, he exercised only part of the powers of a service commander. He neither supervised nor controlled the selection and advancement of officers. Indeed, there were no clear lines of such control. Ship commanders often appointed their own Marine officers, as in the case of John Paul Jones's appointment of Samuel Wallingford in 1777, but so did America's diplomatic agents in France and the Navy Boards established by the Continental Congress in coastal cities. Congress retained the power to confirm or reject such appointments, but in those times of slow communication a man might serve for months and Congress might take weeks before appointments received what were usually routine acceptances.[34]

Likewise, orders were issued to Marine officers through various channels. When at sea, they came under the direct command of the ship's captain, but even when ashore orders were not usually delivered through Nicholas. Congress itself might direct individual officers or Navy boards might, as was the case when William Vernon, acting in the name of the Navy Board of the Eastern Department, ordered Lt. William Waterman to join the frigate *Deane* at Boston.[35]

Congress did not establish formal rules and regulations for the Marine Corps as it did for the Continental Navy, leaving that task to the Board of Admiralty, which seems to have done so without consulting Nicholas. Congressional committees, likewise, planned strategy, again without consultation with Nicholas or any senior naval official. Nicholas's title, "senior marine," was not as lofty as George Washington's or Esek Hopkins's, both of whom were commissioned commander in chief, but the powers he did actually exercise were very similar to theirs. Both Washington and Hopkins commanded the forces serving directly under them, but not those serving in other areas. Washington was consulted, but he did not control strategy and he advised Congress on, but again did not control, officer promotion.[36] Hopkins was appointed commander in chief of the Continental Navy soon after its establishment in 1775, but his failure to follow Congress' instructions in January 1776 and his failure to take action during most of the year that followed led to his suspension from command in March 1777 and, finally, to his formal dismissal from the Navy on 2 January 1778. At no time during his tenure, did he exercise control over vessels not serving directly under him and no one was appointed to the position of commander in chief following his dismissal.[37] In short, none of the armed forces had a single commanding officer in the modern sense of the phrase.

The roles of the Continental marines were more limited than those of their descendants. Afloat they served to maintain discipline and provide small-arms fire during battle. They joined landing parties, but they were never formed into a permanently organized tactical unit for expeditionary employment. It can be argued that the congressional resolution of 10 November 1775 contemplated the formation of such a force, but it was never raised, and the clear implication is that if the battalions were formed, they would remain part of the Continental Army. Lastly, marines served in support of Army units. In 1776, three Marine companies reinforced Washington's hard-pressed Army during the Trenton-Princeton campaign and others served with George Rogers Clark in the Ohio Valley.

When America's independence was won and a treaty signed with Great Britain, Congress disbanded the Continental Navy and with it the last elements of the Continental Marine Corps. In eight years of service afloat, in amphibious operations, and in land operations with the Army, the precedent was set in terms of roles for the later establishment of the U.S. Marine Corps. Samuel Nicholas did not fulfill all the functions which would later be assigned to the commandant of the Marine Corps, but as the "senior marine" he did personally command marines on board ship, the most successful amphibious landing carried out by American forces during the war, and the marines who supported Washington's army. He commanded the companies raised to guard naval prisoners, supervised recruiting in Philadelphia and handled various administrative duties, including the supply and pay of marines. Robert Morris's request for a "return of Marines Officers now on pay" shows that the civilian head of the Navy considered Nicholas to be the Marines' commanding officer, and his 1782 memorial to Congress in behalf of all Corps officers demonstrates that he continued to view himself as their leader even following his official retirement.

2
William Ward Burrows

1798–1805

MAJ. BRENDAN P. RYAN, USMC (RET.)

The vulnerability of American shipping after independence to piracy and the navies of the European powers eventually resulted in the formal establishment of both the United States Navy and Marine Corps. The lack of an inherent ability to provide maritime protection was not immediately felt because for ten years American ships enjoyed the benefits of European naval actions against the most predatory of the North African corsairs. In 1794, Portugal, the last European naval power not to have come to terms with the Barbary states, signed a treaty with Algiers. Almost immediately, corsairs reentered the Atlantic looking for prey. Aware of this danger and spurred on by their threatened business constituents, Congress passed a naval bill on 27 March 1794 authorizing six frigates. The antipathy toward a federal military was strong and the commitment to a navy half-hearted at best, so that the lengthy negotiations with Algiers were completed long before any of the frigates were launched. As a result, in the interest of economy and the pursuit of peace, three of the ships were canceled outright. The other three, launched between 9 May and 22 October 1797, suffered from additional congressional parsimony which delayed their fitting out. The necessary stimulus came from the renewed war between England and France, in which American ships were seized in large numbers. Three frigates, *United States, Constellation,* and *Constitution,* were fitted out, and additional money was appropriated for the resumption of construction on the other three ships authorized three years earlier.[1]

As had been done for the Continental Navy, and in keeping with the practice of other naval powers, a Corps of Marines was authorized on 28 May 1798 to number 33 officers and 832 enlisted marines. All marines for American warships would be drawn from this Corps. Congress also recommended that this Corps be annexed "to the existing military establishment" and that it be supervised by one field-grade officer, a major commandant. President John Adams signed the bill into law on 11 July and appointed

Lt. Col. William Ward Burrows, second commandant.
Oil painting by Lt. Col. John Joseph Capolino, USMCR (Ret.), after a pastel by Miss Edith McCartney, 1944. U.S. Marine Corps Photo.

as the first commandant William Ward Burrows, "a gentleman of accomplished mind and polished manners."[2]

Burrows was an urbane South Carolinian of staunch Federalist politics. His father, a native of England, had emigrated to Charleston, where he married Mary Ward, daughter of a prominent family. William Ward was their second child, born 16 January 1758.[3] William senior prospered as a lawyer and desired the same for his son, sending him to study in England. In 1772, young William was admitted to the Inns of Court. In the dynamic capital of the British Empire, Burrows undoubtedly heard the debates of Pitt,

Fox, Sheridan, North, and the other leading statesmen on the best policy for his homeland. As hostilities approached, Burrows returned to Charleston in 1775.[4] There is only scant evidence of his service in the War for Independence, but enough to suggest that he served in the militia during 1780–81.[5] In 1783, Burrows married Mary Bond, daughter of Thomas Bond, later surveyor general of the United States.

After the war, Burrows prospered as a lawyer and businessman in Philadelphia, dealing in land speculation and other financial ventures. The extent of these activities is unknown, but some indication is given by the lawsuit he brought against William S. Smith. Smith had apparently borrowed a large sum of money from Burrows and for security pledged land that had already been pledged to another. Burrows sued for $194,000, exposing Smith's financial difficulties and causing a scandal that prevented Smith's appointment to the Collectorship of Customs at New York City.[6]

Burrows's activities in Philadelphia in the 1790s included prominent participation in civic activities and in circulating among the political elite of the Federalist party. He developed contacts with Robert Morris, Alexander Hamilton, John Adams, the Pickneys, and Rutledges. He was considered for several appointments but never took office, on one occasion being opposed because of "probable want of industry."[7] Apparently few others doubted his ability or industry, for when the office of commandant of the Marine Corps was created, he was President Adams's known choice. No doubt this was due to Burrows's standing with the Federalist party, but also in part to the political influence of the South Carolina faction, particularly John Rutledge Jr.[8]

Until the creation of the Navy Department in 1798, the Department of War and its secretary, James McHenry, had handled naval affairs. Initially providing marines for naval vessels by drawing upon Army units, McHenry soon began to recruit specifically for service with the Navy. He established a height requirement of "five feet six inches . . . without shoes" and excluded "Mullatos, Negroes, and Indians."[9] The difficulty of administering and controlling the separate detachments convinced McHenry of the need for at least a separate infantry regiment tasked with the responsibility of serving as marines.[10]

The creation of the Marine Corps and Burrows's appointment as commandant answered the need for a central administration. Burrows embarked on a vigorous recruiting campaign to fill the ranks. He established recruiting rendezvous in the major seaports, staffed with Corps officers, to enlist men for ships fitting out in those ports. Burrows's correspondence indicates that the many obstacles to recruiting drove his officers to distraction.[11] Marines were assigned the Army pay scale but served on board ship with the better-paid sailors. The miserable two-dollar enlistment bounty could not match those of the other services. Burrows soon found that he had to modify the enlistment standards established by McHenry, reducing the height requirement to five feet four inches and admitting one foreigner for every three native Americans. The only exceptions were made for drummers and musicians, who were signed on regardless of age, size, or nationality.[12] One recruiting officer confessed to Burrows that the "total stagnation" in recruiting was enough to "baffell [*sic*] the utmost exertions of any Marine recruiting officer."[13]

Authorized a strength of thirty-two officers, Burrows was often forced to accept political appointees with little or no military experience or, what was worse, aptitude. Some were appointed by the president, others by the secretary of the navy, and many through the influence of powerful Federalists.[14] As a result, many of these officers were a burden on the commandant. Burrows was, on several occasions, confronted with an unsatisfactory officer who refused to leave the Corps.[15] Lt. Stephen Geddes, whose drunkenness was well known, was ordered to send in his resignation. This tactic having failed, Burrows charged him with disobedience, neglect of duty, and "ungentlemanlike conduct, in degrading himself by keeping company with a Lieut. of Artillery, and for being seen drunk." Found not guilty by court-martial, Geddes later deserted.[16] Some of Burrows's officers soon found, like Lt. Benjamin Strother, that the service was "in every way disgusting" and resigned.[17]

The major task that confronted Burrows, once the marines were enlisted and serving on board ships of the new Navy, was to give the Corps an institutional identity. The office of the commandant had been created to provide centralized supervision for the recruitment and administration of the widely dispersed Marine detachments. Burrows, however, was determined to do more than that. He had very little military experience himself, but he was sufficiently astute to recognize that this new Corps required military professionalism, stature in the eyes of Congress, and a good public image if it was going to survive. Burrows approached this challenge on three separate levels: within the Corps, where high standards of appearance and conduct were set; within the operating Navy, where the duties and status of the Marines had to be established; and within the Department of the Navy, where the independence and integrity of the Corps had to be asserted.

The task of policing the Corps was Augean. Burrows's officers were sometimes faced with motley detachments that signed on for a myriad of reasons. A year after the Corps was formed, Capt. Daniel Carmick still found the detachment on board the *Constitution* a "shabby set of animals."[18] Desertion was rife among the detachments stationed in the port cities, and Burrows was finally driven to offer bounties to his officers for apprehended deserters.[19] As desertion continued to plague the Corps, Burrows's response to it escalated. In 1798, he advocated "100 lashes . . . will have great effect," but within the year he despaired, admitting that while two hundred lashes had been administered to one deserter, "we will never cure this evil till we can shoot one or two of them."[20]

Marines were often of disgraceful appearance due to a cumbersome supply system dependent upon Navy agents. Lt. Reuben Lilly pointed out that winter clothing was a "very considerable inducement and if provided . . . would greatly facilitate the recruiting service." But Burrows could only promise him one watch coat for every three recruits.[21] Burrows moved Headquarters Marine Corps out of Philadelphia and into a camp on the outskirts of the city to not only reduce the cost of rented quarters but also escape the distractions of the city and to be able to drill and more closely discipline the recruits.[22] Burrows insisted that the officers commanding detachments establish appropriate standards of conduct, repeating in his letters to each of them that "every sentry be fully dressed and powdered if possible" and that no sentry be relieved without the presence of a noncommissioned officer. He understood the importance of the sergeant's role, cautioning officers that "if the authority of the sergeant is taken away by disgracing him, he must lose all authority over his men."[23]

While continuing to raise the Corps's military professionalism, Burrows applied his social talents to establishing the Corps's public image. Beginning with a ten-dollar contribution from each of his officers, he provided the Marine Corps with fifers and drummers and established the Marine Band at Headquarters, where it entertained the citizens while the Marines paraded. Burrows also lent the band to perform for other organizations and events.[24] In the summer of 1800, when the government moved to Washington, D.C., Burrows overcame his reluctance to leave Philadelphia and relocated Headquarters and the band to the new federal city. With the Marine Corps at the center of "the mysterious web of party politics, personal feuds, gossip, newspaper stories, boarding house associations, and land speculation," the band continued to provide the "amenities that had existed in Philadelphia" with outdoor concerts and accompanying church services in the House of Representatives.[25] Burrows rented temporary quarters for himself and his officers from which he conducted the business of the Corps, although he disliked having to be "under the same roof as [his] officers." In 1801, he was instrumental in selecting the site of the new Marine Barracks and Commandant's House, which, despite Jeffersonian economies, were funded as part of the improvement of the city. Burrows's friendship with President Jefferson was unquestionably useful to the commandant and his Corps, although the remainder of the Democratic party had little use for the Federalist appointee.[26]

Burrows's campaign to improve the appearance and reputation of the Marine Corps was successful in the long run. A far greater task was carving out the Corps's status and duties within the Navy. The basic problem was ignorance: no one knew what marines were supposed to do. Aside from the obvious duties in battle of providing small-arms fire and boarding parties, Burrows could only draw on the experience of the Continental and British Marines to insist that his men be "excused from going aloft." Even this attempt to establish a peacetime distinction between marines and sailors was uncertain. Eventually, Burrows settled on ensuring that his marines were not ordered into the rigging but that "for the good of the service" (i.e., smooth relations with the ship captains), they could be permitted and even encouraged to do so.[27]

The issue was simple: ship captains prescribed the duties of the crew, regardless of their service, and when able seamen were in short supply, marines filled the ranks. Lt. Robert Harwood voiced this general lack of knowledge among Corps officers when he wrote to Burrows: "When I came aboard the ship [*Baltimore*] I was entirely at a loss to know the Marines' duty on board a ship of war, nor did I know who to apply to for information on the subject . . . When I arrived here in Hampton Roads I made it my duty to go to Norfolk to get, if possible, some information . . . but could not obtain any."[28]

Burrows could only reply with the simple prohibition on allowing marines to be ordered aloft. While unsure of what his marines were supposed to do, Burrows was sure of what he did not want them doing. He was incensed by reports that marines were being used to perform a wide variety of sailors' duties, which often resulted in the ruin of their uniforms, and, on occasion, acting as servants to ships' officers.[29] He struggled against the overall attitude of the Navy officers toward marines, demanding just treatment and respect. Marine officers did not share in prize money at the same proportion as Navy officers of equivalent rank, but rather, as Burrows saw it, "with the men who were always kept out of danger," that is, the purser or chaplain. He argued, "There is no officer on board the ship more approved of in action than the Marine officer, and therefore ought to be rewarded accordingly."[30] A source of constant irritation to Burrows and his officers was the treatment of the marines' uniforms. Duty on board ship could reduce a detachment's uniforms to tatters and its men to a state of undress. The sailors' harassment of marines increased these difficulties. Despite all precautions, uniforms were damaged when the marines performed sailors' duties, hats blew away, and the ship's crew often "as a matter of amusement" threw the marines' belongings overboard on the pretext of clearing the ship for action.[31]

Such rough conditions inevitably led to friction and hatred between the Marine Corps officer who tried to protect his men and the officers of the ship. On several occasions, Marine officers, interceding on behalf of their men, were insulted and struck by Navy officers, with the inevitable result of a duel. Although he detested duels fought unnecessarily, Burrows encouraged the defense of honor, charging his officers "to put up with no ill usage from any of them." Few Marine officers needed such encouragement to defend their honor or the rights of their men. The most famous of these incidents involved Lt. Henry Caldwell of the USS *Trumbull.* Burrows was outraged that Caldwell had been struck by a Navy officer. Caldwell was advised to bring charges against the officer, but with regard to personal honor and the Corps's reputation that would not suffice. "It is my duty," Burrows wrote, "to support my Officers and I will do it with my life, but they must deserve it." To be worthy of this support, Caldwell was expected to demand satisfaction and was abjured by his commandant: "Don't let me see you 'till you have wiped away this disgrace." Burrows commended to Caldwell the example of Lt. Anthony Gale (who became the third lieutenant colonel commandant) who, when "struck by an officer of the Navy . . . called the Lieut. out, and shot him."[32] Burrows urged the secretary of the navy to intervene in the conflict between Marine officers and their Navy counterparts, pointing out that it was important to "introduce humanity and politeness" into the relationships between officers, "as our Navy is in its infancy; we had better begin early with these qualities, that these form the basis of our future conduct, or disgrace must follow."[33]

Burrows fought his greatest battle for the independence of the Corps within the Department of the Navy. For the office of the commandant to have any meaning or justification, Burrows recognized that he had to insist on freedom from interference in matters of personnel and duties. He resented the Navy assuming that the Marine Corps detachments on ships were part of the crew and therefore at the disposal of the ship's officers. When a marine in the *Baltimore* was enlisted into the Navy over the objections of the detachment commander, Burrows wrote to the secretary of the navy that such conduct was unacceptable and suggested "a power I conceive was never intended to be rested in any Navy officer. My officers can have little encouragement to enlist men and be at the trouble of instructing them in the Manual Exercise if they can thus be taken away from them."[34]

Such an issue was only a skirmish compared to the battle Burrows fought with Capt. Thomas Truxton, not only over personnel issues, but eventually over the survival of the Corps. Truxton was the first important architect of the American naval tradition, instilling in the infant United States Navy concepts of organization, discipline, and duty which became the bedrock of future growth and performance. He was also an egoist, jealous of his rank and influence within the Navy, and his frigate victories in the Quasi-War with France encouraged a dangerous conceit. Truxton had not waited for the Marine Corps to define the duties of the shipboard detachments, but had devised his own, directing the marines on his ship to train with and exercise their small arms twice a day; remain fit and clean; post sentries and be prepared to form a landing party; and when necessary "pull, haul, and heave at the Capstan."[35] These were the clearest instructions issued to the Marines in the early period, but Truxton considered his authority over the detachment to be more extensive than just issuing standing orders. Upon returning from the Caribbean in 1801, he intended to take with him to his new command Lt. Bartholemew Clinch, who had commanded with distinction in action the Marine detachment of the *Constellation.* Burrows, determined to preserve administrative control over his Corps, insisted that he "would never allow an [*sic*] naval officer to change [Burrows's orders] . . . nor would [he] submit to it even in the Secretary." Burrows assigned another officer to Truxton, who responded by insisting that it was the commandant's "province to furnish the officers of Marines and Marine privates," and that was the limit of his duty, but he must never "attempt to dictate to the Commander of a man of war, who is answerable only to the President of the United States."[36] Burrows recognized the inherent danger to the Corps, and to the commandancy, in such an assertion. He protested to the secretary that "if Navy officers can displace [Marine] officers" without his consent, there would be no need of a commandant or a Headquarters staff. He insisted, therefore, that all decisions regarding the disposition of the Marines be made through his office.[37]

Burrows's dogged insistence on his authority over Marine Corps personnel appointments, coupled with continued friction between Marine and Navy officers over rank and authority, infuriated Truxton and convinced him that the Corps was more trouble than it was worth. Truxton wrote to Burrows of his continued opposition, insisting that "the youngest sea officer in the Navy takes seniority over the oldest Marine officer in service." Blaming marines for disrupting the peace on board ships with "improper ideas of rank," Truxton again criticized Burrows for assigning officers without consulting ship captains. "This is not the way to preserve that harmony so much to be desired," he said. Professing himself "sensible to the unimportance of the Marine Corps, especially in time of peace," Truxton made no secret of his willingness to campaign for the Corps's abolition if Burrows was not "put to right."[38]

The outcome of the conflict was to define more clearly the relationship between the Marine Corps and the Navy. Acting Secretary of the Navy Henry Dearborn, in a circular letter to all ship captains, directed that marines were directly responsible to the commanding officer but would not be ordered to perform any acts of "mere seamanship." Burrows successfully kept control of personnel assignments out of the hands of the ship captains, but only at the cost of relinquishing it to the supervision of the secretary of the navy. Marine Corps officers, however, were to have "no rank on board of a ship of the United States, over any of the officers of such a ship." Referring to the case on *Baltimore,* the circular directed that marines could be transferred into the Navy by ship captains but "subject . . . to the superintending control and ratification" of the department.[39]

In August 1800, Burrows prophesied to a close friend that Thomas Jefferson and his party would win the impending election: "I suppose they will try to ferrit [*sic*] me out of the Corps but I am convinced they will never disband the Corps."[40] Burrows was correct in both cases. Promoted to lieutenant colonel by act of Congress on 22 April 1800, Burrows became the focal point of Jeffersonian attacks on the Corps. Despite his personal friendship with Jefferson, Burrows's "militant Federalism, and his use of it to bind his relationships with his officers had only increased tensions" with the House of Representatives.[41] Burrows's promotion was viewed as Federalist patronage, rewarding him for political loyalty rather than military excellence.[42] The assault on the commandant was postponed while the Barbary Wars continued, but in March 1804, the Jeffersonians moved against the Corps. Burrows was by this time worn out and seriously ill, devastated by the loss of his wife a year earlier. In February 1804, he requested and received permission to go on a leave to recover his health.[43] On 18 February 1804, the House began to inquire into the financial records of the Marine Corps and into Burrows's personal account books. The committee formed to conduct the investigation recommended the abolition of the office of commandant, a reduction in officer strength, and what would have been oppressive financial oversight of the Corps's budget. Burrows was found to have an unexplained deficit of nine thousand dollars. The haphazard accounting of the Corps's early years, and confusion over just what the Marine Corps was authorized to spend and how it was spent, is to blame for the discrepancy. Nowhere was there the slightest evidence of dishonorable conduct on Burrows's part. Several years later the books were deciphered and all but a few hundred dollars were accounted for. Federalist strength in Congress was sufficient to prevent any of the punitive recommendations of the committee from being enacted, but Burrows, unable to recover his health, submitted his resignation on 13 March 1804.[44]

William Ward Burrows died on 13 March 1805 at the age of forty-seven. His greatest accomplishment was the successful establishment of the Marine Corps's identity as a viable, if somewhat circumscribed, military organization. From the beginning of his commandancy he was faced with daunting challenges in all areas of command, and his success in meeting those challenges was varied. His struggle against the threat of absorption of the Corps by the Navy, characterized by his personal conflict with Truxton, won for the Corps at least partial freedom to govern its own ranks. Burrows's outspoken Federalist politics were valuable political capital until 1801, when he entered into an adversarial relationship with the dominant party. Nevertheless, he established an important precedent of close cooperation with and sensitivity to the legislative and executive powers of the government. While his successors were wise to avoid the outspoken advocacy of one political party, they could not ignore his successful orchestration of Marine Corps interests at many different levels of public activity.

3

Franklin Wharton

1804–1818

COL. GERALD C. THOMAS JR., USMC (RET.)

In March 1804, news of his appointment as commandant reached Capt. Franklin Wharton (23 July 1767–1 September 1818) at his post at the Philadelphia Navy Yard. He had completed nearly four years commanding the Marine Barracks since returning from sea duty in April 1800; in fact, he had become a marine there six years earlier. Even before the Marine Corps formally organized in July 1798, the young Philadelphia businessman had accepted a lieutenant's commission and command of the Corps detachment in the 44-gun frigate *United States.*[1]

The summer of 1798 had been an exciting time in the nation's capital of Philadelphia as Congress established the Navy and debated war with France. In all their major seaports, Americans made ready for war, and in Philadelphia orders were issued on 3 July 1798 for the *United States* to prepare for sea. Within the next week, Congress abrogated the treaty with France and, among many other measures, established the United States Marine Corps. Though critical to his future career, this could not have been of any immediate concern to Lieutenant Wharton, as he spent the same week busily recruiting, organizing, and outfitting his fifty-man detachment for imminent action against the French in the West Indies.[2]

First launched of the new frigates, the *United States* was Philadelphia-built, Philadelphia-manned, and commanded by the city's hero of the Revolution, John Barry. Sailing on 13 July, Wharton celebrated his thirty-first birthday on board ship and, unknown to him at the time, on 3 August, was promoted to captain, the appropriate rank for the senior Marine officer of a 44-gun frigate. During the next month, the *United States* cruised off Barbados and on two occasions captured French privateers after exciting chases. But while Wharton and his marines may have gone to battle stations, they only watched as the Frenchmen surrendered as soon as they were overtaken and a few token shots fired. Back to home port with her prizes, the *United States* returned to sea in mid-October but turned back after being damaged in a severe Atlantic storm.

Lt. Col. Franklin Wharton, third commandant.
Artist unknown. U.S. Marine Corps Photo 526643.

During this period in port, Wharton received his promotion to captain, and a new junior officer joined his detachment in November.[3] Returning to the Caribbean in December, the *United States* sunk a privateer in February 1799 and rescued her fifty-eight-man crew. Two attempts were needed to exchange these prisoners for an equal number of Americans held at the French island of Guadeloupe, the first attempt being answered only by fire from the French fort. Later in the month, the *United States* recaptured an

American ship from its French prize crew, and in March it captured both a privateer and her American prize.

By this time, the *United States* was flagship of a seven-ship squadron deployed to protect American ships trading in the West Indies. Relieved in late April 1799, it convoyed home some thirty of these merchantmen, arriving at New Castle, Delaware, on 10 May 1799. Captain Wharton went ashore to take charge of a large detail of French prisoners, some to be exchanged and others to be sent to confinement facilities at Lancaster, Pennsylvania. Here he would have met the officer bringing the prisoner detail from Lancaster, Capt. Daniel Carmick, his junior by one number and the man who became his best friend in the Corps.[4] The summer of 1799 was spent in uneventful cruising off the Atlantic seaboard. In November 1799, the *United States* sailed to France carrying the American envoys to negotiate peace. With negotiations successfully concluded, the ship returned home in April 1800, and Captain Wharton left her to command the Marine Barracks at Philadelphia.

In these twenty months of war at sea, Wharton had a chance to recruit and equip his own detachment, to learn the sound and smell of combat and the intricacies of fighting a warship, to maintain shipboard discipline under conditions of both boredom and danger, and perhaps also to experience prisoner exchange under a flag of truce. These lessons would provide him an invaluable insight into the principal mission of the Corps, and he could hardly have gained this seasoning under a better captain and commodore than the redoubtable John Barry.

Wharton's command at the Philadelphia Navy Yard involved recruiting and training marines, provisioning a variety of security details, and handling much of the procurement for the Corps. As a member of one of Philadelphia's most prominent merchant families, he was well qualified to do this. Early Federal Philadelphia was hailed as the "Athens of America" and was not only the new Republic's most populous city but also its cultural capital and busiest port. In addition, it was the center for manufacturing, overseas trade, and banking and finance.[5] Two months after Wharton's assignment there, the federal government moved from Philadelphia to "Washington City." Marine Headquarters and a small Marine detachment also departed for the new capital. Newly promoted Lieutenant Colonel Commandant Burrows accomplished much in the crude encampment on the Potomac, but it was simply not possible for him to arrange for supply of the Marine Corps in that wilderness. Captain Wharton remained in Philadelphia to tend to these business affairs, and the city became the Corps's chief supply depot, continuing as such for more than a century.[6]

The Philadelphia Navy Yard was located adjacent to the shipyard of Joshua Humphreys, America's most talented ship designer and a prominent commercial builder. By chance it was at the foot of Wharton Street, and the Marine captain was surrounded by Wharton family businesses representing the maritime interests of the city—overseas export trade, shipbuilding, marine insurance, and the like. Franklin Wharton was the youngest of eighteen children of "Duke Joseph," a leading Philadelphia merchant until his death in 1776, and cousins and older half-brothers had been prominent in state and national government since the Revolution.[7] Before joining the Marines, this youngest family member was associated with half-brother Samuel's business on Second Street. He also served in the minor post of city water inspector and made an unsuccessful run for elective office in May 1798.[8]

Now launched in an independent career, duty as Philadelphia's senior marine must have been a happy time for Wharton, as he married in October 1800 and his first two children were born there. During this same period, older brother Robert was elected to the second of fifteen terms as Federalist mayor of Philadelphia, and other family members continued to prosper in business and finance. There can be little doubt that Wharton brought to the Corps commercial contacts and a social status as high as that of any commandant before or since.

Elevation to the commandancy brought new problems for Franklin Wharton as he entered the political world of a capital controlled by President Jefferson's Democratic-Republican party. The populist, antimilitary Republicans had opposed creation of a federal Navy in 1798 and were very reluctant to support it once they came to power in 1801. Soon after his inauguration, Jefferson reduced the number of privates authorized for the Marine Corps from 890 to 400, and for their first year in office his administration planned to reduce the Navy budget by two-thirds. Federalist appointees in all branches of the government were replaced by Republicans, and Jefferson personally supervised the dismissal of a number of Army officers suspected of anti-Republican loyalties.[9]

At the time of Wharton's appointment in 1804, partisan harassment of Federalist-appointed judiciary by Congress reached new heights with the investigation of Associate Justice Samuel Chase in the House and the impeachment trial of Judge John Pickering by the Senate. A similar effort the year before had sought dismissal of Federalist Burrows by eliminating the position of commandant of the Marine Corps. That measure passed the House but failed by four votes in the Senate.[10] The commandancy was saved, but in February 1804, Congress began a new investigation of Burrows. With both health and personal finances already in ruins, the commandant resigned from the Marine Corps. Wharton's nomination as his replacement was based only on his being the next officer in seniority, the "motion for abolishing the Office . . . having been rejected." It remained to be seen how the politically inexperienced Federalist Wharton would fare in Washington.[11]

First, there was the trouble with the Barbary states. The primary mission of the Marine Corps was to supply detachments for the fleet, and first priority was given the squadron deployed to the Mediterranean. For the first fifteen months of Wharton's commandancy, the chief operational mission was to support the sporadic fighting involved in the blockade of Tripoli. Almost as soon as Wharton became commandant, President Jefferson decided to send out a second squadron and extraordinary efforts were required to find marines for the additional deploying ships.[12] Marines engaged in several of the small actions against Tripoli in August and September 1804 and, notably, in the seizure of Derna the following April. Peace finally came in June 1805, but a squadron remained deployed to the Mediterranean for the next several years, a significant number of Wharton's marines always with it.

Even before the second squadron sailed for the Mediterranean in the summer of 1804, Wharton was required to send a large detachment to New Orleans. This new post proved to be nearly as challenging as Tripoli, flanked as it was by the two Spanish territories of Mexico and West Florida. The latter was a particularly troublesome neighbor, as weak Spanish rule allowed it to become a haven for pirates, hostile Indians, fugitive slaves, and troublesome American squatters. The man selected to lead the New Orleans detachment was Wharton's close friend and contemporary, Capt. Daniel Carmick. The detachment was to have a confused history of being established in the spring of 1804, recalled in May 1805, reestablished at reduced strength in November 1805, reinforced in December 1806, reduced the following summer, and finally established in 1809 as a three-hundred-man garrison commanded by newly promoted Major Carmick. Such were the conditions of the Marine Corps mission as Congress struggled to deal with the security requirement posed by this remote yet strategic territory.[13]

The first problem raised by establishment of the Marine command in New Orleans was a confused chain of command, with Captain Carmick reporting initially to the Army commander, then to the local Navy officer once a base was established, and later to the territorial governor for special missions. The Corps in New Orleans manned defensive works outside the city, provided guards for the gunboats which began service there in 1806, and took part in campaigns against pirates and renegades in nearby West Florida and in the occupation of Baton Rouge, when the United States annexed that portion of West Florida in 1810. Establishment of this garrison ashore was the first "as the President may direct" mission, and Wharton, ably assisted by Carmick, was careful to keep it on those terms.[14]

Such missions may have been portentous for the evolution of the Corps, but the new commandant's most important work was to set his own house in order. In his first week, Wharton issued orders reemphasizing discipline, which he recognized as the hallmark of the Corps and one of the prime factors distinguishing marines. Compared with either soldiers or sailors, marines were far more likely to be assigned in small, isolated detachments with only a junior noncommissioned officer in charge and therefore a high state of discipline was crucial to their performance. This inherent challenge was only reinforced by Jefferson's attempt to restructure the Navy into a fleet of small gunboats. Generally, each gunboat was assigned a guard of a sergeant, a corporal, and eight to twelve privates, but some had only a corporal and four privates. These gunboats were dispersed to all of America's coastal cities without provision for Marine officer supervision.[15]

Following Burrows's example, Wharton kept up a flow of correspondence to his far-flung commanders, monitoring their problems and issuing instructions as necessary. One of the most vexing difficulties exacerbated by Marine Corps dispersion was uniform supply, a chronic problem and not a trivial one in view of the importance of ceremonial duties in the Marine mission. On extended deployments to the Mediterranean or to the bayous of Louisiana, Marine leaders were hard put to keep their men presentable. Wharton, fresh from duty as the Corps's principal uniform procurer, demonstrated how important he regarded the matter by issuing the Marine Corps's first uniform regulations within a week of taking command. Uniforms were standardized, and the new commandant even persuaded the secretary of the navy to authorize "fatigue dress for the private Marines."[16]

One of the consequences of Jefferson's anti-Navy attitude was to make it difficult to find men of suitable stature to serve as secretary of the navy.[17] This was of critical importance to the commandant, since the secretary was his immediate superior and, under Jeffersonian concepts of extreme civilian control, personally managed the day-to-day administration of both the Navy and Marine Corps to an unusual degree. The secretary had both operational and administrative authority over the Navy, writing basic instructions to deploying commodores as well as directly supervising ship captains, yard superintendents, naval purchasing agents, and, through the commandant, the operation of the Marine Corps. That this authority was exercised only through the commandant was crucial to the integrity of that position, and each of the four secretaries under whom Wharton served in his fourteen years as commandant extended him that respect. Not all of his successors were so fortunate.

Mismanagement of government funds was among the charges Congress had brought against Burrows, and now Wharton had to account for the admittedly chaotic Marine Corps funds with particular care. Here his business background must have been useful, as his staff was limited to three lieutenants: an adjutant, a quartermaster, and a paymaster. During these first few years of Wharton's commandancy, he brought accounting under control and established a solid reputation for frugality and sound management.

This success came about through his detailed supervision of all procurement, especially of the construction of barracks buildings for the marines of the initial navy yards. Throughout his commandancy, Wharton assumed personal responsibility for all Marine Corps construction and, based on a War Department precedent, was allowed a 4 percent commission on the contracts he supervised.[18] Perhaps because of Wharton's known abilities, the yard superintendents did not interfere in his supervision of these activities within their yards. He also kept the armory for the Washington Navy Yard and assisted in the management of the Navy hospital there.

The secretary of the navy expected Wharton to be a very active supervisor of barracks construction, and this duty required very frequent travel to Philadelphia, New York, and Boston. During most of Wharton's commandancy, Headquarters correspondence was often signed by the senior officer present, who actually became acting commandant for routine administration. The correspondence shows the large amount of time demanded by personal supervision of construction at widely separated sites.[19] Thus Wharton's business background was put to good use serving an administration which begrudged every dollar spent on the military. Perhaps this was only his way of maintaining cordial relations with his political superiors, but it proved an effective one and made best use of the resources provided him to the long-term benefit of the Corps.

Another of Wharton's contributions was to establish the Marine Corps and its commandant in the ceremonial life of the nation's capital. For more than a decade he ensured that the Corps was a prominent participant in the president's celebration of New Year's Day, Washington's birthday, the Fourth of July, and in the inaugural parade and other ceremonies of state. Wharton's private means and high social background assured that the lieutenant colonel commandant was among the key organizers of every major social event. It was also during his commandancy that the Marine Band became solidly entrenched as the "President's Own." With a place in the business community due to his extensive investment in rental properties and as a prominent member of Washington society, Wharton was called to serve on numerous boards and organizing committees as churches, banks, a subscription library, and the like were established in the growing city.[20] Nor did partisan politics chill the commandant's personal relations with President Jefferson or his successors. Following his initial purge of the most extreme Federalists, Jefferson adopted a wise policy of winning over the moderates, and with the amiable Wharton he succeeded.[21]

But Wharton's duties were by no means confined to social Washington. By 1808, he had established the barracks as the effective center of the Corps. Here officers returned from sea duty to the staff, for detail as diplomatic couriers, or other such assignments where he could personally observe their performance and where they might even have opportunity to serve as acting commandant. Whatever troops were available at the Washington Barracks were paraded daily. In this way, Wharton's headquarters served as a training center for both officers and enlisted marines.[22] Marine commitments remained heavy throughout his commandancy, and as soon as Mediterranean operations slacked, they were replaced by Indian fights and response to disorders in both East and West Florida. Since marines were operating ashore in these situations, local Army commanders generally assumed they were subject to Army orders, often contrary to the prior orders of the secretary of the navy. This became a particular problem for Capt. John Williams in the Patriot's War at Amelia Island in 1812.[23] But the lieutenant colonel commandant was also able to exploit this ambiguity on occasion by claiming for the Corps such Army benefits as enlistment bonuses and prohibition against flogging.

Wharton's greatest trial came with the War of 1812, for which the nation was so notoriously ill-prepared and during which his own conduct was uninspired. Great events occurred on three widely separated fronts—the Atlantic, the Great Lakes, and New Orleans—and on each, the Marine Corps made a small contribution. Yet even that was made with difficulty as Congress established unprecedented recruiting incentives for the Army and overlooked the Marine Corps; thus, during the entire war, it was never possible for Wharton to achieve his authorized strength.[24]

The question of the Corps's relation to the Army came up on every front during this confused, incompetent war but was never really resolved. An example was the Great Lakes front, where there was considerable Army–Marine Corps interaction. There the secretary of the navy's detailed instructions to his overall commander, Commodore Isaac Chauncey, made no mention of the Marines, despite the fact that he set forth specific guidance for Army-Navy cooperation.[25] Marines and soldiers did cooperate, and when marines were not available, Army units provided men to fulfill their function on board ships on the lakes, but all of this was accomplished by lower-level commanders without definitive guidance from Wharton or any other Washington-based authority.

In the second year of the war, the commandant suffered a personal loss with the death of his wife in August 1813 after a long, painful illness. Six motherless children added to Wharton's burdens. One year later, he suffered through the evacuation of the capital and its seizure and burning by the British. He incurred severe criticism for simply evacuating along with the rest of the government rather than joining his Headquarters detachment in the field. In fact, the detachment had been formed for some time under command of the adjutant, Capt. Samuel Miller, and Wharton had not previously accompanied them on local deployments. However, Wharton made no effort to join them when battle was imminent. Ever the efficient manager, he was seeing to the care of Miller's casualties from the fighting at Bladensburg earlier in the day when "some balls began flying about" as the British troops entered Washington. He led the small barracks guard in an orderly evacuation via the navy yard, in the course of which he saved the Headquarters' funds and records.[26] But the tale of his retreat grew in the telling, and some of his own officers accused him of deliberate cowardice.

Some of these wounds seemed less bitter in the joy and national celebration of an honorable peace, but for the Corps it was soon business as usual. More marines were again needed as Decatur's squadron deployed in a new war against Algiers and other marines fought pirates in Florida and along the Texas coast. It took some time following the war to settle into a new peacetime posture, but in January 1816, Wharton was required to reduce enlisted strength to one thousand while the number of officers remained constant. The real postwar definition of the Marine Corps came with the Peace Establishment Act of 1817, which reduced officer strength to 50 and set enlisted strength at 924. The difficult part of implementing this was in the forced dismissal of excess officers as both majors and eleven of the Corps's twenty authorized captains were eliminated in April.

Only one major remained after Major Carmick's death in 1816, and there was little question that Wharton could dispense with his services. This was Maj. John Hall, a contemporary who was commissioned less than a month after Wharton in the summer of 1798. Hall had an exemplary record in the fighting around Tripoli and had served with distinction in a number of important posts, not least of which was command of the guard in *Chesapeake* during her destruction by the British, where he was one of the few officers to escape public censure. Hall became the leader of the critics of Wharton's 1814 performance and was sent to the Mediterranean with Decatur's squadron in 1815. But his outspoken criticism continued, and he was recalled.[27]

As the Corps shrunk and Wharton showed no readiness to resign (there being no such thing as retirement), six brevet majors were looking at a long future without hope of promotion. It developed that the most ambitious of these, Archibald Henderson, precipitated a crisis by preferring charges of neglect of duty and conduct unbecoming an officer against the lieutenant colonel commandant. Both charges struck at Wharton's leadership style, the first charging him with not taking personal command of the small groups of marines then available for drill and training at Headquarters, a role he considered suitable for a captain, and for several misunderstandings in routine Headquarters administration. The second was vague but was understood to refer to his aversion to dueling and failure to call out a junior who questioned his leaving the capital in 1814.

The court-martial of senior officers was not uncommon in the early 1800s and matters which in later years might well have been referred to inquiries or formal investigations were tried by court-martial. Still, this incident can only be assessed as bizarre in all its aspects.[28] First, the ambiguous status of the Corps was apparent as a Navy court was convened, but found to lack jurisdiction and the charges against Wharton were referred to an Army court. Under then-current regulations, Army courts allowed members junior to the accused and the court was composed of two Army colonels and five lieutenant colonels. Uncomfortable in its lack of Marine Corps members, the court delayed for ten days while this membership question was referred to the attorney general of the United States. He found no such requirement but passed the question onto President James Monroe, whose decision was to add additional officers of both the Army and Marine Corps. Two more Army officers were added, along with Bvt. Maj. Richard Smith and Capt. of Marines Robert Wainwright. Wainwright, knowing he would be called as a prosecution witness requested to be excused, but was denied by the court!

The lieutenant colonel commandant surrendered his sword to the president of the court, Col. William King, 4th Infantry, and with Brevet Major Henderson acting as prosecutor, the trial finally began on 20 September 1817. The court quickly dismissed the charge of conduct unbecoming an officer (a duel being in itself an illegal act) and, after hearing only three prosecution witnesses and Wharton's dignified and cogent rebuttal, acquitted him of both charges.

This was a vindication for the aging commandant, but also more than he could bear. His health failed, and much of the spring and summer of 1818 was consumed in medical consultations and visits to curative springs. Returning from Saratoga in late August, he reached New York City but was unable to go on. He died there on 1 September 1818 and was buried at Old Trinity Church following an elaborate military funeral.[29]

The legacy of Franklin Wharton is clear: he presided over the Marine Corps during fourteen of its most turbulent years, inheriting a sound foundation, building on it, and passing on a Marine Corps that was small, efficient, and already possessed of a record of military smartness, usefulness, frugality, and heroism. The individual marine was a disciplined, brave, and reliable soldier, his officers were both gallant and competent, and his Corps was managed with a careful frugality. Wharton himself was an effective peacetime manager but lacked the warrior spirit, a character trait that was, in the eyes of some of his officers, especially those who coveted his position, his fatal defect.

4

Anthony Gale

1819–1820

LT. COL. MERRILL L. BARTLETT, USMC (RET.)

The death of Franklin Wharton in September 1818 laid bare the factionalism among senior officers of the Corps. One clique, led by the indefatigable Archibald Henderson, charged that Wharton's faintheartedness in the face of the British advance on the capital during the War of 1812 had disgraced the Corps; the same group alleged that Wharton and other officers devoted themselves to their private lives and business ventures, ignoring their professional duties. Another important coterie consisted of officers, close to the now-deceased, who had achieved their positions and rank by currying favor with shore-based politicians and senior officers of the Navy. A third group of field-grade Marine officers fell into another category, senior officers commanding barracks who only wanted to be left alone by everyone. Bvt. Maj. Anthony Gale belonged to this last group.

An immigrant from Ireland in 1793, Gale traced his paternal lineage to Col. Oliver Gale, who came from England in the train of British forces sent to occupy Ireland during the reign of Henry VIII (1509–47). Born in 1761 to Ann Delany and Anthony Gale, he left his parents, two sisters, and four brothers to seek his fortune in the New World. When the fledgling U.S. Marine Corps sought applicants for commissions in 1798, Gale became one of the sixty-three successful candidates who served during the Quasi-War with France. His commission was dated 26 July 1798. Until December of that year, Gale served with the Marines, guarding and moving French prisoners of war from New Castle, Delaware, to Philadelphia. As the New Year approached, Gale's superior, Capt. James McNight, reported that after a forced march of eighteen miles, "Lieutenant Gale is very hearty and begs me to make his respects to you."[1] Following his initial tour of duty ashore, Gale received orders to sea during the winter of 1798.

Few records survive concerning Gale's brief tenure as commandant, and we have no image or portrait.

Gale's first tour of sea duty was in *Ganges,* a 24-gun frigate. The U.S. government purchased the former merchant vessel on 3 May 1798 as the first man-of-war for the fledgling Navy in the face of increasing hostilities with revolutionary France. On 11 May, Secretary of War James McHenry ordered the *Ganges*'s prospective captain to enlist one first lieutenant, one second lieutenant, one sergeant, two corporals, twenty-one privates, and two musicians for a twelve-month cruise. *Ganges,* under Capt. Thomas Tingley and with a complement of 220 men, sailed to the Caribbean to take up station in protection of the Jamaica trade; Gale commanded its Marine detachment beginning in December 1798 after the transfer of 1st Lt. Daniel Carmick. Returning to Philadelphia for repairs in March 1799, *Ganges* then sailed again to the Caribbean, capturing the French privateers *Vainquere, Eliza, La Rabateuse, John L'Eugene,* and *L'Esperance.* Gale left the ship on 15 November 1799 aglow with praise from the commandant of the Marine Corps over an untoward incident involving one of the *Ganges*'s officers.

When Navy lieutenant Allan MacKenzie relieved a Marine sentry from his duties and placed him in irons, Gale called MacKenzie a rascal and struck him. A duel followed, and Gale killed MacKenzie. Gale's conduct earned Burrows's approval: "On board the Ganges, about 12 mo[nths] ago, Lt. Gale, was struck by an officer of the Navy. The captain took no notice of the business and Gale got no satisfaction on the cruise. The moment he arrived he call'd the lieutenant out, and shot him; afterwards, politeness was restored. . . . It is hoped that this may be a lesson to the Navy officers to treat the Marines as well as their officers with some respect."[2]

Whether Burrows ordered Gale from the *Ganges* to another ship because of the duel with MacKenzie is unknown; however, on 15 November 1799, he left the ship with orders to report to the *Portsmouth* in April 1800 in New York Harbor. A warship similar to *Ganges* with a complement of 220 and a small Marine detachment, *Portsmouth* sailed for Europe in October to return the U.S. envoys who had conducted peace negotiations with France. Following the cruise, Gale left the ship in October 1801. Of the 63 Marine Corps officers receiving commissions during the Quasi-War with France, only 23 were retained following hostilities; Anthony Gale was one of them, promoted to first lieutenant as of 2 March 1799. As a first lieutenant, Gale numbered 9 out of the 18 officers holding that rank. In addition, the officer corps included Lt. Col. Cmdt. William Ward Burrows, 4 captains, and 18 second lieutenants.[3]

After this tour in *Ganges,* Gale married Catherine (Kitty) Swope, the daughter of a Philadelphia physician, on 4 January 1800. Following his marriage, Gale established his residence in Philadelphia, and his children were born there. A daughter, Amelia, died after only four weeks, but a son, Washington Anthony, and another daughter, Emily K., survived into adulthood. After commanding the Philadelphia Barracks from October 1801 to February 1803, he again received orders to sea.[4]

Gale sailed in the frigate *President* from the Washington Navy Yard on 2 April 1804, arriving in Malta on 5 September 1804. In July of the following year, the *President* made ready to return home, but Gale, Presley O'Bannon, and fifty enlisted marines joined the frigate *Constitution* to continue their cruise in Mediterranean waters. On 31 October

1805, however, Gale received orders transferring him to another frigate, the *John Adams.* Continuing his service at sea, Gale and the *John Adams* returned home that fall arriving at the Washington Navy Yard on 3 December 1805. Earlier, on 24 April 1804, the new lieutenant colonel commandant of the Marine Corps, Franklin Wharton, informed Gale that, as the senior first lieutenant in the Corps, the latter had been recommended for promotion to captain and brevet major pending approval by the Senate.[5]

By this time in the early history of the Corps, officers of Gale's new rank commanded barracks ashore, recruited marines, and readied recruits for duty at sea. Assigned to his beloved Philadelphia, Gale commanded the Marine Barracks there once more, from April 1807 to July 1817. With Burrows at the helm, Gale appeared to enjoy success in his career. But after Franklin Wharton became commandant, Headquarters Marine Corps began to take a sharper view of Gale's irregular administration.[6]

In late 1815–early 1816, Capt. Henry H. Forde of the Marine Corps submitted a lengthy correspondence to Wharton in which he demanded Gale's arrest and trial by court-martial. Forde charged Gale with countenancing and encouraging mutiny (three specifications), bargaining and dealing in a commercial venture with his orderly sergeant (two specifications), and conduct derogatory to the character and honor of an officer (five specifications). Wharton ordered a court of inquiry to convene in Philadelphia on 9 March 1816 to (1) gather evidence and render an opinion into Forde's allegations and (2) to inquire into Gale's general military character.

Maj. Richard Smith, a Wharton protégé, headed the court which also consisted of Capt. John M. Gamble and 1st Lt. Frances A. Bond. Over the next two weeks, the body obtained testimony about the circumstances surrounding the construction of the officers quarters at the Philadelphia Navy Yard. The witnesses—eleven civilians, eight Navy officers, four Marine Corps enlisted men, and two civilians employed by the Navy—all claimed to have no knowledge of wrongdoing on Gale's part with respect to allocation of government funds intended for on-post construction. Furthermore, each of the witnesses received sharp questioning from the court with regard to Gale's military character and all testified in his behalf in the most positive manner. On 25 March 1816, Smith and the court reached their conclusions.

Anthony Gale had let his home to a Navy lieutenant who then subleased it to a former Marine Corps sergeant and his brother. Gale received nothing more from the venture except his rent as before. Construction in the navy yard had been completed according to regulations, and none of the materials or labor had been used in Gale's private residence. As for his general character, the court concluded that Gale's military conduct had always been above reproach. After a careful reading of the entire transcript of the inquiry and the charges brought by Forde, it appears that these resulted from a fit of pique from a disgruntled subordinate. Nevertheless, Gale's exoneration at the hands of a Wharton favorite set off further maneuvering to prevent Gale's accession to the Corps's highest post.[7]

Gale's successor in Philadelphia, John Gamble, the hero of the *Essex,* made no secret of his dismay regarding the state of the barracks. Moreover, as a member of

Archibald Henderson's clique, his criticism of Gale served to fuel the controversy surrounding Gale's possible accession to the commandancy. Gamble's charges against Gale finally reached the secretary's office after Wharton's death, and another court of inquiry followed.

On 14 February 1819, the adjutant and inspector general's office ordered a court of inquiry into Gale's military conduct. The members of the court, directed to convene on 17 February, consisted of two field-grade Army artillery officers and a Marine Corps captain. An Army judge advocate served as recorder. The witnesses against Gale included Archibald Henderson, who admitted that his knowledge of Gale's misconduct in Philadelphia was based on hearsay. Gamble's testimony, however, contained firsthand damaging information.

Gamble charged that upon relieving Gale in Philadelphia, he found stores and liquor for sale by the sutler mixed with goods kept and owned by the government. Then, Gamble launched into a litany of complaints against his predecessor: "His [Gale's] command was in a very bad state. I confined a number of men immediately afterwards, for theft and had a great deal of trouble for a length of time restoring discipline and order. The Naval officer commanding stated likewise to me that sentries were often drunk on post."[8] But upon sharp questioning by the court, no evidence could be obtained from Gamble indicating that Gale had profited from the sale of public liquor or otherwise acted improperly. Neither Archibald Henderson nor Samuel Miller could testify as to firsthand knowledge of anything untoward in Gale's character.

A Navy purser, stationed in New Orleans, testified that Gale had a reputation for being intoxicated on duty, but that he had never personally seen him drunk. Upon being recalled, Samuel Miller remembered vaguely that Gale had "transmitted an unofficerlike and ungentlemanly" letter to the former commandant of the Marine Corps. When requested by the court to produce the correspondence, however, Miller and his office failed to find the letter. After pondering the evidence, the court concluded that no evidence had been provided to confirm the reports of Gale's misconduct. One member of the court, nevertheless, dissented, citing several errors in the proceedings: witnesses against Gale did not appear and additional charges of improper conduct on his part had not been addressed. The secretary of the navy ignored the dissent and the matter was put to rest. In hindsight, the entire affair appears to have been a feeble attempt to discredit Gale.

A glance at the lineal list made most Marine Corps officers shudder with the knowledge that Gale might assume the commandancy after Wharton's death. With a reputation for a fondness for the bottle, a hot Irish temper, little combat experience, and a casual indifference to administrative procedures, Gale seemed ill suited to head the Corps. Moreover, he apparently displayed few of the qualities of a gentleman, and samples of his correspondence suggest that he was not well educated. His lackluster record and questionable character precipitated a flurry of political machinations as some hoped that in this instance strict seniority would not be observed.

The adjutant and inspector at Headquarters Marine Corps, Maj. Samuel Miller, the hero of Bladensburg, considered himself well suited for the commandancy. Like the commandant, he maintained close ties with the capital's politicians and bureaucrats. He lost no time in requesting the Corps's highest post for himself. On 4 September 1818, Miller notified the secretary of the navy, Benjamin W. Crowninshield, of Wharton's death. Two days later, he wrote the secretary to suggest that he conduct the affairs of the commandancy until President Monroe had made a decision for a successor to Wharton. Meanwhile, several members of Congress wrote to the president extolling Miller's professional qualifications for the commandancy. Miller's machinations did not go unnoticed, however.

Maj. Richard Smith wrote excitedly to the chief clerk of the Department of the Navy to inquire if Miller was in charge. Then Henderson leaped into the fray by arriving at Headquarters on 7 September 1818, declaring that as the senior line officer present, he should be acting commandant. Apparently, Gamble considered Henderson a better choice than Miller because he began to address all of his correspondence to him with the title "Lieutenant Colonel Commandant." By that fall, the sides in the dispute over succession and seniority had fallen into place with Henderson appealing directly to Secretary of the Navy Smith Thompson. In his correspondence, Henderson laid claim directly to the commandancy, citing his gallantry, compared to Wharton's faintheartedness, in the War of 1812. No one seemed to take Gale's claim for the post seriously.[9]

Much to the dismay of most observers, President Monroe and Secretary Thompson chose to follow the custom of seniority despite whatever criticism they may have heard about Gale's professional character. While the political maneuvering continued almost up to the announcement of his appointment, Gale assumed that the post would be his and wisely remained aloof from the bickering. On 3 March 1819, he received the appointment and was sworn in as the fourth commandant.

Gale inherited only 47 officers and 875 enlisted marines, mostly assigned duties among detachments serving with the Navy's fleet of fifty-eight ships or in barracks at the navy yards in Washington, D.C.; New York City; Portsmouth, New Hampshire; New Orleans; Sacketts Harbor, New York; and Erie, Pennsylvania. Gale's duties had been defined for the House of Representatives in 1803 and had not changed since: recruiting then outfitting the new marines; providing sentries for ships and stations; disciplining marines ashore; maintaining small arms for marines when ashore; and administration of the Corps's pay and accounts with the Department of the Navy.

In contrast, the Navy received most of its direction directly from the office of the secretary of the navy. Although the Navy's Board of Commissioners had been in operation since January 1815, its duties remained outside of operational and personnel matters. The secretary and senior Navy officers appeared to pay little attention to the fledgling Corps, provided that the commandant and barracks commanders supplied sufficient guards to maintain discipline among the Navy's enlisted force. Few men appeared attracted to a sailor's life plagued by bad food, low pay, dangerous work, and lengthy voyages at sea. Thus, those who did enlist usually were recent immigrants who could find employment nowhere else, riffraff from the waterfronts, or fugitives from wives and families, debts, or the police. Most Navy officers and government officials of Gale's era believed strongly that only the threat of the lash and a Marine Corps guard could keep such a motley rabble in check.[10]

Whatever personal and professional shortcomings Gale possessed, he appeared sufficiently perceptive to address a problem that had plagued the fledgling Corps almost from its creation. By selecting its officers largely from the educated and socially prominent sector of the population, it only followed that most chose to devote an inordinate amount of their time and energy on personal business. Worse, when an officer wanted a particular assignment or an extension of leave, the secretary of the navy or even the president might receive the request rather than the commandant. Barely more than a month after Gale had assumed office, the restless and ambitious Henderson wrote directly to Secretary Thompson requesting permission to join Gen. Andrew Jackson in Florida.[11] Whether news of Henderson's request prompted Gale to storm the administrative barricades or whether he had planned to address this pesky problem as a first priority during his commandancy is unknown. In any event, Gale took the problem directly to the secretary of the navy.

An attorney, Thompson became the secretary of the navy on 1 January 1819. President James Monroe had sought an appointee with some knowledge of naval matters. When Commodore John Rodgers, president of the Board of Commissioners, declined the position in Monroe's cabinet, Thompson accepted it with great reluctance. From March until December 1819, he even remained absent from his desk for some unexplained reason. Gale's professional relationship with the new secretary did not begin until almost the end of the calendar year. While Thompson might be unenthusiastic about his appointment, he appeared determined to exercise his prerogatives as secretary, and he and Gale came quickly into conflict.[12]

In August 1820, Gale wrote Thompson a long and rambling letter outlining the problems of the command authority of the commandant. In it, Gale asked simply that the limits of his office be defined. If the secretary bothered to answer Gale's clumsy correspondence, the letter has not survived.[13] In any event, Gale had other problems. Apparently unnerved by the weighty problems of his post and inability to deal with Thompson, Gale resorted to the bottle for comfort. Miller reported his superior's drunken binge to the secretary of the navy.[14]

From 20 August until the order confining Gale to his quarters on 7 September 1820, Miller signed all correspondence coming from Headquarters Marine Corps. The adjutant and inspector's administrative action suggested that Gale remained intoxicated and incapable of performing his duties during that period. Together with orders for Gale's confinement came specific charges: charge one: habitual drunkenness; charge two: conduct unbecoming an officer and a gentleman; charge three: signing a false certificate.

Although the order appointing the court came from the office of the secretary, it is impossible to tell who supplied the strange list of participants for Thompson. Brig. Gen. Thomas S. Jesup, U.S. Army, headed the court, joining two field-grade Army officers, three company grade Army officers, and two Marine Corps captains. Although Lt. Richard M. Desha would be a witness for the prosecution, he received orders as a supernumerary while Miller, who had preferred the charges, prosecuted the case.[15]

When Gale's trial convened at the Marine Barracks on 18 September 1820, an additional charge had been added: violation of the order for his arrest. Between 7 and 11 September, Gale had apparently left his quarters to seek legal counsel and witnesses in his defense. Two of the officers detailed as members of the court failed to appear, and General Jesup adjourned the trial until the following morning.

Noting the absence of the two officers again, Jesup ordered charges preferred and called for two of the supernumeraries. Desha, a witness for the prosecution, now sat on the court. He objected to being called because of personal differences with the accused, but the court overruled him simply because he, not Gale, had objected. The charges and specifications were read by Miller, who noted that they had been ordered by Secretary Thompson.

Charge one included three specifications: being disgracefully intoxicated in the streets of the nation's capital to the point of being incapable of performing his duties. Charge two accused Gale of visiting a house of ill-fame near the barracks, calling Lieutenant Desha "a damned rascal and coward," threatening him and then challenging him to a duel, and declaring in the streets that "he did not give a damn for the President, Jesus Christ, or God almighty." Charge three alleged that Gale had signed a certificate swearing that he had not used a Marine Corps private as a waiter and coachman, when in fact he had. And then there was the additional charge of violating the confinement to the arrest. Gale plead not guilty to all charges and specifications.

As the prosecution produced its witnesses, the trial counsel extracted statement after sworn statement supporting the government's contention that Gale had indeed been on a drunken binge, disgracing his office and uniform. Gale requested permission again to leave his place of arrest and confinement in order to obtain counsel and witnesses in his defense. The court referred the matter to Thompson for a decision. As the witnesses for the prosecution testified, Gale managed to cast doubt on their accounts. None could say for certain that they had seen the commandant drink to excess, while Gale attempted to gain support for his argument that he had been mentally deranged. When the witnesses for the government had finished, the trial counsel's case appeared tissue thin. Then, one of Gale's defense witnesses destroyed his plea.

Upon direct examination for the defense, the Navy surgeon attached to the barracks testified that he had known Gale for two or three months, considered him a madman and drunkard, and, most important, suggested that his mental disorder may have resulted from intemperance. The next five witnesses for the defense failed to sway the court after they had heard from the Navy physician. Then, as a sad postscript to the sorry affair, the District police arrested Gale because of a civil debt. On 28 September 1820, the last day of the trial, Gale read a rambling defense of several pages. Unmoved, the court found him guilty of all charges and all but one of the specifications.[16]

On 19 October 1820, Samuel Miller informed the still-confined Gale that President Monroe had approved the findings of the court and ordered the fourth commandant of the Marine Corps dismissed. In a postscript to his letter, Miller hoped that Gale would "correct a habit [drunkenness]."[17]

Following the trial, Catherine Gale appealed directly to the secretary in her husband's behalf, and she reported that the former commandant's mental condition had worsened, resulting in his confinement to a mental hospital. In her letter, she claimed that Gale's mental instability had first become apparent in 1817 and wondered why after his long years of faithful service his country would turn its back on an adopted son: "His head is silvered with age and service . . . [and he] never neglected his duty until it pleased heaven to visit him."[18]

In 1826, Gale abandoned the Philadelphia area for the frontier. Purchasing 158 acres of land on the Dicks River in Lincoln County, Kentucky, he moved his family and lived out his days there in poverty and ill health. Although he received no pension at the time of his dismissal, Gale's repeated requests for relief resulted in first a small monthly stipend of fifteen dollars, later increased to thirty dollars. The amount never exceeded the last amount, despite Gale's pleas directly to the president: "[My] children compelled to daily labor to procure a scanty subsistence. . . . This is a hard case after devoting the prime of life to the service of my country. . . . An old soldier now on the verge of his grave. . . . My dear children, keep them from want."[19]

After 1840, Gale's fortunes worsened. Failure to repay a small loan resulted in foreclosure proceedings, and the courts seized his meager possessions and a side of bacon. Turning to alcohol again, his dipsomania drove him to a mental hospital. A last letter pleading for an increase in his modest pension revealed the poor health and broken spirit of the fourth commandant: "I cannot remain long in this vale of tears. I am now on the verge of the grave."[20]

Anthony Gale died on 12 December 1842 of either tuberculosis or lung cancer. The location of his grave remains a mystery, and the former commandant of the Marine Corps probably lies in a potter's field somewhere in Dicks County, Kentucky. Catherine survived him by four years. The children continued to live in poverty appearing periodically in hope of receiving their father's pension.[21]

The other participants in this sorry tale suffered far less. In 1824, Thompson received an appointment more to his liking. From that date until his death in 1843, he served as a justice of the Supreme Court. Samuel Miller served with distinction during the campaigns against the Seminole Indians in Florida, 1836–37. Promoted to brevet lieutenant colonel, Miller commanded the barracks in Philadelphia and then Boston. He died in 1855, never achieving the commandancy he sought.

Anthony Gale's brief tenure left no mark on the history of the Corps's highest post except for the stain of his sad personal behavior. However unsophisticated and uneducated he might have been, he realized at the outset that the authority of the commandant had yet to be established firmly. His feeble attempts to correct this flaw only exacerbated the political scheming afoot among the senior officers of the small Corps. To a moralistic jurist like Smith Thompson, Gale must have been an anathema. Gale's behavior and bouts with the bottle, worsened perhaps by mental illness, only made a change easier to accomplish.

5
Archibald Henderson
1820–1859

COL. JOSEPH H. ALEXANDER, USMC (RET.)

No man contributed more to the perpetuation and development of the United States Marine Corps in the nineteenth century than Archibald Henderson, the fifth commandant, who headed the Corps for an unmatched thirty-eight years. Of the many legends that surround the Henderson era, the most familiar has the redoubtable colonel commandant leaving his headquarters for field duty with this apocryphal note upon the door: "Gone to fight the Indians. Will be back when the war is over." The historical truth behind the legend is scarcely less colorful. Colonel Henderson in the summer of 1836 had the panache to drop literally everything—the endless struggles with the secretary of the navy, Congress, and his own rivals—and lead half the Marine Corps in a prolonged field deployment in support of the U.S. Army. This incident represented Henderson's defining moment as commandant and marked a major turning point for the Marine Corps. In one masterful stroke, he established for the Corps a national reputation for readiness and military utility. If the ensuing Creek and Seminole Wars proved less than exemplary for America's fledgling military establishment, few policy makers would ever forget how Henderson mustered from a dozen scattered posts a fully armed and equipped force of four hundred regulars at the port of embarkation within ten days.

As a junior officer, Archibald Henderson survived his own personal doldrums, proved his mettle under fire, then emerged as an unofficial, outspoken crusader for professionalism and accountability within his own officer corps. He served well as acting commandant, energetically sought the legitimate appointment, endured literal exile during Anthony Gale's tempestuous tenure, then became, at age thirty-seven, the youngest officer to attain that office.

Henderson inherited a tiny Marine Corps in disarray, a marginal naval auxiliary discredited by the scandalous conduct of his predecessor and crippled by low esteem and ambiguous purpose. In less-capable hands, the Corps of 1820–21 would surely

Bvt. Brig. Gen. Archibald Henderson, fifth commandant.
Oil painting by Reuben LeGrand Johnston, 1916, from a photograph by Henry Ulke. U.S. Marine Corps Photo A413173.

have failed to survive another decade. Henderson's strength of character, leadership, unyielding professional standards, unbounded energy, courage, political astuteness, and sheer longevity made the critical difference. His stewardship, known since as the "Henderson era," enabled the Corps to survive and grow in usefulness to the nation. Arguably, his postmortem influence conveyed sufficient momentum to enable the Corps to endure its undistinguished Civil War performance and the recriminations that followed. It is impossible to understate the personal impact this man had on his institution.

We know that Henderson did not suffer fools and that he was somewhat a martinet in dealing with his high-spirited officers. We also know he was paternal and kindly to his enlisted marines and obviously affectionate toward his younger wife (to the extent of producing nine offspring), so presumably his forbidding official countenance occasionally relaxed into humor and tenderness. He was, in all, a well-bred, broadly educated, thoroughly disciplined man who managed to avoid the excesses in food, drink, and ego which plagued so many of his contemporaries.

Archibald Henderson was born 21 January 1783 in Colchester, Prince William County, northern Virginia, near the small town of Dumfries. His birth date, occurring after the Declaration of Independence and a matter of weeks before the Treaty of Paris, makes Henderson the first American-born commandant. He was the fourth son of Alexander and Sarah ("Sally") Moore Henderson, whose children eventually included four daughters and six sons.[1] Alexander Henderson (1738–1815) migrated from Scotland to Virginia in 1756 and settled in Colchester. Within a few years he became a prominent merchant in the region. As a vestryman for Truro Parish in 1769, he was at odds with George Washington over the proposed site for Pohick Church. The two overcame their differences. Henderson served two terms as a delegate to the Virginia General Assembly and later campaigned with some distinction as a colonel under Washington in the Continental Army during the Revolutionary War. In 1785, the elder Henderson participated in the "Mount Vernon Convention" with George Mason, Edmund Randolph, and James Madison, along with delegates from Maryland, an interstate meeting which eventually led to the Constitutional Convention.[2]

Archibald Henderson's parents lived long enough to see their Marine Corps son attain national recognition for valor for his role in the 1815 sea battle between the USS *Constitution* and HMS *Cyane* and *Levant.* Alexander Henderson died on 22 November 1815 in Dumfries while Captain Henderson was home on furlough. Sally Henderson died the following year.

In the custom of his times, Archibald Henderson received an informal but intensive education, beginning with his Scottish governess and extending through private academies at Bladensburg and Frederick, Maryland. By his late teens, he was working at an ironworks in Antietam (partly owned by his family) and learning French from a private tutor. After two years he returned home to Dumfries, unemployed. At this point, doubtlessly with strong encouragement from his father, he began to apply for a commission in the armed forces. By fate, the Marine Corps favored his application and appointed him a second lieutenant on 4 June 1806. He was twenty-three years old.

Henderson seemed to thrive from the start as a Marine Corps officer. He received a promotion to first lieutenant after only nine months' service. By April 1807, he was commanding a detachment of twenty-three marines on board USS *Wasp* in time for a three-month cruise to England and the Mediterranean.[3] By December of that year, he had transferred to USS *Constitution,* whose Corps guard included three sergeants, two corporals, one drummer, and forty-seven privates, plus a certain sergeant, "a prisoner for mutiny."[4]

Henderson spent 1808 ashore, first at the Marine Barracks in New York, then in Washington. In February 1809, Lt. Col. Cmdt. Franklin Wharton assigned him to Headquarters for service as the adjutant of the Corps. Henderson held this position less than four months before resigning the staff billet for a field command, but this brief tour put him in good stead for later service in the capital. Despite his low rank and inexperience, he immediately began to take part in the activities of the city. Within weeks he had joined one committee to celebrate Washington's birthday and another to arrange the inaugural ball for President-Elect and Mrs. James Madison. He also joined the United States Military Philosophical Society.[5]

Henderson left Washington in mid-1809 to become the second commanding officer of the new and short-lived Marine Barracks in Charleston, South Carolina. The term "barracks" was a misnomer. Henderson organized the move of his small post from Sullivan's Island to Fort Mechanic, but neither site consisted of more than a few temporary hovels. The command consisted of two dozen enlisted marines, whom Henderson assigned in small detachments to the flotilla of gunboats then engaging pirates along the Georgia–South Carolina coastline.[6] These intermittent skirmishes, spiced by rumors of filibustering intrigues along the border with Spanish East Florida, held Henderson's interest for nearly two years. On 1 April 1811, Congress approved his promotion to captain of marines. He was twenty-eight years old.

Captain Henderson left South Carolina in late 1811 to command the Marine detachment on board the 44-gun frigate USS *President* but arrived too late to participate in the ship's celebrated prewar battle with the British sloop-of-war HMS *Little Belt* off Sandy Hook. Disconsolate at missing the action, and restless amid rumors of a full-fledged war to come with Great Britain, Henderson went so far as to approach the U.S. Army about transferring his commission. News of his unofficial negotiations for an interservice transfer brought a stern rebuke from Navy Secretary Paul Hamilton. Henderson wrote an apologetic letter to Hamilton and promised to be more content with his lot.[7]

Henderson spent the first fifteen months of the War of 1812 in command of the Marine Barracks at Charlestown (Boston). His frustration at missing so much of the action became evident in a May 1813 letter to his brother John in which he vowed to resign at the end of the war if he was not promoted.[8] Two months later, his fortunes took a significant turn for the better with news that he would be assigned to command the Marine detachment on board USS *Constitution,* the 44-gun frigate already known as "Old Ironsides." Henderson reported for duty on 9 September 1813, glad to be back on a man-of-war but fearful that he had missed too much of the action already. Indeed, by that time *Constitution* had already won two stirring victories over HMS *Guerrière* and HMS *Tava.* When the Royal Navy extended its blockade to include Boston in early 1814, Henderson despaired of ever getting the chance to prove himself in close combat.

Ironically, the war was officially over when Henderson earned his spurs. Earlier, Capt. Charles Stewart had sailed *Constitution* through the blockade for one final cruise on the high seas. On 20 February 1815, at a point 180 miles east of Madiera, Stewart encountered HMS *Cyane,* a 34-gun frigate, and HMS *Levant,* an 18-gun sloop. Unaware that Congress had ratified the Treaty of Ghent three days earlier, Stewart cleared for action. By skillful seamanship, he split the two British ships, outfighting and capturing each in turn. With much of the fighting executed at ranges as close as 250 yards, Henderson's marines maintained effective, well-aimed musket fire that raked the weather decks of both British vessels. The range, Henderson would later testify, was "so close that the marines were constantly engaged almost from the beginning of the action."[9] The detachment suffered two killed and three wounded.

While tactically insignificant, *Constitution's* last victory produced a political windfall. Combined with the American victory over British regulars at New Orleans five weeks earlier, the capture of the two enemy men-of-war restored some of the luster to the nation's armed forces, for whom the War of 1812 had provided too many embarrassments. Archibald Henderson, in particular, benefited greatly from this one engagement. The first benefit was the lasting admiration of the ship's commander, Captain Stewart. In a general order dated three days after the battle, Stewart announced that "to Captain Archibald Henderson and First Lieutenant W. H. Freeman, commanding the Marines, he owes his grateful thanks for the lively and well-directed fire kept up by the detachment under their command." Stewart further assigned Henderson the enviable task of delivering to the secretary of the navy the captured battle flags of the two British ships, "as an evidence of the veracity of the late enemy."[10] Six years after he quit the post of adjutant of the Corps, Henderson had returned to Washington in temporary glory.

Henderson reaped other benefits from the *Cyane/Levant* engagement over the years, including a silver medal from Congress, four hundred dollars in prize money, and an engraved sword from the state of Virginia. Of prime importance to the ambitious young officer was a brevet promotion to major, backdated to August 1814. As a field-grade officer, and having renounced any further intentions of transferring to the Army, Henderson took it upon himself to cleanse the somewhat ragged reputation of the Marine Corps in the postwar years. By his standards the Corps had been dishonored by the less-than-courageous actions of Lieutenant Colonel Commandant Wharton during the British invasion of Washington, and Henderson did not hesitate to prefer charges of cowardice and malfeasance against his direct superior.[11] Six days after Wharton died, in September 1818, Navy Secretary Benjamin Crowninshield, to whom Henderson had delivered the *Cyane/Levant* battle flags in 1815, selected Brevet Major Henderson to serve as acting commandant.

Henderson turned over command of Marine Barracks, Portsmouth, New Hampshire, on 10 September 1818 and journeyed to Washington to commence a six-month tour as acting commandant. He worked well within the system, endeavored to keep the Corps solvent and acceptable during the turmoil, and learned valuable lessons. He was a natural selection for the permanent post, but such decisions were strictly based on seniority. Maj. Anthony Gale would remain the front-runner as long as he could clear his name of the various charges being brought against him. There was little love lost between Henderson and Gale. Henderson attempted to sway official opinion of Gale on at least two occasions during this period. On 18 November 1818, he wrote President James Monroe asking for the permanent position should the government decide the "present senior officer is incompetent to discharge the duties of the Commandant of the Corps." In a long letter to new Navy Secretary Smith Thompson the following February, Henderson relayed hearsay evidence that a certain naval officer "has frequently seen Major Gale intoxicated in New Orleans."[12]

Henderson's worst fears became reality on 3 March 1819, when the Monroe administration selected Gale as commandant. The younger officer left Washington immediately on an extended furlough. Eight months later, Gale, doubtlessly with relish, ordered Henderson to the remote post at New Orleans "by the nearest and most expeditious route." Henderson replied somewhat loftily from his brother's house in "George Town" that he would proceed "either by sea from one of the northern ports [or] across the Allegheny and down the Western Waters."[13] The journey took ten weeks.

Henderson's tour in command of the Marine Barracks in New Orleans represented the low point in his career. Having tasted the power and responsibility of the commandant's office, he found it difficult to adapt to mundane duties on the frontier. He was thirty-seven, had no wife or children, and seemed to be serving in exile at the hands of Anthony Gale. The Louisiana climate affected him badly. A Navy surgeon advised him to move to a more northern station due to "an evident predisposition to disease in your liver."[14]

Duty in New Orleans seemed to bore Henderson. Twice he volunteered for combat action, asking the secretary of the navy for active employment "on the Southern frontier" and to Gen. Andrew Jackson "should there be a forcible occupation of the Floridas." Meanwhile, he endeavored to maintain currency in Marine Corps issues being considered by Congress. At one point he wrote Secretary Thompson from New Orleans to ask for a better consideration of the Marines, saying, "Our isolated Corps, with the Army on one side and the Navy on the other (neither friendly), has been struggling ever since its establishment for its very existence."[15]

As Gale's short-lived commandancy began to unravel in disgrace, Henderson realized that he did not necessarily have a clear shot at succession. There was talk of bringing Maj. John Hall back from involuntary retirement. Among officers on active service, Henderson had four other competitors, all, like himself, captains serving as brevet majors: Richard Smith, Robert D. Wainwright, William Anderson, and Samuel Miller. Of these, Miller seemed to have the inside track. He had served many years at Marine Headquarters as adjutant, taking the field to fight with distinction against the invading British at Bladensburg, and was now acting commandant in Gale's enforced absence. Henderson often disparaged Miller's worth as a field marine, ignoring Bladensburg, emphasizing that he had never been to sea. The two officers would be implacable rivals for decades, but the rivalry did neither man credit. Miller served the Corps well, fighting with undeniable valor in the Seminole Wars as well.

This time the seniority system worked to Henderson's benefit. The Monroe administration, stung by the Gale scandal, needed a quick, credible replacement with acceptable political credentials. There was no time or much interest in recalling Major Hall to duty. Samuel Miller was two years junior to Henderson in terms of initial commissioning and fully three years behind Henderson's date of rank as a captain. Henderson similarly held seniority over Smith, Wainwright, and Anderson. With the approval of the president and the advice of the Senate, Navy Secretary Smith Thompson appointed Henderson "Lieutenant Colonel Commanding and Commandant, United States Marine Corps, vice Anthony Gale removed," to rank from 17 October 1820. Henderson received these orders in New Orleans on 10 November and left the next day for Washington. He was thirty-seven years old.

While Henderson owed his success to the seniority system and to the modest political clout of his family, he had attained the commandancy more on the basis of his proven record of valor, probity, patriotism, and leadership. Although on active service for just fourteen and half years at the time of his selection, he had experience with each aspect of his profession. His career to date had been divided in this fashion: 19 percent sea duty, 58 percent on barracks duty, and 6 percent at Marine Headquarters (the balance, some thirty-one months, consisted of furloughs, travel, and miscellaneous brief assignments).

Thus Henderson began his long odyssey as fifth commandant of the Corps. During his tenure he would serve eleven different presidents and eighteen secretaries of the navy. While the Marine Corps as a profession of arms would benefit immensely from his enlightened leadership, the overall size of the Corps would hardly flourish. He had the distinction of doubling the authorized number of marines, but there were still less than two thousand officers and men on the rolls when he passed on. Henderson's protean efforts notwithstanding, the nation simply had no major role for its Marine Corps throughout much of the nineteenth century.

The record of Henderson's commandancy was therefore one of prolonged wrangling with each succeeding administration over the purpose, role, size, and authority of the Marines. Two of the earliest and most serious threats to abolish the Corps altogether emerged during his tenure. His voluminous correspondence files reflect an unflagging effort to protect and enhance the Corps, unabashedly seeking to publicize deeds of daring-do and masterfully mobilizing support from a cadre of senior naval officers and congressmen. Significantly, he almost always respected the chain of command. The times that he opted to bypass the secretary of the navy and appeal directly to the president probably numbered less than half a dozen in all thirty-eight years. And with each new secretary of the navy, Henderson would begin again—patiently, courteously, insistently—to state the nature and needs of his small Corps. Yet Henderson exercised some practical restraint with this tireless advocacy. He realized and respected the greater roles in national defense filled by the Army and the Navy. His clashes were almost entirely with the service bureaucracies; with the fleet commanders and field generals he scrupulously maintained courteous relations.

Henderson's most significant contribution to Corps and nation between 1820 and 1859 therefore proved to be the establishment of a legitimate role for the Marine Corps, supported by congressional legislation and enhanced by emerging traditions. Providing this basic foundation of identity, purpose, command relationships, and operational concepts for such a small, hybrid, naval-military force represented a singular achievement.

Henderson's first step was to establish legitimacy for the office of the commandant. The disarray of the past decade had produced a situation in which most in the Corps routinely dealt directly with the secretary of the navy on matters down to the most mundane detail. Henderson reasserted the rightful role of the commandant. When President Monroe countermanded his orders sending Captain Miller to sea duty, Henderson wrote the president to warn him that such a decision would cripple internal discipline. While asserting that "it is my most ardent wish to preserve the confidence of the source whence my commission was derived," Henderson offered his resignation if the president in fact lacked faith in his judgment.[16] The effect was polite, low-key, and deadly serious. Henderson never had this problem again.

Henderson likewise sought to enhance the role of Marine Corps Headquarters. The Peace Establishment Act of 1817 created the billets of adjutant and inspector, quartermaster, and paymaster, staff positions that would endure until the start of World War II. Henderson placed officers of his choosing in these billets upon assuming the commandancy, although President John Quincy Adams reversed this authority in 1828 in one of the few turf battles Henderson ever lost. Thereafter, appointment of the three staff billets would remain the prerogative of the president with the advice and consent of the Senate.[17] But Henderson also saw the role of Headquarters in a more innovative light. From the start, all newly commissioned officers began their tour in the Corps by undergoing a period of instruction at Marine Barracks, Washington, the office and home of the commandant. Henderson also endeavored to maintain a disproportionate force at Headquarters (albeit usually a skeletonized battalion at best) for "such service as the President may direct." Though this practice often undercut the legitimacy of his repeated pleas for more men to man the ships, the ready availability of even a small force of trained regulars in the nation's capital would produce recurring dividends during the riots, insurrections, and small wars to come.

Another immediate initiative established and maintained by the new commandant involved an abiding insistence on professionalism. Henderson sought first to raise the Corps above the unbecoming scandals of the past decade. He did this first by setting the standard himself of personal appearance, military courtesy and discipline. He demanded the same of his officers and noncommissioned officers. He would do everything in his power to punish and chastise any marine suspected of mishandling public funds, wasting government property, falsifying reports, or engaging in immoral behavior. This proved to be a daunting task, as many of his officers had received their commissions based more on political patronage than strength of character or military qualifications. His repeated requests to the various secretaries of the navy for a proportionate share of West Point graduates never reached fruition. He literally spent the rest of his life trying to instill a sense of duty, accountability, and self-discipline in his officers.

From the start, Henderson perceived the primary role of the Marines to be service with the fleet. Based on his early experiences at sea on board the frigates *Wasp, President,* and *Constitution,* he believed the Corps contributed most effectively to a man-of-war by providing a disciplined body of riflemen during close engagements with enemy ships and an interior guard force at all other times. As he would proclaim to various secretaries of the navy, "The Marine Corps is the military arm of the Navy."[18] This operational concept applied sensibly to the War of 1812. But naval technology and tactics changed significantly over the ensuing forty-five years, and Henderson's traditional perception gradually phased behind. He was an intelligent man who routinely corresponded with naval officers as well as his own seagoing marines, but there is little evidence of wholesale adaptability to radical changes.

The period of Henderson's commandancy coincided with a series of significant developments for the Navy. In 1820, the year of Henderson's effective assumption of command, the Navy deployed a squadron to East African waters to discourage the slavery trade and dispatched its first ship to visit China. These were the years of the emergence of steam-propelled ships, beginning with the first "combat" deployment of a steamship, the converted paddlewheeler ferry *Sea Gull* in antipiracy operations in the Caribbean in 1823, to the development of screw-driven, iron-reinforced, casemated men-of-war capable of steaming in every sea. In 1830, the sloop USS *Vincennes* became the first U.S Navy ship to circumnavigate the globe. In 1838, Lt. Charles Wilkes, USN, launched a four-year "Exploring Expedition" which charted 280 Pacific islands and covered some eighty-five thousand miles. In 1847, the Navy executed a flawless amphibious operation at Veracruz, landing eighty-six hundred troops in less than three hours without a loss. Six years later, Commodore Matthew C. Perry led a squadron of steamships into Tokyo Bay, forcibly opening up that nation to western influences and trade. By 1858, the Navy could deploy a fleet of nineteen ships to Paraguay in response to a perceived political crisis.[19]

The U.S. Marines took part in each of these naval landmarks, but while Archibald Henderson proved swift to exploit newspaper coverage of the Corps' participation, he was less responsive to the operational changes the event often heralded. At a time when improved ordnance and steam propulsion mandated greater ranges and lethality of sea fights, he persisted in configuring his marines as riflemen trained to man the fighting tops and lead boarding parties as in the days of sail. In fairness, the commandant did make a point to listen to the appeals of his junior officers, and there is plenty of evidence to reflect more than a little interest in their suggestions for greater emphasis on landing party operations or providing crews for the great guns. But his most animated correspondence reflected the traditional roles as a ship's master-at-arms force and sea snipers. Shortly after the Navy abolished flogging in 1850, for example, he wrote Secretary of the Navy William A. Graham, stating that now more than ever was the time to increase the number of marines who exacted discipline among sailors, pointing out that the Royal Navy, which still retained corporal punishment, had three times as many Royal Marines on their ships. As Henderson somewhat snidely concluded, "Are not the habits of sailors of Anglo-Saxon origin pretty much alike?"[20]

The Marine Corps actually had two roles in support of the Navy throughout this period. In addition to providing Marine detachments for every frigate and sloop (and frequently for seagoing gunboats as well), the commandant was responsible for providing security guards at seven navy yards, typically located in Washington, Philadelphia, New York, Boston, Portsmouth, Gosport (Norfolk), and Pensacola. Command relations clouded the relationships at the yards. While Henderson and most in the Corps could understand and accept the special need of a ship's captain for absolute authority over all hands embarked, they were equally unwilling to grant that same deference to naval officers commanding shore establishments. Bad blood existed between the yard commanders and their semiautonomous "commanding Marine officers" throughout virtually the entire Henderson era. Henderson never succeeded in solving this inevitable conflict. In his view, the Marine Corps existed at the navy yards as much to train detachments for future sea duty as to guard the gates and warehouses. Imperious yard commanders felt unconstrained in using the Marines in whatever capacity desired, from personal bodyguards to cooks or carpenters. The equally imperious Marine commanders, typically lieutenant colonels far removed from sea duty and well established in these sinecures, fought every perceived threat to their own autonomy. The interminable squabbling discredited both services.

Henderson did his best to mediate. One of his most admirable practices as commandant was his willingness to leave his Headquarters every year and inspect each barracks command. Each tour took weeks, but these visits brought him in intimate contact with every shore-based officer and noncommissioned officer, gave him firsthand knowledge of the conditions in which his marines had to live and work, and reaffirmed his role as commandant to most of the Corps. Henderson was still conducting these annual inspection tours as late as the fall of 1858, a matter of weeks before his death.[21]

Stern as he appeared, the officers and men sensed that Henderson truly cared for them. They appreciated his personal attention to their welfare during his annual visits and frequent correspondence. In 1836, a group of his officers presented the commandant with a commemorative sword-cane, whose scabbard had been fabricated using wood from the old HMS *Cyane,* the ship he helped capture twenty-one years earlier.[22]

For his part, Henderson gave over much of his personal life to the establishment and maintenance of Marine Corps traditions at the Washington Barracks just northwest of the navy yard. He encouraged the Marine Band to give concerts on the grounds, open to the public. As early as 1822, the commandant ordered the barracks commander to conduct two parades each week, one on Sunday mornings, the other on Wednesdays.[23] On 16 October 1823, following his wedding in Alexandria, Virginia, to Anne Maria Cazenove, he hosted a formal reception on the grounds behind his quarters at the barracks. This was but the first of many receptions the Hendersons would host there, sometimes for distinguished visitors such as the Marquis de Lafayette (in 1824) but more often for their fellow officers and U.S. Navy counterparts.

Henderson was forty and his bride twenty at the time of their wedding. Anne Maria was the second daughter of Anthony C. Cazenove, an Alexandria merchant and importer. She was pretty, vivacious, a charming hostess, a popular favorite of the Washington marines, and the apple of her husband's eye. Soon the austere Commandant's House began to reflect a little humanity—children and governesses and pets. Anne Maria delivered nine children (five sons, four daughters) between 1824 and 1845. Three died in infancy, including young Archibald Murray Henderson, born when the commandant was sixty-two.

Not surprisingly, the Marine Corps influenced most of the surviving children. Charles Alexander, the eldest son, received a commission as a second lieutenant in time to join the joint expedition to Mexico City in 1847. There he was wounded in action and received a brevet promotion for gallantry under fire. Charles Henderson served in the Corps for fifteen years until the outbreak of the Civil War, when he resigned his commission. A second son, Richard Henry, fought for the South in that war, accepting a commission as a lieutenant in the Confederate States Marine Corps at age thirty.[24] The Henderson's second daughter, Eliza Gardner, married 2d Lt. Edward Jones, USMC, in 1853.

Archibald Henderson meanwhile resumed in Washington the same level of civic involvement he had established as a junior officer on his first tour. In 1833, he became one of the founding members of the Washington National Monument Committee. This enterprise took fifty-two frustrating years, from concept to grand opening of the towering obelisk, and Henderson served the committee for exactly half that duration. As committee president in 1848, he escorted the widows of James Madison, John Quincy Adams, and Alexander Hamilton as they laid the monument's cornerstone. In sadder times, Henderson commanded the eight-man military escort which accompanied the body of President William Henry Harrison back to his home for burial in 1841; eight years later he served as a pall bearer at the funeral of his longtime friend Dolly Madison.[25]

Henderson as commandant also established traditions in uniforms and accouterments. He was the first commandant to publish detailed uniform orders. He listened to his junior officers who complained that the full ensemble of dress uniforms, with their enormous shakos and brass fittings, was far too expensive to procure and maintain at their pay grade. Sympathetic to this problem, Henderson within the first year of his commandancy established an "undress" version of the uniform code, which was more comfortable and functional for most seagoing requirements.[26] Henderson, however, was never the final arbiter of the uniform regulations. Most navy secretaries tended to make minor adjustments. In 1833, President Andrew Jackson got into the act, directing all services to return to their Revolutionary War colors. For the parsimonious Marines, this meant a nine-year return to the green-and-buff uniforms of the Continental

Marines, which then had to be worn out in service before reverting to the much more popular blue-and-red uniforms of the pre-Jackson edict.

Henderson also noted the preference of many officers for the ivory handled saber with Mameluke hilt after the style of the one presented years earlier to Lt. Presley N. O'Bannon for his exploits in Tripoli. In the spring of 1825, Henderson directed the official adoption of "the Mameluke Sword": "All officers when on duty either in full or undress uniform, shall wear a plain brass scabbard sword or saber, with a Mameluke Hilt of White Ivory & a gold Tassel, extreme length of sword three feet one inch & a half curve of blade half an inch only, to serve as cut or thrust."[27]

Overall procurement restraints forced a temporary suspension of Henderson's sword directive that December, but he reissued the order to take effect 1 May 1826. Most did not wait. The officers at the New York Marine Barracks were ready to pay the steep price of nine dollars each for their new swords as early as February. "These swords are high," admitted Henderson, "but I presume [they] are of the very best materials."[28] The tradition endured. Except for a sixteen-year interlude around the Civil War period, the Mameluke saber described and adopted by the fifth commandant has remained the official dress sword for Marine Corps officers for over 150 years.

Henderson also maintained a professional interest in the weapons the Marines Corps acquired. The small Corps invariably had to accept the weapons acquisitions of the larger services, but the commandant's preference influenced the selection. In terms of sidearms, the Marines began the Henderson era equipped with the North Model 1808, a single-shot, flintlock pistol of .64 caliber, and progressed to the widely popular Colt Navy .36-caliber Model 1851 percussion revolver. In long arms, Henderson at first found many marines still using the U.S. Model 1795 .69-caliber flintlock musket, a copy of the pre–Revolutionary War Charleville used by the Continental Marines. A Marine Corps test board initially rejected the innovative breech-loading flintlock rifle designed by John H. Hall and adopted by the Army in 1819. But Henderson admired both the rate of fire and the economics of the Hall rifle, and when further Army development improved its reliability, he asked Navy Secretary Samuel Southard for twenty-one thousand dollars to rearm the Corps with fifteen hundred Hall rifles. "On a recent visit to Fortress Monroe," he wrote in 1827, "I made particular enquiries in relation to the . . . efficiency of Hall's Rifle, and its being . . . useful to the soldiers of the Marine Corps." Thus equipped, Henderson's marines made a good account of themselves in the landing party operations against Sumatran pirates at Quallah Battoo in 1832. Later, Henderson acquired the Marines' first percussion rifle, outfitting his seagoing detachments in the 1840s with the Jenks .54-caliber ("Mule Ear") Navy carbine, a breech-loader like the Hall.[29]

Henderson also took measures to improve the undeniably bleak lot of enlisted marines in the early decades of the nineteenth century. He abolished flogging ashore, declared Sundays to be nonworking days, reduced the liquor ration, and fought with limited success for increased pay and allowances. He also established training programs for noncommissioned officers and did not hesitate to give them increased responsibilities. By 1833 sergeants commanded four of the eleven Marine detachments serving on board deployed men-of-war, including two of the three ships on the Brazil Station.[30]

With his energy, intuition, and proactive leadership, Henderson gradually improved the pride and professionalism of his small corps. Unfortunately, the press of executive business in Washington continually distracted him from full concentration on purely internal matters. Like every commandant since, of necessity he spent most of his time engaged in prolonged debates with the Navy Department, its Board of Naval Commissioners (replaced in 1842 by the various bureau chiefs), and Congress. The central themes of this intermittent discourse would persist for decades and indeed be familiar to each succeeding commandant: the roles and mission of the Corps and the related "force/mission mismatch." In Henderson's view, neither Congress, the White House, nor the Navy Department ever authorized enough marines to meet legislated and customary requirements at sea and ashore.

Congress enacted the Peace Establishment Act in 1817 essentially as a delayed economic measure to "downsize" the military establishment following the conclusion of the War of 1812. Regarding the Marine Corps, the act legislated an authorized strength of 49 officers and 865 enlisted men. Henderson inherited this ceiling in 1820, found it inadequate, and argued ever after for increases, especially for privates. In this crusade he was only marginally successful; legislated increases occurred roughly once every decade and these were unremarkable. More often than not, Henderson had to assume the defensive against assorted efforts to tinker with or outright abolish the Marines.

Henderson faced the first of these attacks on the relevancy of the Corps not long after taking office. In a special report to Congress in February 1821, the Navy Department's Stevenson Archer complained that the Corps was the "size of an infantry regiment" but cost three times as much to operate and maintain. Archer perceived the Marine Corps as an aggregate of separate attachments without need for institutional organization; the Headquarters, including the office of commandant and quartermaster, could thus be eliminated at considerable savings. The duties of the commandant, he argued, were of a "civil character" and could be assumed by the secretary of the navy.[31]

Henderson's response during the preparation of Archer's report reflects an early emphasis on the military utility of the Marines. While justifying the size of his Headquarters establishment on the basis of guard, band, training, and contingency requirements, Henderson pointedly reminded Navy Secretary Smith Thompson of the primary mission of trained marines: to serve "on board the Ships of War in distant seas for the protection of our widely extended commerce."[32]

Archer's proposals went nowhere in Congress, but Henderson was alarmed by the Navy Department's willful effort to dismantle the Corps in the spirit of fiscal economy. He set out to provide a more substantial underpinning for the mission and strength of the Marines. Comparing the Corps to an infantry regiment was specious, he argued. The Marines needed more junior officers and NCOs than an army regiment because of the fragmented nature of providing detachments to a dozen different ships and half a dozen far-flung posts. He prevailed upon Commodore William Bainbridge of the Board of Naval Commissioners to establish a manning scale similar to that used by the Royal Navy, essentially requiring one marine for every major gun on a man-of-war. The so-called Bainbridge Scale, announced in 1825, provided such a ratio. Using this scale, each three-deck ship-of-the-line would rate ninety privates; at the lower end, each armed sloop would rate eight. Although never adopted by Congress, and therefore not binding on the secretary of the navy, the Bainbridge Scale served Henderson well during years of supplications for increased manpower.[33]

Not everyone agreed with Henderson that he had insufficient marines to carry out his mission. Naval reformers and congressional budget cutters often looked askance at the large percentage of Marine Corps officers, the senior captains and above, who no longer went to sea. This was a valid point. Taking the distribution of Marine officers in February 1833 as one example, only two captains (John Harris and Thomas S. English) and ten lieutenants served at sea; the other thirty-seven officers, more than two-thirds of the authorized strength, occupied shore billets. For all his leadership skills, Henderson never succeeded in convincing his more senior officers of the intangible benefits of sea duty.[34]

Debates over the continued need for a Marine Corps came to a head during the early years of the Jackson administration, taking on both fiscal and operational overtones. Despite Henderson's strenuous efforts, the expenditures of the Corps remained tainted, due in part to the propensity of the Marines to shift artfully between jurisdictional loopholes of both Army and Navy regulations. Navy reformers argued that Marine Corps guards on ships had grown anachronistic, that modern sailors, having enlisted voluntarily, no longer posed a mutiny threat. To prove the latter point, the captain of the sloop *Erie* deployed in 1829 without his customary Marine detachment, an experiment watched with considerable interest by fellow reformers. At this point, Amos Kendall, fourth auditor of the Treasury Department and a personal friend of Jackson, submitted the results of his extensive investigation into "the pay and emoluments of the officers of the Marine Corps" to Congress. Kendall cited evidence of unauthorized expenditures, extravagances, and executive privileges. He saw little use for most senior officers—"there is generally the greatest pay for the least service"—and recommended legislation to clarify the legal position of the Corps within the Department of the Navy.[35]

President Jackson, aware of Kendall's ongoing investigation, did not wait for the formal report. On 8 December 1829, he recommended to Congress that "the Marine Corps be merged in the artillery or infantry, as the best mode for curing the many defects in its organization. But little exceeding any of the regiments of infantry, that corps has, besides its Lieutenant-Colonel Commandant, five brevet lieutenant-colonels, who receive the full pay and emoluments of their brevet rank, without rendering proportionate service. Details for Marine service could well be made from the artillery or infantry, there being no peculiar training required for it."[36] Whereas future commandants would turn to Congress and the public for support against such threats, Henderson turned to the U.S. Navy. At first the Navy reformers seemed to take the side of the president. An officer from the sloop *Erie* claimed success for the ship's deployment without the Marines, reporting that Corps guards were "superfluous" and wondering rhetorically "why such an absurdity had been so long tolerated." Other ship captains, including Isaac Hull, argued that the Marines' role had grown obsolete. One naval officer disparaged his marines as "objects of mere pageantry," but other, older, more experienced captains weighed in on the side of the Marines, including Henderson's former commanding officer Commodore Charles Stewart, who cited the usefulness of embarked marines as military examples, guards, infantry, gun crews, and components of the landing force.[37]

Henderson would refine the technique of amassing support from fleet commanders over the years. A quarter of a century later, during yet another public questioning of the need for the Corps, he would repeat the process. In all cases he chose to let the Marines' cumulative record speak for itself—with the help of a few pointed reminders. In 1833, for example, encouraged by the performance of the Marines in the landing party at Quallah Battoo, Henderson pointed out to Navy Secretary Levi Woodbury that "the attack on the Malays found the Marine Guard fully sufficient for the perilous duty assigned it."[38]

The 1830s debate actually proved beneficial for the Marine Corps. It led directly to landmark legislation enacted by Congress in 1834 "for the better organization of the United States Marine Corps," the first major modification to the Corps since its initial charter in 1798. The act clearly stated the position of the Marine Corps as a separate sea service within the Department of the Navy and fully subject to Navy Regulations. At all times the Marines would serve under the command of naval officers at sea and under the control of navy yard commanders on shore (a bitter pill). The good news for the Marines came in an increase in authorized strength to 58 officers and 1,224 enlisted men—and a raise in rank to colonel for the commandant. Henderson assumed his new rank on 1 July 1834.

The 1834 legislation contained one significant caveat. The president of the United States could henceforth order the Marines to support the Army on special occasions. Two years later, amid continued wrangling about overextended commitments and ongoing sour relations with navy yard commanders, Henderson saw a golden opportunity to exercise this legislation to further justify the Corps.

With much of the U.S. Army bogged down in fighting the Seminoles in Florida in 1836, the Creek Indians went on the warpath throughout southern Georgia and Alabama. Sweeping virtually unopposed throughout the region, the Creeks burned Roanoke, Georgia, and threatened Columbus and Tallahassee. Thousands of settlers became refugees. The Army, now stretching to fight on two fronts, clearly needed help. Taking advantage of the 1834 legislation, Henderson promptly offered President Jackson the service of a Marine regiment. "Old Hickory" accepted immediately.

Henderson moved with alacrity to mobilize half the entire Marine Corps for this mission. This was a remarkable achievement, one that set an example of readiness and adaptability which would come to characterize the Corps. Nor did Henderson hesitate to take to the field in command of the improvised regiment. While he did not exactly leave the legendary "Gone to fight the Indians" sign on his door, his parting letter to Lt. Col. Robert D. Wainwright was nearly as terse. "During my absence on the Campaign against the Creek Indians, I leave you in command at Head Quarters. There will be little other than bureau duty to attend to." Henderson left only a dozen privates and four NCOs to guard the navy yard and assigned the Marine Band to guard the barracks. With that, Henderson departed for field duty, no doubt grinning in anticipation.[39]

The Marines deployed to Georgia in two movement groups: Henderson led the first battalion on board the chartered steamer *Columbus* at Fortress Monroe on 2 June; the second battalion, comprised of troops from the northernmost barracks and posts, followed three days later. The Marines disembarked at Charleston, proceeded by rail to Augusta, and then commenced a 224-mile march to Columbus over the next two weeks. Hard-pressed Gen. Winfield Scott avidly welcomed the fully equipped regiment of regulars.[40]

The reality of the subsequent counterguerrilla campaign against first the Creeks and then the Seminoles quickly dispelled any thoughts of a swift campaign. Henderson and his troops were undeniably useful in the fighting, helping subdue the Creeks then redeploying into northern Florida. Henderson eventually commanded an Army brigade, including his marines, and led this force to the small victory at Hatchee-Lustee in January 1837. Then the war bogged down. By April, Henderson was ready to come home. As he wrote in his journal, "I do not wish to be premature in this request [for orders to Washington]. . . . I am anxious to leave Florida & our connection with the Army without the shadow of a stain on our escutcheon." He admitted to difficulties with certain "unquiet spirits among ourselves." The next passage revealed an abiding personality trait: "we must take care to be right, & then they are powerless."[41]

Henderson returned to Washington to much public acclaim after a year in the field. Congress and the administration rewarded him with a brevet promotion to brigadier general, effective 1 January 1837. Extracting his marines from the Army of the South proved another matter. Some remained engaged against the Seminoles for five years, although most returned by mid-1838. Henderson greeted these marines with a proclamation at once congratulatory and apologetic. "Soldiers! Two years ago you left your stations as volunteers," he began, then reminded them that he had been "your Commander in your first campaign against the Seminoles in their unexplored morasses," thanking them for their subsequent campaigning in his absence and assuring them that they had "elevated their Ancient Corps in the estimation of the Country."[42]

Significantly, the Marine Corps did not abandon its traditional role of service with the fleet in this rush to join an Army campaign. Plenty of marines served on board the ships of the West Indies Squadron and the "Mosquito Fleet" throughout protracted riverine operations against the Seminoles. The Seminole War may have been an unmitigated military-political disaster, but the Marine Corps earned invaluable acceptance and appreciation by a generation of Army and Navy officers in the experience.

Similar developments occurred during the Mexican War in 1846–47. Fleet marines served with distinction in protracted amphibious campaigns along the coasts of California, Baja California, and eastern Mexico. The commandant likewise tendered the services of a provisional Marine regiment for deployment with the Army. President James K. Polk accepted the offer and ordered the regiment to join Gen. Winfield Scott's army in its campaign against Mexico City in the summer of 1847. Although Congress had authorized an increase in the Corps of twelve officers and a thousand men the preceding March, most of the men who deployed to Mexico were untrained recruits, unlike the troops mobilized to fight the southern Indians. There was another critical difference this time. Bvt. Brig. Gen. Archibald Henderson, now sixty, did not take the field to lead his marines. The performance of the marines assigned to Scott's army reflected his absence.

Lt. Col. Samuel E. Watson commanded the Marine regiment (downgraded to a battalion upon arrival in Mexico); Maj. Levi Twiggs served as second in command. Both officers had served in the War of 1812 and were now somewhat long in the tooth. In the crucial assault on Chapultepec on 13 September 1847, Twiggs was killed and Watson showed little initiative. Lacking senior leadership on the scene, most marines missed the initial action, waiting in defilade for attack orders that never came. Only a handful of officers, such as Capt. George H. Terrett, 1st Lt. John D. Simms, and 2d Lt. Charles A. Henderson, rose to the occasion and fought with élan. The marines who followed these officers fought in the highest traditions, but on balance Chapultepec was not a shining moment.

Back in Washington, Henderson waited impatiently for the kind of field reports from Watson he had come to expect. What he got instead was confusion and recrimination. Watson died of illness shortly after the battle. The remaining field-grade officer, Maj. William Dulany, got himself arrested for drunkenness and looting in occupied Mexico City. Most other officers seemed at war with each other, leveling charges and countercharges about cowardice and poltroonery. (Indeed, public recriminations between Brevet Maj. John G. Reynolds and 1st Lt. John S. Devlin continued in the tabloid press for five years after the battle.)[43]

It took Henderson nearly a year to collect enough favorable information about Terrett, Simms, and his son at Chapultepec to be able to provide a "full account" to the secretary of the navy. The report, which said nothing of Watson's inertia or the confusion that slowed the advance of most of the battalion, emphasized that a marine had raised the national colors within the citadel at the conclusion of the fighting. When the citizens of Washington presented Henderson with a commemorative flag inscribed with the words "from Tripoli to the Halls of Montezuma" the legend was immortalized. Soon after, officers and NCOs began wearing a scarlet stripe down the leg of their blue trousers to honor, tradition has it, the blood of the fallen Chapultepec heroes.[44]

Henderson's desire to report the performance of the Marine battalion in the assault on Mexico City in a positive light is fully understandable, but in doing so he missed a great opportunity to realign the operational focus of the Corps. The instructive example of the Mexican War for the Marine Corps was not the extended commitment of a battalion of raw recruits to an inland campaign in support of the Army but the performance of Marine landing parties under the energetic leadership of a new generation of Navy officers. The achievements of Commodore Robert F. Stockton and Capt. Jacob Zeilin of the Marines in the Pacific Squadron, and Commodore Matthew C. Perry and Capt. Alvin Edson of the Marines in the Gulf Squadron, heralded a bright future for sustained landing force operations. The conquest of California and the east coast of Mexico reflected the potential tactical value of mobile, seaborne forces, trained and equipped to land at will along a hostile coastline. This was the kind of mission that would have put the Corps in good stead for the Civil War. Henderson, for all his foresight and professionalism, missed the implications.

In truth, marines and sailors conducted fifty armed landings "under conditions short of war" during the Henderson era. These small landing excursions occurred all around the globe, from the Falkland Islands to Liberia, from Fiji to Uruguay. Marines splashed ashore at Nicaragua, Tarawa (Wilkes Expedition), and Okinawa nearly a century before the bloodier, more notable engagements to follow. Each of the landings during Henderson's commandancy involved a combined force of sailors and leathernecks, typically under the command of a naval officer, assisted by the lieutenant of marines.[45] Henderson seemed to regard these missions as routine business. Despite being an avid booster of Marine Corps accomplishments throughout his career, he opted to highlight only two of these many landings—Quallah Battoo in 1832 and the amphibious seizure of the Barrier Forts in China in 1856—in his correspondence with the Navy Department.

Henderson persisted in perceiving the main function of seagoing marines as disciplinary guards. This had been his experience during the period from 1807 to 1815, when he went to sea, and thus it would be ever after. The increasingly effective use of squadron-sized landing parties, as epitomized during the naval war with Mexico, never struck him as the mission of the future. In Henderson's view, the two most significant events in the U.S. Navy in his later years as commandant were the *Somers* mutiny of 1842 (a ship without a Marine Corps guard) and the abolition of flogging at sea in 1850. When the commandant solicited ship captains for comments to reinforce his perpetual request for more Marine guards in 1852, he received a prescient response from Cdr. David G. Farragut: marines were helpful in maintaining discipline at sea, he stated, but their greater value existed in "the important duty of landing to act against the enemy, when they became the nucleus: and in fact, the chief reliance of the Commanding Officer for the formation of the landing forces, when an efficient guard, commanded by a good drilled officer would prove a most substantial comfort."[46] True to his bias, Henderson collected the first point and overlooked the remainder of Farragut's argument.

Nor was Henderson the only senior Marine officer to be seemingly blind to the possibilities of an expanded amphibious mission for the Corps. In 1852, Maj. John Harris (Henderson's eventual successor) assembled a board of officers for "the preparation of such regulations . . . as we deem necessary for the Government of the Marine Corps, on shore and afloat." Predictably, most of the findings and recommendations concerned perceived inequities in command relations between commanders of the navy yards and the commanding Marine officers as specified in the act of 1834. Proposed regulations for seagoing marines remained pallid and traditional: "Marines are to be frequently exercised by their own officers so they may become proficient in the use of their arms," and "upon beating to quarters for action, the Marine officers shall place themselves at the head of their men and occupy the position on the deck designated." Landing party operations received no mention.[47]

To his credit, Henderson did show an early and abiding interest in developing a combined arms capability for the Corps. In this case he listened to the petitions of his junior officers for artillery training and endeavored for decades to gain the Navy Department's approval. In 1823, he stated his desire to "introduce a knowledge of artillery duty" and proposed the establishment of a "Corps of Marine Artillery." In 1841, responding to an inquiry from Navy Secretary George E. Badger concerning the impact of steam-powered vessels on the Corps, he suggested his marines be "regularly instructed in the Artillery and Infantry skills," ready indeed for "operations on land" using those same skills. As usual, he linked this suggestion to yet another request for force augmentation, and it went nowhere. In 1848, following the Mexican War, Henderson requested "four light artillery pieces for training purposes." He submitted a similar request in 1853. In 1856, 1st Lt. Israel Greene wrote the commandant requesting artillery instruction for junior officers. Four years later, Henderson sent Greene to West Point for the summer to acquire "a knowledge of artillery for the purpose of introducing it into the Marine Corps." Finally, ten months after Henderson's death, the Navy Department notified his successor that the Bureau of Ordnance would provide Marine Headquarters with "two 32-pound guns and four pieces of light artillery for training at Marine Barracks in the use of ships' guns and field artillery."[48]

Henderson lived long enough to have a memorable experience in direct confrontation with a loaded artillery piece in the nation's capital. On 1 June 1857, Washington erupted in an election-day riot. One of the factions imported an armed band of Baltimore toughs, the infamous Plug-Uglies. President James Buchanan authorized the employment of a Marine company from the barracks to help quell the disorder. Having given the necessary implementing directives to the barracks commander, Henderson, age seventy-four, dressed in mufti, strode downtown to supervise the action. He found his company and the Plug-Uglies confronting each other at the Northern Liberties Market. Seeing a small brass cannon aimed at his advancing troops, Henderson swiftly crossed the square, placed his body in front of the muzzle, and quietly stated, "Men, you had better think twice before you fire this piece at the Marines." In the melee that followed, Henderson collared one pistol-waving rioter, disarmed him, and hauled him off to the police. The Marines sustained several casualties but scattered the rioters and captured the artillery piece. The action, breathtakingly reported that day by the *Washington Star,* captured the imagination of the public and enhanced the perceived utility of the Corps.[49]

The "Plug-Uglies Incident" illustrates the vigor with which the aging commandant continued to exercise his duties. In his last years he worked even harder to improve professionalism and quality-of-life issues for the Marines. He reiterated his frequent earlier requests for West Point graduates, engineer and artillery training for officers, and continuing military education for NCOs. He standardized recruiting, published recruiting regulations ("No man is wanted who does not come voluntarily to the standard of his country"), and created the first supply depot (Philadelphia, 1857). Yet his personnel problems remained staggering. He could not convince the Navy Department to establish an involuntary retirement policy for over-aged senior officers, and his ossified barracks commanders continued to block the growth and development of impatient junior officers who had earned their spurs in the Mexican War or in fleet operations around the globe. Sea duty for enlisted men continued to be bleak and protracted, causing high desertion and low reenlistment rates.

On 28 October 1858, the Henderson's youngest daughter, twenty-three-year-old Charlotte Shepherd, married E. Irenee duPont at the commandant's house. General Henderson then departed on an inspection tour of the various barracks. His final report to Navy Secretary Isaac Toucey reflected many of his original themes of the early 1820s: the Corps needed more officers and men, more emphasis on drill and other military skills, and urgently needed "a standard of education for officers of the Corps."[50]

On 2 January 1859, Henderson presided over a meeting of the Washington National Monument Committee. Four days later he abruptly died. As officially reported by the adjutant and inspector to Secretary Toucey, "It becomes my painful duty to announce to the Department the demise of Brevet Brigadier General Archibald Henderson, late Commandant of the Marine Corps, who died on the afternoon of yesterday the 6th inst. at quarter past 4 o'clock, while reclining on his sofa."[51]

Archibald Henderson died fifteen days before his seventy-sixth birthday. He had served continuously on active duty as a Marine Corps officer for fifty-two years, seven months, and two days, and as commandant for thirty-eight years, two months, and nineteen days—both records of longevity unlikely to be surpassed. He was buried in a vault in Washington's Congressional Cemetery on 10 January. President Buchanan and his entire cabinet attended the service. Nine days later, his widow Anne Henderson, fifty-six years old and a semi-invalid, died. Young Capt. Charles A. Henderson, USMC, deployed to Paraguay with the Atlantic Squadron, missed the deaths of both his parents.

Henderson's principal contribution in his long years of leadership was to establish formal legitimacy and informal legacy to the Marine Corps. In the process, Henderson indelibly shaped the once and future Corps as a multimission, combined-arms, force-in-readiness, a distinctly naval service, rich with customs and traditions, with unique capabilities to offer the nation. One measure of his lifelong contributions came posthumously, in Secretary Toucey's Annual Report for 1859. "The Marine Corps," stated Toucey, "is an indispensable branch of the Naval Service. . . . It is a gallant little band upon which rests the most widely extended duties at home and in every sea and clime, without sufficient numbers to perform them."[52] Archibald Henderson would have treasured this accolade.

6

John Harris

1859–1864

COL. JOSEPH H. ALEXANDER, USMC (RET.)

In the early spring of 1837, a seasoned veteran of the Florida Seminole Wars arrived in Washington in a hurry, bearing important news of treaty agreements with several tribal chiefs. The Seminole War, it seemed, was over, a quick victory for the young United States. The courier, Bvt. Maj. John Harris of the U.S. Marines, was exultant. For the forty-three-year-old Pennsylvanian, the short campaign had been rewarding. His command of a company of mounted marines throughout the expedition in Georgia and Florida had resulted in favorable reports by the colonel commandant, Archibald Henderson, to the secretary of the navy. Best of all, he had just been cited for gallantry in action in the battle on the banks of the Hatchee-Lustee River, his second brevet promotion in the past twelve years.[1] Some of his juniors were already whispering that he appeared a likely candidate to replace Colonel Henderson, eventually, at the head of the Corps. For Bvt. Maj. John Harris, it was an early and welcome spring.

Unfortunately for Harris, and for the nation, his perceptions represented a false spring. The Seminole War was not over; it had merely become a deadly insurgency which was to frustrate and embarrass the United States for another five years.[2] And while Harris eventually replaced Henderson as commandant, it was not for another twenty-two years—half a lifetime in terms of early-nineteenth-century longevity. By the time he moved into the commandant's quarters in southeast Washington, John Harris was nearly sixty-six, bald, stale, and deskbound.

On balance, John Harris appeared to have all the qualities to lead the Corps forward in hard times. He was, if nothing else, a survivor. For one thing, he was the last active Marine Corps veteran of the War of 1812. His nearly forty-five years of service had included three wars, as well as twenty years of sea duty throughout the world. He had fought the British, the Barbary pirates, the Creeks and Seminoles. He had also commanded Marine Barracks at Erie, Boston, Philadelphia, Washington, Norfolk, and Brooklyn. And while not exactly a protégé of Henderson, he had served the legendary

Col. John Harris, sixth commandant.
U.S. Marine Corps Photo 308347.

commandant throughout all thirty-eight years of his tenure and was at least imbued with the same sense of discipline and naval orientation as his more distinguished predecessor.[3]

John Harris's problems throughout his commandancy were twofold. First, lacking the broad vision of Henderson, he failed to sense the opportunities for change and growth offered by industrialization and the oncoming Civil War. Second, he was simply too old and stale to meet anything but the bare minimum requirements of his office.

It had been twenty-three years since his last sea duty, eleven since his last field deployment.[4] In truth, the Hatchee-Lustee skirmish that far-off winter of 1837 was the peak of his career as a fighting marine. His subsequent assignments were almost entirely a succession of routine barracks commands, where he served without distinction, trying to outlive the dynamic Henderson.

What was John Harris really like? Most historians of the Corps use the words "lethargic" and "disorganized" in describing his commandancy. Clyde R. Metcalf called him "an old man of none too great ability."[5] His chief rival and only capable field commander, Lt. Col. John G. Reynolds, wrote Secretary of the Navy Gideon Welles that Harris was "coarse, vulgar, ungentlemanly and insulting."[6] These may each be apt descriptions, but a study of Harris's correspondence as commandant also reveals a man with pride in his Corps, an abiding sense of duty, a refusal to suffer fools, strong affinities with the Navy, and an admirable, if unimaginative, determination to protect the Corps from corrosion of discipline within and institutional takeover from outside.

Harris was born on 20 May 1793 in East Whiteland Township, Chester County, Pennsylvania. We know little of his early years, education, or, indeed, his private life throughout his career. He was twice married, but there is no record of children from either union.[7] His second marriage occurred in 1845 to Mary Gilliat Gray, daughter of a British diplomat. He was not without political allies in Philadelphia, but was never considered to have significant influence within Congress or either the Buchanan or Lincoln administrations. Indeed, the dearth of reference to any Marine Corps activities throughout Navy Secretary Welles's otherwise loquacious diaries reflects quite clearly the low political profile maintained by John Harris throughout much of his tenure as commandant.[8]

Forty-five years earlier, when a hostile army likewise threatened the nation's capital, John Harris was appointed second lieutenant of marines. The date was 23 April 1814. Two months later he was promoted to first lieutenant, an exigency of the war. He clearly fought against British major general Robert Ross's expedition against Washington and Baltimore, although the tradition that young Harris fought with the Marines at Bladensburg may not have been the case. Orders signed by Lt. Col. Cmdt. Franklin Wharton on 9 August 1814 directed Harris to report to Baltimore for duty aboard USS *Guerrière.*[9] The fight at Bladensburg occurred on 24 August. Harris more likely fought with the Marines at Sparrows Point and Fort McHenry from 11 to 13 September. His performance in either case appears to have been unremarkable.

First Lieutenant Harris was in charge of the thirty-seven marines assigned to the USS *Macedonian,* which sailed from New York in May 1815 as part of Stephen Decatur's squadron to punish the Barbary pirates. It was but the start of nearly twenty years of service afloat for Harris. Subsequent seagoing assignments took him to sea on board the *Franklin, Java, Delaware, Philadelphia,* and (again) *Delaware.* For unspecified gallantry on board USS *Franklin* in 1825, he earned a brevet promotion to captain.[10] He was then thirty-one years old.

Fourteen years later, Harris joined Henderson at Fort Monroe, Virginia, as part of the joint expedition to fight the Creeks and Seminoles in Georgia and Florida. "While in Florida," wrote Henderson to the secretary of the navy, "Captain John Harris had command of Mounted Marines and did good service in that capacity."[11] There followed the skirmish on the banks of the Hatchee-Lustee, the brevet promotion to major and the short-lived glory of his return to Washington that spring of 1837.

The intervening years of barracks duty seemed to take much of the fire out of John Harris. Unlike most of his contemporaries, he was reluctant to take the field in the Mexican War. In a revealing letter to General Henderson in 1847, Harris stated, "If you could not give the Command of the Battalion to me . . . I would rather stay at home than go second to an Officer of my own Grade." Further, he wrote, 'I have no desire to go, but if you think the good of the service requires it, I shall not hesitate to do so."[12] Harris was then fifty-four years old and comfortably in charge of the two officers and twenty-nine men stationed at Marine Barracks, Gosport (later Norfolk), Virginia.[13] Ten months later, his request for command was granted, and he sailed from New York with a Marine Corps battalion bound for Mexico. By the time of his arrival in Veracruz, however, the war was over.[14] The Archibald Henderson era ultimately ended with this somber memo from Maj. Henry B. Tyler, adjutant and inspector, Headquarters Marine Corps to Secretary of the Navy Isaac Toucey, dated 7 January 1859: "It becomes my painful duty to announce to the Department the demise of Brevet Brigadier General Archibald Henderson, late Commandant of the Marine Corps, who died on the afternoon of yesterday the 6th inst. at quarter past four o'clock, while reclining on his sofa."[15] Selection of Henderson's successor was easy. John Harris, then a lieutenant colonel, and the only officer above the rank of major, was clearly the senior claimant. His nomination by Secretary Toucey was routinely endorsed by President Buchanan. Harris left Marine Barracks, Brooklyn, for Washington the same day as Tyler's announcement. He was promoted to colonel and sworn in as commandant on the eighth. Harris inherited Henderson's Headquarters staff of four officers: Major Tyler, adjutant and inspector; the politically connected Maj. William W. Russell, paymaster; Capt. A. T. Maddox, assistant paymaster; and Maj. Daniel I. Sutherland, quartermaster.[16] The strength of the Corps in January 1859 was 60 officers and 1,895 enlisted, the latter figure representing a small increase over the monthly average of the previous twenty years. About 60 percent of the fifty-two company-grade officers were assigned to sea duty.[17]

Judging from the tone of his initial correspondence, Harris was determined to run a taut ship. In an endorsement forwarded to Toucey his second week of office, he wrote, "Captain Doughty has reported Pvt Robert B— as a skulking, worthless character and recommends that he be discharged and not enlisted again in the Corps. I join in the recommendation."[18] All well and good, but in truth the office of the commandant had very little authority vested in it for military leadership. Legislation enacted in the early 1830s, plus general practice in subsequent years, placed major limitations on the commandant's freedom to run the Corps. The commandant could not select his own staff officers, grant or extend leave, approve discharges, answer letters of indebtedness, obligate large sums of money, or authorize simple repairs to barracks without referring each case to the secretary of the navy.[19] John Harris—phlegmatic, unimaginative, and dutiful—could handle this in peacetime, but with war and the preoccupation of new secretary Gideon Welles and his galvanic assistant, Gustavus V. Fox, with naval operational matters on a near global basis, Harris was hard-pressed to influence the Navy Department on any important Marine Corps issues.

The few occasions when Harris dared to exercise his own authority usually proved negative. Early in his tenure he ordered 2d Lt. Henry B. Tyler (his adjutant's son) to Norfolk from the African Squadron. Young Tyler responded directly to the secretary of the navy: "I did not anticipate that I was to be ordered in such hot haste to perform duty on shore," pointing out that the orders were issued by the colonel commandant without the secretary's approval and concluding rather breezily that "orders to Norfolk at this particular time will be inconvenient and annoying to me."[20] Harris's orders were overruled.

This is not to contend that the authority of the secretary of the navy over the commandant was necessarily counterproductive. Indeed, the single successful deployment of a sizable Marine Corps unit to a field mission ashore during the Harris years—the capture of John Brown at Harpers Ferry in November 1859—occurred under exactly these restrictions. The "initiating directive" for this operation was given directly by a Navy Department clerk, Charles W. Welsh, to 1st Lt. Israel Greene, officer-of-the-day at the Washington Marine Barracks. In an early example of combat readiness and tactical mobility, Greene had his troops armed, provisioned, and embarked on the train for Harpers Ferry in three and a half hours. Their movement was in fact so rapid that the Army regulars from Fort Monroe, summoned initially to quell the insurrection, had their orders canceled while en route.[21] Greene's subsequent performance under Col. Robert E. Lee's direction at Harpers Ferry was arguably a preview of late-twentieth-century missions for the Corps—detailed planning and violent execution for a successful hostage rescue. To relate both sides of the story, Greene was also beset with some twentieth-century micro-management as well. Colonel Harris, for example, insisted that Greene be accompanied by the paymaster, Major Russell, to "prevent undue bloodshed."[22] And both the secretary of the navy and the secretary of war came to the Washington train station to give Greene his orders.[23] Harris, however, stayed at home.

With the nation obviously drifting toward civil war, Harris began efforts to increase both the numbers and the lethality of the Corps. In words that he would repeat plaintively throughout his commandancy, Harris wrote Secretary Toucey in late 1859, "Our little Corps is hard pressed all the time, and these frequent calls [from ships] show the absolute necessity of an increase of our numbers."[24] He also deplored the lack of training opportunities due to the increasing commitment to provide more and more men to form Marine guard detachments in the rapidly growing Navy: "We find it impossible to instruct the men as Infantry, and as Light and Heavy Artillery as much as they should be."[25] Pointing out that the Corps was equipped with muskets of three different calibers, he requested authority in early 1860 to purchase one thousand .58-caliber Springfield muskets.[26] He got the muskets, but not the people, and he never had enough time to train throughout the war.

The favorable public reaction to the Corps following Greene's successful operation at Harpers Ferry soon faded as officer after officer tendered his resignation to serve the newly established Confederacy in 1860–61. All services were hit hard by these defections, the Army losing Robert E. Lee, Albert Sidney Johnston, and Joseph E. Johnston, and the Navy losing Matthew Fontaine Maury and Franklin Buchanan. Defections from the Marine Corps were not as well known, but they took the heart out of the Corps's real strength, the company grade officers. Sixteen of the thirty-one captains and first lieutenants under Harris went South, including Israel Greene; John Simms, hero of Chapultepec and the Barrier Forts in Canton, China; and Robert Tansill, who had served well with Jacob Zeilin in California during the Mexican War. Both Major Tyler, Harris's adjutant, and his son, the same Lieutenant Tyler who put Harris on report for ordering him to Norfolk, opted to fight for their native Virginia. So did Maj. George H. Terrett, commander of Marine Barracks, Washington, and a veteran of Mexico City and Quallah Battoo.[27] To compound their embarrassment, the Marines then learned that the late Archibald Henderson's son Richard had joined the Confederate States Marine Corps from civilian life.[28]

It is difficult to determine whether strong, enlightened leadership on the part of John Harris might have turned the tide of these defections. He seems to have been devoid of redeeming social graces in dealing with his younger officers and likely held no bond of fealty from them which might have overridden state and regional loyalties. He was, at any rate, soon left with a huge gap between a large number of second lieutenants and a handful of senior officers almost as old as himself. It was with these latter officers—Majs. William Dulany, James Edelin, Ward Marston, and John Reynolds—that Harris began to spar and snipe, becoming increasingly distracted by what became a running fight with his senior barracks commanders at the expense of supporting the war. For new secretary of the navy Gideon Welles, taking office barely a month before the Confederate attack on Fort Sumter at the beginning of the war, it must have been both astonishing and depressing to have to officiate time and again in these internal quarrels.

The earliest and perhaps longest running of these disputes between the commandant and his senior commanders occurred when Harris relieved Maj. Ward Marston of command of the Barracks in Philadelphia for "the careless manner in which you render the important returns of your Command, and the continuing differences you have with the Naval Officers of the Philadelphia station."[29] Marston howled in protest. He besieged the commandant, Secretary Welles, and even President Lincoln with long letters of injured pride. Contained in all the rhetoric was a nugget of tradition. Marston contended that the Marine Corps Act of 1832, as implemented by the Navy Department, conveyed command of the five largest Marine Barracks—typically Boston, Brooklyn, Philadelphia, Portsmouth, and Washington—to the five senior officers of the Corps (aside from the commandant) according to rank. Therefore, argued Marston, only the secretary of the navy could deprive a member of the "Top Five" of his command, and then only for good and sufficient cause.[30] Given the limited authority held by the commandant in those years, Marston was probably right, but Secretaries Toucey and Welles backed Harris, and Lincoln refused to answer Marston's petitions. Marston remained on active duty, but in suspended duty status throughout the early years of the war, eventually gaining a promotion and assignment to yet another command, where he was to embarrass a subsequent commandant.[31]

Meanwhile, the Department of the Navy geared up for war, the Navy expanding and modernizing rapidly, the Marine Corps still sluggish and reactive under John Harris. He continuously bristled at perceived attempts by Army general Winfield Scott to deploy the Marines, arguably the only regular infantry in the capital during the early days of the war. He doggedly sought continued service for the Marines with the fleet, but he was essentially blind to developments within the Navy and to improved use of the Corps afloat. The requirement to provide marines as marksmen aloft, to lead boarding parties and repress potential mutinies, had passed with the days of sail. What the Navy really needed were seagoing regulars who could stand interior guard and man some of the big guns in the broadsides to come against Confederate forts and cruisers.[32]

Years after the war, Capt. Louis E. Fagan of the Marines, a veteran of the abortive assault by the Naval Brigade against Fort Fisher, wrote Lt. Henry Clay Cochrane: "The [Civil] War was our great opportunity and we owlishly neglected it."[33] The Marine Corps truly had the opportunity in 1861 to articulate a bold new mission, that of amphibious operations with the fleet against an enemy whose greatest vulnerabilities lay in thousands of miles of unprotected coastline and hundreds of navigable rivers penetrating into his interior. Revolutionary as such a concept may have been, it was not without precedent. Barely fifteen years earlier the United States had executed a highly successful amphibious assault at Veracruz. The marines under Commodore Samuel F. DuPont along the California coast likewise demonstrated the successful application of combined landing party operations. It was a natural progression, but it was not to be. John Harris and his senior subordinates were simply too old, too much at odds with each other, and too beset by increasing demands for small increments of troops for sea duty to formulate any new roles and missions. Those imaginative naval officers and junior marines who later tried to experiment with amphibious operations were never able to present their case convincingly. Marines in the Civil War provided commendable service afloat in small units. When they went ashore, however, especially in battalion formation, their performance ranged from mediocre to abysmal.[34]

This shortcoming was demonstrated during the first battle of Manassas in July 1861. A Marine battalion was formed for detached service with the Army over Colonel Harris's strong misgivings. Command was given to Major Reynolds, the longtime antagonist of the commandant but the only senior officer with enough vigor and experience to take to the field. There was nothing deficient with Reynolds's sense of duty or bravery under fire. Unfortunately, most of his troops were the rawest of recruits. "Of the 350 officers and enlisted men under my command," Reynolds later reported, "there were but two staff officers, two captains, one first lieutenant, nine Non-Commissioned Officers and two musicians who were experienced from length of service." The remainder, he observed, were recruits with less than three weeks' service who had "hardly learned their facings."[35] Like most of the other units in McDowell's army, they fought bravely but were eventually swept up in the rout which carried them in disorder all the way back to Washington. Their forty-four casualties represented 12 percent of the command, but the Corps as an institution had suffered a greater loss. Colonel Harris forwarded Reynolds's report to Secretary Welles with the sad observation that this represented "the first instance in [Corps] history where any portion of its members turned their backs to the enemy."[36] He also repeated his insistence that the Marines not be detached for service with the Army.

Shortly after the debacle at Manassas, Congress approved legislation which slightly enlarged the Corps and, of more importance to the commandant's senior subordinates, established new billets for one colonel and several lieutenant colonels. There was immediate interest in who would receive the colonelcy and thus become the heir apparent to the aging incumbent. Intrigue, alliance making, and secret petitions then ensued among the three obvious contenders—Majs. Dulany, Edelin, and Reynolds—and their supporters. There also appeared a surprise contender in the form of the enigmatic paymaster, Maj. William Worthington Russell. Staff officers were prohibited by law from command billets, but Russell had enough influential friends in Congress perhaps to overthrow that ruling. A veteran of many more years in Washington than afield or afloat, Russell had twice served as aide-de-camp to Archibald Henderson and performed with some distinction at Harpers Ferry. Influential and ambitious, his whispered candidacy for the new colonel's billet would dominate the Corps's attention throughout the winter and spring of 1862.[37]

Against this background, Major Reynolds again deployed with a Marine battalion, this time as a landing party with Flag Officer Samuel F. DuPont, in what was arguably the last chance for the Corps to develop some amphibious credibility. The expedition, however, was snakebit from the start. First, the troopship, the *Governor,* sank in a storm off Cape Hatteras, keeping the battalion out of the landing at Port Royal. Then, every time DuPont wanted to employ his battalion, notably for amphibious raids up the St. Johns River to Jacksonville and St. Augustine, the Army preempted him, sending its own forces under a superior officer to take charge. Frustrated, DuPont gave up and relinquished command of the battalion with regret.[38] Reynolds returned to Washington where he was promptly relieved of his command and ordered to stand a general court-martial under charges preferred by Colonel Commandant Harris.

The Reynolds court-martial in May 1862 epitomized all that was wrong with the Corps in the early years of the war. The case reflected all the rivalry, jealousy, and bitterness that marked so many of the relations among the senior officers. Reynolds was charged with drunkenness upon reembarkation of the battalion at Port Royal after the *Governor* incident and, more significantly, with disrespect to the commandant in a letter written at the same time. In it, Reynolds avowed that "the Glove of Major Reynolds is at the feet of any officer who aspires to supersede him in rank."[39] Reynolds was not challenging Harris to a duel, it turned out, but venting his frustration over reports of political lobbying of Major Russell to obtain the newly established colonel's billet. That issue had meantime been resolved. Dulany was awarded the new billet; Edelin, Reynolds, and even Marston received promotions to lieutenant colonel; and Major Russell had begun a downward spiral which was to lead shortly to reprimand and suicide.[40] But the court that convened in Marine Barracks, Washington, on 7 May 1862 was keenly sensitive to the issues of succession and politics. Dulany was the president; Edelin and Marston were members; and Reynolds introduced witness after witness to discredit the commandant and Major Russell. Harris himself was on the witness stand for four days of the proceedings, and the grilling was rough. Reynolds was acquitted of both charges, although Welles refused to approve the findings.[41]

Reynolds was not through with Harris. In an amazing letter directly to Welles on 23 July 1862, he sought to bring charges against Harris for perjury, dereliction of duty, playing favorites, and assaulting a Marine Corps private and a drummer boy with his fists.[42] Welles had heard enough. He sent letters of reproof to both Reynolds and Harris, remarking in his diary that "almost all the elder officers [of the Corps] are at loggerheads and ought to be retired."[43]

It is sad to realize that nearly a third of the officers of the Marine Corps were directly involved in this twelve-day trial in Washington at the identical time when the largest amphibious operation of the war, General McClellan's Peninsula campaign, was under way and such signal events as the recapture of Norfolk and the sealing of the Elizabeth River (which effectively ended the short violent life of the Confederate ironclad *Virginia,* née *Merrimac*) were occurring. Significantly, the day following Colonel Harris's testimony for the prosecution, a young enlisted marine stepped into the carnage wreaked by Confederate batteries on Drewery's Bluff against USS *Galena,* restored order out of chaos, removed the dead, and began directing return fire of the ship's great guns against the enemy. Cpl. James Mackie's actions may have escaped the attention of his commandant, but not that of his president. Abraham Lincoln himself awarded Mackie the Medal of Honor, the first ever won by a marine.[44] It was to be that kind of war for the Corps: business as usual among the "Old Guard" back in Washington and most of the barracks, but a steadily emerging "New Corps" of junior officers and troops who did what had to be done in a hundred small unit actions at sea and along the inland rivers.

There was one more attempt at battalion-sized landing operations in the summer of 1863, and once again Admiral DuPont and Lieutenant Colonel Reynolds were teamed together. The target was Fort Sumter, symbol of secession and formidable guardian of Charleston harbor. Heavy bombardment by the Union fleet was followed by a daring, and doomed, night amphibious assault by a naval regiment in small boats. The few marines and sailors who actually made it to the base of the walls of the fort were cut to pieces. The defeat was such a setback that DuPont was relieved in disgrace and Reynolds returned to barracks duty for good.

Colonel Harris began to show signs of the stress of being a wartime commandant. He continued to struggle against the rising tide of desertions within the ranks, pleading with Secretary Welles and the few members of Congress he knew for more men, greater enlistment or referral bounties, and permission to enlist Confederate prisoners. His final Annual Report, submitted to Secretary Welles in October 1863, repeated his request for more troops to meet the incessant demands for Marine Corps guards. He concluded with the request that, given the tripling of the Corps's strength from twelve hundred to thirty-six hundred, the billet of commandant be upgraded to brigadier general. The request was "more for the good of the service" than his own advancement, he added. "For . . . the honor, if conferred, can remain with me but for a short period."[45]

There remained, however, one more obstacle to overcome. Congress, in December 1863, mounted one of its recurring attempts to legislate the Corps out of existence, in this case by transferring it to the Army for assimilation. Harris rose to the occasion in what was arguably his finest work as commandant. First, he set straight the thinking of his own officers. He admonished Maj. Addison Garland, commanding officer of Marine Barracks, Mare Island, with these sharp words: "It appears to me that you are unwilling to be associated with the Navy. . . . This cannot be, and it is this very idea which has in some way gained ground, and is now giving us so much trouble here, and induced the recommendation that we be transferred to the Army. We are of the Navy; are governed by Navy Regulations on shore and afloat; have nothing in common with the Army except forms of parade, inspections, guard mounting and drill."[46]

Harris then borrowed a page from Archibald Henderson's recourse when under congressional attack by soliciting help from the Navy. Eloquent responses poured in from experienced Navy flag officers, including Farragut, DuPont, Wilkes, Balch, and Schley. A masterpiece came from Adm. David Dixon Porter of the Mississippi Squadron. "When they take away the Marines from the Navy they had better lay up all large vessels," he wrote. "I wish anyone could see the difference between the Marines out here and the people they call soldiers; they would not talk of abolishing the Corps."[47] The positive endorsement by the illustrious flag officers carried the day; there would be more congressional attempts to alter or abolish the Corps, but not on John Harris's watch.

The end for Colonel Harris came in early May 1864. One of his last acts was to request relief of the Marine guard on the USS *Minnesota:* "They have served faithfully for three years."[48] With all the shortcomings Harris may have had, faithful service was certainly an attribute he manifested until the end. On the morning of 12 May, after what was described as a "short illness," John Harris died in the Commandant's House. His passing was hardly noticed. General Grant's Wilderness campaign was just under way in Virginia, and total war was about to be unleashed against the South. Harris was buried in Georgetown's Oak Hill Cemetery on 14 May with little fanfare. Gideon Welles released a cursory announcement, then began casting about in his mind for a suitable replacement.[49] The obvious candidates were not appealing. The billet could lay vacant for awhile. After all, there was a war on.

Future historians of the Corps may hypothesize as to what Archibald Henderson, or for that matter John Archer Lejeune, would have done in Harris's place given the opportunities and challenges of the oncoming Civil War. Harris, however, probably did the best he could. While the Corps missed opportunities and suffered grievous setbacks under his leadership, it at least survived as a military institution. This itself was no mean accomplishment. The fact that Harris was able to perpetuate the Corps as a professional force amid the waves of volunteerism, antielitism, and industrialization is very much to his lasting credit. His mobilization of naval support to preserve the Corps was masterful. On the other hand, his cold reserve, petty squabbling, and overall lethargy did the Corps a lot of harm in those dynamic times. There is no record, for example, of Harris ever visiting his troops in the field, in the hospitals, or at the various ports of embarkation or debarkation. Even his annual visits to his barracks were abbreviated, consisting of hasty trips to Boston, Brooklyn, and Philadelphia without a single visit to the recaptured barracks at Norfolk or Pensacola or the newly established posts at Mare Island or Mound City, Illinois. He was a cold, unimaginative, reclusive, desk-bound commandant. It was clearly time for a younger, more personable, more vigorous leader.

7

Jacob Zeilin

1864–1876

COL. JOSEPH H. ALEXANDER, USMC (RET.)

"Attended the funeral of Colonel Harris," confided Navy Secretary Gideon Welles in his diary for Monday, 14 May 1864. He noted that Harris's death "gives embarrassment as to a successor. The higher class of marine officers are not the men who can elevate or give efficiency to the Corps. To supersede them will cause much dissatisfaction. Every man who is over-slaughed and all his friends will be offended with me for what will be deemed an insult. But there is a duty to be done."[1]

Who should become the next commandant? It is instructive to imagine what Welles's thoughts on the subject of succession may have been during the month following the death of Colonel Harris. First, there was no rush. Regardless of who occupied the commandant's office, the administrative reins of the Marine Corps were still very much in the hands of Gideon Welles and his assistant, Gustavus Fox. The two officials held approval authority over most major Marine Corps issues, including appointments, transfers, leave, discharges, procurement, maintenance, disciplinary policy—even selections of uniforms, weapons, and equipment. Operationally, deployed marines were under the command of naval officers who in turn reported to the Navy Department. And there had been no marines deployed in conjunction with the Union Army since the first year of the war. Picking a new commandant was hardly a matter of high priority to Secretary Welles. He may have brooded about it during the Harris funeral, but his primary focus throughout May 1864 would have been elsewhere.

Second, the Lincoln administration was facing a severe test in the upcoming presidential election. At risk was whether the nation retained enough faith in Lincoln, after three years of frightful costs and dubious gains, to see the ordeal through to its end. The administration desperately needed some breakthrough victories. Welles's Navy Department could point to earlier successes—New Orleans, Vicksburg, the *Monitor*—but there were obvious shortfalls. The Union blockade had yet to seal the ports of Wilmington, Mobile, and Charleston, and Confederate commerce raiders like *Alabama* and

Jacob Zeilin, seventh commandant.

Shenandoah continued to roam the high seas. Recent failures of combined expeditions up the Red River and against Fort Sumter were also injurious to the president's reelection campaign.

Third, Welles did not like the traditional option of simply picking the next senior officer. Nor were most of the other candidates appealing to him. These were the field grade officers of the line on duty at the time of Harris's death, listed by order of seniority:

Colonel William Dulany, Commanding Marine Barracks, Norfolk
Lieutenant Colonel Ward Marston, Commanding Marine Barracks, Boston
Lieutenant Colonel John G. Reynolds, Commanding Marine Barracks, Brooklyn
Major Jacob Zeilin, Commanding Marine Barracks, Portsmouth
Major Addison Garland, Commanding Marine Barracks, Mare Island, California
Major Isaac Doughty, Commanding Marine Barracks, Philadelphia
Major William L. Shuttleworth, Commanding Marine Barracks, Pensacola.[2]

Welles probably reviewed the strengths and weaknesses of each candidate. Dulany, the obvious prime contender, had sent Welles a telegram three days after the Harris funeral reminding the secretary of his seniority and requesting assignment as commandant.[3] But Dulany was abrasive and unpredictable; court-martialed for drunkenness and looting after the assault on Chapultepec, he was currently facing grave charges from the commander of the Norfolk Navy Yard. Marston? The worst of the hidebound barracks commanders, still whining about being relieved for cause by John Harris four years earlier, too selfish and lethargic to run the Corps. Reynolds? A warrior no doubt, but he was forever tainted by his long-running feud with the late commandant and his obvious maneuvering to gain power and prestige within the Corps. Zeilin? A legitimate contender yet an enigma. Garland? Promising but best known for his ignominious surrender of two Marine companies without firing a shot when *Ariel* was captured by *Alabama;* another barracks commander unable to maintain harmonious relations with his naval counterparts and superiors. Doughty? Good Mexican War record but unremarkable in the eighteen years since and too old. Shuttleworth? Good record but an unknown quality; Pensacola in those years might as well have been on the moon. That left Zeilin.[4]

Secretary Welles at this point probably reflected on what he knew about Major Zeilin. Who, really, was he? Was he the energetic military professional with West Point training and a splendid combat record in California and Mexico, the officer who had sailed into Yokohama with Perry and voluntarily served as a Marine company commander at First Manassas? Or had he perhaps been too weakened by the hepatitis he contacted in the Far East and the wound he sustained at Manassas; had he perhaps grown stale and old with too many intervening years on the barracks circuit? Welles could not have known for sure, but he did know that Zeilin was the best of the lot.

There was one more factor. Zeilin had the best political connections of any of the candidates, and there was a critical election ahead. That cinched it. Welles's diary entry for Thursday, 9 June 1864 (two days after Lincoln had barely won the nomination of the Republican convention in Baltimore) reflected his decision: "Concluded to retire the marine officers who are past the legal age, and to bring in Zeilin as commandant of the Corps. There seems to be no other alternative."[5] Zeilin was notified the following day. On 11 June, Welles had the Corps adjutant and inspector send identical letters to Colonel Dulany, Lieutenant Colonels Marston and Reynolds, and Major Doughty: "The President has been pleased to direct that your name be entered on the Retired List of

Officers of the Marine Corps from the 9th Inst."[6] Although the blow was softened by each of the officers being permitted to remain at their posts for the duration of the war in a "retired on active duty" status, Welles's decision was still revolutionary. It was the first "deep selection" of a commandant, a rare occurrence even in the twentieth century.[7]

While the rest of the Corps digested the news of his selection, Zeilin quickly turned over command of the Portsmouth Barracks and moved to Washington. His appointment confirmed, he sent this telegram to the secretary of the navy: "I have the honor to acknowledge your communication of this date, concerning my commission as Colonel Commandant of the Marine Corps, and, in obedience to your instructions, I shall at once enter on the duties of that office."[8]

Who indeed was Jacob Zeilin? He was fifty-eight years old when he assumed the commandancy, and he brought thirty-three years of active service to the office. Born on 16 July 1806 in Philadelphia, he became the second of three consecutive commandants from that area. His father, a prosperous tavern owner, was able to send his son to the prestigious Washington Academy for seven years. The headmaster of that institution endorsed Zeilin's subsequent application to the U.S. Military Academy with the prediction that "into whatever profession he may enter, diligence and zeal will not be wanting on his part."[9] Influential family friends petitioned John C. Calhoun, then secretary of war under President James Monroe, for an appointment to West Point.

Jacob Zeilin was barely sixteen when he became a West Point Cadet in 1822, and the academic requirements became too much for him. While his deportment was satisfactory, his performance in mathematics, French, chemistry, and philosophy was marginal, and after his third year, he was discharged. There was no disgrace—only 41 members of the original 103 cadets in the class of 1826 actually graduated—but Zeilin was chagrined.[10] He was to spend the next six years seeking a regular commission.

Back home in Philadelphia, Zeilin became acquainted with the junior officers assigned to the Marine Barracks and through them became inspired to apply for a direct commission in the Marines. There ensued years of petitions and appeals from Zeilin, his family, and friends to three consecutive secretaries of the navy, the secretary of war, and the president. In an 1827 appeal to Secretary of the Navy Samuel L. Southard, Zeilin stressed his "three years attentive apprenticeship to Military business at West Point" and the "favorable manner in which my military conduct was uniformly reported."[11] Four years later, Zeilin appealed directly to President Andrew Jackson, observing that "being just 24 years of age, I am yet young enough to enter into Commission and to learn by study all that I have not acquired by action and hard practice."[12] His perseverance paid off. Zeilin was finally commissioned a second lieutenant of marines on 1 October 1831.

While Zeilin's three years at West Point surely gave him an initial advantage over most other new lieutenants, there is nothing in his early records to portray him as an overachiever. He had the same mixture of barracks and sea duty assignments as his contemporaries. He served briefly in New York under the legendary Lt. Col. John Marshall

Gamble before having to go home on extended sick furlough. He served on board the sloop *Erie* and the frigate *Columbus,* both of them assigned to the South Atlantic. In 1845, he married Margaret Freeman in Norfolk and eventually fathered three children, William, Margaret, and Annie. When the Mexican War erupted the next year, Zeilin was in command of forty-six marines on board the frigate *Congress* off the coast of California.[13]

First Lieutenant Zeilin's performance as commanding Marine Corps officer and adjutant of the Naval Brigade for Commo. Robert Field Stockton's Pacific Squadron was exemplary, clearly the finest sustained execution of field duty in his career. The brigade was deployed imaginatively by Stockton, and the mixed group of sailors, marines, and volunteers made a series of successful landings throughout southern California during 1846–47. Zeilin was prominent in the relief of Stephen W. Kearny's beleaguered forces in December 1846, then fought bravely in the sharp skirmishes with the Californians at Rio San Gabriel and La Mesa the following month. His heroism in the former fight earned him a brevet promotion to major. He also served several months as the military commandant of San Diego. Reembarking with the Pacific Squadron when it was ordered into action along the western coast of Mexico, Zeilin—by then holding a regular promotion to captain along with his brevet rank—participated in the landings at Guaymas and Mazatlán. He finished the war as military governor of Mazatlán.[14]

In 1852, Zeilin began an extraordinary cruise as fleet marine officer on board the flagship *Mississippi* when Commodore Matthew C. Perry led the East India Squadron to force open the closed doors of Japan. Zeilin organized the Marine detachments of the various ships into a ceremonial battalion and was in fact the second American ashore at Yokohama (behind Perry) at the historic landing in Tokyo Bay on 14 July 1853. Contemporary accounts of the impressive formation of marines in full-dress uniform convey only a sense of what was likely both a tense and proud moment for the forty-six-year-old brevet major. Unfortunately, Zeilin contracted hepatitis on this deployment and was ordered home by Perry in the spring of 1854.

Jacob Zeilin commanded the Washington Navy Yard in 1857, when the "Plug Ugly" riots erupted in the capital. He commanded a company of marines under the overall leadership of Archibald Henderson in the urban fighting that ensued.[15] During the next two years, he served at sea on board the frigate *Wabash* in the Mediterranean. It was his final sea duty assignment; at that point in his career he had spent almost exactly half of his twenty-eight years as a marine on board ship. Returning to the United States just before Christmas 1859, he found Colonel Harris in place as commandant and the nation on the brink of the Civil War.

Zeilin's initial assignments in the 1860s reflected the unsettled times. He first was ordered to Philadelphia to relieve Maj. Ward Marston, removed from command by a vindictive John Harris. With the outbreak of the war five months later, he was ordered to take command of Marine Barracks, Washington, a key billet abruptly vacated by Maj. George H. Teretes's decision to fight for the Confederacy. When Major Reynolds was given command of a provisional Marine battalion in support of McDowell's army for what was perceived to be the climactic battle of the insurrection, Zeilin volunteered to serve as one of the four company commanders. It was an understandable, even commendable, gesture on his part, but it had disastrous consequences. He experienced all the confusion, exhaustion, and frustration of trying to lead raw recruits in the bewildering melee that was First Manassas. Late in the day he was wounded and left on the field for dead while the entire battalion ingloriously fled to Washington. His hospitalization coincided with news of permanent promotion to major, but it is not difficult to imagine the impression this experience gave him of combined operations with the Army or the quality of recruits in the New Corps.[16]

With one exception, Zeilin was effectively out of the war from this point on. He returned to his command of the Barracks in Philadelphia, then took command of the larger unit in Brooklyn. He was a member of the general court-martial which convened in Washington in May 1862 to hear charges of drunkenness and disloyalty against John Reynolds; the trial became a public vendetta of the senior officers of the Corps against Colonel Commandant Harris. The record of trial indicates that Zeilin himself had been approached by one of the conspirators involved in trying to nominate Paymaster Russell for the new rank of colonel and thus heir apparent to Harris. To his credit, however, Zeilin appeared to have sidestepped that squabble.[17]

Major Zeilin had one more opportunity for combat action. In July 1863, Secretary Welles directed that he be placed in charge of a Marine battalion for service with Adm. John Dahlgren's South Atlantic Squadron for an amphibious expedition against Fort Sumter. It could have been a fortuitous assignment, but Zeilin had a frustrating time even getting the battalion formed and embarked. Sickness and desertions reduced the battalion from 400 to about 250, and the number of effectives dropped even more after a month of hurried training on Morris Island near Charleston.[18] "I have 150 men," he notified Admiral Dahlgren in disgust, "such as they are."[19] The strain was too much. Zeilin became sick and had to be relieved. John Reynolds took command and the battalion went on to ignominious defeat in an abortive night attack against the fort, but none of the subsequent recrimination reflected against Zeilin.

In fairness, it should be noted that Zeilin was fifty-seven years old at the time of the Charleston expedition. At that time of the war, many battalion and regimental commanders in the Union Army were in their twenties. Zeilin was in fact one year older than Gen. Robert E. Lee and fifteen years older than Gen. U. S. Grant. Nevertheless, this was the fourth time in his career he had to be sent home on sick furlough.[20] Like Manassas, this experience also seemed to take something out of Zeilin. His subsequent performance in command of the Brooklyn Marine Barracks was ineffectual. Colonel Harris rebuked him about the great number of desertions at that post: "So much dissatisfaction must be strong presumptive proof that things are badly conducted unless an improvement is made at once, a radical change will be made."[21] When improvements failed to appear, Harris ordered Zeilin relieved and sent to the smaller post at

Portsmouth. It was in that obscure corner of the Corps four months later that Zeilin received the startling news of his selection by Gideon Welles to become the seventh commandant.

The Marine Corps that Colonel Commandant Zeilin inherited on 1 July 1864 numbered in excess of thirty-eight hundred men and was committed principally in the form of small detachments on nearly one hundred different ships. The support of this primary mission became at once a full-time job. There were not nearly enough troops to meet operational commitments; recruiting was difficult, the desertion rate embarrassing, and systematic training was nonexistent. Zeilin's West Point training and field experience in amphibious landings notwithstanding, there was probably no time or motivation to experiment with other roles and missions. Zeilin himself had experienced directly the negative results of battalion-sized operations in support of both the Army and Navy; there is no evidence that he was inclined to pursue that path.

Zeilin's Headquarters staff included Maj. A. I. Nicholson, adjutant and inspector; Maj. William B. Slack (who had served under Zeilin on the expedition to Japan), quartermaster; and Maj. John C. Cash, who had replaced Major Russell as paymaster. These three staff officers served Zeilin throughout the next twelve years. Of his officers of the line, only four of the nineteen captains were at sea.[22] Combat leadership within the Marine Corps had devolved by this time to the level of lieutenants and sergeants. It was Zeilin's function to recruit, equip, train, and supply the many ships' detachments. It was a daunting task. The Navy had expanded exponentially during the war, from 42 vessels and 11,000 men in 1861, to 671 vessels and 50,000 men in 1865.[23] Zeilin's office was beset by requests for even more ship's detachments.

Actually, providing marines to the fleet was beginning to be very much worth the investment. Seagoing marines gave impressive accounts of themselves while manning some of the great guns in the destruction of *Alabama* by *Kearsage* off Cherbourg, and with Farragut in the storming of Mobile Bay. A small provisional battalion of ship's marines served under 1st Lt. George G. Stoddard (he was the only officer; each company was ably led by a sergeant) in the mildly successful Broad River expedition. Even the barracks marines bestirred themselves for once. Capt. James Forney took command of a hastily organized battalion out of Philadelphia to help thwart Confederate general Jubal Early's raid north of Baltimore in July 1864, earning a brevet promotion for himself and restoring a bit of luster to the Corps's inland fighting ability.

In other respects, however, it was business as usual. Lieutenant Colonels Reynolds and Marston feuded over assignment of a particular carpenter to their barracks to the point that Zeilin had to write an angry letter citing their "unabated animosity" toward each other and "the lack of obedience and want of respect" to their new commandant.[24] Zeilin subsequently had to sack Marston for gross misappropriation of his recruits' bounty money, a case which hardly endeared the Corps to the secretary of the navy.[25]

While "Old Guard" marines continued to bicker and gripe, the Lincoln administration toiled for reelection. The military equation had changed that summer and fall of

1864. Farragut had seized Mobile, Sherman had captured Atlanta, Sheridan had driven Early from the Valley of Virginia, and Grant appeared to have finally brought Lee to bay at Petersburg. In the 8 November election, Lincoln prevailed by a significant margin over General McClellan.

It was not to be a straight road to victory, however. Fort Fisher, gateway to Wilmington, was captured by a combined expeditionary force in January 1865, but the assault by the sailors and marines of the Naval Brigade was a spectacular failure. Adm. David Dixon Porter's plan to launch a direct assault by seamen armed only with cutlasses and revolvers, supported by Marine riflemen, was at best a seagoing version of Pickett's charge, in execution "sheer, murderous madness."[26] The bluejackets were cut to pieces before the confused marines could get into position to support them, a bloody debacle very similar to the assault of the Naval Brigade on the second day at Veracruz fifty years later. Although the Army took advantage of the suicidal charge to invest and capture the fort from the north, no one felt good about the operation. The Navy was quick to blame the Corps; even Admiral Porter took up the hue and cry. Capt. L. L. Dawson's report as the senior marine described the conflicting and impossible orders given by various naval commanders, but it received no press. It was an undeserved black eye for the Marines, one that set back the development of American amphibious operations as much as Gallipoli did in 1915.[27] Admiral DuPont, himself on the sidelines and in disgrace following the earlier failure of a naval brigade to capture Fort Sumter, reflected the mood of the sea services with these remarks: "That silly storming party of sailors and marines, in order to have a 'share in the assault.'"[28]

Zeilin agonized over this public flogging of his Corps but got no sympathy from Welles. The end of the war was perceived to be in sight, and no one in the Navy Department particularly cared if the Marine Corps had its collective toes stepped on unjustly. After a while, Zeilin dropped the issue. He was terribly worried about the skyrocketing rate of desertion in the Corps. His adjutant was reporting a total of 993 deserters in the final year of the war, more than a quarter of the enlisted strength of the Corps.[29] A shameful development for any proud military organization, the rate of desertion also compounded the problems Zeilin faced in meeting the ever-increasing demand for ship detachments. As late as two weeks before Appomattox, he had to reject the request for more marines from 1st Lt. Henry Clay Cochrane, commanding Marine Corps officer on USS *Blackhawk,* flagship of the Mississippi Squadron: "The pressure for seagoing vessels is so great that I have but few men to spare."[30]

The Civil War was finally over. The Corps had sustained very modest casualties compared to the other services: 148 killed in action, 312 deaths from other causes.[31] But the Corps as an institution had sustained greater casualties: the large-scale defections, the rout at Manassas, the capture of the Marine battalion on *Ariel,* the intermittent feuding between the senior officers of the Corps, the disastrous attacks on Fort Sumter and Fort Fisher, and finally, the desertion rate. The Marine Corps would be in for some serious questions by Congress and the Administration. Fortunately, Zeilin, already intelligent and energetic, was gaining confidence in the execution of his office.

Zeilin could deal with public indifference to the regular establishment (the popular perception, hardly overstated, proclaimed that "the volunteers won the war!"), but he was hobbled throughout by Gideon Welles's continued disregard for the Corps. Welles seemed simply to ignore the Marines. With one small exception, Welles's diary entry of 9 June 1864 about his selection of Zeilin to be commandant was the last mention of the Marine Corps for the remaining four years of his office. On the dark side, Welles may have become actively prejudiced against the Corps. Historian Robert Debs Heinl found evidence in an 1892 report of the House Committee on Naval Affairs that Welles had suppressed the Marine names from a list of Navy and Marine officers recommended for accelerated promotion for combat bravery at war's end.[32] The assistant secretary held similar views. In a letter dated 1 June 1865, Gustavus Fox listed eight postwar objectives of the Navy Department; item number four was "marines to go to Army, where they belong."[33]

This combination of negative perceptions—ragged wartime performance, uncertain future roles and missions, inconsistent support from the Navy Department leadership—produced yet another attempt by Congress to disestablish the Corps. A House resolution in June 1866 suggested "abolishing the Marine Corps, and transferring it to the Army."[34] Zeilin was ready for this. Just as Harris and Henderson had done before him, he went right to the fleet. There were plenty of grateful commanders on hand who weighed in with their personal endorsements of the value to the Navy of a Corps of Marines, among them such national heroes as Farragut, Foote, Dahlgren, and even Porter. To this stout defense, Zeilin added his own Pennsylvanian political connections with the House of Representatives. It worked. The House Naval Affairs Committee not only succeeded in killing the bill but also issued a ringing reaffirmation of the worth of the Corps: "No good reason appears either for abolishing it or transferring it to the Army; on the contrary, the Committee recommends that its organization as a separate Corps be preserved and strengthened . . . (and) that its commanding officer shall hold the rank of Brigadier General."[35] This was welcome news. On 2 March 1867, Zeilin became the first marine ever to hold the regular grade of brigadier general. (Henderson's rank had been a brevet appointment.)

Zeilin then turned with relish to other postwar problems within the Corps: professional training, modernization of weapons and equipment, quality and quantity of recruits, the growing schism between field grade and company grade officers, long neglected repairs to barracks and armories. It was an uphill struggle in each case. There were never enough troops; the largest concentration of marines in any single place in those years never exceeded two hundred; there was little interest on the part of either Congress or the Navy Department to fund repairs; and there was little incentive during the antimilitary atmosphere that prevailed for young men to turn from profit seeking to the hard sacrifices of sea duty and barracks guard.

Zeilin's first significant act after his promotion was to direct the adoption of Emory Upton's *Infantry Tactics* as the basis for military education for all Marine Corps officers. It was a good initiative but tough to implement, given the fragmentation of the

Corps into such small units. Zeilin had no real way of institutionalizing this reform except through the annual visits by himself and his Inspector. Some officers took it to heart; many others chose to ignore it.[36]

The commandant had more success in procuring improved firepower for his riflemen. Zeilin had earlier resisted the temptation to recommend adoption of the Plymouth rifled musket, highly touted in some inner sanctums of Washington, because a board of his officers reported that the existing Springfield musket was four times as accurate at three hundred yards and was the only weapon that registered any hits on target at all at five hundred yards.[37] Zeilin was particularly interested in obtaining breech loaders for the Marine Corps. While the Marines would be issued certain experimental or limited-quantity breech-loaders during his commandancy—the .50-caliber Ward-Burton M1871, .50-caliber Remington "Rolling Block" M1870, and .45-caliber Remington-Lee M1882, for example—Zeilin was most enthusiastic about a simple conversion process for his existing muzzle loading, percussion muskets developed by Erskin S. Allin, master armorer of the Springfield Armory. The weapons were remilled to accept a rising breech block, solid hammer, and firing pin. Allin performed a series of improved modifications to the Springfield in the immediate postwar years which benefited the Marines.[38] The 1870 Allin Conversion Springfields issued to the Corps that year so delighted the commandant that he declared that there was "nothing left to be desired in the military equipment of the Marines."[39] Distribution of the new weapons to the scattered fleet marines was slow, however, and Capt. McLane Tilton, who had evaluated the Plymouth musket in 1864 and the prototype Remington "Rolling Block" in 1869, complained to the commandant that his men had to use the "blasted old Muzzle Fuzzel" muskets during his sparkling assault against the Salee River forts in Korea in June 1871.[40]

Tilton's letter serves as a reminder that a large majority of Zeilin's marines were deployed afloat and engaged in continuing incidents of nineteenth-century power projection around the world. Marines participated in landing operations in China in 1866; Formosa, Japan, and Nicaragua in 1867; Japan and Uruguay in 1868; Mexico in 1870; Korea in 1871; Panama in 1873; Hawaii in 1874; and Mexico again in 1876. The Korean expedition was a good revalidation of the usefulness of Marine Corps landing parties. Captain Tilton's company led a large naval battalion ashore against Kwang Fort in the Han River under the protective guns of Commodore John Rogers's squadron. The fighting was spirited, marksmanship noteworthy, and six marines received the Medal of Honor.[41] All in all, the fight helped purge some of the ghosts of Fort Fisher from the emerging Navy–Marine Corps team.

During those same years, the Corps was called out to combat major urban riots in Baltimore, Boston, New York, and Philadelphia. "Whisky riots" in the Irish shanties of Brooklyn were fairly common, and the Marines were better received by the rioters than were the police. Zeilin commended Capt. Richard S. Collum after one such confrontation for his "firmness and discretion" in achieving "successful and bloodless" termination of the situation.[42]

Zeilin looked for ways to improve professionalism and esprit. He was the first marine to become a member of the Naval Institute. He sent Captain Forney to England to learn from the Royal Marines and later tried to adopt their motto—Per Mare, Per Terras—as had Henderson. He was aware of the rising discontent of his junior officers and tried to accommodate some of their wishes. In November 1868, for example, he forwarded their recommendation for a new cap ornament in the shape of an eagle, globe, and fouled anchor with a favorable endorsement. That same month, however, he only reluctantly forwarded a petition of his officers to return to the brass-milled Mameluke sword. He cited the lack of serviceability of the metal scabbard, the susceptibility of the brass fittings to saltwater corrosion, and the lack of a hand guard as reasons to retain the regulation Civil War saber. The younger officers, however, associated the "Army sword" with the Harris years; it had been adopted less than a month after the previous commandant had taken office and was virtually indistinguishable from the Army version. They yearned for a return to the distinctive Mameluke of Presley O'Bannon and Archibald Henderson. Welles sided with the petitioners. The Mameluke sword was readopted for officers over Zeilin's objections, although NCOs retain the M1859 model to this date.[43]

Zeilin also fought for improved quality in recruiting. Doubtlessly recalling his adverse experiences with poor quality recruits at First Manassas and Morris Island, the commandant took his chief recruiting officer to task with words that were resurrected one hundred years later in a similar period of postwar doldrums: "A few good men are preferable to a number of recruits of inferior material."[44]

Zeilin was energetic and caring, but he was unable on his own to steer the Marine Corps clear of deeply troubled times that affected the military establishment in 1874. These were particularly dark times for the Corps. Two-thirds of all enlisted marines were at sea on extended deployments, and public opinion was at an all-time low. Desertions increased proportionately to the same alarming levels as 1864–65. To make matters worse, yet another congressional attempt to abolish the Corps took root and became worrisome. Although Zeilin was once again adept at mobilizing support among his political friends and the Civil War naval officers, this crisis was a near thing. The Corps survived, but its operating budget was slashed by a third, officers were reduced from ninety to seventy-eight, privates capped at fifteen hundred, and the brigadier's rank for the commandant rescinded.[45]

Morale of the junior officers took a nosedive in the mid-1870s, partly as a result of the extended postwar doldrums and the accompanying cutbacks, but also as a result of certain grievances which had been percolating for years. The most outspoken of the lot was 1st Lt. Henry Clay Cochrane. He and his friends wrote a disgruntled pamphlet in Annapolis in the fall of 1875 for circulation among the company grade ranks. Cochrane was not one to mince words. "That there is a deep seated and wide spread antipathy towards the Marine Corps only the blind and imbecile can doubt," he began. His object was to "arouse every officer to the necessity of some action that will make us respectable and useful." He went on to list twenty-five reforms, including "more rapid and certain promotion, and a system of examinations for each step"; an end to drunkenness and fraud; a brigade organization with regiments, battalions, and companies; equitable berthing on board ship (complaining that lately "even a Fleet Marine Officer with gray hairs and grown children" had to sleep in a hammock and "make a morning exhibit of the shape of his legs and the sheer of his shirttails to gaping servants").[46]

Cochrane met later that winter in Norfolk with a group of other reformers, including Capt. (and Bvt. Lt. Col.) Charles Heywood and Capt. (Bvt. Maj.) Louis E. Fagan. Their product was a draft bill for enactment by Congress which codified twenty-three separate reforms.[47] This was a forlorn hope in the political atmosphere of the time, but within the Corps it was an early clarion call for professionalism, unity, and esprit.

Zeilin's exhausting struggles to preserve his small Corps had unwittingly made him a defender of the status quo. He turned a deaf ear toward the reformers, insisting to the end that the "present organization of the Marine Corps is the best that can be devised."[48] He was tired and increasingly ill, and it was time to pass command to a younger man. Earlier, in 1871, he had shown foresight in bringing his logical successor, Col. Charles G. McCawley, to Headquarters to serve an extended apprenticeship. Zeilin surely sought to avoid the embarrassing political fights among candidates for the top billet which occurred during John Harris's declining years, so he did the right thing. On 1 November 1876, he became the first commandant to retire in office. He was seventy and had attained forty-five years of active service to his Corps.

Jacob Zeilin died four years later, officially of complications from the same hepatitis which had afflicted him since his expedition to the Far East with Commodore Perry. His family attributed his death to another cause. The apple of the old commandant's eye during his later years was his son, Willie, a second lieutenant of marines. On 4 June 1880, young Zeilin was on a picnic near Norfolk when he learned of his selection for first lieutenant. Exuberant, he galloped his horse back to the barracks. The horse collided with a tollgate, throwing the lieutenant and killing him instantly. News of his son's death was devastating to the general. He sank into melancholy and died a few months later at the Washington Navy Yard.[49]

At Quantico, Virginia—the "Crossroads of the Corps"—the streets and buildings are appropriately named for the great Marine heroes of the past. The names of Lejeune and Russell and Barnett and Butler are prominent. There are also two parallel streets named for John Harris and Jacob Zeilin, but they are predictably obscure thoroughfares, two old, out-of-the-way streets between the railroad tracks and the ancient warehouses. The sixth and seventh commandants deserve a better fate. Both did their best to keep the Corps intact during painfully tough times. Zeilin, in particular, provided energetic and innovative leadership at a critically low point in Marine Corps history. Whatever malice Gideon Welles may have borne toward the Corps, he certainly did the Marines a lasting favor by his courageous decision to "deep select" Jacob Zeilin as commandant in the dark days of 1864.

8

Charles G. McCawley

1876–1891

JACK SHULIMSON

In the autumn of 1876, as Brig. Gen. Jacob Zeilin, after twelve years as commandant of the Marine Corps, spoke openly of stepping down, several officers jockeyed to succeed him. The frontrunner was Lt. Col. Charles G. McCawley, commander of one of the Corps's most prestigious posts, its Washington Barracks. A son of a Marine officer and veteran of both the Mexican and Civil Wars with a distinguished combat record, the forty-nine-year-old McCawley had friends in high places and maneuvered carefully behind the scenes to place himself in a strategic position. In mid-October, Secretary of the Navy George M. Robeson announced that General Zeilin would retire at the end of the month and that on 1 November 1876, Lieutenant Colonel McCawley would become the next commandant of the Marine Corps.[1]

Zeilin had left the Marine Corps in much disarray. In successive years from 1874 to 1876, Congress had reduced the rank of commandant to colonel, cut the enlisted strength from about three thousand to two thousand men, and authorized no further second lieutenant appointments until the officer corps was down to seventy-five, a reduction of some twenty-five officers. The chairman of the House Naval Affairs Committee wanted to either abolish the Marine Corps or transfer it to the Army. Even Lt. Henry Clay Cochrane, a leader of the reform element among the younger officers, called either for a "funeral or a resuscitation" for the Corps.[2]

The Marine officer corps was badly divided with many of the younger officers in almost open revolt. Several of the more "progressive" junior officers had met secretly and exchanged communications. In a letter that Capt. Robert Huntington circulated among the reform group, he declared that the Marine Corps consisted of two elements, the progressive and the conservative, largely divided by age and seniority: "To the one, the present is the best moment; the other looks to the future. It is the irrepressible conflict between conservatism and progress."[3]

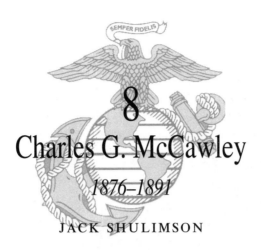

Brig. Gen. Charles L. McCawley, eighth commandant.
U.S. Marine Corps Photo 515338.

Cochrane pushed for a complete reformation of the Marine Corps. He demanded mandatory retirement at age sixty-two, examinations for promotion, officer vacancies to be filled by Naval Academy or West Point graduates, a brigade organization with permanent regiments, and the fleet marine officer to have the rank of major while serving in that position. Cochrane also referred to the possibility of redesignating the Marine Corps, the United States Naval Artillery: "I feel that at present we have no motive or special incentive to anything beyond the mere mechanical performance of a monotonous routine and the ideal gratification of social instincts."[4]

Despite the agitation of the reformers, General Zeilin had defended the status quo until the very end. In his final annual report, he had declared "the present organization of the Marine Corps is the best that can be devised." For the Marine Corps, like the Navy, reaction and reform continued to coexist in an uneasy relationship. The transition from the old to the new Navy and Marine Corps would be a tortuous and circuitous one.[5]

With a reputation as a traditionalist and strict disciplinarian, McCawley was neither the first nor last choice of the reformers. Robert Huntington, for example, had written to his father several years earlier that he believed McCawley as a commandant would "not be bad although he is pretty mean." Not necessarily privy to the confidences of the reform group but sharing with its members some similar goals, McCawley desired to improve the officer corps and to make the Marine Corps a more efficient organization. He supposedly had remarked to a junior officer in 1873 that if he became commandant, he would "work hard for the Corps and try to bring it up to that standard where it should have been." Relatively conservative, however, McCawley foresaw no new mission for the Marine Corps and remained satisfied with its ad hoc organization. Thus, a McCawley commandancy promised some reform but limited, if any, change in the traditional mission and organization of the Corps.[6]

The Marine Corps that McCawley inherited was an organizational anomaly. Dispersed into small ships' detachments and navy yard guards of usually one hundred or fewer men, it had no formal company, battalion, or regimental structure. Its commandant was responsible for the training, equipping, and assignment of personnel. Yet outside of the Headquarters staff, he had no troops under his command except those assigned to the Washington Barracks and the Marine Band. The commanding officers of the Marine Corps ship detachments reported directly to the Navy captain of the ship, and the marines at most shore installations came under the authority of the commandants of the various navy yards, usually a senior naval officer. Although also a land service and occasionally serving with the Army, the Marine Corps by tradition and law, came under the authority of the secretary of the navy and for most matters was "subject to the . . . regulations for the government of the Navy."[7]

The Marine officer corps was held in rather low repute. Entrance into it had been largely through influence and political connections. Officer aspirants, similar to candidates for the Military and Naval Academies, required either congressional or presidential sponsorship. When openings occurred, nominees would have to pass a perfunctory examination before a board of officers that included a Navy doctor as to their physical, mental, and moral qualifications. Of the thirty officers appointed after the Civil War through 1876 on active duty four years later, ten had attended West Point or Annapolis and failed to graduate. Sons of military officers and members of prominent social and political families dominated the lists of successful selectees.[8]

Enterprising journalists found the Marine officer corps an inviting target. One Philadelphia newspaper devoted an article to what it called the "social Marines." The author observed that both the Army and Navy had developed aristocracies centered around West Point and Annapolis: "But the simon-pure, superaesthetical, ultra-social concern is the Marine Corps." He then listed the names of several officers who were the "sons and nephews of army and navy officials and of Senators and of high officials." Thus, whether deserved or not, the Marine Corps had a "Captain Jenks" popular image which McCawley would have to overcome if he were to attain his agenda.[9]

Just before assuming the commandancy, McCawley drew up a list of thirty-some changes that he wanted to make in the Corps. Many of the items on the list dealt with relatively mundane matters such as the number of men at the navy yards, relations with the staff, prohibiting the sale of "malt-liquor" in post traders' canteens, musical instruments, and barracks furniture. Yet a consistent theme of modest reform runs through this rather ordinary listing, representing a real desire to better conditions for the enlisted men, to improve the quality of both enlisted and officer personnel and training, to increase the status of the commandant, and to have the Marine Corps Headquarters staff answer to him.[10]

In his first months, McCawley took several steps to implement these measures. In May 1877, he issued a circular to all Marine commands directing commanding officers to drill their troops in the "School of the Company" and "School of the Battalion" using Upton's *Tactics* as the text. All commanders were to "at least once a week, inspect personally their commands under arms, and will also visit the different parts of the garrison to assure themselves that they are in good order." At the end of every month, each commanding officer was to report to the adjutant and inspector that he had carried out the provisions of the directive.[11]

Despite resistance, McCawley persisted in efforts to improve the caliber of the individual marine. He berated officers who enlisted poorly qualified men into the Corps. He bluntly told one commander that the fifteen recruits he provided were of low quality and one was "so very stupid . . . I doubt if he will be of any use." He urged his officers to enlist only the best men. McCawley obtained from the secretary of the navy the approval power for all enlisted promotions and believed this would eventually lead to the creation of a capable cadre of noncommissioned officers. Rather than award promotions and grant reductions at the caprice of a single commanding officer, he established an examining board of officers to submit recommendations to the commandant. McCawley argued, "We have today a better class of non-commissioned than we have had before, and the order has given great satisfaction in the Corps."[12]

The commandant did not limit his efforts to improve the Corps only to enlisted men. With the 1876 legislation that suspended officer appointments until the number of officers reached seventy-five either through dismissal, retirement, or resignation, McCawley attempted to cleanse the service of several of its chief mischief makers. One of the principle transgressions among several of the junior officers appeared to be the nonpayment of debts. Wanting to make an example for others, McCawley pressed court-martial charges against the worst offenders. In March 1877, McCawley recommended charges against 2d Lt. Julius C. Shailer, who not only borrowed money from his fellow officers without repaying but also did the same with enlisted men. Within a month, Shailer proffered his resignation, which McCawley accepted. The commandant also forced the resignation of 1st Lt. Edward T. Bradford, who, McCawley observed, had been "reported more frequently [than any other officer] for not paying his debts." 1st Lt. Andrew Stevenson, described by a fellow officer as "a liar with the lowest instincts" and "unfit to associate with gentlemen," escaped the commandant's dragnet, however, by first offering his resignation and then withdrawing it once charges against him were dropped. Nevertheless, the *Army and Navy Journal* accessed McCawley's first year in the commandancy as one that contributed to a marked improvement in the morale of the Marine Corps and observed that in the officer corps, "three old offenders will not appear in next year's registers."[13]

Notwithstanding his modest success in winnowing out the chaff among the officers, Colonel McCawley quickly learned the limitations of his power relative to officer assignment. In early 1877, soon after becoming commandant, he attempted to appoint Col. M. R. Kintzing, the Corps's most senior officer, to the much sought-after command of the Brooklyn Navy Yard Marine Barracks. Maj. John L. Broome, who had held this prized position for over ten years, was not about to give up his post voluntarily. He quickly appealed to influential patrons to take his case to the secretary of the navy. In April 1877, the leading Democrat senator on the Naval Affairs Committee, James McPherson of New Jersey, wrote to Secretary of the Navy Richard Thompson asking that Broome be retained at Brooklyn, because he "had the esteem of the most prominent men of Brooklyn of both political parties." Despite the vehement protest of Colonel Kintzing, the navy secretary overruled McCawley and kept Major Broome at Brooklyn. Secretary Thompson denied that his action reflected negatively on Kintzing's reputation as an officer and a gentleman, but merely indicated the desire "not to disturb the present arrangements at Brooklyn." It would take more than a year for McCawley finally to get Broome out of New York.[14]

Yet during his first year in office, McCawley had established himself as a forceful leader and an able administrator. In the summer of 1877, he organized two Marine battalions that were deployed in Washington, D.C., and later sent to Baltimore, Philadelphia, and Reading, Pennsylvania, during labor unrest in the nation's railroads and mines. Having restored order, the two battalions returned to Washington and, on 17 August, paraded before the secretary of the navy and disbanded. In the immediate aftermath of the crisis, the Corps basked in public accolades. During a burst of initial enthusiasm, Thompson assured McCawley of the department's willingness "to cooperate in the adoption of any measure necessary to their [the marines'] comfort and an increase of their efficiency." McCawley issued a general order in which he quoted the complimentary phrases about the officers and men of the two battalions made by the Army commanders under whom the marines had served. He then ended with a grandiloquent flourish: "Such conduct cannot fail to impress upon the whole country the fact that the Marine Corps now, as in the past, well sustains its old reputation of 'ever faithful,' and proves its value as a reliable military organization." By November, however, these words were largely forgotten, and Colonel McCawley himself made only passing reference in his annual report to the Marine strikebreaking role.[15]

Still under the legislative dictum to reduce the officer corps, McCawley continued with his efforts to prune the number of officers down to seventy-five. By 1879, forced resignations and retirements of more senior officers brought the number of officers to the desired size. McCawley complained, "The constantly decreasing number of second lieutenants will shortly render the duties of all lieutenants much more onerous, and at the same time cause more difficulty (as it already does) in making agreeable details for shore duty."[16]

In 1880, for the first time in four years, the Marine Corps commissioned seven second lieutenants. These new officers were hardly an exception to those that preceded them: one was the son of a prominent Indiana politician, another had attended the Military Academy for two years, while a third was the son of a socially prominent Virginia family. This latter officer, Littleton W. T. Waller from Norfolk, had actually wanted a commission in the cavalry, but was too short. His father, a friend of Senator Wade Hampton from South Carolina, asked the Senator to intercede for the younger Waller. According to one account, Hampton received assurances that the Marine Corps did not have such "foolish standards" as the Army. In response to his request, Secretary Thompson replied, "Certainly Senator, we'll appoint him. Mr. Cushing make out a commission of Marines for Mr. Waller." This story may be apocryphal, but it indicates the importance that political influence continued to play in officer appointments.[17]

The most flagrant use of political patronage, however, continued to be in the selection of staff officers. In early 1880, Capt. William A. T. Maddox retired as an assistant quartermaster in a career marked either by dishonesty or gross incompetence, and probably a little bit of both. Many senior lieutenants with strong qualifications for the position applied. Yet, the appointment went to a relatively junior lieutenant, Woodhull S. Schenck, whose stepfather was active in New York Republican politics and a good friend of Secretary Thompson. According to Schenck, Thompson had told him, "Wood, you shall have it." The Senate Naval Affairs Committee recommended disapproval of Schenck's appointment but was overridden by the full Senate. Supporters of Schenck had pointed out during the debate that, only a few years earlier, Major Goodloe, the paymaster and a son-in-law of Senator Beck of Kentucky, went from a junior lieutenant to his present position under similar conditions. One disgruntled Marine Corps officer wrote, "Where the current of promotion resembles the flow of Puerto Rico Molasses in winter, simple humanity would dictate a cessation of advancing favorite juniors over faithful seniors." Colonel McCawley in his annual report referred to the need of legislation "to define the manner for staff appointments."[18]

A major scandal, in 1880, also pointed to the need for reform within the officer corps. Col. Thomas Y. Field, commander of the large Brooklyn Barracks and the senior officer in the Corps outside of the commandant, engaged in a series of feuds with his subordinate officers, mostly about the cleanliness of their quarters. During August and September, he conducted several inspections of these quarters at unusual hours of the day and night. In one extreme case, he directed a police party of enlisted marines to knock down the door of one of the lieutenants and search the room. Field told his subordinates that he had been ordered "to the different yards to clean them out and put them to rights; and now he was ordered to the Marine Barracks at the New York Yard to put that right." To some of the junior lieutenants, he denounced the officers under him and most other Marine officers as "ungentlemanly and immoral, . . . whoremongers, blackguards, liars, and scoundrels." A Navy court-martial found Field guilty of "Conduct to the prejudice of good order and discipline [and] Conduct unbecoming an officer and gentleman." Due to Field's long service, the court recommended clemency and the secretary of the navy ordered him "released from arrest, relieved of command of the Marine Barracks, Brooklyn," and to "be regarded as waiting orders."[19]

Marine Corps officers also had to contend with what amounted to a second-class relationship with their Navy counterparts. On both land and sea, marines normally served under naval authority. At sea, of course, it was the fleet or squadron commander or ship's captain, while on shore it usually was the naval commandant of a navy yard. Navy officers often viewed the Corps as an inferior service and referred to marines on board ship as "idlers." An occasional piece appeared in naval professional journals about reducing the number of marines or taking them altogether off naval vessels. On shore, navy yards were walled self-contained small military enclaves, usually located in a major American city. Here the naval commandant reigned, and, as one officer remembered, "in the old days his only superior was God."[20]

Throughout his commandancy, McCawley engaged in a constant struggle to maintain his prerogatives and that of his officers against what he perceived as usurpation on the part of many naval officers. He realized that "some Naval officers consider everything done by the commandant of the Marine Corps as 'an assumption of authority.'" In June 1880, nevertheless, the secretary of the navy permitted McCawley to issue minor orders relative to transfer of men between duty stations and ships without first submitting them to the department for approval. Two years later, the secretary expanded the authority to include the detailing of Marine officers in the "same manner as is now done in regard to the enlisted men." To a complaint from a navy yard commander about officer assignment, McCawley replied, "I respectfully submit that the Commandant of a corps of 2,000 men (while not holding the rank to which he is fairly entitled, both by custom and precedent), should have as much authority over the officers and men of his corps, wherever stationed, as a commodore commanding a navy yard has over his command."[21]

Inherent in McCawley's ambitions for the Marine Corps was the buildup of the prestige of the commandancy. Part of this prestige lay in pomp and ceremony and in the parlors of the capital city. Although his young and fashionable wife on occasion referred to McCawley as "too old for her," she proved a gracious hostess. She held afternoon teas for the Washington social set, and the Marine Corps Band provided entertainment. The band also often played concerts for the public at the Marine Barracks. Both the band and marines at the barracks took part in the inauguration of President James A. Garfield in 1881 and received favorable attention from both spectators and press. The Marines also participated in ceremonial parades on several other state occasions. Indeed, the band became so popular that McCawley had to reject some invitations.[22]

McCawley, of course, understood that prestige depended on more than outward show. One of the basic thrusts of his commandancy was an effort to standardize training and drill. He monitored the inspections of Marine Corps shore barracks and insisted that commanders conduct battalion drill and teach tactics and permitted no exceptions. The commandant convinced the secretary in August 1881 to issue a general order that directed commanding officers of ships entering ports where there were barracks to have their marines train twice a week with the shore garrison. The entire purpose was "to ensure uniformity in the drills of the U.S. Marines."[23]

McCawley's leadership style allowed little room for delegation. He often engaged in what we would now call "micromanagement" with his subordinates and emphasized the carrying out to the letter an order or regulation. The commandant wrote to one commander, "It is my fixed attention that Commanding, as well all other officers in the Marine Corps shall do the work assigned them by orders and regulations, and I cannot in justice, permit any Commanding Officer to hold himself as too high a rank to do his proper duty." This demand for detail often involved McCawley in disputes with his subordinate officers and several navy yard commandants.[24] The commandant took quick umbrage at what he considered dereliction of duty on the part of senior commanders. For example, in August 1882, he scolded Lt. Colonel Hebb of the Boston Barracks for confining several NCOs in cells prior to their trials. After receiving an inspection report that described the barracks as "streaked with tobacco juice, and the rooms untidy," he observed to the secretary that a change of commanding officers was in order.[25]

McCawley faced a persistent problem with political involvement in officer assignments and personnel decisions in general. In one example, a young man joined the Marine Corps "in a fit of desperation," and the family or friends of the family brought his case to the attention of the president. The secretary of the navy told the commandant that the president "has directed his discharge. You will see, therefore, that it is done immediately." In this case, McCawley had little choice but to do as he was told. More often, however, the influence was more indirect, and the commandant often circumvented the political pressure. As could be expected, McCawley's difficulties with his officers often involved assignment to sea duty or to unpopular shore posts. McCawley once complained to the secretary of the navy that "for the honor of the Marine Corps and, even for their own interests, its officers should be required to obey orders without regard to other considerations."[26]

Both Secretaries of the Navy William S. Hunt and William E. Chandler during the Garfield and Arthur administrations largely supported McCawley in the latter's efforts to blunt congressional or political interference with officer assignments. Secretary Chandler replied to Senator Nelson W. Aldrich of Rhode Island, who had written on the behalf of one Marine officer, "Attempts on the part of officers to evade duty are so frequent that a general statement by a Member of Congress, like that of your letter, is never deemed sufficient." To 2d Lt. Frank S. Denny, who had written a letter to the postmaster general to use his influence to countermand a McCawley order, Chandler had a subordinate write, "Your action in thus appealing to the Head of another Department is highly unofficerlike and unproper, and deserves severe censure." The censure in this case was merely a warning not to repeat his action.[27]

Colonel McCawley had a running feud with the official Marine Corps staff, especially with the Quartermaster Department, that lasted through much of his tenure. From the beginning of his term, McCawley had attempted to curb what he viewed as the unbridled license and inefficiency of the quartermaster. He went so far as to insist that "all staff officers and clerks . . . will be present promptly at 10 a.m. No deviation from the order will be allowed except upon application to the Colonel Commandant." In February 1879, he upbraided the quartermaster, Maj. William B. Slack, for not notifying him of an absence. Thereafter, when Slack departed Washington "on business connected with your office," he was to "make an application for an order to do so to the Commandant of the Corps."[28]

During the early 1880s, the friction between McCawley and the quartermaster officers, if anything, increased. He had several run-ins with Major Slack and reprimanded the new assistant quartermaster, Captain Schenck. In 1884, McCawley and Slack reached a new low in their acrimonious relationship. McCawley ordered Slack to make some minor changes in the annual budgetary estimates. Slack refused on the basis that he considered it "a deception upon Congress" and stalked out of McCawley's office. The commandant called him back with another officer as witness and repeated his request. Once more, Slack rebuffed him. McCawley then took his case to the secretary, stating that he wanted Slack brought up on charges to "enforce discipline, and make the Quartermaster of the Corps an assistance to the Commandant rather than the reverse." Chandler supported McCawley in his authority to direct the changes in the estimates but did not believe that Slack deserved to be court-martialed. The secretary told McCawley that Slack denied that "he intended to be disrespectful, and unless you are prepared to prove that his manner was so offensive that by itself it can be the subject of a specific charge, the whole subject had better end with this communication." Chandler assured McCawley that the department commended his "general management of the Marine Corps and will sustain you on all proper occasions which call for its actions." In May 1885, Major Slack retired from active duty because of age.[29]

Throughout this period, McCawley's attitude toward his formal staff was one of distrust and distaste. He wrote to Chandler, "I have never known the staff to care for anything but its own interests. . . . When they were appointed by the Commandant they were far more efficient, and did not intrigue to be made Commandant and set the whole Corps in disorder, as they have done in late years." McCawley's obvious solution was to make the staff answerable to the commandant of the Marine Corps both for their appointment and to the terms of their service.[30] The struggle against desertion, which had plagued the Marine Corps since its inception, continued as well. Colonel McCawley inaugurated a series of administrative reforms which he hoped would improve enlisted morale and satisfaction. His predecessor, General Zeilin, had viewed the problem as unsolvable.

McCawley believed, however, that more selective recruiting, improved working and living conditions, more regular pay periods, additional recreational facilities, and promotion by merit would cut the desertion rate. Blaming the sutler system, or at least the selling of beer by the sutler or post trader, for much of the indiscipline, he pointed out that widows of former officers held most sutlerships and they hired corporals and sergeants as agents. According to McCawley, "this reduced them [the noncommissioned officers] to mere traders selling to the men and most of the business consists of selling beer." The commandant contended that if the men were paid monthly, there would be no need of sutlers or post traders.[31]

By the early 1880s, McCawley had made many of the changes that he had wanted but with relative little impact on Marine Corps desertions. Having established early in his commandancy promotion standards for the noncommissioned ranks, in December 1878, he forbade the sale of beers "by sutlers or their agents" in barracks. About a year and a half later, he implemented monthly pay periods for enlisted men to replace the quarterly payment system. Yet the number of desertions for the three-year period, 1876–79, averaged 290 men annually as opposed to an annual average of 414 men for the period 1879–82, an increase in the desertion rate from 14 to 20 percent in relation to total enlisted strength. Despite McCawley's best efforts, which included an experiment by Capt. James Forney in Philadelphia to widen the Marine Corps recruitment base, the desertion rate hovered close to 25 percent.[32]

Colonel McCawley's efforts to limit desertions were perhaps doomed from the start. The problems of desertion during this period were endemic to all of the services. The desertion rates for the U.S. Army varied from a low of 6.9 percent in 1876 to a high of 15.8 percent in 1882. As McCawley obviously recognized, many factors over which he had no control largely determined how attractive men found the Marine Corps. Economic conditions certainly played a role. If jobs were plentiful, men were more unlikely to enlist and more likely to desert. Perhaps the most important cause, all other aspects being equal, was the background of the enlisted men. According to one scholar, background and personal attributes of individuals had more of a correlation to desertion rates than a particular military situation. Here, McCawley had few options. Marine recruiters operated largely in the port cities on the eastern seaboard. The only West Coast recruiting office was located in San Francisco. Very often the Marines found recruits from the "sea faring class" of these cities' waterfront areas. As one experienced recruiting officer remarked, "It is impossible to make a soldier out of a sailor." The "rabble from the large cities," he added, "make very indifferent soldiers."[33]

Despite his inability to reduce Marine Corps desertions, McCawley made some real contributions to enhance enlisted life. He encouraged enlisted men to seek out promotions and provided status to noncommissioned officers. More important, he insisted that officers not abuse their power. As he wrote to one commanding officer, "Enlisted men have rights which officers must respect; and it will not do for an officer to talk about a soldier disobeying orders when he himself is disobedient and giving illegal orders." In addition to the reforms he inaugurated at the beginning of his commandancy, McCawley worked to improve the enlisted man's food ration and to provide retirement after an enlisted man completed several years of military service. Congress eventually passed a law that permitted retirement of enlisted men after "30 years of honorable service."[34]

While concerned with the quality of enlisted personnel, McCawley continued to support the efforts of the Marine reformers to improve the caliber of the officer corps. Having relatively little success in making the changes he wanted on his own, McCawley looked to Congress for assistance. Marine Corps officers worked closely with congressional allies. In January 1881, Captain Cochrane and Col. William Remey, the Navy judge advocate general, met with Senator James McPherson, chairman of the Senate Naval Affairs Committee, and largely wrote the bill that McPherson's committee reported out. If the legislation was enacted, it would have provided for eighty-eight officers, promoted the commandant to the rank of brigadier general, and allowed for a fleet marine officer, who would receive the temporary rank and pay of the next highest grade while serving in that capacity. It contained stipulations that called for officer promotion examinations and placed seniority requirements on staff appointments. Furthermore, graduates of the U.S. Military and Naval Academies or deserving noncommissioned officers were to fill all new vacancies in the Marine officer corps. Congress, however, adjourned without voting on the bill.[35]

Although the Corps's congressional friends continued to introduce reform bills in the following sessions of Congress, they all failed. In the summer of 1882, Captain Cochrane wrote McCawley that the Corps "may yet have to come to my plan of getting *a little at a time.*" Yet the appropriation bill, which Congress enacted on 5 August 1882, proved to be one of the most far-reaching pieces of legislation for both the Navy and the Marine Corps. Although best remembered for its authorization of armored ships and the beginning of the "New Navy," the appropriation act had a tremendous impact on Marine officer commissioning.[36]

For the Marine Corps, the most important aspect of the new legislation was the provision that, in effect, limited Marine commissions to Naval Academy graduates. The impetus for this move came not from the Marine Corps, but from the Navy. Over the years, several naval officers had proposed in professional journals the limitation of appointments in all corps of the Navy to actual vacancies and to Naval Academy graduates. The argument was that it would create a homogeneous officer corps and end corps disputes within the Navy. Cdr. Bowman H. McCalla remembered that Congressman Robeson brought Commodore John G. Walker, chief of the Bureau of Navigation, a rough draft of the appropriation bill. McCalla, who at the time was assigned to the bureau, related that he recommended to Walker the language that eventually was incorporated into the bill: "And from those [naval cadets] . . . appointments shall hereafter be made as it is necessary to fill vacancies in the lower grades of the line and of the Engineer Corps of the Navy and of the Marine Corps."[37]

The Marine Corps was to face a more hostile atmosphere in Congress during the following years, especially in the House. In January 1884, Congressman Samuel J. Randall, chairman of the House Appropriations Committee, asked why the Corps was requesting funding for ninety-three officers when the appropriations act of 1876 had reduced the number of officers to seventy-five. Colonel McCawley explained that the "Marine Corps having been reduced below that number [75], the Department held that the law had been complied with, and that no bar to appointments up to the original number of 30 second lieutenants existed." Despite the protests of McCawley and Chandler, the House in its Navy appropriation bill allowed the Corps twenty-two second lieutenants but would not permit any new appointments until the officer corps numbered fewer than seventy-five. After some debate, the Senate, in January 1885, agreed to the House provisions. Despite their best efforts, McCawley and the Marine reformers had reached a dead end in their efforts. Ironically, the 5 August 1882 appropriations act, with which they had little to do, was to have the most impact upon the Marine Corps. For the next fifteen years, all new Marine second lieutenants were to be graduates of Annapolis.[38]

In April 1885, the United States intervened in Panama, then in the throes of a revolution against Colombia, in order to keep the transit across the isthmus open. The newly inaugurated President Grover Cleveland and Secretary of the Navy William H. Whitney sent a naval expeditionary force, eventually consisting of two Marine Corps infantry battalions and a seaman artillery battalion, to restore order. For nearly two months, marines and sailors maintained the peace until relieved by a Colombian military force.[39] Upon the return of the marines, the press and public generally heaped praise on the conduct and readiness of the Corps. Secretary Whitney, on 12 June, added his congratulations to Commandant McCawley, remarking on "the promptness which is in keeping with the excellent reputation that the Marine Corps has enjoyed since its organization."[40]

After basking for a time in the public and official approbation, the Marine Corps soon found itself under attack from an unexpected quarter. In an extended report on the isthmus expedition to the secretary of the navy, Cdr. Bowman McCalla, commander of the naval landing force, while describing the Corps "as highly efficient and admirably disciplined," criticized the Marines for using the tactics "of a bygone day." He suggested that officers needed advanced professional schooling and training in the employment of artillery and machine guns. Moreover, McCalla argued that marines wasted too much time in barracks and recommended summer maneuvers for the entire shore establishment in conjunction with the fleet and the Army. McCalla proposed that the Navy Department purchase its own transports to carry future naval brigades and that the fleet should practice more realistic landing operations. In effect, he recommended the establishment of a naval expeditionary force, with a definable role in such an organization for the Marine Corps.[41]

Commandant McCawley angrily responded to McCalla's report. In a lengthy letter to the secretary, he answered in turn each of McCalla's criticisms. Referring to the comments on Marine tactics, McCawley replied that the Marine Corps used the same tactics as the Army, and if these were wrong, "it is singular that it is left to a naval officer to discover this." He then declared that marines did not waste time in barracks since they faced constant guard duty in the navy yards. The commandant rejected the idea of a summer maneuver, stating that it was his experience after thirty-eight years of service that he "never found the least trouble in having every duty as well performed in camp as in garrison after a few day's experience." Throughout his letter, McCawley emphasized the limited number of officers and men available to him. He defined the main missions of the Marine Corps in the traditional terms of ships' detachments and sentry duty at the navy yards. He made no reference to any future expeditionary role for the Marines.[42]

The furor soon died. The Navy Department published McCalla's report, Secretary Whitney released Colonel McCawley's letter to the press, and there the matter ended. Although the naval expedition to the isthmus consisted of six ships of the North Atlantic Squadron reinforced by two ships from the Pacific Squadron and well over twelve hundred men, including the troops sent from New York and the crews of the ships, the immediate effect on both the Marine Corps and the Navy was relatively slight.

For the Corps, the four years of the first Cleveland administration were mainly a period of marking time. Colonel McCawley, by this time, was not looking for new initiatives. His main concerns remained preserving the traditional missions and increasing both the enlisted and officer strength of the Marine Corps. With the temporary prohibition of new officer appointments, the Corps by 1887 was down to fifteen second lieutenants. In December 1887, McCawley, in what had become an annual refrain, observed to Whitney that this number of lieutenants "was totally inadequate to perform the sea duty." He remarked that the flag ships were down to one officer and "at none of the Shore Stations are there enough men to carry on duty." On the Pacific Station alone, McCawley stated, thirty vacancies existed, and he asked the secretary to recommend suitable legislation to Congress to remedy the situation. He repeated these requests to the secretary again in May 1888, and in his annual report for the year in October. Throughout all of these appeals, the only reference McCawley made to the New Navy was that the newer ships would require larger Marine Corps guard detachments.[43]

Some of the reformers believed that McCawley had become too resigned to desertions and too ready to blame the lack of personnel for all of his problems. One wrote an anonymous letter to the editor of the *Army and Navy Journal* in 1886 that the Corps's enlisted men "now often go to bed, or guard duty, hungry, empty, and mad." He remarked on the poor condition of most barracks, leaving the men with "no comforts, no games, nothing but 'taps' to look forward to as a blessed relief." He recommended a reduction of guard duty, the provision for the Navy ration, and enforcement of the penalties for desertion. The *Journal,* which hitherto seldom took the Marine Corps to task, returned to the subject the following year with an editorial entitled "Reckless Recruiting." First, the editorial applauded McCawley for his "conscientious efforts" to increase the "usefulness and efficiency" of the Corps, but believed that its present recruiting practices were counterproductive. The *Journal* claimed that the Corps, especially in the large cities, haphazardly selected recruits, "oftentimes from the scum of the earth." According to the editorial, many of the new recruits were deserters from either the Army or the Navy and in turn deserted from the Marine Corps. Observing that recruiting in New York and Philadelphia was left to a sergeant, the *Journal* recommended that the commandant appoint a senior officer to head the recruiting service and select only the best men.[44]

Colonel McCawley personally answered the *Journal* with a letter to the editor. He denied that noncommissioned officers were in charge of the recruiting effort in the large cities. McCawley remarked that the commanding officer of each barracks swore in all recruits and was ultimately responsible for them. He admitted, nevertheless, that the Marines were not obtaining the best men. "Every officer knows," he wrote, "that if written testimonials of good character were demanded from recruits, that it would be impossible to enlist men to carry on duty." He observed that "men enlisted in the large cities have always been of an inferior class" and that the Marine Corps did not have funds to send officers into the countryside and rural areas where better men could be obtained. In any event, McCawley asserted the Marine Corps was no worse than either the Army or Navy, both of which had much the same problems relative to desertion.[45]

In its next issue, the *Journal* replied. The article, perhaps authored by Marine captain Henry Clay Cochrane, rejected out of hand each of McCawley's explanations. According to the *Journal*'s writer, the commanding officer could not personally attend to recruiting together with all of his other responsibilities. It believed that McCawley, if he took his case to Congress and the administration, could receive a special appropriation for recruiting since it would result eventually in the saving of money. The *Journal* found it incredible that the Navy Department could spend millions on new ships that would be "manned by men of 'an inferior class.'" Recognizing that the Marines had a shortage of officers, the author maintained that at least one experienced captain or major could be spared for recruiting duty. The *Journal* concluded that the "Marine Corps has now and has always had our own best wishes and support. We would be pleased to see it in the van, but men of an 'inferior class' will never get it there." Colonel McCawley noted in his 1888 report 415 desertions for the year, equaling 22 percent of the Marines' enlisted strength.[46]

Many of the old problems with the officer corps also haunted the McCawley commandancy during these later years. The commandant continued to have difficulty—ranging from indebtedness to alcoholism to insubordination—with several officers. Serious incidents involving Marine officers continued to embarrass the Corps. In 1888, for example, Rear Adm. James A. Greer, commander of the European Squadron, court-martialed 1st Lt. Otway G. Berryman for being drunk on duty. Commanding the marines on the *Enterprise,* anchored at Leith, Scotland, on 22 September 1888, Berryman paraded the guard on the quarterdeck in honor of the visit of the Lord Provost of Edinburgh to the ship. According to witnesses, the lieutenant "was so much under the influence" that he failed to salute the visiting dignitary. The resulting court-martial found Berryman, who had a history of alcohol-related offenses, guilty and directed that he be suspended from duty for two years at half pay.[47]

Throughout this period, McCawley's coexistence with the Marine Corps staff was at best in a state of armed truce. With the retirement of Major Slack, the quartermaster, in May 1885 and the succession to the post by Maj. H. B. Lowry, his relations with that department actually improved. At this point, Colonel McCawley reserved his greatest animosity for his adjutant and inspector, Maj. Augustus S. Nicholson. For several years, the commandant of the Marine Corps, when he departed Washington or took leave, appointed the adjutant and inspector of the Marine Corps as the "acting commandant." Given his feud with Major Nicholson, McCawley changed the procedure, "Experience having convinced me that the Commandant should issue his own orders and not be dependent on an officer who is frequently absent, and whose own duties have then to be performed by another." In the summer of 1887, Major Nicholson protested McCawley's practice of selecting the commander of the Marine Barracks in Washington to act in his stead. The commandant heatedly defended himself, charging that the last time he made Nicholson the acting commandant, the adjutant and inspector turned over the duties to another officer "and went to Europe without my knowledge." According to McCawley, Nicholson "has been at variance with me during my whole term of office." McCawley then suggested that the duties of the adjutant and inspector be better defined and that "the authority of the Colonel Commandant be plainly laid down as regards him."[48]

The commandant and his staff, despite their disagreements over jurisdiction and personal prerogatives, cooperated fullheartedly in an effort to influence Congress. They wanted legislation that would provide promotions for both staff and line officers including a brigadier generalship for McCawley. In February 1888, several of the Washington-based officers formed a committee to lobby for a bill that would substantially enlarge the officer corps and included promotions for both the staff and senior line officers.

Capt. Henry Clay Cochrane, who had led earlier attempts for similar legislation and was one of the leading Marine reformers, opposed the bill. He believed it was designed to benefit certain officers and especially the staff. Cochrane observed that Major Goodloe, the paymaster, "Senator Beck's son-in-law, who has already gained two grades, forty-five numbers, and at least twenty-five years over his brother officers," would be one of the chief beneficiaries. Cochrane, claiming to speak for the interests of the younger officers, wrote to the secretary of the informal lobbying committee: "We need lieutenants more than we need colonels and we need majors on the large foreign squadrons more than [at] a one company shore station."[49]

Cochrane's motivations were actually much less altruistic. The bill added three more colonels, not including the commandant, and two more lieutenant colonels, while the Marine Corps retained the same number of majors. If Congress enacted the legislation, Cochrane feared that several senior officers, who were about to retire, might be induced by the additional rank to remain on active duty, thus limiting the promotional opportunities for their juniors, and his own. In any event, he knew that under present circumstances, the bill provided for promotions for five captains to major and that with his place on the lineal list he would not be one of them. Moreover, under the provisions of the bill, once these new captains became majors, they were not subject to sea duty. As Cochrane wrote to one of his fellow captains, Louis E. Fagan, the others "will be *per terram* officers and you and I *per mare.*"[50]

In his letter to Fagan, Captain Cochrane divulged his frustrations and his unhappiness with the present course of the Marine Corps and with its efforts to influence legislation. He noted that twelve years before he wrote and advocated the provisions contained in the present bill about the fleet marine officer, "but today I am a gray-headed, bald-headed father of a family and no such temporizing, relapsing, and conditional 'rot' suits me." Cochrane exclaimed, "If I have to go to sea, I want to go as a real major." He declared that he was unwilling to "serve twenty-five years as a captain (at sea when required) for the sake of being a *major on shore* for a few years commanding a two-cent post." According to Cochrane, the Marine Corps required ten "at least real, sure enough, come-to-stay majors who will take their sea duty" on the ships of the new Navy and "let the captains take the second rates."[51]

Although reported out by the Senate Naval Affairs Committee, the bill stood little chance of passage in a presidential election year as Congress hurried to adjourn. As the bill was about to come to floor of the Senate for a vote, Democrat senator Francis M. Cockrell of Missouri objected, stating, "Let that go over." The presiding officer agreed that the "bill will be passed over, but retain its place on the calendar." This was the last reference to the legislation, which was never voted on by the full Senate and never got out of the House Naval Affairs Committee. The Marine officer corps remained divided about its organization. Although Cochrane's viewpoints obviously were identical to his self-interest, he probably voiced many of the sentiments of the other officers when he claimed, "We stand well before men, and always seem to have a full hand which we do not know how to play." According to Cochrane, "The Navy is undergoing a complete revolution, but the Marine Corps slumbers." He believed, and was probably correct, that any Marine legislation had to be tied into the "New Navy."[52]

Under Secretary Whitney, the Navy Department continued the building of the "New Navy" that had begun under his predecessors. During his tenure, the government authorized thirty new warships including the "first modern armored cruising ships," later designated the second-class battleships, the *Texas* and the *Maine.* Despite the construction of the new ships, the transition between the old and new Navies occurred at an uneven pace. Monitors and unarmored cruisers coexisted with the laying of the keels of the forerunners of the modern battleships. Officers and politicians who were progressives in one matter could be reactionary in another. Whitney, who generally supported naval reforms, opposed funding the Naval War College. Even Alfred T. Mahan, the so-called Prophet of Seapower, whom Whitney removed as president of the War College in 1888, could be considered a conservative when it came to the new technology. In contrast, younger officers looked to the new technology, managerial reorganization, and efficiency to build the new Navy. The years of the Whitney stewardship were a period of flux in which the old and new blended together creating a renewed emphasis on naval policy and strategy as well as on ship design and weaponry.[53]

Several of the naval trends of the preceding decade came to fruition during the term of Whitney's successor, Benjamin F. Tracy, who served as secretary of the navy during the Benjamin Harrison administration. Influenced by many of the "naval progressives" and possibly by Mahan, Tracy, in his first annual report in 1889 called for an offensive navy, built around a heavily armored battleship fleet. Earlier in the year, at the suggestion of Commodore John G. Walker, he formed under Walker a "squadron of evolution" of the first three steel ships of the "New Navy," the *Atlanta,* the *Boston,* and the *Chicago,* provided for in the Navy Appropriation Act of 1882. At the same time, Secretary Tracy appointed Rear Adm. James A. Greer, the former commander of the European Squadron, to head a Navy board to examine naval organization in light of the needs of the new steel ships now coming into service. The findings of the Greer board would have an impact upon the Marine Corps.[54]

With a new administration in Washington, Colonel McCawley, at this point, decided to reexamine the relationship of the Marine Corps within the Navy. Whether occasioned by the force of events or convinced by two advisers, Lt. Col. Charles Heywood, the new commander of the Washington Barracks, and Capt. Daniel Pratt Mannix, McCawley in October 1889 suggested to Secretary Tracy that the Greer board "consider the Marine Corps in connection with the new navy, and that its duties on board ship be well defined." The secretary agreed, and McCawley appointed Captain Mannix to represent the Marine Corps, stating that Mannix "is a most intelligent officer of large experience, and can fully explain to the Board my views on the whole subject."[55]

A graduate of the Army Artillery School and the Naval Torpedo School, Daniel Mannix had served four years as an adviser with the Chinese Navy and was a member of the reform group. Before his assignment by McCawley, Mannix had written to Cochrane that he was about to offer one more suggestion to "stir the Corps to do something besides hanging onto the skirts of the Army or Navy." He wanted a board of officers "along the lines of the Greer Board" to study the mission and organization of the Marine Corps. Mannix recommended that marines on board ship man the secondary guns, "leaving the sailors for the great guns." He closed the letter with the prediction that if the Marine Corps did not do its own planning, "the Greer Board will do it for us and perhaps not altogether to our liking."[56]

Mannix's closing words proved prophetic. The Greer board, composed of many of the young Navy progressive officers, including Lt. William F. Fullam, voted to take Marine Corps guards off Navy warships. They believed their use as ship police inhibited sailor morale and that marines took up needed space on the new steel vessels. Instead, the board advocated that the Marines establish permanent battalions and regiments ashore that could be quickly formed into a naval expeditionary force on board Navy transports, much the same recommendation Commander McCalla had made after the Panama intervention. Although several reformers agreed that the Corps should have a permanent tactical organization that could be deployed rapidly as an expeditionary force, none supported taking the guards off the ships. Almost all Marine officers, whether reformer or a member of the "Old Guard," viewed the Greer board's proposal as a veiled threat to the very existence of the Corps. As McCawley wrote, the Greer board's recommendation, if implemented, would deprive the Navy of "one-fifth of its combative force, and leaving an essentially military corps in the position of non-combatants."[57]

Much to the relief of the Marine Corps, Secretary Tracy essentially rejected the report by filing it away. The subject of the ships' guards became an issue a year later when Lieutenant Fullam published an article in the Naval Institute *Proceedings* essentially proposing the Greer board's recommendation. Although not receiving official sanction, Fullam's suggestions about the guards caused much acrimony between Navy and Marine officers and served to befog the debate over the role of Marine expeditionary forces and naval advanced bases.

By the time Fullam's article appeared at the end of 1890, Colonel McCawley was on permanent sick leave. Having been in ill health since the beginning of the year, Colonel McCawley relied heavily on Lieutenant Colonel Heywood, commander of the Washington Barracks, to handle the day-to-day running of the Marine Corps. On 4 September 1890, nevertheless, the commandant asked that he be relieved of all of his duties but to be permitted to remain on active duty until his birthday on 9 January 1891, when he would reach the mandatory retirement age of sixty-four. The secretary agreed, and Col. C. D. Hebb, as the next senior officer in the Marine Corps, served out the remainder of McCawley's term. Upon Colonel McCawley's official retirement in January, Secretary Tracy selected Colonel Heywood as the new commandant.[58]

The McCawley commandancy in its own lights was relatively successful. Colonel McCawley was not a visionary and had a very narrow perspective of the role of the Marine Corps, but one can not blame him for being a man of his own time and not foreseeing the amphibious mission and the Marine Corps of today. He had some rather modest goals and he accomplished many of them: he improved conditions for enlisted marines, obtained a slight increase in enlisted strength, and helped provide for a more professional officer corps. McCawley was a transitional commandant during a transitional period of Marine Corps and Navy history.

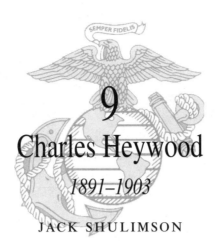

9
Charles Heywood
1891–1903

JACK SHULIMSON

In February 1891, Charles Heywood became the ninth commandant of the Marine Corps. Over six feet tall and broad shouldered, the walrus-mustachioed Heywood brought a sense of renewed vigor to the Corps. Commissioned at age nineteen in 1858, he early won renown as a troop leader. During the Civil War, the future commandant served with distinction and earned two brevet promotions as well as the sobriquet the "boy colonel" because of his relatively tender age. In 1873–74, during the crisis with Spain over the seizure of the American ship *Virginius,* he was the fleet marine officer of the fleet gathered at Pensacola. During the wave of railroad strikes in 1877, he led the Marine battalion sent to keep the peace in the city of Baltimore. Eight years later, in 1885, Heywood commanded the Marine brigade formed to protect the land transit across Panama.

Long identified with the Marine Corps reform group, in 1889, Lieutenant Colonel Heywood took over the Washington Marine Barracks and played a large role in the day-to-day running of the Marine Corps. Indeed, during the last two years of the McCawley commandancy, Heywood often was acting commandant as the incumbent became more and more incapacitated. While taking a back seat since September 1890 during the brief Col. Clement D. Hebb interregnum,[1] Heywood remained the favorite of much of the press and the officer corps. According to the *New York Times,* despite Hebb's own candidacy and that of several other officers for the commandancy, all the New England congressmen and Secretary of State James G. Blaine supported Heywood, who, like Blaine, was from Maine. It was no surprise, then, that on 31 January 1891, Secretary of the Navy Benjamin Franklin Tracy announced the appointment of Heywood, hardly the "boy colonel" at age fifty-one, as the new commandant of the Marine Corps.[2]

When on 10 February 1891, Colonel Heywood assumed his new office, the Marine Corps appeared to be besieged on all sides. An article by Navy lieutenant William Fullam had just appeared in the Naval Institute *Proceedings,* which questioned the very

Maj. Gen. Charles Heywood, ninth commandant.
Oil painting by Louis H. Gebhardt, 1917, from a photograph. U.S. Marine Corps Photo A413182.

existence of the Corps. Following its publication with an answering chorus of approval from much of the Navy officer corps, sailors on board U.S. Navy warships sent a deluge of petitions asking for removal of the marines. To most Marine Corps officers, the relationship between the petitions and the push by the Fullam faction was transparent.[3]

Heywood and his protégé, Capt. Daniel Pratt Mannix, who replaced Heywood as the commander of the Washington Barracks, nevertheless had an agenda of their own.

They decided against a confrontational strategy to meet the challenge presented by the Fullamite Navy reformers. Colonel Heywood rather preferred to act on the priorities that Captain Mannix had outlined two years previously to the Greer board.[4] He wanted to increase the size of the Corps, build up the morale of the enlisted men, carefully define the mission of the marines on board ship, further professionalize the officer corps, and establish a "School of Application" that would both serve as an educational forum and a ready reserve battalion for any unexpected emergency.[5]

As Heywood clearly realized, he could justify the existence of the Marine Corps and its expansion only in terms of its relationship to the Navy. As the new armored ships authorized by Congress during the past two administrations came into commission, the commandant wanted a role for his guards. If the mission of the Marine Corps were closely intertwined with these warships, the pride of the "New Navy," he believed the Marine Corps as an institution would be more secure. Seizing upon Colonel McCawley's recommendation to the Greer board for the Marine guards to man the secondary batteries of the new steel ships, Heywood wanted the secretary of the navy and, if possible, naval regulations to mandate this duty. With more ships, there would be a corresponding need for more recruits.[6]

Before he could persuade the secretary of the navy and Congress to allocate more marines, Heywood first had to convince them that the Corps could do the job. This would be hard to do with the existing enlisted Corps, which still had a desertion rate of over 25 percent. His naval opponents pointedly alluded to the fact that in 1890, the Marine Corps had 948 enlistments, 85 reenlistments, and 520 desertions, for a total enlisted strength of approximately 2,000 men.[7] Heywood's primary need was for a corps of officers and men capable of manning the guns of the secondary batteries. The secondary battery usually consisted of 6-inch rifled guns and smaller-caliber rapid-fire cannon and machine guns as opposed to the 13-inch and 8-inch rifled guns of the main turrets on board the new warships. The commandant had already taken some first steps to ensure that the guards who went on board the Navy ships were properly trained by Captain Mannix at the Washington Barracks.[8]

Heywood had even bolder plans in relation to Marine Corps training and education, all centered on the Washington Barracks. Together with Mannix, he worked out a scheme for the formal establishment at the barracks of a School of Application. Based on Mannix's original proposal to the Greer board, Colonel Heywood, on 13 April 1891, forwarded to Secretary Tracy a detailed course outline and asserted that the school would be established without any further appropriation. Five days later, Tracy gave his approval. On 1 May 1891, Heywood issued General Order No. 1 announcing the formation of the School of Application of the United States Marine Corps, to consist of both an enlisted and officer division. While the school was nominally under the "direct care and supervision of the Colonel Commandant," its actual running was to be the responsibility of the director of instruction, who also functioned as the school commander.[9]

Heywood apparently viewed the proposed School of Application as the flagship for a system of satellite schools that would be established at every Marine post. At this moment, however, all he could do was to ask the cooperation of all officers so that the "Marine Corps will be enabled to keep pace with recent progress in the profession of arms."[10] As far as the School of Application, Heywood had several things already in place. Even before the actual publication of his general order, he had made arrangements with the Bureau of Ordnance for assistance. The Marines would use what weapons and equipment were on hand to keep costs down. This, however, did not rule out future appropriations for specialized engineering and survey instruments. Heywood had also named Captain Mannix, who probably had drafted the general order, as the director of instruction and commanding officer of the school.[11] Heywood and Mannix decided to designate the seven new second lieutenants who had just graduated from the Naval Academy as the first students of the new school. The commandant could assign these new officers to the School of Application without disrupting the rest of the Marine Corps with transfers and reassignments. Moreover, the school could serve as a rite of passage for the new graduates.[12]

Heywood's interest in officer professionalism extended beyond the School of Application and the new second lieutenants. Very much aware of the attacks against his Corps, the commandant on 3 August 1891, with the approval of Secretary Tracy, convened a special board on officer organization and promotion. He also charged the board with a broader mandate "to insure a condition of increased efficiency in the Marine Corps." The board consisted of four officers identified with the reform faction: Maj. Percival C. Pope, in command of the Boston Barracks; Capt. Richard S. Collum, an assistant quartermaster; the ever-present Captain Mannix; and 1st Lt. T. C. Prince, who served under Mannix at the Washington Barracks. Major Pope, as the ranking officer, served as the president of the board.[13]

The board made its recommendations in the form of a congressional bill. It incorporated most of the measures that the reformers had been pushing through the McCawley years. The proposed bill would expand the Marine Corps by four hundred men, make the commandant of the Corps a brigadier general, promote the senior Headquarter staff officers to lieutenant colonels, limit appointments to the staff to senior line officers, and increase the number of officers to eighty-eight. The bill's most important feature was the mandating of physical, mental, and professional examinations for all officers below the rank of major.[14]

In October, Heywood used the board's study as the basis for his own annual report to the secretary of the navy. He referred to the officer stagnation in the Corps, especially at the rank of captain, and made reference to the board's recommendations to relieve the situation. He observed that the Marine Corps was the only service that did not require promotion examinations. The commandant then turned to the board's proposal for a four-hundred-man increase in the enlisted force of the Corps. Like McCawley, Heywood stressed in his report the shortage of personnel and the resulting strain that it placed on the individual marine.[15] Heywood departed from the board's report, which had touched only superficially upon the Corps's mission, to redefine the role of the marine on board ship. According to the commandant, "It is as artillery men aboard our new floating batteries that their importance must be felt." He asked Tracy to approve the practice of the Marines manning the secondary battery with an official Navy Department directive.[16]

On 18 November 1891, Heywood seized upon a request by the Navy commandant of the New York Navy Yard for more recruits to press his demands. Citing his annual report, he insisted to Tracy that "the number of officers and enlisted men in the Corps is too small." Heywood also turned his attention to Congress. He convinced Senators Eugene Hale and James McPherson, the leading Republican and Democrat respectively on the Senate Naval Affairs Committee, to introduce bills which incorporated most of the provisions of the Pope board on Marine Corps reorganization. Heywood, at the end of the year, had reason to hope that his reforms would take hold.[17]

By January 1892, Heywood, however, found himself attempting to fend off an unexpected assault on the core of his planned rehabilitation of the Marine Corps. At the direction of the Bureau of Navigation citing 1880 Navy Regulations, Navy ship commanders were pulling off Marine guards from the guns of the secondary batteries. Denying the applicability of the 1880 regulations to the situation, Heywood argued that marines performed better when together than "when mixed with sailors." He remained "convinced that the majority of the commanding officers of vessels now in commission would express the same opinion."[18]

As the question of the secondary battery remained in limbo, Heywood lost his earlier high hopes for congressional action. He decided to cut his losses and push for enactment of a single bill that would permit examination of officers before promotion. In May, the House Naval Affairs Committee reported out favorably such a measure, which passed both chambers of Congress in July. Under the new law, every officer below the rank of commandant would take an examination before promotion.[19]

Colonel Heywood immediately started to implement the provisions relative to examination for promotion as required in the new legislation. During the past year, there had been a "remarkable" turnover of officers in both the Navy and the Marine Corps. Together both services experienced twenty-three retirements, five resignations, and four deaths. For the Marine Corps this resulted in six vacancies for new second lieutenants and a number of promotions. Even before the enactment of the new law, Heywood refused to recommend one senior captain to the rank of major. In August, Tracy appointed the first promotion board to examine the first three eligible candidates for higher rank, who all passed.[20]

In late 1892, the Navy Department, especially the Bureau of Navigation, continued to give the Marine Corps warning signals about the role of the Marine guards on board ship. On 1 November 1892, the bureau asked the Corps to provide guards for seven new ships coming into commission. A few weeks later, the bureau chief, Commodore Francis Ramsay, told Heywood that no Marine guard would be required for the *Monterey,* one of the largest of the new vessels. Colonel Heywood protested the decision and argued that if berthing space were a problem, the marines could replace an equal number of sailors. The department curtly turned down his appeal.[21]

As President William Harrison's administration came to a close in early 1893, the Marine Corps under Heywood remained in a precarious but somewhat more hopeful situation. Despite the carping of its critics, the Corps had made some real gains. Colonel Heywood observed in his last annual report that the desertion rate was down by 20 percent. Although this reduction was largely due to the economic downturn and the resulting unemployment in the country, Heywood's improvements in the creature comforts of the enlisted man had contributed to the improvement of morale. The professionalization of the officer corps advanced apace with that of the Navy at large. New officers continued to enter the Marine Corps from the Naval Academy; Marine officers now had to pass both physical and professional examinations for promotion; and the School of Application was about to graduate its second class.[22]

Continuing much of the naval policy of his predecessor and while keeping Commodore Ramsay as chief of the Bureau of Navigation, the new secretary of the navy, Hilary A. Herbert, in the second Grover Cleveland administration, supported most of Heywood's reform program. In his annual report for 1893, the commandant could boast that the Corps was only seven men short of its appropriated strength.[23] More important, Heywood's efforts to raise the professional qualifications of his officer corps had met with some success. The new promotion and examination standards had meaning and some bite to them. In the spring of 1893, 1st Lt. George T. Bates failed his examination and therefore his promotion to captain.[24]

Although hardly receiving the elite of the Naval Academy cadets, neither Colonel Heywood nor Captain Mannix protested the quality of the new Marine Corps officers. Because of the 1883 law, there were still fewer openings in the entire naval establishment than there were graduates. Competition for any commission was keen. The young lieutenants for the most part proved to be able and eager students at the School of Application.[25] When Captain Mannix died in February 1894, Colonel Heywood was not about to allow the school to lapse. He appointed Capt. Paul St. Clair Murphy to succeed Mannix. Murphy took over on 8 March, and on 3 May, the School of Application graduated its third class of officers and its second class of noncommissioned officers with the usual final exercises and ceremony.[26]

Like his predecessor, Colonel McCawley, Heywood's relations with the Headquarters staff were often on an uneven keel. Yet at the beginning of his commandancy, he enjoyed a brief harmonious interlude with the staff officers. In contrast to the open hostility between McCawley and the adjutant and inspector, Maj. Augustus S. Nicholson, Heywood and Nicholson were on amicable terms. Often upon his absence, Heywood designated Nicholson acting commandant. Upon the latter's retirement in the spring of 1894, Heywood moved rapidly to replace him with an officer he could trust, Capt. George C. Reid.[27]

In a letter, Heywood observed that the adjutant and inspector would function as the commandant of the Marine Corps in the absence of the commandant. Still feeling the loss of Captain Mannix, who had served as an informal adviser, Heywood wanted an ally in his push for reform. Secretary Herbert acceded to Heywood's request and made Reid the new adjutant and inspector.[28]

Heywood's ties with the other two senior members of the formal staff, the paymaster, Maj. G. C. Goodloe, and Maj. H. B. Lowry, the quartermaster, however, had deteriorated. Goodloe made no secret of his ambition to be commandant. Prior to Heywood's appointment, the paymaster, the son-in-law of the senior senator from Kentucky, had made a serious bid for the post. While correct toward one another, neither Goodloe nor Heywood had any great fondness for the other.[29] At first, Heywood and Major Lowry had little difficulty with one another until the commandant discovered that the quartermaster was addressing correspondence directly to the secretary of the navy. Backed by the department, Colonel Heywood reprimanded Lowry. According to Heywood, the quartermaster stopped "personal intercourse with me and . . . maintained that of only the strictest official character." Like his predecessor, Heywood's efforts to rein in the independent actions of his paymaster and quartermaster met with only half success.[30]

During this period, the Navy and the Marine Corps were caught up in an imbroglio over personnel structure, especially centered around the question of promotions. Congress in early 1894 formed a joint subcommittee from the naval committees of both houses of Congress to study the entire organization of the Navy. The establishment of the joint committee opened a Pandora's box for almost every special interest group in the naval establishment. There was a lack of unanimity among Navy officers, let alone Marine officers, which resulted in "jealousy and strife between the different corps."[31]

Colonel Heywood forwarded a twenty-one-page report for Secretary Herbert to consider. The descriptive title of the report, "Statements and Arguments Setting Forth the Value and Necessity of a United States Marine Corps to the Navy; Showing that It Will Be a Measure of Efficiency, Economy, and Justice to Increase the Corps, Giving It Enough Officers and Men to Efficiently Perform the Duty Expected and Required of It," aptly provides the basic thrust of the document. In a rudimentary form of cost analysis, the commandant enclosed charts that demonstrated that the individual marine was one thousand dollars less expensive than the individual sailor. Using past annual reports and studies, Heywood repeated many of his usual refrains: the need for more marines; the assignment of the marines under their own officers to the secondary batteries on board ship; the increase in numbers of officers; and the creation of higher ranks for the officer corps.[32]

In his testimony before the joint committee, Heywood spoke about the reluctance of the Navy, especially of the Bureau of Navigation, to make full use of the Marine Corps complements on board ship: "As the matter stands now, the Marines are sent on board as sharpshooters . . . and they do not render the service which a body of men who are so well organized and drilled could perform." He declared that the captains of the various ships often assign the Marines to the secondary batteries, but "the guns are taken away from them . . . upon orders from the Bureau of Navigation."[33]

Complicating the relations between the Marine Corps and the Navy was the continuing circulation of petitions among Navy enlisted men to withdraw Marine guards from warships. In the summer of 1894, 1st Lt. Littleton W. T. Waller, assigned to the Norfolk Navy Yard, obtained copies of one such petition there, which he forwarded to the commandant. Colonel Heywood immediately protested to Secretary Herbert, suggesting that the matter "savor[s] of conspiracy."[34]

At the end of July, Herbert issued a circular letter to Navy commanders in which he largely supported the Marine position. Several years later, he stated that at the time there was a "movement then on foot among certain officers of the line, to induce me to favor the abolition of the Marine Corps." According to Herbert, he credited Major Reid, the Marine Corps adjutant and inspector, for convincing him to retain the Corps intact. Despite strong words in support of the Marines, Herbert made no mention of marines manning the secondary batteries on board ship.[35]

In his annual report, Colonel Heywood attempted to renew the issue of the duties of marines on board ship. His original draft contained a statement requesting once more that they man the secondary batteries. Heywood suggested that putting marines on the guns would free approximately one thousand sailors for other duties.[36] Fearing more dissension and disruption in the Navy, Herbert informed Heywood that he thought "it best to revise . . . the portions [of the commandant's report] marked with blue pencil." This portion, of course, was the reference to marines replacing sailors at the secondary batteries. Heywood deleted the offending phrases. Nevertheless, he included an appeal for more marines to assist in the manning of the new ships now entering into service.[37]

While deflecting the Navy attempts to remove marines from ships, Heywood suddenly found the Corps the center of another dispute not of its making. This time the instigators were Army officers. In August 1894, Army artillery reformers, who wished to separate the coastal artillery from the field artillery, induced friendly Senators to introduce a bill that would combine the Army coastal artillery regiments with the Marine Corps for the purpose of harbor defense. Although the bill called for a brigadier general to command this new artillery organization, Heywood and Marine officers recognized the bill as a direct threat to the Marine Corps. Heywood understood that junior artillery officers framed the bill for their benefit without consultation of Marine officers or the commandant. The bill allowed for more promotions, but Marine officers would in general rank below their Army artillery counterparts. Heywood recommended to the secretary of the navy that the latter oppose the bill. Given the opposition of the commandant, combined with that of the old guard of the Army, the bill had no future. It languished in committee and never appeared on the floor of either house of Congress.[38]

As 1894 drew to an end, the panacea of any legislation that would enhance or, for that matter, diminish the Marine Corps, appeared doomed to failure. The much heralded joint committee of Congress had completed its labors and, in January 1895, submitted its final report. It called for no change in the organization or general size of the Marine Corps. The bill's most controversial feature was the infamous "plucking," a forced retirement provision. It divided the Navy officer corps into two antagonistic groups, based largely on seniority, each of which formed its own lobbying association for and against the legislation. Marine officers largely supported the bill but were suspicious of both naval groups. With no consensus in the Navy, Congress remained loath to act.[39]

The question of marines on board the new warships came to a head again in 1895. In October of that year, Capt. Robley D. Evans, commander of the new battleship USS *Indiana,* wrote to Secretary Herbert, asking that no marines be sent to his command. Commodore Ramsay, chief of the Bureau of Navigation, strongly endorsed Evans's recommendation.[40] Alarmed, Heywood protested, repeating many of the same arguments that he had used in his testimony before the joint committee the year before. He commandant compared the "modern man of war" to a "floating fort," which "should be manned more by soldiers than sailors, men who are artillerists and accustomed both to the use of great and small arms." As the *Army and Navy Journal* pointed out, Colonel Heywood was well aware that "should the Department decide to grant Captain Evans' request, it is not probable that Marine Guards will be supplied to any of the other battleships."[41]

Secretary Herbert came down again on the side of the Marine Corps. In his reply to Captain Evans, he wrote that he considered the latter's proposal but "determined that the 'Indiana' shall be supplied with a Marine guard." Moreover, the secretary ordered that, in addition to their customary duties, marines were "to be detailed for service at the guns in such manner as the commanding officer may deem expedient." In an obvious rebuke to Evans, Herbert enclosed in his letter a copy of the circular pertaining to the Marines that he had issued the previous year.[42]

In his annual report for the year, Herbert addressed the subject in even stronger terms: "There has always been more or less objection on the part of some officers of the Navy to Marines on board ship, but as Marines have constituted a part of our naval establishment both on shore and at sea from its infancy it may fairly be presumed that experience has . . . demonstrated the wisdom of maintaining this branch of the service." The secretary believed that the two organizations on board ship "create a healthy competition to excel." He ended with the statement that he had decided to place marines on the *Indiana* and "will put Marines on the other battleships as they are severally commissioned."[43]

Despite the secretary's remarks in his annual report, the Marine Corps's relationship with Navy officers on the role of marines on board ship remained problematical. Navy ship commanders continued to question the status of the Marine officer on board ship. Lt. William F. Fullam once more led the progressive naval officers' counterattack, again using the Naval Institute *Proceedings* to air his views. In the resulting article, Fullam returned to several of his favorite themes first proposed in the Greer board in 1889. He argued, in true progressive fashion, using terms such as "efficiency" and "objectivity," that the Navy reduce the number of all the various staff officers on board ship and remove altogether the marines and paymasters. This time, however, Fullam emphasized the Corps's expeditionary role. He would organize the Marine shore establishment into battalions that could be embarked upon Navy transports for operations on foreign shores.[44]

Colonel Heywood, however, saw the article only in terms of an attack on the Marine Corps. The Naval Institute had sent him, as well as many other officers of the Navy and Marine Corps, a copy of Fullam's article prior to publication for "opinion and criticism." Heywood refused to comment on the draft but instead went to the secretary of the navy asking that the latter suppress the article. The commandant observed that Fullam's would-be policies for the Marine Corps directly contradicted those recently enunciated by Secretary Herbert.[45] Herbert refused to involve the Navy Department in the imbroglio. He stated that while the department "doubts the advisability of discussions of this character relative to different branches of the naval service, particularly while Congress is in session," it would take no action. Herbert noted that the article was to be published in *Proceedings,* and that he did not want to hinder "full and free discussion in said journal."[46]

Colonel Heywood had his own legislative agenda. In his 1895 annual report, the Marine Corps commandant renewed his appeal for more enlisted men, asking for five hundred more personnel. In January 1896, Heywood wrote to Secretary Herbert that the Navy had asked for one thousand more sailors and that the same reasons for the increase in the Navy enlisted strength applied to the Marine Corps. On 20 February 1896, Herbert forwarded the commandant's letter to Charles A. Boutelle, chairman of the House Naval Affairs Committee, and recommended approval.[47]

Colonel Heywood's request for additional enlisted men fared much better than his attempt to expand the officer corps. On 24 March 1896, the House Naval Affairs Committee reported the naval appropriation bill and included a five-hundred-man increase in the enlisted force of the Marine Corps. In explaining the action of the committee to the full House the following day, the chairman, Congressman Boutelle, stated that it was done at the request of both the secretary of the navy and the commandant of the Marine Corps "in view of the increase of the number of our ships afloat." The House passed the bill and the increase without debate.[48]

The Navy progressives saw the House legislation as another setback in their attempt to remove the marines from the battleships. They attempted to recoup in the Senate where they had some influence with certain members of the Senate Appropriations Committee, including Senator Hale, the Republican chairman of the committee. On 9 April, the Senate committee reported the naval appropriation bill without the increase for the Marine Corps. One of Fullam's cohorts gloated that he did not believe the Corps stood a chance to get its five hundred men. Richard Wainwright, the Chief of the Office of Naval Intelligence, was less sanguine about the Senate committee action: "The Marines are very strong in Washington and we will find it hard work getting rid of them."[49]

Action on the floor of the Senate confirmed Wainwright's fears. On 2 May 1896, the appropriation bill came up for debate. Two members of Hale's party, Senators William Chandler and Henry Cabot Lodge, took exception to the deletion of the Marine clause. Both quoted Secretary Herbert that the additional marines were essential, and Senator Chandler referred to the secretary's action in reinstating the marines on the

Indiana. The Senate rejected the committee's recommendation, and the Marine clause stayed in the bill.[50]

With the final passage of the appropriation bill on 6 June 1896, the Marine Corps had its first significant increase of enlisted personnel since the Civil War. In his annual report, Colonel Heywood observed that he had little difficulty in recruiting the additional men and by October the Marine Corps was only ninety short of its appropriated enlisted strength. With the increase of the enlisted force, Heywood now argued that there needed to be corresponding growth in the officer corps. He pointed to the stagnation at the rank of captain and the requirement for new second lieutenants to meet the additional demands for marines on board ship.[51] Despite the continuing shortage of Marine Corps officers, Colonel Heywood sent officers to the Navy War College and continued the Marine School of Application. Obviously the commandant considered the school with its emphasis on artillery and new technology as essential education for Marine officers serving with the "New Navy."[52]

Viewing the Marine Corps's role with the New Navy as manning the secondary batteries of the new warships, Colonel Heywood and Major Reid fashioned a plan that tried to implement earlier reforms. It consisted simply of organizing and training a Marine guard for several months before assigning it to a particular ship. On 21 August, Reid, while acting commandant, apparently without informing the secretary of the navy but with the implicit consent of Heywood, designated forty-five men as the guard of the cruiser *Brooklyn,* soon to be commissioned, and assigned them to the Newport Barracks. Colonel Heywood asserted that this new system would increase the efficiency of the ship guards since it permitted the men to "become accustomed to each other, and there is time to weed out bad elements."[53]

Colonel Heywood suddenly ran into unexpected opposition to his plans. Unaware of the commandant's plans, Secretary Herbert questioned the assignment of the guard to Newport. Heywood defended the action, declaring that it was always his "desire to take this action in the cases of all guards intended for ships, but could not because lack of men." He concluded, "There is nothing exceptional being done, and the only difference between this guard and any other will be that this one will have been instructed as a whole, while the others were not."[54]

The Navy Department, however, accepted no part of the commandant's argument. Although acknowledging that assembling the guard of a ship at one location and drilling them had its advantages, the department ruled that the commandant and Major Reid overstepped their authority in moving marines from one post to another without replacing them. Moreover, the Newport station was under the Bureau of Navigation and there never was an intention for "making it in some sense a school of instruction for the Marine Corps." The department even ordered Heywood to remove any mention of the Newport experiment from his annual report.[55]

Still, the Marine Corps had fared fairly well under Herbert's stewardship of the Navy Department. After several years of requesting additional manpower, the Corps received a significant increase in enlisted strength. The fact that the Corps did not receive a corresponding expansion in officers was due to internal divisions among both Navy and Marine officers rather than any hostility upon the part of the secretary. Herbert encouraged Heywood's attempt to further the professionalization of the officer corps through the Marine Corps School of Application and the Navy War College. More important from Heywood's point of view, the secretary not only vetoed every attempt of the Navy progressives to take the Marine Corps guards off the ships but also approved the incorporation into the 1896 Navy Regulations of an article that marines would serve on board ship as a "distinctive" command under their own officers and assigned to certain guns when practicable. Heywood had astutely used the secondary battery mission to link the Corps to the new battleships coming into service. New ships would require more men to man them. If marines were assigned to the guns, there would be the need for more of them. Thus, the Corps remained competitive with the rest of the Navy for increased manpower and appropriations.[56]

At the end of the Cleveland administration and the start of the new Republican William McKinley administration, Colonel Heywood was engaged in one of his perennial feuds with one of his senior officers or Headquarters staff. Heywood wanted to retire those officers unable to function in their respective positions. Two of his prime targets were Maj. H. B. Lowry, the quartermaster, and Lt. Col. John H. Higbee, now the commander of the New York Marine Barracks. Despite physical infirmities, Higbee refused to accede to pressure that he place himself upon the retired list.[57] Colonel Heywood met equal frustrations with Quartermaster Lowry. Despite official reprimands, Lowry survived both a court of inquiry and a survey board to force his retirement.[58]

In June 1897, after all of the furor of the survey board in February, Major Lowry suddenly announced his retirement. This led to a chain reaction with Lowry's assistant, Capt. Richard S. Collum, becoming quartermaster and upon his promotion, then also retiring. The junior assistant quartermaster, Capt. Frank L. Denny, then became the new quartermaster. Charles L. McCawley, the son of the former commandant, a civilian, and for several years the chief clerk in the commandant's office, received a commission as a captain and filled one of the two assistant quartermaster vacancies.[59]

Patronage politics apparently played a large role in the latter appointment. While President McKinley made a fellow former governor and friend, the rather passive and scholarly John D. Long of Massachusetts, his secretary of the navy, he had appointed as a counterpoint the energetic Theodore Roosevelt as assistant secretary. Ironically, Roosevelt, the former Civil Service commissioner and Republican reformer, apparently engineered the entire McCawley affair. In a strange alliance with Richard Olney, the secretary of state in the Cleveland administration, Roosevelt worked behind the scenes. More than a week before the acceptance of Lowry's retirement, he admitted to Olney that he had interceded with the president and now believed "I have got young McCawley's matter satisfactorily arranged. . . . At any rate, I have done everything that it is in my power to do." The evidence does not indicate that Roosevelt was behind the sudden retirements of Lowry and Collum, but he was certainly aware of the circumstances.

According to Captain Cochrane, who quoted another Marine officer, the "Lowry, Collum deal cost $30,000.00."[60]

Within this setting of political, personal, and bureaucratic juggling, the Heywood reform movement for the Marine Corps continued its uneven progress. New Marine officers still came from the Naval Academy but at a slower pace. In June, the commandant asked that the Marine Corps receive three of the naval cadets from the Naval Academy to fill vacancies in the officer corps. Like the previous year, however, there were not enough graduating cadets to meet the demands of the respective branches of the Navy. Assistant Secretary Roosevelt denied Heywood's request, agreeing only to give the Marine Corps the two cadets already selected by the Naval Academy Academic Board. An underlying reason may have been behind both the secretary's and board's decision: as promotions among the junior officers now lagged behind the Navy line and engineers, most naval cadets attempted to avoid the Marine Corps.[61]

With the continued stress on technical and artillery skills, Heywood pressed the issue over the assignment of marines to the secondary batteries of warships. He found himself fighting a constant battle with naval officers trying to find loopholes in the 1896 Navy Regulations. At the same time, he tried to convince the department to reinstate the training of ships' guards at the Newport Barracks.[62] Although the department did not act upon Heywood's suggestion, Capt. Henry Clay Cochrane, commanding the Newport Barracks, had undertaken several innovations in training and providing for the morale and well-being of his men. He even went further than Colonel Heywood at first was willing to go. Cochrane had established a post exchange at Newport to replace the old post trader system. Heywood, however, did not support the idea and ordered all Marine post exchanges closed.[63]

In this case, however the Navy Department overruled Heywood. On 6 August 1897, Assistant Secretary Roosevelt directed Heywood to reopen the Newport post exchange to compare the "relative merits" of the post exchange and the post trader systems.[64] Colonel Heywood made no mention of the implementation of the post exchange in his annual report, but Secretary Long spoke of the system in glowing terms. He observed that the department had instituted post exchanges at some of the Marine barracks and intended to open them at all of the posts.[65]

In his effort to reform the promotion system to reflect merit as well as seniority, Heywood enjoyed the full support of the department. In September 1897, the department published a new general order pertaining to officer promotion. The order emphasized the testing of the practical application of the officer's knowledge "rather than the committal to memory of equations and data, which, he would, under ordinary conditions, obtain from books of reference."[66]

A few months later, in November, Assistant Secretary Roosevelt headed a special Navy Board to study the officer structure of the entire naval establishment. The board was to draft a bill which would make recommendations relative to the "reorganization of the personnel of the Navy." Consisting of both line and engineers, the deliberations of the board immediately aroused concern among other officer corps. While studying the amalgamation of engineers with line officers, the board also looked at the possibility of the integration of both the officers of the Paymaster Corps and the Marine Corps with that of the line as well. On 9 November 1897, Roosevelt invited Colonel Heywood to testify before the board on such a proposal.[67]

Two days later, Heywood came before the board. He learned that one of the line members had suggested that the Marines, in effect, be dissolved. The board asked Heywood to canvas his officers for their opinion. In a round robin letter, Heywood conducted an informal survey of the Marine officer corps on the subject of the possible integration of the officer corps with the Navy and the possible elimination of Marine Corps guards from warship crews.[68] Marine officers opposed the first proposal, and few showed any willingness to accept doing away with the Marine guards on board ship. In fact, only Lt. George Barnett actually mentioned the possibility of the removal of the guards but quickly observed that marines on board ship served a useful purpose. In somewhat of a minority opinion, Barnett argued that the chief role of the Corps both "on shore and at sea must be considered as an expeditionary force for use in any part of the world and not merely as a collection of watchmen."[69]

On 22 November 1897, Colonel Heywood appeared again before the board to defend his Corps against its detractors. In a long passionate appeal, he traced the history of the Corps. He then spoke about his own forty years of service. He observed that the Marines were specialists and it would be necessary for some other organization to take the service's place without the advantage of Marine pride and esprit de corps. In contrast to Barnett, the commandant defined the main mission of the Marine Corps in the traditional role of ship guards with the added duty of manning the secondary batteries.[70] By this time, the board had decided to confine itself to only two topics, the integration of engineer officers with the line and the forced retirement of senior officers. On 9 December, Assistant Secretary Roosevelt forwarded the final report to Secretary Long, recommending these two provisions. There was no mention of Marines or any other corps of the Navy. The Marine Corps had escaped once more the knives of its enemies.[71]

Following the sinking of the *Maine* in Havana Harbor in February 1898 and the growing sentiment for war against Spain, Secretary Long in March appointed the Advisory War Board. The board recommended that in the event of war, the Navy take the offensive and not be relegated to a passive coastal defense role. Based on the consensus of earlier war planning efforts, the board suggested the close blockade of Cuba and its extension to Puerto Rico. The Navy was to concentrate as well on the poorly defended outposts of Spain's insular empire, including the Philippines.[72]

On 10 March 1898, after congressional passage of an emergency appropriation of $50 million for the Army and Navy, Secretary Long provided Colonel Heywood with guidelines on the use of the Marine Corps's share. The commandant was to incur expenses under the appropriation only after making an estimate of expenses and receiving the approval by Long and the president, "all in writing." All told, the Marine Corps would eventually receive $106,529.64 under the measure. The expenditures included the purchase of one million rounds of ammunition for the newly issued Lee rifles,[73] tents from the Army, various field equipment, and for the installation of the first telephone in one of the offices at Marine Corps Headquarters. As Heywood explained to Long, the only telephone then in use was located in the guard room of the Marine Barracks, "across the parade ground from these offices, which necessarily, results in much delay and unnecessary publicity in the transmission of messages."[74]

Both Secretary Long and the commandant wanted to expand the Marine enlisted ranks by over four hundred men to meet the anticipated increased demands on the Marine Corps caused by the crisis. Long told Heywood, however, that "before any such increase of Marines can be made it must be . . . authorized by action of Congress." Acting on Long's advice, on 11 March 1898, Heywood pled his case before the House Naval Affairs Committee and obtained from it 473 additional slots and permission "to proceed with enlistment." The following day, Heywood informed the secretary that he wanted to visit recruiting stations in Boston, New York, and Philadelphia to expedite the new enlistment drive. Long concurred.[75]

The role of the Marine Corps in any pending conflict was still vague. In his correspondence with the House Naval Affairs Committee, Secretary Long explained the need for more marines in terms of traditional missions. Still, the concept of advanced bases as the "first line of defense" of the battleship fleet with or without specific mention of the Marines was already a familiar theme in the Navy literature of the time. Moreover, the usually authoritative *Army and Navy Journal* carried a story on 12 March 1898 that the secretary had ordered Colonel Heywood to form two battalions ready to deploy at short notice: "Two battalions have been made up on paper, and all the available officers of the Corps assigned to places in different companies."[76]

As well as uncertainty about the Marine role, there was the questionable readiness of its aging officer corps in the higher ranks. Coincidentally, on the same day as the sinking of the *Maine,* Lt. Col. Robert Huntington, the most likely commander of any Marine Corps expedition, described Marine field-grade officers, including himself and several of the senior captains, most of whom had over thirty years of service and were Civil War veterans, as "fit for service in barracks, but age has decreased . . . the power of resisting the hardship and exposure incident to service in the field."[77]

With the passage of a congressional joint resolution on 11 April giving President McKinley authority to use force if necessary for the withdrawal of Spanish forces from Cuba, the requirement for all available military forces became obvious whatever shortcomings existed. Whether influenced by the lack of readiness on the part of the Army or as part of the general mobilization, Capt. William T. Sampson, the commander of the fleet off Key West, asked Secretary Long for the deployment of two Marine battalions to serve with his command. On the sixteenth, Heywood received verbal orders to make the necessary arrangements. The following day, a Sunday, he met with the Headquarters staff and sent out telegrams to Marine commanding officers at the various East Coast navy yards. Planning to mount the first battalion out of New York within the week, the commandant, on the eighteenth, departed Washington to supervise personally the preparations. Back at Headquarters, Maj. George C. Reid, the adjutant and inspector and now acting commandant, asked for and received twenty thousand dollars out of the emergency appropriation to transport and equip the expedition. By Wednesday, the twentieth, the Marines had assembled 450 men from various East Coast navy yards at the New York Barracks. At that point the department decided against the formation of a second battalion. Instead, the Marines increased the one battalion by another 200 men. At the time of its embarkation, two days later, the 1st Battalion, under the command of Lt. Col. Robert Huntington, consisted of 631 enlisted men, 21 officers, and 1 surgeon organized into five infantry and one artillery companies.[78]

The specific mission of the Marine battalion still remained unclear. At the time of the formation of the unit, Major Reid wrote that the Marines "are to have no connection whatever with the army, and are to report, and be at the disposal of the Commander-in-Chief of the North Atlantic Fleet." In any event, on 29 April, four days after the declaration of war, the battalion joined the fleet at Key West. It remained there for more than a month. On 23 May, its transport departed leaving the battalion in effect marooned on the beach. As one senior battalion officer remarked, "When I think that war was declared on the 25th of April . . . , and that we embarked on the 22d, organized, equipped, and ready for duty, it annoys me that so little benefit comes from it."[79]

While Huntington and his officers vented their frustrations against their forced inactivity on the white sandy beaches of Key West, Heywood and his staff in Washington busied themselves in placing the Marine Corps on a wartime footing and lobbying for permanent legislation to benefit the Corps. Heywood and his Headquarters had every reason to take pride in their accomplishment of mobilizing and equipping a full battalion with its own artillery in less than a week. Heywood also attempted to uniform the battalion in "campaign suits of brown linen" and the wide-brimmed "campaign hats" but was unable to do so until later because of the "great demand for these articles . . . by the Army." He authorized the purchase at Key West of tent floors to keep the men off the ground. At the same time, the commandant and the quartermaster, Maj. Frank L. Denny, ensured that the battalion received ample medical supplies, including quinine and a barrel of whiskey.[80]

While meeting the needs of the battalion, the commandant and his Headquarters staff also attempted to satisfy the demands placed upon them by an expanding wartime Marine establishment. The Quartermaster Department made some innovations in outfitting the Marines. It provided intermediate sizes in coats and trousers that improved the fit of enlisted uniforms. Moreover, the Corps introduced a more durable shoe for field conditions. The transition of the Marine Corps from the old Springfield to the new Lee rifle, however, remained an unresolved problem for the Headquarters staff, with most shipboard marines retaining the old Springfields. Still, with this one exception, which was really the fault of the Bureau of Ordnance, Colonel Heywood and his Headquarters performed well in coping with the wartime buildup.[81]

At the beginning of the crisis, Heywood and his staff were in hopes of obtaining from Congress a significant increase in the number of enlisted men and a restructuring of the officer corps. As events turned out, the commandant settled for much less than he wanted, due in part to the legislative strategy of the McKinley administration. When informed that the recommendations of his Personnel Board for the reorganization of the Navy officer corps would not be incorporated into the appropriation bill, Assistant Secretary Roosevelt informed the House Naval Affairs Committee that he then wanted no personnel provisions added to the measure.[82]

A few days later, 28 March 1898, Colonel Heywood submitted a formal request for proposed legislation to Secretary Long for the restructuring of the Marine officer corps. The recommended bill contained many of the same provisions that the Corps had pushed through the years: higher ranks and more officers. It contained one new wrinkle, however, in that it permitted the appointment of new second lieutenants from the ranks of "meritorious non-commissioned officers." Long forwarded the bill to the House Naval Affairs Committee, which in turn incorporated it with the reform measures suggested by the Roosevelt Personnel Board.[83]

The incorporation of the Marine bill with the broader Navy personnel legislation, however, had its disadvantages, in that Congress would not consider any of its provisions in the appropriation bill. In the appropriation legislation, as a result, the Marine Corps realized only some minor expansion in its enlisted ranks and in the number of temporary officers. Congress authorized the inclusion of the already approved 473 temporary enlistments into the Corps and allowed the recruitment of another 1,640 men for the emergency. The final appropriation measure signed on 4 May 1898 contained a stipulation that allowed the president to appoint "if an exigency may exist" such officers to the Marine Corps as may be necessary from civilian life or from the ranks of meritorious noncommissioned officers. These officers could serve only through the emergency and could not be appointed above the rank of captain.[84]

Colonel Heywood miscalculated in his legislative stratagem. He went along with the Navy Department policy to divorce the wartime mobilization from the permanent reform of the officer corps. The commandant apparently believed that Congress would pass the Navy Department sponsored personnel bill which would amalgamate the line and engineers. Despite assurances from Heywood that the legislation was "sure to go through," many Marine officers remained skeptical. The skeptics proved correct. Congress was not about to touch the controversial measure in the midst of the war when more pressing matters diverted its attention. Despite last-minute efforts on the part of Heywood and his staff to separate the Marine legislation from the overall naval personnel bill, the attempt failed. There was no major wartime reformation of the Marine officer corps.[85]

With the temporary officer appointments permitted by the appropriation act, however, the Marine officer corps at least gained some wartime increase. The Navy Department and Marine Corps were inundated with young and some not so young applicants who wanted to go to war as Marine second lieutenants. To weed out the unfit, the department established an examining board to test the applicants for physical, mental, moral, and military attributes and then ranked each candidate by merit. By 21 May, the commandant wrote Long that he had sufficient candidates to appear before the board.[86]

By early June, examining boards had selected twenty-four men from civilian life to serve as Marine Corps second lieutenants. Although the law actually left the number of temporary commissions open, Long and Heywood had decided upon twenty-eight new officers for the time being. With the completion of the selection of the officers from civilian life, the remaining four officers were to come from the ranks of meritorious noncommissioned officers. Eventually the Navy Department raised the quotas so that forty-three officers served as temporary second lieutenants through the end of the war. Of this total, forty were from civilian life and three were former noncommissioned officers.[87]

The selection of the new lieutenants from the enlisted ranks was somewhat different from that of the officers from civilian life. A noncommissioned officer who wanted an appointment needed to submit his application through official channels to the commandant. Based upon the endorsement of the man's commanding officer and other factors, Heywood made his recommendation whether to permit the candidate to take the officer examination.[88] The training of the new officers was quick and pragmatic. With the outbreak of the war, the Marine Corps School of Application graduated its class in April 1898 at the Washington Barracks and temporarily suspended operations. The Corps then used the barracks and school's facilities to indoctrinate the new officers. As Heywood observed, "The newly appointed officers were hurriedly drilled and otherwise prepared for duty as rapidly as possible."[89]

In the war, the Marines served with both Commodore George Dewey's and Sampson's fleets in the victories over the Spanish in the battles of Manila Bay in the Pacific and Santiago Bay in the Caribbean. Still, it was Huntington's battalion and its seizure of Guantánamo that caught the public eye and also signaled portents for the future. As Colonel Heywood was quick to remark, the Marine battalion with the fleet "showed how important and useful it is to have a body of troops which can be quickly mobilized and sent on board transports, fully equipped for service ashore and afloat, to be used at the discretion of the commanding admiral." The refusal of the Army to participate in a proposed joint Army-Marine amphibious operation against the fortified heights that dominated the entrance to Santiago Harbor posed questions about interservice cooperation in future campaigns.[90]

Upon the return of the Marine battalion from Cuba, Colonel Heywood was not slow to exploit the Corps's record in the war and kept the unit together at Portsmouth, New Hampshire, for over three weeks, ostensibly to permit the men "to rest and get the malaria" out of their system. On 10 September, Heywood visited the Marine encampment and reported to Secretary Long that "the men are looking very well, none of them being sick, and there has not been a death by disease since the battalion left for Cuba." As would be expected, the Navy Department and the press both compared the 2 percent sickness rate of the Marine battalion with the ravages that malaria and yellow fever caused among the Army troops.[91]

Finally, before disbanding in mid-September, the 1st Battalion paraded before the president in Washington. Despite a downpour, a large crowd turned out to cheer the marines, dressed in their campaign uniforms, as they passed in review to the strains of a "Hot Time in the Old Town Tonight." President McKinley praised the troops, stating, "They have performed magnificent duty and to you, Colonel Heywood, I wish to personally extend my congratulations for the fine condition your men are in."[92]

Despite the accolades, Heywood persisted in his efforts to call attention to the role of the Marine ship detachments. Even before the end of the war, on 9 August 1898, Heywood sent out letters to selected ship commanders and to Marine detachment officers for reports on the effectiveness of Marine gunnery in the sea battles. In his annual report, Heywood boasted that the secondary batteries manned by marines did the greatest damage to the Spanish ships at Santiago.[93]

The accounts by both Marine Corps and Navy officers were much less conclusive. For example, Marine Captain Littleton W. T. Waller on the *Indiana* related that no more than a third of the marines manned the guns. The *Indiana*'s commander, Capt. H. C. Taylor, explained that the marines on the secondary battery fired about half the number of rounds as the seamen because the marines manned the "port battery of 6-pounders, while the starboard battery was the one engaged." In fact, naval gunnery during both the battles of Santiago and Manila Bay was notoriously poor. As one naval study concluded, "War ships of the present day will generally be placed hors de combat by conflagration and the destruction of their personnel before they are sunk by gun fire."[94]

Still, neither the public nor Congress was overly concerned with the technicalities of naval gunfire. In fact, the inadequacies of the aimed firing during the two sea battles did not come out until several months later, and then appeared only in professional journals and published official reports. Heywood's report containing lists of marines breveted for gallantry in action and glowing accounts of marines in battle on both land and sea served to satiate the nation's appetite for heroes.[95]

Colonel Heywood had already anticipated new demands on Marine Corps manpower. On 9 November 1898, he asked Secretary Long for a Corps of 6,000 men, an increase of 1,268 over its wartime force. The commandant argued that this "would give the Navy a well-organized and well-drilled body of men, who would be always available for any duty, to act in conjunction with the Navy, in any service they may be called upon to perform." He also insisted that the Marine officer corps needed to be restructured and referred to the bill for the reorganization of the Marine Corps that he had submitted in the spring. Although the bill was still on the House calendar for action, the commandant stated that its provisions were no longer valid as they were "based on the requirements of the Navy before any large increase was contemplated." He asked permission to submit a new bill that would include his present recommendations to Congress. In his annual report, Secretary Long supported an increase of the Corps "to at least 5,000 men and necessary officers."[96]

Still not satisfied, Heywood pursued his efforts to obtain more for the Corps. He asserted that altered circumstances because of the war and its outcome required "at least 6,000 men at the present time" but warned that this number would only be adequate for five years. He then enclosed a copy of his proposed bill, which, among other things, provided for doubling the officer corps, including sixty second lieutenants. The new lieutenants would come from the Naval Academy, the temporary lieutenants appointed during the war, meritorious noncommissioned officers, and from civilian life.[97]

Although originally expecting to retain the temporary officers appointed during the war, Colonel Heywood soon learned differently. As early as October, Long had written Heywood, "hostilities having been suspended it is desirable to reduce the volunteer officers as rapidly as circumstances will permit." By 17 January 1899, after releasing several of the temporary second lieutenants, Colonel Heywood suggested that the secretary reconsider. Long denied the request, stating that it was "the plain requirement of the law" that officers could only be retained until peace is concluded. He nevertheless permitted the Marine Corps to keep the officers until the official ratification of the Paris Peace Treaty. With that ratification by the Senate on 6 February 1899, Long ordered Heywood to "discharge the second lieutenants in the U.S. Marine Corps, appointed for temporary service." This was to be a very temporary demobilization.[98]

In the meantime, the secretary had forwarded Heywood's proposed legislation to the House Naval Affairs Committee, recommending approval. On 17 January 1899, the committee then incorporated into the naval personnel bill an amendment which included the changes wanted by Heywood. Although the full House agreed to the amendment, it took out a provision which would have made the commandant a major general. It would, however, promote Heywood to the rank of brigadier general. The House then passed the entire personnel bill, which included the amalgamation of the Navy line with the Navy engineer corps.[99]

The full Congress quickly acted on the measure. By the end of February, the Senate passed the bill and a House-Senate committee resolved the differences between the two chambers. On 3 March 1899, McKinley signed the bill into law. The new law provided the Marine Corps with the 6,000 enlisted men and with an authorized officer corps of 201 line officers, including the new rank of brigadier general commandant. In addition, it permitted the Corps 5 new staff officers and promoted the paymaster, adjutant and inspector, and the quartermaster to the rank of colonel. As a result, the authorized number of Corps line officers was one brigadier general commandant, five colonels, five lieutenant colonels, ten majors, sixty captains, sixty first lieutenants, and sixty second lieutenants.[100]

The new law completely transformed the Marine officer corps. Heywood, of course, became a brigadier general. Two officers received promotions from lieutenant colonel to colonel and one a promotion of two ranks, from major to colonel. Another three officers went from major to lieutenant colonel and two from captain to lieutenant colonel. In more junior ranks, ten captains became majors, and all the lieutenants, both first and second, became captains. Of the forty-three temporary officers, thirty received commissions as first lieutenants, bypassing the rank of second lieutenant. Out of the three noncommissioned officers who took advantage of the law to apply for a commission, only one, Sgt. Thomas F. Lyon, passed the qualifying examination and became a first lieutenant. Except for General Heywood, all of the newly promoted officers, except the former temporary officers, passed a written and physical examination.[101]

The new law now allowed the appointment of forty-five new second lieutenants in 1899 and fifteen more after the new year. General Heywood immediately proposed guidelines in accordance with the legislation for the appointment of the new officers. He recommended to Long selection procedures and a uniform examination for all officer aspirants including a barrage of written tests in English, geography, history, constitutional law, surveying, and math to encompass plane trigonometry and logarithms. Long approved these recommendations and issued a Navy circular which incorporated the new provisions.[102]

The result was a relative explosion of Marine officer appointments and promotions. By May 1900, the Corps consisted of 171 commissioned officers, 107 appointed or promoted in the past year, as opposed to the 211 authorized by law. Notwithstanding valiant efforts by Heywood to maintain officer professionalism, the result was an obvious deterioration of standards. While directing that new Marine officers receive some formal instruction at the various barracks, the commandant had initially neither the manpower nor financial resources to reopen the Marine School of Application. With the continued accelerated rate of promotions, the Navy Department, over the protest of Heywood, permitted as a temporary measure the advancement of certain officers, without formal examinations, based solely on their past records. Such measures hardly raised the prestige of a Marine commission. One Naval Academy midshipman successfully argued against assignment to the Marine Corps by mentioning that there were officers in the Corps who had entered the Naval Academy after him but had failed to graduate and would now be senior to him.[103]

Despite these drawbacks to officer professionalism, Heywood took several initiatives to improve the quality of his officer corps. At the request of the Navy War College in June 1900, he detailed six Marine officers there. While the School of Application remained closed for most of the year, Heywood established a summer camp in Annapolis for the training of new officers and enlisted recruits. In November 1900, he reopened the School of Application at the Marine Corps Barracks in Washington.[104]

In its second term beginning the following November, the school consisted mostly of those officers who had failed their examinations. While the eligible Marine officers had received promotions based upon their record, the Navy Department still required them to pass the written examinations within a year of their promotion. In November 1901, Heywood observed to the secretary of the navy that several officers had failed their examinations and needed to be reexamined or lose their rank or even possibly their commissions. Stating that the new officers recently appointed from civilian life had now ample "opportunity to prepare themselves," he again sought to impose the requirement that Marine officers pass written qualifying examinations before being promoted. Upon

Heywood's insistence that it was of the "utmost importance that this standard of qualification for Marine officers . . . [the same as for Army officers]" be maintained, the Navy Department approved this last request. By May 1903, Heywood moved the School of Application to Annapolis, where he believed the new barracks and other buildings erected there afforded "exceptional facilities" for instruction. The school opened in July with a class of fifteen new second lieutenants as a result of the law of 3 March 1903, which once more expanded the Marine Corps.[105]

Throughout this period, despite the growth of the Corps, a major concern for Heywood was the continuing pressure for the Corps to man the new foreign outposts in the Far East. Since the spring of 1899, at the request of Admiral Dewey, the Marines deployed to the Philippines to garrison the Cavite naval base. By November of that year, the Marines had three battalions at Cavite consisting of 43 officers and 976 enlisted men. While taking only a marginal role in the suppression of the Filipino resistance, these battalions were the first American troops inserted into China during the Boxer emergency in the spring and summer of 1900. In October, the Marine forces withdrew from China after participating in the taking of the city of Tientsin (Tianjin) and lifting the siege of the foreign legations in Peking (Beijing). Still, nearly 2,000 marines, or one-third of the entire Corps, remained in the Far East through the Heywood commandancy, including a 1,500-man brigade in the Philippines.[106]

The Marine brigade in the Philippines remained largely in garrison, with the notable exception of the battalion commanded by Maj. Littleton W. T. Waller in the Samar campaign of 1901–2. In what Marine Corps historian Allan Millett called a "monument to human endurance and poor planning," Major Waller led fifty-four marines of his command supported by native scouts and porters in an ill-fated reconnaissance march. Suffering substantial casualties, a weary and fever-racked Waller ordered the summary execution of eleven of the Filipinos whom he believed betrayed his troops. Although operating under Army orders, an Army court-martial acquitted Waller on the technical grounds that it did not have the authority to try the Marine officer. In a separate memorandum to the secretary of the navy, General Heywood refused to express an opinion whether the Samar battalion was subject to Army or Navy court-martial. He did state, however, that it would appear that Waller and his command "were serving under the immediate command" of an Army general. The commandant, in his annual report, quoted approvingly the words of the naval commander on the scene that Waller's battalion "performed its duty in a most efficient manner." Upon the return of Waller and his battalion to the United States in June 1902, Heywood sent him a letter of commendation praising "the splendid service which has been rendered by you and the officers and men who have served under you, both in China and the Philippines." The Samar march would enter into Marine mythology, but the incident would remain a blemish on Waller's record and probably barred his possible ascendancy to the commandancy.[107]

Despite the Samar incident, the first years following the Spanish-American War were a relatively auspicious time for the Marine Corps and one of expanding missions. Much of the rancor between the Navy progressives and the Marines had dissipated.

With the colonial acquisitions in the Pacific, the commandant noted as early as December 1898, "prominent naval officers . . . [believe] there should be a force of 20,000 well drilled and equipped Marines, who could be placed on board naval transports, at very short notice, . . . without the necessity for calling on the Army . . . [and] without the conflict of authority that must necessarily result from the co-operation of Army troops with the Navy." In testimony before Congress in February 1900, he elaborated: "Naval officers are almost a unit as to the necessity for a larger number of Marines to act in cooperation with the Navy, especially now, since our outlying possessions will in all [make] such cooperation necessary."[108]

Throughout this period, the Navy looked to new roles for the Marine Corps. At its first meeting in the spring of 1900, the newly formed General Board, the nearest thing to a Navy general staff, under the leadership of Admiral Dewey, assigned its Marine member, Col. George Reid, the Marine Corps adjutant and inspector, to come up with the "number and organization of a force of Marines sufficient" to defend several proposed bases in the Caribbean. With the volatility of the situation in China, the board also studied the attaining and defending of an advanced base off the Chinese mainland. On 6 October 1900, Dewey signed a memorandum from the board to the secretary of the navy recommending the immediate formation of a four-hundred-man Marine battalion that could serve as the nucleus for a one-thousand-man Marine force, in the event of a war, to defend of an advanced base in support of a naval campaign in Asiatic waters. The board suggested that "the Marines would be best adapted and most available for immediate and sudden call" for the establishment of such a base and the throwing up of hasty defenses and gun positions and the laying of mines to channelize the approaches. If more permanent defenses were then decided upon, Army units could be sent to relieve the Marine force, which then would be available "for other duty." General Heywood agreed to the proposal but warned that the preparations would "necessitate very careful consideration, and considerable time will be necessary for accomplishing it."[109]

Although the General Board directive referred to an advanced base force in Asia, the Marines in the Philippines for the most part stayed scattered in some fifteen naval facilities in the Manila and Olongapo sectors. As Colonel Reid testified before Congress, the final disposition of the Marines in the Philippines would not be resolved until Congress determined "some definite policy there about naval stations." This issue would remain a matter of dispute for several years between Army and Navy leaders.[110]

It was on the U.S. eastern coast and in the Caribbean that the Marine Corps took the first measures to implement its advanced base mission. The most important initiatives occurred at Newport, the home of both the Navy Torpedo School and the Naval War College. In May 1901, General Heywood ordered Maj. Henry C. Haines, one of the Marine officers assigned to the War College, to take charge of a special Marine detachment of five officers and forty-five enlisted men sent to the Torpedo School. At the school, they underwent advanced base training, including communications and torpedoes. While Haines returned to his other duties on the Naval War College staff, the detachment in July joined the North Atlantic Squadron for its summer maneuvers off Nantucket Bay, Massachusetts. In July, some two hundred marines of the fleet, including the Newport detachment, landed at Greatpoint in Nantucket.

The troops immediately set up "lines of defense," including a mine field; mounted guns on shore from the fleet; established a communications network; and successfully "repulsed" an imaginary enemy. The troops then reembarked for a ten-day rest and then landed once more near Nantucket. Breaking camp on 18 August 1900, they returned to their ships and the specially trained advanced base detachment proceeded to the New York Marine Barracks. The detachment, however, left its equipment at Newport for maintenance and safekeeping. In his annual report in October, General Heywood stated that he desired to repeat the advanced base training and maneuvers the following year.[111]

Despite his acceptance and apparent support of the advanced base mission, Heywood had reservations about the implications that it had for the deployment of Marine forces. He especially objected to a proposal by the General Board that he organize a contingency force to consist of four Marine companies with each company to be kept at its full strength of slightly over one hundred men. Each company would be assigned to a separate barracks or post and prepared to consolidate into an expeditionary or advanced base force upon call. The equipment of this force would be maintained at Philadelphia "ready for instant use." Heywood argued that he did not have the manpower to keep that number of marines at these posts and limit their use to the expeditionary and advanced base missions. He pointed to the example of the Spanish-American War, during which the Marine Corps was able to organize an expeditionary battalion on short notice. The commandant suggested instead that the Corps establish schools of instructions at four different posts and bring the men together periodically for practical exercises. Heywood then declared that although the Marine Corps had some expeditionary stores at Philadelphia, it did not have the appropriations to obtain the necessary supplies for the size force suggested by the General Board.[112]

While accepting in part Heywood's explanation, the General Board still insisted that the Marine Corps form some sort of advanced base force. Seeing the handwriting on the wall, Heywood tried to make the best of the situation. Stating that he had no intention of structuring the Marine Corps around permanent battalions or even companies, nevertheless, he agreed to "organize and maintain one or more companies at the full company strength, according to the strength of the command" at six major posts, including Mare Island in California. According to Heywood, these personnel would be trained in both expeditionary and advanced base duties and "equipped for mobilization into battalion organization at a moment's notice." He asked that the Navy be required to provide a transport "capable of accommodating 1,000 men together with full equipment, including ordnance and military stores, for expeditionary duty." While conceding that Philadelphia was an obvious site for the storage of equipment, Heywood repeated his observation that this would require additional appropriations. Moreover, he used the opportunity to call attention to all of the duties required of the Corps, including the providing of guards for both the Navy's ships and shore installations. According to Heywood's calculations, the carrying out of the advanced base mission as outlined by the General Board would require an immediate additional four thousand men for the Marine Corps. In the meantime, the commandant proposed further exercises in the "landing of troops, guns and other military stores, at the base of operations," stating that the staff of the Navy War College had already a "complete scheme, in detail, covering the subject."[113]

Indeed, the General Board had already suggested to the secretary that the North Atlantic Station carry out a landing at Culebra, a small island just east of Puerto Rico. Approving the recommendation in mid-November 1901, the secretary ordered Heywood to assemble "without delay" an expeditionary force of one hundred enlisted men and four officers to report to the commander of the North Atlantic Station to carry out the mission. Heywood was to provide this force with the necessary equipment for field fortifications, gun emplacements, field telegraphs and telephones, and searchlights, while the Bureau of Ordnance would supply mining and countermining outfits. General Heywood selected Major Haines because of his previous experience the year before and his general duties with the staff of the Navy War College to command the Marines.[114]

Arriving on New Year's Day 1902, the small force established their temporary base. Through January and into early February, the Marines participated in various exercises, including the landing of guns and the laying of mines, with the fleet offshore. When the fleet departed on 2 February the detachment remained at Culebra and continued to carry out various tests of their equipment. Haines and his detachment remained on Culebra until late April, when ordered home, leaving behind a caretaker party of one officer and ten enlisted men.[115]

Culebra as an advanced base assumed additional significance as the General Board and the Navy initiated planning for the 1902 and 1903 winter fleet exercises. Underlying the preparations for the maneuvers was the growing crisis between the United States and several European powers, especially Germany, over the failure of the Venezuelan dictator Cipriano Castro's government to repay its debts to foreign nationals. The untried, new president, Theodore Roosevelt, who had replaced William McKinley in September 1901 after the latter's assassination, appeared to accept with equanimity, a German government note two months later that it might have to use force to collect the debts. He, nevertheless, had the U.S. Navy undertake several steps that showed concern over possible European naval actions in Latin America. The General Board immediately began to gather intelligence about the situation in Venezuela. In January 1902, the department requested an additional $120,000 appropriation from Congress to cover expanded fleet maneuvers. In June 1902, President Roosevelt asked Admiral Dewey, the president of the General Board, to assume personal command over the upcoming winter fleet exercises. From November 1902 into early January 1903, one of the largest concentrations of U.S. warships up to that time, divided into battleship, cruiser, and torpedo divisions, practiced fleet maneuvers in the Caribbean off Puerto Rico and Culebra. How much a possible Roosevelt ultimatum in December 1902 or the

U.S. maneuvers caused the Germans to arbitrate their differences with the Venezuelan government remains a matter of some conjecture. There can be no doubt, nevertheless, that the United States show of force demonstrated American naval prowess, in effect making the Caribbean in the words of Admiral Dewey, "the American Mediterranean."[116]

The Marine Corps was part and parcel of this buildup of naval strength in the Caribbean. In July 1902, at the behest of the General Board, the new secretary of the navy, William H. Moody, ordered General Heywood to form five companies of over one hundred men each, four infantry and one artillery, to take part in the proposed winter maneuvers. Heywood directed that two of the infantry companies be organized at Annapolis, the third at the Brooklyn Marine Barracks, and the fourth at the League Island Barracks in Philadelphia. The commandant organized the artillery company at the Washington Barracks. Their mission was clear. They were to establish and provide protection for an advanced base of the fleet at Culebra while preventing any enemy landing force from establishing such a base for the opposing fleet. The plans were for the five companies to form a battalion at either Philadelphia or Norfolk in November and embark on board the Navy transport *Panther* for Culebra.[117]

Circumstances forced some alterations in the original plans. A revolution broke out once more in Panama, which at this time still belonged to Colombia. In the previous year and earlier in 1902, when civil unrest had occurred in Panama, Marine ship detachments from the fleet had landed and secured the peace. This time, the U.S. government determined a larger force was necessary and ordered a Marine battalion to sail from the United States. General Heywood organized the battalion at Philadelphia from one of the units slated for the advanced base maneuver and from a draft of replacements for the Philippines. On 14 September, the battalion consisting of 16 officers and 325 enlisted men embarked on board the *Panther,* and two days later the ship departed for Panama. The battalion arrived in Panama on the twenty-second and landed the following day at Colón. One company remained at Colón while the other three traveled by train to Panama City and thus secured the rail transit. The Marines quickly ended the outbreaks. On the twenty-sixth, the U.S. troops using their rifle butts prevented Panamanian rebels from removing a Colombian officer from a train. As one reporter wrote a few weeks later, "The arrival of the Marines has had a salutary effect . . . as no indignities are now committed." On 18 November, with relative calm restored, the Marine battalion reembarked upon the *Panther* and departed Panama for Culebra.[118]

During the initial period of the Panamanian crisis, Colonel Heywood ordered the mobilization of even a larger Marine battalion at Norfolk, Virginia, consisting of nearly six hundred men organized into six companies. This force included the remaining elements of the original advanced base force and whatever manpower reserves that were left on the eastern coast. At this point, it was not clear what role the Marines would play in the forthcoming winter maneuver. When it became apparent, however, that this battalion would not be required for service in Panama, the Navy Department ordered it to Culebra to take part in the maneuvers. Under the command of Col. Percival C. Pope, the overstrength battalion boarded the U.S. Navy transport *Prairie* at Norfolk and on 5 November set sail for Culebra, arriving there on the twentieth.

Originally, the idea was for the Marine battalion at Panama to join the Marines at Culebra, but this proved infeasible. Yellow fever and malaria wreaked havoc at Panama. When the Panama battalion, which had reembarked on board the *Panther,* arrived off Culebra on 24 November, the medical officers quarantined the ship and would not authorize the Marines to land. Lt. Col. Benjamin R. Russell, the battalion commander, reported eighty-three men of his command on the sick list. The *Panther* departed Culebra on 30 November 1902 and returned to the U.S.[119]

Colonel Pope's marines on Culebra soon set to work to improve the island's defenses against a possible attacking fleet or landing force. Reformed into a regiment with Pope still in command, they established two separate camps, each manned by a battalion. In a repeat of much of the effort of the year before, only on a larger scale, they manhandled large guns, dug a canal between two harbor sites, established both telegraph and telephone lines, and built new roads. The exercises lasted through 3 January 1903 and ended with a visit ashore by Admiral Dewey, who praised their labors. Shortly afterward, the regimental headquarters together with one of the battalions reembarked on board the *Prairie* and returned to the United States and disbanded.[120]

While leaving a small detachment on the island on 7 January, the remaining marines under the command of Major Haines boarded the transport *Panther,* which had returned to Culebra. The *Panther* with the battalion embarked became part of the newly formed Caribbean squadron, which included four cruisers, the *Olympia, Atlanta, Machias,* and *Marietta,* and the ship tender *Vixen.* As Admiral Dewey's second in command during the maneuvers, Rear Adm. H. C. Taylor explained to the secretary of the navy, the squadron operating from Culebra would "serve two purposes; one of being ready for service anywhere, and the other that of improving the base and harbor." As for the marines on board the *Panther,* Taylor asserted they were "a most valuable adjunct" and could be "landed on the Isthmus or anywhere else they may be needed."[121]

As Major Haines, the battalion commander, observed to General Heywood, "the assignment of a battalion permanently to a ship is a new departure in our service." He asked Heywood for guidance relative to the status of his battalion remarking that as he understood his mission "it is to have a mobile military force ready to be thrown at any point needed." In peacetime, the Marines were "to suppress disorder and protect American property"; in wartime, the battalion was "to attack, seize, and hold any desired tactical or strategical point." He believed that the only way that the battalion could accomplish both missions was to spend much of its time ashore where it would "become accustomed to camp life . . . and be trained in such exercises as would be necessary in actual service." Haines viewed the battalion's assignment to the ship as merely a means to provide "a mobile base of supplies, and a means of transportation to any threatened point." According to Haines, the battalion was not under ordinary circumstances to remain on board ship. He also wanted more authority while embarked over his own men, much the same relationship as that of a commander of a Marine barracks to a commander of a navy yard or station.[122]

Unfortunately for Haines, Heywood had little authority to ameliorate any of his relationships with the Navy. The Marine battalion was assigned to the *Panther* and, while on board ship, was subject to the authority of the ship's captain. The chain of command was entirely naval, extending from the secretary of the navy, who was advised by the General Board, to the commander of the North Atlantic Station, then to the commander of the Caribbean commander, down to the ship's commander. In an exchange of views, the commander of the *Panther* and Haines agreed to a large extent about the situation of the marines on board ship. They both believed that the battalion required a larger ship to accommodate the men comfortably for any extended period. Such a ship, according to them, required "cargo ports, booms and winches for hoisting in and out stores rapidly" and a large number of small boats for the embarkation or landing of the battalion. More important, both commanders maintained that the battalion commander should have more authority over his men while embarked on board ship. They recommended that the department issue a general order "which would do much to make the duties of both the captain of the ship and the Marine battalion commander much easier, and tend to settle questions which are liable to arise in the absence of specific orders governing them."[123]

Despite the unanimity of views of the two commanders, both the squadron and fleet commanders refused to alter the existing command relationships. Rear Adm. J. B. Coghlan, the Caribbean Squadron commander, recommended against giving the battalion commander any more authority on board ship and suggested waiting to see how the present circumstances worked out. In any event, he pointed out that when the battalion went ashore, the ship's commander no longer had any authority over the battalion. The commander in chief of the North Atlantic Station was even more adamant. "It would be unwise in the extreme to take from the captain of the ship the responsibility for assigning punishments and giving [it] to another officer," he wrote. "If allowed on such a ship as the *Panther,* the same would be demanded on every ship where there was a guard in command of a Marine officer." Finally, after the *Panther* returned to U.S. coastal waters, Admiral Coghlan denied the contention of the ship's commander that "the vessel carrying a force of Marines should be more of a transport than a man-of-war." Neither the General Board nor the secretary of the navy had any desire to overrule their senior commanders. The board referred the matter back to the squadron and fleet commanders for further study, observing that it was not convinced that "the experience thus far gained is sufficient to justify any departure from existing practice."[124]

The Navy Department, nevertheless, felt the assignment of the Marine battalion to a transport a successful experiment and one that should be continued. Despite Major Haines's initial objections, the battalion remained embarked on board the *Panther* for the most part of its tour. The ship remained with the Caribbean Squadron in West Indies waters until late July, when it departed for Frenchman's Bay, Maine, where the battalion landed and took part in Army-Navy joint maneuvers. The battalion then reembarked and sailed for League Island Philadelphia. Haines then turned over command of the battalion to Maj. John A. Lejeune. Under Lejeune, the battalion was transferred from the *Panther* to the Navy ship *Dixie* to begin preparations for the 1903–4 winter maneuvers. Once more circumstances altered events, and Lejeune's battalion was later in the year, under a new commandant, to be diverted to the Panama crisis of 1903–4 over the building of the Panama Canal.[125]

Both the experiments with the cruising battalion and the Culebra maneuvers would have portents of a growing debate within the Marine Corps and the naval establishment. Was there a clash between the advanced base mission and the expeditionary one? While this dichotomy was not examined during the Heywood commandancy, the Marine Corps was aware that its new missions and activities were costing more money. In September 1903, the Marine Corps quartermaster noted that the organization of both the Panama battalion, the previous year, and the battalion with the Caribbean squadron cost a total of seven thousand dollars each. These costs were borne by the Corps without any increase of funds, which required reductions and economies throughout the Corps.[126]

While the Marine Corps discovered expanded roles abroad in both the Pacific and Caribbean, General Heywood continued to fight some of the same battles in Washington that he had encountered from the beginning of his commandancy. His efforts to expand the Corps met with only grudging consent in Congress. The Marine Corps received no additional personnel in either 1900 or 1901. Congress did allow for 750 more enlisted men in 1902, but no increase in the officer Corps. The 1902 appropriation did contain a provision promoting Heywood to major general, but the commandancy would again revert to the rank of brigadier general upon Heywood's retirement. Finally, in 1903, Congress approved a further augmentation of 720 enlisted men and 67 more officers including 12 additional second lieutenants. Heywood, while still calling for a Marine Corps of 10,000 men, apparently was not unhappy about the gradual increase so "that the new officers and men may be better assimilated into the Corps."[127]

With the approach of Heywood's sixty-fourth birthday and his mandatory retirement, Marine officers began to maneuver for position to succeed him. As early as 1901, rumors spread that General Heywood was in ill health and might retire early. Much of the early speculation had centered around Colonel Reid, adjutant and inspector of the Marine Corps. Since Reid's appointment to the position of adjutant and inspector, Heywood had relied heavily on him for much of the day-to-day administration of the Corps and for his successful dealings with both the Navy and Congress. When the Navy General Board came into being in 1900, Heywood once more turned to Reid to be his personal representative.[128]

Sometime between 1901 and 1903, the relationship between Reid and Heywood had definitely cooled. The reasons for this can only be a matter of conjecture. Heywood may have resented what many in the Marine Corps perceived as Reid's overriding ambition to succeed him. At the court-martial of Col. Robert L. Meade in November 1901 as a result of a dispute between him and the Headquarters staff, Heywood testified that he had no intention of retiring before he reached the mandatory age limit and that he knew of no conspiracy among the staff to eliminate Meade as a candidate for the commandancy. Still, these rumors about a conspiracy seem to have colored Heywood's perception about the entire relationship between the Headquarters and senior line officers. Moreover, Heywood may well have believed that Reid as the Marine Corps representative to the General Board and the author of many of its memos on the advanced base may have placed too much emphasis upon the restructuring of the Marine Corps for the advanced base mission.[129]

Whatever the factors, despite strong bipartisan political backing for Reid by such influential figures as former Democrat secretary of the navy Hilary A. Herbert and Republican senator Mark A. Hanna of Ohio, the adjutant and inspector did not receive the appointment. According to Col. Henry Clay Cochrane, Reid believed that the commandant in effect dealt treacherously with him by throwing his support to Lt. Col. George Elliott, who commanded the Washington Barracks. In June 1903, President Roosevelt officially announced that Lieutenant Colonel Elliott would succeed Heywood. On 3 October 1903, Heywood retired and George Elliott became the tenth commandant of the U.S. Marine Corps. A little more than eleven years later, on 26 February 1915, Charles Heywood died in Washington of chronic heart disease at the age of seventy-five.[130]

In his last report, Heywood made an extensive listing of the accomplishments that occurred during his tenure. He included in these the introduction of officer promotion examinations, the establishment of the School of Application, the appointment of Marine officers to the Naval War College, barracks improvements, the assignment of Marine detachments to both the secondary and main batteries on board ship, the movement of Marine Headquarters from the Washington Barracks to buildings in downtown Washington closer to the office of the secretary of the navy, the formation of Marine overseas battalions in the Philippines and Guam, and of course the rapid expansion of the Marine Corps following the Spanish-American War. Ending his report in a mild self-congratulatory vein, Heywood wrote, "Considering the fact that at the time that I assumed command of the Marine Corps on 30 January 1891, it consisted of but 75 officers and 2,100 enlisted men, stationed at eleven posts in the United States and on board ships in commission, and the corps now consists of 278 officers and 7,532 enlisted men, stationed at twenty-nine posts in the United States and in our colonial possessions, and on board ships in commission, I think I may be pardoned for stating that the corps is at the present time in much better condition than when I was appointed Commandant."[131]

Heywood left unmentioned other of his achievements during his commandancy, including the practice of opening recruiting offices in inland cities to meet the increasing demands for an expanding manpower base. He encouraged the participation of the Marines at most public ceremonies. Marine guards protected the Navy exhibit at the Pan American Exposition in Buffalo in 1901 and formed part of the funeral escort for President McKinley's body after his assassination there in September of that year. Under Heywood, there was a new emphasis upon marksmanship, and the Corps successfully introduced two new rifles: in 1897 and 1898, the Lee "Straight-pull" 6-mm rifle and in 1900–1901, the .30-caliber Krag-Jorgenson rifle.[132]

Curiously, Heywood remained silent in his final report about what later observers might consider the two most important initiatives of his commandancy: the acceptance of the advanced base mission and the deployment with the fleet for an extensive period of a Marine battalion on board a Navy transport. Again this may indicate the stronger commitment of Heywood to the more traditional secondary battery and guard missions of the Marine Corps rather than to either the advanced base or expeditionary roles. Moreover, it may indicate that others such as Mannix, Reid, and Haines may have been more responsible for these new enterprises than the commandant himself. Still, Heywood saw the merit in such men and appointed them to positions where they could influence the renovation of the Marine Corps. If Colonel McCawley was the transitional commandant, General Heywood was the first modern commandant and, literally and figuratively, the first twentieth-century commandant. As the *Army and Navy Register* observed in April 1903, he was "intimately linked with the prosperity and fame of the Corps."[133]

10

George Frank Elliott

1903–1910

ROBERT J. CRESSMAN

At noon on Saturday, 3 October 1903, George Frank Elliott, as a brigadier general, relieved Maj. Gen. Charles Heywood and thus became the tenth commandant of the Marine Corps, assuming his duties in a simple ceremony in the sixth-floor offices of the Mills Building at Seventeenth Street and Pennsylvania Avenue. At that time, the Marine Corps enjoyed the highest number of officers and men, about eight thousand, in its history.

Elliott, born on 30 November 1846 in Eutaw, Alabama, to Gardner Edward and Anne Bryant Elliott, moved to New Hampshire as a boy, where he heard Revolutionary War tales from his grandfather. During the Civil War, Elliott, deemed too young for soldiering, nonetheless "served the government in a civil capacity" and ultimately received an appointment to the United States Military Academy from the 2d District of New York. He took the oath of office as cadet on 2 July 1868. Although he survived the rigors of plebe year at West Point, he was later found to be "deficient" in mathematics and French and was honorably discharged on 30 June 1870.[1]

On 14 October 1870, he received an appointment as a second lieutenant in the United States Marine Corps and reported to the Marine Barracks, Washington, D.C., to commence his instruction. He then served at the Marine Barracks at Portsmouth, New Hampshire, where Cdr. Jonathan Young, U.S. Navy, who had performed distinguished Civil War service, apparently took a paternal interest in the young Marine officer and, unknown to him, told his father that his son was coming under the "bad influence" exerted by a certain, but unspecified, family at Portsmouth. Gardner Elliott promptly implored Col. Cmdt. Jacob Zeilin to transfer his son, preferably to the New York Navy Yard in Brooklyn, presumably to get him away from Portsmouth. Whether or not Gardner Elliott's letter to Colonel Zeilin prompted it, Lieutenant Elliott was soon ordered to the Marine Barracks at the New York Navy Yard.[2]

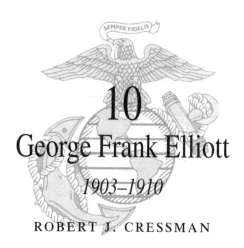

Maj. Gen. George P. Elliott, tenth commandant.
U.S. Marine Corps Photo.

Elliott then served successive tours in the receiving ship *Vermont,* in the *Frolic* (a "special duty" flagship at the New York Navy Yard), and in the *Monongahela,* a screw sloop assigned to the South Atlantic Station. During his time in the latter, he demonstrated devotion to duty in the face of trying circumstances when yellow fever felled much of the ship's company at Rio de Janeiro, Brazil, and Elliott voluntarily assisted the ship's doctor in caring for the sick. Later, during Elliott's time in that ship, his father's death compelled him to ask for duty at Norfolk so that his mother could reside near him. Colonel Zeilin complied with Elliott's request, and after his tour in the *Monongahela,* Elliott went to the Marine Barracks at Norfolk.

He next commanded the Marine Corps guard of the steam sloop *Alliance* and was in that ship when she searched Arctic waters for the ill-fated DeLong Expedition's *Jeanette.* During her cruise, the *Alliance* performed scientific duties, in which Elliott participated with gusto. Cdr. George Wadleigh, commanding the *Alliance,* later commended his Marine officer, an accomplished hunter, for bagging "several specimens of birds and animals" as examples of the fauna of the region.[3]

Following that sea duty, Elliott served at the Boston Marine Barracks and again at Norfolk. While he was serving in the latter, a revolution occurred in the Colombian province of Panama in the spring of 1885. When marines and sailors were sent to "maintain order, open communications, and protect American lives and property" in the region, Elliott, then a second lieutenant, commanded the post established at San Pablo in the Matachin district. There, although he saw no combat, he showed that he could exercise independent initiative. More important, he again came under the favorable gaze of a senior naval officer. "Thrown upon his own resources, he [Elliott] at once established an excellent set of regulations for the government of the post," wrote Cdr. Bowman Hendry McCalla, U.S. Navy, commander of the sailors and marines of the second battalion sent to Panama. Not easy to please, thought a martinet by some, but possessing as fine a grasp of Navy–Marine Corps operations as any of his contemporaries, McCalla considered Elliott "a remarkably good officer."[4] Following that expeditionary service, Elliott returned to the Norfolk Navy Yard.

He then went to sea in the *Vandalia,* on the Pacific Station, and in the *Mohican,* before he joined the *Lancaster,* the flagship of the Asiatic Squadron, on 29 August 1892 at Nagasaki, Japan. When the cruiser *Baltimore* relieved the *Lancaster* as flagship, Elliott transferred to her, on 16 January 1894, to serve out the remainder of his tour. A captain by then, he was assigned the collateral duty of fleet marine officer, in addition to commanding the flagship's guard.

Growing tension between China and Japan found the *Baltimore* lying at Chemulpo, Seoul, Korea's outlet to the sea, when, on 23 July 1894, American Minister to Korea, John M. B. Sill, reported that the Japanese had seized the palace and the King of Korea. Sill then reiterated an earlier request for a guard for the American Legation. During the ensuing conference on board the *Baltimore,* most of her officers agreed that a march to Seoul could not be made at night, and that going by day, in the oppressive summer heat, would endanger the men. Elliott disagreed and believed that the situation dictated sending a guard immediately. Impressed by Elliott's willingness, Capt. Benjamin Franklin Day of the *Baltimore* ordered him to proceed.

Landing at Chemulpo at 8:45 the night of 24 July 1894, the guard ultimately reached Seoul the next morning, having covered thirty-one miles in eleven hours. Sill considered its arrival "very timely," since Japanese soldiers and disorderly Koreans garbed as Japanese were looting homes near the American legation. Augmented on the twenty-sixth by a bluejacket detachment from the cruiser, the *Baltimore*'s marines spent three months at the legation, preserving order and providing security for not only the eighty Americans in Seoul but also other foreign nationalities.[5]

Elliott's marines then spent the period from December 1894 to February 1895 in Tientsin (Tianjin), poised to move to protect the foreign enclaves in Peking (Beijing) should Sino-Japanese hostilities have threatened them. In February 1895, Elliott traveled alone to Peking, where he conferred with the American minister, Charles Denby (father of the future secretary of the navy). They discussed arrangements to resupply the guard, if necessary, and to determine how to protect American missionaries in the event that the Japanese moved against Chinese forces there. Later during Elliott's time in the imperial capital, he served as military attaché for Denby during an audience with the emperor of China.

Detached from the *Baltimore* on 6 June 1895, Elliott traveled back to the United States and, after two months' leave, reported to the Marine Barracks, Brooklyn. He was still serving there when the battleship *Maine* blew up in Havana Harbor on the night of 15 February 1898. As part of the preparations for war with Spain, the commandant was ordered to organize a Marine battalion for expeditionary service in Cuba. Accordingly, the force, drawn from East Coast barracks and receiving ships, was formed at New York and embarked in the transport *Panther,* with Elliott commanding Company C.

Under Lt. Col. Robert W. Huntington, a veteran of the Civil War, the force landed at Guantánamo Bay, Cuba, on 10 June 1898 and established Camp McCalla; the following day, the Marines entrenched atop the hill overlooking the beach. The Spanish, however, sniped at and probed the Corps's defenses over the ensuing days. To relieve pressure on the Marines, the senior officer present, Captain McCalla—who had praised Elliott's abilities in Panama thirteen years earlier—ordered an offensive against Cuzco Well, six miles away and the only Spanish water supply within a twelve-mile radius. The well's existence, McCalla believed, enabled the Spanish to keep up their "annoying attacks."[6]

On 14 June 1898, Companies C and D, with Elliott in command, set out for the well, augmented by a force of fifty Cubans and supported from seaward by the guns of the dispatch boat *Dolphin.* After a brisk and spirited engagement, Elliott's men drove off the numerically superior Spanish force—estimated later to have contained at least four companies of regular infantry and two companies of guerrillas, some five hundred men all told—and destroyed the objective. The expedition succored Camp McCalla, and Huntington considered the captain's gallantry and skill as essential to the success achieved, and recommended advancing him one number on the captain's list. Ultimately, Elliott was advanced three, for "eminent and conspicuous conduct under fire."[7]

Elliott remained with the Marine battalion of the North Atlantic Squadron until 22 September 1898, at which time he was detached to command the Marine Barracks at the Washington Navy Yard. While serving there, in December 1898, Elliott represented the Marine Corps on a joint Army-Navy board charged with considering the question of adopting a standard and uniform caliber for small arms and machine guns.[8] He was promoted to major on 28 March 1899.

By the time Elliott was nearing the end of his time in Washington, the Marine 1st Battalion had been formed for service in the Philippines, an area that required substantial numbers of both Army and Marine Corps troops for pacification and garrison duty, and was based at Cavite, the former Spanish naval station near Manila. The commander in chief of the Asiatic Fleet, Rear Adm. John Crittendon Watson, U.S. Navy, had deemed one battalion insufficient, and had, on 26 July 1899, requested another. On 4 August, Elliott was detached, and traveled to New York, where he joined the newly designated 2d Battalion three days later. After a transcontinental train trip, the battalion embarked in the Pacific Mail Line steamship *City of Sydney* and sailed on 18 August, reaching Manila on 11 September.

With the establishment of the 1st Brigade, command devolved upon Lieutenant Colonel Elliott (who had been promoted while en route to the Philippines) when illness incapacitated the original commander, Col. Percival C. Pope. Elliott commanded the force as it supported Army troops in the attack upon Insurrecto fortifications at Novaleta on 8 October 1899. With the gunboat *Petrel* providing gunfire support, Elliott and his men, in the teeth of heavy fire, ultimately carried the Insurrecto outposts and the town in a frontal assault—"a most difficult task" that Admiral Watson considered accomplished in a "highly creditable manner." Surprisingly, the Marines lost only one man outright, although two died later from wounds. Heat stroke, however, temporarily disabled at least fifty; Elliott himself suffered vertigo and, briefly, became unconscious.[9]

Over the ensuing months, Elliott suffered what regimental doctors diagnosed as two subsequent bouts with headaches, insomnia, and mental depression. Consequently, a medical survey board on 22 March 1900 ordered him home to the United States, as temporarily "unfit for duty . . . incident to 29 years' service in the Marine Corps, and especially during exposure to the climates of Cuba and the Philippines."[10] Accordingly, Elliott traveled home in the U.S. Army Transport *Sherman,* and arrived at San Francisco on 26 April, to undergo treatment at the Naval Hospital at Mare Island. Subsequently commanding the Norfolk Marine Barracks, arriving there to take up his duties on 1 October 1900, he was detached to duty in Washington on 26 February 1903 and assumed command of the barracks at "Eighth and Eye" two days later. Promotion to colonel soon followed.

Elliott's career had followed a pattern similar to his contemporaries, even down to the glacial pace of promotion. Significantly, he had distinguished himself on expeditionary duty and had proved himself brave in battle. The expansion of the Corps, together with its senior officers reaching retirement age, meant a rapid turnover in its high command. Those factors, together with his past record, and perhaps recognition by influential seniors within the naval establishment as he went along, commended him. As the *Army and Navy Journal* declared, "He has had almost fourteen years of sea and foreign service and has always rendered a good account of himself."[11] And, although his service for two decades in the grade of lieutenant explains it, his rise from company commander to commandant in just five years seems, by modern standards, nothing short of meteoric.

Elliott, at the time he relieved Heywood as commandant, stood half an inch over six feet tall and weighed 157 pounds, with hazel eyes, gray hair, and a ruddy complexion. He cut a dashing figure, and Washington's military society warmly welcomed him and his wife. As the *Army and Navy Journal* expressed it, the Elliotts were "well known and deservedly popular."[12] Elliott's wife, Annie Mansfield Elliott, was the sister of Capt. Charles J. Badger, U.S. Navy, and the union had resulted in one daughter, Daisy, who would marry a Marine officer, Harold C. Reisinger (who later became paymaster of the Marine Corps). The Elliotts moved into the recently renovated Commandant's House that November.

Expeditionary service, however, soon called the new commandant away. Exactly one month after Elliott had relieved Heywood, the people of Panama proclaimed independence from Colombia and instituted a republic. As in 1885, the Corps was sent to stabilize the situation. Two days after Christmas 1903, 635 officers and men embarked in the transport *Dixie* and sailed from League Island (Philadelphia) Navy Yard, reaching Colon on 3 January 1904. Elliott, who had taken passage in the transport, upon his arrival established his Headquarters at Haute Obispo and assumed command of all the Marine forces on the isthmus (two battalions had already preceded the two that had arrived in the *Dixie*). He thus became the first commandant since Archibald Henderson to lead a Marine expeditionary force in the field and the only one to do so in the twentieth century.

While rumored offensive action by Colombian troops never materialized, Elliott, a vigorous man, did not let his brigade lose its fighting trim, keeping it active in "drilling, hiking, rifle-shooting, and map-making." The Marines remained in Panama until conditions there warranted the withdrawal of three of the four battalions, and Elliott, himself, sailed for home on board the *Dixie* on 16 February 1904. A little less than two weeks later, the Republic of Panama—its coasts guarded by U.S. naval vessels operating under war conditions and its capital patrolled by the Marines—was proclaimed and its first president inaugurated. The groundwork was laid for the building of the Panama Canal.

During the remainder of his first year as commandant, Elliott inspected shore stations and took stock of the status of the Corps. Although he had not testified at the Jan uary 1904 appropriations hearings since he had been in Panama, he nevertheless set forth his perception of the needs of the Corps that October in the commandant's annual report. He did not mince words as he reported the Corps to be undermanned, a refrain that he would reiterate often during the rest of his commandancy.

At the end of his first year at the helm of the Corps, Elliott lamented the fact that it was too small to carry out the missions he had seen develop over the years. During Elliott's first year, the Corps consisted of 278 officers and 7,532 enlisted men. He urged the secretary of the navy to secure from Congress authorization to recruit an additional

2,480 enlisted men, the necessity for this action being made apparent, he argued, when one considered that "every post of the Marine Corps is now short of the strength required" to protect properly government property at the various navy yards and naval stations. The posts in the field barraged him with requests for more men. On top of that, as the Navy expanded its forces afloat, a significant number of new ships assigned marines would need men.

During 1904, troubles abroad, particularly in the Dominican Republic and in the Far East relative to the Russo-Japanese War, had prompted the landing of Marine detachments. Marines also escorted a diplomatic mission to Abyssinia and, furthermore, garrisons had been established at Honolulu and Midway. A Marine detachment landed in Morocco to protect the American consulate in Tangiers.

In January 1905, Elliott went before Congress for the first time as commandant. His predecessor, Heywood, had promised that the number of marines he had would be sufficient for years to come. Congressman John E. Rixey, recalling Heywood's promise, asked the new commandant to explain why he wanted more men. Elliott responded that, among other reasons, new ships were being built that required Marine Corps guards. By the same token, Elliott insisted on setting training standards: "I can not enlist a man today and put him aboard a ship tomorrow. . . . It takes six or eight months to get a man so that he is fit to go to sea. These men are held so that we can carry them immediately, in twenty-four hours, to any part of the country [*sic*]—Panama, the West Indies, or anywhere else."[13] He declared that the Corps could best carry out the advanced base mission because the Marines "can get there quicker than the Army can" and could seize the advanced bases the Navy wanted.[14] Despite Elliott's entreaties, however, the Corps only received authorization for half of the men asked for. It would be the last increase in enlisted strength for three years.

During fiscal year 1905, Elliott conducted the usual inspections of posts and stations, and in his annual report on 25 September 1905, he declared that he was generally pleased with the state of the Corps, considering the fact that his officers and men were performing arduous duty. He blamed the necessity for that upon the concurrent expiration of the four- and five-year enlistments, a continuing deficiency in the number of officers in the Corps, and upon a two-month suspension of recruiting during the summer of 1905, factors that combined to reduce the strength of the Corps.[15] If Congress authorized the full desired quota of enlisted, however, Elliott insisted that the Corps would have had a difficult time housing them. He argued that should the Corps be brought up to authorized strength, the Spanish American War vintage barracks would barely be able to house them adequately.

To that end, he directed the quartermaster to provide estimates for sufficient funds to commence a building program for officers' quarters and barracks. Among other things, he also complained (as he would in succeeding years) about the crowded conditions that existed at Headquarters, where, in his own offices, for example, eleven clerks, ten desks, ten file cases, and six typewriter tables vied for space in three rooms, each of which measured fourteen by eighteen feet. On top of that, the records sometimes needed to carry on the day-to-day business at Headquarters were stored at the Marine Barracks, necessitating a time-consuming cross-town trip to bring them back.

During fiscal year 1905, Elliott requested an additional 1,200 men, an increase which Secretary of the Navy Charles J. Bonaparte considered "absolutely necessary for the efficient discharge of its duties." The Corps's "sphere of usefulness has greatly expanded" within the past decade, the secretary declared, and although it had been increased simultaneously, "it is barely strong enough for the work it has to do."[16] Such work included further expeditionary duty in Santo Domingo, the replacement of Army troops with Marine troops at the legation in Peking, and ceremonial tasks such as escorting the body of naval hero John Paul Jones back from France and participating in the ceremonies at Kittery, Maine, where Russia and Japan signed the treaty that ended the Russo-Japanese War. Furthermore, on the question of relative rank, Bonaparte did not believe that the ranks of Marine Corps officers corresponded with their duties. With bureau chiefs possessing the rear admiral's rank, it seemed to the secretary that the head of the Marine Corps was entitled to a higher rank than that which corresponded to commodore, and suggested placing a major general at the Corps's head.

In February 1906, Elliott again pressed for more men in his testimony before the House Naval Affairs Committee. He asked for additional officers because the Corps was short of them; those who had served in the Philippines were clamoring for leave—some had not a month's total leave in five years. The new ships then building, which amounted to fourteen of the twenty-three then under construction, would require officers for the additional Marine detachments. When Chairman George E. Foss asked Elliott to justify the number of men requested, Elliott shot back, "You cut us off last year. We asked for 2,480 men, and you divided it up, giving us half that, and we now come back and ask for the other half." When Foss noted that that was an increase, Elliott responded, "Yes; we will want all—1,100 men—by October for these new ships."[17]

Elliott's testimony on 2 February 1906 reiterated his complaint that marines served guard duty more often than soldiers (the soldiers one day in six, the marines every other day), helped coal and clean the ship, and manned a portion of the ship's secondary battery. On top of those duties, there lay the mission of protecting American lives and property, and backing up American foreign policy abroad. With all of the United States' possessions, the Marines could be sent to any one "to do duty and there is no talk in the papers about a foreign invasion, because the sailor or marine can go anywhere around the world without bringing up any question on this subject."[18]

At that point, when queried as to whether or not the Marines comprised part of a standing army, Elliott seized the opportunity to reiterate the character of the Corps's advanced base mission. "If we should go to war anywhere, we would be obliged to hold some port," he began, "so that the torpedo boats might have some place to rest. The ships of the fleet can go into a harbor that is not thoroughly protected, and they would put the marines ashore from the transports and then the marines would get together and throw up a temporary fortification." Trained to use a 3-inch gun, small arms, and automatic guns, marines could prevent the enemy from harassing the fleet. Holding a harbor of refuge for the Navy, he maintained, was an important job; furthermore, steam transportation, in enabling marines to get to where they were going faster, had enhanced the Corps's usefulness.[19]

Circumstances at home and abroad underscored Elliott's appeals for more men. The Marines provided assistance for civil authorities in San Francisco after the disastrous earthquake and fire devastated the city, and unrest in Panama required the dispatch of an expeditionary battalion. Assembled at League Island on 20 May 1906, that force sailed in the cruiser *Columbia,* reaching the Canal Zone nine days later. Later in the year, revolutionary disturbances in Cuba prompted the Corps's presence. On 13 September, marines and sailors from the cruiser *Denver* and the gunboat *Marietta* went ashore at Cienfuegos on the same kind of duty. On 18 September, a Marine battalion originally earmarked for duty in the Dominican Republic landed at Cienfuegos. A detachment of sailors and marines from the *Marietta* landed three days later to protect a railroad; one week after that, a small Marine detachment was landed at the request of the Cuban government to guard the treasury at Havana. In the meantime, a provisional battalion of 804 marines was thrown together and sailed in the battleships *Kentucky* and *Indiana,* arriving at Havana on 1 October. The experiences in Cuba, Secretary of the Navy Bonaparte observed later in his annual report, showed that the Corps was "clearly insufficient in numbers to satisfactorily discharge all the multifarious duties now imposed upon it." Gathering the Cuban expeditionary force, for example, necessitated stripping the ships of the Atlantic Fleet and all the East Coast shore stations of their Marine Corps guards. Although no serious consequences resulted, "it was a source of embarrassment and might have had undesirable results."[20]

As with every troop movement, there arose the problem of transport—the men cramped on board ships that had been built with other duties in mind than hauling troops and their equipment. The need for a transport to carry an expeditionary force, Elliott felt, was acute. Over the next few years, he regularly appealed for such a ship.[21] Elliott had pressed for more men but despite his appeals, the Corps received none.

The year 1907 saw the Marines assisting in rescue work at Kingston, Jamaica, in the aftermath of a severe earthquake that devastated that port in January, and the following month the Marines landed from the *Marietta* at Truxillo, Honduras, to protect the American consulate amid political unrest. When hostilities between Honduras and Nicaragua threatened American lives and property at Laguna, Honduras, the gunboat *Paducah* landed marines to protect them.

By the beginning of Elliott's fifth year as commandant (1908), the Corps consisted of 267 officers and 9,100 enlisted men. Roughly a third of that number was serving on board ships of the fleet, a third at shore stations in the continental United States, and a third overseas on expeditionary duty. On 13 February 1908, Elliott went before the House Committee on Naval Affairs to ask for an increase in officers and men. He complained that some of his "best young officers" were resigning, or desiring to, because of the "hard duty [the younger officers, in particular, having officer-of-the-day duty every other day] and the slow promotion which they know accrues to them in the future." He went on to reiterate the arduous duty stood by the enlisted men, again referring to Army regulations that forbade, by law, a soldier standing guard duty more than once in five days. His stations were so very short of men that "no station has enough men to do the duty required and give the men a proper time off." Elliott declared that commanding officers of posts and commandants of naval stations were daily writing him for more men.[22] This time, however, the entreaties bore fruit, and despite the fact that it was not for the number requested, Congress authorized an increase of 755 more men "to further increase the efficiency" of the Marine Corps. In addition, the act of Congress of 13 May 1908 advanced the rank of commandant to major general. Elliott assumed that rank eight days later.

While the Corps continued to grow, albeit not at the pace Elliott desired, a movement was afoot again seeking to eliminate what some naval officers considered the Corps's anachronistic mission of ships' guards. In the forefront of that movement stood Cdr. William F. Fullam, commander of the Naval Training Station at Newport, Rhode Island, who saw in the Marines' shipboard presence an affront to the "self respect and efficiency" of sailors. Fullam also stood among the "reformers" who sought to remodel the Navy by abolishing the bureau system and establishing a general staff akin to that recently instituted in the Army.[23]

Apparently, Elliott, a blunt and open man, had adequately combated the efforts of those who championed removal of the Marines. Fullam complained in exasperation, "It is wrong that a Major General and his staff in Washington, should, by this influence, maintain a stranglehold on the enlisted men of the Navy."[24] Elliott's heretofore successful defense of the Corps's shipboard mission prompted Fullam's lament: "General Elliott goes to the Secretary and combats the proposition [removal] every time—successfully." He continued, "Our organization is such that one man, a 'General' in Washington—can defy the whole Navy and perpetuate a wrong." He asked the president's naval aide, Cdr. William S. Sims, to bring the matter to Roosevelt's attention.[25]

Sims did so, emphasizing Fullam's arguments that marines serving as ships' policemen undermined the discipline and morale of the sailors. He observed that a large majority of senior naval officers favored the removal of the marines, as opposed to the small coterie of junior officers who initially had supported them.[26] "The juniors of 20 years ago," Sims declared, "are now the seniors, and the sentiment has accordingly changed." Sims cited the fact that two successive chiefs of the Bureau of Navigation, Rear Adm. John E. Pillsbury and Rear Adm. George A. Converse, had recommended removal of the marines, but that Elliott had gone to the secretary of the navy and secured their retention. Sims then echoed Fullam's complaint that "one man, a general, can defy the sentiment of the whole military branch of the navy and perpetuate conditions which we have long since outgrown." He urged Roosevelt to sever this Gordian knot by wielding executive authority to *order* the guards off ships, declaring that the effect of taking them off "would be electrical, because the demand is universal."[27]

Thoughtful and perceptive men noted that Fullam and those of like mind did not want to abolish the Corps, only redefine its mission. If the Corps was relieved of its shipboard duties, the reformers argued, it could concentrate on forming permanent battalions to be moved to potential trouble spots in their own designated transports, instead of in the makeshift arrangements that had often plagued them.

Using the Marine Corps in the expeditionary role was, of course, nothing new. The Navy's General Board had formally assigned the Corps the advanced base mission in 1900. Over the ensuing eight years, despite shortages in men and materiel, temporary advanced base and expeditionary units had been organized and exercises carried out. The Marines did not quarrel with the advanced base mission, but by the same token did not want the diminution of the shipboard mission. Service in ships, the Corps maintained, kept marines in close touch with the Navy and provided them with skills necessary for the expeditionary and advanced base duty.

The latest effort at removal came upon the heels of the defeat of the Navy's reformers at the Newport Conference, when they had attempted to have a hand in the design of the newest Navy battleships. Fullam, in his disappointment, complained that the "Marines and the bureau system [that had defeated the reformers] are twins." If the Navy were to be prepared for war, he declared bitterly, the Corps and the bureaus would have to go.[28]

On 16 October, the chief of the Bureau of Navigation, Rear Admiral Pillsbury, urged Secretary of the Navy Victor H. Metcalf to substitute sailors for marines in the ships that then had Marine Corps guards. The marines, Pillsbury suggested, could be formed into regiments and battalions and given their own transports. Roosevelt approved the proposal, and on 23 October, the secretary of the navy directed that the plan be implemented. None of the parties involved, including the president, secretary of the navy, and chief of the Bureau of Navigation, had deigned to broach the issue to General Elliott. The commandant, however, perceived hints that forces inimical to the Corps's shipboard mission were again at work when the battleship *Iowa* was recommissioned with a reduced Marine guard. Elliott asked Metcalf to restore it to a larger size.

One week later, Elliott informed Sims that he (Elliott) intended to ask the president to stop the pressure to delete the Marines' shipboard duties. Before he could so, however, Secretary Metcalf informed him that the guards' mission would soon be a thing of the past. Having accomplished nothing in meeting with Pillsbury, Elliott appealed directly to Metcalf, declaring, in a memorandum of 7 November, that "the proposed removal of Marines from vessels of the Navy is . . . contrary to the long established and uninterrupted custom of the service . . . to all precedent and rulings of the Department . . . to the wishes of the Congress, and is based on no argument which is cogent or potent."[29] Although Metcalf informed him that the president's mind was made up (guards would be removed), the undaunted Elliott was allowed to take up the matter with Roosevelt himself.

On 9 November 1908, Elliott met with the president himself. While he found Roosevelt sympathetic to the Corps, he also found him committed firmly to removing Marine guards from warships. Elliott related that all of the Marine officers he had contacted saw in the abolition of the guards the "death knell" of the Corps. To Roosevelt's query as to whether or not Elliott shared that view, the commandant bluntly replied that he did not. "We are overworked now," he declared, "and . . . could be assigned to duties of great importance."[30] Roosevelt then instructed the general to draw up a statement of the Corps's mission after the ship guard function was abolished.

Over the next two days, Elliott's Headquarters staff drafted an executive order defining the Corps's duties. The proposed order stated that the Marines would garrison navy yards and stations, "both within and beyond the continental limits of the United States," as well as the Isthmian Canal Zone, and would "furnish such garrisons and expeditionary forces for duties beyond the seas as may be necessary in time of peace." Once the ships' guards were withdrawn, the Corps would consist of nine permanent regiments of eleven hundred men each: four on the East Coast, one on the West, one in Hawaii, two in the Philippines, and one in the Caribbean. The duties assigned the Marines were those that (1) "naturally" belonged to the Corps, which had always served with the Navy, and (2) did not interfere with the duties of the Army.[31]

On 12 November, ironically only two days after the Corps's 133d birthday, Roosevelt incorporated the wording of Elliott's memorandum into Executive Order 969. Although it neither deleted ships' guards nor called for their removal, all, including the commandant, knew that that was its intent. Over the next several months, the Bureau of Navigation began removing the shipboard marines. By early 1909, about eight hundred of the nearly twenty-seven hundred marines serving in shipboard detachments in November 1908 had been removed.[32]

Some Marine officers perceived in Executive Order 969 the abolishment of the Corps. When disgruntled Marine officers were rumored to begin lobbying Congress to reverse Roosevelt's decision, Elliott declared optimistically that the order would be the "making of the Marine Corps" and forbade such activities that, he posited, violated regulations and were "offensive to military discipline." Furthermore, he also deemed it "contrary to the motto of the Corps, for 'Semper Fidelis' would be but a meaningless term if it shone only on the sunny side of life or duty."[33] Then, accompanied by an aide, Capt. William C. Harllee, Elliott journeyed south to inspect the naval stations at Port Royal and Charleston, South Carolina.

Even as Elliott optimistically embraced the "new" mission for the Marine Corps, a new player entered the drama. Maj. Gen. Leonard Wood, one of Roosevelt's confidants, proposed to incorporate the Corps into the Army to expand the latter's infantry regiments. Once that was accomplished, he explained, details of transfer could be worked out with Congress at a later date. Wood's planting the seed found fertile soil in the mind of the chief executive. Marine Corps's lobbying irritated Roosevelt. The Marines' "influence," he complained to his military aide, Capt. Archie Butt, "which they have gained by pandering to every political influence, has given them such an abnormal position for the size of their corps that they have simply invited their own destruction. They should be absorbed into the Army," Roosevelt declared, and "no vestige of their organization should be allowed to remain."[34]

Wood had discussed the matter with other high-ranking Army officers, and, after telling them that he (Wood) favored amalgamation (a view supported by the president), asked two Marine Headquarters staff officers, Col. Frank L. Denny, the quartermaster, and Lt. Col. Charles L. McCawley, the assistant quartermaster, to sound out Marine opinions. On 23 November, the two officers, "behind closed doors and in confidence" told Elliott, who had just returned to the capital from his inspection trip, about their talk with Wood, particularly how "complimentary he was about the Marines and how much the Army would like to have the corps" incorporated into it. They also told the general of the president's support of the idea.[35] Elliott could not believe his ears. He reacted by protesting to Wood, the next day, that neither he (Elliott) nor the secretary of the navy had been apprised of transferring the Corps to the Army. "I would as soon believe there was a lost chord in heaven," Elliott declared, "as that he would ask any one to have us transferred to the Army after defining our duties in a general order and without stating to the secretary of the navy or myself that for good and sufficient reasons he had changed his mind in regard to our duties."[36]

Wood responded to the commandant's missive by reiterating support for Marine Corps–Army amalgamation but denied that he had spoken for the president in the matter. Further heated correspondence ensued. Elliott declared that Wood, an Army general, had no right to discuss disposition of the Marines, and that both the Army and the Corps would be bitterly opposed to amalgamation. Wood, for his part, scolded the two Headquarters staff officers for violating a confidence in mentioning the president's view to the commandant. He also apologized to Roosevelt for having mentioned his name, but the chief executive remained adamant: "I think the marines should be incorporated into the Army. It is an excellent corps and it would be of great benefit to the services that the incorporation should take place."[37]

Wood then informed Elliott of the president's formally endorsing the transfer of the Corps to the Army. Elliott, who had in good faith acquiesced in the removal of the guards from Navy ships to enable the Corps to concentrate on its expeditionary mission, could justifiably feel that Roosevelt had double-crossed him. "While we had been following quietly our duties," he later declared, "elimination and absorption were casting unknown to us their shadows at our heels."[38] Although Elliott had been among the last to learn of Wood's scheme to incorporate the Corps into the Army, speculation on the subject began appearing in the media.

On 11 December 1908, Elliott, accompanied by three members of the Headquarters staff, Colonel Denny, Col. Charles H. Lauchheimer, the adjutant and inspector, and Lt. Col. George Richards, assistant paymaster of the Corps, appeared before the House Naval Affairs Committee. A key moment in the hearings came when, in response to the question whether it cost more or less to maintain a marine on board ship than a sailor, Denny responded, "It costs very much less." If 2,766 marines (the number afloat) were replaced, man for man, by sailors, Richards pointed out, the cost to the service was estimated at $497,000. In retrospect, Richards's timely producing of the table, even if the figures would later be reduced, was a "master stroke."[39]

Subsequently, Elliott and the Marine Corps mobilized congressional support, and lobbying efforts by the Marines, heretofore prohibited, proceeded unhindered. Between 9 and 15 January 1909, twenty naval officers, thirteen marines, and Secretary of the Navy Truman H. Newberry, who had replaced the ailing Metcalf, testified before Congressman Thomas S. Butler's subcommittee. Butler, known to oppose removing Marine Corps guards from warships, had a son (Capt. Smedley Darlington Butler, who had served under Elliott at Novaleta) in the Corps. A bitter Fullam later complained that Elliott and the Marine Headquarters staff seemed indistinguishable from members of the committee as the marines exhorted, objected, and cross-examined during the course of the hearings. Marine officers to a man supported the retention of guards on board ships, while their naval counterparts stood evenly divided. Among the naval officers supporting the guards' retention was Elliott's brother-in-law, Capt. Charles J. Badger, superintendent of the Naval Academy.

Although the legislators seemed to concern themselves chiefly with matters of economy, the matter of Army absorption of the Corps came up during the hearings. Some of those opposing Executive Order 969 warned that, ultimately, the Army would gain the Marine Corps if the guards were taken off Navy ships. Even those who advocated removal emphasized the importance of keeping the Corps a sea service. "If I were king . . . ," Fullam declared, "I would preserve the Marine Corps in its present numbers, and if necessary increase it . . . to use it . . . as a splendidly organized, mobile force, to serve with the Navy."[40] Secretary Newberry testified that rather than lose the Corps to the Army, he would prefer to return the Marines to sea duty. Those who supported Roosevelt wanted to leave it up to him as to whether or not the Corps would serve at sea but balked at amalgamating the Marines into the Army.

On 16 January 1909, the Naval Affairs Committee recommended restoration of Marine guards to ships. Vigorous White House and Navy Department lobbying set back the efforts at restoration, as the House passed the appropriation bill without language decreeing the return of the Marine Corps to ships. This proved to be a temporary victory, since in the Senate, a majority of Democrats, strongly backed by many conservative Republicans, added to the naval appropriations bill a rider that marines comprise 8 percent of the enlisted men assigned to battleships and armored cruisers. By a vote of fifty-one to twelve, the Senate put Marine guards back on ships.

Shortly before Roosevelt left office, though, on 3 March 1909, he loosed a parting shot in directing the return of the Marines to shipboard duty with the proviso that ships' commanding officers would determine the duties of their Marine detachments. This, in effect, was a reduction of responsibility, since the Corps's shipboard duties before Executive Order 969 had been quite specific, including manning some of the guns in a warship's battery. The General Board, however, recommended to the new secretary of the navy, George van Lengerke Meyer, who had taken office on 6 March 1909, and to the new president, William Howard Taft, that that part of the order signed by the outgoing chief executive be changed. Taft agreed, and on 26 March directed Meyer to restore the old regulations.

While the removal controversy had shown how the Corps could put up a spirited fight to those forces who threatened it from without, before the year was over, personality conflicts at Headquarters led to an incident that threatened it from within. On the morning of 14 December 1909, Elliott burst into the office of Colonel Lauchheimer, and berated him for the latter's perceived efforts to restore a junior officer to the Corps after the man had been dismissed for theft. Although Lauchheimer's explanation elicited the commandant's apology, the colonel complained of the incident to Secretary of the Navy Meyer. Elliott again confronted Lauchheimer over the issue, which prompted the latter to complain once more of the commandant's treatment of him. Mindful of past controversy attached to the lobbying effort by Navy (and Marine Corps) officers with Congress and mindful of what the press would do if it perceived a scandal in the making, Meyer censured both Elliott and Lauchheimer. Assistant Secretary of the Navy Beekman Winthrop called the entire affair "this disgraceful controversy."[41]

Although the secretary had censured both Elliott and Lauchheimer for their conduct, the "disgraceful controversy" ultimately led to Meyer, on 5 March 1910, ordering a board of inquiry to look into the conduct of Elliott and Lauchheimer, not only toward each other but toward their respective offices. More importantly, it was also to determine what effect the recent incidents had upon the discipline and efficiency of the Corps.[42]

In the meantime, on 24 March 1910, soon after the board began its work, Secretary Meyer entrusted the Marine Corps with the responsibility for the custody and care of all advanced base material. On 18 April 1910, Elliott proposed the course of instruction for the advance base school earmarked for establishment at New London. Although primarily concerned with the training of officers there, he called for enlisted men to be assigned to the first course beginning in July 1910. Until the Navy designed its own mines, its use of Army equipment prompted Elliott to assign two Marine officers to the Army School for Submarine Defenses at Fort Monroe, Virginia. In addition, the burgeoning field of wireless telegraphy resulted in the assignment of two Marine officers to attend the Army's Signal School at Fort Leavenworth, Kansas.

Considering the Advance Base School a postgraduate level course, Elliott deemed necessary a "good working knowledge of . . . elementary professional subjects" such as those pertaining to the attack on and the defense of advanced bases. "In order to obtain the best results," Elliott declared, such instruction had to be "both theoretical and practical, systematic and progressive." He considered that, with the subjects so varied and comprehensive, a year's study—of gun, mobile, and mine defenses as well as "general governing considerations"—would be required. Elliott stressed the importance of naval ordnance and gunnery, including the study of the use of field artillery to provide direct and indirect fire support for infantry; the types and use of explosives and projectiles, construction of fortifications, and the development of communications systems to meet the needs of the Corps in the advanced base mission. He also urged the study of past advanced base operations, so that the Corps could learn from history. The roles Elliott and his staff envisioned presaged the combined arms aspect of the modern Marine Corps.[43]

In the meantime, the board charged with looking into matters at Headquarters finished up its work, and on 26 April 1910, reported its findings. If he perceived that "the facts had the least bearing on the question[s]" posed to him, Elliott had proved unhesitatingly candid with the board, even if his testimony proved detrimental to his own case. While "he worked for the good of service and accomplished much," Elliott, the board believed, had failed to maintain discipline at Headquarters and enforce the proper respect due himself and his office. The investigators opined that while the controversy did not appreciably affect discipline of the Corps beyond Headquarters, it decidedly created havoc within the Mills Building. The board recommended holding no further judicial proceedings, and since both Elliott and Lauchheimer had been censured for their actions, concluded that Elliott's offenses were not grave enough to warrant a court-martial. Only "prompt and decisive disciplinary steps," the Bureau of Navigation, believed, would restore order. It recommended detaching Colonel Lauchheimer and another officer, and that even other officers at Headquarters who had not been party to the disturbances be replaced. Acting Secretary of the Navy Beekman Winthrop approved the board's findings on 15 July 1910.[44] Commenting on this case in his annual report, Secretary Meyer recommended that for the betterment of administration, discipline, and organization, that Congress limit the commandant's tour to only four years, and that line officers be detailed to the post of adjutant and inspector.[45]

While the troubles at Headquarters to some extent sullied the end of his career, reflecting an apparent inability to keep order in his own "house," Elliott nevertheless in his final report continued to outline the needs of his Corps. He reiterated the refrain that its enlisted men were called upon to perform "arduous duty" and that six newly established posts further strained Marine manpower resources. Recruiting had not been successful, either—which did not help—due to "increased economic activity" throughout the country. He urged that the Corps be equipped with the new-model Springfield rifles and reported an increasing interest in target practice within the Corps. He pointed with pride to the fact that, due to the efforts of the Marine Corps Rifle Team, the members of which had been distributed among the various posts and stations, about 30 percent of the enlisted men were drawing increased compensation for scoring well in target practice.[46]

Having reached the age of sixty four, Elliott retired from the Corps on 30 November 1910. His retirement years passed quietly; he enjoyed hunting until advancing age prohibited it. He remained interested in the Corps, and his memory continued to be sharp, amazing those who called upon him with his grasp of past events. His son-in-law, Col. (later Brig. Gen.) Harold C. Reisinger, interviewed him often at his Washington, D.C., home during the 1920s. Those recorded reminiscences emerged in the *Marine Corps Gazette,* the closest thing to a published "oral history" of the time. Elliott evidenced his unfaltering loyalty to the Corps in remarks delivered at a surprise party given in his honor on Thanksgiving Day 1922. "The time is coming close when I must pass over the Great Divide," he mused, "and, you know, when I do I want to sit on the cool side. So I have been doing a lot of thinking lately, and have been reading my Bible. And I can tell you of a text that points directly to our Marine Corps—it is in Revelations [*sic*]. 'Be ye faithful unto death . . . ' That is our motto isn't it," he asked the assembled guests, "'faithful unto death'? Yes, the Marine Corps has been faithful. It has always been that, it has always done what was expected of it. And we must always live up to that motto of ours and be 'faithful unto death.'" Faithfulness, he concluded, "took us—the Marine Corps—through the war. The Old Marine Corps—and the New. God bless them."[47] Ultimately, in 1928, Elliott developed arteriosclerosis and apoplexy. Three years later he contracted pneumonia, and the combination contributed to his death at his Washington home on 4 November 1931. Two days later, he was laid to rest in Arlington National Cemetery.

Elliott's tenure as commandant reflects the fact that whereas he had excelled as a field soldier, and had gained much practical knowledge of the Corps's expeditionary duties, he was more at home on the battlefield, rather than in the political arena. What he may have lacked in terms of finesse and polish, though, he compensated for in determination. Elliott exemplified the Corps's motto, "Semper Fidelis." Dogmatically loyal to the Corps, his performance of duty throughout his career mirrored that motto. No intellectual, he exhibited a single-minded devotion to duty throughout his career. He battled those who sought to separate the Corps from its seagoing element but was outmaneuvered. The Marine Corps remained a seagoing branch of the Navy, not simply an expeditionary corps and never amalgamated into the Army. That, however, may have owed more to the opposition that Theodore Roosevelt had amassed for himself in his dealings with Congress than the retention of a mission that was, in retrospect, a minor one. Elliott's difficulties with the Headquarters staff, on the other hand, stemmed from his own blunt and frank nature, but also, apparently, from clashing ambitions and temperaments within the staff itself.

11

William Phillips Biddle

1911–1914

BRIAN MCALLISTER LINN

During the first decade of the twentieth century, the U.S. Marine Corps began the process of transforming itself from a naval constabulary into a modern military force charged with seizing and defending overseas naval bases. The Corps's eleventh commandant, William Phillips Biddle, was a transitional figure in this process. Biddle's controversial selection as commandant and his conservative approach to the advanced base force mission have led some writers to dismiss him as a passive mediocrity, yet his corpulent frame and lethargic demeanor concealed both a practical intelligence and a fiery temper. Faced with external attacks on the Corps's existence and with a variety of daunting internal problems, Biddle pursued a slow and cautious policy of reform which left the Corps better prepared for the more visible and dramatic policies pursued by his successors.

William Phillips Biddle was born on 17 December 1853 in Philadelphia into a prominent and powerful Pennsylvania family that had included a number of naval officers. After graduating from the University of Pennsylvania, he accepted a commission in the Marine Corps on 22 June 1875. For the next two decades he served in a variety of roles, commanding detachments on board ships and in navy yards. Promoted to first lieutenant in 1884, and to captain ten years later, he led the Marine detachment on board the USS *Olympia* at the Battle of Manila Bay in 1898. His early service reports indicate he was a solid, competent, and efficient officer who was commended by a number of his superiors.

Biddle's career accelerated with America's new imperial commitments. After achieving his majority on 3 March 1899, he was assigned to the 4th Marine Battalion on 22 June 1900, and from 5 August to 9 October 1900, he was with the battalion in China during the Boxer Rebellion. He was then assigned to the 1st Brigade in the Philippines from 25 October 1900 until January 1903. Promoted to lieutenant colonel on 23 March 1903, he served on the Marine Examining Board and as an umpire in the combined

Maj. Gen. William F. Biddle, eleventh commandant.
U.S. Marine Corps Photo.

Army-Navy maneuvers of 1903, which featured amphibious landings in New England. After a brief tour of duty in Panama, he returned to command the barracks at League Island, was promoted to colonel on 14 March 1905, and chaired the board which drafted the new regulations for administering the Marine Corps. In August 1906, he returned to the Philippines to command the 1st Brigade, and, with commendable prescience, he encouraged Maj. Eli K. Cole's pioneering experiments in "advanced base" training in

Subic Bay in 1907.[1] Returning to the United States in May 1908, Biddle briefly commanded the barracks in New York City before being detailed to an expeditionary brigade for duty in Panama between 14 December 1909 and 22 March 1910. He then returned to Marine Corps Headquarters in Washington, where, because of Cmdt. George F. Elliott's declining health, he assumed charge of all business conducted by the office of the commandant.

Biddle's selection as commandant on 10 February 1911 followed a long and controversial period of political maneuvering. According to President William Howard Taft's secretary, Maj. Archie Butt, U.S. Army, the position was originally to go to Col. Littleton W. T. Waller, but Senator Boies Penrose of Pennsylvania threatened to sabotage Taft's policies if Biddle was not selected. Most historians accept Butt's view that Biddle's was a political appointment, and some argue he was chosen primarily as a safe mediocrity with no significant enemies.[2] Marine Frederic M. Wise, a Waller partisan, sneered that Biddle's "dominant characteristic was love of a comfortable chair" and nicknamed him "Sitting Bull."[3] Yet, in fact, Biddle's career, if devoid of heroics, had demonstrated his competence in both staff and command duties. His fitness reports had been consistently either excellent or superior, and he had been commended on several occasions for his efficiency and skill.[4] Wise's disparaging remarks to the contrary, as a line officer Biddle had participated in numerous expeditions in Asia and Latin America. He had administered Marine barracks at various navy yards and served for almost thirteen years on sea duty. In short, he was what Eli K. Cole would later term an "all around Marine." Moreover, Biddle was one of the few senior officers with any experience in advanced base work at a time when this part of the Corps's mission was becoming increasingly controversial. Perhaps most significantly, his career had been remarkably free of controversy or bad judgment, and his apprenticeship as Elliott's assistant had given the president, the Navy Department, and Congress ample opportunity to evaluate his fitness for the task.

Although Biddle possessed the qualifications necessary to become a commandant, his appointment also may have been due to the absence of competitors. Two potential rivals, Col. Charles H. Lauchheimer and Colonel Waller, were even more "political" than Biddle. Lauchheimer's long service as the Marine Corps adjutant and inspector had given him very close connections to Congress. Waller's family were prominent Virginia Democrats, and his own mentorship of Smedley Butler had secured him the patronage of Pennsylvania congressman Thomas Butler. Yet despite their political strengths, both Lauchheimer and Waller had probably disqualified themselves. As a staff officer, Lauchheimer had virtually no chance of becoming commandant, and he was further hampered by his feud with Elliott, which had thrown Marine Headquarters into disarray. When he had finally been disciplined, Lauchheimer's supporters had wrongly claimed he was a victim of anti-Semitism, much to the embarrassment of both Taft and his secretary of the navy.[5] The charismatic Waller was popular with such field marines as Wise and Butler, but he was also a bigoted, tactless, and erratic dipsomaniac who on one occasion had been suspended from duty after assaulting a naval officer in a drunken brawl. Court-martialed for his retaliatory execution of Filipino civilians on Samar Island during the Philippine War, Waller was publicly censured by President Theodore Roosevelt. Taft, who as governor of the Philippines had championed a policy of benevolent assimilation, had even less reason to appoint the "Butcher of Samar" as commandant. Indeed, it is possible that Taft encouraged Senator Penrose's support of Biddle as a means of countering Butler's pressure for Waller.

Biddle's tenure as commandant, from 13 February 1911 to 24 February 1914, coincided with one of the more traumatic and unhappy periods in Marine Corps history. Despite an increase of nearly two thousand men since 1900, the Corps by 1909, as Biddle's predecessor complained, was "being strained to the utmost, and some action looking toward relief must be taken in the very near future."[6] Moreover, critics attacked the very existence of a separate Marine Corps under Navy Department authority. Reformers had made similar attacks in the past, but rarely had they been able to secure such powerful support as in the first decade of the twentieth century. In 1908, President Roosevelt ordered the removal of Marine Corps guards from the Navy's capital ships, thereby robbing the Corps of one of its primary functions. To the Corps's chagrin, most of the Navy's officers, including Adm. George Dewey, vigorously applauded this action. Although Congress forced the Navy Department to reinstate the guards in 1909, Navy reformers viewed this as only a temporary setback and continued to push for their permanent removal. Other attacks on the Corps's independence were launched by military officers who wanted the Marines incorporated as a special unit within the Army. The Army's smooth and efficient occupation of Cuba in 1906 and the equally impressive mobilization of the military forces in the Philippines for possible intervention in China threatened the Marines' role as an expeditionary elite. Finally, the Corps itself was prey to factionalism based both on personal cliques and the historic line-staff rivalry. Under Lauchheimer, the Headquarters staff had grown more competent, but also more insubordinate, prompting a court of inquiry in March 1910.[7] Among the line officers, Waller headed his own group of anti-intellectual colonial warriors, whereas Maj. Dion Williams served as a spokesman for those who stressed professional education and technical competence. Both within and without, the Corps needed stable leadership until its mission was clarified.

Central to Biddle's tenure was the problem of the Corps's involvement in the advanced base mission. The creation of new steel battleships and the imperial expansion overseas had made the U.S. Navy dependent on overseas stations where it could secure coal, supplies, and repairs. As the United States had no major overseas facilities, naval planners concluded that in wartime the Navy would need special troops not only to seize such bases, but especially to defend them from enemy attack when the American fleet was engaged elsewhere. This "advanced base force" would need to master the functions of coast artillery, to defend itself against a hostile fleet, as well as those of a mobile field unit, in order to defend itself against a land attack. It would require personnel highly skilled in "fixed defenses"—the use of heavy artillery, communications, mines, and fortification construction—who could also operate as conventional infantry. Obviously, such a specialized group could not be created overnight; moreover, its personnel and its essential armament and equipment, referred to as the "advanced base outfit," would henceforth need to be maintained as a special unit both for training and for immediate deployment.

The Marine Corps approached this new mission in fits and starts. Many feared that the adoption of any new missions would result in the loss of their historic functions and the rapid disbandment of the Corps. Throughout the first decade of the twentieth century, soldiers were found as often as marines in overseas expeditionary missions. Not until 1907 did the Army agree to turn over its own advanced base equipment to the Navy. That same year the U.S. Navy's General Board determined that there should be an advanced base brigade on both the Atlantic and Pacific Coasts. With Biddle's encouragement, Maj. Eli K. Cole established an experimental base on Subic Bay with a Marine company and an advanced base outfit of artillery, tackle, and building materials. In 1910, the board reiterated its recommendation that there be two advanced base forces, and in partial response, the Marines founded an Advance Base School at New London. Shortly afterward, the school was moved to Philadelphia, where officers could balance their theoretical instruction with practical work with the navy yard's garrison. In the Philippines, the site of the Corps's largest permanent overseas force, Capt. Earl H. Ellis's company mounted a number of artillery pieces both as a response to a war scare with Japan and to test the best ordnance for future advanced base deployments.[8]

But, in fact, much of this activity was more cosmetic than real, and there is little evidence of any sustained commitment to the advanced base mission by either the Navy or the Marine Corps. The Navy Department consistently deleted funds for advanced base equipment, and the General Board subverted its demands for permanent advanced base units by requiring that these specialized forces also serve on expeditionary duty. Nor, with the exception of a small but vocal faction, was there much interest for advanced base work within the Corps. Commandants Heywood and Elliott were either unwilling or unable to establish a permanent advanced base force for training and deployment. Moreover, except for Major Williams's articles, there was little theoretical writing on the subject within the Corps. In 1910, Capt. Alexander S. Williams of the Marines delivered a devastating critique of the advanced base outfit in the Philippines, at that time the only one in existence and the sole source of advanced base training. According to Williams, the advanced base outfit was little more than a motley collection of obsolete and impractical material of little use either for practice or combat. Because no Navy or Marine administrative bureau would acknowledge responsibility for the outfit's maintenance, it was impossible to acquire suitable equipment. Not surprisingly, Williams reported that advanced base training was "extremely unsatisfactory to all concerned." He also denigrated Cole's famous 1907 Subic Bay experiments, pointing out that notwithstanding the presence of the Olongapo Naval Station in support across the bay, an unopposed landing, and Army assistance, the Marines had still taken almost three months to mount the outfit's assorted collection of artillery. In an insightful comment on both the complexity of advanced base duties and the haphazard manner in which the exercises were carried out, Williams noted that although the Corps had finally emplaced its guns, it had neither established a fire control system nor conducted fire exercises.[9]

A similarly dismal picture emerged in the United States, where Commandant Elliott estimated in 1910 that it would take almost two years for the Advance Base School to develop a cadre of officers. Yet even Elliott's modest attempt to develop skilled personnel was frustrated by the requirements of the Corps's other duties as expeditionary forces. Thus for much of 1911 and 1912, the majority of the Advanced Base School's students were detailed overseas. Between 1910 and 1913 only thirty-two officers passed through the school, some of them in less than two months. The school's curriculum was unclear, its concepts and doctrine largely borrowed from Army and Navy manuals, and its facilities so limited that Biddle had to scrounge books from various navy yards to provide it with a rudimentary library. When the director of the school wrote to Biddle's assistant, Eli K. Cole, requesting that all information on the Corps's advanced base work be forwarded, Cole discovered that the only file in the commandant's office was his own 1907 report of the Subic Bay landings.[10]

This sorry record assumed greater importance when Navy captain William F. Fullam, the secretary of the navy's aide for inspections, demanded that the Corps fully commit itself to this new mission. Fullam earlier had led the campaign to remove the Marine Corps guards from capital ships on the grounds that they were both useless and demoralized the crews. Defeated by Congress on that issue, he returned to the attack, arguing that marines' duties as ship guards prevented them from fulfilling their advanced base mission. Fullam's arguments had some merit: as late as 1913, Biddle's own statistics demonstrated that out of the Corps's total strength of 10,021 officers and men, only about 20 percent were available for either advanced base or expeditionary work. That same year, a high-ranking Marine officer confessed that the Corps lacked sufficient men to do its assigned tasks, much less comply with the General Board's demand that it now furnish 3,200 men for two advanced force brigades. To Fullam, the solution was clear: the Corps must abandon its historic role as ship guards on the battleships and cruisers and devote its full attention to the vital advanced base mission.[11]

Fullam received new ammunition in 1913, when Assistant Secretary of the Navy Franklin D. Roosevelt ordered a combined Navy and Marine commission to inspect the Philadelphia Navy Yard, devoting special attention to the Marines' advanced base facilities. The commission's 19 April 1913 report was highly critical both of the state of the advanced base outfit and the "spasmodic efforts" to train men in this mission. Although the inspectors found fault less with the Marine Corps than with the Navy, they pointed out that the advanced base equipment was scattered from Philadelphia to the Philippines, that there was virtually no consensus on material or organization, that there were no officers qualified to oversee such vital tasks as the transportation of the force, and that it would take between twelve and eighteen months of uninterrupted work to establish even the basic procedures for advanced base deployments. The report concluded that "with the present strength of officers and men of the corps, systematic instruction and preparation is impossible. It also appears, relating to personnel, that in consequence of lack of material and the many interruptions due to expeditionary service, no adequate steps have been taken to secure or educate the large number of men who will be required to perform manifold technical duties in connection with the fixed defense regiment."[12]

Fullam immediately used the report to lash the Corps. He informed Secretary of the Navy Josephus Daniels that the Marine Corps had consistently failed to devote sufficient attention to the advanced base mission, that it was completely unprepared for the tasks it would have to undertake in war, and that currently most of these duties could be better performed by sailors than marines. To Fullam, the causes of this were clear: the Marine Corps was widely dispersed, poorly organized, and insufficiently trained, and, perhaps most important, its insistence on placing unnecessary guards on board warships rendered it incapable of advanced base duties. Fullam accused the Corps of devoting more attention to defending its antiquated methods and "self-considered interest" than to the advanced base mission and urged that the Marines be formed into permanent advanced base battalions.[13]

Commandant Biddle responded with a stinging rejoinder that blamed the Navy for the sorry state of affairs. Biddle made it clear that he viewed the report as a continuation of Fullam's earlier efforts to remove the Marine guards. With some justification, Biddle argued that not until 1910 had the Marine Corps been given exclusive control over the advanced base mission. Since then, the Marines had made a "concerted effort" to get men and material together for specialized education at the Advance Base School in Philadelphia. Taking issue with Fullam on the specifics of advanced base organization, Biddle defended the decision to organize the Marines into "semi-permanent" companies rather than permanent regiments as more flexible and better suited to expeditionary and naval service. To Biddle, the Philadelphia inspection proved that the main problems faced by the Corps were not internal weaknesses but a lack of Navy support, of manpower, or equipment, and/or storage facilities.[14]

The commandant received valuable support from his officers. His assistant, Eli K. Cole, defended the existing organization before the Navy's General Board, claiming that Biddle's establishment of semipermanent companies allowed for a variety of duties. Cole also reiterated Biddle's contention that Marine Corps guards on board ship were essential to ensure that the Corps remained part of the Navy. Declaring that advanced base training was only part of their mission, Cole argued sea duty and base duty were also needed, so as to produce "all around" marines; and he even claimed such generalists were best suited for advanced base duties as well.[15] Responding to an article in the Naval Institute's *Proceedings* supporting Fullam's position, Col. George Richards declared that sea duty provided skills essential for expeditionary and advanced base training. Even Maj. Henry C. Davis, who believed that the majority of Marine Corps officers were "coming to realize that the proper function of the Marine Corps is advanced base work and expeditionary work," criticized Navy officers for constantly interfering in shore operations and ignoring the Marine officers' expertise in this field.[16]

Biddle also received assistance from the Navy's General Board, which had been among the most vocal organizations in demanding that the Marines focus on the advanced base mission. In June 1913, Secretary Daniels sent the board a questionnaire asking it to determine whether the Corps was able to fulfill its advanced base mission, whether sea duty was interfering with its capabilities, and whether its manpower should be increased. The board responded that service on warships allowed marines to acquire the "sea habit" and to practice with artillery, searchlights, and the handling of boats. The board's president, Admiral Dewey, also criticized Fullam's suggestion that a special flotilla of older warships and transports be permanently assigned as an escort for the advanced base regiments since this would both divide the fleet and prevent those ships from being used for other purposes. Dewey further declared that an increase in the Corps was unnecessary since the advanced base personnel could be obtained by shifting marines between Navy bases. Moreover, the assignment of permanent forces to advanced base duty was undesirable because it prevented such troops from serving as expeditionary forces.[17]

Predictably, the General Board's report did not satisfy Fullam, who on 22 September responded with a devastating point-by-point critique of its contradictory reasoning. So long as the Corps tactical units remained provisional, they would never be adequately trained. Sea duty was of little use: most warship captains refused to allow marines to handle either boats or searchlights. Fullam also commented on something that the Corps itself had found: training with fixed ship's guns was of limited use for troops using mobile artillery ashore. Although Fullam's position was both more realistic and better reasoned, Daniels chose neither to support his aid nor to force either the General Board or the Corps to implement the reforms.[18]

To Biddle's credit, he recognized the merit of much of Fullam's argument, and he made substantial improvements in the Marines' existing advanced base capacity. During his tenure, the Corps conducted five special studies on advanced base ordnance and equipment. Biddle not only disseminated Maj. Dion Williams's writings on advanced base organization but also implemented many of the suggestions therein. Foremost among these was Williams's contention that the advanced base force should be of brigade strength and divided into a fixed defense and a mobile regiment, each of 104 officers and 1,248 men. The fixed defense regiment would be a permanent organization with special companies of artillerymen, searchlight operators, engineers, and signal troops, whereas the mobile forces would be provisional organizations of infantrymen drawn from navy yards and ships' companies.[19] In 1911, Biddle attempted to organize the Philadelphia advanced base personnel into a semipermanent fixed base regiment along those lines, but the 1912 deployment to Cuba prevented this. By the end of his tenure, Biddle was urging the secretary of the navy to concentrate upward of 2,000 marines each into two major camps on the Atlantic and Pacific Coasts, where they could be trained for both advanced base and expeditionary service.[20]

Biddle also strongly supported the first major test of the new training, the 1913–14 exercises in the Caribbean. After consulting the commandant, on 5 February 1913, the General Board urged that the upcoming Navy maneuvers be used as a test of both the advanced base concept and the Corps's ability to implement it.[21] As had occurred so often previously, other responsibilities immediately threatened the mission. President Woodrow Wilson's contemplated intervention in Mexico in mid-February forced Biddle to deploy most of his available manpower to the Guantánamo Bay Naval Station. Pleading that the remaining personnel precluded his furnishing a full brigade for the Caribbean maneuvers, Biddle proposed initially to use only six companies, or about 800 men. By April, the diminishing prospect of action in Mexico allowed him to comply with the board's demands for more manpower. The commandant could now promise a provisional brigade composed of two skeleton organizations: a fixed defense regiment of 810 men to include artillery, signal, engineer, and mining companies, and a mobile defense unit of about the same size composed largely of infantry. Making clear his objections to the converted ship's guns the Navy had issued, Biddle demanded ordnance suitable for the fixed defense regiment's special needs. He also requested the permanent assignment of an adequate transport vessel for practice in loading supplies and disembarking troops. The maneuvers, held at Culebra Island near Puerto Rico, lasted from November 1913 to February 1914, and "demonstrated that the Marines could organize an advanced base force on short notice and carry out all the complex steps of an advanced base operation."[22] Although Biddle retired before the triumph of the Culebra maneuvers was fully apparent, he deserves credit for the planning, organization, and staffing which made them a success.

Because he left limited official correspondence and no personal papers, it is difficult to assess Biddle's own views on the importance of the advanced base mission. He clearly was unwilling to sacrifice any of the Corps's traditional missions, and he fought hard to retain its ship detachment, navy yard, prison, and overseas duties. In retrospect, his resistance to Fullam's reforms was mistaken, as Fullam foresaw that the Marine Corps's future lay with the advanced base force. Biddle's insistence that the Corps retain its traditional roles was in effect a mandate for further dispersion, inefficiency, disorganization, and scrambling for men and equipment.

Nevertheless, in Biddle's defense, it must be said that his caution had some justification. Throughout his tenure, the Navy withheld tangible support for the advanced base mission; indeed, in 1908 it had appeared willing to abandon the entire Corps. To give up the Corps's tried and true duties in favor of a possibly transitory task was not in Biddle's temperament. Moreover, he recognized, more clearly than most, that the advanced base mission was a highly complex task, requiring far more manpower, training, and support than the Marines' traditional missions. On 24 February 1913, as once again the advanced base school was gutted to provide a provisional expeditionary force, he protested that it was "absolutely essential" that the Navy Department understand that the advanced base forces' specialized skills demanded as much training as those of a battleship's crew.[23]

Although he temporized on the major issue of his tenure—the advanced base mission—Biddle achieved some success in organizational reforms. He apparently stabilized the situation at Headquarters, for there is little evidence of the demoralization and insubordination that characterized his predecessor's tenure. His appointment of Eli

K. Cole as an assistant to the commandant in charge of training was astute and progressive: Cole, an early convert to the advanced base mission, worked steadily and competently to establish it. Biddle sought to concentrate scattered detachments into two major posts, one on the East Coast and one on the West, to allow for training sufficient forces for expeditionary or advanced base duty. He advocated the withdrawal of most of the brigade from the Philippines, and he sought to diminish the number of Marine guards at prisons, navy yards, and miscellaneous shore details, pointing out that this was a constant and unnecessary drain on manpower.[24] In 1911, he initiated a policy of dispatching marines to Annapolis for special training as ships' detachments, and throughout his tenure he sought to establish four major depots at Port Royal, Philadelphia, Mare Island, and Puget Sound, where recruits could be given three months of training before being assigned to duty.[25] His establishment of semipermanent tactical companies, although unsatisfactory to Fullam, was clearly superior to the improvised and provisional organization that had characterized earlier Marine Corps forces. Biddle also maintained and strengthened contacts with other services, soliciting and profiting from Army and Navy doctrinal manuals and sending a few selected officers to advanced schools.

In one progressive cause he fought long, but unsuccessfully to secure Marine Corps representation on the Navy's General Board. Like many marines, Biddle believed that the Navy Department paid insufficient attention to the Corps's needs or opinions when it made policy. Biddle was aggrieved that the agreement which dealt with marines serving with the Army, was decided by a board composed exclusively of Army and Navy officers. He questioned the Navy's adoption of its regulations for small arms and artillery without consulting the marines who would have to fight with them. He also contested the Navy Department's policy of concentrating advanced base forces without allowing the Corps to make suggestions or objections. In his last official action as commandant, Biddle trenchantly informed Secretary Daniels that "the Marine Corps can never realize its highest efficiency as a branch of the Navy under a system of naval administration which excludes it from being well grounded in proper Naval doctrine—which prevents its officers from possessing intelligent initiative in matters of Naval policy, and which restricts the formulation of policy to methods that fail to produce proper coordination of effort and unity of action between the Marine Corps and the Navy."[26]

Biddle was in poor health when he became commandant. He had already failed one fitness test and his health had been one of the few questionable marks on his later fitness reports. The tumultuous events of 1913, when Biddle had to defend himself against Fullam, both organize an expeditionary force for Mexico and for the Caribbean maneuvers, and comply with the Navy Department's often contradictory demands, appear to have exhausted him. Almost as soon as the Culebra advanced base force had deployed in November 1913, Biddle petitioned to be allowed to retire. He remained in office until 24 February, when his successor, Col. George Barnett, officially assumed his duties. Called back to active duty during World War I, Biddle served as president of a general court-martial before being allowed to retire again on 23 May 1919. On 25 February

1923, a decade after he had retired, the eleventh commandant of the Marine Corps died at Nice, France.

Biddle is almost forgotten within the Marine Corps, and his contributions to Marine reform are barely acknowledged. His fellow officers appear to have respected him, but he was neither admired nor loved. A portrait of Biddle painted when he was commandant shows an aging, unhealthy looking, corpulent man. In over three decades as a field officer, he proved a competent, cautious, and prudent commander who either never received or never seized the opportunity to distinguish himself on the battlefield. Certainly he was not cast from the same heroic mold as such colorful contemporaries as Butler, Waller, Hiram Bearss, or Joseph H. Pendleton. Yet in his own way, Biddle proved an adept leader who could identify capable subordinates and delegate responsibility. Frederic M. Wise, who idolized Waller and was often critical of Biddle's leadership, acknowledged that Biddle was a good commander who treated his junior officers well. Wise also testified that Biddle would refuse to compromise over matters of principle and that those who pushed him too far found that behind his pleasant demeanor was a furious and explosive temper. The commandant's correspondence confirms Wise's observations; once aroused, Biddle would defend both his own and the Corps's interests with considerable force. These latter characteristics certainly emerge in some of Biddle's battles as commandant.

Biddle has been characterized as "lethargic"[27] and a commandant whose duties were "mainly of routine character."[28] He was certainly not a great executive, but his critics have been overly harsh in portraying him as a do-nothing mediocrity. It is more charitable, and more accurate, to characterize Biddle as a transitional commandant who was well suited to guide a Corps itself in transition. A quarter of a century's service with the "Old Corps," consisting largely of guarding navy yards, commanding ship's guards, and occasional expeditionary duty appears to have left him with the conviction that such duties should continue to figure prominently in the "new" Corps of the twentieth century. Yet Biddle was no moss-backed reactionary. During his tenure as commandant, the Marines moved cautiously but firmly toward securing their claim as the Navy's advanced base force, which in turn provided the ultimate justification for the Fleet Marine Force. Given the absence of acceptable candidates for commandant, the disarray of the Corps, and the impossible demands of the Navy Department, he did a commendable job. Commanders who demonstrate their competence in defensive warfare are seldom as glamorous as those who go on the attack; much of Biddle's tenure was one long holding action against Fullam, the General Board, and the Navy Department. But Biddle's steadfast defense of the Marine Corps's interests and his refusal to stake it all on a new mission until his superiors made an equally firm commitment should not be slighted, for they provided a solid foundation for his successors to build on.

12
George Barnett
1914–1920

LT. COL. MERRILL L. BARTLETT, USMC (RET.)

George Barnett's quest for the commandancy began in earnest in 1910, when Maj. Gen. George F. Elliott applied for retirement. Although all of the Corps's colonels, even lieutenant colonels, could apply for the post, the list of potential candidates dropped quickly to three from among the eight colonels of the line: Littleton W. T. Waller, who carried the clout of the Virginia congressional delegation along with an impressive record of lengthy expeditionary service; William P. Biddle, who came armed with his famous Philadelphia name and the support of powerful Pennsylvania senator Boies Penrose; and Barnett.

Representative John Weeks of Massachusetts supported Barnett, his Naval Academy roommate. At the time, Colonel Barnett commanded the Marine Barracks in Philadelphia. Secretary of the Navy George von Lengerke Meyer escorted each of the supporters to the White House, where President William H. Taft allowed everyone to argue for their respective candidates. Then Taft excused everyone except the senator from Pennsylvania. Penrose reminded Taft that he owed him a political favor and failure to nominate Biddle might result in Penrose's decision not to support current legislation Taft desired. Thus, Biddle came to hold the Corps's highest post in 1910.[1]

President-elect Woodrow Wilson's secretary of the navy, Josephus Daniels, arrived in 1913 determined to bring order and efficiency to the department. A year with Daniels convinced Biddle of the advantages of retirement, and in late 1913, the quest for a successor began. A glance at the lineal list of that year revealed that the roster of contenders had not changed appreciably. Waller's record book arrived on the secretary's desk with a letter from Senator Claude A. Swanson of Virginia to President Wilson containing the endorsement of all thirty-one Democrats in the Senate. Weeks, now a senator, championed his old friend Barnett again, but the names of two newcomers also appeared. Lt. Col. John A. Lejeune, the commanding officer of the Marine Barracks, New

Maj. Gen. George Barnett, twelfth commandant.
U.S. Marine Corps Photo.

York, and a recent graduate of the Army War College, threw his hat into the ring, while Commandant Biddle supported Col. Lincoln Karmany, commanding officer of the Marine Barracks, Mare Island. A veteran campaigner like Waller, Karmany, who like Weeks was a Naval Academy classmate of Barnett, had a reputation for hard drinking and womanizing.

As Secretary Daniels considered his choices and prepared to make a recommendation to the president, he found little alternative but to select Barnett. Although attracted to Lejeune, considering him the best qualified candidate of the lot, his rank eliminated him at the outset, and Karmany's recent, messy divorce in order to marry another woman made him unacceptable. Waller lost out simply because the Wilson administration had just announced a new and progressive program with regard to the administration of the Philippines, and it made poor political logic to appoint an officer who had been accused of inhumane treatment of the Filipinos. Thus, Daniels's choice narrowed to Barnett, although the secretary felt far from comfortable with the selection.

Daniels later recalled reservations about choosing Barnett, but at the time it made good political sense to nominate an officer with strong Republican support to serve in a Democratic administration. Moreover, Barnett had an excellent record—albeit with few powder burns or tropical sweat stains on his uniforms—and he had a diploma from the Naval Academy. On 25 February 1914, Barnett took the oath of office as the twelfth commandant of the Marine Corps.[2]

Barnett was a descendant of Joseph Barnett, who migrated from England in 1740 and served as an officer in Washington's army during the Revolution. In 1850, Andrew and Mary Benton Barnett, the new commandant's grandparents, moved from Pennsylvania to Lancaster, Wisconsin. Their son, James (1828–1907), married a local girl, Elizabeth A. Collis (1831–1921) in 1855, and George's older sister, Martha (1858–1910), was born there. George Barnett was born on 9 December 1859 in Lancaster as well. Barnett's family soon moved to nearby Boscobel, where his father worked as a small businessman. He had a younger brother and sister, Charles H. and Mattie. Early in his youth, Barnett seemed attracted to the life of a soldier, but he took the opportunity to join the naval service when the opportunity presented itself.

While still in high school, Barnett expressed an interest in an appointment to the U.S. Military Academy and pressed his father to speak to their neighbor, Congressman George C. Hazelton of Wisconsin's Third District. His father, however, demurred. But one day in the spring of 1878, Barnett encountered Hazelton, and the congressman offered him an appointment to the U.S. Naval Academy. He boarded the train for Annapolis with the well wishes of the local citizenry: "Of all the young men whom Wisconsin has chosen as representatives of her in the naval forces [George Barnett] carries with him a good disposition . . . and as good an education as any."[3]

Although not a particularly good scholar, Barnett's academic performance improved steadily following a nervous start during his plebe year, especially in mathematics. After two years, his average had risen to 2.9 out of 4.0, placing him thirtieth in a class of seventy-nine survivors among the original 120. When the class of 1881 received their diplomas from President James A. Garfield on 10 June 1881, Barnett stood twenty-ninth out of a class of seventy-two, his worst grades appearing in navigation and marine engineering—hardly harbingers of future excellence for a Navy officer. In deportment, Barnett's transgressions from the numerous and petty regulations reflected more of a youthful sense of humor than a rebellious spirit, and the number of his offenses on the conduct roll of cadets never approached the limits for which expulsion might follow.[4]

The Navy that the class of 1881 hoped to join, however, had fallen on hard times. Although in 1865 the U.S. Navy claimed to be the largest in the world with 671 ships, post–Civil War demobilization took its toll. Two years after the conflict, only half that number remained in service with the balance rotting at pier side or rusting at anchor; however, the Navy continued to train and educate future naval officers in the same numbers. By Barnett's time, naval cadets became "passed midshipmen" upon graduation and served as such at sea until an ensign's vacancy became available. In 1880, the Navy counted one graduate for every four sailors; two years later, the secretary of the navy reported that he had 1,817 officers to man thirty-seven small ships. The average graduate might spend eight years in the fleet before a vacancy appeared, and some graduates resigned in disgust. As Barnett and his classmates cruised the seas from 1881 to 1883 (Barnett sailed in the *Essex* to Africa and South America), Congress stepped in to take administrative action to solve the dilemma.[5]

Because the Navy could not reduce the number of naval cadets entering Annapolis, and seemed unable to prune the ranks of its officers of deadwood, Congress applied a surgical solution. On 5 August 1881, a proviso appeared on the annual naval appropriations bill stipulating that for every midshipman commissioned, there must be two vacancies at the top of the lineal list of officers. Thus, when Barnett and his classmates returned from their cruise in the late spring of 1883, they realized that many among them would be leaving the Navy to start life anew after six years of hard work. The only positive feature of the legislation was that for the first time, graduates could accept commissions in the Marine Corps instead of the Navy.[6]

The academy's Academic Board computed composite scores for the class of 1881 based on each cadet's undergraduate academic and deportment record, fitness reports from the postgraduate cruise, and post-cruise examination results. The board recommended only twenty-three cadets for commissioning in either the Navy or Marine Corps, with the remaining sixty-three to be discharged. Barnett appeared on the list of naval cadets destined for the Corps along with nine others. In his unpublished memoirs, Barnett claimed that the Marines had been his first choice; in reality, it was his only choice. Faring poorly in the post-cruise examinations, he slipped to twenty-third in order of merit for commissioning. Thus, with only one position on the merit roll left, Barnett was saved from the disgrace of discharge and an uncertain future in rural Wisconsin.[7]

The Annapolis experience shaped Barnett's worldview and left perspectives that endured for the rest of his life. Whatever the young man from Wisconsin was when he arrived in 1878, six years later he identified with America's post–Civil War naval aristocracy: Protestant, ultraconservative, and Republican in political thinking, extremely patriotic, and so pro-Navy as to appear myopic at times. Common experiences as plebes and the mild hazing, the rigorous academic regimen, pranks in defiance of the administration, and adventuresome cruises became important parts of the emotional attachment of the Annapolis years. The intensity increased over the decades as Barnett and his classmates felt the loss of their fellow graduates denied the opportunity to join them in the naval services.[8]

Barnett's commission as a second lieutenant, dated 1 July 1883, reached him at home in Boscobel, and with it came orders for all of the new Marine Corps officers from the class of 1881 to report for initial training to the Marine Barracks, New York. That fall, Barnett and his classmate, Franklin J. Moses, received further orders to report in October to the barracks at Mare Island, California, for additional instruction. Barnett then received orders transferring him to the *Pinta,* an old screw tug that served as the Navy's garrison ship in Alaska. Barnett commanded its marines until 1887. After a short tour ashore at the barracks in Washington, he received orders to the *Iroquois* in 1889 as the commanding officer of the small ship's detachment. The *Iroquois* steamed from California to Hawaii and then into the South Seas. In February 1892, the deployment ended in the region, and the ship returned to San Francisco for decommissioning on 12 March 1892.[9]

Barnett again received orders to Marine Barracks, Washington, reporting on 30 July 1892. He had been promoted to first lieutenant effective 1 September 1890. As a change from the usual round of barracks duties, Barnett joined a Marine detachment sent to the World's Fair in Chicago in 1893, detailed to guard valuable government documents sent there for display. Returning to Washington after the fair closed, Barnett received orders transferring him to the barracks in Portsmouth, New Hampshire, in March 1896, then to the receiving ship *Vermont* in New York, and finally to command the marines in the cruiser *San Francisco.*

Traveling by commercial steamer across the Atlantic and through the Mediterranean to Athens, Barnett arrived by train in Smyrna, Turkey, to join his cruiser on 12 December 1897. The ship then steamed west, stopping at Naples, the French Riviera, and Lisbon. At its last port call, news of the sinking of the *Maine* and possible war with Spain reached them, and the *San Francisco* sped north to England. There, the crew took possession of the Brazilian cruiser *Amazonas.* Renamed the *New Orleans,* the ship steamed across the Atlantic, and Barnett remained part of its crew after hostilities began against Spain.

During the U.S. landings in Cuba and Puerto Rico, the *New Orleans* provided fire support. With the end of hostilities, the Navy took the *New Orleans* out of commission, and Barnett began to cast about for another seagoing assignment. Promoted to captain on 11 August 1898, Barnett transferred to the cruiser *Chicago* and for the next year and a half steamed across the Atlantic and Mediterranean, around the horn of Africa, and then to South America. Detached in April 1900, he explained to his classmates his reason for not marrying. Until almost the turn of the century, only junior Marine Corps officers served at sea, while field grade officers remained mostly in shore-based billets: "I always thought it would be a good time to get married after having finished sea service."[10]

From 19 October 1901 until 13 September 1902, Barnett recruited marines in the Philadelphia area. Following this short stint ashore, he commanded a battalion deployed to Panama from 23 September to 18 November 1902. Promotions came more quickly as the Corps expanded following the Spanish-American War; Barnett pinned on the insignia of a major effective 3 March 1901. With the new rank came increased responsibilities. Late in 1902, Barnett formed a Marine battalion at the Philadelphia Barracks and sailed with them to the Philippines in January 1903. Upon arrival at Subic Bay, he turned the unit over to the commanding officer of the Marine Corps brigade in anticipation of orders transferring him to another assignment. In July 1903, Barnett became the Marine Corps officer on the staff of the commander, Asiatic Fleet. Promoted to lieutenant colonel effective 28 February 1905, Barnett had orders in hand to become the commanding officer, Marine Barracks, Washington, effective July 1905. In Washington, Barnett met and married the woman who would change his life.

On 9 December 1906, Barnett hosted a supper dance at the Washington Navy Yard to celebrate his forty-seventh birthday. As he stood by the entrance to greet his guests, two fashionable belles from among his circle of friends stepped forward to introduce the beautiful and wealthy Lelia Montague Gordon. Claiming later to be smitten on the spot, Barnett unleashed all of his polish and charm on the recently widowed Mrs. Gordon. Lelia Montague was born in 1871 in New Rochelle, New York. As a child, her family moved to Baltimore, where she attended local schools. Introduced to a member of Virginia's landed gentry, Basil Gordon, in 1892, Lelia was swept off her feet even though he had been stricken with tuberculosis of the spine the year before. Tremendously wealthy, Gordon stood to inherit a vast country estate in the foothills of the Shenandoahs, Wakefield Manor. The two married, but Gordon died in 1902, leaving Lelia with four small children. Returning to her family in Baltimore after the death of one of the children, Lelia attempted to put her life back together. In 1905, she took up residence in a fashionable town house on DuPont Circle in the nation's capital and quickly entered the city's social set. While Barnett pursued her as if he was assaulting a military objective, the beautiful Mrs. Gordon appeared unhurried to marry again, especially since she enjoyed the attentions of several titled European diplomats. Nevertheless, Barnett pressed his case by showering the lovely widow with daily deliveries of flowers and demonstrating his considerable charm, exquisite manners, and skill as a dancer. But when Barnett appeared likely to receive orders for transfer in late 1907, he had not yet gained Mrs. Gordon's hand.

Barnett tried to obtain a decision from Mrs. Gordon. He informed her that he had been to see the commandant of the Marine Corps and Major General Elliott had offered him two choices of duty: Marine Corps officer accompanying the Great White Fleet around the world or commanding officer of the Legation Guard in Beijing. If Mrs. Gordon was not ready to accept his proposal of marriage, then Barnett would opt to sail with the fleet and see the world; however, if she would agree to marriage, then it would be China. Still hesitant, Mrs. Gordon agreed only if the wedding could be put off until the late winter. On 11 January 1908, the couple exchanged vows in a Baltimore church. Congressman John Weeks served as best man for his former roommate, and Major General

Elliott sent part of the Marine Corps Band. Not easily impressed, the new Mrs. Barnett commented tartly that "the natives probably thought a circus had come to town."[11]

In China, Barnett seemed to have few military or diplomatic duties, and he and his bride spent most of their days in endless rounds of social activities. More than a platoon of Chinese servants attended to their every need, and the obvious decay of the Ch'ing Dynasty and the Manchus failed to dampen their spirits. All too quickly, the adventure ended with orders for Barnett to command the barracks in Philadelphia in October 1910 with the new rank of colonel. The social whirl that Mrs. Barnett maintained in Beijing continued unabated in Philadelphia for the next three years. At the barracks, George Barnett trained marines for duty at sea or deployment overseas in a ritual that had changed little from the days of sail. Three times during his tour, he commanded a hastily formed regiment deployed to Cuba to quell domestic disturbances. During this last tour before assuming the commandancy, the Barnetts devoted themselves to cultivating important social liaisons as Lelia pushed her husband with fierce determination to seek the Corps's highest post.

In Barnett's opinion, an important factor in determining his suitability for the position would result from his leadership during the most important peacetime maneuver of the Marine Corps. Shortly after the turn of the century, the Navy's new General Board addressed the obvious requirement for support to the fleet in worldwide operations. For the fleet to operate any distance from the shores of the United States, it required either an extensive supply train or a force to establish advanced bases for the provision of supplies, munitions, and repair facilities for the ships and amphibious forces. Originally conceived as a four-hundred-man battalion of infantry composed of marines and bluejackets, by 1912 the force—in theory—had grown.

On the eve of its first major maneuver, the Advanced Base Force consisted of two thirteen-hundred-man regiments: one, a fixed defense regiment composed of coastal artillery, searchlights, and mining companies, augmented with machine guns and harbor defense mines; the second, a mobile defense regiment consisting of light infantry reinforced by field artillery guns and machine guns to repulse an enemy landing force. In theory, the force remained organized, trained, and equipped for immediate deployment. In fact, it had never really existed except on paper because Congress failed to allocate the necessary funds. Moreover, the Marine forces allocated to man the two regiments were also required on board ship, as guards at various barracks at Navy stations and yards, or deployed overseas as "colonial infantry." Pressure emanating more from Navy circles than from Congress or from the Marine Corps resulted in the requirement to test the concept in 1914 as part of the annual fleet exercises.[12]

In July 1913, Barnett and Assistant Secretary of the Navy Franklin D. Roosevelt together chose the tiny island of Culebra, sixteen miles east of Puerto Rico, as the site for the maneuver. Although the staff of the Atlantic Fleet prepared the overall scheme for the fleet maneuver, the Advanced Base School in Philadelphia drew up the plans for the exercise of the Advance Base Force. The scenario envisioned a declaration of war by an unknown European nation (clearly, Germany) on 15 December 1913; the Atlantic

Fleet would concentrate on Culebra to meet the enemy fleet and then steam north to defend the east coast of the United States.

On 27 November 1913, the Mobile Defense Regiment commanded by Lt. Col. John A. Lejeune steamed out of Philadelphia in the transport, *Prairie,* prepared to either deploy to Culebra for maneuvers or to Mexico in the event of hostilities. On 18 December 1913, the Fixed Defense Regiment under Lt. Col. Charles G. Long began its embarkation in the same port. On 3 January 1914, another ship left Philadelphia with Long's regiment, Barnett and the brigade headquarters, a small aviation detachment, and a field hospital.

On 7 January 1914, the amphibious task force dropped anchor off Culebra and began to fortify the small island in earnest. Two weeks later to the day, the opposing fleet arrived on schedule and the Advanced Base Force defended the island vigorously. The chief umpire, Capt. William S. Sims, declared a victory for the defending forces and trumpeted success for the concept of defending advance bases. As the ships turned away, the force spent the next two weeks camped on the small island to engage in target practice and other training. Finally, on 9 February 1914, its odyssey ended, the Advanced Base Force returned to New Orleans in anticipation of possible deployment to Mexico in the face of heightened tensions in the region.[13]

Barnett left the force in New Orleans and journeyed north by train to take up his new post as the twelfth commandant of the Marine Corps, basking in the warm glow of numerous letters and telegrams of congratulations. Ahead lay a never-ending series of personnel shortages with which to cope, increasing requirements for the Corps in overseas expeditionary commitments, service for the Marines in a land war in Europe, and subordination to the most difficult and obstinate public servant to hold the office of secretary of the navy since the office was created in 1798.

Born in 1862, Josephus Daniels established himself through his small newspaper as an articulate spokesman for the New South, progressive reforms in government, and prohibition. From 1896 until 1916, he served continuously as a Democratic national committeeman, and in return for his support of presidential hopeful Woodrow Wilson, became a member of Wilson's cabinet in 1913. Calling on the outgoing secretary on 5 March, Daniels received advice that he would carry throughout his tenure in office. As he prepared to make his departure, the patrician George von L. Meyer offered guidance from his experience as secretary: "I do not wish to give you any advice, but merely to suggest that you keep the power to direct the Navy *here.*"[14]

Convinced that waste and inefficiency abounded within the department, Daniels brought to the office a stubborn evangelical fundamentalism. One Navy Department official later described Daniels as "a queer character, a combination of ignorance, kindheartedness, and shifty opportunism."[15] During his first official visit to a ship, Daniels set the tone for his administration which sent shock waves throughout the Navy and Marine Corps. Waving aside the guard of honor assembled on the quarterdeck, Daniels mounted a wooden box and asked all of the sailors to gather around him. He then informed the crew that he intended to run the Navy for *them* and henceforth their persecution at the hands of the officers would cease. To begin his progressive reforms, Daniels moved to oust the collection of "headquarters toadies" that had made a career of service in the nation's capital.

Correspondence in Daniels's personal files suggests that the stimulus for removal of the career bureaucrats within the Department of the Navy came from the indefatigable reformist William F. Fullam, aide for inspections. Fullam's criticisms stemmed in part from the conclusions of the court of inquiry resulting from the conflict between Major General Elliott and Col. Charles H. Lauchheimer, the adjutant and inspector at Headquarters Marine Corps. The court had concluded that the lax administration in certain offices resulted from too long a tenure in office among the Headquarters staff officers of the Marine Corps.

On 5 April 1913, Daniels recommended to President Wilson that the tours of duty of the commandant of the Marine Corps and his principal staff officers be limited to a period of four years unless reappointed. Winning speedy approval for his ukase, Daniels then asked for a list of Corps officers who had been on duty in Washington longer than four years. To his alarm, he learned that the colorful Lauchheimer had served at Headquarters Marine Corps for almost twenty of his thirty years in uniform.[16]

Whatever reformist goals the indefatigable Daniels had in mind for the Corps, few reached fruition. Barnett served most of a second tour as commandant, Lauchheimer stayed on as adjutant and inspector until his death from cancer in 1920, and the quartermaster and paymaster that Barnett inherited in 1914 continued on through his tenure at the helm of the Corps. Daniels also inherited a clumsy ad hoc staff system devised by Meyer, which he discarded after a year in office.

In 1909, Meyer created the Council of Aids, composed of the chiefs of the Bureaus of Operations, Personnel, Material, and Inspections, to advise him on naval matters and otherwise to reduce the numbers of subordinates reporting to him. Early in 1914, Daniels added Barnett to the council, but a year later he determined that the arrangement was inefficient and limited his span of control. For the remainder of his tenure, Daniels preferred to deal with the chiefs of the various bureaus and Barnett directly; in the secretary's opinion, the commandant of the Marine Corps was just another bureau chief.[17]

During Barnett's tenure, no issue came to dominate his commandancy more than personnel increases. In his last annual report to the secretary of the navy, Barnett's predecessor, General Biddle, had underscored the increasing number of commitments for the Marines without a concurrent rise in manpower. Ever since the Spanish-American War and America's increasing willingness to become involved in overseas affairs, both Congress and successive presidents appeared willing to commit naval forces as the spearhead of neocolonialism. From an overly committed small force numbering approximately ten thousand in 1914, the Marine Corps grew to more than seventy thousand by the end of World War I. For casual observers of the Corps's administrative scene, the increases appeared tied to the commitment on the western front; however, long before "over there" became a household phrase in the United States, Barnett and his staff had argued successfully for significant increases in numbers.[18]

In October 1915, Barnett told Daniels of his concerns about personnel shortages. On the heels of a demand by the Navy for an increase of seventy-five hundred men, Barnett argued for an increase in his ranks of fifteen hundred using the figure of 20 percent of Navy strength for the Corps, which he cited in his Annual Report. On 3 February 1916, a special personnel board headed by Assistant Secretary of the Navy Franklin D. Roosevelt made several far-reaching conclusions: the overall strength of the Marine Corps should be 20 percent that of the Navy, officer strength should be 4 percent of enlisted strength, staff and line officers should be on the same list when considered for promotion, and there should be one brigadier general for every four colonels.[19]

Even before the board met or reported out, Barnett appeared optimistic. The previous fall, he indicated to his close friend and fellow Naval Academy graduate Col. Joseph H. Pendleton that he anticipated an increase of approximately two thousand officers and men along with authorization of two brigadier generals. In January 1916, Barnett testified before the House Naval Affairs Committee, which liked his plea for increases. The commandant noted that without the increases and authorization for more rapid and timely promotion of the officer corps, most officers would be too old to keep pace with their young and more fit troops. Barnett informed the House committee that unless company grade officers received promotions at a more accelerated rate, the average captain would spend thirty-five years in uniform before becoming eligible for advancement to major. In just five more years, he would be forced to retire for age. While the representatives appeared to agree with Barnett's argument, one member of the committee appeared ambivalent over at least one aspect of the commandant's proposal.[20]

Representative Thomas S. Butler argued against merging line and staff officers and spoke out strongly against allowing staff officers to become eligible for promotion to brigadier general. Doubtless the elder Butler reflected the histrionics of his restless son, the colorful Maj. Smedley D. Butler, winner of two Medals of Honor. When news of the commandant's proposed legislation traveled to Haiti, Butler lost no time in venting his spleen in a letter home: "Tell him [father], the line officers . . . look upon this proposed Marine Corps personnel bill with suspicion. . . . It promotes practically no one but staff officers who went into a staff department because they preferred an easy life."[21] Barnett received even less support from Daniels and Roosevelt. Testifying on 28 February 1916, both officials agreed with the proposed increases in the size of the Marine Corps but expressed reservations over the figure of officer strength of 4 percent of enlisted numbers. Both the secretary and assistant secretary doubted the need to promote so many colonels to brigadier general.

On 12 May 1916, the House Naval Affairs Committee reported out its bill for naval appropriations for the following fiscal year to the floor of the House. Much to the surprise of Barnett and his staff, it called for an increase of 3,079 enlisted men for the Marine Corps, approximately 700 more than requested. In June, the House passed the measure and sent it on to the Senate. Before the Senate could take up action on the measure, however, a fit of wartime hysteria appeared after Mexican revolutionary Pancho Villa's raid into New Mexico. Following Gen. John J. Pershing's punitive expedition into Mexico, the Senate passed a naval appropriations bill on 22 July 1916 specifying an enlisted strength for the Marine Corps of 14,940, approximately 5,000 more leathernecks than called for in Barnett's estimates. The bill also allowed the president to increase the size of the Corps to 17,400 men without further legislation in the event of hostilities.

Much to the delight of Barnett and the Corps's colonels, the Senate measure authorized the creation of eight brigadier generals, including three from among the Headquarters colonels. When the bill became law on 29 August 1916, Barnett received immediate authorization to recruit an additional five thousand men, to promote eight colonels to flag rank, to combine the line and staff officers on one list for the purposes of promotion, and to establish the Marine Corps Reserve. In his first term in office, Barnett had presided over a greater increase in the size of the Marine Corps than in any similar period in its history. However, the legislation of 1916 would only be the beginning of the expansion of the Corps as America drifted closer to war with Germany.

Barnett took immediate steps to involve his leathernecks in the conflict. In testimony before the House Naval Affairs Committee, he took the unusual step of arguing with Adm. William S. Benson, chief of naval operations. Barnett cited the existence of three brigades of Royal Marines then serving with the British Expeditionary Force in France; Benson countered vigorously by claiming that the Marines should be used solely for naval purposes. Barnett's argument that every trained fighting man must be made available in time of war or national emergency, regardless of armed service, won the day. On 20 May 1917, the naval appropriations bill for fiscal year 1918 became law; significantly, it included provisions for an increase in the number of men wearing forest green to more than thirty thousand.[22]

Barnett convinced a less-than-enthusiastic Secretary Daniels to offer a Marine brigade to accompany Gen. John J. Pershing and the initial contingent of the American Expeditionary Forces (AEF) to France. Anxious to participate, Barnett agreed to several administrative changes so as to outfit and organize the token leatherneck force along Army lines. Because the typical Marine Corps brigade numbered approximately the same number of men as in an Army regiment, Barnett ordered the 6th Marines combined with the 5th Marines for the deployment. To give the outfit polish and grit, the CMC ordered eight companies of veteran leathernecks home from the Caribbean to form the backbone of the regiment and infuse it with characteristic Marine Corps eccentricity and toughness. From the outset, however, the Marines were made to feel unwanted, as Secretary Daniels noted in his memoirs: "When war was declared, I tendered, ready and equipped, two regiments of Marines to be incorporated in the Army. Senior Army officers were not keen to accept them."[23]

Despite wails of protest and claims of discrimination by senior leathernecks, Pershing ordered the 5th Marines to guard duty along the lines of communications while the doughboys began a rigorous program of training. Barnett complained bitterly to Daniels and any congressman who would lend his ear. News of the meddling reached Pershing's ears, irritating him and his staff, who considered the interference a patent example of attempts by the Department of the Navy to muscle in on the Army's show.

Pershing then moved to end further Marine deployment to the AEF. Despite the AEF commander's request that "no more Marines be sent to France," the adjutant general of the Army informed him that another regiment and a machine-gun battalion were en route. He even directed an assignment for the unwanted forces as one of the two infantry brigades in the 2d Division, AEF. For almost the next year, Pershing paid scant attention to the token force. But when the brigade's commander, Brig. Gen. Charles A. Doyen, Barnett's Naval Academy classmate, fell afoul of the AEF's medical examiners, Pershing assigned Brig. Gen. James G. Harbord, his chief of staff and an old friend, to command the leathernecks on 6 May 1918.[24]

While the assignment of an Army officer to command the brigade sent shock waves through Headquarters Marine Corps and naval circles, the talented Harbord quickly gained the allegiance of his senior leatherneck officers and led them through one of the most famous battles in Marine Corps history. Between late May and early June 1918, the 4th Brigade (Marine) dug in along the Paris-Metz highway to block the main thrust of the German spring offensive. After entering Belleau Wood and ejecting the enemy forces, the leathernecks were forced to return again to complete the final defeat of the Germans after the Army regiment sent to relieve it failed. But along with the sweetness of victory came an outburst of intense interservice rivalry and acrimony that persisted throughout the war. Although Pershing had issued strict orders that American war correspondents were not to identify specific units in their dispatches, those covering the Battle of Belleau Wood (6 June–6 July 1918) reported the attacking AEF units to be Marines. To the consternation of the AEF staff and the soldiers of both the 1st and 3d Divisions, as well as the doughboys in the 2d Division's other infantry brigade, the Marines had reaped a public relations bonanza. As Pershing and his senior officers continued to simmer over this brouhaha, Barnett chose to suggest that even more Marine units deploy to France.[25]

Brig. Gen. John A. Lejeune reported to the AEF just as this simmering cauldron of animosity and interservice rivalry reached its crescendo. As instructed by Barnett, he broached the matter of employing additional marines with Pershing. The unyielding commander in chief repeated his conclusions with regard to commonality of units and equipment, leaving no doubt that he could do without the impediments of an entire division of leathernecks. After meeting with Lejeune and rebuffing his request, Pershing cabled the secretary of war in hopes of ending the matter once and for all: "I am of the opinion that the formation of such a unit [a Marine Corps division] is undesirable from a military standpoint. Our land forces must be homogenous in every respect. . . . While the Marines are splendid troops, their use as a separate division is inadvisable." Maj. Gen. Peyton C. March concurred and added, "If you are called upon to send any troops from your force to Italy or any other place, they will be selected from the army and will not be chosen from the Marines."[26]

Meanwhile, Pershing had grown increasingly disconcerted by and wary of the leadership of the 2d Division. Maj. Gen. Omar Bundy appeared to be yet another doddering senior officer who "lacked the grasp." In a pungent diary entry, Pershing noted his disappointment: "General Bundy disappoints me. I shall relieve him at the first opportunity."

First, Pershing shunted Bundy off to command a corps not likely to play a significant role in future offensives; next, he promoted Harbord to major general and gave him command of the 2d Division while Lejeune assumed command of the 4th Brigade (Marine). Subsequently, however, Harbord moved to command the Services of Supply and Lejeune took the division. Perhaps not coincidentally, Barnett's able assistant commandant received another star and retained command of the division throughout the remainder of the war and the period of occupation duty in Germany.

Even before Lejeune's fateful meeting with Pershing, Barnett persuaded Daniels to accompany him to offer the remaining elements of a Marine Corps division to the secretary of war. On 30 March 1918, Barnett and Daniels met with the assistant secretary of war. From the outset of the conference, it appeared that Benjamin Cromwell had been briefed by the chief of staff of the Army on the subject of commonality and the undesirability of accepting further leathernecks in the AEF. Barnett agreed to whatever changes Cromwell wanted. The 4th Brigade (Marine), AEF had already turned in its trusted Lewis machine guns for the Army's less-reliable Hotchkiss model; when Marine Corps uniforms wore out, the leathernecks donned Army brown—but sewed on their own buttons. The marines in the AEF had even learned the Army's style of close-order drill, much to their disgust. Still, Cromwell continued to resist the offer. Daniels's diary entry for that day mirrors the frustration and resentment he and Barnett felt: "Saw [the] Assistant Secretary of War about sending Marines to France. . . . Question [is] whether [the] Army desires them."[27]

Barnett continued to hope for an entire Marine division in France. He ordered the organization of the remaining elements necessary, and the units formed and trained all that summer at Quantico. As the first leaves of autumn appeared, Cromwell informed Barnett that he was "sorry to have to tell you that it will be utterly impossible for the War Department to furnish transportation for a Marine [brigade] in the [forthcoming] sailing." Just as forthrightly, and more than a bit smugly, Barnett informed the Department of War that it had already arranged for transportation on the Navy ships escorting the draft to France. Despite his gloating, however, Barnett failed to obtain permission to deploy the remaining elements at Quantico: two regiments of artillery, an engineer regiment, and a supply train. And just as determinedly, AEF Headquarters disbanded the 5th Brigade upon its arrival in France and used its personnel as replacements or for duties along the lines of communication.

The swagger and élan of Barnett's marines rubbed Army sensibilities raw; by the end of the war, doughboys took delight in singing the following doggerel when marching past a group of marines:

The Marines have won the croix de guerre, parlez-vous
The Marines have won the croix de guerre, parlez-vous
The Marines have won the croix de guerre,
But the sons-of-bitches were never there,
Hinky-dinky, parlez-vous.

Even at the officer level, animosities appeared occasionally. In the 2d Division, many Army officers found service with the leathernecks troubling. After the cease fire, one of Lejeune's Army regimental commanders vented his anger to another senior officer after transferring out of the division, referring to the marines as "a bunch of adventurers, illiterates, and drunkards."[28] Fittingly, Harbord placed the animosities in perspective in his published memoirs: "The Marines have been taunted with having thought they had won the war, and there have been some unkind comments from Army officers of high enough rank to be above such pettiness. . . . The wounds inflicted by publicity received by someone else do not rate a wound stripe, but they are a long time healing."[29]

Whatever the Army thought of its comrades in arms, the Corps returned home with a fresh reputation for superb performance on the battlefield and more than its share of honors. Approximately 30,000 marines were in France at the end of the war out of the 72,963 leathernecks on active duty. Of the number "over there," almost one-third suffered wounds; the brigade received more than 1,300 individual decorations for bravery, including five Medals of Honor. The brigade participated in eight major combat operations, including the epic battle for Belleau Wood, in which it suffered more than 50 percent casualties. Barnett had every reason to be proud of his marines.

At the outset of Barnett's plea to include marines in the American Expeditionary Forces, he insisted that traditional Navy commitments would be met first. Leathernecks continued to provide ships detachments and security forces just as they had during the age of sail. Larger Marine forces deployed to Haiti and the Dominican Republic in the Caribbean before the United States entered the war in Europe. While attention remained focused on the war across the Atlantic, the Corps performed at home and throughout the world to the satisfaction of the president, Congress, and senior Navy officers.

Although Daniels appeared pleased with the performance of the twelfth commandant and continued to write outstanding fitness reports on Barnett, their relationship became increasingly strained beginning in early 1918. As Barnett's first four-year term of office neared its end in 1918, the senior officers of the Navy and Marine Corps expected him to be reappointed. Although Daniels had announced at the outset of his administration that he planned to limit the commandant and bureau chiefs to single four-year terms in office (his "single-oak" policy), changing so many key officers in the middle of a war made no sense. Daniels summoned each of the incumbents and asked for an undated letter of resignation which he intended to use upon the cessation of hostilities. While each senior Navy officer complied, Barnett hesitated.

According to Barnett's version of the incident, he refused to sign such a letter, claiming that as an officer he served at the pleasure of the president. When the commander in chief no longer required his services, he would leave office. Later, Daniels told him to forget the matter. The secretary's version differs. On 25 February 1918, when Daniels made his request to Barnett, the commandant agreed. However, the following day he telephoned and asked to be allowed to reconsider. Barnett then gave his word as an officer and a gentleman that a resignation would be forthcoming any time that Daniels wished it. Sensing a stubborn streak in a subordinate usually subservient, Daniels told Barnett to forget the matter. An undated letter of resignation in his case would not be required. Later, the secretary suggested that Mrs. Barnett had probably goaded her husband into refusing Daniels's request. For the first time, Daniels used the expression "if Barnett was an Indian, his name would be 'the-man-who-is-afraid-of-his-wife.'"[30]

While Mrs. Barnett might have enjoyed a reputation as one of the most sparkling hostesses among the smart set in the nation's capital, her charm failed to impress Daniels. Scorning inherited wealth, the secretary found Mrs. Barnett more irritating than amusing or clever. Shortly after Daniels announced that alcoholic beverages would no longer be served at official functions at naval installations ashore, Mrs. Barnett obtained his permission to continue to use liquor in cooking. She then served the secretary a dinner which he and the guests would remember: every course except the roast beef came laced with alcohol!

Other than a populist's scorn for Mrs. Barnett's social position and inherited wealth, Daniels had no reason to dislike her. From the outset, she provided yeoman service to her husband's office in a variety of areas. Early on, she established herself as a champion of the downtrodden enlisted man, something that should have warmed the heart of Daniels, who had the image of himself as the standard-bearer of egalitarianism in the naval services. Often her inquiry into confinement resulting from conviction by courts-martial resulted in reduced sentences. Mrs. Barnett lectured and wrote on the responsibilities of wives and mothers during the war, winning the affections of Washingtonians.

Not limiting her interest to the enlisted ranks, Mrs. Barnett insisted that the commandant's home be made available on weekends as a sort of meeting place and club for the young officers then training at Quantico. Perhaps this last burst of generosity came from her son, 2d Lt. Basil Gordon Jr., reportedly one of the most undisciplined young officers in the Corps. On one occasion, Gordon served a period of confinement to quarters and asked his mother to have him released, which she attempted to do. (The appeal did not work.) Whether this incident came to Daniels's attention is unknown. Other family matters frequently did, adding to the secretary's growing distrust of the commandant.[31]

In the summer of 1919, Daniels learned that a young Marine Corps second lieutenant had filed suit for divorce after a brief marriage and was unwilling to pay the alimony dictated by the courts. Confusing the matter further was the fact that the officer involved was Mrs. Barnett's nephew, Arthur I. Caperton, the son of an admiral. Daniels apparently refused to believe that Barnett could adjudicate the matter responsibly because of the family relationship and turned the file over to Lejeune, in confidence, to sort out. Meanwhile, Barnett ordered Caperton to begin making alimony payments through him, to ensure payment, and in the same letter counseled Caperton to "lay off women and rum for once and straighten up." The fact that Daniels turned to Lejeune to investigate such a minor matter reflected a growing lack of confidence on the part of Daniels in the commandant.[32]

In May 1918, Barnett's Republican supporters in the Senate attached a proviso onto the annual naval appropriations bill calling for the promotion of the commandant of the Marine Corps to lieutenant general and each of the principal staff officers at Headquarters to major general. Once again, news of the legislation reached the restless Smedley D. Butler in Haiti, and he lost no time in sharing his outrage with his father. Even before the bill reached the House, Congressman Butler learned of its offending aspects, and he instructed the assistant secretary of the navy on the "selfishness of these men who are endeavoring to take care of themselves only."[33]

More important, when Congressman Butler learned that Daniels knew nothing of the proposed promotion before the Senate Naval Affairs Committee passed it, he rose in the House to denounce the legislation. Pointing to the visitors gallery and Barnett, his wife, and the principal staff officers at Headquarters Marine Corps, he referred to the commandant as a "rocking chair warrior" and added, "When the rewards are handed out for service in the war, they will go to men that have earned them, and not to those who may perchance be favored by certain social surroundings in the Capital of the United States." Sensing blood, another representative jumped to his feet and suggested court-martial for Barnett because he had attempted to gain a promotion by going around Secretary Daniels. Later, Barnett insisted that the proposed legislation had not been his doing, but sufficient evidence existed that revealed a third star had been on his mind for some time, and he had used all of his influence with his Republican friends to gain the promotion. Sadly, this incident coupled with the difficulties over Barnett's reappointment months before fueled Daniels's convictions that Barnett had become just the sort of entrenched bureaucrat that he sought to remove when taking office in 1913.[34]

On 20 September 1919, Daniels summoned Lejeune to his office. After an exchange of pleasantries, the secretary informed him that he intended to remove Barnett from office; the new commandant of the Marine Corps would be John Archer Lejeune. In the conversation, which Daniels charged be kept confidential, he told his candidate of the circumstances surrounding Barnett's reappointment in 1918. At the time, Daniels had decided on Lejeune once he returned from France. The only matter left unsettled was the approval of the president. The secretary planned to gain that as soon as Wilson returned from his speaking tour in the western states. But the president's subsequent illness and debilitating stroke prevented any decision, and in mid-October, Daniels summoned Lejeune again and informed him that the plan to remove Barnett had gone awry. After the conference, Lejeune motored back to Quantico with Smedley D. Butler, who confided that Daniels had informed his father of the plan and gained his enthusiastic approval.[35]

The elder Butler's dislike for Barnett stemmed from his impatient son's continual criticism. Throughout Smedley D. Butler's career, his father's political position as a member of the House Naval Affairs Committee had propelled the younger Butler's career along. Every commandant from Heywood to Barnett had treated Smedley with kid gloves, and the young man never failed to use his father's influence to better his career. In 1915, he gained assignment to the Marine brigade in Haiti and then to the

Gendarmerie d'Haiti, a native constabulary directed by the U.S. Marine Corps. Although only a major at the time, Butler received a local promotion to Haitian major general and appeared satisfied. The ambitious and frenetic Butler had obtained the assignment because of his considerable political influence. In his next letter home, he commented, "Thank him [father] for his share in my fine vacation."[36]

But for some observers, Butler as an "instant" major general appeared a bit much. Butler's brigade commander, the veteran campaigner Waller, found his subordinate entirely too pompous with the temporary promotion and he confided his irritation in his next situation report to Headquarters Marine Corps: "He [Butler] asked me where he should sit if he came to my mess. I told him that if he came as a major of Marines he would take his place according to rank and if he came as a Haitian general, he would feed in the pantry."[37]

Butler's histrionics over Waller's failure to gain the commandancy in 1914 had run their course by the time he came to Haiti. His abrasive manner and obstructionism appeared likely to result in Adm. William B. Caperton (commanding the Naval Mission to Haiti) cabling for the recall of his enfant terrible marine as well as that of Waller. Probably speaking for Barnett, Lejeune cautioned Waller at one point to cease ruffling the Navy's feathers for fear that it might jeopardize his promotion to brigadier general. Although Butler's requests for assignment to a combat unit in France left with each mail boat from Haiti, Headquarters Marine Corps turned him down with equal regularity. The restless and ambitious Butler believed that his continual antagonism of Barnett and his coterie of "headquarters toadies" lay at the root of the negative endorsements to his requests. Butler's superiors, however, continued to believe that despite his eccentrics, he had performed in a superlative manner in Haiti.[38]

Privately, Barnett admitted that he had no positive feelings for the mercurial Butler and supposedly remarked that the latter had used all of his political pull to get the assignment in Haiti and could just remain there! Such rhetoric aside, the commandant of the Marine Corps could not shoulder off the political pressure of Smedley's father forever. In the spring of 1918, Daniels told him to issue orders transferring Butler to Quantico to command the 13th Regiment in preparation for deployment to France. According to one interested witness to the scenario, Congressman Butler intervened with Daniels to obtain the transfer for his son. Butler trained and sweated through the hot and humid Virginia summer of 1918. Before he left Quantico, Butler attached an important young man to his personal staff, 2d Lt. Jonathan Daniels, the son of the secretary of the navy.

Shortly after arriving in France, Butler wrote home excitedly of his friendship with young Daniels and his plans to make him his aide-de-camp coincident with his expected promotion to brigadier general. Lejeune had the same idea and apparently for the same reason. Before Butler could cement his plan, Daniels received orders transferring him to the 2d Division and assigning him to Lejeune's personal staff, precipitating a bitter letter to his important father: "Somebody is playing politics over here. . . . [Lejeune] had GHQ order me from here to the 2nd Division as his aide-de-camp. . . . I don't want to go and Gen. Butler does not want me to leave him for that job either. . . . When the time comes to pick the next MGC [major general commandant of the Marine Corps], you will see why this major general [Lejeune] is doing me this way."[39] But Butler's worries over the abrupt transfer of young Daniels paled next to the machinations of Headquarters, AEF, and General Pershing. They ordered the 5th Brigade broken up to be used for rear-area duties and to provide replacements. Butler then became the commander of the AEF's personnel processing center, Camp Pontanezen, on the Atlantic coast near Brest. He continued to blame Barnett for his failure to get to the front, and in one letter home referred to the commandant of the Marine Corps as a "weak old woman." Butler's hatred for the commandant grew as his morale plummeted: "I feel at the present time and have felt for the past five months that my days of soldiering are over. For over twenty years, I worked to fit myself to take part in this war which has just closed, and when the supreme test came my country did not want me."[40]

After returning to the United States in the late summer of 1919, Butler vented his frustrations to his father. Thus, when Daniels informed the elder Butler of his plan to oust Barnett, he found a ready ear. No political fool, Daniels knew the importance of enlisting the support of a powerful congressional Republican if he planned to remove an appointee of a Democratic administration who enjoyed substantial Republican patronage on Capitol Hill.

In May 1920, Daniels summoned Lejeune to his office and informed him that he had approved Barnett's request for a tour of inspection to the West Coast only to get him out of town and set the machinery in motion for Barnett's ouster. On 17 June 1920, Daniels met with the ailing president and gained his approval for the plan. At the meeting, the secretary apparently informed Wilson of Barnett's promise to step down. In his office two days later, Daniels dictated a letter of dismissal, then he packed for a business trip out of the capital, leaving instructions for a messenger to deliver the correspondence to the commandant of the Marine Corps.

Ill with influenza, Barnett received news of his removal from office at "Eighth and Eye" at approximately 1:30 p.m. on Friday, 20 June 1918. The messenger had instructions to remain for an answer: did Barnett wish to retire effective on the thirtieth as a major general or remain on active duty as a brigadier general? Stunned, Barnett summoned his wife and together they penned a response: the commandant elected to remain on active duty and requested promotion to major general (a vacancy existed because of Lejeune's elevation to the commandancy), assignment to Quantico, and extended leave because he had not used any since the beginning of the war.[41]

Daniels may have expected Barnett to bow out, but he underestimated his opponent and Mrs. Barnett's fury. That evening the Barnetts held a council of war in their home, and President Wilson's personal physician, Adm. Cary Grayson, attended. A close friend of the Barnetts, Grayson apparently witnessed Daniels's meeting with the chief executive on the previous Tuesday. From the Barnetts' view, Daniels's request to seek the commandant's removal reeked of duplicity. Grayson pledged the Barnetts to secrecy for his part in the revelation of what he had witnessed at the White House, and

Barnett took the name of his informant to the grave. However, Mrs. Barnett revealed Grayson's name, unwittingly, in the table of contents to her unpublished autobiography. By the end of the evening, both Barnett and his wife had decided to fight the order of dismissal.[42]

On Capitol Hill, Barnett turned to his considerable array of Republican friends to seek redress, and they turned out in force. Henry Cabot Lodge indicated his support, and even a Democrat on the Senate Naval Affairs Committee, Claude Swanson, tried to help. Barnett's old roommate from the class of 1881, Senator John Weeks, led the charge. The chief of naval operations, Adm. William S. Benson, while congratulating Lejeune on the one hand and offering advice to Barnett on the other, suggested that the ousted commandant call on Daniels to confront him. When Barnett had his painful audience with Daniels, the secretary refused to discuss the matter or answer Barnett's questions and dismissed the commandant curtly. Meanwhile, events moved closer to the change in office.

Barnett's letters of sympathy and concern came mostly from Republican friends, classmates from the class of 1881, and relatives. Lejeune's mail burst with warm notes applauding his appointment and were sent by every important senior officer in the Marine Corps and Navy except one: only Brig. Gen. Joseph H. Pendleton expressed sympathy for Barnett's plight and remained aloof from the controversy. Others, such as Charles H. Lyman and Ben H. Fuller, dashed off letters of condolence to Barnett then wrote to Lejeune to congratulate him. Meanwhile, the Butlers reveled in the event, and Congressman Butler's letter of congratulations to Lejeune exuded warmth and promised a smooth relationship with the House Naval Affairs Committee: "We are going to have a Marine Corps and it is [?] commanded by a real soldier. My I am pleased with your appointment & mean to assist you in any way to make your administration a great success. . . . The right thing has been done. Tell me always when I can serve you."[43]

Mrs. Barnett ordered a party for their close friends on their last day in the historic home of the commandants. All of the Barnetts' possessions had gone, and the furniture and trappings of the old mansion had been put away; the walls remained bare except for a photograph of Daniels inscribed affectionately to Barnett. None of the guests missed the point. The next day, Lejeune arrived at Headquarters at 11:30 a.m. for the change in command. Two versions of the strained event survive.

One aide-de-camp, Clifton B. Cates, recalled that Barnett asked Lejeune why as an old friend and fellow officer, he had failed to inform him of the plot. Lejeune only replied lamely that his hands were tied. The other aide-de-camp, Charles I. Murray, recalled that Barnett ordered Lejeune to stand at attention in front of his desk, refusing to give up the office until twelve o'clock sharp and accusing his successor of disloyalty. As the clock struck noon, Barnett ordered Murray to remove one star from each shoulder and he walked outside a defeated man. Across the street, Smedley Butler sat in a parked car to relish the scene, a bit of petulant behavior recorded by his own aide-de-camp.[44]

Meanwhile, Daniels refused Barnett's request for a promotion and assignment to Quantico and penned a negative endorsement to the ousted commandant's letter of grievance to the president. Senator Weeks gathered support for Barnett as best he could. Lejeune sought to end the controversy fairly and with dispatch by suggesting to Daniels that (1) Barnett be assigned to a new post as commander, Department of the Pacific in San Francisco (and far from his seat of political power) and (2) receive a promotion to major general. Righteous in his wrath, the secretary agreed to the transfer but not to the promotion.

Barnett took up his post in San Francisco alone; Mrs. Barnett would have none of his exile, and the general spent the next two years living at the Bohemian Club. When a new administration took office in 1921, Secretary of the Navy Edwin H. Denby approved Barnett's promotion to major general. In 1923, Barnett reached the mandatory retirement age of sixty-four and retired to the Barnetts' new home in Washington. In his final years, the former commandant worked on his memoirs, but in 1929 he suffered a debilitating stroke. His last year was spent mostly in the Naval Hospital, and his wife probably completed much of the autobiography for him. Kidney failure followed the stroke, and the twelfth commandant of the Marine Corps died on 30 April 1930. Mrs. Barnett survived her husband by twenty-nine years and continued to lash out at her enemies while attempting to salvage his reputation.[45]

Whatever charges the Barnetts levied against Daniels and the Butlers, no evidence exists to prove that the secretary and a cabal schemed to oust Barnett. Daniels apparently thought to get Lejeune into office while he had the power to do so. The secretary had envisioned Lejeune as commandant of the Marine Corps for four years, then succeeded by Butler; three successive Republican administrations put the plan asunder.[46]

George Barnett was the last of the traditional commandants. The world war years marked a watershed in the history of the Corps. By the end of the conflict, all of the Marine forces in the Western world had disappeared except for the British Royal Marines, and they lost their organic capabilities for combined arms operations. By insisting that the Corps take an active part with the AEF in France, Barnett proved that Marine Corps units could and should play a role in conflicts largely nonnaval in nature. Wisely choosing to keep his three personal staff officers in office, supporting them with promotions to flag rank when the opportunity presented itself, and otherwise allowing them to operate with reasonable independence, Barnett avoided the in-house controversies that befell many of his predecessors. His adept leadership of the Corps through the pitfalls of 1914–20, dominated by concerns over personnel matters and difficulties with a meddling secretary of the navy, made it easier for his successor to keep the U.S. Marine Corps healthy in the lean years of retrenchment to follow.

13
John A. Lejeune

1920–1929

LT. COL. MERRILL L. BARTLETT, USMC (RET.)

The officer whose name is synonymous with the Corps's highest post, John Archer Lejeune, traced his paternal ancestors to migrants from Brittany to Nova Scotia in the 1730s. When the Seven Years' War spread to North America, the Lejeunes fled France's bleak maritime colony to find refuge in Louisiana. The grandson of these determined pioneers, Ovide Lejeune, married the descendent of French Huguenots, Laura Archer Turpin, in 1859. Two children came of this union: a daughter, Augustine Lejeune, on 22 March 1860, and a son, John Archer Lejeune, on 19 January 1867. Ovide Lejeune prospered as a sugar planter, but the Civil War brought financial ruin.

Finding affordable schooling for their son remained a persistent problem for the Lejeunes. At first, they enrolled him in his Uncle James Archer's boarding school in nearby Nachez, Mississippi. The secluded, rural environment failed to provide the intellectual stimulus they thought he needed, so in September 1881, they enrolled him in the preparatory program at Louisiana State University. Continuing economic problems at home, however, forced Ovide Lejeune to seek a less costly alternative to his son's education. Attracted to a military career and taught to revere the leadership of the Confederacy, John Lejeune hoped for an appointment to the U.S. Military Academy. Although his senator did not have a vacancy for another cadet at West Point, he offered the young Louisianan an appointment to the U.S. Naval Academy. Lejeune left LSU in April 1884 to spend a month studying for the entrance tests awaiting him in Annapolis.[1]

Academic preparation at his Uncle Archer's school and at LSU resulted in Lejeune passing the entrance examinations. For the next four years, he maintained high marks in every area except deportment. Lejeune considered the numerous regulations petty and the Navy officers who insisted on enforcing them martinets. By the time the class of 1888 graduated, Lejeune stood thirteenth in a class numbering thirty-two naval

Maj. Gen. John A. Lejeune, thirteenth commandant.
U.S. Marine Corps Photo.

cadets, survivors of the original ninety. Although ranking second academically, his poor record of deportment lowered his overall standing.

The Annapolis experience failed to affect him, unlike many of the naval cadets of the era. Lejeune arrived at the Naval Academy a determined southern Democrat; four years' association with the sons of mostly northern Republicans failed to alter his political perspectives. Raised an Episcopalian, he found most of his classmates to be of the same faith. Although of an economic station considerably lower than most fellow naval cadets, his intellectual prowess more than made up for any shortcomings he felt. Knowing that his class standing offered little chance for a commission in a Navy with too few openings for the Annapolis graduates, Lejeune spent the following two years considering alternatives to a naval career.[2]

As a passed midshipman, Lejeune reported to the *Mohican* at Mare Island, California, in the fall of 1888. When diplomatic unrest in the South Pacific islands of Samoa attracted renewed U.S. interest, several of the officers and crew of the *Mohican* received orders to join the *Vandalia* for a speedy voyage to the troubled region. Shortly after Lejeune arrived in Apia in March 1889, a violent storm lashed the region. As fifteen-foot waves crashed over the ship, Lejeune manned his station on the forecastle and earned his first commendation in the naval service. The ordeal probably put the capstone on his decision for a naval career: for the remainder of his days as a midshipman, his record reflected little interest in seamanship. By this time, Lejeune was determined to obtain a commission in the Marine Corps.

Returning to Annapolis in the late spring of 1890, Lejeune and the class of 1888 crammed for the post-cruise examinations. When the results were announced, Lejeune had risen to a position of sixth among the class of 1888 for the purpose of service selection. Earlier, however, the chief of the Bureau of Engineering had requested a share of the graduates standing high in their class to fill the ranks of new assistant engineers. Because Lejeune alone among the top graduates failed to select Navy line or engineering, Academy officials attempted to force him into Navy blue. Outraged, the feisty Louisianan sought the assistance of the senator who appointed him.

A meeting with Senator Russell L. Gibson led to an introduction to Secretary of the Navy Benjamin F. Tracy. Navy officials found themselves outgunned and overruled, and Lejeune received a commission in the Marine Corps, effective 25 July 1890. The new second lieutenants reported to Maj. Robert W. Huntington at the Marine Barracks, New York, for indoctrination and instruction. Mostly, they had themselves fitted for uniforms and learned the duties of a guard officer by inspecting the sentries twice during the hours of darkness.

Lejeune believed that he had made a wise choice for a career because Marine Corps second lieutenants earned considerably more money than their counterparts in the Navy. An assistant engineer earned seventeen hundred dollars a year, and an ensign received one thousand; while ashore waiting for a vacancy in a ship or on leave, the ensign's pay dropped to eight hundred dollars and the assistant engineer's to fourteen hundred dollars. In contrast, a second lieutenant's salary remained fixed at fourteen hundred dollars per annum whether at sea, in the field, or at a barracks.[3]

When asked for choice of duty for his next assignment, Lejeune requested the barracks in Philadelphia or Washington. Ignoring his wishes, the commandant selected the small barracks in Portsmouth, Virginia. Reporting on board on 3 November 1890, Lejeune found the routine more boring than demanding. He inspected sentries as the guard officer and usually had the duty one day out of three: when the barracks suffered a shortage of junior officers, he and another lieutenant carried the load by taking the duty every other day. The only respite from the dismal routine was the weekly dances in one of the receiving ships in Norfolk Harbor. At one such social gathering, he met Ellie Harrison Murdaugh, the stunning daughter of a Portsmouth judge. Smitten, he pledged his troth just as the colonel commandant issued him orders to sea.

For the first decade of his career, Lejeune served in assignments typical for the nineteenth-century Marine officer. A three-year stint in the *Bennington* (1 October 1891–28 July 1893) preceded another barracks tour in the Tidewater area, this time at the larger barracks in Norfolk. While stationed there, he renewed his courtship of Ellie Murdaugh and married her on 23 October 1895. From 2 August 1897 until 17 February 1899, Lejeune commanded the marines in the *Cincinnati.* When the ship went into the yards for overhaul following the Spanish-American War, he received orders to the battleship *Massachusetts.* The short, satisfactory conflict with Spain came and went with Lejeune's involvement limited to duty at sea in the Caribbean and a brief, uneventful foray ashore in Puerto Rico.[4]

Promoted to captain on 3 March 1899, Lejeune received orders to command the Marine Corps recruiting station in Boston that summer. In the fall, he assumed command of the small barracks in Pensacola. Expecting orders to join a battalion forming for duty in the Philippines, a case of appendicitis resulted in hospitalization in Baltimore, followed by a new assignment as the officer in charge, Marine Corps Recruiting Station, New York.

In the summer of 1903, six months after being promoted to major, Lejeune assumed command of the battalion on the transport *Panther.* That fall, Lejeune and his marines transferred to the *Dixie* and steamed to the Caribbean. When the United States became embroiled in the affairs of Panama in an attempt to gain a cross-isthmus canal, Lejeune landed with his battalion to enforce President Theodore Roosevelt's policy that Panama remain independent from Colombia. On the last day of 1904, the troops returned home. He commanded the Washington Barracks for his next tour, punctuated by a short return to Panama from May to July 1906. From April 1907 until May 1909, Lejeune served overseas in the Philippines, commanding the battalion at Cavite. Unlike most Marine Corps officers of his year, Lejeune chose to bring his family with him to the inhospitable tropical environment. A devoted husband and father, he could not bring himself to accept separation from his wife and three daughters: "I shrink from the thought of two and one-half years out there alone."[5]

In conferences with Maj. Gen. Cmdt. George F. Elliott over his next assignment, Lejeune expected to receive orders as commander of a small barracks or as executive officer at a larger post. Instead, Elliott suggested assignment as a student at the Army War College. Returning to the classroom for the first time since leaving Annapolis twenty years before, Lejeune earned a reputation as a bright and articulate scholar. Many of his classmates and instructors would be the Army's senior officers in the world war to follow. The diligent application to his studies resulted in a glowing letter of commendation from the college president.[6]

In November 1910, Lejeune assumed command of the New York Barracks. The largest barracks in the Corps, the post had earned the undesirable record of also having the largest desertion rate. Its new commander brought the scandalous absentee rate down. During the four years he served there, Lejeune deployed once with a regiment to Cuba. Another expedition to the Caribbean followed, this time with an entire brigade to test the concept of the Advanced Base Force. With Col. George Barnett's elevation to the commandancy following the second deployment, Lejeune received a summons to become the assistant to the commandant of the Marine Corps. Before he could take up his new post, however, diplomatic estrangement with Mexico resulted in a significant deployment of naval forces to Veracruz. From 22 April until 15 November 1914, Lejeune commanded a regiment in the naval expeditionary force ashore. In January 1915, he took up his post as Assistant to the commandant, and appeared content to serve at Headquarters Marine Corps (HQMC). The entrance of the United States in World War I, however, caused him to request an immediate posting to the American Expeditionary Forces (AEF) in France.

Barnett appreciated the yeoman service Lejeune performed at Headquarters and did not relish the thought of losing him to Pershing's command. At one point, the commandant admonished his subordinate for the repeated requests for a transfer to France by implying that further combat or expeditionary duty was unnecessary. Barnett considered Lejeune his logical successor in the Corps's highest post. Lejeune persisted, however, and in the fall of 1917 received orders transferring him to Quantico. He had been promoted to brigadier general the previous summer.[7]

Although the return of Brig. Gen. Charles A. Doyen from France indicated a vacancy for a Marine Corps general officer, the Headquarters of the AEF said that no replacement was requested. Lejeune opted to take his chances for an assignment. He reported to Pershing's headquarters on 19 June 1918 and was sent on a short tour of orientation and observation with the 35th Division. On 5 July, he received orders to command the 64th Brigade of that division. But after only ten days in his new assignment, the promotion of James G. Harbord to major general and assignment to command the 2d Division made command of the 4th Brigade (Marine) available. Lejeune took command of his fellow marines on 15 July 1918.

Before the month was out, however, Pershing had convinced Harbord to accept command of the muddled Services-of-Supply. As the senior brigadier general in the division, Lejeune assumed command pending assignment of a replacement for Harbord. Personnel legislation passed during World War I authorized an additional major general for the Corps. With the enthusiastic support of Barnett, Congressman Thomas S. Butler, and Secretary of the Navy Josephus Daniels, Lejeune took the new position on 31 July 1918. Pershing left him in command of the 2d Division.[8]

Four days before Lejeune's promotion, Pershing ordered the formation of the First American Army and directed it to be operational by 10 August 1918. The 2d Division received assignment to I Corps, commanded by Lejeune's Army War College classmate, Maj. Gen. Hunter Liggett. On 1 August 1918, Lejeune supervised the movement of his division to Pônt-a-Mousson in the valley of the Moselle for an intense period of training with the French Army. From 12 September until the night of 15–16 September, the division participated in the first major offensive for the American Army, the attack to take the St. Mihiel salient.

Territory that had been seized by the attacking Germans in 1914, the salient threatened the flanks of the French Army, and prevented future offensive action in the Loraine and Meuse-Argonne. The German high command had already decided to abandon the territory before the offensive, and Lejeune's soldiers and marines had little difficulty taking the disputed terrain. Prisoners and supplies lined the roads to the rear after the brief offensive. A disgruntled German major, marching to the rear with a column of prisoners of war, underscored the state of the enemy forces by the fall of 1918: "These men are all young and fresh and vigorous. . . . We can't do it, but I wish I had had a 1914 battalion behind me. You wouldn't have had such a pleasant afternoon."[9]

When attacking French forces failed in repeated attempts to seize the heights of Mont Blanc, the Allied high command appealed to Pershing for assistance. Reluctantly, Headquarters, AEF released the 2d Division to the Fourth French Army. Gen. André Gouraud then assigned Lejeune's command to the XXI Corps. In a daring frontal attack using both of his infantry brigades, Lejeune took the heights. Although facing a considerable array of German forces holding the disputed terrain, the starch had left most of the enemy force. On the eve of the Mont Blanc offensive, a German general reported to his higher headquarters: "I can no longer guarantee that during a surprise attack, they [200th Division] will continue to hold their position."[10] Lejeune's command captured 48 officers and 1,915 enlisted Germans as they stormed over the top of the massif. In October, control of his sector passed to the 36th Division, and Lejeune returned to the First Army carrying the praises of his French superiors.

On 25 October 1918, operational control of the 2d Division passed to the U.S. V Corps. Its commanding general, Maj. Gen. Charles P. Summerall, displayed a threatening style of leadership which troubled Lejeune. Lejeune endured a difficult period under Summerall, who more than once reminded him that officers who failed to measure up would be relieved! As the Allies forced themselves through the weakened German lines during the Meuse-Argonne offensive, Lejeune performed to the satisfaction of the exacting Summerall and Pershing. Although all of his Army superiors heaped praise on him in the form of glowing fitness reports, letters of commendation and praise, and decorations, privately some senior army officers criticized his performance.

Even before the cease-fire on 11 November, Pershing had ordered his senior commanders to prepare candid and confidential fitness reports on the major generals. Lejeune's appraisal at the hands of Hunter Liggett contained only praise, but Summerall's report suggested shortcomings in his professional character. Lejeune's former corps commander found his subordinate to be argumentative; worse, he often decided for himself when a mission had been completed. Lejeune's regular fitness reports, written by Liggett and Summerall, contain only positive markings and comments. A fitness report written by Maj. Gen. John L. Hines, while not extant, contained sufficient unfavorable material to cause Lejeune to request its removal from his Officer Qualification Record.[11] Although Lejeune never served under Lt. Gen. Robert E. Lee Bullard, Bullard had his own opinion and reservations about Lejeune, which he shared in an essay published after the war: "Through three changes of commands and three battles [2d Division], [Preston] Brown [chief of staff] stood forth as the striking, dominant personality of the division."[12]

Whatever criticism his seniors might have had for Lejeune, the 2d Division earned an impressive record during the conflict. During the world war, the 2d Division suffered more than twenty-four thousand casualties, 10 percent of the total suffered by the entire AEF. Lejeune's command captured more than fourteen thousand German prisoners and an impressive array of ordnance and supplies. The 2d Division advanced farther than any division in the AEF—sixty kilometers; its members earned 7 Medals of Honor, 675 Distinguished Service Crosses, 10 Distinguished Service Medals, 6 Belgian Crosses, 17 Legions of Honor, 42 Medals Militaire, and 2,740 croix de guerre. To his Sampson Medal, Marine Corps Expeditionary Medal (with three stars), and Mexican Service Medal, Lejeune added the Distinguished Service Medal (Army), World War Victory Medal (with clasps for St. Mihiel, Meuse-Argonne, and Defensive Sector), Legion d'Honneur (commander), and croix de guerre (Bronze Palm).[13]

Although Lejeune and his division hoped for a train trip to an embarkation port and transport home, Pershing and his staff selected the 2d Division as part of the American Army of Occupation in Germany. After only five days of rest, Lejeune and his division began a march through Belgium and Luxembourg, crossing into Germany on 13 December 1918. Until the following July, it occupied billets along the Rhine before returning home. After a triumphant march through the streets of New York City, the doughboys and leathernecks returned to their respective camps. Lejeune took up his old command at Quantico.

Although Lejeune expected to be the next commandant, Secretary Daniels's plan to oust the incumbent before his second term of office had elapsed bothered Lejeune. The duplicitous nature of the plan ran against his personal honor and integrity. His suggestion of a promotion to assuage Barnett's ego was a wise one, and it served to put most of the rancor to rest. Even though the Senate set aside his nomination because of the election of Warren G. Harding in November 1920, Lejeune took the reins of the Corps as firmly as if he intended to remain commandant.[14]

The organization of HQMC received Lejeune's attention immediately, and he affected changes that altered the traditional arrangement and functioning of the Corps's highest post. The act of 11 July 1798 authorized additional officers to assist the commandant. The act of 3 March 1903 increased the numbers of assistants, while increasing the ranks of some of them. The passage of significant personnel increases during the World War I years resulted in the promotion of the commandant's three principal assistants—adjutant and inspector, quartermaster, and paymaster—to brigadier general. Not surprisingly, by the time the thirteenth commandant entered office, the incumbents on the staff had established their own fiefdoms.

Lejeune moved immediately to reorganize his Headquarters staff and make it more responsive to the commandant. While serving as the assistant to the commandant, he had urged Barnett to form a Planning Section. On 1 December 1920, Lejeune ordered the expansion of the Planning Section into the Division of Operations and Training. The new organization had responsibility for operations, training, military education, intelligence, and aviation. Significantly, the new director of the Division of Operations and Training, Lt. Col. Robert H. Dunlap, reported directly to the commandant via his assistant. Three new sections appeared at HQMC together with the Division of Operations and Training: Personnel, Education, and Recruiting. Their heads also reported directly to the commandant via his assistant. Clearly, Lejeune had moved to eclipse the power of the traditional Headquarters staff, especially the adjutant and inspector. Wendell C. Neville became assistant to the commandant, while Lemuel C. Shepherd Jr. and John Craige served Lejeune as aides-de-camp.[15]

Lejeune envisioned the Division of Operations and Training as the springboard for Marine Corps doctrine and planning. To it, he brought a bright and articulate officer, Lt. Col. Earl "Pete" Ellis, early in 1921. The mercurial Ellis had performed to Lejeune's satisfaction during the world war and returned home wearing the Navy Cross earned for meritorious service as the adjutant of the 4th Brigade (Marine), AEF. With Lejeune's encouragement, Ellis began a monumental and far-reaching study of the potential for amphibious operations in the Central Pacific in the event of an implementation of War Plan Orange. He foresaw the requirement to seize the mandated islands in the region given to the Japanese after the war with the Marine Corps providing the amphibious forces for the naval campaign.

Ellis's study, "Advanced Base Operations in Micronesia, 1921," appeared on Lejeune's desk coincident with a strange request from its author. Ellis asked for permission to visit the Central Pacific to see for himself what fortifications the Japanese had erected in the islands. Lejeune gave his approval to the venture, even accepting Ellis's undated letter of resignation and assisting his subordinate in the establishment of a covert identity. Traveling to Japan and then taking passage to the Central Pacific, Ellis continued his frequent bouts with the bottle. His presence in the Caroline Islands became known quickly to both Japanese and U.S. Navy authorities, and he apparently died of disease on 12 May 1923. Lejeune's prompt and forthright admission to having knowledge of Ellis's ill-conceived mission prevented the affair from becoming a cause célèbre.[16]

From his desk in Washington, the thirteenth commandant encountered an intense period of retrenchment as severe as that facing the Corps following the Civil War. Antiwar apathy resulted in the citizenry demanding less involvement in overseas affairs and, obviously, fewer soldiers, sailors, and marines. Before Lejeune had spent a year in office, he saw his beloved Corps reduced to fewer than twenty-one thousand men. To his dismay, traditional leatherneck commitments with the fleet and in overseas stations remained the same. The potential for overseas deployment of an amphibious force remained.

With the aid of the indefatigable Brig. Gen. Smedley D. Butler, Lejeune kept Marine Corps prowess and élan prominent in the eye of the public. Quantico became the showplace of the Corps in a series of events designed to please the citizenry and Congress. Renewed emphasis on marksmanship appeared—a Corps tradition dating from the age of sail—and leatherneck sharpshooters dominated the annual interservice matches during Lejeune's commandancy. More colorful and entertaining, Quantico's athletic teams, with the base band thundering in the background and Butler acting as head cheerleader, competed successfully against college teams in baseball and football.

Between Butler and Lejeune, an even more spectacular display of leatherneck prowess emerged. Beginning in the fall of 1921, the Quantico-based East Coast Expeditionary Brigade participated in reenactments of Civil War battles. The first such display took place near Chancellorsville, the site of the Battle of the Wilderness. Butler's marines marched along the Washington to Richmond highway in a column five miles long. While Butler considered the maneuvers a combination of fun-filled physical fitness training and excellent public relations, Lejeune hoped to demonstrate that tactics in modern warfare had changed considerably due to technology and modern weaponry. The Quantico marines used the weapons and equipment of the 1920s but carried out the scenario of 1864. Large crowds of spectators, including prominent politicians, attended the events, giving them a gala, festive air. Following the success of 1921, the reenactments continued: Gettysburg (1922), New Market (1923), and Antietam (1924).

During the same years, the role of the Marines in guarding the U.S. mail provided the capstone to claims of being a "corps d'elite." Alarmed over the growing number of robberies of railway mail cars, Postmaster General Will H. Hays requested assistance in the form of federal troops. President Harding responded immediately by directing Secretary of the Navy Edwin H. Denby to employ the Marines. On 8 November 1921, the initial contingent of leathernecks, fifty-three officers and twenty-two hundred enlisted men, began their new duties. Denby sent them off with stirring orders: "If attacked, shoot, and shoot to kill."[17] As expected, the sight of heavily armed marines riding the rail cars put an immediate damper on attempted thievery.

While the Quantico marines in their public relations efforts and their comrades riding shotgun on railway mail cars served to keep the public's acclaim and esteem for their leathernecks high, Lejeune knew that ultimately he answered to a miserly Congress. Fiscal restraint dominated hearings of both the House and Senate Naval Affairs Committees. On 21 January 1921, he told the House Naval Affairs Committee that his first step as commandant would be to reduce expenses in fiscal year 1921 by 40 percent, and in fiscal year 1922 by 50 percent. While Lejeune's promise suggested catastrophic reductions, he knew the lower numbers could be achieved by simply closing most of the recruiting stations. Given the sharply reduced personnel strength mandated earlier, he ordered a halt to all new enlistments; only requests for reenlistments would be honored.

Given Congressman Butler's admiration of Lejeune, the thirteenth commandant experienced little difficulty with the House committee. No such easy sailing, however, occurred in the Senate Naval Affairs Committee. Despite his frugal management policies, members of the Senate committee often took turns sniping at Lejeune over matters of minor detail, usually involving personnel. During one exasperating period of testimony, Lejeune reminded the committee members of an increasing tendency to employ naval landing parties as an international police force. Unmoved, the Senate committee refused to pass on Lejeune's plea for an increase in numbers.

To both officers and enlisted men, Lejeune maintained an image of uncompromising professionalism. An inspiring and stimulating speaker, he spoke without notes. On 12 January 1922, he addressed the officers at Quantico to explain the goals of his administration. Trumpeting his program—"in time of peace, prepare for war"—Lejeune admonished his audience to assist in his goals. In an emotional plea, Lejeune referred to the Corps's priceless heritage and reminded his listeners that it had come to them from the heroic dead. In closing his address, the commandant offered advice on leadership, a favorite theme: "Discipline must be maintained; military punctilio observed; but there is also the obligation to deal justly, fairly, kindly, and honorably with those who are under our command; and to serve loyally and faithfully those who command us. This obligation is mutual."[18]

Most of Lejeune's commandancy under President Harding focused on internal changes and reforms. Because of America's reluctance to become involved in world affairs, only the Corps's traditional commitments remained. During the first year of his tenure, Lejeune ordered Neville to chair a board to examine uniform requirements and recommend changes if needed. Reporting on 16 September 1921, the ad hoc group made numerous recommendations. The sharp-eyed and tradition-minded commandant, however, turned down most of the proposals before sending the list on to Secretary Denby. Lejeune agreed to retain the overcoat but eliminated the old officer's special social uniform. Mess jackets returned, but the commandant balked at eliminating the differing insignia for line and staff officers, and he refused to do away with the traditional dress blue uniform. Such minor administrative matters proved to be light tasks for the thirteenth commandant, but the search for an efficient and prudent system of officer promotion and retention appeared bothersome and elusive.[19]

In April 1917, only 341 officers wore forest green; by the end of the war, their ranks had increased to over 2,400. To fill the vacancies, HQMC turned to meritorious noncommissioned officers and applicants attending colleges and universities. Many of these temporary and reserve officers sought to remain in uniform. First Barnett and then Lejeune faced the unpleasant task of deciding who should remain while mustering others out of uniform.

A board convened during the closing weeks of Barnett's commandancy stunned the officer ranks by "plucking" or reducing in rank many officers with distinguished combat records. Disappointed observers charged that the board had concentrated too heavily on education and pedigrees. Sensing a sharp division among his officers, Lejeune ordered a new board. Chaired by Neville, the new group included Butler and the former commanding officer of the 6th Marines in France, Col. Harry Lee. When this board reported out in May 1921, its recommendations surprised few observers: officers who had demonstrated courage and decisiveness under fire received preference for retention and promotion.

While the Russell board, named after its chairman, Col. John H. Russell, appeared to have overcompensated in favor of gentlemanly and educational qualities, the Neville board leaned in another direction to favor officers with combat decorations. Many of the temporary and reserve officers who received the nod from the latter possessed limited education or were simply too old and lacked the potential for professional growth. The failure of both boards underscored the inadequacies of the officer promotion system, a problem that perplexed Lejeune in all his years at the helm of the Corps.[20]

Lejeune sought to replace the Corps's antiquated custom of promotion by seniority with a selection system. He proposed a regimen of examining boards and presented his plan first to the House Naval Affairs Committee. As expected, Lejeune's plan won speedy approval because of the strong endorsement of Congressman Butler. The commandant did not foresee any wholesale pruning of the officer ranks but merely a thinning out of the aged and redundant: "There is a class of officer of mediocre practical ability who, by reason of some limitation of character or accomplishment, is by lack of marked efficiency in the performance of the more exacting duties, are usually continued in the performance of the minor duties, in which they are able to establish fair records."[21]

Lejeune hoped to force out those officers who had failed selection for at least five years, or when they became too old to lead troops on maneuvers or into combat. Legislation affecting Marine Corps officer promotions had remained essentially unchanged since 1892, allowing HQMC only the prerogative to purge the ranks of the professionally and physically unqualified. Lejeune thought that colonels over age fifty-six and lieutenant colonels reaching age fifty should be retired, while officers in the ranks of lieutenant through major should not be retained beyond their forty-fifth birthday.

Lejeune's proposed legislation passed quickly through the House Naval Affairs Committee but failed to survive senatorial scrutiny. In sharp questioning, one Senator after another wondered just how such a system could remain equitable. Lejeune attempted to mollify his skeptical audience by promising to retain any officer who had completed ten or more years of service until he would be eligible for retirement benefits. The commandant reminded detractors, only the Marine Corps remained tied to an inefficient seniority system. Nevertheless, his critics seemed convinced that the proposed plan invited a callous misuse of administrative power.[22]

Although no evidence of his wrongdoing could be found during the scandals of the Harding administration, Denby submitted his letter of resignation in early 1923. Following Harding's death that summer, President Calvin Coolidge selected Curtis D. Wilbur, a California jurist, to be secretary of the navy. Lejeune welcomed his former classmate from the Naval Academy class of 1888. Privately, they addressed each other by their nicknames from plebe year at Annapolis: "Gabe" and "Magic."[23]

Neither Wilbur nor Denby before him shared Daniels's distrust of bureaucrats in uniform, leaving Lejeune to manage the affairs of the Marine Corps without interference. Daniels had assigned his assistant secretary of the navy, Franklin D. Roosevelt, almost full-time duties overseeing leatherneck affairs. Denby's assistant, Theodore Roosevelt Jr., spent his tenure in office monitoring the progress of the Washington Naval Arms Limitation Conference, leaving him little opportunity or inclination to tamper with the Corps. When a Roosevelt cousin, Douglas Robinson, became the assistant secretary, Wilbur assigned him general duties throughout the Department of the Navy, leaving Lejeune and his staff unfettered by civilian interference.

The restless and mercurial Butler could prove to be irksome at times to Lejeune. A plea from the mayor of Philadelphia to President Coolidge for the loan of a general officer to help rid the city of vice and corruption attracted the immediate attention of the Corps's enfant terrible. Lejeune warmed to the proposal to send Butler, already bored with Quantico, off to Philadelphia to fight demon rum and municipal corruption.[24]

The commandant had more important worries than Butler's frustrated ambitions. Although hoping to redirect the focus of HQMC toward operations planning, personnel and fiscal matters dominated his commandancy just as they had those of his predecessors. In 1920, he counted 17,047 marines in uniform; by 1926, the number had increased only slightly to 19,153.

The parsimonious annual appropriations, however, did allow Lejeune to raise standards. In late 1923, Lejeune ordered the minimum height of recruits raised to sixty-five inches. The following spring, he decreed that only native-born Americans or naturalized citizens could enlist. On 1 April 1924, he ordered the minimum enlistment raised from three to four years. Despite the surplus of young men available for service in uniform, Lejeune noted that in 1923, 1,595 of his marines had deserted; 269 had been captured and sentenced to long terms of confinement.

Lejeune's term of office, his appointment by Denby and Harding, came to an end in 1925. Although the progressive Daniels had advocated single four-year terms of office for the commandant of the Marine Corps and Navy Bureau chiefs, the edict had disappeared into the dustbin of history. Congressman Butler led Lejeune's reconfirmation through the House Naval Affair Committee swiftly and without a dissenting vote, sending it on to Wilbur claiming that the committee's "action [was] largely induced because of [Lejeune's] conspicuous service rendered this country during the great war."[25]

Perhaps rejuvenated by such a vote of confidence, Lejeune sought legislation permitting an increase in the number of major generals. In testimony before the House Naval Affairs Committee, he noted that the Army had one officer of that rank for every thirty-two hundred soldiers while the Navy counted one rear admiral per every three thousand sailors. Lejeune asked only for one major general for each thirty-five hundred marines. As the measure passed through Congress, idle gossip over the possible recipients of the promotions began to trouble Lejeune. In letters of caution to every command, he admonished his senior officers to stop the irresponsible chatter. Undaunted, the restless Butler informed Lejeune that if his chances for another star seemed unlikely, then he would not urge his father to support the legislation![26]

Concern over personnel matters in 1926 prompted Lejeune to lecture the House committee rather sternly. He reminded it of a predilection to use the Marines for almost any overseas commitment, without a concomitant increase in numbers. Too many tasks and too few leathernecks to assign to them made Lejeune fear for the morale of his Corps, a concern he shared with Wilbur: "To reduce the Corps would be highly detrimental to its morale and efficiency. All marines know that the Corps is now too small and consequently overworked, and they would feel that any further reduction of its strength was an indication that those in authority did not regard very highly its value to the nation."[27]

In testimony before the Senate Naval Affairs Committee on 10 January 1927, Lejeune continued his plea for a restored or increased budget. One senator wondered why just marines and not soldiers seemed to be sent off on these expeditionary duties. The commandant then took the opportunity to remind the senators of the conventional wisdom accepted at the time, that the employment of naval forces amounted to nothing more than ordering in a fire or police department. Most people did not object, especially in the underdeveloped countries, but to send in soldiers made it an act of war.[28]

As the internal political situations in the Dominican Republic and Haiti stabilized to some degree, the United States sought a reasonable date for a mutually satisfactory exit. Lejeune's marines left Santo Domingo in September 1924 and seemed likely to depart Haiti before the end of the decade. But across the Pacific, traditional commitments continued. A sizable Marine force remained in the Philippines to provide security for naval bases there, and to maintain an expeditionary force in support of the Asiatic Fleet. Periodic domestic turmoil in China made the employment of landing parties composed of leathernecks and bluejackets more than a remote possibility. Although heading an elite fighting force, Lejeune hoped that none of his marines would receive the call. Certainly no pacifist, he did not want to send young men to fight and die: "I wish to impress on all who hear me that of us who have seen war close up and who know its horrors, carry a bitter hatred of it in our hearts. We love peace and we yearn for its continuance, but nevertheless while working and praying for peace, it is our highest duty to be ready to protect and to defend our country should the dread calamity of war once again burst upon us."[29]

Lejeune's rhetoric, perhaps emotional and a bit bombastic, underscores the emphasis on "readiness" that dominated his commandancy. He faced considerable opposition. Caught up in the spirit of arms limitations during the 1920s, many politicians came to believe that America's small amphibious force should be reduced as well. Lejeune had Wilbur's ear on the subject, and the secretary wrote to President Coolidge citing the areas of the world that could conceivably require the presence of American naval landing parties in the near future: Cuba, Mexico, Nicaragua, Dominican Republic, and China. Earlier, Assistant Secretary of the Navy Theodore Roosevelt Jr. vented his frustration in a pithy diary entry: "The [House Naval Affairs Committee] is perfectly willing to grant us a good Navy, but is not willing to stand against the Appropriations Committee. In other words, they mean well weakly."[30]

By 1929, Lejeune could boast triumphantly that he had completed the orderly separation of administrative and operational functions at Headquarters Marine Corps. As a seemingly unimportant aside to the reorganization, leatherneck aviation had grown considerably. In 1920, only one hundred officers and barely one thousand enlisted served in aviation duties. Under Lejeune's commandancy, the Aviation Section of the Division of Operations and Training coordinated Marine Corps aviation requirements with the Navy's director of aviation. By 1922, Quantico housed the First Aviation Group, a force of twenty-five aircraft organized into five squadrons. Two years later, Lejeune ordered the establishment of a second aviation group at San Diego.

Whether to fly the planes or to lead marines on the ground, Lejeune sought the highest quality officers. He continued to express belief that the best officers came from his alma mater. When Navy officials claimed most graduates of the Naval Academy, he turned to other sources. Meritorious noncommissioned officers from the ranks continued to have the opportunity to become officers. Beginning in 1925, HQMC accepted applications from distinguished military graduates of the nation's Army Reserve Officers Training Corps (ROTC). In the first year of the program, eighty-six young men from civilian colleges and universities applied; Lejeune and his staff selected only twenty to join the sixteen Naval Academy graduates entering the Corps as second lieutenants that year.[31]

Once in uniform, Lejeune believed strongly that his officers be trained well. Early in his commandancy, he ordered the establishment of a Basic School for new officers at Quantico. Courses for company and field grade officers followed. More senior officers attended either the Army or Navy War Colleges. More and more promising officers attended the latter, as Lejeune sought to correct shortcomings observed during the amphibious portions of the fleet exercises of the 1920s.

In 1922, the East Coast Expeditionary Brigade joined with the U.S. Fleet for its annual maneuvers, held in the Caribbean in the waters off Puerto Rico and Guantánamo. Marines wrestled huge naval guns ashore and prepared emplacements to repel an imaginary invader much like their predecessors had in the scenario of 1913–14 involving the Advanced Base Force.

A year later, however, Brig. Gen. Eli K. Cole led the Marines in the first attempt at a modern amphibious assault on the island of Culebra. From all accounts, the exercise underscored major difficulties: boats landed on the wrong beaches, landing craft became lost in the surf, sailors and marines loaded boats and landing craft poorly, and the Navy failed to provide adequate naval gunfire support. Cole's only positive report came with news that the Navy had begun to undertake serious development of a suitable landing craft.

Two years later in April 1925, a Marine force simulated a much larger landing force in the joint Army-Navy maneuvers in Hawaii. This time, students and staff from the field grade course at Quantico participated as an ad hoc staff. Luminaries like Cole and

Dion Williams carried Lejeune's blessing and encouragement in such endeavors. Other faithful subordinates, like Butler, believed that the Corps had no future as the amphibious army of the Navy and thought amphibious warfare to be an anachronism left over from the Age of Sail.[32]

Lejeune and his staff participated in conferences with the General Board of the Navy, but the records of that group for the 1920s reveal scant concern for amphibious warfare. The commandant of the Marine Corps did not sit on the Joint Army-Navy Board, although a Corps officer served on its planning staff. Nevertheless, Lejeune's commanding influence contributed to the board's codification of the Corps's roles and missions in 1926: to provide and maintain forces "for land operations in support of the fleet for the initial seizure and defense of advanced bases; and for such limited auxiliary land operations as are essential to the prosecution of a naval campaign . . . as an adjunct of the Army . . . to perform such duties on land as the President may direct."[33] Predictably, just a year later, the requirement for another traditional naval landing expedition materialized.

Although President Coolidge resisted pressures from American commercial firms and congressional critics to intervene directly in the civil war in Nicaragua, the murder of a U.S. businessman and the plunder of American holdings in late 1926 forced him to act. In early 1927, Lejeune's marines formed the major part of a landing force streaming ashore in hopes of bringing stability to the troubled Central American nation. Although desperately short of marines, Lejeune's staff managed to find approximately two thousand men to reform the 5th Marine Regiment. Choosing its commander carefully, Lejeune selected Brig. Gen. Logan Feland, a trusted and capable subordinate.

Shortly after meeting this new commitment, Lejeune faced a new requirement for the Corps halfway around the world. Domestic violence in China resulted in a plea from the considerable American population residing there for protection under the U.S. flag. On 25 January 1927, President Coolidge approved the assembling of the 4th Marine Regiment at San Diego. On 3 February, the force sailed for China. Three weeks later, Brig. Gen. Smedley D. Butler, a brigade headquarters, and additional marines followed. The deployment further depleted Lejeune's diminishing manpower assets. Earlier, a second rash of railway mailcar robberies resulted in another requirement for the Marines to guard the U.S. mail.

As Lejeune approached the end of his second term in the Corps's highest post (5 March 1929), he had serious misgivings about the state of his Marine Corps. Continued reductions in manpower levels despite increasing commitments plagued him. Although the House Naval Affairs Committee supported his plea for legislation authorizing officer promotion and retention by the action of selection boards, the Senate committee continued to oppose the concept. Finally, domestic political considerations, including the loss of two significant supporters, forced him to a decision.

On 26 May 1928, Congressman Thomas S. Butler died, taking with him Lejeune's influence with the House Naval Affairs Committee. The elder Butler had supported Lejeune for over a decade; just a month before his death, the feisty Quaker from Pennsylvania's Eighth Congressional District sought to perform one last favor for Lejeune. On 27 April 1928, Butler sent House Resolution 13341 to the secretary of the navy. The proposed legislation called for the promotion of the commandant of the Marine Corps to the rank of lieutenant general. But it made little sense, given the small size of the Corps. Wilbur condemned the proposal immediately, providing a death knell by reminding Butler and his colleagues that an increase in rank for Lejeune meant an increase in pay; no means of appropriation had been included in the legislative bill. Wisely, Lejeune remained distant from the maneuvering, recalling all too well the bickering over Barnett's maladroit attempt to gain a similar promotion a decade before.[34]

On the heels of Butler's death, Herbert C. Hoover took the White House in the election of 1928. The arrival of yet another Republican bothered Lejeune, a lifelong Democrat and not the least hesitant to display his political colors. Worse, Hoover indicated no willingness to retain Wilbur as secretary of the navy. Failure to gain congressional approval for changing the Corps's archaic system of officer promotion and retention added to his frustration: "The lack of promotion tends to deaden ambition; and excessive age in grades lessens efficiency, especially in junior grades . . . no opportunity is given to the exception that is not given to the ordinary."[35]

Stunning most friends and observers of Washington naval politics, Lejeune announced on 7 February 1929 that he intended to step down on 5 March, the day before Hoover's inauguration. A day after the announcement, the Department of the Navy released a bulletin to the press indicating that Hoover had approved the nomination of Neville to succeed Lejeune. A handful of Smedley D. Butler's supporters cried foul, but the endorsement of Lejeune and the conspicuous silence of former secretary of the navy Daniels eased the transition. Nevertheless, in a letter written years later to President Franklin D. Roosevelt, the wily former secretary indicated that for some reason he expected Butler to succeed Lejeune.[36]

Although anxious to step down from the Corps's highest post, Lejeune at age sixty still had four years remaining before reaching mandatory retirement age. He appeared willing to accept assignment to the Department of the Pacific, an unimportant post created mainly to ease the troublesome Barnett out of Washington in 1920, but the opportunity presented itself for more worthwhile employment of his talents. On 11 March 1929, Brig. Gen. William H. Cooke, USA (Ret.) notified the Board of Visitors, Virginia Military Institute (VMI) in Lexington that he intended to retire as superintendent on 1 July of that year. When announcements of both retirements became known, several Marine Corps officers who were alumni of VMI—including a former aide-de-camp, Lemuel C. Shepherd Jr.—urged Lejeune's appointment as the new superintendent. On 20 March 1929, the Board of Visitors traveled to Washington to interview Lejeune and three days later offered him the position. The post carried an adequate salary of eight thousand dollars a year, with quarters and utilities provided. Lejeune went on terminal leave and retired from the Marine Corps on 12 November 1929.

The change proved both suitable and comfortable. Increasingly, Lejeune found the "roaring twenties" and the Age of Jazz disturbing. Through the years, his religious beliefs had intensified and, like Butler, he had become a militant prohibitionist. Surrounded by patriotic young men who chose to wear a uniform offered him respite from a troublesome world.

On campus, the new superintendent seemed to have renewed energy. Lejeune appeared at cadet functions, meals, and at athletic and social events. He spoke to them often, usually extemporaneously, in the same ringing tones that had made him such a popular speaker during his Marine Corps career. His special contribution to the institution, however, came about because of a friendship with President Franklin D. Roosevelt.

Lejeune worked tirelessly to obtain government funds through the various public works programs of the 1930s, bringing in grants totaling over $200,000. Four new buildings appeared on campus, while four others were rebuilt. VMI had never experienced such an ambitious program. Lejeune also sought the creation of an endowment fund, a system of recruitment to attract promising students, and the establishment of a retirement plan for members of the faculty.[37]

Shortly before his retirement from the Marine Corps, Lejeune agreed to write his memoirs for publication. The origins of the idea appear a bit hazy. By his own account, his family urged him to "tell his story." Lejeune hesitated, believing that few would be interested or likely to purchase such a book. A Marine Corps officer of the world war era, Maj. Gordon Dorrance, head of the Philadelphia-based publishing company of the same name, pressed a contract into his hand, and Lejeune began to write. For most of 1929 and into 1930, he filled pages, mostly from memory because he kept few personal papers. A first printing of sixteen hundred copies sold almost immediately, and Dorrance ordered a second printing. A newspaper chain published portions of the autobiography as a serial. Its publication reminded Marines that Lejeune remained the "grand old man" of the Corps despite his retirement. For the rest of his days, his commanding influence affected the Marines.

When Neville died on 8 July 1930, President Hoover had his choice of the irrepressible Butler, Feland, or Maj. Gen. Ben H. Fuller, the assistant commandant and a Naval Academy classmate of the new chief of naval operations, Adm. William V. Pratt. At Butler's request, Lejeune penned a folksy and low-keyed letter of support for his former protégé and sent it to Hoover's personal secretary. Privately, Lejeune urged the Feland candidacy. Much to the surprise of most observers, Hoover and his secretary of the navy, Charles F. Adams, selected Fuller.

When Fuller approached retirement age in 1934, Lejeune remained aloof from the selection process. Given President Roosevelt's friendship with Maj. Gen. John H. Russell, it appeared wise. When an angry Butler attempted to mobilize support to prevent Russell's promotion to permanent major general the following year, Lejeune ignored his old friend's plea to join him at the barricades: "Now [we] have the opportunity to return the Corps to that of you and Neville."[38]

Lejeune attempted to influence the choice of a future commandant of the Marine Corps one last time. When Russell neared retirement age in 1936, Lejeune gathered support for a wartime comrade. Despite the formidable array of recommendations for Hugh Matthews, Roosevelt honored Russell's choice for a successor and picked Thomas Holcomb to head the Corps. Butler remained silent this time, perhaps content because the succession of Naval Academy graduates to the commandancy had ended.

From the beginning of his retirement, Lejeune distanced himself from the increasingly irrepressible and controversial Butler. Fuller asked Lejeune to sit on the court-martial planned after Butler's gaffe relative to Italian dictator Benito Mussolini, but Lejeune declined. When Butler elected to retire shortly thereafter, Lejeune claimed the press of his new duties at VMI to turn down an invitation to attend the retirement festivities.[39]

Except for appendicitis in 1902 and occasional bouts of malaria, Lejeune's health had been remarkably good. On 29 September 1932, he fell and fractured his skull while inspecting new construction at VMI. Unconscious for nearly a week and unable to participate fully in his administrative duties for almost a year, Lejeune never recovered his ability to speak extemporaneously. For the remainder of his life, he read addresses and speeches from prepared notes rather than delivering the stirring talks so admired by all who heard them. The accident added to a medical problem that had plagued him since his days as assistant commandant of the Marine Corps.

In 1917, doctors had discovered that Lejeune had an enlarged prostate gland. The condition seemed to disappear, however, because his medical record reveals no further complaint with the malady. During his years as commandant, his aides-de-camp met him each morning at "Eighth and Eye" with horses, and together they rode to work as a form of exercise. At VMI, he played golf every day. Even during the rigorous period of World War I, Lejeune never complained of illness. A lifetime of temperance and moderation left him remarkably fit. He weighed 160 pounds upon graduating from the Naval Academy in 1888; when Lejeune applied for retirement in 1929, he weighed only ten pounds more.

After the accident in 1932, the old problem with his prostate returned. As increasing discomfort prevented him from applying himself fully to administering the affairs of VMI, Lejeune informed the Board of Visitors that he intended to step down on 1 October 1937. Moving to Norfolk, he continued to maintain an active interest in and correspondence on Marine Corps matters and with old comrades through the Second Division Association.

A grandson, James B. Glennon Jr., became the son he never had. A proud grandfather basked in the knowledge that his grandson had an appointment to the Naval Academy class of 1939. In what must have been déjà vu for the distinguished marine, he learned that Naval Academy officials planned to tamper with traditional service selection procedures to prevent graduates, such as his grandson, standing high in the class from selecting the Marine Corps over the Navy. Marshaling political support, just as he had done in 1890, Lejeune succeeded in deflecting the Navy's plans. Gracious in defeat, Navy officials invited Lejeune to the graduation ceremonies and offered him a seat of honor. Doubtless it gave the former commandant added pleasure to note that the commander of the midshipmen battalion and number two graduate in the class of 1939 was Edward L. Beach, the son of his Naval Academy roommate.[40]

That fall, the disturbing news of Hitler's invasion of Poland prompted Lejeune to write to the commandant of the Marine Corps requesting immediate active duty. Holcomb refused the gallant gesture, gently but firmly. The following year, Lejeune wore his uniform one last time, donning his dress blues and Sam Browne belt to attend the Marine Corps birthday ceremony at the Norfolk Barracks. Finally, a grateful nation and Corps paid him an honor that many considered long overdue.

Lejeune learned that Congress had passed the act of 23 June 1938 allowing the promotion of any officer to the next higher rank if he had been commended or decorated. Because the legislation applied only to those officers still on active duty, Lejeune sought assistance from a variety of political supporters. On 8 April 1942, he became the second Marine Corps officer (Holcomb was the first) to wear the three stars of a lieutenant general.

Through that summer, his health worsened. In the early fall, he entered Baltimore's Union Memorial Hospital for treatment. When surgeons removed his prostate, they confirmed what had been suspected for some time: the gland had become malignant and metastasized, spreading deadly cancer cells throughout his body. Lejeune's kidneys began to fail, and he developed uremia. In the early morning hours of 20 November 1942, he died.

A grateful nation honored his devoted and distinguished service to the Marine Corps, VMI, and the nation. After a funeral service in Washington, a military cortege—commanded by the commandant of the Marine Corps—formed at the monument to the 2d Division, AEF; and sailors, marines, and VMI cadets escorted Lejeune's body to Arlington for burial. Pershing's message of sympathy reflected the thoughts of his wartime comrades: "I shall ever cherish the memory of our association in France during the World War in which his talents and force contributed so largely to the victory of our armies."[41]

Lejeune's naval career encompassed the most important era in the history of the U.S. Marine Corps. As the new American Navy embraced the technology of the twentieth century, leatherneck participation in this modernization became tenuous at best. Clinging to the traditional task of providing ships' guards and small landing parties no longer justified the existence of a separate naval service. The colonial infantry mission, believed to be the raison d'être for the Corps by such "bushwackers" as Littleton W. T. Waller and Butler, passed quickly into history. When the Joint Army-Navy Board codified the amphibious assault assignment as a mission for the Marine Corps during Lejeune's commandancy, it marked the end of the era of the bushwackers and the beginning of the golden age of amphibious warfare. Lejeune's professional life encompassed these far-reaching changes and linked his name with the evolution of a modern Marine Corps.

Equally as significant for the future of the Marine Corps, Lejeune unified the officer corps. When he assumed the commandancy in 1920, its ranks had been divided by professional and personal disagreement. One group of officers, symbolized by the outspoken and controversial Butler, sought a future in small-unit actions void of Navy participation. Contemptuous of officers with diplomas from the Naval Academy or the war colleges, this coterie argued that overseas campaigning and service under fire be the barometer of professional growth and promotion. Another important faction consisted of officers with Naval Academy class rings or who had matriculated from colleges and universities. These officers often found intellectual talents more important in the performance of military duties and bridled under the supervision of senior officers lacking their educational backgrounds. Annapolitans, especially, found it easier to work and deal with educated contemporaries, while outspoken stormy petrels like Butler rubbed bluejacket sensibilities raw.

A third important faction demanding its place of prominence crossed over both "intellectual" and "bushwacker" classes. Officers who fought in France came to demand more and more prerogatives over their peers. Although not every Marine officer had the opportunity to serve in the AEF, any of those who did believed themselves deserving of special privileges. In 1920, all factions in this dispute found John Archer Lejeune's appointment as the thirteenth commandant of the Marine Corps satisfactory. The success of his commandancy resulted in many respects because of this acceptance.

Despite the unflagging support of Congressman Butler, and Secretaries of the Navy Daniels, Denby, and Wilbur, Lejeune never succeeded in using political allegiance as adroitly as his predecessor. He never demonstrated the same skill in steering personnel and budgetary legislation through Congress that had marked Barnett's tenure at the helm of the Corps. Attempts to establish an efficient system of officer promotion and retention eluded him.

To his credit, however, Lejeune deflected the primary concern of Headquarters Marine Corps away from personnel and material matters, and toward operational planning. With his urging, the Corps embraced the amphibious assault mission, although it would be left to successive commandants of the Marine Corps to complete the transformation of a tradition-bound elite corps of light infantry into a modern amphibious force.

14
Wendell C. Neville

1929–1930

LT. COL. MERRILL L. BARTLETT, USMC (RET.)

The fourteenth commandant of the Marine Corps, Wendell Cushing Neville, was born on 12 May 1870 in Portsmouth, Virginia. The son of Mary Elizabeth Cushing and Willis Henry Neville, he grew up in a bustling lower-middle-class home with five brothers and a sister. His parents raised him as a Methodist. Neville's father, a ship's carpenter, succumbed to dysentery on 19 January 1883, but an older brother, George, provided for his education. After graduating from Norfolk Academy in 1885, he took an option not unlike the sons of other poor southern families of the era—an appointment to one of the service academies.[1]

In later years, Neville recalled that he received the nomination to the Naval Academy for the Second Congressional District simply because no one else wanted it. Reporting to Annapolis on 10 September 1886, he managed to satisfy the institution's examiners and became one of the eighty-one naval cadets in the class of 1890. Only thirty-four of the young men survived the rigorous physical and mental demands of Annapolis during the next four years. Not a particularly good scholar, Neville graduated twenty-fourth in his class. As was the custom of that era, he then served two years at sea as a midshipman, first in the *Kearsage* and then in the *Newark.* Returning to Annapolis in the late spring of 1892, he and his classmates took the post-cruise examinations and made their choices for service selection. Neville's mediocre standing offered him only two options: the Marine Corps or discharge to civilian life and the uncertain economic future of the Tidewater area. But years later, he told his daughter that the only reason he selected the Marine Corps over the Navy was a strong dislike for standing deck watches at sea. Neville—along with Albertus W. Catlin, Lawrence H. Moses, Cyrus S. Radford, and Thomas C. Treadwell—became second lieutenants on 1 July 1892.[2]

Neville and the new officers entered the Marine Corps during a period of the most intense reformist efforts since its founding. Following a lackluster performance during

Maj. Gen. Wendell C. Neville, fourteenth commandant.
U.S. Marine Corps Photo.

the Civil War, plagued with desertions and morale problems in the postbellum years, and buffeted by demands from some Navy officers for the removal of leathernecks from the ships of the fleet, Col. Cmdt. Charles G. McCawley sought to improve the effectiveness of the Corps during his tenure, 1876–91. Commissioning better-educated new officers became an important part of the reforms. Between 1883 and 1897, all of the

Corps's fifty-one second lieutenants came from the Naval Academy. His successor, Brig. Gen. Charles Heywood (1891–1903), took the reforms for the officer corps a bit further. On 1 May 1891, Heywood announced the establishment of a School of Application to prepare junior officers and NCOs for their duties.[3]

Heywood continued these efforts into the twentieth century. Following the success of the class of 1891–92 at the School of Application, the commandant ordered the next group of accessions from the Naval Academy, including Neville, to the class of 1892–93. Although ranking in the middle of the graduates receiving diplomas on 24 April 1893, Neville received orders retaining him at the school for duty as an instructor in the NCO division. That fall, another group of students, six young officers and 24 NCOs and privates, reported for duty under instruction. Neville remained at the School of Application until the summer of 1894, receiving his promotion to first lieutenant on February fourth of that year.[4]

During this era, junior Marine Corps officers alternated between tours of duty at sea and ashore. Neville began a three-year period with the fleet, reporting to the *Cincinnati* on 16 June 1894 to command the ship's Marine detachment. When the vessel went into the yards for overhaul the following summer, Neville reported to the *Raleigh* for similar duties. Then, when this ship went out of commission in July 1896, Neville resumed his seagoing stint in the *Texas.* Detached on 2 June 1897, he reported to the Marine Barracks, Washington as a guard officer. While there, he met and wooed Frances Adelphia Howell, the daughter of the commandant of the navy yard, Rear Adm. John Adams Howell. The couple exchanged marriage vows on 4 January 1898; their only child, Frances Howell Neville, was born on 6 June 1899.[5]

On 16 April 1898, four days before the United States declared war on Spain, the CMC ordered Lt. Col. Robert W. Huntington to form an expeditionary battalion at his barracks in New York. Neville reported along with other marines from the Washington Navy Yard. The hastily organized force, reinforced with marines from the *Oregon* and *Yosemite,* disembarked and established an expeditionary camp at Guantánamo Bay. On 11 June, Huntington sent Neville with a small party to take charge of the crossroads post flanking the valley running north and south of the base. His platoon joined Capt. George F. Elliott's celebrated action in destroying the Spanish water point at Cuzco Well. Pleased by Neville's performance, Huntington cited him in dispatches and he received a promotion by brevet to captain on 13 June 1898.[6]

Neville next served as the officer-in-charge of the Marine Corps Recruiting Station, New York. He had been promoted to captain on 3 March 1899. In response to open rebellion and a threat to the foreign community in northern China, Neville joined a hastily formed battalion under Maj. Littleton W. T. Waller on 22 June 1900. The force steamed to East Asia, ostensibly to protect American lives and properties threatened by an antiforeign peasant uprising, led by the Society of Righteous and Harmonious Fists, or Boxers. By 20 June 1900, the Boxers had been joined by forces of the imperial government, and the capital of Peking (Beijing) was under siege. Waller's battalion landed at Taku (Dagu) on 20 June 1900 and joined an international force, taking first Tientsin (Tianjin) and then Peking. Neville participated in four pitched battles and was again commended in dispatches for gallantry.

In September, the force deployed to the Philippines. From June 1901 to September 1902, Neville served as the military governor of Basilan Province. When tensions in the islands appeared to subside in the following year, Waller's battalion returned to the New York Barracks. By then, Neville had earned a deserved reputation as a tough and capable tropical campaigner. Known as "Buck" to his friends and family, he had long discarded the nicknames of his youth: "Wen" at home in Portsmouth, and "the kid" to his Naval Academy classmates.

During a short period of temporary additional duty at Headquarters Marine Corps (HQMC), Neville learned of the act of 3 March 1903, which provided for several increases among the officers of the staff. Apparently hoping to take advantage of the increased rank that went with the appointments, he applied for one of the vacancies as an adjutant and inspector but was rejected.[7]

In 1903, Neville served as an umpire during exercises conducted at the Naval War College. He was promoted to major on 4 June 1904. From 1 July 1904 to 11 August 1905, he commanded the small barracks at Narragansett Bay, Rhode Island. From August 1905 until November 1907, Neville served as the fleet marine officer embarked first in the battleship *Maine* and then in the battleship *Connecticut.* In 1906, Cuban liberals, upset because of losses during the national election, brought the island nation to the brink of anarchy. As American lives and property appeared in jeopardy, President Theodore Roosevelt ordered in U.S. troops. Eventually, a brigade of leathernecks and bluejackets landed in Cuba under the aegis of the Platt Amendment. Neville commanded a battalion, formed from the ships of the Atlantic Fleet anchored off Cuba, which occupied Havana on 1 October 1906. Returning home, he commanded Marine Barracks, Washington from 1907 until 1908. From there, he took a Marine battalion to Panama and Nicaragua, 1 December 1909 to 30 April 1910.

On 14 November 1910, Neville established the Marine Barracks at Pearl Harbor, Hawaii. Three years later, he took command of Marine Barracks, Charleston, South Carolina. On 25 February 1914, Neville became a lieutenant colonel. During the landing and occupation of Veracruz, Mexico, of that year, he earned the Medal of Honor:

> In command of the Second Regiment of Marines, Lieutenant Colonel Neville was in both days' fighting and almost continually under fire from soon after landing, about noon on the 21st, until we were in possession of the city about noon of the 22nd. His duties required him to be at points of great danger in directing his officers and men, and he exhibited conspicuous courage, coolness, and skill in the conduct of the fighting. Upon his courage and skill depended, in great measure, success or failure. His responsibilities were great and he met then in a manner worthy of commendation.[8]

Coincident with receipt of the nation's highest award for bravery, Neville received a critical fitness report. For the period 1–21 April, the commanding officer of the *Prairie* wrote, "Forceful, active, exceedingly excitable indicated by exceedingly loud and strident tones when aroused." Nonplussed, Neville responded to the unflattering comment: "Concerning the unfavorable portion of a report of fitness made by Commander H. O. Stickney, U.S. Navy. I desire to state that if there was any excitable temperament shown it was more than likely due to having been nearly two months on the *Prairie* anchored off Veracruz." In his official report, Neville compared the troop and officers quarters in the aged vessel to a "cheap bowry lodging house."[9]

Ordered overseas a year later, Neville commanded the Legation Guard in Peking, December 1915 to October 1917. He was promoted to colonel on 29 August 1916. Returning from China, he sailed to France and assumed command of the 5th Marines. Until his promotion to brigadier general on 1 July 1918, he led the regiment through the battles of Belleau Wood and Soissons, earning an Army citation, two regimental citations, a croix de guerre, and the Legion of Honor. When John A. Lejeune assumed command of the 2d Division, AEF, Neville led the 4th Brigade (Marine) for the remainder of the war and during the occupation of Germany. Under his leadership, the brigade participated in the St. Mihiel, Mont Blanc, and Meuse-Argonne offensives. Lejeune's comments on one of Neville's fitness reports serve to underscore his leadership in combat: "This officer has commanded the 4th Brigade, U.S. Marines, under the most trying and difficult circumstances and during the stress of battle. He has on all occasions not only fully met requirements but has exceeded them." Lejeune then added: "He is an officer of unusual ability and is exceptionally well fitted for high command in time of war. The brilliant successes of the Second Division have been largely due to this officer's courage, and fine qualities of leadership."[10]

To his other decorations, Neville added both the Army and Navy Distinguished Service Medals, and two additional Croix de Guerre. A year after returning home, Secretary of the Navy Josephus Daniels, in a pointed slight to Maj. Gen. Cmdt. George Barnett, solicited Lejeune's recommendation for the name of a brigadier general for promotion to major general. Lejeune recommended Neville enthusiastically and, consistent with Daniels's dictum of "rewarding those who have been at the cannon's mouth," Neville pinned on his second star on 26 March 1920. Until July 1923, he served as the assistant to the major general commandant.[11]

Believing that his wife, a semi-invalid since the influenza epidemic of 1918, might be more comfortable in a warm climate, Neville requested orders to command the Department of the Pacific in San Francisco. In the early summer of 1927, Neville and his wife returned to Quantico, where Frances Adelphia Neville died on 3 December of that year. Their daughter, who had married Ens. John P. Vest two years earlier, took up the duties of official hostess for her father.

Although Lejeune's request to step down from the Corps's highest post surprised and stunned official Washington political and naval circles, President Herbert C. Hoover and Secretary of the Navy Charles F. Adams moved quickly to fill the void. Former secretary Josephus Daniels had hoped to have Brig. Gen. Smedley D. Butler succeed Lejeune. But Daniels remained silent over the issue of a successor to the popular Lejeune, knowing that as a Democrat he had no influence with the new Republican administration. Butler appeared to allay fears that he would challenge Neville's nomination in a letter to Lejeune: "I can do no good in the Marine Corps after you have gone . . . and I would never be any good as Commandant myself, as I simply could not get along with politicians. Their insincerity and duplicity would eat my vitals out, and there would be nothing but fighting, with consequent decimation of our Corps."[12]

Lejeune's preference for Neville to succeed him was well known, and neither Hoover nor Adams considered anyone else seriously. The only other major general on the active list, after Lejeune's retirement, was Eli K. Cole. But Cole, commanding the Department of the Pacific, lay ill and near death in a San Francisco hospital. Brig. Gen. Logan Feland made a feeble attempt to gain the commandancy, as did Col. William C. Harllee, but neither candidacy amounted to much. Neville became the fourteenth commandant on 5 March 1929. Like General Lejeune's reappointment in 1925, Neville's selection to head the Marine Corps had been made without controversy, rancor, or bitter political infighting.[13]

Neville came to the Corps's highest post as Lejeune's hand-picked successor and no one expected him to deviate from Lejeune's goals: refinement of the amphibious assault mission, continuing to meet traditional Marine commitments worldwide in support of the fleet, and securing congressional passage of an efficient means of officer promotion. To assist him at the helm of the Corps, Neville chose his senior officers and staff wisely. Capt. Frank B. Goettge became his aide-de-camp as well as a social aide at the White House. At HQMC, Brig. Gen. Ben H. Fuller remained as assistant to the CMC and de facto chief of staff. Although Brig. Gen. Cyrus S. Radford relieved Brig. Gen. Charles L. McCawley as quartermaster on 24 August 1929, Neville replaced him with Brig. Gen. Hugh Matthews, a comrade from the 2d, AEF when Radford retired that fall. Lt. Col. Thomas C. Turner became director, Marine Corps Aviation.[14]

In shuffling his general officers of the line, Neville dictated assignments that proved both beneficial to the Corps and which served to curtail much of the intraservice political schemes as senior officers maneuvered for selection of the next commandant. Col. Robert H. Dunlap, considered by most senior Marine Corps officers to be the best-qualified successor to Neville, received orders to attend the prestigious École Supérieure de Guerre in Paris. Brig. Gen. John H. Russell returned from almost a decade of detached duty in Haiti for the Department of State to command the small West Coast Expeditionary Brigade based in San Diego; most of its marines remained in China with the 4th Regiment commanded by Col. Charles H. Lyman. In Nicaragua, Brig. Gen. Logan Feland relinquished command of the 3d Brigade (5th and 11th Marines) to Brig. Gen. Dion Williams and returned to the United States to command the Department of the Pacific. Neville chose Brig. Gen. Harry Lee to command the recruit depot at Parris Island.

Finally, Neville ordered his enfant terrible, Brig. Gen. Smedley D. Butler, to command the East Coast Expeditionary Brigade at Quantico. Lejeune's retirement and

Cole's death created two vacancies for major generals; Neville recommended that the promotions go to Butler and Feland, the two most senior of the Corps's six brigadier generals of the line. The same recommendation included the addition of Dunlap to the list of brigadier generals, filling the vacancy resulting from Feland's promotion. Perhaps Neville assumed that Butler might behave himself at Quantico if he received a promotion; if the Corps's stormy petrel really believed himself to be Neville's successor at the helm of the Corps, he might begin to act like it. But it was not to be.[15]

On 5 December 1929, Butler delivered a stirring anti-imperialist speech in Pittsburgh, claiming that he and the Marines had rigged elections in Nicaragua and Haiti. President Hoover and Secretary of State Henry Stimson interpreted the mercurial leatherneck's oratory as nothing less than an attack on the administration's policy in Latin America. Following a severe dressing down by Secretary of the Navy Charles Francis Adams, Butler recanted much of his earlier oratory. Speaking to an American Legion audience, he retreated into a Darwinian explanation: "God made us the most influential nation in the world for a purpose. . . . It is our duty to keep our neighbors from murdering one another."[16]

Whatever conversations Adams had with Neville regarding Butler are lost to history. At Quantico, Butler—with the tacit approval of Neville—gained newspaper headlines with his persistent attempts to rid the nearby town of bootleggers. First, he threatened to cut off Quantico's water supply. Then, he placed the unattractive garrison town off limits; local merchants quickly lost 90 percent of their business following Butler's edict of 14 September 1929. In a stirring but scathing renunciation of civil liberties, Neville's commander at Quantico promised to court-martial any leatherneck who violated his restriction with regard to Quantico town: "I understand that there is some difference of opinion among civilians concerning the right and wrong of Prohibition. Some of it got into the Corps, but those on the negative side are in the brig. It's a closed question for the military and as long as you wear those uniforms don't get opinionated."[17]

Apparently, Neville chose to allow Butler a free hand at Quantico and thus focus his own attention on the duties of the commandancy. He inherited a Marine Corps that had not changed appreciably in size in almost a decade, despite a steady increase in commitments overseas. On 30 July 1920, Lejeune could muster 1,104 officers and 16,061 enlisted marines; on 30 July 1929, Neville reported 1,181 officers and 17,615 enlisted. As had been the case since the turn of the century, a sizable portion of the leathernecks served overseas or at sea with the fleet. The 5th Marines and the headquarters of the 2d Brigade remained in Nicaragua, maintaining an uneasy peace between competing factions in local politics. The 11th Marines left Managua on 31 August 1929 to be disbanded. In Nicaragua, a number of leathernecks opted for the advantages of double pay to serve as officers in the Guardia Nacionale. The 4th Marines appeared to be a permanent fixture in north China, scattered between Tientsin and Shanghai, to protect American lives and properties. Following its return from China in 1929, the headquarters of the 3d Brigade and the 6th Marines folded their colors and reverted to cadre status. In addition, Marine detachments served on board all twenty-eight of the Navy's capital ships.[18]

Although Neville hoped for an end to the Marine Corps commitment in Haiti, a reasonable withdrawal date failed to materialize. By the time of his commandancy, the once-sizable Marine force had been reduced. But many observers, especially in the Department of State, believed that only the Marine Corps contingent provided sufficient stiffness and resolve to keep the troubled nation from descending into anarchy. Despite pressures from the United States, the client-patron president of the island republic refused to increase native participation in the government.

In the fall of 1929, student unrest widened into a general strike of the population. On 6 December 1929, fifteen hundred angry peasants surrounded a detachment of twenty marines near the village of Cayes, demanding the release of prisoners from the local jail. When a rebel bit him, an angry marine bayoneted the Haitian. The detachment then opened fire, killing twenty Haitians and wounding twenty-three. Although the government of Haiti sputtered its outrage and liberals in the United States protested, the incident disappeared into the dustbin of history; the detachment commander received a Navy Cross.[19]

As commandant of the Marine Corps, Neville faced a president (Hoover) and a secretary of the navy (Adams) determined to reduce the armed services in size and at the same time increase their usefulness to the nation. While Hoover kept his distance from intraservice affairs, Adams—the scion of a famous political family and a Boston Brahman—found the rough manners of Neville's officers, especially Butler, particularly unnerving. In one celebrated exchange, Butler responded to a frustrating day-long visit by Adams to Quantico by introducing him to a group of officers as "Gentlemen, I want you to meet the Secretary of the goddamn Navy."[20]

Butler's outburst mirrored leatherneck frustrations with the Hoover-Adams style of management. Both politicians considered Neville's Marine Corps little more than a quaint anachronism that the country, in the depths of the worst economic depression in its history, could ill afford. While Neville and his marines never balked at lengthy periods of overseas duty or with the fleet, the declining amenities and salaries rubbed professional sensibilities raw. As the depression gutted the nation's economy, Congress imposed a 15 percent salary cut, reducing compensation to the military below that of 1908. Only half of the buildings and barracks at Quantico contained central heating. Less than a year in office, Neville lashed out in the pages of the influential U.S. Naval Institute *Proceedings:* "In the field and on foreign duty, the Marine realizes that he must endure certain hardships, but when he returns home he has a right to expect some of the comforts and conveniences enjoyed by civilian friends."[21]

In testimony before the House Naval Affairs Committee for the FY 1931 appropriations, Neville continued his quest for additional recruits to meet existing operational commitments and for funds to rebuild many of the Corps's decaying buildings. He reminded his congressional audience that although a regiment and a brigade headquarters had departed China, the 4th Marines remained in Shanghai (63 officers, 1,145 enlisted men). A legation guard in Peking, established in 1905, required 15 officers and 485 men. Even though the Marine force in Haiti had been reduced to less than 700 leathernecks, 300 marines released from duties in Haiti were transferred directly to Nicaragua as replacements for the brigade serving there.

The significant overseas commitments resulted in a sharp reduction in the number of officers attending Marine Corps Schools. The Basic School in Philadelphia continued to operate at full strength with fifty-three second lieutenants—newly commissioned officers could not be ordered overseas without completing the course—but at Quantico, only seventeen captains and majors were counted at the company and field officers courses. Of his small force, Neville had seventy-six officers and twenty enlisted marines serving as naval aviators. Another eleven hundred enlisted men performed aviation duties, and Neville planned to increase that total to twelve hundred by January 1931.

Although the retrenchment of the Hoover administration eliminated any possibility of meaningful participation in the fleet maneuvers or enhancement of the Marine Corps Schools at Quantico, Neville chose, nevertheless, to continue Lejeune's quest for an efficient means of officer promotion and retention. For too long, his officers had advanced through the rank of colonel in a system tied to rigid seniority. Following a period of rapid expansion, such as World War I, a surplus or "hump" determined that junior officers would spend the best years of their careers in the company grades. In one of his last appearances before a congressional committee, Lejeune argued anew his plea for revision of the traditional officer promotion and distribution system. As had been the case for almost every year of his commandancy, the House Naval Affairs Committee sent the resolution on to the House, where it received speedy passage. As before, the Senate Naval Affairs Committee refused to pass the bill. Neville also requested authorization for the promotion of at least one more major general from among the Headquarters staff. He argued that such an incentive would encourage superior officers from the line to volunteer for staff duties.

On 19 December 1929, Neville began the quest again with the House Naval Affairs Committee. And just as in Lejeune's case, the legislation passed through the committee and then to the full House. Neville noted ruefully that he commanded a Corps led by officers too old to perform at sea or in the field. If the present system did not change, the Marine Corps would have fifty-seven-year-old lieutenants and captains. Sadly, at least a quarter of the Marine Corps's field-grade officers opposed any change in the traditional system of promotion. Neville and his supporters argued that these officers were selfish and motivated by fears that their mediocre records would force them into retirement. Despite his pleas, and those of Lejeune before him, legislation affecting officer promotion in the Marine Corps failed to survive senatorial scrutiny. The Corps's only ally on the Senate Naval Affairs Committee continued to be Eugene Hale, who argued forcibly, but in vain, for passage of the bill.[22]

Neville continued his predecessor's method of securing superior qualified junior officers for the Marine Corps. In his first year as commandant, fourteen meritorious

NCOs became second lieutenants along with nineteen recent graduates of the Naval Academy. To fill the remaining vacancies, HQMC solicited nominations from Army ROTC graduates; 1,118 applications arrived, but only twenty-five of the college men joined the Corps. But in the following year, severe budgetary restrictions allowed only fourteen meritorious NCOs and twenty-eight Naval Academy graduates to receive commissions as second lieutenants. No applications from civilian colleges and universities were accepted.[23]

Plagued by chronic hypertension, Neville's physicians told him repeatedly that he had to get his blood pressure down. An active man, fond of leading by shouting and bullying—admittedly in good humor—the fourteenth commandant failed to heed the warnings. On 26 March 1930, he suffered a stroke. An examination at the Washington Naval Hospital revealed that Neville's blood pressure had risen to 210/130, his electrocardiogram showed significant myocardial damage, and he had partial paralysis of the right side of his body. Spokesmen for the Department of the Navy were quick to describe his illness in mild terms with only a small loss of hand and foot movement. Others close to Neville knew better; he would never regain the use of his leg. Still, he maintained a cheery disposition throughout his lengthy hospitalization and convalescence. In a personal note to Lejeune, Neville urged him to maintain good health, reminding his predecessor that "he was the only commandant of the Marine Corps not in captivity." Elliott and Barnett occupied the Washington Naval Hospital with Neville—all three would be dead within a year.[24]

Recovering at his daughter's home in Edgewater Beach, Maryland, Neville suffered a second stroke and died of coronary sclerosis on 8 July 1930. Although his family expected Neville's passing, it responded with prolonged grief and limited the funeral, held in the commandant's house, to only members of the immediate family. Neville was laid to rest in Arlington Cemetery; subsequently, Frances Adelphia Neville was reinterred and laid to rest next to her husband.[25]

Neville's short tenure at the helm of the Marine Corps left little mark. It is difficult to speculate as to what changes he might have brought about had he the opportunity to serve for a full term in office. Given the impact of the depression and the Hoover-Adams quest for reductions in the armed forces—especially in the Corps—it seems unlikely that significant changes in the composition of the Corps or repairs to its aging physical plant would take place. It would be up to Neville's successors to complete the codification of the Marine Corps's amphibious assault mission.

Known for his gruff exterior and personal dynamism, Neville led by good-natured directness and honesty. The number of older enlisted marines who walked with the funeral cortege at Arlington Cemetery bore witness to the affection in which he was held. An obituary in the *Washington Post* spoke reams about the fourteenth commandant with few words: "An indomitable will, a sense of humor and conspicuous courage were joined with personal magnetism to make [Neville] a soldier of heroic mold."[26]

15

Ben H. Fuller

1930–1934

LT. COL. MERRILL L. BARTLETT, USMC (RET.)

On 9 July 1930, Ben H. Fuller became the fifteenth major general commandant of the Marine Corps after a bitterly contested competition. From the perspective of the Fourth Estate, the most prominent and likely contenders appeared to be Maj. Gen. Smedley D. Butler and Brig. Gen. John H. Russell. A popular veteran with a reputation for colonial combat, and two Medals of Honor, Butler commanded the East Coast Expeditionary Brigade at Quantico. Russell, a graduate of the Naval Academy class of 1892, had recently returned after almost a decade as the High Commissioner in Haiti and was slated to command the West Coast Expeditionary Brigade at San Diego. Observers of the internecine drama considered it merely another fractious chapter in the competition between Naval Academy graduates and officers commissioned directly from civil life that had erupted periodically since 1914. As the political infighting intensified, Butler sputtered in a letter to his brother that "even the lowest ranking privates know that this is a show down between the Naval Academy element and those from civil life and the ranks."[1]

Meanwhile, Russell, knowing that he had no chance for selection after his lengthy absence on detached duty, remained silent. Maj. Gen. Logan Feland, then commanding the Department of the Pacific, made a concerted effort to gain the post by attempting to make the selection a feud between leatherneck veterans of the 2d Division, American Expeditionary Force, and those who did not serve on the Western Front. Feland, commissioned directly from civil life like Butler, enlisted the aid of Maj. Gen. James G. Harbord, USA (Ret.) and Mark L. Requa, a close friend and political confidant of President Herbert Hoover. Both Feland and Butler sought the support of John A. Lejeune, but the circumspect former commandant only offered remarkably tepid support for Butler and no show of enthusiasm for Feland. Ultimately, however, Hoover and Secretary of the Navy Charles Francis Adams bowed to the entreaties of the senior officers of the Navy and selected Brigadier General Fuller; the overriding consideration for his selection was

Maj. Gen. Ben H. Fuller while still a colonel. Fuller was fifteenth commandant.
U.S. Marine Corps Photo 520353.

his diploma from the Naval Academy. By avoiding controversy, and playing his trump card as assistant to the commandant and de facto commandant during his predecessor's lingering illness, Fuller outmaneuvered his rivals.[2]

General Fuller was born on 27 February 1870 in Big Rapids, Michigan, one of the seven children of Circuit Judge Ceylon Canfield Fuller and Francis Morrison. His parents raised him as a Presbyterian. In 1885, Fuller received an appointment to the Naval

Academy from the Ninth Congressional District. Seventy-eight young men began the grueling course that fall and Fuller survived the next four years to join thirty-eight midshipmen for the postgraduation cruise following matriculation on 7 June 1889. Serving first in the *Iroquois,* he narrowly escaped death when the old screw sloop's engines failed, and it drifted across the Pacific. In an interesting coincidence, 1st Lt. George Barnett commanded the small ship's marines.[3]

Fuller completed his cruise in the *Alliance* and returned to Annapolis for the postgraduation examinations in the spring of 1891. He failed to improve his class standing of twenty-fourth and accepted a commission in the Marine Corps rather than face the ignominy of discharge to civilian life. All seven of the marines in the class received orders to attend the first session of the School of Application at the Washington Barracks. While there, Fuller wooed Katharine Heaton Offley, the daughter of a Washington banker, Holmes E. Offley, and the couple exchanged wedding vows on 26 October 1892. Two children came of the union, Edward Canfield Fuller, on 4 September 1893, and Dorothy Nelson Fuller, on 2 October 1896.[4]

After his graduation from the School of Application in the spring of 1892 until the Spanish-American War ushered in a period of colonial infantry duties for the Marine Corps, Fuller's career followed the usual pattern of junior officers—barracks assignments punctuated by duty in command of marines in the warships of the fleet. Following tours at the barracks in Boston and New York, Fuller reported to the *Atlanta* on 2 April 1894. He became a first lieutenant on 7 September of the previous year. Detached from the ship on 28 September 1895, Fuller returned to Marine Barracks, Boston. On 15 March 1898, he began another posting at sea, this time in the *Columbia,* but Headquarters Marine Corps (HQMC) curtailed his tour in December of that year because of a shortage of officers needed to satisfy expeditionary requirements in the Pacific.[5]

Detached on 17 December 1898, Fuller reported to Marine Barracks, New York and joined a battalion formed for duty in East Asia. Arriving in the Philippines on 23 May 1899, he learned that Brigadier General Heywood had ordered his promotion to captain effective on 28 March. On 8 October, Fuller participated in the Battle of Novaleta against insurgent Filipinos resisting American rule and received a commendation in dispatches. He distinguished himself again during the relief of the siege of Tientsin (Tianjin) the following summer. But during the time he served in the Philippines, Fuller apparently succumbed to a problem common to marines who served lengthy periods in the tropics and overimbibed in alcoholic spirits. From February to May, Fuller underwent treatment for neurasthenia at the Naval Hospital, Yokohama. The entire experience, especially the association with heavy-drinking and often-unruly marines, convinced Fuller to avoid friendships with more colorful officers such as Littleton W. T. Waller and Smedley D. Butler. The latter's drunken antics so alarmed him that he even recorded them in his personal papers.[6]

Returning to the United States in 1901, Fuller served first on recruiting duty in Manhattan and then at the Barracks in New York. On 9 January 1903, he began another tour of overseas duty, this time in command of the Marine detachment assigned to the battleship *New York*. With his promotion to major later that year, HQMC posted him first to Mare Island and then to command the Honolulu Barracks. In September 1906, Fuller ended his tour in Hawaii and assumed command of the School of Application, Annapolis, early the next year. From June 1908 to 31 January 1910, until invalided home suffering from a variety of tropical ailments and another bout of neurasthenia, he commanded a battalion in the Canal Zone. His promotion to lieutenant colonel was effective 3 February 1911, and he assumed command of Marine Barracks, Charleston, South Carolina, on 1 August of the previous year.

Unlike many contemporaries, Fuller sought assignments that furthered his professional education. Early in 1913, he completed the Field Officers' Course, Fort Leavenworth as a precursor to attending the Army War College course, 1913–14. After graduation, he assumed command of Marine Barracks, Norfolk on 25 May 1914. On 22 December, however, the commandant selected him for duty as fleet marine officer, Atlantic Fleet, and Fuller followed the admiral's flag in a succession of battleships for the next two years. On 30 June 1916, he reported to the Naval War College as a student and received his promotion to colonel the next August. Following graduation the following summer, Fuller assumed command of Marine Barracks, Philadelphia, but with his promotion to brigadier general on 1 July 1918, he deployed to Santo Domingo to command the Marine brigade there. Although he held that post until 3 December, postwar retrenchment cost him his star and Fuller reverted to colonel on 5 August. Secretary of the Navy Josephus Daniels had interjected himself into the demotion process and insisted that only those brigadier generals with the most overseas service retain wartime general officer rank. Fuller ran afoul of the admiral commanding in Santo Domingo, and he received an unflattering fitness report that described him as "calm, even-tempered, painstaking, but easygoing, trusting too much to subordinates." Meanwhile, he served as secretary of state, interior, and police on the staff of the military governor in Santo Domingo until 25 October 1920.[7]

Returning to the United States in October 1920, Fuller served first at Headquarters then on the staff at the Naval War College, and finally on temporary duty in Santo Domingo. For a short period, he commanded the 1st Brigade in Haiti. During this time, Fuller employed what political leverage he possessed to regain his lost star. His daughter, Dorothy Nelson Fuller, had married the son of Michigan congressman Joseph W. Fordney. The elder Fordney pressed another Michigan Republican, Secretary of the Navy Edwin H. Denby, for Fuller's promotion. At first, Congressman Fordney sought the appointment of Fuller as a replacement for Brig. Gen. Charles G. Long, adjutant and inspector, but Lejeune demurred. On 8 February 1924, Denby ordered Fuller's promotion to brigadier general of the line after Fordney took the matter directly to President Calvin Coolidge.

Fuller assumed duties at Headquarters, and Lejeune named him assistant to the commandant on 2 July 1928. Fuller remained in that post through Neville's debilitating illness and death, earning a reputation for steady and unflappable performance among the Headquarters staff and senior officers within the Department of the Navy.[8]

When Fuller assumed the commandancy in July 1930, the Hoover-Adams program of naval retrenchment had reduced the assets of the Department of the Navy just as the depression had gutted the nation's economy. Nonetheless, worldwide commitments for the Marine Corps remained the same and traditional missions in support of the fleet continued. At that time, the strength of the Marines stood at only 19,380 men. Although brigades had deployed to Nicaragua and China in 1927, only a Marine regiment remained as a semipermanent fixture in each troubled country. Meanwhile, marines continued to serve in the warships of the fleet, man the two skeletonized expeditionary brigades at Quantico and San Diego, and provide sentries at Navy stations at home and abroad. Despite these burgeoning commitments, the number of Marine Corps personnel was only slightly more than a decade before.

Herbert Hoover came to the Oval Office determined to bring efficiency to the government and reduce expenses. The worldwide depression only fueled his fervor to cut federal outlays. Secretary of the Navy Adams proved a zealous subordinate in whittling away at the perceived excesses in the naval services. Although Fuller, like Neville before him, argued that the minuscule personnel figures forced an inordinate number of marines to serve overseas, neither Hoover nor Adams responded to the entreaties of the commandant. Although in the second year of Fuller's tenure, the Department of State called for a sharp reduction in the size of the Marine force in Nicaragua, the numbers in-country remained fairly constant. In 1931, the personnel strength of the Corps dropped to 18,782 men. The nagging from the administration irritated Fuller, and he shared his frustration with Lejeune: "This is some job now with the Secretary telling me not to spend $700,000 of our appropriations for this year."[9]

The curtailment continued into Hoover's third year in office. Although the legal strength of the Marine Corps was 27,400 enlisted men in 1931, Congress had only appropriated funds to pay for 18,000. The secretary of the navy even recommended cutting the daily enlisted allowance for rations from fifty-two and one-half cents to forty-eight! Fuller reminded Hoover, Adams, and the congressional Naval Affairs Committees of his dismal statistics: 9,014 marines in the United States, 4,657 men on foreign duty, 2,093 in the ships of the fleet, 1,073 leathernecks in aviation duties, and 355 men in sick or casual status. Ruefully, he noted that most of his marines were either overseas or with the fleet, or coming from or going there. Still, Hoover and Adams pushed for further reductions. Half of the Navy and Marine Corps recruiting stations closed, Navy bands were abolished, and Parris Island was placed on reduced status. Ominously, the Hoover administration recommended closing Parris Island and establishing a single recruit training facility at Quantico. Appearing more sympathetic, Congress raised Marine Corps personnel levels to 17,500, but Adams just as forthrightly reduced them back to 16,000. Fuller and his senior officers testified before Congress that any further cuts, reportedly to 13,600 as hinted by Hoover and Adams, would devastate the Corps. In the last year of Hoover's administration, Fuller exclaimed to the House Naval Affairs Committee that the reductions in the Corps "have made it impossible to carry out its primary mission of supporting the United States Fleet by maintaining a force in readiness to operate with the fleet."[10]

Meanwhile, as manpower cuts threatened to gut the Marine Corps, Fuller faced continuing problems with his ambitious and frenetic senior officers. Although Butler claimed at the time of his failure to achieve the commandancy that he would remain in uniform to lead the Marine Corps, he began almost immediately to cast about for a civilian position. Increasingly, the Corps's enfant terrible became embarrassing to the administration because of his irresponsible public utterances. Butler had earned the ire of Adams and Hoover by suggesting that the Department of State rigged elections in Latin America. Although appearing subdued after a severe dressing down in the secretary's office, Butler then insulted Italian dictator Benito Mussolini in a speech to a private club. In the imbroglio that followed, Butler faced a threatened court-martial, accepted a letter of reprimand, and marched noisily into retirement.[11]

Other officer personnel problems plagued Fuller, just as they had troubled Lejeune and Neville. The stagnation of the lineal list that had persisted since the end of World War I continued, and Congress appeared reluctant to authorize the creation of selection boards in order to remove the aged and redundant. Although in 1931, President Hoover approved a plan to retire officers who had failed selection for promotion, he reneged when advisers informed him that it required an additional $170,000 beyond existing costs to fund the plan. Fuller and his staff testified that graduates of the Naval Academy class of 1906, then serving in the Marine Corps, were still captains while Navy officers of the Naval Academy class of 1918 would become lieutenant commanders on 1 July 1931. Their Marine Corps counterparts were not due for promotion to major for another ten years at the present rate of promotion. Although the House Naval Affairs Committee approved HR 5344, Congress failed to pass the promotion bill.[12]

Not satisfied with emasculating the personnel strength of the Marine Corps, Hoover and Adams then began steps to disband the smaller of the naval services and transfer its assets to the Army. By 30 June 1932, Fuller counted only 1,196 officers and 15,365 enlisted men in his ranks. But Hoover and Adams sought to inflict further reductions. The Oval Office worked through a compliant Gen. Douglas MacArthur, who apparently harbored little affection for the Marines as a result of the Corps's unwarranted publicity during World War I. A MacArthur protégé, Maj. Gen. George S. Simonds, prepared a proposal that argued that the Marine Corps duplicated much of the Army's function. Simonds proposed that the Army could easily absorb the Corps's overhead and avoid unnecessary duplication. His position paper contended that a savings of twenty-five million dollars was attainable: "It represents a clear possibility of saving money without impairing national defense."

Unknown to Fuller, the triumvirate of Adams-MacArthur-Simonds had enlisted the support of an unlikely ally. Adm. William Veazie Pratt had, by that time, come under the MacArthur spell and agreed with the argument that the Marine Corps should be limited simply to traditional duties on board ship. The chief of naval operations, Fuller's

Naval Academy classmate, agreed that the combined arms aspect of Corps organization overlapped and duplicated that of the Army. But this time, congressional supporters of the Marine Corps rose to the challenge and the proposal died.[13]

The year before Fuller noted in his annual report that the personnel situation could not become worse: he had marines serving in thirty-three ships plus aviation detachments on the carriers *Lexington* and *Saratoga.* Early in January, a Marine battalion was formed at Cavite and Olongapo and then sent hurriedly to reinforce the 4th Marines in China. The proposed reduction in end-strength, from the 18,000 approved by Congress to the 15,343 recommended by the administration, made the Corps's position untenable. On 30 June 1932, Fuller counted only a slight increase to 16,561, and a year later that number dipped to 16,068. "With the present enlisted strength, the Marine Corps is not prepared to perform its allotted task in the event of a national emergency," Fuller warned in his annual report to the secretary of the navy. Then, as if to underscore the crisis, he issued a terse statement to the troops: "I wish to record my appreciation of the efforts put forth by all ranks during a trying year."[14]

In 1933, the dismal outlook for the Marine Corps took an upturn. Entreaties by the Department of State and congressional criticism had convinced the president to begin withdrawing the Marines from Nicaragua and otherwise implement a "Good Neighbor Policy" in Latin America. The election of Franklin D. Roosevelt, an unabashed supporter of the Marine Corps, buoyed hopes at HQMC for relief of the dismal personnel situation. Fuller took the opportunity to begin major shifts in senior personnel. The departure of the troublesome Butler in 1931, and the disappointed Feland in 1933, cleared the way to realign the ranks of general officers. Brig. Gen. Robert H. "Hal" Dunlap, a promising and popular officer considered by many as a potential commandant, lost his life in an accident. He had been detailed as a student to the prestigious École Supérieure de Guerre and died attempting to rescue a French woman from a landslide on 19 May 1931. To fill the major general's slot vacated by Feland, the commandant nominated Dion Williams. Fuller sent forth the name of another Naval Academy graduate, Charles H. Lyman—a protégé of Maj. Gen. Joseph H. Pendleton—to become a brigadier general and fill Williams's vacancy.

Fuller's foes had either departed the scene or muted their disappointment in his selection. From nearby Lexington, Lejeune remained distant and occasionally badgered the commandant for additional commissions for graduates of the Virginia Military Institute. From retirement, Butler observed the progression in the ranks of general officers with scorn and dismay. Obviously, Fuller had undertaken a shuffling of senior officers to prepare the ascension of an heir to the commandancy. Worse, the officers elevated possessed diplomas from the Naval Academy. Butler lost no time in storming the barricades, this time in a characteristic diatribe to President Roosevelt. He observed tartly that upon the retirement of Williams for age in January 1934, Fuller planned to elevate John H. Russell to the vacant major generalcy. Clearly, this move paved the way for the despised Russell to succeed Fuller. Butler argued passionately for Brig. Gen. Harry Lee for promotion to major general and referred to him as a member of a group "which is fast passing out, discouraged and broken in spirit." Butler then added, "The class to which I refer is composed of those officers who did not have, at least, some Naval Academy education, but who, notwithstanding this handicap, is . . . almost entirely responsible for the proud record of the Marines." Butler and his coterie hoped for Lee, ranking one number senior to Russell in 1931, to retain seniority and succeed Fuller as commandant.[15]

President Roosevelt and Secretary of the Navy Claude A. Swanson ignored Butler's protestations. Russell commanded at Quantico from 1 December 1931 until assuming the position of assistant to the commandant in February 1933. Fuller finally had his team in place, then he began to focus on a major realignment of the Marines as expeditionary forces in support of the fleet. Beginning in 1931, the General Board of the Navy had intermittently studied the role of the Marine Corps in support of the fleet. In that year, the CNO demurred with the commandant's request to increase the number of aircraft at the expense of personnel assigned to fleet or shore activities. Fuller hoped to increase the assets of VO-7M from six to twelve aircraft, thus giving the Marine Corps a total of seventy-four operational planes, plus twenty-one spares. Then, in the following summer, the War Plans Division made a significant recommendation to the General Board concerning the organization and establishment of the Marine Corps.

In its conclusions, the body emphasized that the Marine Corps must only be responsible for the seizure and defense of advanced bases; subsequent operations ashore would then pass to the Army. Planners argued that the Marines must only be employed as an adjunct to the Army if necessary, because in any likely scenario the Marine Corps would be busy supporting the fleet. Prophetically, the director of the War Plans Division posited that Marine Corps air assets should always remain an integral part of naval aviation and never be allowed to operate as a separate component; otherwise, it would allow criticism from the Army Air Corps "which has for its purposes the abolition of all Marine Corps air activities, and the diversion of the present appropriations for this component to its purposes."[16]

Knowing of the board's deliberations, Fuller and his staff invited its attention to an important study, "History of Advanced Base Training in the Marine Corps." As the General Board appeared increasingly to dwell on the marines with the fleet as the primary source of expeditionary forces, Headquarters argued emphatically for the separate organization and maintenance of marines intended primarily for deployment overseas: "Marines in ships' detachments be not considered available for duty with expeditionary forces." In the same study, the board made several recommendations and observations that failed to garner the attention of HQMC and attain some measure of agreement.

The use of the Marine Corps as part of a field army, such as in World War I, was considered a special case. In future wars, planners anticipated the requirement for all Marine Corps assets in support of the fleet. Marine aviation assets must be considered as part of naval aviation and never deployed separately from the fleet. Planners scored the inclination toward indoctrination of the so-called Leavenworth scenarios, because potential deployments appeared most likely to be in naval and not land warfare: "The idea that the Marine Corps is an amphibious organization should not be lost sight of in the composition, organization, training, and equipment."[17]

Late in 1932, another study by the General Board arrived at Headquarters. Fuller repeated his objection to counting Marine ships' detachments as part of available expeditionary forces. The commandant wondered if such detachments could be available to deployment, then who performed their normal duties on board ship. But a statement relegating the Corps to an obscure, secondary role to that of the Navy raised Fuller's ire. He took umbrage with the suggestion that naval strength had priority over that of the Marine Corps. In the Navy's view, manning the ships of the fleet should be given priority; if the Corps lost numbers in the process, so be it. Then, in an obvious rebuke to the director, the War Plans Division, and General Board, Fuller informed him that he intended to conform solely to the requirements resulting from Naval War College Advance Base Problem No. 1. Just a week earlier, Fuller informed the same admiral that he had ordered a study of the organization of the Advanced Base Force to support the major strategic plan—obviously War Plan Orange.[18]

A year later, however, the General Board appeared more supportive of the Marine Corps's position. The board reported that the strength of the Corps should be 21,000 men to support the fleet adequately; however, the chief of naval operations increased that figure to 27,400 in his endorsement of the study. Fuller and his staff objected to the Navy's position that any artillery larger than 3-inch caliber reduced the mobility of the landing force; experience had shown the requirement for 155-mm guns or howitzers. Finally, the CNO expressed concern over the shortages of marines assigned to the fleet; specifically, he wanted detachments in the new light cruisers and more leathernecks assigned to the battleships. Both the CNO and the commandant agreed that the time-honored figure of Marine Corps strength being one-fifth that of the Navy no longer appeared valid. Less than a month later, Fuller asked the secretary of the navy to approve the assignment of a Marine Corps officer to the General Board because of the increasing number of matters of interest and vital importance to the Corps.[19]

Fuller's final step, one that altered the operating forces of the Marine Corps substantially, was to recommend the dissolution of the various Marine expeditionary forces and replace them with the Fleet Marine Force. These troops would come under the operational control of the fleet commander. As part of the process, he scored the lack of suitable doctrine, as evidenced by the gyrations of the General Board of the Navy over the previous two years. Fuller ordered the commandant, Marine Corps Schools, to "proceed as expeditiously as practicable to prepare for publication a manual for landing operations." Fuller directed Quantico to begin work no later than 15 November 1933 and authorized the suspension of classes to use the staff and students to work on it.[20]

Fuller spent his final days at the helm of the Marine Corps in tidying up personal affairs, ensuring that his changes occurred, and deflecting criticism of his creation of the Fleet Marine Force. To the uninitiated, it appeared as if the commandant had merely agreed to the wholesale transfer of the Marine Corps to the Navy. On 28 February 1934,

Fuller reached the mandatory age for retirement, and he passed the colors to Russell. In the annual report to the secretary of the navy for that year, marines continued to serve in the 4th Marines in Shanghai and at the legation in Beijing; a brigade of reduced strength remained in Haiti with orders to withdraw by 15 August; but battalions remained deployed in Florida, Guantánamo, and on board the battleship *Wyoming* off Cuba. On 30 June 1934, the new commandant counted only 16,361 marines to meet these commitments and other traditional missions in support of the Navy.[21]

In his retirement years, Fuller divided his time between Washington and a country home in Hamilton, Virginia. He enjoyed reading and playing cards, appearing often at the Army-Navy Club. General Fuller never recovered from the sad loss of his son, killed as an infantry company commander at Belleau Wood in 1918. Ted Fuller was interred in the cemetery at the Naval Academy, and his father requested a plot next to him. The years of tropical campaigning had taken their toll on the former commandant, and his few years in retirement were marked by increasingly ill health. On 7 June 1937, Fuller was admitted to the Naval Hospital in Washington with lumbar pneumonia and arteriosclerosis. In addition, his physicians diagnosed gouty arthritis, liver congestion, and prostate problems. A day later, General Fuller died in his sleep.[22]

Surpassing the meager expectations of his critics, Ben H. Fuller proved a stellar commandant of the Marine Corps. At the time of his surprise selection to head the Corps, the venerable Lejeune sniffed despairingly that "at least he is a lively fellow," and Feland called Fuller "one of the most worthless men we have ever had in the Marine Corps." Harbord appeared to applaud the selection of MacArthur to head the Army, but saw in the selection of Fuller a contradiction: "one rule for selection of a chief of staff applied in the Army and another rule applied in the Navy for selection [of] a major general commandant of the Marine Corps." Nonetheless, Fuller steered his Corps through the shoals of the Hoover-Adams naval retrenchment, deflected the estrangement among many of his officers, avoided an erstwhile attempt at amalgamation with the Army, and began the process to codify the amphibious assault mission in support of the fleet.[23]

16
John H. Russell
1934–1936

LT. COL. DONALD F. BITTNER, USMCR (RET.)

On 10 November 1936, the secretary of the navy announced that the sixteenth commandant of the Marine Corps, Maj. Gen. John H. Russell, would retire and be succeeded by Brig. Gen. Thomas Holcomb. Russell could look upon his two-and-a-half-year tour as commandant, plus over a year as assistant commandant, with a sense of accomplishment. He had shifted the focus of the Corps from its traditional mission to amphibious warfare. He also induced Congress to pass a new officer promotion law which changed the obsolete system of advancement based on seniority and vacancy to one which would reward ability and merit through selection. Furthermore, Russell backed continued changes in the professional military education system of his service: the officer corps would be better prepared to execute the new type of warfare which would become its recognized specialty. His success was such that Marine Corps historian Robert Heinl could write, "Russell laid the essential foundation for much of its effectiveness in the war which was to come."[1]

Such accomplishments surprised many, for when Russell assumed office little was expected of him. Although the *New York Times* noted that he was very qualified to be commandant, *Time* magazine had another view: "If Commandant of the Marine Corps, Good Soldier Russell will probably institute few far-reaching changes, but his smart, svelte, active wife Mabel will make things social hum in the comfortable red brick commandant's quarters of Washington's Marine barracks."[2] But who was John Henry Russell Jr.?[3] Before 1930, he had a traditional career pattern for officers of his era, with tours at sea, with Marine barracks, and in colonial occupations. The latter included thirteen years in Haiti between 1917 and 1930 in military and diplomatic postings. There were two significant exceptions, assignments at the Naval War College and with the embryonic Office of Naval Intelligence.

Russell began his military career at the U.S. Naval Academy. But his grandfather, himself a former naval officer, opposed his going there, for he believed that the naval

Maj. Gen. John H. Russell, sixteenth commandant.

service was “too big,” and no longer a “gentleman’s profession.” His father, Naval Academy class of 1847, also disapproved of his son’s quest for an appointment to the academy. Thus, Russell used his own initiative to secure it: at the age of fourteen, he met with President Grover Cleveland at the White House and asked for one. Cleveland was reluctant. His recent nominees had not done very well, and the chief executive was hesitant to appoint any more. However, Russell persevered, assuring the president, “I will succeed. You can put your trust in me."[4] On 18 May 1888, Russell received the appointment.

John H. Russell Jr. was born on 14 November 1872 at Mare Island, California, the son of Rear Adm. John H. Russell, USN. He entered the Naval Academy in the summer of 1888, a youngster of only fifteen. His record at the Academy was unexceptional. After four years, he finished twenty-eighth of thirty-four on the Order of Merit List in the Line Division.[5] In June 1892, he reported to the USS *Atlanta* for his mandatory two-year tour at sea. While on board, he received his initial press publicity in September 1893 for saving the life of a mail orderly in a boating mishap.[6]

Two years later, on 1 July 1894, Russell was commissioned a second lieutenant in the U.S. Marine Corps. In that grade he served for two years on board the battleship USS *Massachusetts.* While a signals officer during the Spanish-American War, he received commendation from the captain for "standing alongside me on the bridge under fire and displayed the greatest gallantry and coolness in the execution of the duties of his office." The commandant then recommended to the secretary of the navy that Russell be given the brevet rank of first lieutenant for his actions in combat.[7]

Other duty proved more hazardous than combat against the Spanish fleet. On 21 April 1899, Captain Russell joined the Marine battalion on Guam. He served there until 8 December 1899 but spent as much time in the Naval Hospital, Yokohama, severely ill. The doctors simply noted he was "unfit for duty" as a result of "gastro-enteritis . . . due to dietetic and climatic conditions incident to service at Guam" and recommended that he be ordered home and given three months' sick leave.[8] Seven years later, Major Russell arrived in another place noted for illness and death: Camp Elliott, Canal Zone, Panama. Between 13 July 1907 and 26 July 1908, he served as commanding officer, Marines of the Canal Zone and Wireless Station, Colon, Panama. Tours of duty there were often only one year due to rampant malaria and yellow fever, but his ended abruptly for another reason: on 21–22 July 1908, a dog entered the Marine compound and bit ten marines, including Russell, before being killed. Medical examination revealed the dog had rabies, and the bitten marines had to be medically evacuated to Washington. Russell received appropriate treatment in August, followed by a month of medical leave.[9]

During this period, Russell also had diverse assignments. He served three tours with the School of Application after his attendance there as a student in 1894–95. In 1895, he took charge of a class of thirty-two noncommissioned officers; in 1900–1901, he served as the officer in charge, curriculum director, and primary instructor for a class of eleven officers; and again between 1904 and 1906, he served as officer-in-charge and curriculum director, but this time with subordinate instructors and sixty-five officers in attendance at one time.[10] He also held a significant post in Asia. Between 1910 and 1913, he commanded the Marine detachment at the American legation in Peking (Beijing), China. This assignment brought him into contact with Chinese culture and the Japanese military in Peking. While there, he developed the ability to write and read "fairly good" Mandarin and an oral fluency in Japanese. He also acquired an insight into oriental culture, value systems, and psychology.[11]

Between 1914 and 1918, Russell experienced expeditionary service. From April to November 1914, he commanded the 2d Battalion, 3d Regiment, 1st Brigade, during the Veracruz operation in Mexico.[12] Next, between March and November 1917, he commanded the 3d Marine Regiment in the Dominican Republic. Then, one month after his promotion to colonel in October 1917, he moved to Haiti, a country in which he would serve almost continually between then and 1930, to command the 1st Provisional Brigade.

One interruption occurred, however. In December 1918, he served as Head, Planning Section, Headquarters, Marine Corps. In 1919, the "Russell Board" selected the officers who would be retained in the Corps after the Great War, what rank they would hold, and where they would be placed on the lineal list. The results were controversial, as this board placed more reliance on education and potential than on service in France during the war. Furthermore, none of the board's members had served in Europe, including Russell, although he had requested such duty.[13] He was also charged with commenting to the board that the officers retained in the Corps would be those who would be entertained in their homes and might marry their daughters. Maj. Gen. Smedley Butler challenged the board results, championing the cause of the veterans of France, many of them former, older noncommissioned officers. Hence, the results of the Russell board were discarded; a second board, chaired by Wendell Neville but run by Butler, prepared a new list.[14]

Russell, however, had a short tour at Headquarters. At the specific request of the Haitian government he returned to that country in October 1919. From then until February 1922, he commanded the 1st Marine Brigade, and then until November 1930 served in the diplomatic post of high commissioner as the representative of the United States.[15] Russell, now working for the State Department, experienced accomplishment and trial. The government and social elites of Haiti responded well, but during his early years there, the Marine Corps, the Department of the Navy, and the Senate investigated his role in implementing U.S. policy in that country. His tour also ended in an inquiry. In late 1929, opposition to U.S. presence there resulted in riots and demonstrations, culminating in the Cayes Massacre, during which marines fired on Haitians, killing at least twelve and wounding twenty-three. These incidents reopened the issue of American policy in the region. Russell's employment in Haiti was terminated on 12 November 1930, and he returned to Marine Corps duty.[16]

But his career was not hurt by this troubled tour. An investigation of the incident in 1930 not only absolved him from blame for any negative aspects of U.S. policy in Haiti, but cited his duty and cooperation.[17] In 1922, Russell was promoted to brigadier general, and he was also decorated twice, receiving the Navy Cross in 1920 and the Distinguished Service Medal in 1930, while the Haitian government awarded him its Haitian Medaille Militaire. The State Department also gave him its support for promotion to major general, but this did not help. He had become too identified with that department's interests, and many officers viewed him as being too far removed from Marine Corps affairs.[18] But because of his extra-Corps assignments, he was not directly involved with various factions within the Corps concerning its proper role and mission.[19]

Despite Russell's apparently "normal" career for an officer of his era, two assignments were pivotal in shaping his ideas on the mission and nature of the Marine Corps: service at the Naval War College and duty with the Office of Naval Intelligence. Between 26 September 1908 and 24 September 1910, Russell served on the faculty of the Naval War College. He arrived there at a time when that institution was reforming its professional military education program. This included regular hours, noon meals, and the study of application problems.[20] More important, Newport was also addressing various aspects of the seizure and defense of advanced naval bases, and the roles and responsibilities of the services in such endeavors. Russell wrote four papers on the defense of advanced naval bases. In these, a number of themes emerged, including his projected role for the Marine Corps, tactical concepts, and required equipment. He believed that it would be necessary to seize and defend *temporary* advanced naval bases, with such landings linked to fleet operations; an advanced base force should be part of the Fleet. The future commandant further stated that such bases were only a temporary refuge for friendly ships, for the naval objective remained the enemy's battle fleet.

How were such bases to be defended? In a December 1909 paper, Russell divided the defense into three parts: gun defense against water approaches, mine defenses or water obstructions, and land defenses. In tactical concepts, he had learned well the lessons of the Boer and Russo-Japanese Wars. He advocated the use of machine guns, attack trenches, obstructions, submarines, plows (to build trenches quickly), telephones, and airships. Russell cogently commented that "the efficiency of the machine gun as an element of defense can scarcely be overestimated." The construction of trenches had to change, for "the old hasty type were of little use; now, they had to be deep and narrow so as to give shelter and reduce the target." In May 1910, he further developed some of these ideas, recommending the construction and use of field fortifications ("in general it may be said that too much stress cannot be laid on the advantage to be derived from invisibility and the proper construction and use of cover"); formidable trenches (bomb proof, head protection, elbow rests, traverse every twenty yards, ammunition rets, clear fields of fire, communications to the rear); and the use of obstacles ("barbed wire, which forms part of the Naval Advanced Base Outfit, has when used as an entanglement, proved to be the most effective of all obstacles, being almost insurmountable and withstanding artillery fire exceedingly well"). Russell's last paper in May 1910 drew two final conclusions. First, he stressed that "the Advanced Base Outfit is suitable for the protection of advance or temporary bases only and should not be employed for the permanent defense of bases such as Guam or Samoa." Second, the looming threat had become Japan: "Today, the nation which in 1904 loaded, by means of lighters and sampans, 100,000 troops on transports in four days, is better prepared than any other world power to wage amphibious warfare, its army being organized and equipped for overseas expeditions."[21]

After his return from China, between 1913 and 1917, Russell had a nontraditional assignment in the Office of the Director of Naval Intelligence. He arrived during a major reorganization which focused on war planning, the collection and dissemination of information, and service to a two-ocean Navy which might have to confront threats from both Japan and Germany. He led a group which reorganized the office, eliminating duplication of work. His team also suggested reforms in the collection of intelligence and closer cooperation with other agencies. More important, Russell expressed concern about Japan. On a report of a proposal by Britain to sell battleships to Japan for help against Germany, he commented that Tokyo would be free to venture against the Philippines, Hawaii, or lower California, without British opposition. He concluded on 20 January 1916 that "Japan would switch sides in the war anyway and join Germany in a coalition against Britain and the United States."[22]

Then, in June 1916, Russell published a significant article in the *Marine Corps Gazette,* "A Plea for a Mission and Doctrine." Using examples from military history and the social sciences of the era, he articulated the concerns previously addressed at the Naval War College. He stated that the Corps lacked a mission, hence it did not have a doctrine. He called for a clearly stated doctrine which all marines would learn upon entry into the Corps. Efficiency was linked to this socialization, for without it organization (material and personnel), policy (the system of management to accomplish a mission), leadership (trained in professional military schools), discipline, and morale could not be obtained. The current mission of the Marine Corps could not accomplish this goal, for it was too vague: "To cooperate with the Navy, in peace and war, to the end that in the event of war the Marine Corps could be of greatest value to the Navy."[23]

Russell's views meant many things to many officers, as his article produced an intense reaction. In a December 1916 *Gazette* rebuttal, Earl Ellis commented that the Corps had its mission, policy, and doctrine, and if Russell doubted it, all he had do was visit the West Indies and see marines at work.[24] But Ellis missed the key point of the piece. Russell had correctly identified the real issue: "The Marine Corps may be called on in the near future to face trained, seasoned, highly disciplined and indoctrinated troops. Lacking a doctrine, no matter how good our organization, equipment, personnel, discipline, and morale, we would unquestionably be handicapped, perhaps fatally. We have no creed . . . ; we are as helpless as a ship without a rudder." In a subsequent response, he further articulated the reason for a mission and doctrine. The Marine Corps must develop and indoctrinate its personnel with it, "thus infusing the Corps with a new life. In so doing, we prepare in peace for the war which will come, for when it starts we fight with what we know, i.e., learned in peace."[25] Russell had stated the goals which would reappear when he became commandant.

By 1930, Russell was a contender for commandant. After General Lejeune retired in 1929, the Corps had three commandants in seven years. In 1930, as Wendell Neville neared death, there were four possible successors. In July of that year, a White House staffer reported Navy Department views to President Hoover: Ben Fuller. Navy and Marine officers were "unanimous for him." Logan Feland was "probably the second choice" and had a good record of cooperation with the Navy, although he was not an Annapolis graduate. As for Butler, "I can find no backing for General Butler in the Department." With regard to Russell, "neither the Navy or Marine Corps believe he should be placed at the head of the Corps after thirteen years on detached duty," although he was "generally liked and respected but there is a pronounced feeling that his appointment would be an injustice to the officers who have served continuously with the Corps."[26]

Thus, Fuller in July 1930 became commandant, and Russell finally served with the Marines as a general officer. In December 1930, he became commanding general, Marine Corps Base, San Diego, California. A year later, he assumed duties as the commanding general, Marine Barracks, Quantico, Virginia. Next, in February 1933, he became assistant commandant, serving until appointed commandant of the Marine Corps in April 1934. Thus, because of the untimely death of Neville and the subsequent retirement of General Fuller, Russell suddenly found himself the head of his Corps.[27] By then he had the support of the Navy. In the maneuvering for the post of commandant, the CNO, Adm. William Standley, supported Russell. In September 1933, Standley wrote to President Roosevelt on Fuller's successor relative to the factionalism in the Marine officer corps: "There is no intention, as far as I can find out, of having Harry Lee succeed Fuller as major general commandant of the Marine Corps. There are many reasons why Lee should not get this and reasons why Russell should, and none of these are because Lee is not a Naval Academy man and Russell is."[28]

Russell experienced three major successes between 1933 and 1936. He supported the creation of the Fleet Marine Force (FMF) and development of amphibious warfare doctrine and, as best he could within the constraints of the time, the means to implement it. He also achieved reform of the officer promotion system by persuading Congress to pass legislation authorizing advancement by merit through selection. Russell then implemented the law and purged the corps of officers unfit, for whatever reason, for the rigors of what he foresaw as the looming war.

Russell's initial accomplishment was the establishment of the Fleet Marine Force. In the annual report for fiscal year 1934, he stressed that the FMF was an integral part of the U.S. Fleet under the operational control of its commander in chief, and that this had resulted in "simplicity and increased efficiency in the event of an emergency requiring the use of Marine Corps forces with active fleet operations." In 1936, he also identified conflicting commitments, which precluded the faster evolution of the FMF by consuming manpower, maintaining ships' detachments and garrisons on foreign stations, and performing guard duty at naval shore stations. He declared, "The Marine Corps under present strength cannot maintain component units of FMF required by its mission with the Fleet."[29] Thus, the realities of the mid-1930s placed limits on the evolution of the Fleet Marine Force.[30]

But was such a force necessary? Russell thought so and, in 1946 recalled his own views: "For many years, it had been my opinion that the Marine Corps should have a striking force, well equipped, well armed, and highly trained working as a unit under the fleet under the direct orders of the Commander-in-Chief." This force did not exist in 1933. Marines trained in small arms but little else. Even the old expeditionary force lacked senior staffing and planning as well as fully manned and trained units. Troops assembled only when needed, and only then did organization and training commence, resulting in hasty and incomplete plans. Russell called this process as providing "the body without the head or brains." Such a "crude force was organized and whipped into shape to make a successful landing against light opposition" to safeguard some American interests and suppress revolutions in small nations. It was, however, "not an organization capable of meeting situations such as would develop in a war with a major power."[31]

Published memoirs of marines depicting conditions before 1934 support Russell's comments. For example, retired lieutenant general Pedro del Valle, one of the key officers who worked on amphibious warfare doctrine in the 1930s, held similar views. He described a planned 1933 landing in Havana, where another revolution was occurring. The hastily assembled landing force disembarked in Colon, Panama, to check itself, and after an inspection of men and equipment and acquisition of ammunition, they embarked for Cuba, although "the sad condition of our landing force was made shockingly obvious." Although a plan had been prepared to restore order in Havana, "thank God we never had to make this crazy landing," del Valle wrote.[32]

Russell's creation of the Fleet Marine Force occurred not while he served as commandant, but as assistant commandant. He assumed these duties in February 1933, and proclaimed his intentions in an August 1933 *Marine Corps Gazette* article titled "A New Naval Policy." Marines were part of the fleet, just as any division of ships were; the United States was a naval power with global interests; and the fleet needed bases from which to operate to defend those interests. Hence the Corps had to focus on the seizure and defense of advanced bases. A Marine expeditionary force on transports was equal to a division of battleships or a squadron of destroyers. If bases could be seized and defended, this enhanced naval power because more ships could remain in the area of operations; also, if the enemy lost bases, then his sea power was crippled. If the United States possessed such bases, in peace and war they had to be manned and protected. In war, where there were no such facilities, they had to be seized and defended by the Marines. His charge to the Corps was simple: "I believe that when the Marine Corps itself is completely saturated with the subject, as it should be, and eats, sleeps, dreams, thinks, acts, and exudes advanced bases, there will be a marked advancement. My advice is to make advanced bases and shore operations for the fleet your Bible."[33]

As assistant commandant, he took action. In February 1933, Russell recommended to General Fuller the creation of a permanent staff at Quantico which would work with mobilization plans and be prepared to mobilize troops on short notice. But more was needed: "a permanent striking force, well equipped, well armed, and highly trained working as a unit of the fleet under the direct orders of the Commander-in-Chief." That summer he turned his ideal into reality. As acting commandant, he showed Fuller his proposal, received approval for it, and on 17 August 1933, over *his* signature, recommended this policy to the chief of naval operations. Russell began by noting that four missions were assigned to the Marine Corps, and "the fourth and most important of these is to 'provide expeditionary forces in immediate readiness.'" The Corps's most important contribution for the Navy was an expeditionary force which "has as its principal mission the establishment of an advanced base. In time of war, this force advances with the fleet in offensive operations. It gives the fleet essential striking power against land objectives that it otherwise would not possess. It should be considered an integral part of the fleet." Russell recommended that such a force be made a permanent part of the fleet, maintained in a state of readiness by either "Fleet Base Defense Force" or "Fleet Marine Force." Finally, it would "be included in the Fleet organization as an integral part thereof, subject to the orders for tactical employment, of the Commander-in-Chief, U.S. Fleet."[34] He achieved his goal. On 7 December 1933, the Navy Department issued General Order 241 with the new entity designated the Fleet Marine Force. The next day Marine Corps Order 66 implemented the Navy Department order. On 13 December 1933, the Marine Corps Expeditionary Force Staff at Quantico became Headquarters, Fleet Marine Force.[35]

Russell then ensured that it had requisite publicity. On 15 December 1933, the *New York Times* reported the birth of the FMF: "This new policy unifies the Marines as an offensive arm of the navy at the disposal of the Commander-in-Chief of the fleet."[36] Russell used many means to communicate his message to the Corps. At Quantico, the home of the FMF, the base newspaper continually stressed this new focus. In February 1936, the *Quantico Sentry* informed its readers that a "modern fleet can operate efficiently only from a suitable base. The securing of such bases is the primary mission of the Fleet Marine Force. The gunfire of the fleet can disorganize an enemy on shore, but the enemy's capture and the organization of the advanced base can be consummated only by the landing force." The *Sentry* also noted the difference between ideal and reality: "The organization of the Fleet Marine Force into one of the units of the U.S. Fleet progresses systematically but slowly during the past year because of a shortage of personnel." Speakers from Headquarters were also used to spread the new gospel. In March 1936, the *Sentry* reported the remarks of Maj. Gen. Louis McCarty Little, assistant to the commandant, who pointed out "the essential part played by the FMF in seizing advanced bases during fleet operations."[37]

In October 1936, just before his retirement, Russell used *Proceedings* to address the officer corps of the maritime services. His theme remained the same: "lacking bases for distant operations, the fleet would have to seize them." The FMF was formed to do this as efficiently as possible. But the tasks were now more complicated: "You can no longer hit the beach with some navy landing guns, some pushcarts, and your rifles and bayonets"; special equipment and capabilities were also needed, and the troops "can neither be improvised overnight from the recruit depots nor called up short notice from the reserves." All the parts needed to work efficiently together, and cooperation between the naval and military was essential for success. Preparedness was necessary for "it is not likely that time will be granted for the assembly and training of a fleet unit." With respect to the FMF, he concluded that "it is the Marine Corps' most important contribution to the great cause of national security."[38]

Russell knew that ideal and reality were not the same, as evidenced in his published articles and official reports. In his October 1936 *Proceedings* article, he stated that "owing to the fact that the supply of Marines is exceeded by the demand for them, the Force is substantially below strength." But training was still stressed. In his report for fiscal year 1936, Russell noted that FMF landing exercises were conducted, supported by artillery and air units. Although at an early developmental level, these exercises addressed the proper issues: "training of combat teams, infantry and artillery with air support, with special emphasis on liaison and communications between the arms is carried on in the Fleet Marine Force." In his final report as commandant, Russell called for more recruits, the procurement of needed equipment, and, equally important, an assault force, two Navy transports specially designed and built for the FMF.[39] One of Russell's aides recalled the conditions of the time. The Corps had little, and had to fight for that. Requested aircraft and tanks were disapproved; Quantico had five tanks in two or three different models, and several of these were inoperable. The question always arose: "How can we train with less than one unit of everything?" And Russell used many means to obtain additional funding. As Gen. Julian C. Smith recalled, although defense of advance naval bases was not the primary focus of the Corps, he explained the rationale: a defense task was a request that the administration could support and was used as a means to obtain more troops and money from Congress.[40]

Most important, Russell's Fleet Marine Force would require a doctrine by which to operate and be led by officers nurtured by him through advocacy of amphibious warfare doctrine and advanced by his reform of the promotion system. Officers such as Holland M. Smith rewarded their patron by turning his concepts into reality and executing them in World War II. By 1945, theory, development, and experience had merged. In a series of articles for the *Marine Corps Gazette* on amphibious warfare after World War II, Smith's definition of the term reflected the changes that had occurred: "The art of conducting an operation involving the coordinated employment of military and naval forces despatched by sea for an assault landing on a hostile shore." The foremost trainer and commander of amphibious troops in the war made the following key point: "It was only when the naval phase of our amphibious operations—the seaborne approach and the ship-to-shore or shore-to-shore movements—was visualized, not as a ferry boat ride, but as a tactical movement, culminating in an assault, that successful landing operations were possible." As Smith succinctly stressed, "The concept of assault is therefore elemental."[41] To achieve this goal, Russell provided support from the top of the command structure.

Before he became a direct player, efforts had already begun. In March 1931, four officers were tasked at Quantico to work on a formal text devoted to landing operations.

The team consisted of Majs. Charles Barrett, Lyle Miller, and Pedro del Valle, and Lt. Walter Ansel, USN. The group was charged with drafting a manual for attacking a defended shore from the sea, integrating both Navy and Marine operations. Work continued on this project for the next four years, with varying degrees of support.[42] It built upon a small base of the previous decade at the Marine Corps Schools at Quantico. A small harbinger of the future rested in the Field Officers Course. By the 1930–31 academic year, it devoted 216 hours to "landing operations." Still, most of its operational problems were based on Army doctrine, organization, and equipment.[43]

But change soon occurred. In December 1931, Russell became commanding general of the Marine Barracks, Quantico, of which the Marine Corps Schools were a part. Then, on 15 August 1932, Col. Ellis B. Miller, the director of the Field Officers Course, proposed that the schools and their curricula be linked to the naval service and not the Army. He stated the implications: what the officers were taught "must involve Marine organizations, Marine equipment, Marine problems, Marine operations, with a Naval, not Army, background." He also recommended that the schools devote themselves to preparing a manual on landing operations and to have a course for 1933–34 based solely upon Marine Corps oriented matters.[44]

For the 1932–33 academic year, Gen. James C. Breckinridge, commandant of the Marine Corps Schools, and Colonel Miller planned to collapse the Field Officers Course into a "Committee of the Whole" to work on the proposed projects. This, however, did not occur until November 1933. In the meantime, Barrett's committee continued to work during the 1932–33 academic year. The Marine Corps Schools studied the Gallipoli campaign, dissecting all of its many missteps; they also produced Advanced Base Problem I. Then Russell intervened. Walter Ansel later recalled the possible triggering event. He had been transferred from Quantico to California as flag lieutenant to Adm. Ridley McLean. In the summer or autumn of 1932 or 1933, he and McLean "were working on some sort of an operational exercise. The Admiral complained that the naval doctrine or manual (perhaps the Landing Force Manual) was inadequate." Ansel replied that "there was a much improved doctrine floating around HQMC. The admiral said, in effect, I'll write my friend General Russell about it.[45] On 14 November 1933, in accordance with orders issued by General Russell on 30 October, classes were discontinued so the Schools could produce the "rules and doctrine covering landing operations." Between 28 March and 13 June 1934, the initial draft was completed. From this came the conceptual basis of the offensive amphibious assault operations of World War II: the *Tentative Manual for Landing Operations.* It focused upon the key elements of command relationships, naval gunfire and aviation support, the ship-to-shore movement, the tactics of securing a beachhead, and logistical support of the operations.[46]

But the new "doctrine" was only a draft. Throughout the rest of Russell's term as commandant, and that of his successor, Gen. Thomas Holcomb, revisions were made, based upon the lessons learned from fleet landing exercises. World War II refined the techniques, but the basic doctrinal concepts remained as developed. In 1936, Russell pointed to this achievement with pride in his final report to the secretary of the navy. The schools' "routine work" had been suspended to devote their full attention to this task, with a group of experienced officers finishing it. This "was completed in 1935 with the issue of the new 'Tentative Landing Operations Manual,' now published and distributed to the naval service and to certain interested branches of the Army by the Chief of Naval Operations." In this process, Russell also looked forward to how his creation might be used. His aide for 1932–34 recalled in 1984 that Russell "evidenced keen interest in, and familiarity with, the 'island hopping' strategic concept later employed against Japan. . . . He mentioned this concept with me on a number of occasions."[47]

One additional element remained to be added to the major changes Russell envisioned for his Corps: properly selected officers to lead it in a forthcoming war. As soon as he assumed office, Russell addressed this through reform of the officer promotion system. With his success on this issue, he achieved a goal that had even eluded Lejeune. For this, he received both praise and criticism. By 1934, a potentially critical situation existed in the officer corps. Due to immediate post–World War I policies and the overturning of the results of the 1919 Russell board by the 1921 Neville board, many of the aging officers of the Corps were hardly capable of fighting a major war against a first-class foe. For many, the solution to this problem lay in promotion by selection based on merit and elimination of advancement by vacancy and seniority. General Lejeune had advocated this reform coupled "with an annual, automatic elimination of a certain percentage of non-selected officers." Upon his retirement, he commented "that his greatest disappointment as commandant was that he could not leave a selection law behind."[48]

Lejeune's last attempt had died in the Senate in 1928. Russell, upon assuming office, made this an immediate priority. On 20 April 1934, he testified before a subcommittee of the Senate Naval Affairs Committee in support of proposed legislation that would produce the desired reform. The commandant described the "grave condition" of the officer corps as "the most serious problem confronting the Marine Corps since I joined in 1894." He stated that officers in every grade but second lieutenant were generally overage and physically unfit. He stressed that troops had to be led by physically able and active officers, equal to or in better condition than their men. But the opposite situation existed: the ages of colonels ranged from fifty-two to sixty-two, lieutenant colonels from forty-nine to fifty-seven, and majors from thirty-eight to fifty-six. For company grade officers, 70 percent of the captains were over forty, and 37 percent of the first lieutenants over thirty-five. Russell emphasized "the over-age condition of these grades strikes at the very heart of the efficiency of the corps: namely its fighting effectiveness." In responding to questions, he said that these officers were too old for both service in war and in the United States. Early in the hearing, he stated his desire for a system which would "reward ability and merit" and promote "only the fit," and later he said, "We [shall] promote the efficient." His staff provided additional details. Without any change, conditions would get worse in the ensuing decade. Without reform, by 1946 all officers above the rank of major and 81 percent of the captains would be over fifty years of age, with some spending over thirty years as a company grade officer. The commandant noted at the end of the hearing, "I think it is understood, sir, that our only method of promotion now is by retirement, resignation, or death."[49]

Supporters of this reform expected opposition, and the Senate and House committees were told that some officers opposed the proposed new law. To circumvent this, Russell saw President Roosevelt on 25 April 1934. Later, the president's Marine aide, Maj. Joseph Fegan, wrote to his secretary soliciting support from the chief executive. Fegan described the situation: "What a pathetic condition our personnel situation is and has been for years."[50]

But what was the reality behind this view? Officers could serve until age sixty-four forced retirement, and annual attrition amounted to only 2.5 percent a year; hence, stagnation resulted. As the *New York Times* commented on 15 January 1934, under the current system and promotion rate, an officer would serve 140 years before being eligible for general officer rank. Two Marine officers stationed at the Portsmouth Navy Yard came to a similar conclusion: "We'd have to be 102 years old by the time we made major." By the early 1930s a Naval Academy jibe reflected the problem; midshipmen who elected the Navy taunted their peers who opted for the Marine Corps: "I'll see you in 20 years when we're both captains."[51] By the 1930s, newly commissioned officers could realistically expect to remain a company grade officer for two decades: Gen. Robert Devereux served as a second lieutenant for over five years and as a first lieutenant for over ten years. The lot of a captain was similar. Col. John Thomason served in that grade for fourteen years, and Gen. O. P. Smith for seventeen. Junior field-grade ranks were no different: Gen. H. M. Smith was a major for fourteen years and Gen. Roy Geiger for over thirteen.[52]

In his final report as commandant, Russell addressed the real problem in the old system: "another serious defect of the seniority system was that an able, zealous, active and efficient officer could not be promoted over the head of another who lacked such qualifications." The remedy: "reward for merit and elimination for unfitness."[53] Russell now succeeded where his predecessors had failed. On 29 May 1934, the Marine Corps personnel bill was enacted into law, providing for promotion based on merit and by selection board and eliminating advancement by seniority and vacancy. The entire bill provided for the distribution, promotion, discharge, and retirement of officers. The law also included a provision giving second lieutenants in the Corps the same status as ensigns in the Navy, thus ensuring their automatic promotion to first lieutenant after three years of service. In his annual report for 1934, Secretary of the Navy Claude A. Swanson called this "a wise provision and fulfills a need which has existed for a number of years."[54]

The results were immediate. On 25 June 1934, the secretary appointed a senior officers promotion board (to lieutenant colonel, colonel, and brigadier general) and a junior promotion board (to captain and major). Russell personally chaired the senior board. These boards met and did their work thoroughly. Gen. John Letcher later would write that the boards affected the "incompetent officers of the Marine corps like scythes cutting through ripe grain. . . . There was wailing and gnashing of teeth and bitter words especially from the wives of officers who were not selected." Gen. Merrill B. Twining later succinctly commented that "the first board rid us of a heavy concentration of alcoholics, functional illiterates, and incompetent slobs. It was ruthless and intended to be."[55]

For the Marine Corps, the names on the promotion lists of the initial senior officer boards reads like a "who's who" of the leadership which led the Marine Corps during World War II. Russell intended talent and ability to rise, and the selections ensured this. The first brigadier's list contained the name of Col. Thomas Holcomb, who in 1936 would succeed Russell as commandant; the colonel's board for 1934 included Clayton Vogel, H. M. Smith, and Charles F. Price; and the lieutenant colonel's list had Julian C. Smith, Joseph C. Fegan, A. A. Vandegrift (the eighteenth commandant), Roy S. Geiger, Charles Barrett, Harry Schmidt, William Rupertus, and Pedro del Valle. The total numbers revealed what was occurring: two of eleven colonels selected for brigadier, eleven of forty-five lieutenant colonels for colonel, and fifty-three of ninety-nine majors for lieutenant colonel. Russell reported to the secretary of the navy on 25 June 1934 that those selected were "the best fitted of all those under consideration to assume the duties of the next higher grade." The process continued the next year: in 1935, J. C. Fegan, A. A. Vandegrift, Roy Geiger, and Charles Barrett were selected for colonel, while another board picked Julian C. Smith and John Marston for that grade; those two boards also recommended for advancement to lieutenant colonel two future commandants, Clifton B. Cates and Lemuel Shepherd, plus Graves B. Erskine, Maurice Holmes, and Leo Hermle, all future general officers.[56]

The company grade boards had an even more drastic effect. In 1934, only 92 of 259 captains were recommended for promotion to major, and only 89 of 198 first lieutenants to captain. The officers not selected, if physically or professionally able to perform their duties, would be retired. Future commandant Holcomb commented to another officer that many of these former NCOs had performed valuable service, but younger college-educated officers had surpassed them. More important in the emerging "new" Marine Corps, these newer officers "did not have to *unlearn* how we used to do it in Haiti. . . . I believe all the junior officers were . . . tired of hearing about Belleau Wood."[57]

The new system also had administrative effects. With the new promotion system, records considered by the boards had to be complete. Also, promotion board members thoroughly evaluated fitness reports, which were required even under the old system, both on their content and who wrote them. A recorder for a selection board considering first lieutenants to captain recalled an example: twelve officers had an entry in their fitness reports, each signed by Gen. Smedley Butler, calling each "the best officer in the Marine Corps."[58]

Russell achieved many of his goals, but a personal ordeal soon unfolded. This occurred in 1935, when his name was forwarded to the Senate for promotion to permanent major general. This gave his opponents an opportunity for a personal and professional attack on him. They took advantage of the general officer promotion system and the office of major general commandant. By law, any officer of the grade of colonel and above could be nominated to serve as major general commandant; if not a major general, he would wear the rank and receive the pay and allowances of that rank. But if not promoted to that grade, upon leaving office he would revert to his permanent one. Also, the general officer promotion pattern was advancement to temporary and then permanent brigadier general, followed by the same sequence for major general. When Russell became commandant, he held the rank of temporary major general. When advanced to both that position and rank in 1934 and 1933 respectively, no opposition surfaced and Senate confirmation quickly followed. In 1935, conditions, however, had changed: opponents of the newly enacted promotion reform, aided by Senator Hugo Black of Alabama and retired major general Butler, opposed his promotion.[59]

Russell had expected some reaction but was surprised by its intensity. In a letter to the secretary of the navy on 30 August 1934, he wrote that "promotion by selection is new in the Corps, and officers passed over have not yet had time to reconcile themselves to the fact, if reconciliation is ever possible under such circumstances."[60] What had changed since 1934? In 1935, Russell supported legislation which would close an anomaly in the law of 1934. A first lieutenant, captain, and colonel if not selected for promotion would be retired after reaching specified years of service. However, under the 1934 legislation, majors and lieutenant colonels, even if not promoted, could continue to serve until reaching the age of sixty-four. Russell intended to close this loophole, which he viewed as seriously limiting the effect of the new promotion system. His opponents wrote senators, congressmen, and even President Roosevelt; their champion was Senator Black, who took their cause to the floor of the Senate in February and March 1935.[61]

The real issue can be simply stated: promotion as a reward for past service or advancement predicated on future potential. Amid the personal attacks on Russell, this became clear. On 5 March 1935, Senator Black articulated the view of promotion as a reward for *previous service:* for nonselected officers, the new system "will cut off their military careers and send them out of the service, even though they wear the decorations of American service in the form of bullets and the ravage of disease." Addressing the issue of too many officers, Black articulated his main concern: he demanded that the situation be "handled in a humane way and not unjustly." He continued, "Which is more important—a 'hump' or justice to men who fought the war . . . 'to make the world safe for democracy.' . . . A rank, outrageous injustice is about to be perpetrated upon men who fought on the battle front. . . . It is proposed that these men shall be kicked out, they will be removed from the Marine Corps. Their chances to earn their daily bread will be taken away from them."[62]

Such concerns, however, were not linked to the needs of the Corps. Russell's defenders in the Senate presented the alternative arguments. Senator Park Trammell of Virginia led this effort, aided by Millard Tydings of Maryland and Peter Gerry of Rhode Island. On the same day that Black presented his view of the promotion system, Gerry gave the opposite, commenting that "while a man might have a brilliant record as a Second Lieutenant, and be a man of great bravery, it would not necessarily follow that he was qualified to become one of the high-ranking officers in the Marine Corps, where other qualities such as judgment, and so forth, are necessary. . . . The main point is to promote efficiency in the Corps so that the very best perform their duties." And echoing Russell's August 1934 letter to the secretary of the navy, to the person not selected for promotion, "it is always an injustice to that officer in his own estimation."[63]

In this affray, Black engaged in a solo effort, albeit abetted by General Butler. To attack Russell, they impugned his chairing the Russell Board in 1919, assailed his performance of duty at Veracruz in 1914, charged an affront to Senatorial dignity while serving as high commissioner in Haiti, and alleged misuse of government funds and property. They even claimed that he conducted a "reign of terror" in the officer corps through his use of the boards to conduct a personnel purge. Ultimately, all of these attacks were refuted. Even their efforts to enlist the aid of General Lejeune, ironically, aided Russell. Lejeune wrote to Senator Trammell on 14 February 1935, supporting promotion by merit based on selection and repeating his oft-uttered lamentation that he had been unable to achieve this reform. The former commandant stated, "I rejoice that the present law was enacted, as I believe, if perfected in accordance with General Russell's recommendations, it will work a beneficial revolution in the officer personnel of the Marine Corps." He supported the new system and attacked the previous one: "the system of promotion by seniority, I believe, has been far worse. The meritorious, the energetic, and the able have been smothered, very often, by the worthless, the lazy, and the stupid. To return to the old system of promotion by seniority . . . would be destructive to the morale of the officer personnel."[64] Russell later received public support from the assistant secretary of the navy. Speaking in October on NBC radio's *Washington Star* program, Henry L. Roosevelt said that the proceedings of the boards "have failed to please everybody . . . [but] as far as the principle of selection, it is so sensible and logical that I do not even consider it to need extended comments. . . . Ability and initiative are made eligible for reward. I find it in no way unreasonable that competence be the basis for naval promotion."[65]

The Senate confirmed Russell's promotion. Black later confided that his purpose had been to delay or postpone legislation, which would have forced the retirement of majors and lieutenant colonels not selected for promotion. In this he succeeded for one year. Those officers retained one more year of service and eligibility for promotion; under the new law, after 30 June 1936, if they were not on a selection list and had completed twenty-one and twenty-eight years of service respectively, they would be retired with appropriate pension.[66] Russell endured this ordeal in silence. However, on 18 February 1935, he reminded the former commandant of his lament before leaving office: if "personnel legislation was not enacted within the next five or six years the Corps was virtually lost." Russell also commented on his tribulation: "The disgruntled element has singled me out for attack. For the past week I have been called everything in the category. I felt greatly ashamed that officers of our Corps could and did fall so low. It clearly proved to me the wisdom of our selection system and the extreme necessity for it."[67]

Russell bequeathed other permanent achievements to his Corps. He ensured that the barracks at "8th and Eye" became the public showplaces of the Corps. To do this, he turned the barracks over to Col. Lemuel Shepherd, with the guidance to make it "more of a military organization than it has been for a number of years. . . . It's the oldest post in the Corps and it should be the best."[68] Limited financial support and manpower compounded by competing roles plagued the Corps in these years. On 30 June 1936, Marine Corps strength stood at 17,224 (officers, 1,074; warrant officers, 150; enlisted, 16,000). To recruit marines, Russell's recruiting service used the "modern methods of publicity, press, radio, and correspondence."[69] The old methods of street recruiters and itinerant recruiting trucks were abandoned. To further augment the regular forces, the Marine Corps Reserve was reorganized on a battalion basis, and beginning in 1934 reservists attending drills began to receive financial compensation. Legislative authorization was also obtained for the issuance of better year-round uniforms and places to drill.

Russell also expanded officer recruitment. In 1935, he recommended to Congress the creation of the Platoon Leaders Class program, a system of officer procurement and training, which would produce officers for the Marine Corps Reserve and form the nucleus of the junior officers for an expanded Marine Corps whose regular lieutenants would be rapidly promoted in time of war. In addition, at the end of fiscal years 1934 and 1935, he reported that the Corps had joined its first officers from the Naval ROTC program; this resulted from an agreement that the Corps could obtain a maximum of 20 percent of all NROTC graduates.

The number of regular officers, however, remained small: 1,070 as of 15 June 1936: major general, 4; brigadier general (line), 7; brigadier general (staff), 3; colonel, 41; lieutenant colonel, 86; major, 160; captain, 321; and first and second lieutenants, 448.[70] Russell recommended that the officer strength be 6 percent of the enlisted. The commandant also wanted those men physically and professionally unfit for modern war purged from the service, stressing that "the duties of a Marine officer require special training in the principles and practice of both land and sea warfare" and this took years to acquire. Increased numbers of officers were needed for expansion in case of war, to plan, train, and lead marines. Thus, the fiscal year 1936 increase in officer strength from 1,023 to 1,074 went where he deemed more important, to the FMF and aviation duty.

Significant changes in professional military education for officers also occurred. A theme appeared in all of Russell's annual reports: the Marine Corps Schools would focus on the techniques and tactics of amphibious operations. In his final report of September 1936, he wrote that the curricula of the schools had been expanded and improved, "particularly in the field of landing operations," and that they now met the requirements of the officer corps except in practical work. The outgoing commandant then recommended that the land west of the Quantico reservation be purchased for this purpose. Even if the men and equipment were not yet available, the theory and techniques of landing operations could be taught so the officer corps would be prepared when the expansion occurred.

For general officers, more reform was necessary. There were too few annual retirements at flag rank, and in years when none retired, this blocked advancement for younger officers. Thus, Russell recommended that legislation be passed to ensure two annual vacancies per year. In accordance with the provision of Navy Regulations, he also wanted a Marine general officer to serve on the General Board, since "it often deals with problems materially affecting the Corps." With respect to selection of major generals, Russell recommended a change in the law, which at the time permitted mixed selection boards of Navy and Marine flag officers. He noted, however, that the Navy admirals comprising the major general selection boards during his tour had performed their duties in a most satisfactory manner. Finally, Russell recommended that no commandant should serve more than one tour of four years, with his selections based "on the sole ground of present and future efficiency," and that his rank should be increased to lieutenant general.[71]

In 1936, there appeared to be four contenders to succeed Russell: Maj. Gen. Louis McCarty Little, the assistant commandant; Maj. Gen. Charles Lyman, commanding general, FMF; Brig. Gen. Hugh Matthews, the quartermaster of the Marine Corps; and Maj. Gen. James Breckinridge, commanding general of the Department of the Pacific. But Russell chose someone else: Brig. Gen. Thomas Holcomb, the ninth ranking of eleven general officers in the Corps and a flag officer only since February 1935.[72]

On 12 November 1936, Roosevelt approved Holcomb, and Russell retired on 1 December 1936.[73] As a retired general officer, what would he do? Col. and Mrs. Ira Copley, owners and publishers of the Copley newspapers, desired a military commentator and suggested that Russell become the military writer for the *San Diego Union.* Russell accepted, and he and his wife moved to Coronado, California, where he commenced his career as a journalist.[74] There he remained until his death on 6 March 1947. He died the day after his last column was due for the *San Diego Union;* his family found it, and it was duly published the following Sunday.[75]

John Henry Russell was one of the most significant commandants of the Marine Corps in the modern era. His accomplishments laid the foundation for the transition of his service from a small force linked to sea service, performing traditional and unessential missions of ships' guards, landing parties, and manning guns, coupled with small war intervention forces, to that of a modern military force with a mission, doctrine, and embryonic force structure and equipment. However, he could only lay the foundation of this change. Limited resources due to the conditions of the time, coupled with the competition for resources for traditional missions, restricted what could be done between 1934 and 1936; his successors would have to build upon what he bequeathed to them.

When Russell retired, a private comment by Maj. John Thomason candidly assessed the achievements and stress of Russell's commandancy:

> The last two and a half years, I have been in an excellent position to observe Naval and Marine Corps matters. General Russell is going out, a very tired man, with

some solid achievements behind him. He has put through the selection legislation, and he has set up the Fleet Marine Force—both of them great things for us. . . . He has never been popular, and he has not enjoyed the full confidence or loyalty of all his officers. Indeed, the conduct of some Marine Officers under him has been revolting to see. Heavy blows have been struck at him by the very people who should, by every decent standard, support him. His endurance and resolution have been entirely admirable. . . . A man of less rigidity would not have had to endure so much, but such a man would have accomplished less.[76]

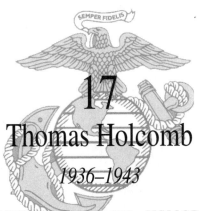

17
Thomas Holcomb
1936–1943

COL. JOHN W. GORDON, USMCR (RET.)

When Thomas Holcomb became seventeenth commandant in December 1936, the United States stood midway between the worst year of the Great Depression and the start of World War II. He was the second of Franklin D. Roosevelt's three appointees to the Corps's highest office and eventually became the first marine to win the four stars of a full general. Serving during three of FDR's four presidential terms, Holcomb achieved a record for longevity as commandant surpassed in this century only by John A. Lejeune's nine-year tenure. Yet it was the expanded power, size, and quality of the Fleet Marine Forces (FMF) as the combat elements of the Corps that above all testified to Holcomb's success. His contribution as commandant was to be nothing less than the builder, the organizer, and the trainer of the Marine Corps that fought World War II.[1]

Though the linkage of the Marine Corps to the Navy reaches back to the age of sail, that linkage developed into full partnership only during World War II. On Holcomb's watch, his service achieved a partnership with the Navy that made it possible to project sea power ashore in a way that had previously existed largely on paper. He neither at the time nor later made claim to be the original thinker who conceived either the overall strategy or the main concepts by which the amphibious mission would be accomplished. Rather, what he did was to take plans and concepts and join to them the actual forces of men, weapons, and proven techniques that would carry them out.[2]

To do this, Holcomb essentially had to reforge, and in some respects reinvent, the Marine Corps, taking it from a small peacetime professional nucleus of less than a division in strength to a force of nearly half a million men and women. The Corps not only had to go through a quantum expansion in size but had to do so with no dilution of the old aggressive, assault-minded, fight-in-every-clime-and-place esprit that stamped the professional leathernecks. In other words, Holcomb had to ensure that the hundreds of thousands of young men who poured into Parris Island and San Diego and Quantico

Gen. Thomas A. Holcomb, seventeenth commandant.

U.S. Marine Corps Photo.

and Pensacola after Pearl Harbor were remade in that same way. And he did. They became not World War II GIs but marines. To the prewar cadre of veteran leathernecks and the as-yet-untried doctrine of the amphibious assault, he added the infusion of wartime volunteers who in turn helped transform the Marine Corps into the instrument that would prevail in every amphibious assault.

At the point Holcomb took over, the Marine Corps had already altered course to begin preparing for an operation fundamental to the strategic contingency plan for conflict with Japan, War Plan Orange. The architect of the wartime mission was John A. Lejeune, the thirteenth commandant. Under its sixteenth commandant, John H. Russell, it had established the structure that would carry it out, the Fleet Marine Force. But it was left to the seventeenth commandant, Holcomb, to build this initial infrastructure into forces equal to the challenge of war in the Pacific. The numbers speak for themselves. In seven years' time Holcomb expanded his service from 16,000 to 400,000 (including Women Marines)—from just under 1,200 to more than 20,000 commissioned officers, from 158 to more than 8,000 aviators, and the initial FMF from two understrength brigades into an amphibious striking arm of three balanced divisions (with another in preparation) and four full aircraft wings, numbering some ninety-five fighter, bomber, and observation squadrons of high-performance aircraft.[3] Finally, Holcomb directed the final shaping of what British armored-warfare theorist and historian J. F. C. Fuller called "the most far reaching tactical innovation" of World War II, the amphibious assault.[4]

His role was not unlike that of his fellow service chief and sometime bitter rival, Army Chief of Staff George C. Marshall, "the true organizer of victory." Holcomb himself functioned in a like capacity on a lesser scale. Coping with smaller numbers of men and resources, but against the vast geographic sweep of the war in the Pacific, he prepared the formations needed to storm the island strongholds guarding the long sea route to Japan. If World War II was indeed "the golden age of amphibious warfare" and the Pacific theater its most trying arena, then Thomas Holcomb was for the Marine Corps the true "organizer of victory."[5]

The man whose task it was to prepare his service to meet the challenges of World War II was born on 5 August 1879. The son of the elder Thomas Holcomb and the former Elizabeth Barney, he was brought up in New Castle, Delaware, and reared an Episcopalian.[6] A distinguished ancestor on his mother's side—Joshua Barney, a highly regarded man-of-war captain in the Revolution and, by the War of 1812, a commodore in the U.S. Navy—made a career in the seagoing services seem a calling.[7]

Holcomb himself needed some of his ancestor's brand of courage in joining the Marines. He tried first in 1898, only to be rejected as "too slim." "Youngster," the recruiting officer told him, "better go home and forget about the Marines—you'd never stand the gaff." Holcomb regrouped and called up the heavy artillery for his second attempt. The result was that a U.S. senator and family friend put through the paperwork necessary for him to take the competitive examination to earn appointment as a second lieutenant. Holcomb passed easily. Not quite twenty-one, he was commissioned in April 1900. His initial physical examination noted that he had brown hair and blue eyes, was five feet seven inches tall, weighed 155 pounds, and possessed excellent sight and hearing. The Navy doctors further certified that he was "fit to perform active duty at sea or on foreign service."[8]

He attended the prescribed officers' School of Application at the Philadelphia and Port Royal (Parris Island), South Carolina, Navy Yards. Until his introduction to formal small-arms training at this time, he had never shot a rifle of any type, far less the newly adopted .30-caliber Krag-Jorgenson with its potent recoil. But in a service which regards marksmanship with the rifle as a fundamental skill, Second Lieutenant Holcomb very soon distinguished himself.[9] He won a coveted place on the newly formed Marine Corps Rifle Team and participated in a series of national competitive matches. He became team captain and was chosen for the international matches at Bisley in England. There he shot fourth highest among the American participants, with the Americans defeating all comers. Eight years later, at the national matches of 1911, the Marine Corps Rifle Team, now equipped with the .30-06-caliber Springfield rifle Model 1903 that Holcomb with affection always regarded as "a wonderful weapon," shot better than ever. A byproduct of these matches was that many of the techniques used in training for them soon found service-wide application, particularly after Holcomb was named to the commandant's staff with the overall responsibility for marksmanship training. By 1940, when Holcomb's picture appeared on the cover of *Time,* that magazine could pronounce the Marine Corps "the keenest rifle-shooting outfit in the world . . . today." As a young officer, thirty years before and during the period when the world's armies were perfecting and institutionalizing techniques for large-scale marksmanship training, Holcomb had played a direct and personal role in making his service a force of riflemen par excellence for the twentieth century.[10]

But most of Holcomb's time, between the big matches and tours of sea duty, was spent on the far side of the Pacific. Promoted to first lieutenant and wearing now on his blouse the gold medal of Distinguished Marksman, an honor since obtained by only one other commandant, he soon embarked upon the first of many tours in China. He was stationed with the Legation Guard in Peking (Beijing), a post which served to awaken his interest in the people of that vast land. And, as did the U.S. Army's 1st Lt. Joseph W. Stilwell in those same years, he demonstrated a rare talent for speaking the Chinese language. Acting on his own and with long hours of patient study, he worked to pass the State Department's demanding series of examinations in Mandarin Chinese. Eventually, in the final report forwarded back to the secretary of the navy, Holcomb was described as having acquired a "most extensive" vocabulary, one that would permit him to converse effectively with a Chinese of the Mandarin class. Many junior officers served in China; few, however, bothered to take on its complex language. But Holcomb by sheer hard work had managed to build for himself a reputation as a competent linguist, even within that exclusive diplomat-missionary-merchant-officer community of "Old China Hands."[11]

His next assignment demonstrated his growing reputation within the Marine Corps. In 1907, as President Theodore Roosevelt was flexing American naval muscle and sending the Great White Fleet around the world, Holcomb returned to Washington and was promoted to captain and made a White House military aide. But he took up his duties at a trying moment for his service. There were rumors in circulation that the hero of San Juan Hill was sympathetic to a move that, in the name of Progressive efficiency, would shift the Marine Corps from the Navy to the direct control of the U.S. Army.[12]

In the end, none of this came to pass. Nor could Holcomb, promising junior officer or not, have played any great role in the effort which finally anchored the Marine Corps's home firmly in the Navy Department. Still, in choosing him to serve as White House aide, Holcomb's superiors had picked their man well. He had outshot the British and nearly everyone else at Bisley, and had, in his last China tour, hunted in big-game expeditions under the auspices of the Smithsonian Institution. He seemed thus precisely the sort of young officer who fit Roosevelt's ideas about the "strenuous life." And certainly for Holcomb himself the term as aide was a profitable experience. It brought poise, seasoning, and the chance to learn about the kinds of men whose business brought them to the Oval Office. It brought him also his first meeting with the president's young cousin, twenty-six-year-old New York attorney Franklin Delano Roosevelt.[13]

Other tours included service as aide-de-camp to the commandant, more sea duty, and a series of inspections to gauge the quality of the Corps's training and preparation for war. Holcomb did, however, find time to discover Miss Beatrice Miller Clover, daughter of Rear Adm. Richardson Clover. A recent Washington debutante, she was twenty, and Holcomb, by now a major, was thirty-seven. But the seventeen-year difference in their ages apparently proved no obstacle, and the two were married in November 1917.[14] They were to have little time to themselves. A Marine officer's professional calling is to command in combat. When the Holcombs married, the United States was six months into the great European war that had raged since 1914. Maj. Thomas Holcomb now had the chance to show just what kind of Marine officer he really was.

Holcomb secured a command in one of the two Marine Corps regiments earmarked for the American Expeditionary Forces embarking for France. Reporting to the Corps's newly acquired training base at Quantico, he assumed command of the 2d Battalion, 6th Marines, or "Two-Six." A new unit formed from the Parris Island–trained volunteers, who had answered the call to be "First to Fight," the 6th Marines also contained a small core of "old-time leathernecks," the men with the "drilled shoulders, bone-deep sunburn . . . [and] speech flavored with navy words" whom Col. John W. Thomason, "the Corps's Kipling," described as the "Old Breed." Late in 1917, the whole unit shoved off for France to join its sister regiment, the 5th Marines, already "over there." Three days off the ship at St. Nazaire, Two-Six commenced additional training under veteran French officers and noncommissioned officers (NCOs), and then moved up to the front lines. Forming the 4th (Marine) Brigade of the U.S. Army's 2d ("Indian Head") Division, the Marines were given a quiet defensive sector. It did not stay quiet for long. The campaign of 1918, which followed, produced some of the most vicious fighting of the war. This not only established the Marines as able to beat the best elements in the German Army but also caused President Woodrow Wilson to pronounce them "a splendid body" whose record "the entire nation has reason to be proud of."[15]

After several unsuccessful offensives against the British, in May 1918, the Germans mounted the all-or-nothing offensive by which they intended to smash open the way to Paris and win the war. After the Germans punctured the French lines, the Marine brigade, including Holcomb's battalion, along with the rest of the 2d Division and the 3d Division, rushed forward to hold the Marne River line. The Germans were trained in the stormtrooper assault tactics they had perfected on the Eastern Front, and their advance would have daunted veteran troops. Few of the marines were veterans, but they waited for the enemy to come into range. All marines sent to France had qualified as at least "Marksman" with the Model 1903 rifle; they now met the Germans with intense, highly accurate fire that mowed them down as they advanced across open farmlands. The Marines then shifted over to the offensive. Their objective, the Bois de Belleau, was a place thick with underbrush and German trenches. It was the hard-fought, back-and-forth action for this blighted game preserve that established the Corps's reputation in the war. Advancing in a counterattack on 6 June, the Marines were ravaged but unhalted by enemy fire. Despite tremendous casualties, they managed to fight their way into the broken ground and smashed trees. Holcomb's battalion gained the key village of Bouresches on the right flank and just outside of the woods. Ordered to hold, Two-Six was able to keep the village in the face of repeated German counterattacks. At the heart of the defense was Lt. Clifton B. Cates, another future commandant. In the end the enemy fell back with heavy losses in four different divisions, and the Marines had won their first battle in France.[16]

For Premier George Clemenceau, the fight had "saved Paris." The French Army published an order officially renaming the site the Bois de la Brigade de Marine. Visiting the front, Assistant Secretary of the Navy Franklin D. Roosevelt reported that Allied commanders "could not say enough" about the Marines' "magnificent showing." As for Holcomb himself, his conduct in the action won him France's croix de guerre. Emphasizing his "untiring energy . . . , judgment and tactical knowledge," the citation noted that he had personally led the assault and had then managed to "maintain his battalion" on a front that was being "violently attacked" by large and determined enemy formations.[17]

In the next four months, Holcomb played a conspicuous part in virtually every action in which the Marines fought. In these campaigns he was wounded, promoted to lieutenant colonel, and twice more awarded the croix de guerre. He was also made a chevalier of the Legion d'Honneur, France's highest decoration. He became the executive officer of the 6th Marines. An additional duty "in charge of infantry weapon training" for the entire 2d Division also permitted him to apply many of his proven techniques for marksmanship training on a broad scale. His work impressed the division's new commander, Maj. Gen. John A. Lejeune, the first marine ever to command a division. By the time the war was over and he marched across the Rhine with the Army of Occupation forces, Holcomb had not only made a name for himself as a combat commander, but had gained invaluable firsthand experience of working directly with senior officers. These included the U.S. Army's Maj. Gen. Charles P. Summerall, John J. Pershing's most trusted corps commander, and two future commandants, Lejeune and Wendell C. Neville, the Marine brigade commander. Summerall, who became U.S. Army chief of staff in 1926, and other Army officers had to admit that Marine officers had certainly demonstrated a capacity for maneuvering large forces in advances characterized by "great dash and speed."[18] By the point when, in mid-1919, Holcomb finally returned to the United States, he had seen his Corps meet the test of combat against a first-class enemy and achieve a reputation far beyond anything it had known before.

He came home to his wife and to the infant son who was also a future Marine officer, Franklin Porteous.[19] But short periods at home were soon followed by long periods away—serving at Guantánamo Bay in Cuba and as an observer with the fleet's East Coast Expeditionary Force. This last assignment was particularly important. It reflected both the commitment of Lejeune, now the commandant, to the development of the amphibious mission as the ultimate raison d'être of the Corps, and his faith in Lieutenant Colonel Holcomb as an officer who could play a useful role in that result.[20]

For the Marine Corps between the two world wars, War Plan Orange, the contingency plan for a potential war with Japan, provided the overall guidance for service plans and policies. Based on concern over Japan's naval strength and developed by the U.S. Navy's General Board and the Naval War College, Orange laid out the basic strategy to be used in such a conflict. Over the years, improvements in weapons-system capabilities—the aircraft carrier, for example—were gradually incorporated and the plan updated accordingly. The central concept, however, remained largely intact. Assuming the Japanese would strike first and then use their Micronesian island bases (taken from the Germans in World War I and assigned as League of Nations mandates) as an outer ring of defense, Orange called for the U.S. Fleet to attack west across the Central Pacific. The payoff to this long thrust would be the great sea battle to be fought against the enemy fleet somewhere east of the Philippines.[21]

Orange was indeed the big picture. But significant blank spots—how to seize the islands that lay in the path of the Central Pacific drive, islands which the Americans would themselves need as advanced naval bases to carry out the counteroffensive—had yet to be painted in. This was where the Marines came in. Lejeune used Orange as the mandate to drive the development of a full array of amphibious-assault tactics and techniques to seize these islands. On a map the islands seemed little more than dots in the Pacific, but the harsh reality was that the enemy would be able to defend them at virtually every possible landing point.[22]

Certainly the prevailing military wisdom held that no such assault could prevail against well-entrenched troops equipped with modern weapons. But as Holcomb and his peers came more and more to analyze the Gallipoli campaign and previous landing operations, the Quantico-based Marine Corps Schools emerged as the central institution for the study of the operational requirements of amphibious warfare. Yet Lejeune was never content to rely solely upon Quantico for honing the professional skills and expanding the horizons of his most promising officers. For that reason Holcomb would find himself, over the next dozen years, winning sought-after assignments to the very top professional schools offered by the American military establishment. In the end, this experience helped to produce an individual equipped to meld the latest military theories and concepts of the Army and Navy to the particular institutional needs of the Corps.[23]

Holcomb's crucial educational process commenced with a tour at the U.S. Army's Command and General Staff School at Fort Leavenworth, Kansas. Reporting in 1924, he joined two other Marine officers, Maj. Roy S. Geiger and Maj. William P. Upshur. All three were to become general officers. Lasting a full academic year, the course was, as the Army's Maj. Dwight D. Eisenhower later recalled, an "unrelieved grind." But the Marines did well. By the end of the course, Holcomb, competing with the Army's best, finished as a Distinguished Graduate, an achievement that won him an official commendation from Lejeune and guaranteed that he would go on for additional educational assignments of a demanding nature.[24] Certainly the one that came next took him to the best possible location for studying the operational components of Orange, the U.S. Naval War College. Newport, however, gave Holcomb little opportunity to indulge narrow service interests. In the various war games that went on, he frequently found himself shifting make-believe battleships, cruisers, and destroyers around the globe with his Navy colleagues. By the close of the year-long program, he had succeeded in developing a solid theoretical grasp of the role that sea power, particularly naval aviation, would have to play in the conduct of the Central Pacific effort.[25]

The assignment that came next was an even greater plum. Only a select handful were chosen to represent the Corps at the apex of naval professional education. But immediately after finishing one war college, Holcomb was tapped to represent his service at still another, the U.S. Army War College, Washington, D.C. If anything, this latter selection was an even more telling indication of the esteem with which Holcomb was now regarded by senior officers. With the memory of General Pershing's animosity toward the Corps still fresh in its institutional memory, Headquarters Marine Corps would not have considered anyone but the very best officer as an emissary to the enemy camp. Certainly Holcomb was one of only a small elite of Marine officers to attend the Army War College in that era. Of the Army officers who went through their service's highest school between 1920 and 1940, over half would achieve general officer's rank. But the figure for the Marines was even higher, amounting to at least six out of every ten who attended.[26]

Holcomb's graduation in 1932 would climax a long and intensive course of study concentrating on "the conduct of field operations of the Army and higher echelons," as well as those "political, economic, and social matters which influence the conduct of war." Education at the Navy and Army colleges exposed him to the latest concepts in two modes of warfare: warfare on land and warfare at sea. It was a complementary form of education which indeed helped to make him, in Kipling's old tag about the Royal Marines, more completely the "soldier an' sailor too."[27]

His new knowledge was quickly put to use. Assigned to Washington for the next three years, he was called upon to help incorporate into the Navy's planning the new concepts in amphibious warfare. A crucial achievement was the creation in 1933 of the Fleet Marine Force. The FMF was intended to be not merely an ad hoc assemblage of expeditionary units but a permanent, organized, and carefully balanced combat or "type" command of fundamental importance to the Navy. This new force would be "included in the fleet organization as an integral part thereof," and would function as the fleet's amphibious striking arm to seize advanced naval bases. As study and refinement of the new techniques went forward, Holcomb was the officer picked to head the place where the emerging doctrine was being hammered out, the Marine Corps Schools at Quantico. This prestigious assignment at the Corps's intellectual center represented quite a step in Holcomb's career. John H. Russell, who became commandant early in 1934, had himself previously been head of the Schools, and he, like Lejeune before him, viewed their function as vital to the forging of the new wartime Corps. Holcomb took over in early 1935. Two months later, at age fifty-six with thirty-five years' service, he pinned on his first star.[28]

Promoted to major general after only a year, Brigadier General Holcomb was chosen by Russell to head several selection boards. This gave him an opportunity to evaluate and choose many of the officers who would be promoted to key command and staff slots in the crucial years ahead. Russell also sent him to make speeches to veterans' groups, brought him up to Headquarters for frequent consultations, and assigned him to carry out liaison visits to the Navy, including various exercises held at the Naval War College.[29] These were followed by a period at the Navy Department, for which Holcomb was officially commended for his "able presentation of the Landing Force Problem," explaining to the secretary of the navy and the chief of naval operations the whole range of techniques which the Marine Corps had developed for amphibious operations.[30]

That Holcomb, a junior major general, enjoyed Russell's personal trust and esteem was obvious to all. What came next, however, proved a major surprise even to those who prided themselves on being close observers of service politics. A longtime personal friend of FDR's, Russell, now approaching retirement age, was due to step down at the end of 1936. The odds-on favorite to succeed him was Maj. Gen. Charles H. Lyman. Like Holcomb a graduate of both war colleges, Lyman had also been Russell's first choice to command the FMF. Moreover, the commandant tended to favor those officers who, like himself, had not won combat honors in France because of assigned duties in the Caribbean. But Russell did not make what seemed to be the obvious choice. Instead, he recommended as his successor not the rumored heir apparent but the far more junior Thomas Holcomb. Perhaps Lyman's age (he was already sixty-one) and Holcomb's ability to get along well with the Navy influenced the decision. Certainly this last was a factor which could only grow in importance in advancing the fortunes of the FMF.

For his part, Lyman, swallowing whatever disappointment he may have felt, admitted to friends that the decision was personally "a matter of surprise. . . . I had really expected to be appointed." But Holcomb was "the logical man unless they appointed me. . . . Tommy is a fine man [and] a good friend."[31]

Eleven days after Roosevelt was reelected to a second term, he appointed Thomas Holcomb the major general commandant of the Marine Corps. The Corps's new leader and Mrs. Holcomb moved into those "quaint, spacious . . . quarters at Eighth and G Streets Southwest, alongside the Marine barracks," where, as *Time* magazine noted, "Commandants have lived in unbroken succession since the house was built in 1805."[32] It would be their home for the next seven years, their longest stay in any one place in all of Holcomb's forty-three years of service.

The new commandant immediately turned his attention to building up the three-year-old FMF, whose understrength Atlantic Coast brigade was based at Quantico and the Pacific one, also understrength, at San Diego. A series of full-scale fleet landing exercises (FLEXs) had begun in 1934 to test in practice the techniques laid down in the *Tentative Manual for Landing Operations.* But with the nation's economy slumping anew, Congress was in no mood to fund offensive forces intended to seize enemy islands in a war that no one wanted. Even the money that supported the Navy's new warship-building program proved a two-edged sword, since each new cruiser, carrier, or battleship required its own Marine detachment and thus further deprived the FMF of needed men.[33]

Also, the Navy lacked crucial transport vessels and had done little to develop the kinds of small craft needed to land the Marines on a hostile shore. This is not to suggest that the Marine Corps enjoyed some sole-proprietor, visionary role regarding development of these craft soon to figure so prominently in the war ahead. Such was not the case at all. The U.S. Army was interested in amphibian vehicles, for example, although more for river-crossing operations than attack from the sea. Likewise, in England, the Royal Navy and British Army cooperated in a series of experiments with landing vessels. So also did the Imperial Japanese Navy. More particularly, the Japanese were first to develop a drop-ramp bow for landing craft, an innovation Western military officers would not see until six months into Holcomb's tour and the start of the Sino-Japanese War in 1937. But Holcomb had by then already started the Marine Corps on a course that focused intensively on acquiring vessels capable of solving the problem of ship-to-shore movement. He recognized very clearly that accomplishment of the mission hinged on getting suitable craft, and gave personal attention to the acquisition, preferably under Navy auspices, of several main types. A key first step was to transfer the Marine Corps Equipment Board from Washington down to Quantico. This meant that the board, placed under a succession of aggressive officers, was co-located both with the place where the operational techniques and doctrines were being worked out, the Marine Corps Schools, and with the elements that would carry out much of the actual field testing, the units of the East Coast FMF.[34] With the field testing of various types of new launches and vehicles given this sort of strong new impetus, the information so developed could then be used to prompt the Navy to greater efforts.[35]

Ultimately, the most successful of these experiments concerned the famous "Alligator," an amphibian tractor designed by Donald Roebling, as well as a drop-ramp landing craft developed by Andrew Jackson Higgins of New Orleans. In the case of Roebling's experimental vehicle in particular, Holcomb recognized a good thing when he saw it. Essentially a boat with tracks, it could handle open water, swamps, or crawl up to operate on dry land with equal facility. Roebling originally designed his amphibian to bring help to hurricane victims stranded in the outlying bayou country. When a *Life* magazine article praised the tractor's performance, Holcomb ensured that the Equipment Board immediately commenced a thorough investigation of its potential as an assault vehicle. It was this "alligator boat," as Holcomb called it, that eventually became the amphibian landing vehicle tracked (LVT), or "amtrac," so crucial to the operations in the Pacific. Holcomb also invited the deputy chief of staff of the army, George C. Marshall, down to Quantico to see the pilot model in 1937. He told Marshall, "We believe that this vehicle will be of definite value in landing operations."[36]

The Higgins boat evolved at about the same time from several shallow-draft vessels able to operate in rough surf. It outclassed previous types of Navy-developed lighters employed for moving men and equipment ashore by the addition of a droppable bow ramp, which greatly facilitated landing on the beach. This sound design—the basis of the plywood LCVP, or, officially, the landing craft/vehicle personnel—was eventually adapted to a whole variety of larger, all-metal landing craft capable of carrying heavy vehicles, artillery, and tanks to shore.[37]

Marshall and his officers were impressed by these craft, especially the "alligator boat." At the moment, however, with the war in Europe still two years off and the ability of Britain and France to withstand Germany an article of faith, Army officers were more interested in vehicles that could help Army units dash across rivers. There seemed to be little point in developing a whole family of specialized vehicles for ship-to-shore movement. Even should the United States again become involved in a European war, Army officers remained confident of their access to French ports by which to unload men or materiel administratively, as in 1917–18. They were impressed by the Navy and Marines' hard work in developing a forced-entry, land-from-the-sea capability to establish a force on a hostile shore, but saw little in it for themselves.[38]

Still, Holcomb was able to use Marshall's visit and further Army interest to good avail. Indeed, he soon lobbied the secretary of the navy into establishing a special Navy Department board that would concentrate solely on the development of landing craft. This, of course, represented a considerable bureaucratic coup for Holcomb and the Marine Corps and was a way to get Equipment Board recommendations quickly to government contractors. It materially aided the study and acquisition of these essential craft in ways that would ultimately benefit not just the two sea services but also the Army and indeed any Allied force eventually to be engaged in landing on an enemy shore in any theater of World War II.[39]

Other efforts went forward on somewhat less conventional fronts. Holcomb was a shrewd enough politician to make good use of every available ally, especially when these included the president's son, James Roosevelt, lieutenant colonel, U.S. Marine Corps Reserve. Holcomb's predecessor, Russell, had arranged for the younger Roosevelt to be commissioned at FDR's request and thus gained an advocate in the Oval Office. The seventeenth commandant occasionally asked the president's son's advice at particular moments. He also set it up so that Roosevelt, in civilian life a vice president of the Samuel Goldwyn motion picture company, could serve as a special observer on a number of FLEXs. And never one to miss a good public relations opportunity, Holcomb was aware that the president himself had "told James that we must have, if we would search our files, a number of interesting and stirring episodes, which could be made into a good movie" about the Marine Corps.[40] Holcomb began this project by enlisting Lt. Col. John W. Thomason. His combat record and vivid writing style made Thomason a "legend in the armed forces and literary world," with best-selling books and frequent short stories to his credit. The best-known work was *Fix Bayonets!* a classic account of the Marines in World War I. Holcomb was convinced that merely having Thomason's name on the film would guarantee considerable "box office appeal" since his literary brother officer already had "quite a public of his own." Despite these efforts, however, the Goldwyn Company decided to pursue other movies and the project was dropped.[41]

Holcomb continued to build the Corps as World War II approached, doing everything possible to promote good relations with two secretaries of the navy and two chiefs of naval operations. By the time German tanks rolled east into Poland in 1939, Holcomb had in hand the broad outlines of a plan by which to expand the infrastructure of bases which supported the Marine Corps—but no money to buy the land or to build the buildings. Aside from a recruit training depot at Parris Island and the various Marine barracks located at the principal Navy installations, a full regiment, the 4th Marines, was stationed in China. By far the largest contingent of Holcomb's field force was concentrated in the FMF—an FMF for each coast, each comprising a brigade and its aviation combat elements. The East Coast units were at Quantico, whose airfield accommodated the fighter, bomber, and observation aircraft that supported that brigade's ground elements. The West Coast brigade was at San Diego, with its attendant aircraft operating out of the North Island Naval Air Station. These and other naval facilities on the West Coast had been built up in the 1920s to support War Plan Orange.[42] Basic equipment, however, was little changed since the last war. The individual marine still carried the Model 1903 rifle and still wore, on field service, either the campaign hat or the Model 1917 tin-hat helmet. In the field, the wool forest-green, winter-service uniform was worn in cold weather and the cotton khaki summer-service one in hot. Knee-high canvas leggings were worn with both, except that officers wore leather puttees. The defense budgets ensured that both air and ground FMF units were manned at less than peacetime table-of-organization strength.

Virtually all the aircraft compared unfavorably with those that the Germans and Japanese flew. It was this nucleus which Holcomb was about to carry into the huge and unprecedented program of American military expansion for World War II.

That program began incrementally as FDR endeavored to shape U.S. security policy to meet the challenges implicit in first the "China Incident," then the formation of the Rome-Berlin-Tokyo Axis, and finally the actual outbreak of war itself. In 1940, the fall of France and the Low Countries and, earlier, the German conquest of Norway and Denmark, at length induced FDR to sign a "two-ocean navy" expansion bill intended to deal with the growing menace to the United States of war in Europe and Asia simultaneously. Economic sanctions against the Japanese for the war in China were backed up by leaving the U.S. Pacific Fleet in the Hawaiian Islands. By that point American defense planners had begun blending the various prewar "color" plans, of which Orange was one, into a workable and coherent whole. Ultimately, the product of their labors and the blueprint for U.S. strategy would be the version called Rainbow Five.[43]

In the midst of these determinations, the Joint Army-Navy Board considered what to do should the Germans try to seize an island in the Atlantic or perhaps the Caribbean as a base for U-boat operations. This remote possibility soon produced a key recommendation from the board that Holcomb turned to advantage for the Marine Corps. The threat that the Germans might try something in the Western Hemisphere led the board to emphasize the need to create a ground-combat force of at least corps size and amphibious in capability. The raids into the Atlantic by the German warships *Bismarck* and *Prinz Eugen* seemed to lend urgency to such preparations. The planners directed that a two-division force be set up within Adm. Ernest J. King's U.S. Atlantic Fleet, and that the overall commander of this amphibious corps be an experienced Marine officer. This last point alone represented a considerable achievement for Holcomb, since no marine had ever commanded a joint or any other kind of force at that level. The second advantage came because one of the divisions was to come from the Army and the other the Marine Corps, and this required the Corps to establish its first full, balanced, combat-arms Marine division.[44]

Having lobbied to get the strong-willed, sulfurous, but highly talented, Maj. Gen. Holland M. Smith appointed the amphibious corps commander, Holcomb was also able to win authorization to form the 1st Marine Division. Authorization to form a second division, this one on the West Coast, soon followed. The commandant watched carefully over the design of the Marine division to ensure that its structure combined both new ideas about organization and deep-rooted Marine Corps concepts regarding firepower and maneuver at the small unit level. He was not content to proceed merely by expanding the two existing FMF brigades into something larger. Rather, he was convinced that the Marine division needed some particular capabilities. A major requirement was that it would have to be capable both of mounting the amphibious assault—and then holding on until relieved, even in the face of enemy air, naval, and ground counterattack. In determining the appropriate mix of units and capabilities, he took careful note of the excellent work and rigorous experimentation with infantry forces by the Army's Maj. Gen. Lesley J. McNair. Like the McNair-designed Army infantry division, the Marine division that Holcomb soon fielded was "triangular." It was based, that is, on three-infantry maneuver elements supported by artillery and tanks, and had, generally speaking, essentially the same array of weapons as the Army organization. Also, the combat service-support structure was ostensibly the same.

But Holcomb's division was different in three respects. Marine infantry units incorporated the fire team–based rifle squad (each fire team a nucleus of riflemen organized around an automatic weapon, the squad a multiple of teams) concept under evolution since the Banana Wars. They were also bigger than comparable Army units. Put simply, they had the ability to deploy greater numbers of riflemen in the assault or to hold a position on the defensive. The division also packed a greater wallop in terms of its own artillery—a full regiment (five howitzer and gun battalions) of artillery as against the Army division's "Divarty" of three or four battalions. A third difference was the strength and weight of the engineer effort. Instead of the Army's divisional battalion of combat engineers, the Marine division contained three battalions of Marine engineers, plus a Navy mobile construction battalion of SeaBees. There were additional differences in terms of numbers of vehicles, quantity and availability of antiaircraft, and antishipping artillery. Overall, the Marine division that Holcomb brought into being was larger than its Army counterpart, had plenty of depth, and carried a big punch. When task-organized into amphibious elements called regimental landing teams, it had with naval gunfire support, the power to hurl itself onto the hostile shore—and stay there and win.[45]

Elements of this new, first-of-its-type division began training exercises early in 1941. Holcomb used these exercises to push for more money for men, equipment, and bases. Likewise, the establishment and early training exercises of the Atlantic-based amphibious corps, of which the 1st Marine Division was part, ultimately benefited all parties concerned. Marine officers now had a vehicle by which to acquire competency in training, maneuvering, and supporting their new divisions. For the Army, which supplied the 1st Infantry Division, the experience proved an eye-opener and a catalyst. It provided the Army its first direct exposure to the new amphibious techniques so long evolving in the Navy and Marines. Exercises took place off the Virginia coast and in the Chesapeake. Now in the throes of burgeoning expansion (Congress had passed the first peacetime draft six months before), the Army observed, evaluated, and then began training in these techniques, using both the 1st Infantry Division and overall corps structure as the platform. Eventually these techniques were incorporated into McNair's training program as Army divisions prepared for landings that would be conducted from New Guinea to France.[46]

At another level, however, joint amphibious corps also resurrected the Army–Marine Corps rivalry of 1918. In the end this proved the catalyst to a good decision. Few who observed Maj. Gen. "Howlin' Mad" Smith would have identified diplomacy as his paramount trait. Senior Army officers, finding their service a newly apprenticed third party to the close Navy–Marine Corps amphibious partnership, both prickled over Smith and likewise resented the control which these other two services exerted over key decisions. But there was more to it than that. American military planning had in 1941 embraced the concept that, should war come, Europe was the vital theater and Germany must be defeated first. The Germany-first decision appeared tidy and clearcut, seemingly permitting a full effort in Europe. Diplomacy, it was hoped, would in the meantime keep Japan at bay on the far side of the Pacific. But should war erupt in that theater as well, Marshall's officers, already concentrating on the role that ground forces would have in a European war, believed that landings designed to pierce Hitler's Festung Europa would be fundamentally different from those in the Pacific. The War Department told Holcomb that landings in Europe would be on a massive scale and merely the prelude to standard maneuver operations ashore. Those against the Japanese, on the other hand, Army planners dismissed as "small and part of a distinctly naval campaign." Finally, Army officers regarded the whole idea of an Army–Navy–Marine Corps command structure as "a nightmare."[47] They resolved to be clear of it at first opportunity.

By year's end, the Japanese strike at Pearl Harbor would provide that opportunity. The War Department proposed a geographic division of amphibious effort: the Army would take on the landing operations in Europe, the Marine Corps those in the Pacific. This proposal delighted Admiral King, who "wanted the war against Japan to be a Navy-dominated campaign." For Holcomb, this decision allowed him to get back to the business of preparing the Corps for the great test in the Pacific.

He had worked hard all along to maintain good relations between his service and the Army. But the bitter truth was that he often had to compete with Army Chief of Staff Marshall in order to win what the Corps needed. Writing to Representative Carl Vinson (D-Georgia), chairman of the House Naval Affairs Committee, he laid out requirements which included new weapons, more men, and acquisition of places where "better training facilities are available."[48] This last requirement followed the decision to create the 1st Marine Division. Quantico was too small and would in any case be needed to train new officers. The purchase of the base at New River, North Carolina, later named in honor of General Lejeune, made it possible to train the division's full complement of infantry, artillery, engineer, tank, and other units on the East Coast. Equidistant between Los Angeles and San Diego, Camp Pendleton provided a huge training and maneuver area on the West Coast for the new 2d Marine Division. Holcomb's concept was to use the battalion as the basic building block, with each, once trained, to be formed into larger units, as additional resources became available.[49]

If building up the Corps's ground forces required Holcomb to vie with Marshall for scarce materiel as well as for quality manpower, an even more difficult task was building up Marine aviation elements. This effort entailed not just the acquisition of first-line aircraft but also competition with both the Army Air Forces and the Navy's air arm for young men who could meet the rigorous standards for pilot training. As late as 1939, the Marine Corps had only about two hundred qualified aviators. The old method was to send lieutenants, after seasoning as ground officers, to Pensacola to become naval aviators. This approach would never yield the number of pilots needed in the time required. Holcomb therefore worked out a system for a set quota for Marine pilot-training slots authorized under the newly expanded Naval Aviation Cadet Program. By the time he stepped down as commandant, more than eight thousand pilots had been trained in this way.[50] The promotion of prewar flyers with infantry experience proved sufficient to ensure that Marine aviation maintained its commitment to support ground units. Virtually on the eve of the war in the Pacific, Marine squadrons finally received the same models of Grumman F4F Wildcat fighters and Douglas SBD Dauntless dive bombers as their Navy counterparts.

Indeed, by late 1940, when *Time* put Holcomb's picture on its front cover, the Corps whose development he had so carefully shaped could be characterized as, "the Navy's professional fighters," an elite service whose ranks comprise, "a small, well-integrated army (the Fleet Marine Force) equipped with tanks, airplanes, machine guns, artillery." And when the Japanese onslaught finally smashed into the U.S. Pacific Feet at Pearl Harbor, Holcomb's Marine Corps was, as the *New York Times* later noted, "the one member of the armed forces . . . prepared for immediate action."[51]

Yet disaster after disaster in an unbroken sequence befell the Americans over the next six months. In succession, marines were lost on Guam, Wake Island, and Corregidor. The defense of Wake Island, however, and in particular, the excellent account given by a single pair of Wildcat fighters against overwhelming numbers of enemy aircraft, could only strengthen the public image of marines as heroic fighters. Holcomb did not, however, concentrate his efforts solely on the crucial task of preparation for war in the Pacific. In these early days of 1942, there was no shortage of ideas for dispatching the Marine Corps everywhere there was trouble. One of them called for landing the 1st Marine Division in North Africa to help the British finish off Rommel. To Holcomb's relief, that idea and others fell away in the face of logistical and operational realities. One that would not, however, vexed the commandant mightily and transcended his abilities to defeat it. Despite his deep conviction that all available resources must go into building the Marine amphibious divisions, men more powerful than he soon forced the experimentation with very different types of forces. Thus, despite his strenuous objection, the type of hit-and-run raiding unit which the British described as a "special force" would also make its appearance in the Marine Corps.[52]

The chief advocates of forming units on the pattern of the British commandos were President Roosevelt, himself, and Secretary of the Navy Frank Knox, a Chicago newspaper magnate and former Rough Rider. A key proposal had come from Holcomb's old acquaintance from the China days, Capt. Evans F. Carlson. As commander of the Marine guard detachment at the president's Warm Springs retreat, Carlson gained FDR's regard. Carlson was considered a dangerous eccentric by some; he had, nonetheless, studied the guerrilla warfare techniques of the Communist Eighth Route Army in China. Another plan for a special unit came from the president's son, James, now on active duty serving as "military adviser and liaison officer" to FDR's Columbia Law classmate, William J. Donovan. Of the various projects submitted, it was the one offered by Donovan, a Medal of Honor winner from World War I and a celebrity attorney on Wall Street, that ultimately forced Holcomb into forming commando-type Marine units. Once Donovan was able to gain Knox's backing, Holcomb's balking did no good. The secretary of the navy effectively trumped him by threatening to raise Donovan, then technically a colonel, U.S. Army Reserve, to the rank of brigadier general in the Marine Corps Reserve and chief of Marine commandos. Holcomb had no choice, but to give in; the Marine Corps would have to create special operations forces after all. His one stipulation was that the Corps "not have to go outside . . . its ranks to secure leaders [i.e., Donovan]," and that only Marine officers be permitted to command Marine commandos.[53]

Thus the Marine "Raiders," the first American special force raised in World War II, were formed. Carlson was promoted to lieutenant colonel and made commander of one of the Raider battalions with James Roosevelt as his executive officer. Donovan himself wound up not with the threatened Marine brigadier general's star but with an assignment rather more ambitious in scope: head of the new Office of Strategic Services, modeled after the British Special Operations Executive and predecessor to the Central Intelligence Agency. The Raiders' primary function was to carry out strategic reconnaissance and hit-and-run attacks. The men and women of the OSS were to act in conjunction with local resistance forces. To Holcomb, nevertheless, all the "specialized training" required by raiding, parachute, or glider troops was at best "in the nature of post-graduate training for a Marine." He saw little that these various elite units could add to the capabilities of the standard units and much that they could take away. Paralleling the British experience, they threatened always to "skim off the cream" by pulling "the best men" out of the battalions and regiments that Holcomb knew would do the lion's share of the fighting.[54]

But there were issues far larger than these to fill the hard months following Pearl Harbor. In the new year, Hong Kong, Malaya, Singapore, the Philippines, and the Dutch East Indies and Burma fell as the Japanese rampage continued unchecked. Convoy losses to U-boats in the Atlantic climbed, and in Russia the German drive toward Stalingrad appeared unstoppable. Not until the Japanese fleet was turned back in the Coral Sea did the balance in the Pacific war begin to shift. A month later, in June 1942, it shifted still more when the Japanese lost four carriers and hundreds of skilled pilots off Midway. Throughout these various turns of fortune, Holcomb enjoyed a seat that permitted him to witness the formulation of American strategy at the highest military levels. Early in 1942, the body which had been called the Joint Army-Navy Board was redesignated the Joint Chiefs of Staff. One of its new purposes was to parallel the British body called the Chiefs of Staff Committee. When the two acted together, they were called the Combined Chiefs of Staff. Holcomb had been permitted to function as one of the "full and equal members" both of the original body and the JCS. In that capacity he had served on the U.S. delegation to the Anglo-American Combined Chiefs of Staff, "dealing with Winston Churchill and the British [service chiefs]." He, along with

Admiral Stark and General Marshall, "participated in all the basic British-U.S. strategic planning for 1942, acting in general as the amphibious warfare expert."[55]

Early in the same year and in recognition of the Corps's growing size, Congress approved the appointment of Holcomb as "Lieutenant General and Commandant," the first marine ever to wear three stars. He needed every bit of influence the new star brought. Holcomb was personally stunned by the high losses sustained by the Marine Corps pilots sent up to blunt the wave of enemy planes flying against Midway Island. The engaged Marine squadrons were equipped with aircraft that were no match for their Japanese opponents and Holcomb pressed hard to win his aviators better machines out of the naval aviation pipeline. The new star also came in handy in his other main task of that year, laying the foundation for the first American ground offensive of World War II—the landing in August, of the 1st Marine Division on Guadalcanal in the Solomon Islands chain.[56]

In all the prewar planning for Plan Orange, the South Pacific had figured not at all. But for Holcomb, the Marines, and the Navy, Guadalcanal was a little like the old tag about reality being what happened to you while you were busy planning your future. Notwithstanding that their fleet had been turned back at the Coral Sea in May, the Japanese had continued to push down the Solomons; they now were close to completing an airfield on Guadalcanal. Once completed, it would be a base from which their planes could fly to cut the sea-lane that led from the United States to Australia. For the Americans, Guadalcanal was the strategic reality of the movement that had to be dealt with.[57]

Only with difficulty, however, could an offensive be prepared. The 1st Marine Division was in actuality only partially available. An infantry regiment short, it would have to land reinforced by special force Raiders, a Marine parachute battalion, and a 2d Marine Division battalion. Nonetheless, early in August 1942, the Marines stepped ashore into a green jungle paradise—and into a battle that became a test of all that Holcomb had worked to accomplish. For the next three months, Maj. Gen. Alexander A. Vandegrift's Marines and the Navy offshore had to withstand Japanese attacks that seemed almost certain to destroy the Americans. As the battle opened, Holcomb spoke on the *March of Time* radio program to express his "firm conviction that . . . the valor of our forces will prevail."[58] At home, however, the impression quickly mounted, as the ferocity of the struggle increased, that Guadalcanal was a fiasco and the Marines were out on a limb. The president became "fearful that his troops might be driven out," and many were convinced that the beleaguered Marines might be defeated by the same jungle-trained enemy who had proved unstoppable in Malaya and the Philippines. Indeed, as the battle raged on, members of a group called the Marine Fathers' Club sent a telegram to FDR, demanding that he, as "the father of a Marine, act at once to prevent any further . . . losses of life among our boys . . . before we face another Wake Island or Bataan."[59]

The situation was sufficiently grim for Roosevelt to dispatch the commandant himself out to check on matters. Even as Holcomb arrived, however, the situation was actually already well in hand—or nearly so. Reinforcements were on their way, and the Navy had come back swinging from earlier losses in carriers and cruisers. In addition,

Marine, Navy, and Army Air Forces pilots daily flew from Guadalcanal's crude airfields to wage a campaign of aerial attrition that further crippled Japan's naval air arm. Although stricken by tropical diseases, the Marines on the ground prevailed in the jungle, beating back attack after enemy attack. By the time Holcomb returned from the island, he could report great progress. Sharing his findings at a special press conference held on the Corps's birthday in November, Holcomb told the reporters just what they wanted to hear. "There is no question about it," he said. "The young men of the Marines . . . are individually superior to the Japanese soldier. . . . They will win."[60]

For win, of course, they did. After a bitter half-year's air-sea-land campaign, the last Japanese troops finally quit the island early in 1943. Yet not before Holcomb had come close to letting an extremely important cat out of the bag. He had very nearly given away the priceless secret of "Ultra," the ability to decrypt and read some of the most vital of Japanese radio messages. At the official press conference held upon his return from the islands, he talked too fully about American accomplishments, saying something to the effect that "we had captured the Japanese landing code." There had never really been a cause for worry, he said, since the Americans had always known what the Japanese planned. The commandant's statement was reported in the *Washington Post.* Had Holcomb's slip been detected, it might have destroyed not just the Allied ability to read Japanese but also German and Italian radio transmissions, since these Axis powers all used variants of the same Enigma encoding machine. After some tense weeks, the flap abated when it became clear that Ultra had not been compromised after all. Holcomb went back to the business of sending Marine divisions and aircraft wings to the Pacific.[61]

The campaign for Guadalcanal had revealed a number of critical shortcomings and problems. A continuing irritant was the Raiders. Even before the Raiders' diversionary raid on Makin Island (a Japanese outpost in the Gilberts, distant to the north and west of Guadalcanal) had almost turned into "a complete fiasco," the commandant had already begun taking steps to get "this Raider business . . . straightened out." The effort had taken on even greater importance when the Navy's Rear Adm. Richmond Kelly Turner, commander, Amphibious Force South Pacific, actually began trying to expand the Raiders, not do away with them. Turner's contention was that the Marine division, in its present form, was too cumbersome for the job at hand. Rather, it should instead be broken down into small, lightly armed forces like the two Raider battalions already formed. Without bothering to check with the Marines first, he took it upon himself to order the immediate conversion of all available infantry units into Raider battalions. Holcomb and his fellow general officers had great respect for Turner's ability as a Navy thinker and planner, but they also knew that his expertise stopped at water's edge. Turner's meddling raised questions about the larger issue of Marine Corps control of landing forces ashore. Indeed it seemed to threaten the integrity of the whole structure and doctrine for amphibious operations.[62]

To deal with Turner, Holcomb finally had to win the support of Turner's Navy superiors, Admiral Nimitz in the Pacific and Admiral King, the CNO. When King agreed that standard Marine units were already "fully capable of Raider-type operations and that no fundamental alteration in Marine organization was presently either feasible or called for," Holcomb had won his case.[63] Moreover, as American strength in the Pacific grew in 1943, and as the nature of operations began to shift toward the large-scale assaults essential to the Central Pacific drive, it became increasingly apparent that Raider units could be assigned only to lesser, subsidiary tasks. Holcomb's argument, defeated the year before, this time triumphed. The Pacific war was about to enter a new phase, one in which special forces could have had no major role. A CNO staff subsection soon produced the memorandum which sealed their fate. Declaring that any operation "so far carried out . . . could have been performed equally well" by standard units, it specified that the Raider program be terminated, "so as to make all . . . organizations uniform and to avoid . . . [an image of] elite or selected troops."[64] The ex-Raiders were reassigned to conventional infantry battalions. Thus, an experiment influenced by the British experience with the commandos finally came to an end.

There remained for resolution, however, the rather larger problem of Navy–Marine Corps command relationships during the conduct of an amphibious campaign. Going into Guadalcanal, the doctrinal bible had been Fleet Training Publication 167: Landing Operations Doctrine, U.S. Navy, essentially a refined, more detailed version of the original *Tentative Manual.* Left unspecified in that document, though, were the actual powers to be exercised by the Marine general commanding the force once it went ashore. From the Marine perspective, the Navy still had too much influence, and the recent experience was not encouraging. Admiral Turner had felt free to meddle with Vandegrift's troop dispositions during some of the most critical stages of the fighting on Guadalcanal; with the present arrangement, the same thing might occur again later. Holcomb, therefore, wanted to have the respective boundaries of authority clearly laid out. Proceeding carefully just as he had in the Raider issue, he approached the key admirals one by one. The commandant proposed, first, that the Marine general (the landing force commander) should be empowered to function as an equal to the Navy admiral (the amphibious task force commander) during the planning stages of an amphibious operation. Thereafter, during the actual prosecution of operations ashore after the assault phase, the Marine general should return to a position of equality with his Navy counterpart. Holcomb argued that any disagreements should be submitted directly "to the common superior (presumably a Navy theater commander) for resolution."[65]

For the Corps, the benefit of this set-up was obvious. It had the effect of granting the Marine general a parallel, not a subordinate, relationship to the Navy amphibious force commander during two very crucial stages of an amphibious operation. Also, the set-up made sense. Indeed King proved receptive to Holcomb's ideas, which seemed a good way to divide along the lines of expertise and function, and yet retain effective unity of command. The concept was also a concession to the Corps's growing strength and significance in the war in the Pacific. Another concession was to give Marine generals the additional authority they needed. Thus, in the South Pacific, Vandegrift was given command of a new I Marine Amphibious Corps, and, at Pearl Harbor, Holland

M. Smith was given charge of Amphibious Corps, Pacific Fleet, for the impending effort in the Central Pacific.

Holcomb was successful also in improving the strength and power of his aviation elements. For the first time, Marine Corps pilots gained a first-class fighter plane. The adoption of the gull-winged Vought F4U Corsair, principally allocated to Marine rather than Navy squadrons because the first models had defects that impaired their use in carrier operations, provided the Corps with a superlative aircraft. Fast and maneuverable, it became the Marines' mainstay multirole fighter for attack, air-to-air combat, and close-air support for the rest of the war. Marine air represented a unique blending of both carrier- and land-based qualities. In the role of close-air support, Marine aviators pushed to achieve a level of performance never matched by the Navy or the Army Air Forces. Inheriting a handful of squadrons in 1936, the commandant by mid-1943 had built the Corps's aviation strength to more than sixty squadrons. Holcomb was not an aviator, yet he successfully presided over the emergence of Marine aviation and saw it forged into a weapon that proved its lethality through three more wars in the next fifty years.[66]

Nor was Holcomb's success restricted to Marine air alone. His various recruiting programs rapidly swelled the size of the Corps yet preserved its character as an elite fighting force. By mid-1943, he had three divisions and four aircraft wings trained and deployed or deploying to the Pacific. A fourth division was assembling. New equipment—jeeps, deuce-and-a-half trucks, radios, Sherman tanks, amphibian tractors—arrived to Marine divisions. The M1 bowl helmet replaced the Model 1917 model, and Marines now carried as their service rifle the semiautomatic caliber .30-06 Garand that replaced the "Oh-Three" Springfield of nearly forty years' service. Others carried the .30-caliber M1 carbine or fired 60-mm and 81-mm mortars that took the place of the antiquated Stokes models with which the original FMF had been equipped. The artillery battalions gained powerful 75-mm pack and 105-mm howitzers for their batteries. Flame-throwers, 2.36-inch rocket launchers, and satchel-charges of plastic explosive were lethal new items that would make it possible for teams of infantry and engineers to attack the well-fortified, dug-in positions with which the Japanese would defend the islands of the Central Pacific. Finally, early in 1942, the long-standard forest-green and khaki service uniforms gave way to a new battle dress for marines in the field. The sage green, herringbone twill, cotton "utility" or "dungaree" uniform, stamped with "USMC" and the eagle-globe-and-anchor emblem on the breast pocket, became distinctive markings of the Marines for the rest of the war. So, too, did a "green side out" and "brown side out" camouflage helmet cover.[67]

Ultimately, Holcomb fought for and won, despite Army opposition, the permission of the JCS to build a 478,000-man Corps. This strength would allow a fifth and sixth Marine division. But this welcome expansion in size also brought changes in the social character of his service, changes the commandant did not personally welcome. Holcomb found himself the first commandant of the Marine Corps forced to make real concessions to some increasingly important domestic political and social realities of twentieth-century American life. For despite his strong efforts to keep them out—and, when that failed, to limit their participation—both women and African Americans were brought into the Marine Corps in large numbers where they were employed in important, if not first-line, roles.[68]

Of the two groups, accepting women proved for Holcomb a far less bitter pill to swallow than accepting blacks. Women had briefly served in support roles in World War I. In the new war, Holcomb resisted the pressure to enlist women, with the result that the Marine Corps was the very last American armed service to organize a women's component. Nonetheless, in 1943, women were accepted, but only as wartime reservists, and they were given no training in weapons or field operations, even of a defensive nature. They were recruited under the slogan "Free a Marine to Fight" and assigned to clerical and technical support billets. The Women Marine Reserves remained distinctly an auxiliary element and were viewed by Holcomb as acceptable because they did precisely what their slogan demanded: to free male marines for combat in the Pacific.[69]

Bringing African Americans into the Marine Corps was quite another matter. The commandant's opposition reflected both his own background as well as his assessment of the practical problems arising from having to provide special, segregated training arrangements for black marines. On balance, Holcomb's views on race were those of an officer corps still largely "drawn from an old-family, Anglo-Saxon, Protestant, rural, upper-middle-class background." By neither upbringing nor professional experience was he inclined to be in the vanguard of those pressing for "full participation in the defense program by all persons regardless of color, [so that] . . . the Armed Forces . . . shall lead the way in erasing discrimination over color or race." But these were the words forming the preamble to the executive order, which the president signed in June 1941. Holcomb could resist but so long.[70] Appearing before the Navy's General Board early in 1942, he announced that it "had long been his considered opinion that 'there would be a definite loss of efficiency . . . if we have to take Negroes.'" He stated that "the Negro race has every opportunity now to satisfy its aspirations for combat, in the Army, a very much larger organization than the Navy or Marine Corps—and their desire to enter the naval service is largely, I think, to break into a club that doesn't want them." Had any ambivalence remained, his final statement summed up his attitude. "If it were a question of having a Marine Corps of 5,000 whites or 250,000 Negroes," the commandant announced, "I would rather have the whites."[71]

He had a powerful ally in his views: Secretary Knox. Knox proclaimed that "it is no kindness to Negroes to thrust them upon men of the white race" and promptly directed the General Board to help him show "why colored persons should not be enlisted."[72] President Roosevelt continued to press, however, for some form of integration in the naval service, if only, as he told Knox, to put "some good Negro bands aboard battleships." Finally, and despite Knox's footdragging, the issue was resolved. In 1942, the Navy and Marine Corps alike were forced to accept blacks. Holcomb's response to this unwanted directive was as measured and calculated as he could manage. The first

African American recruits were placed for their training, not at Parris Island or San Diego, but at a separate camp in North Carolina and under a handpicked white officer of long experience, Col. Samuel A. Woods, South Carolina–born and a 1914 graduate of the Citadel. Unwilling to place any real faith in their ability to handle infantry-combat roles, Holcomb directed that the black marines be used to form separate defense battalions. As often as not, however, they found themselves relegated to something less than actual combat support, but service in labor battalions whatever their title.[73] Holcomb might indeed have been forced to accept blacks into the Corps, but he could and did make every effort to ensure that they were kept from the combat roles.

But such issues assumed second-place importance as the autumn of 1943 approached. As the commandant understood full well, his Corps was about to endure its harshest trial-at-arms since Guadalcanal: an amphibious assault, in the third week of November 1943, upon Betio Island, Tarawa Atoll, in the Gilbert Islands. Above all, this effort, unlike Guadalcanal, would be the first real test of the amphibious doctrine twenty years in the evolution since the landings against Betio, a small coral island, would be fiercely contested from the moment the assault forces tried to move ashore. Holland M. Smith, commanding the new V Amphibious Corps, catalogued the hazards. These included a difficult coral reef, tricky tides, a maze of mines and obstacles, and well-entrenched Japanese, most of them elite Special Landing Force troops or Japanese "marines." The 2d Marine Division, which had gained some combat experience on Guadalcanal, would carry out the assault. Everything depended upon coordination, communications, and above all the effectiveness of the Navy's air and naval gunfire preparation. Should these measures fail to smash the enemy's defenses, the assaulting marines would encounter devastating fire as they approached the beach.[74]

Smith's worst fears were very nearly realized. Certainly the first news that reached Holcomb was appalling. Not only had the carefully planned bombardments failed, but also poor intelligence of tidal depths over the reef and inadequate numbers of LVTs (the crucial amphibian tractors) had combined to bring the whole operation close to disaster. While the battle still hung in the balance, reinforcements had at last proved able to land and expand the first meager lodgments. By the time the fight for what war correspondents were already calling "Bloody Betio" ended, it had led to a cost in lives lost (1,085) per square yard of ground, higher than any previous American battle.

That Holcomb had from the start grasped its significance as the great test was reflected in his message of congratulation to "the gallant officers and men of the Second [Marine] Division." Tarawa, he said "was our first atoll attack and the sort of operation we have always been planning. . . . Your success is therefore particularly gratifying." But as he admitted privately to Vandegrift, "things are in good shape now, but they had a bad time at Tarawa." Indeed, questions about the planning for what *Time* correspondent Robert Sherrod described as Betio's "One Square Mile of Hell" very nearly led to a full congressional investigation. In fact, it was Sherrod's article, even with tight censorship, that had particularly emphasized the horrors of the battle. His account emphasized "the fighting spirit of the U.S. Marines" as the "decisive factor," and he suggested that victory had been snatched from the jaws of defeat by acts of courage and sacrifice by individual junior officers and men, not by the preparations preceding the operation.[75]

Only too mindful of accusations that Tarawa was bungled in the planning and needlessly wasteful of American lives, Holcomb and his generals acted quickly to make operational changes. They could at least, however, take some comfort in the knowledge that most of what had gone wrong had gone wrong in areas which were the province of the Navy rather than the Marine Corps. Chief among these was the failure of the preliminary bombardment to destroy the deeply entrenched Japanese fortifications. Marine planners thereafter used Tarawa to spur the Navy to shift to methodical, targeted shelling rather than saturation bombardment, as well as to make better arrangements for ship-to-shore movement and communications.[76] Not only were its "lessons" grasped quickly, but they would be used to good effect in preparing for what was to follow. Coming the month before he was scheduled to step down as commandant, Holcomb regarded Tarawa's bloody test as the payoff to long years of work and preparation. If the Marines could take Tarawa, any of the island bastions guarding the sea route to Japan could be taken. His response to charges by U.S. Army officers that Marine tactics were needlessly bloody reflected his faith in the Corps's doctrine and style of leadership. Pointing to the conspicuously slow progress of the lackluster 27th Infantry Division in taking nearby Makin Island, Holcomb argued that such "bogged down" tactics left American ships dangerously exposed to enemy submarine and air attacks. The Marine approach, on the other hand, saved lives in the long run. He seemed to be right. While the Army was feeling its way forward on Makin, a Japanese submarine had time to slip in and torpedo the aircraft carrier USS *Liscombe Bay* just offshore. Almost as many Americans were lost (750 deaths) as had died in taking "Bloody Betio."[77]

At some point during 1943 but before Tarawa, Holcomb made his decision to step down. At age sixty-four, however, he was only a year older than Army Chief of Staff Marshall and a year younger than Chief of Naval Operations King. For this reason and because of his high regard for Holcomb's services, President Roosevelt found himself "reluctant to accept . . . [a] request for retirement." During a dinner party at the White House, FDR therefore called Holcomb aside and indicated that he wanted him to stay on into 1944. There was also a hint that the president would seek to have Holcomb made a full-fledged member of the Joint Chiefs of Staff. Holcomb encouraged both proposals and awaited events. He soon learned, however, that the JCS bid in particular had aroused the opposition of Admiral King. A compromise developed that may have disappointed Holcomb, but seemed to satisfy all the other parties concerned. Holcomb, whose resignation was officially tendered at the end of November, would retire as commandant but would be restored to active duty in order to serve the secretary of the navy in a special advisory capacity.

Thus on the first day of December 1943, Secretary Knox wrote Holcomb to accept "with great reluctance" his resignation as commandant. Commenting on Holcomb's "superlative ability . . . in organizing, training and equipping" such a vastly expanded

Corps, he lauded in particular the recent assault on Tarawa, where the Marines "displayed the quality of the soldier and the discipline of a trained fighter in superlative degree." Finally, "as Secretary of the Navy I could have had no finer cooperation and support than that which you have always rendered to me as the civilian head of the Navy."[78]

His resignation thus accepted, Holcomb was succeeded on the first day of the new year by Lt. Gen. Alexander A. Vandegrift. While service rumors noted that Holcomb had gone "way down the line [of seniority] to get Vandegrift," there had long been little doubt that his successor would be the hero of Guadalcanal. Vandegrift had worked closely with Holcomb since 1937, and Holcomb had the highest regard for his abilities. Although Holland M. Smith, now a lieutenant general, had also been a potential contender for the high post, the peppery Alabaman "was always a loud talker." He could, especially when it came to getting along with senior Navy officers, more than live up to his nickname of "Howlin' Mad" Smith. If anything, Smith was perhaps the biggest "Navy hater" of all the Marine generals since the days of the fiery Smedley Butler.[79]

Vandegrift, on the other hand, was a solid "team man" who combined an unmatched experience of operations in the Pacific with an intimate knowledge of the inner workings of Headquarters. He seemed capable of achieving a smooth transition—an important factor, given Holcomb's long incumbency—and working well with the Navy. Moreover, by recommending Vandegrift as his successor, Holcomb could keep Smith doing what he did best: carrying out the difficult landing operations now thrusting ever closer to Japan. Thus it was that Smith was given command of the vastly expanded arm now designated the Fleet Marine Force, Pacific.[80]

Meanwhile, Holcomb's nearly forty-four years of active service were far from over. Assigned to the office of the secretary of the navy in January 1944, the immediate past-commandant was, by act of Congress, promoted in retirement ("tombstoned") to the rank of general. As Knox informed him, "You will be the first officer of the Corps to hold the rank of general—the highest rank in our armed forces. I know of no other officer to whom that distinction more fittingly belongs." Holcomb's promotion was based on a provision which permitted "line officers of the Navy who have been specially commended for . . . duty in actual combat . . . [to be advanced] upon retirement . . . to the next highest grade."[81] The action represented no sudden recognition that the position of commandant had now become a general's post, but Holcomb's advancement in rank did much to advance the status of the Corps. Certainly it helped to establish the idea of having a general as head of that service, on par in terms of rank with the other service chiefs.

For the first four months of 1944, General Holcomb served the secretary of the navy, traveling extensively to bases and supply depots and advising on matters pertaining to organizational structure, manpower, and training. He had, however, very little time left in which to serve the secretary, for late in April, Knox died at seventy and was succeeded by James V. Forrestal. Holcomb had already been given another appointment, this one in the Department of State. Awarded the Distinguished Service Medal and retired from the Corps for the second (and final) time, he was now named United States minister to the Union of South Africa.[82] He served in that capacity from

1944 to 1948, and Holcomb, the first and only commandant ever to hold such a post, enjoyed the tour. Always something of the "foxy old farmer," as one of his generals described him, he seems to have appealed to the Afrikaners. By the time of his return to the United States, Holcomb felt that he could look back upon a period in which he had worked tirelessly and effectively to promote American interests in South Africa.[83]

He and his wife retired to the Maryland country estate, "Rosecroft," which they had purchased years before. There, with Holcomb enjoying the life of a gentleman farmer, they resided until their declining health dictated a move to less demanding quarters. Eventually, after a long illness, Beatrice, his wife of four decades, died at age sixty-six. But in all these years Holcomb kept in constant touch with the Corps whose expanded size and status he had done so much to bring about. The Marine Corps Birthday Ball of 1962 proved for him a particularly memorable event. Now eighty-three, he was both the oldest living commandant and the oldest marine present at a celebration that featured the nation's new astronaut, another marine, Lt. Col. John H. Glenn.[84]

Plagued by a heart ailment, however, Holcomb had to spend increasing periods in the Bethesda Naval Hospital. Yet his health, apart from an early bout with malaria and the wounds sustained in 1918, had always been remarkably robust. His service records reflected the fact that, between 1933 and the end of his tour as commandant ten years later, he had missed, in all that time, a total of only forty-one days "sick in quarters." Indeed his Navy retirement physical examination found him, for a man who was a veteran of two wars and considerable service under harsh conditions, a picture of excellent health. At retirement he was twenty-four pounds heavier than when first commissioned. His blood pressure and pulse readings were "130 over 84," or "extremely good readings for a man of that age." Yet the years at last caught up with him. His difficulties with calcific aortitis resulted in additional trips to Bethesda. He had just returned from one such visit when, late in May 1965, at age eighty-five and less than three months before what would have been his next birthday, he died. Four days later, the seventeenth commandant of the Marine Corps was buried with full military honors in Arlington National Cemetery.[85]

Much of the wartime Marine Corps's achievements must be credited to Holcomb and to his considerable political skill with Congress and the Roosevelt administration. Throughout his tenure he had done a superb job of sensing exactly when, as he wrote Vandegrift on one occasion, "the time was ripe" so that if things were handled properly, a few thousand men "deducted each from the Army and the Navy [quotas], would never be missed." It was these men or some additional allocation of materiel that "would give us the . . . [extra that] we need to round out our . . . Corps."[86]

Yet Holcomb, at least to some of his generals, was never "an easy man to deal with." One of them complained that there "wasn't much of the milk of human kindness" in him. Rather, he simply "played the game," not making "a decision on what was best for the Marine Corps . . . [but on] 'how it will affect me.'" But those who were able to observe most closely his day-to-day sparring with Marshall and King had a different view. They came away impressed by Holcomb's ability to steer through the interservice shoal waters. And unlike Admiral King, Holcomb assiduously avoided dressing down subordinates publicly. Nor did he have King's other habit: relieving promising officers on the spot for some minor shortcoming in performance.[87]

Still, he also managed to chalk up his fair share of aberrations. He resisted the integration of African Americans into his service, and his faith in the virtues of the Springfield rifle delayed the Corps's adoption of the excellent M1 Garand, the robust, simple to operate and maintain weapon that gave Corps riflemen a real advantage on the islands in the Pacific.[88] In addition, his animosity toward raiding and special operations kept the Marine Corps from developing this mode of warfare to its fullest potential in the war against Japan. Although neither Holcomb nor his generals accepted special operations as a part of amphibious warfare, what they were good at was concentrating on the main thing: assembling and training Marine divisions and aircraft wings to fight in the Pacific. Holcomb emphasized stringent quality control throughout this process to ensure that there was no dilution of the Corps's elite standards and values. His influence on stateside training was direct and personal in every aspect, as in the area of officer training. The Marine Corps had historically functioned with the highest officer-enlisted ratios of any of the services; Holcomb saw every reason it should continue that way.

Regarding the enlisted marines, whether ground or air, Holcomb kept all recruit training conducted at Parris Island or the new boot camp at San Diego. No other sites were developed for male recruit training, despite the fact that both sites were severely constrained as to capacity. The exception was the separate camp for blacks at Montford Point. Compared to their Army counterparts, Holcomb's recruits were young and conscious of their elite status. They were patriots and volunteers (even those drafted later had to volunteer for the Corps), and they had joined up to fight the Japanese. They regarded their standards of selection, training, and discipline as far more rigorous than those of other services. Holcomb committed himself to the principle that, no matter how compelling the demand for seasoned NCOs elsewhere, he would at all costs preserve the role of the drill instructor as the most important single element involved in the training of new marines. He made almost the same commitment toward retaining a cadre of handpicked NCOs to serve as firing-line coaches during rifle-range training with the service rifle. The Drill Instructors' School was established at Parris Island. This school, the careful selection of candidates, and preservation of "Old Corps" ways—the campaign hat, for example—assured those key NCOs a standing never present in the training programs of the other services.

New enlisted marines and new officers met each other for the first time, if assigned to ground military occupational specialties, either at Camp Lejeune or Camp Pendleton, when they reported to one of the new battalions being formed. The same was true for those in aviation, except of course that they reported to a squadron rather than a battalion, and to Cherry Point or to El Torro, or one of the other new air stations established in California. Unit training followed for both, carrying units battalion by battalion or squadron by squadron, through a prescribed syllabus whose objective was the achievement of mission competence.[89]

Holcomb oversaw this whole process with close attention to detail, frequent visits to training sites, and great care in the selection and evaluation of commanders. Particularly with regard to the ground units, he employed a mechanism for training and preparing units that was essentially that of the prewar brigade-sized FMFs; he merely acquired the infrastructure of base and personnel requisite to support the process. He did the same for the air units, relying for guidance upon the recommendations of a series of able directors of Marine Corps aviation. Top-quality training was always a paramount goal of Holcomb's, and it was an area in which he achieved unqualified success.[90]

One goal which Holcomb reached would, however, require another four decades before it came within the grasp of any commandant: full and equal Marine Corps membership on the Joint Chiefs of Staff. As the JCS was being formed, Holcomb thought that King could have had "both a senior Naval Aviator and the Commandant of the Marine Corps designated as full members." In fact, seven more years would pass before a commandant was again invited to sit as a member of the JCS. Not until 1952 and in the face of considerable opposition from the Army and the newest service, the Air Force, did the commandant gain that right, and only then because of powerful support in Congress. And still such membership was limited in that he was a nonvoting member only, being permitted to speak solely on matters restricted to his service or to its specialty, amphibious operations.[91]

And yet, Holcomb's time in the Corps's highest position had been successful in ways never before equaled and never since surpassed. The war in the Pacific had presented a set of unique historical circumstances which had offered scope for the employment of large and balanced Marine forces on a scale and with a central role unparalleled in the experience of the service. In the Pacific the Corps whose expansion Holcomb had brought about functioned as a special kind of theater-level army, acting as the elite amphibious shock troops of a drive thrusting toward Japan itself. In preparing his service to meet the challenges of this role, Holcomb had demonstrated a marked ability to exploit to the fullest the inherent status and strength, within the Corps, of the office of commandant. A far older post than either chief of staff, U.S. Army (1903) or chief of naval operations (1916), the eighteenth-century origins of the position of commandant permitted a strong incumbent to function, within his small service, with a firmer, closer grip than could his Army or Navy counterparts in their far larger ones. Both the Army and the Navy contained large, semiautonomous committees and branches shaped around their respective operational functions. A dynamic and forceful commandant enjoyed a considerable opportunity to mold and move his service in ways, which he himself chose. When, as was the case with Holcomb, the period of tenure extended over the best part of a decade, the opportunity to do so was even that much greater.

Above all, Holcomb must be seen as an adaptive traditionalist who took ideas and concepts first advanced during the time of Lejeune, brought them to fruition, and then ensured their successful application on terrible and costly battlefields. He was a pragmatist, a doer rather than a theorist, and ever the wily and intuitive infighter. If in the process the Marine Corps became the acclaimed supreme instrument for the practice of amphibious warfare, it had attained that mantle not least because of the talents and travails of its seventeenth commandant. With John A. Lejeune, therefore, Thomas Holcomb must rank as one of the most important commandants the twentieth century has produced.

18

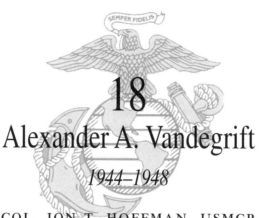

Alexander A. Vandegrift

1944–1948

COL. JON T. HOFFMAN, USMCR

In August 1942, Maj. Gen. Alexander Archer Vandegrift was fifty-five years old and past his physical prime. He had commanded few field units in his thirty-three years of service but had a reputation for training marines for war. He had spent much of his career performing well in high-level staff billets, but mostly with administrative headquarters, so he was not noted for any special skill or flair in planning operations. As a young officer he had participated in a number of combat actions, none of them very large in scale or very fierce. It had been more than twenty years since he had heard a shot fired in his direction. In an era of the Corps marked by flamboyant and quirky leaders, he was almost always calm, even-tempered, quiet, and reserved; he kept his emotions and thoughts to himself. He was cautious for the most part and quick to put the brakes on subordinates he thought too adventurous. He disliked confrontation, preferring to paper over disputes or solve them with compromise. Though inspired as a youth by the valiant deeds of his forebears, he had assumed the air of his father, a modest but prosperous builder and southern gentleman. One commentator later opined that the general could easily be mistaken for "a small town business man who taught a Sunday school class."[1] Vandegrift was perhaps a strange choice to lead the first American amphibious offensive of World War II. The landing on Guadalcanal was a bold, almost reckless gamble launched with weak forces and oftentimes weaker support from higher command. It appeared to need a fire eater such as George Patton or William "Bull" Halsey to make it work, but it got Vandegrift, who brought to the fight quiet resolve, dogged determination, and stubborn persistence. In the months of attrition that followed that proved to be enough.

Vandegrift was born on 13 March 1887 in Charlottesville, Virginia, a small town at the base of the Blue Ridge Mountains. His father was a successful architect and contractor, and young Archer, as he was known, grew up in one of the few houses in town with an indoor bathroom. He was not an enthusiastic student, but he loved reading and

Gen. Alexander A. Vandegrift, eighteenth commandant.
U.S. Marine Corps Photo.

devoured the military historical novels then in vogue. His interest in soldiering was whetted further by the tales of relatives and family friends. His maternal grandfather had died in battle early in the Civil War, his paternal grandfather was wounded at Antietam and Gettysburg, and an older cousin had fought in the Spanish-American War.

His dreams of an Army career faltered when he failed to meet the physical standards for West Point, so he entered college at the University of Virginia and hoped to earn a commission by competitive examination when he turned twenty-one. As luck would have it, there were no vacancies in the Army in 1908, but his congressman offered him a nomination to the Marine Corps. Vandegrift passed the week-long test at the Washington Barracks and fell in love with the Marines as he observed the color and pageantry of daily parades and guard mounts at the Corps's oldest post. He accepted his commission in January 1909, and was only somewhat miffed at the cool reception his dress blue uniform received from Confederate veterans when he returned home.

His career got off to a rocky beginning during his initial training at the School of Application in Parris Island, South Carolina. He inadvertently reported late from liberty and received a court-martial because the commanding officer wanted to make him an example to the group of young lieutenants chafing under the rote instruction. The guilty verdict cost him five numbers on the lineal list, not an insignificant punishment in an era when promotions came exceedingly slow to the 350 officers then in the Corps. Perhaps more important, the conviction and ensuing poor fitness report placed a dark blotch on his record. After graduating fortieth in a class of fifty-five, his first duty assignment was with the Marine Barracks at Portsmouth, New Hampshire.[2] There his senior officers made sure he studied tactics and trained in the field, despite the garrison duties that dominated that small post.

Vandegrift saw action relatively quickly. In May 1912, he joined a provisional brigade deployed to Cuba to protect American plantations from Cuban insurgents. Two months later, he transferred to another expeditionary force in Panama under the command of the renowned Smedley Butler, then a major. In August 1912, Butler's battalion moved to Nicaragua and imposed peace in that nation's civil war. Although the battles were not intense, Vandegrift received his baptism of fire guarding trains and later commanding a machine-gun unit in an assault on an enemy-held ridge. Early in 1914, the outfit left Panama again, this time for Mexico, where Vandegrift took part in the seizure of Veracruz. Butler became his enthusiastic patron, nicknaming him "Sunny Jim" for his optimistic disposition.

After several months of study in 1915 at the Advance Base Course in Philadelphia, Vandegrift went overseas with another provisional force, this time to Haiti. He participated in several small engagements, then joined the Haitian Gendarmerie being formed by Butler. He took rank as a major, trained and led part of the fledgling force, and later served as the quartermaster until the end of 1918. Butler praised his "excellent, untiring, and intelligent" subordinate, while an enlisted marine found Vandegrift "serene, farseeing, wise, always just and always fearless."[3] To his great consternation, however, he had missed "The War to End All Wars." After eighteen months in the States, he returned to Haiti for another tour and played a leading role in repelling a large rebel assault on the capital city.

Although the Corps underwent demobilization following the World War, it was still twice its prewar size and Vandegrift became a major. This was relatively rapid advancement by prior Marine standards, but it would be fourteen more years before he received his next promotion. He left Haiti in 1923 for Quantico and served again under Butler's eccentric and frenetic leadership. Vandegrift participated in several of the general's pet projects, to include the construction of a football stadium by hand labor and the reenactment of Civil War battles, both of which garnered positive publicity for the Corps in an era when the media did not look fondly on the military. Although he served mainly as a battalion commander in the 5th Marines, he was often the sparkplug of the regiment, which was commanded by a lackluster colonel out of favor with Butler.[4] Vandegrift wrapped up this tour by completing the Field Officers' Course in 1926.

That summer, Vandegrift followed Butler to San Diego and participated in the successful Marine effort to stamp out a nationwide rash of mail robberies. He deployed from there the following year in command of a battalion as part of the mission to guard the International Settlement in Shanghai from the turmoil of the Chinese civil war. The United States eventually committed an entire Marine brigade under Butler, who promptly made Vandegrift his operations officer. He became intimately familiar with the China station with service in Chinwangtao, Tientsin (Tianjin), and Peking (Beijing) in addition to Shanghai. He also had the chance to observe the Japanese Army at close range.

In 1929, Vandegrift returned to the States for an unusual assignment. He spent the next four years as the Marine Corps representative to the Federal Coordinating Service, a Depression-era agency charged with preventing waste in the national government's procurement and distribution of materiel. This tour gave him a wealth of experience at the senior policy level and in logistics management. Vandegrift then served as the assistant chief of staff for the East Coast Expeditionary Force in Quantico. His two-year tour happened to coincide with a critical period that saw the creation of amphibious doctrine, the redesignation of his organization as the Fleet Marine Force, and the resumption of annual fleet problems involving amphibious maneuvers in the Caribbean. He thus learned a great deal about a topic that previously had been fairly obscure even to most marines. Another institutional revolution brought promotion by selection to the Corps at this time. The tougher standards for advancement resulted in the forced retirement of many mediocre or superannuated senior officers, and Vandegrift reached the rank of lieutenant colonel in 1934.

The following year Vandegrift reported to Peking, China, as the executive officer of the Legation Guard. Within months he assumed the command of this elite unit charged with safeguarding American lives and showing the flag not only to the Chinese but also to the representatives of the other foreign powers. The billet required the skills of a diplomat as well as a soldier, since tensions were running high with the Japanese as they encroached farther into Chinese affairs and territory. In this volatile situation, Vandegrift emphasized preparation for war and for ceremonies as a means to impress potential enemies with American skill and will. His lieutenants found him a "meticulous taskmaster" in enforcing high standards of training, discipline, and polish.[5] At the same time, he was keenly aware of the welfare of his men, believing that "loyalty down [the chain of command] must occur simultaneously with loyalty up."[6] Vandegrift's performance in this highly visible post and the continued workings of the selection law brought him a promotion to colonel in 1936. When it came time for Vandegrift to return to the States in 1937, he took an unusual step and elected to travel across China, the Soviet Union, and Europe by train, and thence by ship to the United States, rather than sailing across the Pacific. As he crossed Siberia, he saw his first airborne operation, a mass jump by Soviet paratroops.

The major general commandant, Thomas Holcomb, had brought Vandegrift home to fill the newly created position of military secretary. Despite the innocuous title, it was an important billet, since Vandegrift effectively was the chief of staff in the small Headquarters. Traditionally this function had been performed by a senior general serving as the assistant to the commandant, but due to Holcomb's recent elevation over the heads of many other generals, he left that post vacant.[7] When Vandegrift received his first star in April 1940, Holcomb reverted to former practice and named him assistant to the commandant.

From 1939 to late 1941, Vandegrift helped oversee an increase in the Corps from eighteen thousand men to more than seventy thousand, all fueled by the threatening war in Europe. The challenges of rapidly expanding the officer cadre, recruiting tens of thousands of new marines, overseeing a burgeoning budget, acquiring new types of equipment, and finding adequate training areas provided him with an all-around education he could not have gained in any other billet. As the commandant's "right hand man," he performed a wide range of other duties.[8] Holcomb, for instance, called Vandegrift "my publicity man," since the Corps did not yet have a special office to take care of that function.[9] In the small Corps of that era, the commandant and his assistant commandant personally handled many matters, such as fiscal oversight, that would have fallen to the staff of a larger organization.

Many of the problems seemed overwhelming. Brig. Gen. Holland M. Smith's 1st Marine Brigade spent the winter of 1940–41 training in the Caribbean and building a spartan camp there, even as the organization absorbed thousands of fresh recruits and tried to create additional units. Headquarters fought for a new base in the States and with the help of the prominent North Carolinian politician Josephus Daniels (a former secretary of the navy) and some congressmen, succeeded in winning President Roosevelt's approval to purchase a large area on the North Carolina coast.[10] Finding sufficient quality manpower to fill up the expanding ranks was not easy, either, especially since the Corps declined to take draftees when they became available in 1940. One good reason for that was the restriction that they could not serve outside the Western Hemisphere, but another aspect was the desire to keep African Americans out of the Marines, a stand Vandegrift endorsed.[11] Despite his views in that area, the assistant commandant otherwise thought the Corps finally was coming into the modern age and "breaking away from a lot of Civil War ideas."[12] At times he was amazed at the changes: "Little did I think that I would ever live to see the sight of thirty-two transports and cargo ships for the sole use of landing force exercises."[13]

He also learned firsthand about the Byzantine organization of Headquarters Marine Corps (HQMC). The heads of three major staff departments—adjutant and inspector, quartermaster, and paymaster—were confirmed by Congress. Since they served at the pleasure of that body rather than the commandant, they were nearly independent fiefdoms. In addition, the Division of Aviation was entwined closely with the Navy's air arm, which trained Marine pilots, supplied the planes they flew, and paid for maintenance and fuel. Holcomb had complete control only over the Divisions of Plans and Policies and Reserve.[14] The commandant and his assistant commandant also had to deal with senior officers who were not adjusting to promotion by selection. Some of those unhappy with the results of the boards tried to overturn them by appealing to their senators. The ever-cantankerous Smith, one of those whose promotion was being challenged, gave typically blunt advice to Vandegrift to ignore those efforts: "It is unwise to get into a urinating contest with a skunk."[15] After holding hearings on the matter, Congress reaffirmed the system.

The assistant commandant was exposed to the high-level machinations of interservice politics, as well. There were wranglings with the Navy over spending priorities, particularly in regard to transports and landing craft. The Army, on the other hand, began to take a strong interest in the amphibious mission and eventually placed a division each under the command of Marine forces on the East and West Coasts. Some senior marines were apprehensive at this possible encroachment on their turf, but Vandegrift did not consider it significant: "We feel that in a major emergency that all would be needed; that after all this is not a private war. . . . We will so perfect ourselves and be so available for immediate movement, that we would be the first to go in any eventuality, irrespective of how many divisions the Army has available for this purpose."[16] Although his sense about the preparedness of the Corps was prophetic, his lack of concern over interservice rivalry would cause him trouble in later years.

The continued expansion of the Corps and the creation of major amphibious training commands on each coast directly affected Vandegrift in November 1941. Holland Smith moved up to head the 1st Joint Training Force, and Philip H. Torrey picked up a second star and succeeded him as commander of the 1st Marine Division. Holcomb considered it "a great personal sacrifice," but decided to let Vandegrift escape HQMC after four years to become Torrey's assistant division commander (ADC) at New River, North Carolina.[17] This first division in the history of the Corps was only eight months old, it was still far short of attaining the full structure allotted to it, and a large percentage of the officers and men were as new to the Corps as their parent organization. The process of setting up adequate training areas on the new base was progressing poorly, too. Some of these problems reflected the administrative focus of Torrey and his principal confidant on the division staff, a supply officer, and that may have influenced Holcomb's decision to dispatch Vandegrift, a proven trainer. He brought with him Maj. Merrill B. Twining, a skilled staff officer steeped in doctrinal expertise after a tour as an instructor at the Marine Corps Schools. With Torrey's concurrence, the two focused on preparing the small units of the division for war while the commanding general and his staff worried about other pressing matters. Vandegrift and Twining soon laid out suitable firing ranges and drafted appropriate combat problems to challenge the troops and their leaders. The ADC then spent much of each day observing the platoons, companies, and battalions as they operated in the field.[18]

When the United States became embroiled in war on 7 December 1941, the only visible change in training was the disappearance of rigid peacetime safety standards. Vandegrift took advantage of the relaxed rules to habituate the troops to overhead fire by artillery, mortars, and machine guns.[19] More important to the division was the national anger over Pearl Harbor, which brought forth a flood of recruits. With thousands of eager, capable young men enlisting in the Corps each week and charging through an abbreviated boot camp, the division looked like it would finally approach its authorized strength. However, the pressures of war and decisions at higher headquarters sapped personnel and units away almost as fast as they seemed to appear at New River. Holland Smith stole a battalion of the 5th Marines to create a light, fast-moving landing element, which soon became the 1st Raider Battalion to appease Roosevelt's interest in special forces. The Raiders and the parachutists both came hunting for additional volunteers and siphoned off some of the best men in the 1st Marine Division. In March 1942, the 7th Marines became the core of a brigade sent to defend Samoa, stripping off another layer of the best personnel and equipment. Vandegrift and others bit their lips and redoubled their efforts to turn green manpower into trained units.

The 1st Marine Division command element faced potentially more damaging troubles in early 1942. There was a bitter personal feud between two senior colonels and Torrey soon found himself embroiled in the dispute. Accusations of improper public comments about Roosevelt brought an investigation, and Holcomb relieved Torrey, probably more for his lack of focus on training and his inability to impose harmony than for any perceived verbal indiscretion. On 23 March 1942, the commandant gave Vandegrift a temporary promotion to major general and entrusted him with the division. Vandegrift moved slowly to purge and reorganize the senior leadership of the division, but he nevertheless ensured that there were no more debilitating internecine squabbles.[20] The staff changes included the elevation of Lt. Col. Gerald C. Thomas to head the operations section, with Twining as his primary assistant. Jerry Thomas, a talented staff officer who had won a battlefield commission in World War I, had earned Vandegrift's respect in previous tours together in Haiti and China.

Just days after Vandegrift took charge, he learned the division would deploy in May to New Zealand for further training. Over the next few weeks, the division absorbed new men and equipment to bring the 1st and 5th Marines and supporting units to full strength. Although nominally ready for duty, the outfit still was woefully short of training and experienced leadership as it shipped out from ports on the East, West, and Gulf Coasts. The ensuing weeks on board cramped ships at sea worsened things, as poor food and lack of exercise took a toll.

The first echelon, composed of the division headquarters and the 5th Marines, was still getting settled in New Zealand when Vandegrift was informed that his force would spearhead the seizure of Guadalcanal and Tulagi in the Solomon Islands. Everything possible seemed to go wrong as the division girded itself for battle. There was almost no information on the target, too little shipping to carry all of the needed equipment and supplies, and not enough time to load the vessels properly, fully rehearse the landings, or work out problems with command relationships and the plan itself. On 7 August 1942, the Allied task force overcame all these handicaps and achieved its initial objectives, but that night a Japanese fleet attacked and inflicted a punishing blow on the surface ships covering the amphibious operation. The remaining Allied vessel withdrew with much of the landing force's supplies and equipment still on board. Bereft of air and naval support and short of sustainment, Vandegrift called his commanders together on Guadalcanal, confirmed the bad tidings, and, without bravado, put them to work organizing the defense of their newly won possessions.

For the next several months, the 1st Marine Division endured daily air attacks, frequent naval bombardments, and occasional major ground battles. The officers and men became battle hardened and then battle weary, as their combat experience mounted and casualties, malaria, and a host of other tropical illnesses took their toll. Food was rationed to two meals a day for the first several weeks and was never adequate in quality even when it finally arrived in quantity. There were occasional setbacks, such as the abortive Second Matanikau, where Vandegrift allowed a poorly supported, ill-organized force of unrelated battalions to attempt a river-crossing in the teeth of strong Japanese defenses. But for the most part, the division fought like its commander, steadfast in the defense and patient, but sure in the offense. The Americans learned to use their firepower to good advantage, not only integrating it with the infantry, but also reaching out to achieve operational impact with their aviation component. The Japanese ground forces, by contrast, were overconfident in the extreme, often reckless, and frequently unsupported by heavy weapons.

Vandegrift relied heavily on the advice of subordinates such as Thomas, Twining, and Col. Merritt A. Edson (commander of the Raiders and later the 5th Marines), but he never let them usurp his authority.[21] While his staff and subordinate commanders drew up plans, he made the final decisions. He could be very stubborn at times in rejecting their counsel, though cautious in doing so. When Thomas and Edson tried to warn him of an impending attack on the undefended southern side of the perimeter, he refused to overturn a decision to move his command post there, although he did allow Thomas to shift Edson's outfit to the area for a rest, just in time to repel one of the most savage Japanese assaults of the campaign. The general spent much of his day visiting units, not in any showy attempt to boost morale but simply and quietly to see and be seen. His quarters were a humble tent for most of the campaign, but he did have a jury-rigged shower and enjoyed a drink of bourbon with his senior staff officers every evening while his men went weeks with no beer and only muddy rivers for bathing facilities. Despite his patrician attitude toward the perquisites of command, he remained well aware that his marines were not "so many pins to be pushed around" and always took into account the limitations of "troops who have been under a strain for a great many days."[22]

His relationships with other senior officers amply demonstrated his distaste for personal confrontation and the expression of "forthright views." During the preparations for Guadalcanal, he had been dismayed by the decisions of the admirals in charge. In particular, he felt that Rear Adm. Richmond K. Turner's actions, "violated the command concepts so clearly laid down in the official manual for amphibious warfare," but he accepted it and altered his plans rather than arguing the point.[23] Turner's continuing attempts to meddle in the conduct of ground operations throughout the campaign exasperated Vandegrift, but he remained reluctant to contest the matter directly or take the issue to their superior. Even when Nimitz visited Guadalcanal and asked for the general's views on his dealings with Turner, Vandegrift "was extremely circumspect."[24] Nimitz only learned the truth from the Marine Corps planner on his staff, who had received the full story from the division commander and Thomas.[25] The issue was not addressed until Holcomb visited the Pacific in October 1942. Even though he was not in the chain of command, it was he who approached senior admirals in the theater and proposed a solution to the thorny problem of command relationships in amphibious operations.[26] Vandegrift was no more willing to upset his higher-ranking subordinates. Despite the poor or mediocre performance of several colonels, he relieved no one, instead using the promotion of some lieutenant colonels to ship several of the laggards home with the excuse that Headquarters had ordered him to give up excess officers.[27]

Vandegrift was not an imposing presence, but his success and quiet competence bred respect. When the number of squadrons on Guadalcanal warranted it, Maj. Gen. Roy Geiger arrived to head what was dubbed the "Cactus Air Force." Although his nominal boss was the theater air component commander, Geiger did not hesitate to accept his marching orders from Vandegrift. The accumulation of Army reinforcements eventually reached division strength, but in deference to the man who had led the struggle from the beginning, the Army placed the Americal Division under his control. Without ever formally receiving authority over any forces outside his own 1st Marine Division, he ended up in overall command of a joint force of two divisions, an aircraft wing, and assorted naval units. Early in the campaign, Vandegrift had commended subordinate echelons with the statement that "God favors the bold and strong of heart."[28] While no one would have accused him of being excessively prone to the former, he certainly provided a stout spirit at a time when it was sorely needed. Years later, Twining felt that Vandegrift's ability to get on with a difficult task without complaint or apparent worry had taught himself and other subordinates an invaluable lesson.[29]

During Holcomb's visit to Guadalcanal in October 1942, the commandant informed Vandegrift that he was his choice to replace him as the head of the Corps if he (Holcomb) retired in the coming year. Holcomb had been unremitting in using the maximum age provision and medical boards to push senior generals out of active service, and he was reluctant to exempt himself from the same rules.[30] His preference for a successor was not surprising. Among the senior leaders in the Corps, only Vandegrift had led an organization as large as a division in combat, and he had garnered the well-deserved respect of fellow marines and the acclaim of the public for being the first to roll back the Japanese juggernaut. (His picture on the cover of a November issue of *Time* magazine ensured he was a household name around the country.)[31] Almost as important, Holcomb considered him a close friend and "the best assistant I have had," and he frequently sought the junior general's counsel on decisions.[32] Among the other senior officers, the commandant rated only Holland Smith as a serious contender, but he disliked his ill temper, finding him "impossible" and "condescending."[33]

From Vandegrift's long tour at HQMC, he was already well aware that being commandant could be an unrewarding job. Holcomb's letters to the Pacific indicated that things had grown no better under wartime conditions. The commandant lamented his lack of operational information on Guadalcanal: "I do not even see the dispatches, but get the contents via the grapevine." With regard to the 1st Marine Division's assignment after Guadalcanal, the senior marine ruefully noted that he had "argued it out with King; of course, to no avail" and "the decision was made on a much higher echelon than mine." He was having little better luck getting the secretary of the navy and the admirals to support his request for additional lieutenant generals for the Corps (only Holcomb then bore that rank), even though the second sea service was soon to exceed 220,000 men: "They just can't stand seeing us get any rank." (In a mark of Vandegrift's new prestige, the naval leadership was willing to consider making an exception for him.)[34] The commandant also was contemplating another attempt to reorganize Headquarters and gain more control over its feudal departments.[35] He summed up the unattractive nature of the billet: "So you see it's the same old Washington. As I told Nimitz I hated to leave the South Pacific because there your enemies are required to wear a distinguishing uniform; here they are not."[36]

Following the withdrawal of the 1st Marine Division from Guadalcanal in December, Vandegrift was finding his own problems in the war zone. In the switch that Holcomb had opposed, the division came under control of MacArthur's Southwest Pacific Area and found itself in a swampy, malaria-ridden camp in the vicinity of Brisbane, Australia. Initially Vandegrift was reluctant to press for a move after MacArthur expressed a personal desire to keep the Marines in place, but his resolve to look out for the welfare of his men finally drove him to fight the decision. Halsey and Nimitz seconded Vandegrift's plea and MacArthur relented, though his headquarters spitefully made no transportation available to get the division to its new home in Melbourne. The Navy stepped in and provided ships from the South Pacific Area to do the job. After this uncharacteristic confrontation, Vandegrift thought that he would be "looking for a job," but he did not regret it: "The health of these men who put out for me counts far more than anything else."[37]

Holcomb brought Vandegrift home to the States in January 1943 for a well-deserved rest and a triumphal tour. Roosevelt presented him with the Medal of Honor in a White House ceremony and he met with the Joint Chiefs of Staff, congressional committees, and a host of influential groups. A national radio program lauded him in imperial terms as "the Conqueror of Guadalcanal."[38] Holcomb believed that his protégé made "a fine impression everywhere."[39] Although the commandant had not talked yet to FDR about retirement or a possible successor, he had given Vandegrift's potential candidacy a big boost and the two already were planning the handover.

The commanding general of the 1st Marine Division returned to his outfit in February and began preparations for the next campaign. He continued to believe that "too much stress cannot be laid on squad, platoon, company and battalion training," but he also demonstrated a keen appreciation of the operational and strategic level of war in challenging a policy statement by the chief of the Army Air Forces. He declared, "I do not believe that the strategy of pushing in each finger from the end is the way to accomplish the result desired. I think it would be far better to cut him off at the wrist. . . . The only reason I can see for taking these islands is either to take an airfield away from the Japanese, thus denying it to them and acquiring it for our own use . . . or seizing an island on which there is not an airfield for the same purpose."[40]

At the end of June, Holcomb finally broached the idea of his retirement to Under Secretary of the Navy James V. Forrestal. Although the age limit of sixty-four did not apply to three- and four-star generals, the commandant suggested that it might be an appropriate time for him to step aside since he had strictly enforced that limit on everyone else in the Corps. If the president agreed, Holcomb intended to leave office at the end of August. He also recommended that his replacement be someone "who has rendered distinguished service in the present war;" the only general fitting that description was Vandegrift.[41]

Vandegrift's route to Headquarters took a slight detour just a few days later. Halsey and Nimitz had been unhappy with the performance of Maj. Gen. Clayton B. Vogel, commander of the I Marine Amphibious Corps (IMAC), but were not willing to fire him. When Vogel's lack of aggressiveness and diligence caused senior leaders to give direction of upcoming operations in the central Solomons to an Army headquarters, Holcomb himself acted and named Vandegrift to take over the corps. As an additional benefit, the commandant used Vandegrift's elevation to command a force of sixty-six thousand men as further ammunition in the battle to obtain a third star for him. Vandegrift was surprised at this sudden turn of events, but realized soon after he reported on board that the corps was in dire need of a "spark plug."[42] Although he had been guilty of similar behavior with the colonels he shipped home from Guadalcanal, he also was upset to learn that Halsey told Vogel that the transfer was entirely due to HQMC. Vandegrift wrote the commandant: "The longer I live the more I think your remarks about enemies in uniform are correct."[43] His dismay at the sudden change in assignment was assuaged when Holcomb informed him on 14 July that Roosevelt had privately approved him as the next leader of the Marine Corps, though the handover would be delayed till the new year. That decision also seemed to break down Adm. Ernest J. King's opposition to Vandegrift's promotion, and he received his third star at the end of July.[44]

There was much to do to get IMAC on the right track. Vandegrift uncharacteristically began by immediately shipping out the G-4, the same supply officer whose mean-spirited demeanor had helped bring Torrey to grief at New River. He then breathed life into the corps staff by bringing in Thomas, Twining, and a few other trusted officers from the 1st Marine Division. The general barely had his own feet on the ground, however, when the Navy threatened to do away with the corps headquarters. The move began with King, the CNO, and Holcomb suspected it was rooted in the Navy's opposition to promoting more marines to three-star rank. The commandant's initial arguments had no effect and Vandegrift's attempt to get Halsey to register his opposition failed when the usually undaunted South Pacific commander meekly replied that he could only provide a comment if the CNO asked for it. Ultimately Nimitz came down in favor of keeping the corps headquarters, and the issue died.[45]

Although Vogel had been relieved largely for shortcomings in operational planning, Vandegrift soon found the most pressing problems were in manpower and logistics, with the latter being particularly acute. During its entire existence, the Corps rarely had to supply a force in the field larger than a thousand men and never during major combat operations. Now there was a need to maintain widely separated forces totaling in the hundreds of thousands and the Corps so far had failed to create a system capable of managing the vast requirements. In addition, the established practice of Marine units leaving their equipment in place for the Army forces that replaced them was drastically increasing requirements. Holcomb recognized the organizational shortcomings, but also challenged Vandegrift to root out the wasteful attitude held by officers and men, most of whom had never served in the frugal times prior to the war. The corps commander agreed and reinstituted both rigorous materiel inspections and the accountability rules waived at the outset of the conflict. Vogel recently had created the IMAC Supply Service as a central agency to handle Marine logistics in the South Pacific and Vandegrift brought in Brig. Gen. Cecil Long to ramrod it. Problems with the logistics system of the entire Corps were harder to fix, and Vandegrift still would be dealing with them at the end of the war.

The personnel system was inadequate for similar reasons. In the small prewar Corps there were only a handful of marines with specialized skills, and it was relatively easy to manage the few thousand personnel that transferred each year. Now it was necessary to assign every marine a particular occupational track, ensure that he receive the proper training, and get him to a unit requiring that expertise. Headquarters was just then instituting such a system in the States, but it was up to the corps commands in the Pacific to implement it properly in the war zone. There was as yet no way to track the number of men holding a particular specialty in any given unit and the demands of replacing losses in the midst of battle promised to complicate the matter. Another challenge was assessing the wartime performance of senior officers and getting the handful of "spark-plugs" into key billets. An example was Colonel Edson, whom Vandegrift transferred to the 2d Marine Division as chief of staff to "put new life into the outfit."[46]

Vandegrift's designated successor at IMAC was Maj. Gen. Charles D. Barrett, commander of the 3d Marine Division, which would participate in the upcoming assault on Bougainville in the northern Solomons. Since that operation would take place in November after the change of command, Vandegrift placed much of the planning responsibility on Barrett. The future leader of IMAC had been one of the creators of the original amphibious doctrine in the 1930s and was considered a brilliant planner. He also was reluctant to delegate responsibility and disturbed by the prospect of casualties. He officially replaced Vandegrift in mid-September, but too much work and worry soon put him in a state of exhaustion and depression.[47] On 8 October, he fell from the balcony of his quarters in New Caledonia and died from head injuries. Vandegrift was touring the Pacific to familiarize himself with units and installations when word came to assume command of IMAC again. He would lead the attack on Bougainville until Maj. Gen. Roy Geiger arrived from the United States and had time to grasp the reins of the corps. The admiral commanding the amphibious task force breathed a sigh of relief when Vandegrift returned and "brought an atmosphere of calm and decision."[48]

Barrett had created a good plan calling for landings on the lightly defended west coast of the island. The American forces would establish an enclave and build an airfield there instead of storming strong defenses elsewhere to take one away from the Japanese. At Thomas's urging, Vandegrift made only two significant changes. He authorized a diversionary raid against the island of Choiseul by the 2d Parachute Battalion and successfully pressed the Navy to move reinforcing units to the beachhead much sooner than planned. Vandegrift observed the 1 November landing from the flagship and visited the troops ashore that afternoon, then returned to the staging base at Guadalcanal the next day to supervise the movement of subsequent echelons. He turned over command to Geiger nine days later and departed for the States. Vandegrift's imprint on the planning and conduct of the campaign had been minimal, but he did provide a steady hand at the helm of IMAC on two occasions when the prestige of the Marine Corps and its future employment in the South Pacific were at stake.[49]

The IMAC detour had cost Vandegrift much of his inspection tour of the Pacific, but he stopped in Pearl Harbor on the way home to confer with Holland Smith and Nimitz. He and Thomas arrived in San Francisco on 16 November and spent the rest of the month looking at Marine units and installations in California before heading on to Washington. On 30 November, the secretary of the navy publicly announced that Vandegrift would succeed Holcomb on 1 January. Other news dominated the media the next day, however—the casualty figures for the assault on Tarawa Atoll. Holcomb and many others had thought that the 20 November landing would be a "push-over."[50] Instead, in seventy-six hours of bitter fighting for half a square mile of sand, the 2d Marine Division had lost more than one thousand killed and twenty-five hundred wounded, exceeding Marine losses incurred in six months of combat on Guadalcanal. The American public was stunned. Then many were outraged when some news stories incorrectly indicated that most casualties were due to poor planning or inept decision making with regard to the depth of the tides over the coral reef. Shocking photos of the bloated bodies of Americans floating in the shallow water seemed to reinforce the point. One Marine mother wrote Vandegrift in anguish, "I beg of you in the name of all mothers, fathers, and wives of our boys out there to use a few of those block busters that have been used to destroy innocent citizens in Germany, on those islands out in the South Pacific before sending any more of our battalions in to be slaughtered."[51]

The commandant-designate had played no role in the Tarawa operation, but his first order of business was to ensure that its fallout did not adversely impact the war effort or the Corps. Vandegrift sent a lengthy explanation to Congress describing the difficulty of attacking small, heavily fortified islands and worked that theme into speeches. Then he brought home Edson, a well-known hero and media favorite, to carry on the campaign. The 2d Marine Division chief of staff gave a press conference in the commandant's office on 4 January, followed by a whirlwind of appearances. He detailed his outfit's steps to deal with the tide, discussed the adequacy of naval gunfire, and laid out the enemy's strategy to reduce the American will to fight. Vandegrift was so satisfied with Edson's efforts that he referred all future questioners back to the press conference for answers. Edson's blunt, earnest, firsthand accounts soon convinced most reporters and the public that the Corps had nothing to hide. The issue died for the moment, though partisans of MacArthur and the Army filed it for future use.[52]

Holcomb had kept his replacement well-informed since October 1942 and had given him the opportunity to influence many decisions, so Vandegrift was thoroughly prepared to take charge of the Corps on New Years Day 1944. The new commandant then promoted Thomas to brigadier general over the heads of more than a hundred other colonels and named him to lead the Division of Plans and Policies, the heart of HQMC. Despite his predecessor's excellent leadership, there were many problems confronting Vandegrift. Two of the major ones continued to be logistics and manpower. Looming over all other concerns was an emerging threat to the very existence of the Corps.

It seemed paradoxical that marines should fear most for the Corps's future as an institution at a time when the Corps had grown beyond their wildest dreams—to 390,000 officers and men with an approved ceiling of 478,000 authorized for 1944.[53] But it was precisely that unprecedented size which spurred the Army to action, since the Corps was siphoning off both quality manpower and combat missions. The Army had launched its campaign in November 1942, when Chief of Staff Gen. George C. Marshall asked the JCS to consider the unification of the War and Navy Departments. He argued that this would ensure unity of command and efficient use of national resources. That initial thrust got nowhere, but it scared the Navy into serious discussion of consolidation within its own department. By the summer of 1943, the admirals had made several proposals designed "to convince the Army there is no duplication."[54] One was to have the commandant report to the CNO as a subset of the Navy instead of directly to the secretary as an equal of the CNO. Another was to treat Marine bases like Navy installations and place them under control of Navy district commanders. The final idea was to merge Marine air into the Navy's aviation component. Holcomb had fended off these propositions, but it was clear to those in the know at Headquarters that "there is a move on to do away with the Corps."[55] That would not happen while Roosevelt was president, as he considered himself an honorary marine, but it continually influenced the attitude of the Navy's leadership in ways detrimental to the Corps.

The manpower situation was one such problem. Each time Holcomb had sought an increase in authorized strength, King had opposed it. The Corps finally had won its ceiling of 478,000, but Vandegrift found that was not enough to fill out all current units, not to mention the sixth division that many wanted. In addition, the changing nature of the Pacific conflict dictated a need for new formations in the realm of heavy artillery, amphibian tractors, communications, logistics, and higher command echelons. Earlier decisions also were returning to haunt the Corps. The creation of defense battalions before the war had seemed like a good idea at the time, since it was a politically palatable way of adding force structure when isolationism still reigned in Congress. Likewise, Holcomb had instituted the parachute and glider programs of his own accord in 1940 to fill a perceived operational need. Holland Smith had been well on the way to creating the Raiders before Roosevelt decreed that they come into existence. Only the barrage balloon squadrons were shoved down the throat of the Corps. Thomas bemoaned the fact that the service had grown without "any well-developed plan." All of these specialty units and their dedicated training establishments soaked up men, even though they collectively could contribute little by that point in the war. The Corps had too few air transports for the parachutists and gliders, the Raider battalions were too lightly armed, and the defense battalions were mostly irrelevant to future missions. Another major factor was the penchant for rear echelon commanders to pad their establishments. The one complicating factor beyond the control of the commandant involved combat losses, which were rising dramatically as the war progressed.[56]

Holcomb scuttled the glider program in mid-1943, and one of his last acts as head of the Corps was to do away with barrage balloon units, but he was reluctant to disband other formations for fear that the JCS would simply turn the manpower savings into cuts in authorized strength. One of Vandegrift's first deeds in office (in fact, he did it before officially taking over) was to convince King to accept the disbandment of the Raider and Parachute battalions. Although his primary motivation was effective utilization of manpower, he also was opposed to the idea of elite formations skimming off the cream of the Corps, as had occurred to his division during its crucial preparations for Guadalcanal. The Raider regiment became the 4th Marines and eventually would join with another independent regiment already in existence (the 22d Marines) to form the core of the 6th Marine Division. The Parachute regiment dissolved, but its handpicked officers and men (along with those in the 4th Raider Battalion and the Raider Training Center) became the cadre of the three infantry regiments of the 5th Marine Division. Vandegrift next went after the defense battalions and by mid-1944 had cut them from a planned level of twenty-nine and an actual strength of twenty to just five. Some converted to pure antiaircraft or heavy artillery units while others simply ceased to exist and freed up personnel.[57]

The frightening toll of casualties from Tarawa was merely a harbinger of things to come for the Corps. In the Marianas campaign in the summer of 1944, the units engaged lost 21,000 marines in the space of two months. At the same time, Vandegrift wanted to establish a rotation that brought home veterans of two years or more in the Pacific. The commandant resorted to several measures to feed the war's appetite for men. He ordered Thomas on a tour of stateside bases to evaluate their requirements and the brigadier reallocated 10,000 personnel from these bloated establishments. Holland Smith's headquarters in the Pacific likewise sought to decrease the number of billets wasted in backwater locations. As the war dragged on, Vandegrift continued to scour the rear echelons for men who had not yet served overseas. When things got really desperate, Headquarters began closing training facilities considered less than critical. The antiaircraft school met that criterion, since the nearly defunct defense battalions were providing a reservoir of trained personnel for a declining specialty. Finally, in 1945, the Corps won an increase in authorized strength to 503,000 to make up for the large numbers of sick and wounded that were unfit for duty.

Other steps did not deliver real men but did reduce the size of the combat units the Corps needed to support. A 1944 revision of the tables of organization for the division dropped its strength from 19,965 to 17,465. Many in the operating forces opposed these cuts because they decreased fighting effectiveness. (Ultimately the next revision of the tables in 1945 restored the division to just over 19,000 men, but the war was nearly over by then.) Headquarters also encouraged subordinate commands to create necessary new units on a provisional basis, which meant that manpower to fill them had to come from existing formations. By 1945 these ghost units absorbed more than 7,000 men theoretically carried on the rolls of authorized outfits that were thus understrength by that amount. A senior marine in the combat zone gave Thomas his candid opinion of that expedient: "It is akin to the ostrich who hides his head in the sand and fools nobody, including you at Headquarters Marine Corps."[58]

The heavy losses of 1944 paled in comparison to those of the following year. The Iwo Jima landing in February cost more than twenty-two thousand men, which came as "quite a shock" to Vandegrift. The early lack of strong opposition on Okinawa heartened him, and he hoped that minimal losses there would put the Corps "back on easy street," but ultimately nearly another twenty thousand marines were killed or wounded in that battle. The twin charnel houses of Iwo Jima and Okinawa took the Corps to the brink of a manpower crisis. To make matters worse, after the victory in Europe, public pressure grew on HQMC to match Army policy and discharge marines with long service. The Corps had kept its fighting units full through the spring of 1945, but it was a close-run thing. Had the war continued, the system might have broken down during the invasion of Japan.[59]

Senior officers presented a different set of personnel-related problems. The first two years of the war had made it clear that far too many Marine colonels were too old or too cautious to make good regimental commanders or lacked the training to perform effectively on high-level staffs. While a number of generals complained about the available material, they seldom formally relieved anyone for cause, instead taking the easy route out and seeking replacements via back channels. Vandegrift had been guilty of similar behavior on Guadalcanal but was now forced to issue an edict to commanding generals to work with what they had or fire a man with a fitness report that would end his career: "All it requires is the moral courage to go on record as stating that this or that officer is not competently exercising command over his unit and in the opinion of the division commander is not competent or efficient to hold the job he now has." But senior leaders were reluctant to crack down on men who had served with them for twenty years in the small interwar Corps. Despite the commandant's directive, many commanders continued trying to arrange quiet transfers with covert appeals. Thomas admitted that the inability of HQMC to weed out poor performers clogged up the promotion system: "We have from forty to fifty colonels, not one of whom anyone would take. If we could get rid of that group and promote an equal number of youngsters, the overall number of colonels now authorized would be entirely adequate." The dearth of "usable colonels" led Vandegrift to change the table of organization of the division so that lieutenant colonels filled the primary staff billets.[60]

In the same vein, Holland Smith lauded the early promotion of Merritt Edson to brigadier general for the precedent it set: "It will open the gate to many other young officers who demonstrate their ability on the field of battle." But the pathway to advancement remained barred to most. After the beginning of the war, Holcomb had gained the authority to appoint generals without a board. Late in 1943 he was "astounded" to find that his liberal selections had resulted in the Corps having proportionally more officers wearing stars than the Navy. Holcomb then allowed Edson to slip through and Vandegrift promoted Thomas, but thereafter there was no room at the top as the size of the Corps remained static. The commandant tried to implement stricter physical examinations for senior officers as means to clear out deadwood, but soon found "there isn't one darn thing that you can do about it." Vandegrift was able to advance only a handful of colonels for the remainder of the war.[61]

Vandegrift's management of the senior officer population was marred by an uneven ability to judge character and competence. For every superior choice such as Thomas and Edson, he made equally poor ones, usually out of misplaced loyalty. Despite his hope that he always would make decisions "for the best of the Marine Corps," he often let "personal feelings" intrude. William A. Rupertus, for example, had turned in a lackluster performance as the 1st Marine Division ADC at Guadalcanal, but Vandegrift backed his elevation to command the division in 1943 and continued to believe that he was one of the "finest officers" in the Corps even after he made serious errors in the assault on Peleliu. The commandant brought him home to run the Marine Corps Schools in late 1944 and would have recommended him as his successor if Rupertus had not died the following year. Vandegrift also rescued Col. John "Buddy" Knighton from a failed tour on Admiral Turner's staff and gave him a prominent role in policy making at Headquarters, a move which almost cost the Corps dearly in the postwar unification struggles. At the same time, Vandegrift often disregarded or shunted aside outstanding officers, such as Merrill B. Twining, whose personalities were not to his liking.[62]

Another challenge for the new commandant was deciding how to manage the large number of ground units now in the Pacific. Holcomb had created IMAC for the South Pacific theater and V Amphibious Corps (VAC) under Holland Smith as the senior Marine headquarters in the central Pacific. The end of the Solomons campaign in early 1944 brought Geiger's IMAC to the central Pacific as well, where it was renamed III Amphibious Corps (IIIAC). Both corps were mixed Marine-Army at that time. Control of such high-level organizations was still very new to the Marine Corps, and policy makers felt their way slowly in developing a command structure. In October 1943, Smith had proposed creation of a headquarters to be called Marine Forces Pacific, which would command all Marine ground units in the theater. Holcomb rejected that concept. He thought Smith the only logical candidate for such a billet but was unwilling to shift him from VAC for fear that an Army general would take over the organization.[63]

The issue remained unresolved until the Marianas campaign, in which both corps participated. For that operation Vandegrift tried another option Holcomb had discarded, allowing Smith to retain his corps and assume control of all other Marine units. There was no new command; Smith simply took the additional and temporary title of commanding general, Expeditionary Troops, with VAC and IIIAC both subordinate to him for the duration of the operation. With his two hats came two staffs, one to serve him in each capacity. Vandegrift also created the Marine Administrative Command under Maj. Gen. Julian Smith to take care of all noncombat support of ground forces in the Pacific. One of its primary subordinate echelons was the Supply Service, a consolidation of the logistics agencies of both corps. Julian Smith reported to Holland Smith, who now commanded all Marine ground organizations in the Pacific with the exception of the outfits under MacArthur. (Throughout the war, Marine aviation units reported to Navy air commanders.)

Edson, now ADC of the 2d Marine Division, pointed out the flaw in this setup to Thomas in May 1944: "It is just not conducive to smooth operations when one officer has to combine in himself the tasks of a corps commander and an army commander in a combat zone and still retain responsibility over the administrative command in [the rear area]." Holcomb had vetoed that alternative for the same reason: "It is more than can be expected of anyone to command and supply his own corps and be responsible for the supply and administrative arrangements of another corps at the same time. Holland would try to be conscientious, but it just wouldn't work." Following his experiences with IMAC, Vandegrift himself had argued against a scheme that rolled rear echelon and combat functions into one: "I feel that the senior man in the Pacific should be located [in Hawaii with Nimitz's headquarters] and should not be away from it for long periods of time in which it gives others an opportunity to undermine while he is away on prolonged combat missions." Holland Smith, on the other hand, felt that he could do it all, and the new commandant gave him the chance to try.[64]

The misgivings of the critics proved prescient. As soon as IIIAC assaulted Guam in July 1944, Holland Smith found that he could not properly oversee that operation as well as the fighting of his own corps on distant Tinian. He quickly relinquished command of VAC to Maj. Gen. Harry Schmidt and served solely in his capacity as CG, Expeditionary Troops. In August, Vandegrift and Thomas traveled to the Pacific for face-to-face meetings with senior leaders. After consultation with Holland and Julian Smith, they established Fleet Marine Force Pacific (FMFPac) to control administratively all Marine ground forces in the theater. If directed by Nimitz, the new headquarters also could serve in combat operations as a field army echelon over two or more corps. Holland Smith selected Edson as his chief of staff and de facto assistant commander. Although this setup still contained flaws, it would serve the Corps for the remainder of the war.[65]

Vandegrift had as much difficulty trying to find a solution to the logistics quandary. Holcomb knew at the end of his tour that it was getting "more confused day by day." The new commandant had hoped to fix the problem by forming a single Supply Service responsible for all Marine ground forces in the Pacific. That was a step in the right direction, but it did not achieve the goal, in large measure due to personnel shortcomings that began at the top. Holcomb had not been satisfied with Long's performance in the South Pacific, and Thomas felt that he would not improve with greater responsibility. Both Thomas and Edson thought the dominance of quartermaster specialists in the logistics field hurt matters since they had no sense of the "turmoil of war." Moreover, the Supply Service drew more than its share of weak officers as senior leaders shunted poor performers from combat units to rear echelon jobs. The organization was undermanned, as well, possessing just 12 percent of FMFPac's manpower, an exceedingly thin ratio of tail to tooth. In the summer of 1945 Long still was attempting to create standing operating procedures for his command, and his headquarters was not organized along normal general staff lines (G-1, etc.). Its record keeping was so chaotic that no one knew exactly what quantities of supplies were on hand in the theater. One wag at HQMC summed up the situation: "The Supply Service is like a bunch of people working in the bottom of a bucket who have not yet found a way to look over the top."[66]

Events forced Vandegrift to take action. Supply arrangements had not worked well for Okinawa, and the upcoming invasion of Japan would generate far greater demands. In June 1945, he implemented a month-old proposal from Edson and changed the name of the supply organization to Service Command, better to reflect its breadth of duties. Then he replaced Long with a line officer possessing proven staff credentials, a "two-fisted, energetic organizer," again Merritt Edson. Finally he sent a retired general with a logistics background to the Pacific to serve as his representative in revitalizing the entire system from HQMC to the far reaches of the war zone. Edson was just beginning to implement serious changes when the atomic bomb brought the conflict to an end.[67]

While the real war raged overseas, the services continued to fight an internecine struggle at home. Vandegrift was in office less than a week when a senior Army officer challenged the fitness of marines to operate at the corps or higher echelon. That debate came to center stage in the summer of 1944, when Holland Smith relieved Maj. Gen. Ralph Smith from command of the 27th Infantry Division on Saipan. The Army outfit had made slow progress and thus endangered the flanks of two Marine divisions. Vandegrift was convinced that Holland Smith was fully justified, and he hoped that the affair would blow over in short order, but it evolved into a lengthy and sometimes bitter public dispute about service tactical philosophy. Marines willingly admitted that they preferred "bold, hard-hitting, relentless assaults." Some media outlets editorialized that the Army was more cautious and thus suffered fewer casualties. Bloody Peleliu in the fall of 1944 added fuel to the fire. The constant sniping only made Vandegrift "irritable," but one group of marines was so incensed by a critical story in a San Francisco newspaper that they stormed its offices and demanded a retraction. The controversy did more than simply raise leatherneck blood pressure; it likely sank any chance for the Corps to operate a field army. After Saipan, Army leaders were loath to place any of their divisions under Marine command and both IIIAC and VAC soon became Marine-only formations. Despite the pleas of the senior admirals planning the Okinawa campaign, Nimitz gave that two-corps mission to the Tenth Army rather than Holland Smith's FMFPac Headquarters, thus relegating the latter to a purely administrative role for the remainder of the war.[68]

Smith versus Smith potentially had even greater ramifications. In the spring of 1944, the House of Representatives had launched the Woodrum committee to conduct hearings on the Army's proposed unification of the services. Vandegrift thought the ill-timed Saipan incident "raised plu-perfect hell" just when the Army was "busily engaged . . . in trying to cut us down in size if not abolish us." In prepared remarks to the committee in May 1944, the commandant recognized the need for unity of command in operational matters and cited Guadalcanal as a model in that regard. He argued, however, that "parallel employment" did not translate into "unnecessary duplication." In his eyes, history demonstrated the value of a land-air component allied with the fleet, a capability the Army would have to replicate if there were no marines. The hearings droned on inconclusively through November, then adjourned till the new year, which gave Vandegrift and Thomas "two more months to marshal our facts and arguments for why there should be a Marine Corps."[69]

During Vandegrift's May presentation, a friendly questioner raised the issue of the lack of Marine participation in the JCS, but the commandant fumbled it: "We are a subordinate part of the Navy, and as part of the Navy, we are represented by a Navy representative." The Corps was actually a service within the Navy Department, an important distinction that made Vandegrift theoretically the equal of the CNO. But tradition had made many commandants exceedingly deferential to their Navy counterparts. Holcomb passed many matters, to include the nomination of his successor, *through* the CNO's office rather than directly to the secretary. Vandegrift perhaps made things worse. Since he disliked King's abrasive personality, he conducted most business with the CNO's primary subordinates, even after he himself was promoted to four-star rank in March 1945. Many admirals, in turn, felt free to interfere in affairs, such as manpower and organization, that were purely the province of the Corps. A prime example was a 1944 Nimitz order that unengaged Marine divisions provide replacements for losses in other formations. Julian Smith, concerned about the effect on unit cohesiveness, asked for the commandant's intervention. Initially Vandegrift simply told Smith to try to change the policy himself before the next operation. Reports of losses at Saipan revealed the potential scale of the problem and finally spurred the commandant to action, but he was satisfied when the CNO merely forwarded the HQMC memorandum on the subject to Nimitz and left the final decision to CinCPac. Luckily Nimitz rescinded his order. Though Vandegrift usually avoided confrontation with the Navy at all costs, he could be cagey in defeating the power plays of the admirals. At one point the Navy needed more space in southern California and wanted the Marine Corps to turn over its San Diego base. At a meeting convened to decide the issue, Vandegrift casually acknowledged the requirement and offered up nearby, less-desirable Camp Elliott; to the consternation of the Vice CNO, the secretary immediately accepted and closed the matter.[70]

Marine aviation proved to be another bone of contention between the sea services. The CinCPac aviation chief presented a plan to Vandegrift in June 1944 to disband forty-one of the Corps's squadrons to provide additional manpower for Navy air units. The commandant quietly chided him for not seeking the input of senior Marine aviators in the Pacific and politely reminded him: "The question of Marine organization both ground and air was something that deeply concerned the commandant of the Marine Corps as in the last analysis he was responsible for the Marine Corps." The idea died when Vandegrift promised to set forth his concerns in a memorandum to the CNO, but he complained to Holcomb about "our daily fights to keep someone from taking something away from us." Holcomb had admonished him at one point for ignoring Marine aviation, but the twin threats of unification or reduction spurred Vandegrift to tie his air arm more closely to the ground forces of the Corps. After the early battles of Wake Island, Midway, and Guadalcanal, Marine squadrons largely had executed their own missions, while Marine divisions conducted assaults backed by Navy or Army planes. In mid-1944, the commandant told Holland Smith to press Nimitz to focus leatherneck air on support of amphibious landings, launched a campaign at home to get Marine planes onto Navy carriers, and instituted a two-week, ground-combat school for new pilots to familiarize them with the challenges facing their infantry compatriots.[71]

These efforts first bore fruit at Peleliu, where Marine Aircraft Group 11 rendered yeoman service to the 1st Marine Division during the brief period between its arrival on the island and the division's departure. Marine close air support truly came into its own during the campaigns on Okinawa and the Philippines, but it was still mainly limited to participation after the seizure and rehabilitation of airfields on the objective. The Navy finally agreed to provide escort carriers for the sole use of Marine squadrons supporting ground operations, but the ships and planes were not ready to fight until after the last amphibious assault of the war was over. A total of ten Marine squadrons did serve on board large-deck flattops during 1945. They were drafted into the duty when air admirals found they had too few pilots and planes to increase fighter strength to combat the kamikaze threat. Due to previous decisions by both Marine and Navy aviation leaders to end carrier training for leatherneck pilots, this expedient did not work out well; far more Marine planes were lost to flying accidents than to enemy action. In any case, it did not meet the commandant's goal of integrating Marine air and ground components into a combined arms force.[72]

During the course of the Woodrum committee, Vandegrift was ready to concede that there was a danger to the Corps, but he remained certain it would come through the process unscathed: "As long as Marines continue to win, which they will certainly continue to do, we have no reason to worry about our place in any post-war setup." In fact, he thought that the end of the conflict would make the Army's idea "impossible of accomplishment." Despite the Navy's sometimes high-handed behavior toward the Corps, he also was sure that it would always be a trusted ally. With the elevation of Forrestal to the leadership of the Navy Department, he believed that there had "never been a finer Secretary of the Navy or one more keenly interested in the Marine Corps nor more alive to our trials and tribulations." John H. Russell agreed with Vandegrift's optimism and was pleased that the current commandant had gained a positive reputation among the admirals for emphasizing the strong bond between the two services. Other Marine leaders were less sanguine. Thomas believed "the Army is tenaciously pursuing the subject and they mean us no good." Holland Smith informed Vandegrift in late 1944 that Nimitz was leaning in favor of unification and warned the commandant that "either service will sell us down the river."[73]

As Vandegrift fought through current problems, he also kept a wary eye on the future. One of his main concerns was postwar basing. The services had vastly expanded the size and number of their posts, and the commandant expected some states to resent the amount of acreage removed from tax rolls. In mid-1944 he was "worried greatly" about southern California, where the Corps had taken control of large tracts equally valuable to the civilian economy and amphibious training. He especially wanted to hold on to these western bases, as it would keep the Marines close to their primary theater of employment, even if the United States returned to continental isolation. He considered it almost as compelling that the distance from Washington would allow the Corps to "be less conspicuous." His seemingly casual gift of Camp Elliott to the Navy was designed to protect the more vital installations at Camp Pendleton, as well as the sentimentally important base at San Diego. While he fended off the Navy with one hand, he was also dueling with the city of San Diego, which wanted land to expand its airport. His foresight proved critical in the Corps's struggle to retain a major presence on the Pacific Coast.[74]

Through all the troubles of manpower, logistics, organization, basing, and unification, Vandegrift had kept his focus on the one thing he considered most important: the people who made up the Corps. He made two trips to the Pacific during the remainder of the war and traveled often to bases in the States. He never treated these as inspections, instead following the practice he had established at Guadalcanal: getting out to see and be seen. He had a genuine concern for his marines, demonstrated in a number of ways. Shortly after taking office, he discovered a rumor was going round that he intended to disband the Women's Reserve. To repair their morale, he not only visited their home base at Camp Lejeune but also mentioned them frequently and glowingly in speeches for the next several weeks. He cared deeply about casualties and personally signed every Purple Heart award. He made it clear to senior leaders that commanders of battalions and companies would write letters to the families of all men killed in action. "This is not something one cares to get out an order about but it is something that the junior unit commanders should in all decency want to do," he stated. Another constant refrain was the requirement to keep the troops informed in order to build cohesiveness and confidence. He also thought it gave combat units an advantage: "A man fights much better when he has a sense of the common objective, rather than merely a knowledge of how things look from his own foxhole. Time after time, I have seen men carry on when all their leaders have been knocked out, using the knowledge given them in advance of the action." Most of all, in word and practice, he espoused the idea that "loyalty must start from the top."[75]

The atomic bombs brought a quick end to the war in August 1945 and solved some of Vandegrift's most pressing problems, but they also opened up new ones. Instead of six divisions invading Japan, two went there as an occupation force and two others moved into China to oversee the repatriation of imperial forces. A total of three wings also deployed to the Far East. These police missions required much less logistical effort, and Service Command focused on bringing material home and disposing of the excess. By HQMC directive, the intensity of combat training dropped off markedly, although schools at every level for officers resumed their longer prewar curriculums.

Manpower woes were not quite as serious, but they were nevertheless daunting. Vandegrift had set his staff to work months before on a demobilization plan, much of which was complete at war's end. It called for a peacetime Corps of 8,000 officers and 100,000 enlisted men with a Fleet Marine Force of two divisions and two wings. Regrettably, the Navy had not been as farsighted, and now the Marines had to wait for them before submitting proposals for approval by Congress. Vandegrift was upset because delay and uncertainty would cause many young officers to leave the service before the Corps could offer them a chance for a career as a regular. The enlisted picture was no better. Of the 415,000 men on active duty on V-J Day, only 72,000 had contracts requiring them to serve beyond the emergency, and two-thirds of those were due to expire within ten months. To complicate matters, there was an intense public clamor to demobilize immediately.[76]

The Corps adopted the same point scheme as the Army to govern discharges. The transfer of individuals and units home was rapid, and by 30 June 1946, there were only 155,000 marines on duty. During those ten hectic months, Vandegrift continued to stress the need to look after the welfare of the troops. He was concerned about persistent reports of poor food, clothing, and shelter for marines in China and Japan and admonished his generals to instill in all officers "the SOP of looking out for the men first." He was appalled by specific blunders, such as a sergeant sent home from the Pacific to be with his dying wife only to be mistakenly held at Camp Pendleton until it was too late: "It is not a sign of efficiency to be hard-boiled and callous, nor is it a sign of weakness or molly-coddling to be decent and humane." At the same time, he was satisfied with Geiger's quick action to arrest men who instigated a demobilization protest on Hawaii. His racial views softened after the war, and he thought it best to integrate African Americans rather than maintain segregated units, but he was unwilling to press the point in the face of opposition from other senior leaders in the Corps.[77]

The manpower picture improved in April 1946, when President Truman finally signed a bill giving the Corps 7,000 officers and 100,000 men. The loss of 1,000 leadership billets from the postwar plan did not bother Vandegrift, since the 7 percent officer ratio was still much larger than the prewar figure. With definite numbers to go by, HQMC immediately made use of a two-month-old law that established a twenty-year retirement for the first time, reduced the maximum age to sixty-two, and authorized the creation of boards to select officers for involuntary retirement. The commandant was especially pleased with the last provision because it finally would allow him to eliminate those who had been "sitting around taking up room because there was no way to get rid of them." The chopping block started near the very top, with Lt. Gen. Holland Smith and Lt. Gen. Roy Geiger and a three-star admiral serving as a panel to select major generals for involuntary retirement. Other boards reviewed regular officers in each rank for retention while yet another panel picked the best of the reservists for conversion to regular status. Although Vandegrift was not happy with some of the results, he was proud that no one would have to revert to lower rank, and he was certain he had presided over a system more equitable than that used after World War I. His revitalized recruiting service also brought in large numbers of new marines on long-term contracts, which put the Corps 70 percent of the way to achieving its force of 100,000 regulars.[78]

Vandegrift's biggest postwar challenge turned out to be the problem he thought would disappear at the end of the conflict: unification. The new president, Harry Truman, had served as a National Guard artillery officer in World War I and shared the anti–Marine Corps bias of many AEF veterans. Perhaps more important, he was intent on erasing the government's huge budget deficit, and the Army's proposal promised to save money. The dawn of the atomic era also called into question the efficacy of old ways of preparing for war. Despite the changed situation, the commandant was confident: "We have the wholehearted support of the Navy because they are in the throes for the first time in a good many years of being attacked also with the prospect of becoming the very small tail to an Army kite. I believe though that we can beat this game because . . . we have a number of friends on the Hill and innumerable ones throughout the country." He recognized it would be no easy fight: "We have got to forget methods that we have used before because as much as we hate to realize it, this is not the day when knighthood was in flower and it's more like a street brawl than a tilting joust." Regrettably, it was the type of struggle for which he was temperamentally least prepared.[79]

The fight initially did not go well. The unification bills introduced into the Senate were short and mainly left the details of reorganization up to the executive branch, where the Corps had no allies. Vandegrift's October 1945 testimony did not persuade the senators that this approach was wrong, and he soon placed his hopes in the House of Representatives. The severity of the Army's intentions also came into focus at the end of the year when Gen. Dwight D. Eisenhower (the new Army chief of staff) told Nimitz (now the CNO) that the Marines should be limited even in wartime to no more than forty thousand men, possess no supporting arms, and focus solely on landing party, shore party, and landing craft duties like the Royal Marines. The Navy's air arm also faced consolidation into a single national aviation component. To combat the threat, the commandant created a think tank under Twining at Quantico and brought Edson home to serve as his liaison with the Navy. Thomas, Edson, Twining, and their handful of assistants carried the future of the Corps on their shoulders for the next eighteen months.[80]

Vandegrift's greatest contribution to the merger fight came on 6 May 1946. At the strong urging of Thomas and Edson, the commandant used a bold statement prepared by Twining and Lt. Col. Victor H. Krulak in his testimony before the Senate Naval Affairs Committee. He closed with an uncharacteristically emotional appeal: "The Marine Corps thus believes it has earned this right—to have its future decided by the legislative body which created it—nothing more. . . . The bended knee is not a tradition of our Corps. If the Marine as a fighting man has not made a case for himself after 170 years, he must go. But I think you will agree with me that he has earned the right to depart with dignity and honor, not by subjugation to the status of uselessness and servility planned for him by the War Department." In an answer to a planted question, Vandegrift also reluctantly unleashed a bombshell in revealing the existence of classified documents containing the Army's heretofore-concealed intention to render the Corps impotent. The media and the public did not alter their predilection for unification, but neither were they eager to disband the Marines. The Army steamroller ground to a halt as Congress decided to give the issue further consideration.[81]

The commandant was ecstatic at the outcome and believed "we have this merger business licked cold." He turned his attention to fresh problems. Truman launched a "very drastic economy wave," and HQMC was forced along with the other services to deal with budget cuts. Vandegrift "drastically curtailed" spending on equipment and supplies in an attempt to maintain end strength, but a few months later the president ordered a 10 percent reduction in Marine manpower anyway. The election of a Republican Congress in November generated pressure for additional cutbacks. Meanwhile the Army and Navy were both taking an unwanted interest in the amphibious mission. In what Vandegrift suspected was an attempt to back the Corps into a corner over its claims of primacy in assaults from the sea, the War Department requested that the Marines provide amphibious training for a major slice of Army units in the current year and all regular and National Guard formations in the future. The commandant assembled able staffs to begin the program but tried to limit it to select Army outfits since there were too few ships and landing craft to accommodate everyone. In a renewal of the amphibious command dispute, the Navy then stepped in to claim control of the new training commands. Vandegrift disagreed with that move, but did not oppose it. Finally, the Corps had to take a painful look at itself and determine how to adapt to the challenges of atomic warfare. A special board headed by Twining argued that the future lay in dispersing the amphibious fleet at sea, using helicopters or seaplanes to concentrate the landing force at the point of attack. This basically returned the Corps to the mid-1930s, when it had a concept but no equipment designed or built to execute it.[82]

Internal battles preoccupied much of Vandegrift's energy during this respite from interservice struggles. Despite his efforts during the war to meld more closely the ground and air elements of the Corps, Marine aviators were afraid they might lose out on what they considered their fair share of shrinking resources. Among other things, they wanted a fixed percentage of Marine end-strength. The commandant convened a board under Maj. Gen. Graves B. Erskine to evaluate the role of aviation. Erskine's report recommended significant cuts to the air component, but also suggested that pilots rotate through ground assignments and schools to integrate better the two communities. Vandegrift adopted these proposals and also directed that some reserve aviators receive regular commissions as ground officers. These policies assuaged concerns that flying leathernecks might disproportionately bear the brunt of personnel reductions. To ensure further that there would be no resurgent rift, the commandant also decreed that future flight school trainees be drawn exclusively from officers with at least one tour of ground duty.[83]

Another major headache was the perennial debate over reorganization of HQMC. Holcomb had made two significant changes: he had merged the Adjutant and Inspector, Reserve, and Public Relations Offices into the relatively new Personnel Department, while the Quartermaster Department had absorbed the Paymaster. These two superbureaus thereafter gained an inordinate amount of power in the Headquarters constellation. As the head of Plans and Policies, Thomas chafed under this setup from the very beginning. He felt it was the prerogative of his office to develop a road map for the Corps, while the other departments filled out these broad directives with details and implemented them as appropriate within their spheres. In practice, however, each department worked independently and personal jealousies between the leading generals only increased the friction. On a more fundamental level, Thomas also argued that HQMC would never function properly until it was reorganized along general staff lines, and that the vast increase in the size of Headquarters required a chief of staff to assist the commandant in supervising the various offices. Although Vandegrift sometimes got "damnably well fed up with the constant petty irritations of this place," he was generally content with the system he had learned under Holcomb and typically reluctant to impose unwanted change on his subordinates. His only significant alteration of Headquarters was the postwar creation of the inspector general's office, which gave HQMC a badly needed means to reimpose materiel and administrative accountability after the wartime relaxation of rules and the disappearance of the Adjutant and Inspector Department.[84]

Vandegrift remained optimistic about the outcome of unification until the situation changed for the worse in late 1946. In the fall, Truman ordered the Navy and War Departments to develop a compromise bill, and Forrestal named Adm. Forrest P. Sherman to represent him in the negotiations. The Corps played no part in this process, and Sherman had a reputation for overlooking the interests of the Marines when it suited his purpose. The end result of the interservice talks did satisfy many of the Navy's objections, but the commandant did not get the one provision he considered absolutely necessary—inclusion of Marine roles and missions in the language of the law. Instead, the proposed bill left the duties of the services to be spelled out in an executive order, which could be changed at the whim of the occupant of the White House. The president approved the negotiated solution in January 1947 and sent it to Congress despite Vandegrift's personal plea for a change. To make matters worse, in their own version of consolidation, Republicans in both houses of Congress merged the military and naval panels into armed services committees. The reorganization in the Senate left the Corps without any of its traditional supporters on this key panel. Forrestal, content with the compromise, issued a strong prohibition against anyone in the Navy Department speaking against the measure in public or before Congress.[85]

After placing so much faith in the Navy, the commandant felt that his sister service had "sold out" the Corps. In a strange memo to one general, he plaintively noted, "I hope someone in Congress takes exception to this and sees fit to write the executive order [on roles and missions] into law. . . . If not, the price of existence will depend on eternal vigilance and the intestinal fortitude of those in control to stick their necks out to see that we are not run over." Regrettably, Vandegrift was not willing to put his own head on the chopping block and lead the offensive himself. He did sanction a proposal by Thomas to put Edson in charge of a group focused on achieving that end, but thereafter he did more to hobble the effort than help it. He repeatedly rejected offers of lobbying assistance from regular, reserve, and retired marines. He refused to deliver another strong statement prepared by Twining's office and instead made a weak presentation before the Senate committee in favor of an amendment to the bill. Before he would allow Edson's group to circulate a hard-hitting critique of the president's proposal, he insisted that it contain no indication that it came from the Corps and that Edson himself sign it as a personal document. When it came time to testify before the House committee, Vandegrift again offered a watered-down plea for amendment. This panel was much friendlier to the Corps and several questions presented an opportunity for the commandant to highlight the Army's secret designs to emasculate the Marines, but he refused to utter statements critical of other services or their leaders. The result was a half-hearted request to protect the Corps from some unspecified threat. Vandegrift killed the last gasp of hope for victory in the Senate when, at the urging of Colonel Knighton, he endorsed an amendment that provided only cosmetic guarantees for the Corps.[86]

The courtly Virginia general always had been predisposed to avoid confrontation, but several other factors likely accounted for his weakened resolve. One was his focus on problems of immediate concern, in particular, the continued effort by both Truman and Congress to cut all military forces to the bone. In May 1947, when things looked bleakest for the Corps on unification, he told another senior marine that "the most pressing question of today" was a "reversion . . . to post World War I thinking with reference to national defense." The reductions in funding and manpower were such that Vandegrift implemented a new table of organization that did away with regimental headquarters and formed ground combat forces into combined-arms battalion landing teams. In July, he thought that a new promotion bill was "the most important piece of legislation before Congress." The internal squabbling between air and ground and the HQMC departments also took its toll on the commandant. Perhaps even more important was the declining health of his wife. She was sick for much of this period and had a severe heart attack in early June. The constant battles and concern for his spouse placed "quite a bit of strain" on the commandant, who was not well himself. His sight and hearing were deteriorating, and he suffered from rheumatoid arthritis and severe back pain. In the end, a tired, disheartened Vandegrift chose to avoid a bitter battle over a nebulous future threat that might endanger his attempts to deal with the immediate challenges that preoccupied him. To underscore his longing for a quiet end to his term, in June 1947 he disbanded Edson's group, transferred Thomas overseas, and accepted Edson's retirement in protest while the fight against unification still raged in the House.[87]

The unification fight turned out well for the Corps almost entirely due to the efforts of Thomas and the Edson and Twining teams. Edson sacrificed his career to deliver powerful testimony against the bill to both the Senate and House committees. He and the others also worked covertly to influence legislators and obtained success in the House, where the responsible panel amended the president's proposal to include a specific statement listing the roles and missions of the Corps. The public relations program of this small band also bore fruit in forcing the administration to ease its restrictions on naval dissent and in awakening the public and Congress to objectionable features of the original bill. The House version ultimately prevailed in conference and Truman signed the National Security Act of 1947 into law on 25 July. When it was over, Vandegrift felt as if he "had just finished a hard football game." Surprisingly, he wanted to believe that it had been his Headquarters that had overcome "great obstacles and difficulties and secured for the Corps the best deal possible under the circumstances." He was more accurate in his assessment that "the Marine Corps is in a stronger position now than ever before because we do have written down into the law things that we have only claimed for ourselves by custom or some kind of divine right."[88]

As Vandegrift's four-year tenure wound down at the end of 1947, he felt that he had gone through a period that "would try any man's soul," and he looked forward "with a great deal of pleasure to going down home . . . and leading a quiet and, I hope, peaceful life." His tour had been contentious, and he had faltered at a critical time in the life of the institution, but he also had overseen changes that boded well for the Corps. In one of his last acts he took a ride in a helicopter undergoing testing and evaluation at Quantico. Three days after he left office, the first Marine battalion landing team sailed for a long-term, shipboard deployment to the Mediterranean. Both innovations would become hallmarks of the Corps. In his closing remarks to his marines, he challenged them to "retain the vital flexibility of a healthy organism" and search for answers to new operational problems such as atomic weapons, massed enemy armor and artillery, and night warfare. He also encouraged them to keep esprit, quality, and readiness at the forefront. He had done much to create and maintain such an environment and could justifiably proclaim: "I have no fears for the future of the Corps."[89]

In retirement Vandegrift achieved the peace and quiet he desired. He eschewed the lecture circuit and corporate board rooms and enjoyed a well-deserved rest after a thirty-nine-year career. He ultimately settled in Florida and died quietly at Bethesda Naval Hospital in May 1973.

19

Clifton Bledsoe Cates

1948–1952

PAOLO E. COLETTA

Clifton Bledsoe Cates was born on 31 August 1893 into a family that grew cotton along the banks of the Mississippi near Tiptonville, a small town in extreme northwestern Tennessee. After attending a country school two miles from home, he was sent to high school in Spring Hill, Tennessee, and then to the Mexico Military Academy, Mexico, Missouri, from which he graduated in 1910. After a year's postgraduate work at Mexico, he attended the University of Tennessee, where he played varsity baseball and football while studying law. Wanting to get into the Great War, he asked the son of the university president to advise him about any vacancies in the military that might be available. When told that the Marine Corps wanted several second lieutenant reservists, Cates replied, "What the hell is that outfit?" He also said, "Yes, put my name down" and did not finish his law examinations.[1]

After passing qualifying tests at the Marine Barracks in Washington, D.C., Cates obtained his first taste of the Corps at Parris Island on 13 June 1917. On 28 August, he was sent for officer instruction to Quantico. He left Quantico with the 96th Company, 6th Marines on 18 January 1918 to board the transport *Henderson* for a "billy-hell trip" to France that took ten days. From St. Nazaire he was sent to the front lines, where he began a distinguished and probably unique career as a commander of a platoon, company, battalion, regiment, and division—all of them in wartime. With the 6th Marines, he participated in the battles of Belleau Wood, Soissons, St. Mihiel, Blanc Mont, and the Argonne. He was severely gassed, seven times wounded, and once was stripped bare of his uniform by a close shellburst. At Soissons, from a crumbling French trench, he reported in words that entered Marine Corps lore: "I have only two men left out of my company and 20 out of the other companies. We need support, but it is almost suicide to try to get it here, as we are swept by machine-gun fire and a constant barrage is upon us. I have no one on my left and only a few on my right. I will hold."[2] For his services he was awarded the Navy Cross and the Distinguished Service Cross with Oak Leaf

Gen. Clifton B. Cates, nineteenth commandant.

Cluster, two wound stripes, and other French decorations. When called "Lucky Cates," he would retort, "Better to be lucky than good looking."[3]

After duty with the army of occupation in Germany until September 1919, Cates returned home and submitted his resignation. Dissuaded by Maj. Gen. Cmdt. George Barnett, he then served as Barnett's aide and representative to President Woodrow Wilson at the White House. Because the president was incapacitated by a stroke, Cates never saw him. When John A. Lejeune became commandant and Barnett moved to San Francisco, the former commandant took Cates along as his aide. The duty lasted for three years. Though Cates had reverted to the rank of first lieutenant after the war, the Neville board jumped him almost four hundred numbers. After being promoted to captain, he remained in that grade for thirteen years.

On 5 October 1920, Cates married Jane Virginia McIlhenny of Washington, D.C. They had two children, a son and a daughter. In 1923, he began a two-year tour in command of the Marine detachment on the battleship *California,* after which he served as recruiting officer successively at Spokane, Washington, and Omaha, Nebraska. After a year on the American Battle Monuments Commission, he rotated between foreign and home duty: with the 4th Regiment at Shanghai, China, 1929–32; attendance at the Army Industrial College, Washington, D.C., 1932–33; Marine Corps Schools, Quantico, Virginia, 1933–35; duty at Marine Headquarters, 1935–37; commanding officer of a battalion of the 6th Marines, Shanghai, 1937; and then of the 4th Regiment, Shanghai, 1938–39. After attending the Army War College, Washington, D.C., 1939–40, he was appointed director of the Basic School, Marine Barracks, Philadelphia.

Except for a period as commandant of the Marine Corps Schools, Cates fought World War II in the Pacific. As the colonel of the 1st Marines in Maj. Gen. Alexander A. Vandegrift's 1st Marine Division, he fought the entire Guadalcanal campaign, in which his careful tactical leadership paid off with relatively few casualties.[4] He later wrote about his experiences on the island and commented to his son that if the campaign was the turning point of the war in the Pacific, the night battle of Tenaru River, 21 August 1942, was the turning point of that campaign. As a major general, in July 1944 he assumed command of the 4th Marine Division and participated in the latter part of the Saipan operation. His subsequent seizure of Tinian is regarded as the model amphibious operation of the war. His 4th Marine Division—with the 3d and 5th Marine Divisions—then stormed Iwo Jima, a campaign he claimed that would "go down in history as the bloodiest fighting of World War II."[5]

The war over, Cates was assigned successively to the Marine Corps Equipment Board, which tested Marine materials and machines, and as commanding general of the Marine Barracks, Quantico. With his retirement as commandant impending, Vandegrift suggested Cates among three possible successors. From a longer list, Secretary of the Navy John L. Sullivan narrowed the field to Cates and Lemuel C. Shepherd. President Harry S. Truman noted that the records of the two men were similar, but he chose Cates, the senior, as the nineteenth commandant. Truman revealed the appointment at a press conterence on 21 November 1947. Because Congress was not in session, Cates was given an interim appointment until early 1948, when he was easily confirmed by the Senate.[6] A telegram of congratulations that brought a smile to his face came from the retired Maj. Gen. Robert L. Denig, who had served with him in France: "It is a far cry from that day in July 1918, when your pants were shot off, and today when you are called upon to occupy the best pair of pants in the Marine Corps."[7]

With no burning desire to become commandant, Cates neither pulled strings nor maneuvered politically to obtain the post; after his talk with Truman he wondered if he really wanted the billet. He nevertheless was sworn in at ceremonies in the office of the secretary of the navy late in December 1947; on 1 January 1948, he was promoted to general and received his appointment. He later confessed that he had been "damned lucky" because he had a good staff at a time when "we were battling for our lives."[8] He thereby overlooked his own aggressiveness, which he hid behind a calm demeanor and reserved manner. He was not looking for a fight when he entered Washington, and knew next to nothing about Capitol Hill tactics. Chain-smoking, quick-talking, alert, vigorous, and sometimes irascible, he would learn his political tactics and fight well.

During World War II, the Marine Corps had peaked at 485,000 men and women. By early 1946, as a result of demobilization, three divisions had been disbanded and another reduced to a brigade. When Cates took over as commandant, the Corps numbered merely 92,000. When Vandegrift turned over his office, Cates recalled, "I have three problems. The first, of course, is the fight that some people are making to cut the Marine Corps to the bone and the other one was in regard to the publication of General Holland Smith's book, and the other was . . . a commission . . . to a very big man—that had quite a bit of influence and he wasn't qualified physically at all. General Vandegrift left it in my lap to disapprove."[9]

The problem with Gen. "Howlin' Mad" Smith arose out of his recommendation to Adm. Raymond A. Spruance during the Saipan campaign to relieve the commander of the U.S. Army's 27th Infantry (New York National Guard) Division, Maj. Gen. Ralph Smith. The Army's commander in the Central Pacific complained bitterly about the firing of an Army general by a Navy admiral on the recommendation of a Marine Corps general. Adm. Chester W. Nimitz let matters ride, and Adm. Ernest J. King explained the matter to the Army chief of staff, Gen. George C. Marshall. There the matter rested until 1947, when a history of the 27th Division bitterly criticized Smith, who had retired on 15 May 1946 and was writing his memoirs. Knowing that Smith would soon publish, Cates declassified Corps records on the Saipan operation, asked Smith to check his facts, and then invited him to visit. When Smith said he would give his publisher the green light on the next day, Cates urged him not to do so. According to Cates, the following dialogue occurred between the two during their meeting:

[Cates]: General [Roy S.] Geiger was a good friend of yours, wasn't he? One of your best.

[Smith]: Yes, he was.

[Cates]: Well, if he was alive today, he wouldn't want you to publish that book.[10]

"And with that," Cates noted, "the tears started coming down General Smith's cheeks and he looked at me and all of a sudden he jumped at me and I thought he was going to hit me. He said, 'Goddamn it, don't hit below the belt.' I said, 'All right, go ahead and publish it.'"[11]

Cates's objection to having the book published was that it was "more or less past history and we didn't want to bring up old sores and also create, well, you might say, more ill feeling towards the Marine Corps." However, he admitted that Smith's points were valid, all perfectly honest, and proved how long-suffering he had been. There was practically no untoward reaction to the book except in the Army, which bristled at the way he had told the Smith vs. Smith story. Cates rested content because it "actually didn't affect the Marine Corps."[12]

Among the problems that Cates inherited were the following questions: the position of the Marine Corps in the Department of the Navy organization and chain of command, its peacetime size, and its role in the new Defense establishment. He also had to provide marines for sea duty and overseas details with American embassies and legations. Cates needed to institute two diverse training programs, one to give marines the expertise they needed to operate sophisticated weapons systems suitable for atomic warfare, the other to conduct conventional warfare and amphibious operations. In addition, he had to implement President Truman's Executive Order No. 9981, dated 26 July 1948, ending racial segregation in the armed services. The Marine Corps also had to adjust to the Uniform Code of Military Justice promulgated in 1950, and, after 25 June 1950, reverse the downward spiral of Marine Corps strength and rebuild the Corps to meet the needs of the war in Korea.

As secretary of the navy, Frank Knox interpreted President Franklin D. Roosevelt's Executive Order 8802 on desegregation, one thousand African Americans a month needed to be recruited. After the Saipan landings, Commandant Vandegrift said, "The Negro Marines are no longer on trial. They are Marines, period." Soon African Americans won officer commissions, and by June 1949, they were fully integrated into the Corps. After Truman ordered desegregation in the armed services on 26 July 1948, Cates said that segregation was not a problem to be solved by the armed forces, but by American society.[13] Under his direction, however, athletic teams, then recruit platoons, and NCO clubs were integrated, and in September 1949 the first black women were accepted by the Corps. On 18 November, instructions were issued that all individual black marines be assigned to vacancies in any unit in which they could be used effectively.[14] During the Korean War, African Americans in the Corps increased from 2 to 6 percent. Maj. Gen. Oliver P. Smith, commanding the 1st Marine Division in Korea, said, "They did everything, and they did a good job because they were integrated, and they were with good people."[15]

Would atomic bombs doom conventional wars and amphibious operations? Was it true as some official Marine historians posed the question that "the atomic bomb of Hiroshima rendered obsolescent in ten seconds a system of amphibious assault tactics that had been ten years in the making? Obviously, the concentrations of transports, warships, and aircraft carriers that had made possible the Saipan and Iwo Jima landings would be sitting ducks for an enemy armed with atomic weapons."[16]

Having witnessed the atomic bomb testing at Bikini in July 1946, the commander of the Fleet Marine Force, Pacific (FMFPac), Gen. Roy S. Geiger, suggested changes in amphibious doctrine. A special board headed by the assistant commandant of the Corps, Lemuel C. Shepherd, on 16 December 1946 recommended what Col. Robert D. Heinl has called a "breath-taking" rather than "revolutionary" concept—that of vertical envelopment.[17] Vandegrift quickly approved the report, and by December 1947

Marine Helicopter Experimental Squadron One (HMX-1) was established at Quantico Air Station under Lt. Col. Edward C. Dyer, while Cols. Merrill B. Twining and Victor H. Krulak wrote *Phib-31,* the basic manual on helicopter amphibious doctrine.[18] At the time the best helicopter (the Sikorsky) could carry only two passengers in addition to the pilot. "The Marines were responsible for the development of the helicopter," Cates stated. "The Army was lukewarm to it, the Navy didn't want any part of it." By August 1948, the Piasecki HRP-1 "Flying Banana" carried six men, and Cates avidly supported the "New Concept" of using helicopters for ship to shore movement and aircraft carriers as transports.[19] He even invited President Truman to witness a simulated helicopter attack at Quantico on 15 June, just ten days before the Korean War started. Not overly impressed, the old National Guard company commander patted the barrel of a 75-mm pack howitzer and said, "I like this best."[20]

According to Gen. Gerald C. Thomas, "Cates did battle [over unification] but he had a rough time. He had perhaps the roughest time of any Commandant of the Marine Corps. Unfortunately, for that purpose his inheritance from Vandegrift was very small. The apparatus that saw the Corps through the trying 1944 and 1947 period had been dismantled, and its members scattered."[21] Moreover, from the Marine Corps viewpoint, even though its own separate existence had been guaranteed, the Navy Department did not oppose unification strongly enough.[22]

To define service roles and mission the first secretary of defense, Forrestal, called the Joint Chiefs of Staff (JCS) and their aides, but not Cates, to a four-day conference at Key West, Florida, beginning 11 March 1948. His failure to invite him, as Cates put it, "was a real slap in the face to the Marine Corps," and it left the fate of the Corps with the chief of naval operations, Louis E. Denfeld.[23]

Except for his Headquarters public relations people and the Marine Corps Reserve Officers Association, Cates originally had little help in preparing the Marine Corps's defense beyond Col. Hunter Hurst, his representative on the Secretary's Committee on Research on Reorganization, better known by its acronym SCOROR, and Merwyn H. Silverthorn in the office of the CNO. However, Twining's "penetrating and facile hand," as General Thomas characterized it, had returned to Quantico.[24] With Don Weller, Robert D. Heinl, De Wolf "Dutch" Schatzel, Victor "Brute" Krulak, Samuel R. Shaw, James D. Hittle, Gordon Gayle, Lyford Hutchins, and others, Twining organized a think tank. Because Krulak was "five foot nothing" tall, some wag put a sign on his office door reading "L.M.M.A.C.S.," meaning Little Men's Marching and Chowder Society, with "chowder" meaning "fight."[25] But the 1949 efforts of this group, according to Krulak, was "a factor of 1–100 compared with that of 1947 and 1948."[26] Moreover, some of Cates's people "did not agree with some of the vaporings that came out of the Quantico ivory tower thinkers."[27]

A law of 1834 constituted the Marine Corps as part of the naval establishment directly under the secretary of the navy. It also authorized the president to order the Marines to duty with the Army. In 1917, President Woodrow Wilson directed Secretary of the Navy Josephus Daniels to have the commandant of the Corps send troops to serve with the Army in France, thus bypassing the CNO. However, with the creation of the Fleet Marine Force in 1933, according to Navy General Order 2412, the Corps would "be included in the Fleet organization as an integral part thereof, subject to the orders, for tactical employment, of the Commander in Chief, U.S. Fleet." The commandant would designate the units to embark with the fleet; men not so embarked remained under his direct command. But World War II saw FMFPac become a type command, with marines fighting under fleet commanders. No change in this arrangement was made when the FMF was extended to the Atlantic in 1947.

Virulent criticisms of the Corps as an anomaly expressed during World War I were revived by various Army officers as early as the Guadalcanal campaign and continued for several years. Some Army generals, including J. Lawton Collins and Dwight D. Eisenhower, and Army Air Forces generals, including Carl Spaatz, repeatedly affronted Marine leaders by objecting to having "two land armies." Some even wanted to limit the Corps to small landing units and for ceremonial occasions, thus following the lead of the British Royal Marines.[28] While Cates stressed that it was the foot soldier who would take and occupy enemy territory, he would not belittle any service. "It is coordination of all arms that wins battles," he said.[29]

In the reorganization of the Navy Department adopted in 1948 in consequence of the unification act of 1947, no mention was made of the Marine Corps. As provided in the act of 1834, in Navy Department General Order 241, the Navy's judge advocate general in 1946 issued a legal opinion that in the National Security Act as amended, the Marine Corps therefore continued "as a separate service in the Naval Establishment" and its commandant was subject only to the control of the secretary of the navy acting for the president. Whether the CNO could exercise authority over the Marine Corps, as part of the Navy's operating forces was moot.[30]

Vandegrift had obtained a gentleman's agreement, in writing, from Secretary Sullivan, who was backed by CNO Nimitz, that the reorganization did not alter the commandant's direct responsibility to the secretary for his position in the department.[31] After Forrest Sherman became CNO in November 1949, however, he interpreted the National Security Act to read that his purview extended over the Marine Corps as well as the Navy, and he obtained permission from Secretary of Defense Louis A. Johnson "to have a free hand in the organization of Marine divisions." To Cates this meant that Sherman was "attempting to diminish the Marines, by an administrative device, to a position comparable to the Veterinary Corps or the Bureau of Yards and Docks."[32] Heinl recalled: "We were really hemmed in and everybody could see it inside the Corps and General Cates was putting up this magnificent series of rear guard actions, for which he's never gotten adequate credit." The matter remained unresolved until early in the tenure of Sullivan's successor, Francis P. Matthews, who assumed office on 30 May 1949. "You had Secretary Matthews, probably the worst Secretary the Navy has ever had, with Sherman one of the most dangerous CNOs the Marine Corps has ever served with," Heinl noted.[33] Yet Matthews bluntly told Sherman that the commandant of the Marine Corps would continue to report to the secretary of the navy rather than to the

CNO. After "coordinating" with Secretary of Defense Johnson, moreover, Matthews wrote a letter to this effect to Millard S. Tydings, chairman of the Senate Armed Services Committee.[34]

Louis A. Johnson, who succeeded Forrestal on 28 March 1949, after Truman forced the latter to resign, was a politically ambitious former Army and National Guard officer and former assistant secretary of war (1937–40). His economizing on the defense budget, he thought, would help his presidential chances. He also praised Cates's "cooperative attitude," yet told him that the commandant would never be a member of the JCS, although he could be invited to attend when matters concerning the Corps were under discussion. Johnson did get a bit upset, however, in one instance, when General Cates failed to show "proper appreciation." At Cates's request, Johnson had restored four Marine air squadrons, but Cates "immediately asked for one more." Said Johnson, "That wasn't very smart."[35]

A vastly more important consideration was Johnson's reliance upon his staff rather than upon the service secretaries for advice. Moreover, he favored the Air Force, which alone could deliver atomic bombs, over the other services. The defense secretary also spoke of ridding the military of "fat" and improving "muscle." Gen. Gerald Thomas spoke for many in the Marines when he said that "using the butcher knife, [Johnson] whittled away at the Corps's vitals, its combat echelons."[36] Overlooking the fact that the Marines were America's best shock troops and in 1946 cost fifteen hundred dollars per man, whereas an Army soldier cost two thousand, he planned to cut the Corps and eventually transfer its troops to the Army and its aviation to the Air Force.[37] By scrapping the building of a supercarrier the Navy said it needed in order to keep pace with technological advances in aircraft, Johnson drove Sullivan to resign on 26 April. According to Heinl, "The White House staff told one candidate [to replace Sullivan] that the next secretary must give advance assurance that he did not oppose eventual abolition of the Marine Corps or transfer of aviation to the Air Force."[38] As for the amendments added on 10 August 1949 to the National Security Act, Cates thought that they conferred "entirely too much power" on the secretary of defense. "I do not think the National Security Act has been given a fair trial," he added.[39]

Johnson severely hurt the Corps. In fiscal year 1949, he cut the FMF by 14 percent, to 30,988, and in fiscal year 1950 by another 5 percent, to 29,415. In addition he ordered a 48 percent reduction in Marine Corps air strength. In 1950, instead of a war strength of 20,000 men, the 1st Marine Division had only 8,000 personnel, and its only infantry regiment 1,800 instead of 3,900, while the 1st Marine Aircraft Wing had 3,700 instead of 12,000 men.[40] Johnson also planned by 30 June 1950 to cut another 19 percent from the FMF, thereby reducing it to six battalions, and to phase out the remaining twelve air squadrons. In sum, in two years he cut the Corps by a third. Despite Cates's objections, moreover, top level planners in Johnson's office spoke of using only infantry battalion landing teams rather than divisions. The largest unit the Corps could commit was thus a regiment.[41] Only by strictest economy could Cates keep eight battalion landing teams in two divisions. Then for fiscal year 1951 Johnson directed that the eight teams be reduced to six.

Debate over unification had long ranged among Sullivan, Secretary of the Army Kenneth C. Royall, and Secretary of the Air Force W. Stuart Symington. At hearings before the Senate Armed Services Committee in April 1949, Royall had suggested that the president should "make the Marines part of the Army, or the Army part of the Marines." When the chairman of the House Armed Services Committee, Carl Vinson, heard that Johnson desired to transfer Marine Corps forces to the Army, Navy, and Air Force, he got the secretary to agree in writing that he would ask for permission first and discuss the matter with the congressional armed services committees.[42]

On 25 May 1949, Representative James E. Van Zandt, a captain in the Naval Reserve, urged Vinson to investigate Air Force procurement arrangements for the B-36. To head off a special investigation chaired by Van Zandt, Vinson undertook the task himself and prepared an agenda on which he would begin hearings in July. Of special interest to the Marine Corps was the item asking for an evaluation of "the roles and missions of the Air Force and Navy, especially naval and Marine Aviation." At Vinson's request, Matthews forwarded his comments on the agenda while rumors abounded that Johnson meant to cut the Navy out of strategic warfare and reduce it to an antisubmarine and transport force and halve naval and Marine Corps aviation funds. Vinson postponed his hearings on strategy and unification until work on the amendments to the National Security Act was finished. On 5 October, when he resumed hearings, the "Revolt of the Admirals" occurred. Navy representatives testified during the first seven of the twelve days of hearings. For five days the Air Force and Army then held forth, followed by Johnson, Herbert Hoover, and others. On 6 October, Adm. Arthur W. Radford castigated the "atomic blitz theory" of the Air Force and called its B-36 program "a billion dollar blunder." He was upheld by a galaxy of World War II admirals and CNO Denfeld, who, among other things, noted that Johnson usurped the powers of Congress by changing the appropriations it made for the services.

The paper written for Cates at Quantico was extreme. It criticized "lord Louis Johnson," the JCS for having "wheels within wheels," Eisenhower for wanting to cut the Corps so that it would have no unit larger than a regiment, and Army chief of staff Collins for holding that "Marines should be pushed down to Navy yard guards and ship detachments." Cates greatly tempered the statement when he testified on 17 October. He paralleled Denfeld in asserting that unification did not work well. He spoke of the "elimination" of the Marine Corps by severe budget cuts and of the takeover of its amphibious function by the Army, which was not permitted by the National Security Act. He objected to increasing the powers of the secretary of defense and desired that the commandant sit with the JCS. In speaking of Johnson's administrative manipulation of congressionally authorized funds, he said, "It is not merely to be a question of cuts in men and money—although they are severe enough. We are being told in detail—and told by the Department of Defense—*where and how* these cuts are to be made—

by striking into the heart of our combat forces. . . . I cannot agree that a cut so pointedly directed at reducing the combat strength of this highly effective organization is an economy." Last, Marine Corps morale was being eroded by "a continuous feeling of apprehension and annoyance sometimes bordering on outright indignation." Though he was supported by Vandegrift, who followed him, he had pleased Congress, but not the Pentagon.[43]

Gen. Vernon Megee recalled that Cates then "said he wanted it understood that if heads were going to roll around there that he personally took the responsibility and he approved what any other Marine officer had said or would say before that Committee." He had in mind that Denfeld had been removed as the CNO and that he had heard threats that the commandant would be next.[44] The best illustration of Army thought at the hearings was revealed by Gen. Omar N. Bradley, the first chairman of the JCS. Bradley could foresee strategic bombardment and large-scale operations in a future war with a great power, but added that "island hopping" would be of little use and that large-scale amphibious operations "will never occur again."[45]

In his opening remarks to a conference of Marine generals held at Headquarters from 29 November to 1 December 1949, Cates said,

> About three or four weeks ago General Collins invited me to have lunch with him at the Pentagon. General Smith and General Pollock accompanied me. General Collins had General Gruenther and General Andrus with him. In our informal discussion at that time, General Collins stated that he hoped that we could work out some of our mutual problems by direct contact. He stated that he had no objection to a 4-division Marine Corps in time of war. As a matter of fact, he said that he would support us in that position. General Collins did say that he felt that our peacetime proportion of air units to ground units was far too high. He is of the opinion that the Air Force is capable of giving just as good air support as the Marines. . . . [Here someone, perhaps Cates, wrote "Eyewash" in the margin of the manuscript.] [Collins's] principal desire . . . was to provide for a Joint Airborne Center. . . . He does not believe in sea power as advocated by the navy. He is obviously not in accord with the balanced fleet concept. . . . He feels that the Army should concentrate on airborne operations. [In the margin: "Suits us."][46]

Despite Vinson's stating that he would not permit the punishment of witnesses, Matthews dismissed Denfeld as CNO and asked Sherman, who according to Heinl was "the Navy's most extreme advocate of unification,"[47] to succeed him. Secretary of Defense Johnson agreed, but he vetoed Matthew's desire to take action against Cates, saying that "it was politically unwise to bring any pressure whatsoever upon the commandant of the Marine Corps."[48] According to Cates,

> So far as I have been able to determine, the Marine Corps position was not damaged by the recent Congressional hearings by the House Armed Services Com-

> mittee. There seems to be no inclination on the part of the officials of the Department of Defense to consider the Marine Corps as part of the Navy's so-called rebellion. There have been some rather guarded "peace overtures" made to us. Both Mr. Johnson and Mr. Matthews have told me personally that they read the statement which I made to the Committee on 17 October. While, of course, they did not go so far as to say they agree with the statement, they did indicate that they took no violent exception to it. They did say it was a forceful and constructive statement. . . . We didn't change anyone's mind—nor did we expect to.[49]

In its report on the hearings on unification and strategy, issued in January 1950, Vinson's committee recommended that the commandant of the Marine Corps be made a member of the JCS, and Vinson introduced a bill to this effect. Cates was therefore upheld in his view that the life of the Corps depended upon granting its commandant access to not only the secretary of the navy but also the JCS level, where important decisions affecting the Corps were made. Moreover, to prevent the emasculation if not disappearance of the Corps by imposing cuts on it by administrative action, a numbers floor must be established below which no additional cuts could be made except by congressional consent. Upon request, Admiral Halsey suggested that a legally fixed percentage of the defense manpower be given to the Corps in the annual appropriations acts, adding, "Six percent spells security."[50] Four senators and fifty-six representatives backed S. 2177, which incorporated Halsey's views—and would have increased the Corps from 75,000 to 100,000—but Secretary of the Navy Matthews opposed it and neither it nor Vinson's bill passed the 81st Congress. Nevertheless, Vinson's hearings and the proposed legislation had alerted the public to the Marine Corps's problems.

By early 1950, as Heinl put it, Cates, well aware of what was going on and now fully acquainted with the details of his office, began to consolidate operations into his own hands rather than leaving them to his Headquarters staff. Overruling his assistant, Gen. Oliver P. Smith, Cates gave Heinl and Schatzel free rein to travel about and "educate" those who could help the Corps. Prime "pupils" were former Assistant Secretary of the Navy John Nicholas Brown and the manager of the Hearst newspaper chain. With the aid of the Marine Corps Reserve, an editorial crusade was begun on behalf of the Corps, and the cascade of letters that reached the White House and Congress indicated that its plight made the public uneasy.[51]

In answer to a question from the committee whether there was an "interservice fight" over appropriations, Cates replied, "I think there has always been a fight, and always will be. That's what the Department of Defense was supposed to have straightened out but they haven't done it and never will."[52] Vandegrift agreed, saying that, "The whole difficulty, then as now, boiled down to money, or lack of it, the basic reason for service jealousies."[53] As O. P. Smith, who occasionally accompanied Cates to congressional hearings, put it, Johnson was "trying to destroy the Marine Corps, but destroy it by cutting down its appropriations. . . . He was no friend of the Marine Corps."[54] As for Johnson's motives, Cates did not know. "President Truman didn't have any love for us," he said, "but still he was fair and square, he was honest in it." As for Johnson, he "disliked us very much and of course there was a group in the Army with thumbs down on us and they made all kinds of plans to absorb us. . . . I think that maybe some of the Army generals thought by reducing the Marine Corps they would get a little more for the Army and, I don't think there is any question about it, that a lot of it was jealousy and lot of it dated back to World War I when we got a little more publicity than they did."[55]

As in World War I and World War II, however, the Marines would prove their worth in Korea. But first they had to be invited to participate, and in this case, Cates was midwife to the invitation. On 28 June 1950, he proposed to Sherman that the FMF be used in Korea.[56] On the same day, Victor H. Krulak reported as operations officer of FMF-Pac in Hawaii. On the thirtieth, a message Krulak acknowledged was prompted by Cates arrived from Sherman: "How soon can you sail for combat employment in the Far East: (a) reinforced battalion: (b) A reinforced regiment?" Krulak drafted a reply and took it to the chief of staff, who was filling in until Lt. Gen. Lemuel C. Shepherd assumed command in early July of the FMF. The draft read, "(a) 48 hours. (b) five days, including a marine aircraft group." Said the chief of staff, "How do you know we can do that?" The "Brute" replied, "I don't but if we can't, we're dead."[57]

In Washington, meanwhile, no highly placed civilian or military leader paid any attention to Cates for several days after the Korean War started. He failed in an attempt to see Secretary Matthews on 27 June. Two days later, with Gen. Douglas MacArthur's poorly trained garrison troops from Japan and the Army of the Republic of Korea being overwhelmed by North Koreans, he "kind of forced" his way into Matthew's office. Upon seeing Sherman, Cates recalled the following conversation:

[Cates:] Forrest, it looks like the Army's 24th Division is in [a] pretty bad spot over there. We can furnish a brigade by draining our two divisions.

[Sherman:] How soon could you have them ready?

[Cates:] We can have them ready as quickly as the Navy gets the ships.

[Sherman:] All right. I'm going to send a blue flag [message] to Admiral [C. Turner] Joy [commander, U.S. Naval Forces Far East in Japan] and tell him that he can inform MacArthur that the Marines can send a brigade and an air group.[58]

On 2 July, probably not knowing that on that day MacArthur had requested a Marine regimental combat team, Cates, "just playing a hunch," alerted the 1st Marine Division. A few days later, at Shepherd's suggestion, MacArthur requested the JCS to send not a brigade but a division. On the third, when the JCS considered the matter, though uninvited, Cates appeared at the meeting and was "reluctantly" permitted to sit in. The following week, while Shepherd visited him, MacArthur informed the JCS that he intended to land behind the enemy lines and cut the North Koreans off from their base. Shepherd offered the 1st Division. When Cates asked Sherman, "How did you put this over?" Sherman replied, "Well, from Cates to Sherman to Joy to MacArthur to the JCS," which Cates thought was a "hell of a way to have to do things."[59]

At the start of the Korean War, Marine Corps strength was 74,279. Though his two divisions and two aircraft wings had only 27,000 instead of 60,000 men, Cates asked General Shepherd, just returned from Tokyo, his own Headquarters staff, and Marine commanders just how enough men could be obtained for a full division and supporting new air squadrons. Further, he posed the question whether the reserves should be called up.[60] He flew out to Camp Pendleton to watch as marines from Camp Lejeune and other posts and stations reported to Brig. Gen. Edward A. Craig to form the First Provisional Marine Brigade—6,800 ground, air, and service support personnel. "Clean this up [in] a couple of months or I will be over to see you," he said.[61] The troops that sailed from San Diego on 14 July were the first combat troops to leave the continental United States for Korea.

During the third week in July, Cates saw Truman, who realized that MacArthur's ground forces needed bolstering. On 19 July, Truman authorized call-up of the thirty-three thousand marine reservists, and on 7 August he called more men from the Volunteer Reserve. Congress, meanwhile, extended the enlistments of all men for a year. Already, on 4 August, the Marines received the authority to assemble, equip, and load the men of the 7th Marines and to bring the 2d Marine Division, at Camp Lejeune, up to strength as well. In addition, the reinforced infantry battalion afloat in the Mediterranean was redeployed to the Far East via Suez, and the 3d Marine Brigade began to take form at Camp Pendleton. At MacArthur's request, the planning staff of the 1st Division flew to Tokyo; within about two weeks the rest of the 7th had sailed out on whatever naval or merchant ships the Navy could find on the West Coast. From 2 August to 5 September, the 5th Marines fought to defend the Pusan Perimeter. It was then pulled out to take part in the Inchon landing scheduled for mid-September. As early as 7 August, Marine pilots began engaging in combat operations from two escort carriers. At a meeting at Camp Pendleton on 14 August, Cates reminded General Shepherd that the planned Inchon operation was consuming the total resources of the Corps, "but he never faltered in his support."[62]

On 21 August 1950, Representative Gordon L. McDonough (R-California), who detested Truman and his Far East policies, had written Truman about how well the Marines were fighting in Korea and asked that they be given a voice in the JCS. Truman retorted, "For your information the Marine Corps is the Navy's police force and as long as I am President that is what it will remain. They have a propaganda machine that is almost equal to Stalin's. . . . When the Marine Corps goes into the Army it works with and for the Army and that is the way it should be."

McDonough inserted Truman's letter in the *Congressional Record* on 1 September, just a few days before the Marine Corps League held its national convention in Washington. With a bad press, a backlash of public opinion, and cartoonists having a field day at his expense, Truman became embarrassed. Not Cates but Maj. Gen. Melvin J. Maas, USMCR, speaking as head of the League, wrote Truman to express "profound regret" at his diatribe but tried to leave a way out for him while still underscoring the need to have Corps representation on the JCS. To make things right, Truman called Cates to the White House and handed him a letter of apology. Told to return the following morning, he was informed that Truman would address the Marine Corps League. With Cates present and in great glee, Truman apologized to the convention.[63] Cates had an autographed picture of Truman on his office wall. Feeling that Truman had not really recanted his view of the Corps, he took it down and never replaced it. The McDonough incident, he later said, was "one of the luckiest things to ever happen[ed] to the Corps."[64]

At the time of the Inchon landing, Cates went to Tokyo to see MacArthur and very plainly asked him, "General, why are you so down on the Marines?" MacArthur replied, "I'm not down on the Marines. The Marines are the best outfit I had in World War II. When I want anything done, I know I can get it done by the Marines."[65] Because the amphibious landing at Inchon would be "an all Marine show," Cates did not know why MacArthur's chief of staff, Lt. Gen. Edward M. Almond, rather than the much better qualified commander of FMFPac, Shepherd, was chosen to be the landing force commander.[66] However, he was positive that Inchon gained the Corps the support of Congress and of the public that finally made possible the passing of the Douglas-Mansfield bill.[67] Early in 1951, Congress considered adding ten divisions to the Army but only a regimental combat team to the Marines. Heinl got James M. Minnify, the military correspondent of the *New York Herald-Tribune,* to alert his friends, including Senator Paul Douglas. Douglas, a former marine, and another former marine, Representative Mike Mansfield, introduced a bill that provided that the Corps would consist of at least four combat divisions and four aircraft wings with a top personnel ceiling of 400,000, that the commandant would have coequal status with members of the JCS in matters of direct concern to the Marine Corps, and that the Corps was a separate military service serving in the Department of the Navy. Cates testified vigorously for what became PL 416. It provided for not less than three rather than four combat divisions and three aircraft wings. Congress and the public continued to be the best guardian of the Marines.[68]

In his annual report for fiscal year 1951, Cates stressed the positive. Marine aviation had superbly supported ground troops, Marine jet fighter squadrons had been used for the first time in combat, and three Marine transport helicopter squadrons had been formed. The Marine reservists had fought well in Korea, where Cates had visited them on the front line. He was also pleased that the Marine research and development program, formerly under the CNO, was now made a Corps responsibility and that great improvements had been made in cold-weather clothing. Anxious to release reservists as soon as possible, by March 1951 he had plans in hand by which recalled World War II veterans would be released first and then others in accordance with a priority list.

There remained, however, persistent squabbling among the service leaders about the proper use of air power in Korea. While concerned about the Air Force demand that it control all air operations, Cates told Maj. Gen. Oliver P. Smith, who commanded the

1st Marine Division from August 1950 to April 1951, "You can catch more flies with sugar than with vinegar."[69]

What with the battle over unification and then Korea, Cates's first three years as commandant passed quickly. The fourth year, 1951, was "just routine work . . . with these long office hours and a certain amount of social—some of it you can't get away from."[70] His typical day began at 0800 with the reading of dispatches and correspondence filtered to him by his staff secretary. He attended the secretary of the navy's conference at 0900, then received an intelligence briefing and dealt with more dispatches and correspondence until lunch time. In the afternoon, to 1800, he worked with subordinates and received visitors. He then took home a briefcase full of unfinished work. Major aspects of his work of course were his frequent appearances at congressional hearings, telling the Marine Corps story at public gatherings or press conferences, and delivering formal addresses to the National War College and to the annual secretary of the navy's civilian orientation conferences. In addition to making inspection trips to the seven major Marine Corps posts—Parris Island, Quantico, Camp Lejeune, Cherry Point, San Diego, Camp Pendleton, and El Toro—he had to write his annual report. Though he knew that much that affected the Corps was agreed upon by officials and legislators at parties or other informal meetings, he attended and gave the fewest possible parties, though he witnessed the customary formal Friday night parades at Eighth and "Eye" and occasionally threw a congressional stag party. His choice as his successor, he told Truman in May 1951, should be Shepherd.[71]

Able to compromise just this side of principle, Cates enjoyed a few major successes. He established the formal position of the Corps in the Department of the Navy organization and chain of command and he acquired legislative approval for setting Marine Corps strength. While assisting in determining the position of the Marine Corps in the Defense establishment under the National Security Act, he ably defended the Corps at the Vinson hearing. Finally, Cates played a major role in preparing the Marine Corps for the war in Korea. Favorable comments on his leadership for the four years of his commandancy are found in letters from President Eisenhower; Charles Wilson, secretary of defense; Dan A. Kimball, secretary of the navy; Robert Carney, the CNO; and Hanson Baldwin, the military analyst; among others. These paralleled those of Marine generals Gerald C. Thomas and Vernon E. Megee. Kimball's letter of fitness mentioned Cates's "highest qualities of leadership . . . splendid executive ability . . . high quality of proficiency in administering the Marine Corps . . . forceful nature . . . and acceptance of individual responsibility for the action of the Marine Corps." Said Thomas: "He always looked good," referring to Guadalcanal. He was "one of the finest officers the Marine Corps ever had."[72] Megee agreed, saying, "I thought General Cates was a very effective Commandant, a very strong leader, a man who would back up his subordinates, and was above any petty intrigue as far as I ever knew or heard. I think he was one of our outstanding Commandants at a time when we needed a strong hand."[73]

After retiring as commandant, Cates wore three stars while serving at Quantico for two and a half years. As chairman of the National Campaign of the USO for two years following his retirement, he traveled widely but received no pay.

Asked about changes that had occurred in the Corps since he had entered it, Cates praised the introduction of the merit selection system for promotion over that of the old system by seniority. He added that retention tended to vary inversely with the economic situation "outside," and that a college graduate could get all the additional education he needed right in the Corps. How would he sum up his career? He had been "lucky." He had seen the static trench warfare of World War I give way to the maneuvering required for implementing amphibious doctrine in World War II and then in the atomic age. The latter had been "the biggest improvement that was ever made in the Marine Corps," and he believed that the Corps would continue to be the "'lead' outfit that it is right now." At the moment, after having served in static trench warfare in Korea, the Corps had to relearn amphibious warfare.[74] Promoted again to four stars upon his retirement on 30 June 1954, Cates retired after thirty-seven years of service at the age of sixty years.

Early in 1955, Cates bought an old house built on a bank of the South River in Edgewater, Maryland, just outside Annapolis, and added a guest house and boat house to it. There he engaged in his favorite sports, fishing and hunting, and some golf. Late each afternoon during the fall and winter seasons he fed huge amounts of corn to perhaps two or three hundred wild ducks, some of which would eat from his hand. In 1960, he gave his papers to the Marine Corps Historical Branch. A close family man, in letters to his wife and children he addressed them as "Dear Jane, Clif, and Ann" or, more often, "My darlings." He dearly loved his five grandchildren. Clifton Jr., "crazy about ships" since childhood, upon graduating from the Naval Academy wished to stay with the Navy but sought his father's advice. Cates replied that it was the son's decision to make and he would not try to influence him in any way. The son served the navy until he retired in the grade of captain.[75]

Cates died of a combination of atherosclerosis and emphysema—he was never without a cigarette in hand—on 4 June 1970. He was buried with full military honors on 8 June at Arlington National Cemetery.

As a leader of fighting men, Cates did not particularly desire to be the commandant of the Marine Corps, a billet largely involving politics, administration, and socializing. To his credit, he learned how to fight on Capitol Hill on behalf of a Corps being emasculated by post–World War II demobilization and the "economizing" of Secretary of Defense Johnson. He helped to ward off adherents of "unification" who would merge his troops with the Army and his air power with the Air Force. Proving apt before congressional committees and Corps, public, and private gatherings, he succeeded in regularizing the position of the Corps in the Navy's chain of command and in the Defense Department. He trained his people for both atomic and conventional war, the latter including vertical envelopment made possible by the Corps's development of the helicopter, and faithfully carried out orders to end racial segregation in the Corps. In addition, he offered his Corps for the Korean War. His were the only troops trained in amphibious warfare, thus making the Inchon landing possible, and his aviators were specialists in supporting ground troops. The Corps fought so well that it helped to get established in law that it would consist of three combat divisions and three aircraft wings. His civil and military superiors and his own subordinates recognized Cates as a strong executive who had prepared the Corps to serve as the spearhead in any contingency.

20
Lemuel Cornick Shepherd Jr.

1952–1955

LT. GEN. VICTOR H. KRULAK, USMC (RET.)

Lemuel Cornick Shepherd Jr. did not start out to become a marine or, indeed, a soldier of any sort. He had quite a different background. Most of his lineal antecedents were farmers and plantation owners. None exhibited any disposition toward a military life until the Civil War, when Shepherd's grandfather, John Camp Shepherd, volunteered for service in the 1st Virginia Cavalry. He survived the experience and, at the war's end, returned to his land, where he opened a small general store on the property. The store was successful, producing enough income to make it possible to send his son, Lemuel Cornick Shepherd, to medical school.

Young Shepherd, who became a successful Norfolk physician, married Emma Lucretia Cartwright, a schoolteacher who was born and raised in Nantucket, Massachusetts. The marriage produced three children. The eldest, a son, born on 10 February 1896, was given his father's name—Lemuel Cornick Shepherd Junior.

Lem junior had a tranquil childhood. His solid Norfolk family gave him a good primary education at St. George's School and the Norfolk Academy. By age fourteen, he had grown into a slender youngster of medium build with a warm and outgoing disposition that brought him many friends. He showed only a modest interest in academic affairs, but a spirited interest in sports, girls, and the exciting world of radio then in its infancy. He ran on the high school track team, played end on the football team, went to dancing school, dated, and was elected president of his class. His father kept two horses for use in his profession. Lem rode them constantly, developing an early affection for horses that persisted throughout his life.

In 1913, at age sixteen, young Shepherd succumbed to the urging of several friends who had entered the Virginia Military Institute, and then decided to forgo his last high school year and join them. He enrolled in the institute class of 1917, with his sights set on an engineering career. Shepherd met the academic challenge of the Institute with average diligence, but saw the rewarding military aspects of VMI as little more than

Gen. Lemuel C. Shepherd Jr., twentieth commandant.
U.S. Marine Corps Photo.

incidental to his long-range engineer aspirations. He got to be a cadet corporal, but it didn't last. He was restive under the military discipline, ultimately losing his stripes for firing skyrockets from his room on New Year's Eve. At age sixteen and, indeed, at nineteen, too, Lemuel Shepherd was a civilian at heart.[1]

The first time young Lem gave the Marine Corps a passing thought was during his third year at VMI. Maj. Gen. George Barnett, the commandant of the Marine Corps, delivered the commencement address, a spirited talk that, along with the general's dress blue uniform and soldierly bearing, generated much favorable reaction among the cadets. Almost a year later, on the day war was declared, Shepherd concluded that the time had come for him to volunteer, not because he had had a change of heart about a military career, but because he believed that everyone should be involved in the war. Nevertheless, from that moment on, he was to be totally committed to a military life.

All Army and Marine Corps commissions had already been taken, but a personal plea from the VMI superintendent to General Barnett on Shepherd's behalf resulted in the offer of a commission in the Marines, if he could pass the required mental and physical examinations. These would take place in Washington, at the Marine Barracks, in forty-eight hours. Shepherd was expected to get there at his own expense.

He made it, reaching the barracks with just five minutes to spare. He was surprised that the dreaded examinations were so perfunctory. The mental examination amounted to almost nothing; it was oral and took just fifteen minutes. The physical examination consisted only of questions concerning any prior diseases. And that was it. On 15 April 1917, Lem Shepherd, just turned twenty-one, was sworn in as a second lieutenant in the Marine Corps Reserve, with the promise of a regular commission as soon as Congress reconvened.

Returning to VMI to complete the final six weeks of his senior year, Shepherd spent only twenty days at the institute. As a foretaste of behavior he was to see often, the Marine Corps changed its mind, ordered him to active duty, and directed him to report on 15 May to the School of Application in Parris Island, South Carolina. VMI had just time to give him a diploma as he packed his trunk.

The School of Application had little opportunity to teach Shepherd much about the life that lay before him. The Marine Corps changed its mind again. Only ten days after he reported, with nothing more than a brief taste of the rifle range behind him, he was advised that Headquarters wanted volunteers for expeditionary duty overseas. In hopes of escaping the School of Application studies, Shepherd hastened to volunteer. The American Expeditionary Forces were to include a Marine contingent: he was headed for France, mud, bully beef, and more war than he had ever dreamed of.

Orders came within forty-eight hours: proceed immediately to the Philadelphia Navy Yard and report for duty to the 5th Marine Regiment. He arrived on 1 June to find a scene of immense confusion. Within minutes he became a member of the 55th Company, commanded by an old professional, Capt. Henry Mitthoff Butler, who put him to work immediately, helping to shake down a group of 50 veteran marines and 150 recruits. Shepherd and his troops had just three days to get their feet on the ground. On the morning of the fourth, the regiment boarded the USS *Hancock* and set sail for New York, where they transferred immediately to the USS *Henderson.* On the night of 11 June, they were under way for France. Second Lieutenant Shepherd, just six weeks separated from his carefree undergraduate life as a VMI cadet, was commander of a Marine platoon and on his way to war.

Landing in France on the morning of 28 June, Shepherd began an intensive seven-month period of training, largely with the French Army, during which time the young lieutenant slowly learned the functions and responsibilities of a platoon commander on the Western Front. The 5th Marines, including the 55th Company, was initially billeted in a camp near St. Nazaire, where its time was consumed in repetitive individual and elementary small unit training and long hikes.[2] A brief period in the St. Nazaire camp was followed by the first experience with the famous French troop train, with its "40 *Hommes* et 8 *Chevaux*" cars, when the regiment moved to a combat training area at Menacourt, south of Verdun. Here the training took on a more serious and complex character. The regiment was taken under the wing of the 115th Regiment Chasseurs Alpines, the highly respected Blue Devils.[3]

In the late autumn of 1917, the regiment was moved again, to quarters in the village of Damblain, a bleak environment, where the troops were housed in drafty tar-paper shacks. The weather was miserable—cold, rainy, and occasionally snowy. Training was intensive—battalion and regimental field exercises and constant drills in trench systems constructed by the French. Shepherd's battalion commander, Maj. Frederic M. Wise, demanded more and more of his units. "He was always hard," Shepherd said, "but now he was hard as nails."[4] In January, Shepherd was sent to an I Corps, AEF school at Gondrecourt, where emphasis was on hand-to-hand fighting. The chief instructor, a British NCO, played a single refrain: "Blood on the bayonet, boys, blood on the bayonet."

An air of great seriousness descended on the 2d Division in early March. There were no more trips to Paris, very little liberty. Finally, orders came to move out to the front. Troop trains were provided to move the unit to a point about twenty miles south of Verdun. From there the Marines marched throughout the night, in rain and mud, without food or rest. For the first time Shepherd could see, hear, and smell the war: battered equipment, devastated buildings, dead farm animals, shell holes full of water covered by a yellow scum from mustard gas and, overshadowing it all, the somber rumble of artillery in the distance.

No sooner had Second Lieutenant Shepherd arrived in the assembly area in a chill and misty dawn than he was directed to reconnoiter the front line sector to be occupied by the 55th Company in relief of a French unit. A French captain oriented him on a map and then took him through a maze of trenches to an observation post where enemy entrenchments, and even enemy individuals were visible. "I shall never forget the inward thrill I feel to actually be at the front, after so many months of anticipation. Here is the real war, and I am in it," Shepherd wrote in his diary.

In early June 1918, the 55th Company found itself responsible for defending a major German objective west of Château-Thierry. During the first day's bitter fighting, Shepherd was wounded in the neck. Nevertheless, he remained with his unit until the German threat was repulsed three days later.

Moved the next day in the direction of Belleau Wood, the company quickly became locked in combat with German units that occupied the Wood in strength. Shepherd's company commander was killed during the first hour of the historic Belleau Wood engagement, leaving Shepherd in command of the unit. The following day, during the ensuing close quarters fighting, he sustained a serious thigh wound, which required his evacuation. It took five weeks before he was able to walk without crutches. Still using a cane, he returned to the 55th Company in time to take part in the U.S. First Army's offensive at St. Mihiel and, shortly thereafter in the Champaign offensive, where his unit was involved in the seizure of Blanc Mont Ridge.

During the Blanc Mont campaign Shepherd experienced what he characterized as "my worst days of the war."[5] In fighting near the village of St. Étienne, the 55th Company lost 200 of its 250 men and all of its officers other than Shepherd. Just as the depleted company was being relieved by an Army unit, a round from an Austrian 77-mm gun landed nearby and a fragment struck him below the hip. The wound was both serious and painful. While recovering in the hospital, near the town of Blois, Shepherd learned that the armistice had been signed.

His valorous service with a front-line combat unit brought him honors: the Navy Cross, the croix de guerre, and citation in dispatches of the 2d Division. Of even greater importance, the intensive training and the bitter fighting provided him with a firm elementary grounding in leadership. And it convinced him, beyond question, that the Marine Corps was the life for him.

The experience in France also introduced him to the elements of command responsibility in practical terms, which benefited him in later years. Those experiences also stood him in good stead during the ensuing two decades of peace, where his life was far removed from the perils of the battlefield. Two additional years in France, in 1919 and 1920, as part of a detail which prepared relief maps of the scenes of the Marines' World War I combat gave him a sense of the importance of cultivating international relations—an understanding that surfaced later after he became commandant.

There followed a series of peacetime assignments, each of which contributed further to his preparation for the challenges in store for him in World War II, and after. Shepherd served as aide-de-camp to the commandant and as a White House social aide, as commander of a Marine detachment at the Brazilian Exposition in Rio de Janeiro, commander of a seagoing Marine detachment in the USS *Idaho,* and, from 1931 to 1934, as a department commander in the Garde d'Haiti.

In 1934, as a major and executive officer of the Marine Barracks, Washington, Shepherd made an unexpected contribution to Marine Corps history. His commanding officer, concluding that there was a need for a manual for drummer and trumpeters, directed Shepherd to produce one. With no musical background, he prepared a publication that is still in use, half a century later.[6] Two years later, his request for assignment to the Naval War College was disapproved. He appealed to Maj. Gen. Cmdt. John H. Russell for reconsideration, reminding the general that he had himself been permitted to attend the college. The appeal was successful. Following War College, Shepherd commanded the 2d Battalion, 5th Marines, during the period when the Fleet Marine Force was the practical laboratory for development of landing force tactics and techniques. This experience was followed by almost three years on the staff of the Marine Corps Schools at Quantico, teaching the principles he had learned in the FMF.

The twenty years of experience after World War I had prepared Shepherd well for the great test introduced by Pearl Harbor, and as a colonel, he was given the opportunity in 1942 to demonstrate his competence by organizing and training the new 9th Marines. At the end of a year, the regiment, then on Guadalcanal, was finely honed, a product of Shepherd's perfectionism. But he did not have the satisfaction of leading it in the 1943 Bougainville invasion. Instead, he was promoted to the rank of brigadier general and served as assistant commander of the 1st Marine Division in the Cape Gloucester operation, where, using enveloping tactics similar to those employed by the Japanese in Malaya, he led the successful attack on Borgen Bay and Talasea Plantation. Then he commanded the 1st Provisional Marine Brigade in the seizure of Guam, where his repute as a tactician and superior combat leader was enhanced further.

His experience with the brigade set the scene for what Shepherd himself described as one of the most meaningful periods of his professional life—organizing, training, and fighting with the 6th Marine Division. Formed overseas on Guadalcanal, the division's principal components were the 4th, 22d, and 29th Regimental Combat Teams—all battle tested, all fiercely independent. Shepherd had six essentially undisturbed months to weld them into a cohesive unit, which he did in an intensive program of field exercises, schools, and inspections.[7]

When the division landed on the Hagushi beaches at Okinawa on Easter Sunday 1945, it was impressive in its competence and professionalism, a fact underscored by its achievements during the following eighty-two days of combat. Assigned the task of capturing the lightly defended northern half of the island, the division, in a succession of rapid tank-infantry maneuvers, drove the Japanese into a final defensive position in the mountainous Motobu Peninsula. There, Shepherd surrounded and destroyed them.

The division was then quickly shifted to the main front, fifty miles to the south, where the U.S. Tenth Army, with five divisions engaged, were faced by 100,000 determined Japanese. Shepherd's force was committed on the right flank of the American attack, which, for the next twenty days, made only slow progress. The Japanese left flank defenses, facing the 6th Division, were fixed on the Oroku Peninsula, a rocky hill mass touching the East China Sea, and rendered doubly strong by a four-hundred-yard-wide deep-water estuary separating them from the Marines.

Nothing was moving. Twelve days of rain had paralyzed every vehicle, immobilized tanks and artillery. Supplies were short, ammunition running low. The Americans were not able to maneuver and small forays netted little other than casualties. A council of high commanders, including Adm. Chester A. Nimitz, the theater commander, and Gen. Simon Bolivar Buckner III, commander of the Tenth Army, was seriously considering digging in and just waiting for the rainy season to end.

Unwilling to sit and absorb casualties while waiting for better weather, General Shepherd visited his superior, Lt. Gen. Roy S. Geiger, U.S. Marine Corps, commander of the V Amphibious Corps. Shepherd's proposition: "If you can scratch up enough ammunition to provide artillery support, I will manage to get a reinforced regiment to the seacoast and, in my division's amphibian vehicles, make a dawn amphibious attack behind the Japanese Oroku Peninsula positions to outflank them and, hopefully, begin to break the stalemate." Instinctively aggressive himself, Geiger reacted: "It's a good idea. Let's go and see Buckner." Buckner demurred at first. He was not enthusiastic about the idea of an amphibious envelopment, but he finally approved. "I'll find the ammunition," he said. "Go ahead. Do it as soon as you can."

It was not easy. Men, equipment, and supplies had to be moved to the embarkation beaches concealed by the darkness, three miserable miles through calf-deep mud and driving rain. Col. Alan Shapley, commanding officer of the 4th Marines (Reinforced), and selected as the landing force commander, was a practical and altogether professional officer. He had many questions about the enemy and a list of material requirements. Shepherd's reaction: "Alan, I'll get you all the information I can, and I'll try to meet your equipment needs, but at 0400 day after tomorrow morning, we go."[8]

And that is the way it worked. Marshaled in thirty-six hours with great difficulty, Shapley's landing force launched the seaborne attack at dawn in a driving rain. It was both a surprise and a success, beginning a process that was exploited by other American forces as the rains began to abate. It marked the beginning of the end for the Japanese defenders. Twenty days later, the three-month battle was over. In his concept for the seaborne envelopment of the Oroku Peninsula, General Shepherd was exhibiting the characteristics that dominated his entire life: resolution, aggressiveness, resourcefulness, impatience, and perseverance. These, the bedrock qualities of a warrior, served as the foundation of his later stewardship as commandant of the Corps.

Following the Okinawa operation the division enjoyed a brief rest in Guam, during which the world-shattering events at Hiroshima and Nagasaki occurred, followed by word that the unit was going to Tsingtao (Qingdao), China. The force sailed from Guam on 15 September, pausing at Okinawa just long enough to permit Shepherd, an aide, his G-2, Lt. Col. Thomas A. Williams, and his G-3, Lt. Col. Victor H. Krulak, to transfer to a destroyer and take off, at best speed, for Tsingtao. He was anxious to get there in advance of the main force to satisfy himself as to the attitude of the Japanese, and make arrangements for billeting the twenty-five thousand men who would soon be arriving.

A Japanese mixed brigade of eight thousand men had occupied the area, and it was known that the Chinese Communists were very strong throughout the Shangtung (Shandung) Peninsula. Shepherd had no intelligence of exactly who was in command of affairs in Tsingtao and the surrounding countryside. Upon anchoring, he discovered that the power still resided with the Japanese. Surrender notwithstanding, they could be seen patrolling the streets, keeping order and protecting the perimeter of the city from the Communist guerillas.[9]

Shepherd's first interview with the Japanese commander gave an interesting insight into Shepherd's personality. When told, "Tomorrow you will deliver up all of your weapons and all of your ammunition to representatives of the Sixth Marine Division,"

Maj. Gen. Eiji Nagano did not respond. Shepherd asked, "Is the order not understood?" Nagano replied that he understood completely but wanted Shepherd to be aware of the consequences. "If you completely disarm my troops," he said, "the Chinese Communists will kill us." Taken by surprise, Shepherd asked Nagano if he had a recommendation. "Yes," the general replied, "If you will allow my men to retain their rifles and five rounds of ammunition, we can defend ourselves. Otherwise, you will have to protect us."[10] Shepherd pondered for a moment. "Very well," Shepherd said, "I will issue the appropriate orders." The Communists encircled the American perimeter but they made no offensive move toward the Japanese encampment.

Not long after the formal surrender ceremony, cold weather began to affect the marines. The billeting areas all required heat, and the coal had to come from mines some one hundred rail miles distant. The Chinese Communists, unopposed in the hinterland, took to harassing the coal trains by carrying off sections of track. Reenter General Nagano. He requested an audience, told General Shepherd that he was mindful of the coal delivery dilemma, and offered to help. The Japanese commander stated, "My troops have nothing to do while we await transportation to Japan. If you will give me back my artillery and a supply of ammunition, I will secure the rail line for you."[11]

The coal was becoming critical to the division's health, and here was a way to ensure its uninterrupted delivery. Shepherd did not hesitate, assenting on the spot. In Nagano's presence, he sent for his chief of staff and issued the necessary orders. So there they were, only weeks after the surrender, Japanese and American forces united in opposing the Chinese Communists. And the electrifying point is that Shepherd made the decision on his own, without prior consultation with Washington—or with anyone else.

On 1 December, Shepherd's orders arrived: return to the United States, duty in Washington. Now the war was truly over for him. He bade an emotional farewell to his beloved 6th Marine Division, "the most professional fighting unit I have ever seen."[12]

On reporting to the commandant, Shepherd learned that his next assignment would be in Norfolk, as commanding general of the Atlantic Fleet Troop Training Command. He spent eight busy months putting the unit on a forward-looking peacetime basis and then, on 1 November 1946, was moved to Washington to fulfill the assignment of assistant commandant and chief of staff at Marine Corps Headquarters. For the next fifteen months, until April 1948, his dual function in the Headquarters acquired great intensity because of a question President Truman asked Cmdt. A. A. Vandegrift: "How would you handle a massive landing like Iwo Jima or Okinawa if the enemy had an atomic bomb?"[13] His question was underscored by the report of the Bikini Atoll "Crossroads" atomic bomb tests. Marine observer Lt. Gen. Roy S. Geiger concluded that he could not "visualize another landing such as was executed at Normandy or Okinawa" and recommended a search for a new solution, on an urgent basis. General Vandegrift waited only two weeks to appoint a special board, headed by Shepherd, to address the question of "amphibious warfare in the atomic age," acknowledging that "revolutionary measures" might be required.

The board report turned out to be a watershed document, underscoring the total impracticality of the classic, highly concentrated slow-moving assembly of ships and the laborious five-knot ship-to-shore movement. In its place, the board proposed dispersion, rapidity of movement, and sudden concentration at the point of attack. In other words, the solution was to be found in high speed ships and close air support from jet aircraft with the assault burden carried by helicopters. The board report set the tactical design for the Marine Corps, as it prepared for the amphibious operations of the future.

The challenge of Shepherd's activities in Washington were tempered somewhat by the growing realization that the leading candidates to replace General Vandegrift as commandant on 1 January 1948 were he and Lt. Gen. Clifton B. Cates. Friends since World War I, there was none of the competitive antagonism that had previously affected the selection of Commandants Neville, Fuller, and Russell. The issue was resolved by President Truman, who sent for the two officers and declared, "I have studied your records. They are both distinguished, and almost identical. Cates is older, and one number senior, so I have decided to appoint him. Shepherd, you will have your chance next time."[14]

Meanwhile, the task of developing the concept for future amphibious operations and the accompanying tactical doctrine fell to Shepherd since he was assigned, on 1 April 1948, as commandant of the Marine Corps Schools in Quantico. He oversaw creation of the first helicopter tactical doctrine, the organization of the first helicopter squadron, and the conduct of the first helicopter-borne amphibious exercise.

In June 1950, Shepherd was transferred from Quantico to command Fleet Marine Force Pacific, which, at that time, was the largest of the Marine field commands, a large amphibious corps of a Marine division, a Marine aircraft wing, and an assortment of supporting operations and logistic units. What Shepherd found was an anemic shell. Every unit was pitifully understrength. The division, whose war strength was listed as seventeen thousand men, mustered only nine thousand. The aircraft wing at war strength would be ten thousand. In fact, it stood at only fifty-five hundred. Equipment, albeit in good condition, was worn. Supplies were at low ebb. The best that could be said was that the force was well trained and ready to go with what it had. But it didn't have much.

En route to assume command he learned of the situation in Korea, where South Korea and U.S. forces were under severe pressure from the North Korean invasion of 25 June. That whiff of gunsmoke was enough. He sent a message to his superior, Adm. Arthur W. Radford, commander in chief, Pacific, offering to come to Pearl Harbor immediately if his presence were desired. Radford responded promptly: "Consider it preferable that you come at once, and take your leave at a later time."[15] Caught up by the pull of prospective combat, he flew to Honolulu, where he was met by Col. Gregon Williams, serving as chief of staff. Williams handed him a curt message from Washington that launched the FMF toward another war and set the stage for what Shepherd later declared was the most important contribution of his Marine career. "From resources within FMF Pac," it said, "prepare a provisional air-ground brigade for immediate deployment to combat operations in WestPac."[16]

After taking two days to issue the detailed orders to marshal the brigade, Shepherd set out for the Far East to learn firsthand what was going on. During the flight, Shepherd discussed the problems the provisional brigade was likely to face in Korea: "A brigade isn't very big. When it gets to Korea its components will be swallowed up. What we need to do is persuade MacArthur to ask for a full Marine Division, and an air wing too. They are big enough to stand alone."[17] Thereupon, in company with his operations officer, he composed a message that MacArthur might be persuaded to send off to the Joint Chiefs of Staff and put it in his briefcase: "I want this handy when I need it."[18]

Shepherd's call on MacArthur turned into an event of historic proportions. After a sober review of the situation in Korea, MacArthur walked over to his map, pointed to the port of Inchon, and said, "Lem, if I just had the 1st Marine Division right now, I'd land it here at Inchon and break the back of the North Korean offensive."[19] Shepherd was ready. "While the division is under my administrative command," he replied, "I don't have authority to release it. However, if you ask the Joint Chiefs for it, I will do my best to see that you get it, and a supporting Marine Aircraft Wing as well. But you are going to have to ask for it." That was all the encouragement MacArthur needed: "Sit down here at my desk and draft up a message to the JCS and I'll send it."[20] Shepherd took the message he had already drafted out of his pocket, copied it, handed it to the general, who released it, then and there.

Shepherd's eye was on the battle. He knew that building the provisional air-ground brigade, in progress at that moment, would leave very little of the 1st Division and 1st Wing, which he had just volunteered to MacArthur. However, he was confident that Cates would perceive the urgency of the situation, the opportunity it created for the Marines, and scrape up the men and equipment needed to build up the division-wing teams from other Marine Corps formations.

Cates did not disappoint him, although in one conversation said that he would like to see one regiment of the division retained at Camp Pendleton as a nucleus for expansion. This ran counter to Shepherd's grain: "No, Clifton, I believe the whole Division should go. I have already promised it to MacArthur, and the 1st Wing with it." The commandant replied, "Lem, I have to think of our commitment to NATO." Shepherd then countered: "But the fire is out here, not in Europe. Not only should we send the whole division and wing, I think you should start working on organizing another division and wing right behind them." Cates, who did not achieve his renown as a fighter by turning away from a challenge, reacted quickly. "That's probably right," he said, "Go ahead with deploying the full division/wing team."[21]

Fifteen days later, a product of herculean effort, the division and wing were on the way. Then, on 18 August, with the wing and division on the move, Shepherd accompanied Admiral Radford to Tokyo to play their roles in a showdown between MacArthur and the Joint Chiefs of Staff as to the site and date of the upcoming operation.

During the westward flight, Shepherd discussed the concept of a landing at Inchon, noting it embodied almost every conceivable disadvantage. A landing at Posun Myong, about thirty miles south of Inchon, would achieve the same purposes, and would involve fewer problems. MacArthur, however, would countenance no change. Inchon, it was to be.

While in Tokyo, Shepherd was advised by Maj. Gen. L. A. Wright, MacArthur's operations officer, that he had recommended that General Shepherd command the Inchon landing force. This propelled Shepherd to raise the subject with MacArthur. In his most ingratiating way, MacArthur said, "Lem, I'd like to give you the command because of your distinguished record in amphibious combat, but I have already promised it to Ned Almond, my chief of staff. If Ned is killed, I will give you the job." Shepherd's private reaction: "I was disappointed, since I had contributed materially to making the landing possible. However, I couldn't criticize MacArthur for giving the command to his chief of staff—his closest military subordinate."[22]

MacArthur asked Shepherd to accompany him on the operation as his amphibious adviser, saying that Shepherd would have full say in every decision regarding the landing. A lesser man would have politely told MacArthur to forget it. Instead Shepherd accepted immediately, subject to General Cates's approval, not for any influence he might have on Almond's decisions, but because he was "sure the Marines are going to need me."[23]

On 11 September, Shepherd flew with MacArthur to Sasebo and embarked in Admiral Doyle's flagship, the *McKinley.* On the trip to Sasebo, Shepherd had an interesting conversation with MacArthur, who told him that he had encountered great resistance in getting JCS approval for the assignment of the 1st Marine Division to the Inchon undertaking. In his diary, Shepherd quotes MacArthur: "The Army was loathe to let the Marines get into the war with a unit of such size, for political reasons."

On 15 September, D day, the 3d Battalion, 5th Marines struck the offshore island of Wolmi-do, the first objective. By 7:30, a small American flag appeared at the top of the island's highest hill. A few minutes later a message was received that the island was secured, at a cost of four killed and twenty wounded. The main landing, launched late in the afternoon, was not so pretty, but was every bit as successful. Inchon, a fanciful dream by MacArthur only sixty-five days before, was now a victorious reality. He transmitted this message to all hands: "The Navy and Marines never shone brighter than this morning."

Shepherd knew that much of the success was a product of the Corps's philosophy of always being ready to march to the sound of the guns. He was aware also of the part he had played personally, in the victorious operation. Later, he said, with regard to his action in getting the 1st Marine Division and 1st Marine Aircraft Wing into the battle: "I didn't realize it then, but I know now that, in my entire military career, it was the single most significant thing I did for my country."[24]

President Truman kept his promise and appointed Shepherd the twentieth commandant of the Marine Corps on 1 January 1952. The new commandant inherited a

Corps of about 230,000 men and women, triple its size just two years earlier. More than 33,000 of them, the 1st Marine Division and 1st Marine Aircraft Wing, were actively engaged in Korea, where the fighting had already cost the Marine Corps 17,400 casualties. Despite the fact that the United Nations Command had shifted to the defensive, Marine losses continued to run at the rate of 2,000 per month, presenting a major drain on the Corps's personnel resources. Other commitments, at home and abroad, strained the capabilities of the Corps still further. These external demands were clearly of pressing dimensions, but Shepherd was determined first to put his internal house in order.

For several years before being appointed commandant, Shepherd had been critical of the organization of Headquarters, believing that the system was archaic and unwieldy. Basically unchanged for five decades, its principal elements were the Personnel Department, Quartermaster General Department, Adjutant and Inspector Department, Aviation Division, Reserve Division, and Division of Plans and Policies. The latter agency was intended to advise the commandant on policies crossing the total spectrum of Corps activity, and was organized accordingly, with sectional divisions for personnel, intelligence, training, logistics and planning. The Plans and Policies Division, because of its comprehensive advisory charter, was continually in conflict with the other major departments. Each of them saw Plans and Policies as a threat to their functional autonomy and access to the commandant.

Recalling, from his service as assistant commandant in 1947 and 1948, the problems implicit in this system and its adverse effect on efficient functioning of the Headquarters, Shepherd had decided, at that time, that the departmental system should be abandoned in favor of a straightforward general staff organization. When he was nominated to become the next commandant, he made no secret of his determination to accomplish the general staff reorganization at the beginning of his regime.

As he began to plan for the change, he became aware, apart from any institutional resistance, that he would encounter administrative and legal problems—regulation and laws which buttressed the existence and function of the Quartermaster, Personnel, and Adjutant and Inspector Departments, and Department of the Navy regulations linking the Aviation Division with the Office of the Chief of Naval Operations. All of these would have to be reconciled with the general staff system before Marine Corps Headquarters could function properly.

In October 1951, while still commanding general, Fleet Marine Force Pacific, Shepherd visited the 1st Marine Division in Korea, where he conferred on the Headquarters organization subject with the division commander, Maj. Gen. Gerald C. Thomas, and his chief of staff, Col. Victor H. Krulak. Thomas, who as the director of the Division of Plans and Policies in 1944, had made a similar proposal without success, concurred fully in Shepherd's contemplated changes. Particularly, he endorsed Shepherd's conclusion that debate on the basic concept would be unproductive and that he should act promptly. "If you don't do it in the first three months, you won't be able to do it at all," Thomas said. That was exactly what Shepherd wanted to hear. "I'm going to do it at once," was his quick response.[25]

Shepherd's idea of "at once" was to announce his decision on 2 January 1952, the morning after he was sworn in. At 10 he made an address to the Headquarters staff at Marine Corps Headquarters setting the tone for his administration: "I have studied the matter careful[ly] over a number of years and it is my conviction that improvement can be achieved through greater decentralization and by reducing the number of subordinates reporting directly to me. I intend to accomplish this by instituting a simple general staff organization of departmental character." His purpose, he said, was, "to emphasize decentralization in organization and action to the end that business will move forward with a maximum of rapidity."[26]

To the surprise of the affected agencies, he did not ask for comment or recommendations; he simply directed them to draft regulations or legislation to make his decision effective. A new office, chief of staff and assistant commandant, would be created to be occupied by General Thomas, who would be assisted by a deputy chief of staff and a secretary of the General Staff.

The several elements of the Plans and Policies Division would become the classic general staff divisions: G-1, G-2, G-3, and G-4. The departments: Personnel, Inspector, Quartermaster General, along with agencies for Reserve Affairs, Public Information, Policy Analysis, Fiscal Affairs, and Administration, would function as special staff agencies under the chief of staff. In an action that Shepherd believed was long overdue, the head of the Division of Aviation would be elevated to the position of assistant commandant for Air with a third star.

There was some dissatisfaction with the attendant organizational upheaval. Disastrous consequences were forecast, none of which materialized. After a brief time, all of the affected departments and agencies became reconciled to their new relationships, with the exception of the quartermaster general, who, under Shepherd's plan, stood to lose the most influence.

In an arrangement that had persisted for over a century (since the act of 1834), the quartermaster general kept the books, purchased, stored, and maintained supplies and equipment, estimated usage rates, prepared and justified the budget, and paid the bills. He was, as an additional duty, the fiscal director of the Corps. In addition, in 1946, he absorbed the function of the Paymaster Department. In other words, the bookkeeper also had the keys to the safe and, at the same time, discharged wide-ranging operation functions.

Shepherd was resolved to change it all, to make logistic planning, including the calculation of material requirements, a function of G-4 of the General Staff, to create a fiscal director who would take over the bookkeeping task, and to make budgeting a Corps-wide undertaking, integrating the views of field commanders under the overall coordination of the fiscal director. The quartermaster general would be confined to procurement, storage, maintenance, and distribution of material.

Maj. Gen. William P. T. Hill (1895–1965) had been quartermaster general for eleven years and had a total grasp of the quartermaster function. Beyond this, he was a man of diverse and exceptional talents. A World War I Marine aviator, an engineer, geologist, anthropologist, Gobi Desert explorer, and writer on a wide variety of subjects, he was truly a man of parts. And he had an impressive array of non–Marine Corps friends. Most important among these were members of Congress, who respected his frugality, frankness, and legendary memory.

Habituated to the broad power his office had exercised for many years, Hill did not accept the circumscribed function embodied in Shepherd's reorganization. He made his views known to the new commandant in strong and sometimes emotional terms, urging, so far as his department was concerned, that the new plan be scrapped completely. Shepherd had no intention of changing his plan, but he was patient. He heard Hill's arguments, reasoned with him, and, finally, when the time for talking was past, told Hill that the decision was final: "I respected Tom Hill. He and I had been close friends for many years and it was very hard to turn him down. But I had to do it, and I did."[27]

The critical step in the logistic readjustment was the creation of the new Fiscal Department. Shepherd was anxious to see its emergence occur as an evolutionary matter, free of conflict, although he understood this to be unlikely due to General Hill's strong convictions and his persuasive qualities. Accordingly, he told General Thomas that he wanted to name a very strong personality as the first fiscal director, since this individual would have the difficult task of negotiating with General Hill on the withdrawal of fiscal and budget functions from the Quartermaster's Department.

Thomas recommended Col. David M. Shoup for the job. He was convinced that Shoup was both strong enough and bright enough to do battle with Hill. Shepherd did not know Shoup well, and upon learning that he had no fiscal or accounting background, he was not disposed to appoint him. Thomas argued the case, and the commandant ultimately approved the recommendation. Shoup was assigned on 1 April 1952 as Hill's assistant for the transition period, during which the essential documentation for creation of the new office would be prepared. The process did not go smoothly. Hill was opposed to losing the fiscal and budgeting function, and he was unmoved by Shoup's rationalization. The quartermaster repeatedly complained of the error of the idea, to both the chief of staff and commandant. Each time, Shepherd tried patiently to mollify Hill without compromising the principle underlying the division of functions. He had little success.

Finally, in February 1953, following a direction from Thomas, Shoup laid before him, and subsequently the commandant, a book titled *Manual for the Formulation and Execution of the Annual Marine Corps Budget,* describing the office and function of the fiscal director in terms consistent with the original concept. Shepherd liked the manual and discussed it with Hill in two long sessions but was unable to get his concurrence on any significant aspect of it. Nevertheless, the commandant approved the document without Hill's concurrence and, on 17 April 1953, appointed Shoup as fiscal director. The system worked from the start. Shepherd had broken with a century of tradition and, in doing so, had made a historic move in the direction of fiscal maturity in the Corps.

While streamlining his Headquarters was a high priority, Shepherd had many other problems. Money was tight, and the task of redressing the imprudent economies of the

Louis Johnson austerity period was a heavy burden. The Marines' budget for fiscal 1952 was about $1.4 billion, which Shepherd saw as inadequate to support a very active Corps, which had a division and a wing engaged in Korea. Material reserves, which had been at low ebb in 1950, had been further depleted. Shepherd decided to rectify this condition, and that required gaining approval for increased appropriations at every level—within the Department of the Navy, in the JCS, in the Defense Department, and in Congress. He was painfully aware, from his earlier service as assistant commandant, that the Marines' influence in all of these areas, except in Congress, was far less than desirable.

He recalled that the major objective of the Corps, during the congressional debates preceding enactment of the 1947 National Security Act, was to ensure wording in the legislation that protected the Corps's existence as an effective air-ground combatant force. "I agreed with that approach," Shepherd later said. "But I also told General Vandegrift, if our forces were to be properly employed, that something needed to be done to make sure that our viewpoint was fully considered when strategic plans and budgets were under discussion, because if you're not in the plans you're not going to be in the budget."[28]

The enactment of the 1947 act and its amendment in 1949 had left many Marine Corps supporters in Congress dissatisfied on this precise point. They were convinced that both the level and adequacy of Marine representation in the high military councils of the nation were unsatisfactory. They were distressed, first, by the agreement in March 1948 at Key West, where Defense Secretary James V. Forrestal assembled an array of high-ranking officials to add functional details to the National Security Act in the area of service roles and missions. All the service chiefs, other than the Marine commandant, were included.

The results were predictable. The Marines had no friends at the table, and the conferees moved aggressively to limit the provisions of the National Security Act that protected Marine Corps missions. They agreed, specifically, that

1. The Corps would not be permitted to expand beyond four division/wing strength in time of war, despite its obvious capability to do more, as exemplified by World War II;
2. Marines would not be permitted to exercise command above the corps level, evidently to counter what the Army had regarded as a threat in World War II;
3. The Corps would not be permitted to create a "second land army," whatever that might mean.

Apprehensions of Marine Corps friends in Congress were heightened further by enactment into law, in August 1949, of the Reorganization Act, which provided for a Joint Chiefs chairman, doubled the size of the Joint Staff, and removed the secretaries of the Army, Navy, and Air Force from the Cabinet.

At the outset of the Shepherd administration, Senator Paul Douglas and Representatives Mike Mansfield and Carl Vinson introduced legislation that established the basic composition of the Marine Corps at four divisions and four aircraft wings. It also placed the Marine commandant as a member of the JCS in order to ensure respect for his viewpoint in strategic planning and budgeting.

The bill had strong support in Congress and equally vigorous opposition in the Department of Defense, where every key official, including the military chiefs of all the other services, as well as the JCS chairman, Gen. Omar N. Bradley, testified against the bill. The CNO, Adm. Forrest Sherman, did the opposition cause no good when he acknowledged, reluctantly, before a congressional committee that the JCS July 1950 discussions concerning commitment of the Marines to the high-risk Inchon operations were carried on without the commandant.

In its final form, the bill fell short of the aspirations of its sponsors, but it still did a lot for the Marine Corps. As Public Law 416, enacted on 28 June 1952, it provided that

> the Corps shall be so organized as to include not less than three combat divisions and three aircraft wings . . .
>
> The commandant of the Marine Corps shall indicate to the chairman any matter scheduled for consideration by the Joint Chiefs that directly concerns the Marine Corps. Unless, upon request of the Chairman for a determination, the Secretary of Defense determines that such a matter does not concern the Marine Corps, the commandant shall meet with the Joint Chiefs of Staff when the matter is under consideration. While the matter is under consideration and with respect to it, the commandant has co-equal status with the members of the Joint Chiefs of Staff.

General Shepherd, as the new commandant, was thus the beneficiary of an organizational guarantee not enjoyed by any of the other services, as well as a status with reference to the JCS that had no precedent. And he was painfully aware that his associates-to-be had all opposed the bill at every turn: "I was convinced that it was right and would make our job in the budget area much easier. Anyhow, it was the law and now I had to do my best to make it work. I had a feeling that it might not be easy."[29]

His first act was to call on General Bradley and declare his determination that the provisions of Public Law 416 would be complied with to the letter and that the Marines had no intention of insinuating themselves into any matters, strategic or fiscal, that did not fall within the strict purview of the law.

Shepherd recalled that "General Bradley was very cool. He said that he had opposed the bill vigorously, and still believed it was wrong, but it was now the law of the land and I could be assured that he would endeavor to see it carried out."[30] And he did. He offered to provide Shepherd a Pentagon office (Shepherd's Headquarters were in the Arlington Annex, a mile distant) and suggested that the Marines establish a liaison officer in the JCS structure so that the commandant could be fully apprised of day-to-day activities.

Following his meeting with Bradley, Shepherd assembled his key staff officers and laid down the principles under which the Corps would meet the requirements of the new law. He said he did not intend to use the Pentagon office "for anything other than to hang my hat," emphasized that the tendency to create a large bureaucracy would be resisted, and that "we are not going to involve ourselves in matters that do not directly concern us, but this is our guarantee that war plans and budgets are not going to be made without us."[31] Shepherd's philosophy soon became evident to members of the JCS, whose initial diffidence was gradually replaced by acceptance of the Marine presence. As it turned out, only 9 percent of all JCS agenda items were declared by Shepherd to be of "direct concern" to the Marine Corps during the first year of the law's existence.

On 1 March 1953, Adm. Arthur W. Radford replaced Bradley as JCS chairman, a step which altered greatly the operating relationships of the Marine Corps and the JCS. Shepherd, as commanding general, Fleet Marine Force Pacific, in the Korean crisis years, 1950 and 1951, had earned the respect and confidence of Radford, then commander in chief, Pacific. In a JCS session shortly after Radford's arrival, Shepherd arose to depart following consideration of the single item in which he had expressed direct concern. Shepherd recorded in his diary that Radford restrained him: "Please stay, Lem. There are a couple of other items on which I would like to hear your views."

This began an informal arrangement that found the Marine Corps involved, at the insistence of the chairman, in affairs that were often outside its normal sphere. Sometime, in advance of a meeting, Radford would ask the commandant to be prepared to give his views on a subject not, conceivably, of "direct concern" to the Corps.

While pleased to be consulted, the trend worried the commandant. He did not want the JCS members to conclude, erroneously, that he was seeking to influence issues that were not Marine Corps business, and he made a point of telling them so on each occasion. Beyond this concern, Shepherd worried about the increased bureaucracy that his broader participation would generate. He knew he would have to prepare himself for the discussions, with an inevitable increased demand on his staff, which was exactly what he did not want. Nevertheless, this ad hoc arrangement, which persisted through the remainder of Shepherd's term, resulted in the Marines being far more involved in discussions of military affairs than had ever been contemplated in Public Law 416. It formed the basis for the later action (1981) that made the commandant a full member of the JCS.

The Public Law 416 problem was scarcely settled before General Shepherd faced a powerful recurrence of an old family quarrel in the Department of the Navy. Beginning with the law of 1834, which codified the existence of the Corps as a separate service within the department, there was a continuing disagreement as to just how much authority senior naval officers exercised over the Marine Corps. The festering issue came to a climax in 1953, in the middle of Shepherd's term, when Adm. Forrest Sherman, the chief of naval operations, undertook to enlarge and legitimize his authority over various elements of the Department of the Navy. He based his case on the provisions of Public Law 432, 80th Congress, which had been written to define more clearly the relations between the CNO and the bureaus and offices of the Navy Department. The law was not intended to affect the statutory posture of the Marine Corps in any way.

The position which Sherman adopted, however, would affect the Marine Corps directly, unfavorably, and in a manner contrary to the provisions of the National Security Act of 1947. Essentially, he proposed to alter the provisions of Navy Department General Order No. 5 (GO-5), which establishes policies governing the distribution of authority for the administration of the department.

Sherman's theory embraced four propositions where the Marines were concerned:

1. That the Marine Corps does not possess operating forces under the commandant's command. Sherman's position was that all Marine combat units were, automatically, part of the Operating Forces of the Navy.
2. That the chief of naval operations should exercise direct supervision over the Headquarters of the Marine Corps as he did over the various Navy Department bureaus.
3. That the chief of naval operations exercised authority termed "naval command of the Naval Establishment" over the entire department, including the Marine Corps and, of great importance.
4. That the chief of naval operations should establish the personnel and material requirements of the Marine Corps.

Upon becoming aware of the nature of Sherman's proposals, Shepherd went to him and detailed his dissent in several discussions that "got hotter and hotter," as Shepherd put it at the time: "I got nowhere. Sherman would not move."[32] Accordingly, he went to Secretary of the Navy Robert W. Anderson, voicing his view that what Sherman had in his mind violated the National Security Act and other laws as well. He called it "a power play." This got Anderson's attention, particularly as the several bureau chiefs also perceived adverse implications of the move where they were concerned, and had expressed similar concerns to the secretary. Anderson gradually began to see that increasing the power of the CNO would, in some degree, erode his own position as head of the department. Accordingly, he convened a formal committee to examine the entire matter and to bring him recommendations designed to clarify responsibilities and lines of authority.[33]

Chaired by Thomas S. Gates, the Undersecretary of the Navy and no friend of the Marine Corps, the committee was to have eight members, only one a marine. General Shepherd selected Lt. Gen. Gerald C. Thomas, his chief of staff, for the task with Col. Victor H. Krulak as his alternate. The other members were Adm. D. B. Duncan, Vice Adm. John Gingrich, Vice Adm. Earle W. Mills, Rear Adm. R. E. Libby, Hobart C. Ramsey, and Richard M. Paget. Shepherd's instructions to his two representatives were simple and tough: "Stick with the National Security Act. Give away nothing. If you have to make a minority report, do it."[34]

The committee met over a period of six months, issues between the CNO and the commandant of the Marine Corps dominating the discussion. Finally, after much exploration of all applicable statutes and administrative instructions, its published report agreed unanimously that three of Admiral Sherman's positions, concerning the Marines, were not valid.[35] Specifically, the conferees accepted that

1. The Marine Corps *does* have operating forces, other than those assigned to the operating forces of the Navy;
2. The chief of naval operations *does not* have authority over the Headquarters of the Marine Corps;
3. In discharging the task of "naval command of the Naval Establishment" the chief of naval operations performs only as a staff officer, carrying out such duties as are specifically assigned by the Secretary, and that the Marine commandant also exercises a fraction of the "naval command" function.

But on the final controversial point, whether or not the chief of naval operations should establish the personnel and material requirements of the Marine Corps, the committee could not agree on language that would reconcile the divergent Navy and Marine Corps views. Nor could the CNO, now Adm. Robert B. Carney, and General Shepherd, whose friendship did not temper the debate. "It was hot going," Shepherd said.[36]

Here was a bone marrow issue. Clearly, if the CNO possessed authority to establish the Marines' requirements for people and things, he would thereafter have the power "to feed and starve" over the Marines' budget. Shepherd recognized that the issue had reached its crisis point and that the time was at hand for him to make a final stand. He persuaded Secretary Anderson to give him the whole of a Saturday morning, during which meeting Shepherd outlined the entire GO-5 problem, its origins, its legalities, and equities.

Shepherd's presentation was unemotional, salted with historical facts and many examples of what was in store for the Marines were the Navy's position accepted. Anderson heard Shepherd out, asked many questions, but made no commitment. He took all the papers, promising to spend the weekend studying the problem. The answer was not long in coming. Early Monday morning Anderson was on the telephone to Shepherd with a simple message: "I find that you are correct on the one unresolved point in the GO-5 controversy. . . . the General Order will be rewritten to reflect that fact."[37]

Anderson was true to his word. General Order No 5, as reissued, contained the critical words: "The Commandant of the Marine Corps . . . commands the Marine Corps and is directly responsible to the Secretary of the Navy for its administration, discipline, internal organization, unit training requirements, efficiency and readiness." Shepherd had been stubborn in the matter. He had antagonized two chiefs of naval operations and risked the displeasure of the secretary. But his persistence paid off. The new General Order 5 codified correctly, and for the first time in over a century, the statutory position of the Marine Corps in the naval establishment. It was a signal victory for the Corps.[38]

Interspersed among the major issues—realigning the Headquarters organization, support of combat forces in Korea, and resolution of institutional problems such as Public Law 416, and Navy Department General Order 5—the Shepherd administration moved on a variety of other fronts. Seeing the operating forces as the central basis for the Corps's useful existence, Shepherd launched a program, at the outset of his tenure, to channel a higher proportion of the Corps's strength into the FMF. Two years of assiduous attention to this project saw the FMF embracing about 59 percent of the Corps's strength, up from 49 percent in 1951.[39]

This manpower realignment was the more impressive in light of other countervailing undertakings. Shepherd reasoned that the broader the Marine Corps involvement in the nation's military affairs, the greater its overall usefulness would be. One such activity was the Corps's Security Guard program, initiated in 1948, by agreement with the Department of State.[40] Upon review of the program, Shepherd concluded that the standards for selection of Security Guard marines needed improvement, as did provision for their training and supervision. Even though it added to the personnel burden, Shepherd decreed that all Security Guard marines have clean records, complete at least one enlistment, and be personally screened and recommended by his commanding officer. A four-week formal school was established to screen candidates further and provide uniformity to the program, and six regional offices were established to oversee the operation of the several embassy guards. The State Department requirements grew steadily, and Shepherd was willing to meet each additional demand, to the extent that, by 1954, there were 682 carefully selected officers and men in the program, serving in detachments of five to fifty-three, in seventy locations around the world.[41]

As far back as his service in France in World War I, Shepherd was impressed with the importance of establishing and nourishing relations with foreign military forces. At his initiative, contacts were enlarged with the Marine Corps of the Netherlands, Great Britain, and Spain. In addition, he encouraged the establishment of a Marine Corps in Thailand, the Philippines, and the Republic of China (Taiwan), committing small advisory groups to each one.

In the same vein he attended each of the annual exercises conducted by the supreme commander of the Allied Powers at his Paris headquarters. It was Shepherd's view that these exercises, which addressed matters of strategic policy and operational relationships, were a potential forum for portrayal of the Marine Corps's concepts of tactics, techniques, and air/ground relationships in amphibious warfare.

It took two years of persuasion before Field Marshal Bernard L. Montgomery, who was responsible for the exercise, acceded to Shepherd's request that the U.S. Marine Corps be permitted to make a major presentation on the vertical envelopment in the amphibious assault as a part of the 1954 exercise. Prepared by the Marine Corps

Educational Center and reviewed by Shepherd with his customary detailed care, the presentation emphasized the unique quality of the unified Navy–Marine Corps amphibious team. It had a powerful impact on the distinguished group of foreign and U.S. participants.

One of the lasting legacies of Shepherd's commandancy derived from his belief that the Fleet Marine Force always benefits from a modern and well-endowed supporting establishment. To this end, he sponsored the growth and permanence of the major training bases at Camp Pendleton and Camp Lejeune, the combined arms center at Twentynine Palms, California, and the two supply bases at Barstow, California, and Albany, Georgia. And he found money, in 1954, to take over from the Navy and rehabilitate the old Aiea Naval Hospital in Oahu as a new headquarters for Fleet Marine Force Pacific.

As his tenure neared its end, Shepherd had the pleasure of seeing a Corps in good condition, one which had come through the Korean crisis with great credit and whose affairs were adequately represented in high national councils. He had established austerity as the Corps's keynote, with a budget down 20 percent from its 1953 high of $1.5 billion and personnel strength down thirty-five thousand from its Korean War peak.

Shepherd had ample cause for satisfaction, and when asked to characterize his administration in a few words, he said, "We tried to make the FMF king. I think we succeeded."[42]

19
Randolph McCall Pate

1956–1960

V. KEITH FLEMING JR.

If a term as commandant of the Marine Corps is judged solely by the strengths and weaknesses of the incumbent, then that of Gen. Randolph McCall Pate would rate as the least effective of the twentieth century. Pate was, by all accounts, the most controversial commandant of the century. Fortunately, the commandant does not bear the Marine Corps burden alone, and during Pate's tenure, dedicated subordinates protected the Corps's reputation and advanced its interests.

Nothing in Pate's youth or early Marine Corps career hinted at the problems of his later years. In fact, his brilliance as a staff officer earned him the nickname "the Wizard." "Ran" Pate came from an old, distinguished Virginia family for whom military service was a tradition. Many had served honorably in the Civil War. His father was a naval officer stationed at Port Royal, South Carolina, at Ran's birth on 11 February 1898. The boy, the eldest of two children, subsequently spent his childhood at Norfolk, Virginia. As a youngster in Tidewater Virginia, he developed a lifelong love of sport fishing. This avocation even influenced his first choice for a career. He talked of becoming a harbor pilot after learning that pilot boats spent considerable time off the harbor entrance waiting for ships to arrive. Ran reasoned this would give him plenty of time for fishing.

He reached manhood during World War I and spent a brief period as an enlisted man in the U.S. Army before the war ended. Pate then resumed his studies at the Virginia Military Institute. He was a popular, competent student who became a cadet captain and president of his class. He graduated in June 1921 with a bachelor of arts degree.[1]

Pate received a Marine Corps Reserve commission in September 1921 and accepted a regular commission the following May. Peacetime service took him to various posts throughout the United States. His early career also involved expeditionary duty to Santo Domingo in 1923–24 and China, 1927–29. In addition, he attended the Army's weapons school at Fort Benning, followed by a stint as an instructor at the

Gen. Randolph McCall Pate, twenty-first commandant.
U.S. Marine Corps Photo.

schools at Quantico. The latter tour earned Pate a reputation as an "ideal instructor," something he cherished for the rest of his life.[2]

World War II took him to the combat zones, but chance, circumstance, and his notable reputation as a staff officer kept him from tactical command. When the 1st Marine Division landed on Guadalcanal on 7 August 1942, Lieutenant Colonel Pate was the assistant division G-4 officer. This made him a member of the so-called 1st Division Club of senior officers who, many claimed, dominated the Corps in the post-war years. In addition, the near-mythical deference associated with the title "Guadalcanal veteran," combined with the Legion of Merit awarded by the Marine Corps in 1947 for his service on the island, gave Pate a mantle of distinguished combat experience. Ironically, Pate's actual service on Guadalcanal was relatively brief, for he soon contracted a skin disease and had to be evacuated.[3]

The evacuation flight itself ended in an adventure which became part of the Pate legend. Various versions of the story exist regarding Pate's activities. Some say the transport plane became lost during the night. Other accounts, including some later publicity releases with Pate's obvious blessing, are more dramatic. These say the plane, an R4D (the naval aviation designation for the twin-engine Douglas DC-3) took off from Guadalcanal at the same time a Japanese air raid began. Friendly antiaircraft fire disabled the plane's navigation equipment, and the pilot could not determine the proper course for New Caledonia. When the aircraft ran out of fuel toward dawn, the pilot crash-landed on a coral reef out of sight of land. The situation of the twenty-five survivors was precarious. At high tide, they had to move to the top of the fuselage, but could return to the shade of the cabin when the tide dropped. They had only a one-gallon container of water and no food. Rationing and the collection of rainwater kept them from dying of thirst. Raw fish was their only food. They remained on the reef for eleven days until rescued by an American destroyer. Pate lost thirty pounds during the ordeal.[4]

The publicity releases, issued at the time Pate received his nomination as the twenty-first commandant, credit Pate with a heroic role during the ordeal on the reef. The report said he took charge of the group and ensured their survival, including doling out one cup of water per day to each man. On Pate's orders, the party managed to get a radio working, and sent out a message which brought the rescuing destroyer.[5] The episode was something of a turning point in Pate's life. Some of his associates believed he never recovered from the psychological trauma of the ordeal.[6]

Pate occupied important staff billets for the remainder of the war. He rose to the rank of colonel and served as deputy chief of staff of Fleet Marine Force, Pacific. His work earned him a Legion of Merit medal for his achievements in the planning of the Peleliu, Iwo Jima, and Okinawa campaigns. In 1947, he received a second award of the Legion of Merit for his service during the earlier Guadalcanal campaign.

In 1948, Pate became a brigadier general, and in 1951, a major general. He commanded the 2d Marine Division at Camp Lejeune, North Carolina, before taking over the 1st Marine Division in Korea in June 1953. This was his only combat command, and it came during the last few weeks of static trench warfare before an armistice ended the fighting. He remained in command of the division until 1954, when he returned to Washington to become the assistant commandant of the Marine Corps. In late 1955, he received President Eisenhower's nomination as the twenty-first commandant, to take effect on 1 January 1956.[7]

Almost every selection of a new commandant is fraught with internal Marine Corps politics. General Pate, however, had the inside track through the sponsorship of his predecessor, Gen. Lemuel C. Shepherd Jr. Both were Virginians, VMI graduates, and distant cousins.[8] President Eisenhower accepted General Shepherd's candidate and sent

Pate's nomination for a two-year term to the Senate for approval.[9] Pate relieved Shepherd as commandant at a ceremony outside Headquarters on 31 December 1955. The following morning, Pate's first full day in office, began with the traditional serenade outside the commandant's house by the Marine Corps Band.

Pate inherited a Marine Corps on the verge of reorganizing its combat capabilities. Public Law 416, passed in 1952, ensured a force structure of three divisions and three aircraft wings.[10] To give this structure the full benefit of new technology, and to counter criticism that traditional amphibious operations were obsolete, the Corps was changing its organization and tactics to use improved helicopters for "vertical envelopment." Marines earlier had made limited but pioneering use of helicopters in Korea, and had made a thorough study of their potential after the war. This effort, which involved a major reorganization of both the divisions and aircraft wings, would reach maturity during Pate's tenure as commandant.

The Marine Corps's plans for the future were dependent, as always, on its standing in the Washington political arena. Among the Corps's recent victories had been the provision allowing the commandant to participate as a member of the Joint Chiefs of Staff on matters affecting the Marine Corps. However, the Marines had little influence within the Eisenhower administration. The Corps, by necessity, turned to its friends in Congress for support. Some of these, such as Senator Paul Douglas, were former marines themselves. Others, such as Representative Carl Vinson of Georgia, chairman of the House Armed Services Committee, were advocates of a large Navy and a capable Marine Corps. Such allies were vital as the Corps fought for its share of the austere defense appropriations sought by the administration under its "new look" defense policy.[11]

These were difficult times for the Marine Corps, and it needed a firm hand at the helm. General Pate, unfortunately, did not have the strength the Marine Corps needed or deserved. The first public evidence of the nature of Pate's service as commandant came in April 1956. A Marine drill instructor, Staff Sgt. Matthew C. McKeon, took his recruit platoon on an unauthorized night march into the tidal marshes surrounding the recruit depot at Parris Island, South Carolina. Six recruits drowned that Sunday night, setting off a national furor over the nature of Marine recruit training. The tragedy at Ribbon Creek, though immediately cloaked with a wider significance, came from errors in judgment by Staff Sergeant McKeon. He was a conscientious noncommissioned officer, a loving husband and father, and a devout Catholic. He wanted to be a good drill instructor who turned out well-trained marines; unfortunately, in addition to an old back injury which often caused intense pain in his legs, he had a tendency toward impulsive decisions.

New to drill instructor duty, McKeon was assigned as an assistant DI for Platoon 78. On Sunday, 8 April 1956, the platoon was in its barracks at the base rifle range. During the morning, McKeon observed several recruits outside the barracks lying on the grass. Upset by such unmilitary behavior and already irritable from a bout of sciatica, he ordered the entire platoon to scrub down their squad bay. When a marksmanship instructor brought a bottle of vodka into the DI's room later in the morning, McKeon took several drinks from the bottle and then went with the man to the base's Staff NCO Club for more drinks. That evening, the alcohol and his painful sciatica, impulsiveness, and the desire to be a good DI became a deadly combination. McKeon decided that a night march into the tidal marsh would straighten out the platoon. Instead, six recruits drowned, and McKeon headed for a court-martial.[12]

McKeon's error in judgment was not the only error made that night. The base did not release the story until the following day. In the interim, however, a local stringer for the Associated Press had gotten wind of a crisis at Parris Island, and the AP put out a teletype advisory to its subscribers to expect a further story. The advisory reached newspaper editors that Sunday night while they were putting together their Monday morning editions. When no official notification came out of Parris Island until after noon on Monday, newsmen from all the media suspected a cover-up and dispatched reporters to the scene.[13]

There was another reason for sending so many reporters to Parris Island. Marine recruit training had become notorious within recent years for its harshness and frequent physical abuse of recruits. Even senior officers recognized the problem, but there had been no significant effort to end the abuses. The situation, in truth, was a powder keg.[14]

When the base notified Headquarters of the tragedy early on Monday morning, Pate was away on a speaking engagement. As soon as his staff reached him, he decided to fly to Parris Island.[15] His presence at Parris Island added to the newsworthiness of the situation. Worse, he proved he could not be trusted with the Corps's best interests when in front of a microphone. Despite having drafted a statement with the help of the base commander, Pate's off-the-cuff comments to the assembled reporters made headlines throughout the country. He said the Corps itself was on trial, an assertion which proved self-fulfilling because it inevitably brought attention to the Marine Corps's reputation for training abuses. Pate made the situation worse when he in effect pronounced McKeon guilty even before completion of the official investigation.[16]

For the first, but not the last, time, officers at Headquarters saved a situation caused by Pate's public statements. Col. James D. Hittle, the congressional liaison officer, immediately went to Capitol Hill to brief key senators and representatives on the situation. He was careful to give them all the available information, and emphasized the fragmentary nature of the information. Colonel Hittle also promised—and kept his word—that the Marine Corps would keep them informed. Hittle's finesse succeeded in keeping Congressmen from making any public statements which might have committed them to later action they and the Marine Corps might have regretted.[17]

When General Pate returned to Washington, the senior officers at Headquarters Marine Corps persuaded him to set up a crisis management team. At their urging, Pate ordered Maj. Gen. Merrill B. Twining, a brilliant and astute Marine officer, to come to Washington from Camp Pendleton, California, to head the team.[18]

Twining, following his arrival, sought to develop a response to Ribbon Creek acceptable to both his fellow general officers and to Congress. The latter was crucial, for even so staunch a supporter as Representative Carl Vinson had in his files more than two hundred complaints from constituents alleging acts of brutality during Marine recruit training. In short, Congress was in no mood for rationalization from the Marines. Its members told the Twining team in no uncertain terms that it expected prompt, decisive action from the Marine Corps or there would be a full-scale congressional investigation of the widespread abuses in recruit training.[19]

Twining devised a straightforward plan. It involved testimony by General Pate before Vinson's committee. Pate's statement would admit the problems in recruit training and lay out general corrective measures. Eventually these measures included better housing for bachelor DIs (to give them quarters away from the recruits), additional pay and uniforms, free laundry and dry cleaning, and, as a new badge of office, the right to wear the traditional peaked campaign hat. The plan, when implemented, also brought more experienced NCOs to the drill field and provided for more officer supervision of the training. The reforms, however, did not touch the so-called shock treatment, the stressful introduction to military life which so long had been a part of recruit training. Twining's plan was a good one and it was in place and working at Parris Island well before McKeon's much-publicized court-martial. Above all, however, Twining's plan satisfied congressional concerns, and forestalled a full-scale congressional investigation of abuses in recruit training.[20]

The court-martial of Sergeant McKeon revealed again General Pate's unpredictable nature. Despite the entreaties of his staff, Pate agreed to testify for the defense in McKeon's behalf. Pate's decision was a key victory for McKeon's astute civilian defense counsel, Emile Zola Berman, who had worked hard to change the public's initial impression of McKeon as a sadistic killer. He largely succeeded, partly because reporters found him more accessible and forthcoming than the military prosecutors. Inevitably, Berman's statements dominated the news reports about the trial. Another part of his trial strategy involved a special effort to develop good relations with Pate. Berman went so far as to arrange to meet Pate secretly at the latter's family home in Norfolk, Virginia. During that meeting, which occurred after the trial opened, Berman persuaded General Pate to testify on McKeon's behalf. Pate agreed, even though he was in the military chain of command which would have to review any guilty verdict and any sentence imposed by the court-martial. When Pate's staff at Headquarters learned of the agreement, they tried to dissuade him from going to Parris Island. Pate reacted angrily and ordered them to stop trying to talk to him about it.[21]

General Pate's appearance at the trial made spectacular headlines. When called to testify, he stopped briefly beside Sergeant McKeon, shook hands, said he had come to help him, and wished him good luck. Pate then testified under oath that he believed McKeon should not have been brought to trial but only reduced in rank and transferred. In essence, Pate implied the Marine Corps had overreacted.[22]

A few days later, on 4 August 1956, the court-martial found McKeon guilty of negligence, reduced him to private, and awarded a bad conduct discharge and a jail sentence. The secretary of the navy, however, soon suspended the discharge and reduced the length of the confinement to that which McKeon had served prior to and immediately after the trial. The story gradually faded from the nation's editorial pages.[23]

A less sensational, but in the long term more significant, development for the Marine Corps came out of the Hogaboom board, which issued its report in 1956. The board, chaired by Maj. Gen. Robert E. Hogaboom, had studied the Fleet Marine Force's doctrine and organization in light of the changes necessary for the best integration of helicopter mobility into amphibious assaults. The board took into account the reality that neither the ships nor the helicopters were available, or likely to become available, for an all-helicopter assault. In addition, the board recognized there was considerable concern in Washington over the ability of the armed services to move combat units to the world's hot spots quickly by using transport aircraft. Thus, a Marine division had to be capable of landing in both the traditional boat/amphibian tractor combination and in helicopters. It also had to be light enough for most of its elements to be flown anywhere in the world.[24] This meant transferring the division's heavy artillery, tanks, and most logistic support units from the divisions to Force Troops. The latter had been set up to provide the combat and logistic support for multidivision assaults. The goal of transferring heavy assets to Force Troops was to make the divisions air-transportable in cargo aircraft, and to make the assault battalions helicopter-transportable. Tanks, heavy artillery, and other support would be attached to the combat units as required by the mission. This gave Marine combat units enormous flexibility to task organize subordinate units to meet whatever the tactical situation required.[25]

Having the board's report in hand and making its recommendations a reality were not the same thing. There were powerful interests within both the Marine Corps and the Navy that objected to the board's recommendations. In particular, the naval aviation community, as a whole, questioned the proposals which affected pilots and aircraft. The Bureau of Aeronautics, which purchased aircraft for both services based upon the overall needs of the fleet, was among those who raised doubts. It could procure additional helicopters only at the expense of giving up an equal number of fixed-wing aircraft since the number of airframes was fixed by law. More helicopters naturally required more helicopter-trained pilots, and this would require a restructuring of the naval aviation training establishment as well as reducing the number of available fixed-wing pilots. In addition, the new amphibious doctrine called for new helicopters and new technology, and these essentially were still in the early developmental stages. Further, the Navy had a considerable investment in traditional amphibious ships, and the new Marine Corps doctrine would require expenditure of scarce funds for ship conversion or new construction.[26]

Achieving the Hogaboom board's goals would not have been easy under any commandant. Having General Pate as the incumbent made the task even more difficult. Pate was more attuned to the slow pace of the pre–World War II garrison years than the hectic pace of the cold war era. His interests leaned more toward appearances than substance. According to Brig. Gen. Samuel R. Shaw (Ret.), who worked closely with the commandant, Pate had fine ideas but no firm convictions of what the Marine Corps was or should be. His convictions had always been those of his boss, a good attribute in a staff officer. However, as commandant, a position that required strong convictions based upon considerable previous thinking, Pate was beyond his depth.[27]

In addition, he was proving a lightning rod for unfavorable publicity within and without the Corps. Early in his tenure as commandant, he created a degree of ill will within the Department of Defense by publicly disagreeing with a minor policy set by the secretary of defense, Charles E. Wilson. The secretary had issued an order in June 1956 allowing officers to wear civilian clothes to work while assigned to the Washington, D.C., area. Pate objected to this policy on the grounds that it would hurt "pride of uniform." The story reached the press, and the resulting articles did not cast Pate in a favorable light.

Pate, of course, could not override the secretary's order, but he got around that by putting out the word to Marine officers that while they could wear civilian clothes to work, his personal preference was for officers to wear the uniform. Marine officers took the hint. Unfortunately, they soon realized that Pate's policy applied to them but not to Pate himself. He wore civilian clothes to his office any day he considered them more appropriate to his scheduled activities. Marine officers took note and grumbled.

The issue of appropriate attire resurfaced in May of the following year when the Washington press reported that General Pate required his Marine drivers to wear civilian chauffeur uniforms. The news stories said one of the two Marine master sergeants assigned as his drivers had complained to another Marine sergeant that he felt humiliated. He believed that not being in regular uniform robbed him of any authority over lower-ranking marines. Drivers of the heads of the other services, as the press pointed out, wore their services' regular "uniform of the day."[28] When the press asked the Headquarters public affairs office for an explanation, the only response was that the Marine Corps would issue a statement soon. When it appeared, the statement baldly reported that General Pate had found civilian chauffeur uniforms to be more appropriate for his drivers for certain functions the commandant attended. The story in the *Washington Evening Star* pointedly noted that Pate had not specified the kind of functions for which the chauffeur uniforms were more appropriate. It also noted that while the Marine spokesmen had suggested reporters talk to the two Marine drivers, the latter were not available for interviews.[29]

Reporters had no problem finding further related controversy. Many officers at Headquarters Marine Corps were disgruntled by Pate's habit of walking the halls and stopping anyone without an impeccable uniform. One news story said that within the past week he had publicly admonished several officers with the reminder that "trousers must break in front over the shoe laces, be 3/8 of an inch longer in back than in front, and clear the ground by precisely one inch." Wives and local tailors reportedly were very busy ensuring the strictest adherence to the uniform regulations. Reporters had no problem picking up this information from unhappy marines.

The underlying reality was that General Pate and his uniform policies, which included encouraging marines to improve their military appearance by carrying a British-style swagger stick, were not popular with the Washington press corps. The reasons for the newsmen's dislike derived in large part from the members of the press's own experience with the military. Most of them had either served in uniform during World War II, Korea, or the cold war, or they had observed military operations firsthand while serving as war correspondents. Their expectations of senior military leaders had been shaped by generals such as Eisenhower and MacArthur. During World War II both of the latter, aware of the politics of a citizen army, had dispensed with the more decorative elements of the uniform, particularly the "fruit salad" of ribbons and decorations. Newsmen had a deep-seated distrust of generals such as Pate who advocated a more foppish approach to the wearing of the uniform, including the carrying of a swagger stick.[30]

General Pate did not endear himself to President Eisenhower, either. The basic problem was Pate's loose tongue, which opened some sensitive issues to press scrutiny. Among these were some American military moves during the 1956 Suez Crisis. The Eisenhower administration's official position was that during the crisis it had exerted diplomatic pressure only in the form of efforts to get the British and French to stop their attempted reconquest of the Suez Canal. However, in January 1957, Pate revealed in an interview the true extent of Marine Corps activities during the crisis: two reinforced battalion landing teams had secretly put to sea in Navy ships with instructions to proceed to the Mediterranean and the Persian Gulf and stand by for further orders. If necessary, they were to rescue American citizens from Cairo, even if that meant fighting their way through whichever belligerent party—British, French, or Egyptian—stood in their way. Pate also said that a reinforced Marine rifle company had gone to Port Lyautey, Morocco, its mission to prevent a reported plan by Arab extremists to storm the American Navy communication station there. While this company did land, according to Pate, there had been no need to order the two battalion landing teams ashore in Egypt since diplomacy had ended the fighting. No trouble occurred at Port Lyautey either.

If these revelations were not sufficiently embarrassing, General Pate dropped another bombshell in the same interview. He calmly asserted that the Marine battalion landing team routinely afloat with the Sixth Fleet in the Mediterranean was armed with nuclear artillery shells.[31]

These revelations caused a considerable uproar in Washington, for they had serious foreign policy implications. For example, had U.S. Marines forced their way ashore during the Suez Crisis, the United States might have had a nuclear confrontation with two of its closest European allies, Britain and France. The story also raised the possibility that American troops might use nuclear weapons during any confrontation with Arab nations.

When the story broke, Pate would neither confirm nor deny its accuracy. Neither would he confirm or deny that he had even made the statement. The episode angered

Eisenhower, and he decided to handle the situation personally. Other high officials, including Secretary of State John Foster Dulles, received orders from the president to say nothing and to direct all press inquiries to James Hagerty, the White House press secretary. Pate himself received a summons to the White House for a face-to-face meeting with the president. Pate did not reveal the nature of Eisenhower's discussion with him, though he admitted that the situation had been personally embarrassing.

Press Secretary Hagerty issued the administration's official statement on 4 January 1957. He told the press, "I have no comment on the story, other than to say that the President has given no authority for the use of atomic or any other weapons in the Middle East." Thus, he did not explicitly deny that the Marine unit in the Mediterranean had a nuclear capability. In any event, news stories about Hagerty's statement pointed out that it was widely known that American aircraft carriers, at least one of which was always on station in the Mediterranean, carried nuclear weapons. They also noted that the only Marine weapon capable of delivering a nuclear warhead was the Honest John surface-to-surface artillery rocket. In addition, the news reports said there was no information as to whether any of the Honest Johns were in the Mediterranean.[32]

Rumors of problems in Pate's relationship to the president continued to circulate. According to news accounts later in 1957, President Eisenhower was not particularly fond of General Pate, and many in Washington reportedly were aware of his feelings. For that reason, said the newspaper account, there was considerable surprise in September, when Eisenhower nominated Pate for another two-year term as commandant of the Marine Corps. Most knowledgeable people in Washington, the story continued, expected the president to nominate Lt. Gen. Merrill B. Twining, who had performed so well in devising the Corps's response to the Ribbon Creek tragedy.[33]

Twining already had become something of a shadow commandant, operating quietly behind the scenes from his post as commander of the base at Quantico, Virginia. His assignment there allowed the Marine Corps, as a corporate body, to try at least to protect both itself and its erratic commandant from further rash actions by General Pate. Fortunately, Pate quite rightly trusted Twining's judgment and telephoned him often. Many of the advancements which occurred during Pate's tenure, including progress toward implementing helicopter mobility and the related reorganization of the Fleet Marine Force, came more from Twining and other senior Marine officers than from Pate.

The Headquarters staff had other ways of protecting the Marine Corps and Pate. In many ways, the best place for Pate was to "hide" him out in the various field activities and commands. During 1957, for example, he made four extended trips away from Washington between March and October. His destinations included the Far East, Central and South America, and Marine bases on the east and west coasts of the United States. The average duration of each of these trips was three and a half weeks.[34]

This ploy could backfire, of course, as it did over the issue of Marine dependents overseas. The necessary base housing for wives and children did not exist at Marine bases in Japan and the American-administered island of Okinawa. In some cases, there was no space on the bases to build such housing, and, given the fiscal austerity of the period, there was little likelihood the Eisenhower administration would authorize or seek the additional funds for that purpose. Taking the money from funds already appropriated would have slowed the Corps's moves toward modernization. Allowing large numbers of dependents to live off the local economies overseas was not desired either, partly because of the quality of the available housing and the unwanted effect it would have on the American balance of payments.

These reasons were not articulated. To have done so would have placed the Marine Corps at odds with the president and Congress, and might have fostered the image overseas of Americans as racists who looked down upon other peoples, cultures, and nations. In addition, the Corps's dominant concern was to foster the expeditionary mobility of its Pacific-based combat units.

Given the latter conviction, the Marine Corps chose to take a hard-line approach to the question of dependents overseas. Its well-known and publicly stated policy was that combat units in the Pacific were expeditionary forces ready to mount out for combat on short notice. The presence of dependents would only degrade that readiness. Thus, wives who dared to travel at their own expense to their husbands' Pacific duty station met a cold official welcome. Some found their husbands suddenly in receipt of orders to another command in another country. The husbands found they were endangering their careers after such travel by wives became a litmus test of a marine's loyalty to the Corps. Unfortunately, this rationale, while an accepted fact of life for older marines, only angered younger ones. Periodically, there were confrontations which got into the newspapers.[35]

General Pate stepped into the middle of such an episode during one of his trips to units in the Pacific. When asked by reporters about the policy, he reaffirmed the Marine Corps position about dependents outside the United States. His statement caused considerable resentment throughout the Corps, for, at the time, Mrs. Pate was traveling with her husband during his official inspection tour of overseas bases.[36]

Stories of such gaffes circulated among marines worldwide, and reinforced rumors of a commandant with a weak character. Some came to believe Pate an alcoholic and a womanizer. One story held that at a formal dinner he had passed out, face down in his plate. There also were stories that he made frequent trips to New York to enjoy the free food and drink offered by a well-known nightclub owner who was a former marine.[37]

General Pate's reputation was a tarnished one; however, the greater tragedy was that it rubbed off on those officers close to him. Men who were working diligently to advance Marine Corps programs and to compensate for Pate's flaws wound up tarred with the same brush. They became guilty by association. Their loyalty to Corps and country cost some of them their day in the sun. The truth of that became clear when it came time to appoint Pate's successor. The senior generals of the Marine Corps, including General Pate, were advocating Lieutenant General Twining as the next commandant. The senior officers knew of Twining's vital role as backstop to Pate and rightly believed he was highly qualified to be commandant.

Eisenhower would have none of it. He decided to clean house. In making his choice for the next commandant, he reached down the seniority list past every lieutenant general and six of the major generals and chose Maj. Gen. David M. Shoup. The latter, a Medal of Honor recipient for gallantry at Tarawa in World War II, received an immediate promotion to lieutenant general, and, on 31 December, his fourth star and the office of commandant of the Marine Corps.[38]

While the rank and file of the Marine Corps were happy to see Pate replaced, the president's selection meant, in turn, hard choices for those generals who had been senior to General Shoup. If they remained on active duty, they and Shoup would be in a delicate position. In addition, they were confronted with the impending loss of one of the era's cherished perquisites. Federal law permitted those naval service officers decorated in combat to be promoted to the next higher grade upon retirement. This promotion, commonly called a "tombstone" promotion, brought no additional retired pay, but did confer considerable prestige. The law would expire at the end of the year. Inevitably, there was a wholesale retirement of virtually all of those previously senior to General Shoup.[39]

General Pate and his wife began their retirement with a move to the quiet, historic coastal town of Beaufort, South Carolina. There he affiliated with a local real estate dealer who advertised in various service journals. These advertisements invited officers planning a move to Beaufort to allow General Pate to help them find a home.[40] This business relationship did not last long, for Pate soon proved to be a sick man. Approximately a year after his retirement from the Marine Corps, medical tests revealed an extensive intestinal tumor. Pate's health declined rapidly, and by July 1961 he was in Bethesda Naval Hospital, where he died on the thirty-first. He was buried in Arlington National Cemetery with full military honors on 3 August 1961.[41]

Randolph Pate's story and the ramifications of his erratic behavior were not over. The legal settlement of his estate revealed that he had willed his house in Beaufort to his alma mater, the Virginia Military Institute. While the provisions of the will permitted her to continue to live in the house, Mrs. Pate would not be able to improve her financial position by selling the house. That blow was particularly devastating because, legally, General Pate's retired pay ended with his death.[42]

The Marine Corps "family" did not ignore Mrs. Pate's plight. Another general officer alerted Lt. Gen. Wallace M. Greene Jr., the new assistant commandant of the Marine Corps to her predicament. General Greene found a way to help her. He knew that if General Pate had a medical problem prior to his retirement, Mrs. Pate would be eligible for a pension. Therefore, he asked the Navy medical department to reexamine Pate's health records, particularly those related to the physical examination taken at his retirement. The records, including some x-rays, turned up evidence of a brain tumor. This qualified Mrs. Pate for a pension from the Veterans Administration.[43]

Any analysis of General Pate's tenure as commandant of the Marine Corps must take his health problems into consideration. Randolph Pate, whose abilities earned him the nickname of "the Wizard" early in his career, simply was a sick man for at least some portion of his tenure and not up to the physical and mental demands of his office. Whatever the reason, General Pate did not add luster to the office of commandant. It was not, however, a period of failure for the Marine Corps, but it was a time of difficult transition. The Corps was struggling to remodel its combat forces to make best use of helicopters in amphibious warfare. Achieving that goal, as well as maintaining its role as the nation's force in readiness, proved difficult under the austere budgets of the Eisenhower administration's "new look." Money for equipment and people was hard to come by. Since the Navy faced the same budgetary problems, the Marines had to compete with other naval service interests for the scarce dollars needed for a new generation of amphibious ships and helicopters. The Corps got only part of what it wanted during the Eisenhower administration, although it largely succeeded during a "golden age" of defense spending during the subsequent Kennedy years. While the Pate era was not one of failure, sadly, the credit for Marine Corps successes under President Eisenhower belongs not to General Pate but to other loyal, dedicated Marine colonels and generals. They bore the heavy burden of a commandant suffering from an undetected illness, and still managed to serve the Marine Corps and their country with great distinction.

22

David Monroe Shoup

1960–1963

HOWARD JABLON

Gen. David M. Shoup became the twenty-second commandant of the Marine Corps at a difficult time in its history. The Corps needed to be reformed and brought to the highest level of combat readiness. That challenge confronted a man whose background, military experiences, and temperament were well suited to the task. It was ironic that Shoup's birthplace would foreshadow his career. He was born on a farm near Battle Ground, Indiana, on 30 December 1904. Like other farm boys, he combined his schooling with daily chores. The demands of his childhood were always a source of great pride to Shoup, who throughout his life was fond of reminding people, "I'm just an Indiana plowboy."

After graduation from high school in Covington, Indiana, he enrolled in DePauw University, where he majored in mathematics and found diversion in sports. Shoup was a successful marathon runner and participated in wrestling and football but cannot be cast in the role of a "dumb jock." He narrowly missed making Phi Beta Kappa. Shoup's academic and athletic accomplishments were remarkable given his circumstances. He worked his way through college by waiting on tables, washing dishes, working in a cement factory, and enrolling in DePauw's ROTC program. Clearly, he earned the degree he received in June 1926. His college career, like his subsequent military career, was marked with the indelible stamp of his relentless drive.

Shoup never intended to pursue a military career after he graduated from college The only reason he later admitted why he enrolled in the senior ROTC program at DePauw was that "they paid you 30 cents a day for rations. . . . It came out to exactly $9 a month, which was exactly what I paid for my room rent, and in all truth that was the only reason I signed up for senior ROTC."[1] Whatever his initial motives, Shoup later changed his mind. The event, which started him on a career with the Marines, occurred during his senior year.

Gen. David M. Shoup, twenty-second commandant.
U.S. Marine Corps Photo.

Shoup, along with fellow cadets in the ROTC Scabbard and Blade Honor Society, attended a conference in New Orleans, where they heard the keynote speaker, John A. Lejeune, major general commandant of the Marine Corps. After his speech, the general encouraged members of the audience to send him a personal letter if they were interested in getting a commission in the Corps and if they were honor graduates at their college. Shoup was among those in that audience who wrote to Lejeune and who were later offered a commission.

After Shoup graduated, he went on active duty at Camp Knox for a two-week period in the Army Reserve Corps. Once again, his military activity was motivated by his need for money. He later recalled that "due to my financial status, which hovered around the zero point all my life up to this point, I got active duty at Camp Knox for a two-week period . . . [in the] Army Reserve Corps. . . . Every time I could get two more weeks' active duty, I took it, because I got good pay, more money than I ever saw in my life."[2] While he was there, he was asked to report for a physical examination for the Marine Corps in Chicago. Shortly thereafter, he accepted a commission as a second lieutenant in the Marine Corps and resigned his commission in the Army Reserve.

When Shoup's reserve tour was up, he went home to work on the family farm until he received word from the Marine Corps that he was to take his oath and then report for duty in Philadelphia. In Philadelphia on his first day as a Marine officer, he made his first mistake in the Corps. Shoup and sixteen other officers marched in before the commanding officer, Maj. Alley D. Rorex, to receive their assignments. Shoup was assigned to play football. Then the brash second lieutenant made a grave error by saying, "Sir, I didn't come in the Marine Corps to play football." Rorex responded by making Shoup stand at attention for at least twenty minutes and then told him, "From now on, the Marine Corps will tell you what to do, you're not going to tell us what you do."[3]

In addition to playing football during the 1920s and 1930s, Shoup served in a variety of billets both stateside and abroad. At different times he served in Philadelphia, Pensacola, San Diego, Quantico, Bremerton, Tientsin (Tianjin), Shanghai, and Peking (Beijing). His assignments varied a great deal. He served with the expeditionary force in China in 1926–27, worked with the New Deal's Civilian Conservation Corps in the Great Depression, and served with the American legation guard in Peking when the Japanese began their war with China. One of his assignments in the period was a tour on board the USS *Maryland,* which years later, during World War II, was the flagship for the Tarawa campaign. During this period of peacetime service, promotion came slowly. Shoup was promoted to first lieutenant in 1932, to captain in 1936 and to major in 1941. But the deterioration of the international scene transformed Shoup's career. As German victory followed victory, American national security policy slowly moved from isolationism in 1939 to active participation by 1941. Before Pearl Harbor was bombed, Roosevelt moved incrementally toward supporting the beleaguered British and others. One of Roosevelt's actions involved assisting in protecting strategically located Iceland, the way station in the transatlantic shipping lanes. Shoup served with the brigade Roosevelt sent there. While Shoup was there, Japan attacked Pearl Harbor. A year later, Shoup found himself stationed in New Zealand as operations and training officer (G3), 2d Marine Division. Now a lieutenant colonel, he was assigned as an observer with the 1st Marine Division on Guadalcanal and the U.S. 43d Infantry Division in Rendova, New Georgia. At Rendova, Shoup received the first of his two Purple Hearts.

The battle for the Tarawa atoll in November 1943 was the high point of his combat experience during World War II. Shoup helped plan the campaign, for which he was awarded the Legion of Merit with Combat "V," but his greatest service was in the fighting itself. Tarawa was one of the bloodiest campaigns of the war up to that time. As the Medal of Honor citation he received for his heroism stated, Shoup was the man largely responsible for the victory.

After Tarawa, Shoup participated in the Saipan and Tinian campaigns as chief of staff, 2d Marine Division. Gen. Wallace M. Greene, a fellow officer who served with Shoup in Saipan, recalled Shoup's bravery. On one occasion he and Shoup were stranded in a forward observer position during a Japanese tank attack. They had only two weapons, a .45-caliber pistol and a bayonet. Greene remembered his anxiety and how unperturbed Shoup was during that kamikaze-like assault. Shoup, Greene observed, never seemed afraid of anything.[4] In any event, for his work in the Saipan and Tinian campaigns, Shoup received a second Legion of Merit with Combat "V." Three months later, in October 1944, he was back in the United States.

From 1944 to 1956, Shoup served as logistics officer, Division of Plans and Policies, Headquarters Marine Corps; commanding officer, Service Command, Fleet Marine Force Pacific; division chief of staff, 1st Marine Division at Camp Pendleton; and commanding officer, Basic School at Quantico. The most challenging of all his assignments during this period was his tour as assistant fiscal director, Headquarters Marine Corps in 1952, and his subsequent promotion to fiscal director. In his new role in the financial affairs of the Corps, he participated in the dismantling of the quartermaster general's empire and helped create the modern fiscal apparatus of the Marine Corps.

In his position as assistant finance director, Shoup served under the domineering Maj. Gen. William P. T. Hill, the quartermaster of the Marine Corps and now head of the powerful Supply Department. The new commandant, Gen. Lemuel C. Shepherd, wanted Shoup to establish the framework of a new fiscal office independent of Hill's authority.[5] Lt. Gen. Gerald C. Thomas, Shepherd's chief of staff, recalled that Hill fought Shoup every step of the way: "Shoup had a real rough time. It took two years to do that job. But he stayed with it."[6] The result was the establishment of the new, independent Fiscal Division.

In April 1953, Shoup was promoted to brigadier general, and several months later, in July 1953, he was named fiscal director. "As soon as General Shoup started working in the fiscal area," Lt. Gen. Frederick L. Wieseman recalls, "and he started going over for the hearings on the Hill—the budgeting hearings—he realized that we just couldn't go over and talk about a program. . . . It had to be something that was thought out and formulated, and the details had to be worked out."[7] Consequently, at Shoup's insistence, a programming system was initiated, despite substantial resistance to it in the Corps. The battle was not won when Shoup left, and one of the things he emphasized to his replacement, Frederick Wieseman, was to "keep after them, make them do it, make them see that they don't let it die."[8] That innovation and others started modern comptrollership for the Corps. For his contribution, Shoup was promoted to major general in September 1955.

While serving as fiscal director, Shoup was called upon once again to act as a "troubleshooter." In May 1956, Cmdt. Randolph McC. Pate assigned him to the newly created post of inspector general for recruit training. That assignment was made in response to the highly publicized Ribbon Creek tragedy, an episode involving the accidental drowning of six recruits in Ribbon Creek at Parris Island during a punishment march. An investigation of the incident was ordered by Commandant Pate with Brig. Gen. Wallace M. Greene in charge of the probe. When Greene took control of subsequent reform efforts, he looked for support at Headquarters and found his staunchest ally was General Shoup. Shoup wanted no cover-up, and he supported the courageous effort to reform recruit training.[9]

Following his brief tour as inspector general for recruit training, Shoup served in a variety of billets, including inspector general of the Marine Corps, 1956 to 1957; commanding general, 1st Marine Division at Camp Pendleton in 1957; and commanding general, 3d Marine Division on Okinawa in 1958. Then he returned to the United States to serve what appeared to be his "sunset" tour as commanding general, Marine Corps Recruit Depot, Parris Island in 1959. It was during this last tour that he received the surprising news that on the advice of Secretary of Defense Thomas Gates, President Dwight D. Eisenhower had named him the twenty-second commandant of the Marine Corps. He was rapidly promoted first to the rank of lieutenant general, then general, before assuming his duties in January 1960.

Shoup became commandant during a period of transition. He was appointed by President Eisenhower, but he served under President John F. Kennedy from January 1961 until Kennedy was assassinated in November 1963, and he finished his tour under President Lyndon B. Johnson. These presidents had much in common. They sought long-term solutions to the problem of Soviet expansion; they made defense policy an important part of their attempts to contain communism; they refined containment, strategic deterrence, and forward collective defense; they placed the development of nuclear weapons at the center of American strategy; and they were able to implement their defense policies because they enjoyed congressional and public support.[10] But they approached national defense issues differently.

Eisenhower and Kennedy, in particular, pursued markedly contrasting policies. Eisenhower's defense policy was colored by his view that the United States must avoid proxy wars like Korea because such conflicts seriously weakened the economy. Given this outlook, he shaped a defense program that emphasized spending cuts and nuclear deterrence as the more economical way to assure national security. The "new look" of his administration relied upon the threat of nuclear escalation to stop Communist-inspired local wars. Along with the club of "massive retaliation" to deter Soviet expansion, deterrence was supplemented with overtures to secure international arms control agreements and an end to above-ground nuclear testing.[11] Some were skeptical, notably Democratic senators like Johnson and Kennedy, who had presidential aspirations and who sought to make the new look a campaign issue. Their attacks on Eisenhower's defense policy received support from a group of strategic revisionists who advanced an analytical approach based on economic theory, game theory, and psychological modeling.[12]

During the Kennedy administration, strategic revisionism led to a dramatic change in defense policy. Kennedy's conception of military reform, "flexible response," meant that the United States would respond to any Communist military threats with appropriate, matching force which would, in the long run, promote international stability and prevent nuclear war. His approach also involved more centralization and civilian participation in defense policy making. To achieve that end, the Department of Defense, led by Robert S. McNamara, became the principal agency to effect the transformation. McNamara embraced both concepts with great zeal, quickly organizing a team of policy activists, scientist-engineers, and "think-tank" veterans to implement this new approach to defense decision making.[13]

Under McNamara's guidance, decision making became more systematic. He instituted the planning-programming-budgeting system in the defense budget process and organized budget categories by function (e.g., strategic deterrence) instead of "inputs" (e.g., manpower procurement). McNamara also developed the Five Year Defense Plan that coupled defense spending with missions that cut across service lines. His approach made it possible for his advisers to apply systems analysis to establish the "cost effectiveness" (military capability) for different levels of expenditure. As it developed, systems analysis became a formidable weapon to use against service requests.

But it was not McNamara's intention to debilitate the services. Rather, there was a shift from the nuclear deterrence and weaponry of Eisenhower's new look to an emphasis upon improving and expanding conventional forces that would fight without nuclear weapons. McNamara supported the Marine Corps amphibious mission, which allowed for the deployment of two division-wing teams. And he encouraged the Army to increase its firepower and mobility. While the Marine Corps and Army benefited from McNamara's support in the long term, many of his "reforms" had unfortunate consequences.

Shoup was commandant during the transition from the new look to the flexible response, policies designed to correct the presumed mistakes of the previous administration. Similarly, Shoup's appointment was motivated by a conviction that the Marine Corps had been heading in the wrong direction and needed a strong leader to steer it back on course. When the time came to replace General Pate, Secretary of Defense Gates seized the opportunity to recommend a successor that would reform the Corps. From Gates's point of view, the reputation of the Marine Corps had been tarnished by the Ribbon Creek episode; its effectiveness diminished by internal squabbling between "teams" (cliques); and its relationship with other services strained by excessive self-aggrandizement. He remembered that "when it came time to finding a successor we felt that . . . the Marine Corps needed to get back some old-fashioned rules of being real tough fighting Marines and a man with an extraordinary combat record was the kind of man we wanted to run the Marine Corps. We didn't want a fellow who was gonna, you might say, play politics." Gates preferred people with distinguished combat careers, and he selected his own aides, in both the Navy Department and the Defense Department, from combat veterans. He was, moreover, annoyed by what he regarded as the "defensiveness" of the Marine Corps. He observed that "the Marine Corps runs a little bit scared. . . . They always are afraid [that] they'll be too dominated by the Navy or they're afraid they'll be too dominated by the other services." Gates thought that too much time was being spent on unnecessary lobbying in the Corps's behalf: "I never could understand it because I thought their merits . . . were earned in blood over . . . history."[14]

When Gates recommended Shoup, a major general, he passed over three aspirants who were lieutenant generals: Edward Pollock, Vernon E. Megee, and, most prominently, Merrill B. Twining.[15] Gates remembered that dipping down to select a leader was not unprecedented. Admiral Burke was selected to head the Navy, though many were senior to him. Similarly, he bypassed others senior to Shoup because he believed they were less desirable. "As I remember it," Gates recalled, "his main competition was General Twining. And General Twining was a fine officer and his principal assistant and workhorse was General Krulak. And those were the two people who were head of, you might say, the geopolitical side of the Marine Corps. They were always [concerned] about the Marine Corps's position in strategy, the Marine Corps's position in policy; they were always writing papers of substance that argued the merits of the Marine Corps's value and in competition with, you might say other people."[16]

Gates's reservations about Twining and his supporters stemmed from their previous actions during the debate over the merger of the armed services. Twining was an active member of a group organized by General Thomas to prevent the subordination of the Marine Corps in the Navy.[17] A member referred to the group as the "Little Men's Chowder and Marching Society." The entire membership proudly referred to themselves as the "Chowder Society," as they worked tirelessly to secure Congressional assistance and a favorable press. Eventually they succeeded. Their campaign preserved the role of the Marine Corps within the military establishment.[18] After the merger threat passed, the group remained in existence, becoming a powerful clique which some feared and labeled the "First Division Gang."[19]

Twining's behavior also adversely affected his chances for becoming commandant. His vigorous campaign for the position antagonized several high-ranking officers who disapproved of the maneuvering by Twining and his supporters. Shortly after the announcement of Shoup's appointment, General Wieseman wrote Shoup:

> I can't name the exact composition of the Task Force that was organized to conduct the campaign. My belief is that MBT [Twining] himself chaired it. Brute [Krulak] has certainly been executive vice president. Murray was a big honcho and Hittle the big contact man. Many good people became very apprehensive about the situation, but an organized minority can inflict its will on an unorganized rabble any time. . . . Nobody had any fear of Twining's personal behavior, but it was almost a certainty there would be friction with the Navy and at JCS level, that there would be hell to pay, vis-à-vis Marine Corps Aviation and that there would only be one set of views considered in making policy. Furthermore the non-team players could expect to be used for the betterment of the "ins." The efforts of TTF [Twining Task Force] to use that pressure was then pointed out and the people in

> the secretary jobs didn't like it. One last thing. There has been a clear understanding that nobody owns Shoup, that there is no sense busting up one clique if another is established and that the Marine Corps's interests are paramount.[20]

Wieseman was not the only general who welcomed the sinking of the Twining Task Force. There were others who wanted an independent leader.[21] When Shoup's appointment was announced, Twining retired immediately in a symbolic protest as well as an expression of his disappointment. Others retired as well. Some believed they just could not work with Shoup, some wanted a "tombstone" promotion to four-star rank, and some were encouraged by Shoup to leave.[22]

The retirements afforded Shoup an opportunity to place new general officers in key positions.[23] His determination to sweep the decks was apparent immediately. When outgoing commandant Pate suggested that he and Shoup prepare a slate for the general officer billets in the Corps, it precipitated a disagreement. In mid-August 1959, Pate invited Shoup to work with him on drawing up assignments for the generals, noting that "they [the general officers] are trying to G-2 what you and I have in mind. Using [Maj. Gen. Thomas A.] Wornham as an example, I am certain that he is wondering now whether he will be given one of the FMFs with three stars. [Maj. Gen. Joseph C.] Burger probably the same and others likewise. [Lt. Gen. Robert] Bobby Hogaboom, I think, intends to remain on. In fact, I know he does."[24] Shoup responded with a memorandum listing his recommendations, which included retaining General Wornham in his position as commander of the recruit depot in San Diego (a two-star billet), asking one general to retire by 1 January 1960 and leaving Lieutenant General Hogaboom's name off the list.[25] Pate acquiesced to most of Shoup's recommendations but insisted upon an important billet for Wornham. Ultimately, Shoup had to "acknowledge the fact that the secretary of the navy is recommending that Major General Wornham be assigned to duty as commanding general, FMF, Pac."[26] In any case, he had his way when it came to selecting officers for two crucial positions. Shoup selected Lt. Gen. Wallace M. Greene Jr. as his chief of staff and Maj. Gen. Frederick L. Wieseman as his deputy chief of staff.

Clearly, the selection of Shoup signaled a change in direction for the Marine Corps. His distinguished record and a career free of the blemishes of politicking and interservice competition made him the logical choice for Eisenhower. While the president did not participate directly in the process, undoubtedly those responsible for making the recommendation to him knew how Eisenhower and Shoup viewed security matters.[27] Shoup shared, for example, Eisenhower's fear of the undue influence of the military-industrial complex.[28] For Shoup the problem was that the

> United States did not have and does not have . . . a national security policy . . . and I have always thought that that was the genesis of the military-industrial complex, simply because here were the Chiefs sitting down there wondering, what armed forces should we have to meet the requirements of the Commander-in-Chief and

> our nation? When actually it should be the other way around. There should be a national security policy that tells the armed forces what to be able to do. So this annually rolled up into obviously hundreds of millions of dollars that the armed forces said they needed because they didn't have any directive.[29]

Consequently, the military, in its desire to be ready for any contingency, in Shoup's judgment, fell prey to large corporations with their host of scientific experts who argued persuasively for new and expensive military hardware that was not really needed.[30] That conspiratorial view along with Shoup's frugal attitude and his experience as fiscal director made him the logical choice for an economy-minded administration.[31]

When Shoup took over as commandant, he emphasized combat readiness and cooperation with other branches of the military. In his first address to the Corps he announced that he intended to take "the grips of the plow and my furrow will be straight and true."[32] That meant bringing the Corps to the highest standards of combat readiness possible. Shoup knew that while he would have to remind the other branches of the military, the administration, and Congress of the appropriate role of the Corps when planning military strategy, he did not have to act defensively. He cautioned against that "stifling psychology inherent in the slogan 'They're sniping at us,'"[33] and he urged his fellow marines to be more confident. No other branch of the military was better prepared, he reminded them, to carry out amphibious landing operations.[34] With that in mind, he assured them he would insist that the Marines be represented on the Joint Chiefs of Staff and other councils to protect the Corps's interests and have its special skills taken into consideration.[35]

Shoup's plans for combat readiness included curtailing the politicking in the Corps. He was well aware of how "teams" were formed to enhance the position of senior officers and advance the careers of junior officers.[36] When he commanded Basic School, he saw how some young second lieutenants schemed to ensure their future promotions. Shoup observed how they planned a succession of assignments under certain officers who might further their careers and help them avoid assignments that might lead to career-killing mistakes. All that was to end immediately. From now on, Shoup announced, Headquarters would assign "jobs commensurate with your demonstrated potential for future assumption of greater responsibilities."[37] He went on to caution, "I do not expect to see the situation exist where a considerable number of personnel on the official and personal staffs of general officers go with them from post to post and endure the same duty assignments year after year without regard to what may be the best for the Corps or the individual."[38] Shoup reminded everyone that the Fleet Marine Force was the main reason for the Corps's existence and that assignments to the FMF would include a cross-section of the Marines.

Shoup emphasized the importance of training as well. He demanded at the outset that all commanders, regardless of their level of command, undertake training of their troops as a basic part of their mission.[39] Producing combat-ready men with the will to fight was part of the Marine doctrine of vertical assault, a principle that would also involve incorporating new weapons into the arsenal of amphibious forces. But Shoup also said, "You don't overlook the fact that no battle was ever won by Marines in a boat, amphibious tractor, helicopter, ship, or transport aircraft. Battles are won by Marines with their feet on the ground."[40]

But victory on the battlefield did not mean that the Marines had to be experts on communism. When Senator Strom Thurmond criticized the Marine Corps and other branches of the military for not training the troops adequately on the evils of communism, Shoup regarded the criticism as interference. He did, however, acquiesce when the senator demanded that his staff be allowed to administer an examination to test the average marine's knowledge of Marxism. Some marines were tested, and they did poorly. Thurmond then announced to the press that the test proved that the Corps was not teaching the dangers of communism. Infuriated by the charge, Shoup countered publicly and privately. He later recalled, "I didn't feel that we needed to have Strom Thurmond and his henchmen determine for me what I taught the Marines about Communism or what the general position of the individual private was, and the fact that he couldn't define dialectical materialism or something like that shouldn't really determine whether he was a good Marine or whether he wasn't, or whether he could fight for his country or whether he couldn't, and to worry people with things of that kind was really immaterial. I thought it was rather ridiculous. So I went to the Secretary of the Navy."[41] Secretary Fred Korth sympathized with Shoup, and the whole matter was dropped.[42]

Preoccupation with combat readiness made Shoup a demanding commandant. He would not tolerate poor performance or forgive any mistake made a second time. He was particularly hard on senior officers and often cruel to them. General Wieseman remembered that soon after he became deputy chief of staff, he was cross-examined by Shoup on the details of his report. "I didn't know the details," Wieseman recalled, "so he was getting a little bit irked at the fact that I wasn't better informed." Wieseman, annoyed by the interrogation, left Shoup's office and returned with brown bags filled with the supporting evidence for his report. "I don't know what's in them and I don't expect ever to know," Wieseman then said. "If you expect me to know all the details of every one of these papers, you'd better get yourself somebody else right now because I am not." Shoup retreated, saying, "Now, now, now, don't get yourself all excited." Shoup's treatment of Wieseman was typical. He would bully people, testing them to see if they had the courage of their convictions and were capable of independent judgment. If a general was poorly prepared or weak-kneed during staff meetings, he would curse at him.[43]

Some of Shoup's behavior, including the cursing, was staged. He was fond of using theatrical displays of both anger and humor to make a point. He had, for example, a favorite way of discouraging mindless conformity, a weakness he despised. If an officer justified his behavior by saying, "Well, it's always been done that way," Shoup would first unload some choice profanity and then present the officer with a copy of the poem "Cow Path," which he kept on his desk. The poem concerns the origins of highways. It describes how, in the earliest period of our history, cows wandered aimlessly in the woods, beat down the brush, and in time created cow paths. Later these paths became trails for frontiersmen entering the wilderness. When settlers headed west, their wagons widened these trails into dirt roads. Finally the roads were paved and expanded, and eventually they became highways. As the poem suggests, Shoup believed that many accepted practices were originated by bovine minds.

Sometimes Shoup's behavior toward senior officers was unnecessarily abusive and coarse. In staff conferences, he often singled out General Greene, chastising him in front of other officers. General Wieseman witnessed how Shoup would "start in on Wally. Finally, he'd throw the papers [that were on his desk] at Wally and he would turn on Wally."[44] At Headquarters, he constantly referred to one of his general officers with an expletive.[45] And he often swore at senior officers in the presence of junior officers—a serious breach of military courtesy.[46] On one occasion, an officer told Mrs. Shoup, "You don't have to worry about your husband getting ulcers, he just gives them."[47] But if a subordinate performed well for him, Shoup was a warm and supportive person.[48] Even those who suffered most from Shoup's attacks, like General Greene, would say, "I admired Dave because of his dedication. I could put up with his cruelty."[49]

On some matters, like proper military dress, he was particularly exacting. But his concern for proper attire did not include carrying the swagger stick. For Shoup, the swagger stick symbolized elitist affectation, and it reminded him of some unpleasant experiences he had had in China when he was a young officer and observed British officers toss money at coolies and then beat them with their swagger sticks as they bent over to pick up the coins. That display of arrogant cruelty made a deep impression on Shoup and later prompted him to make the swagger stick an "optional" piece of attire. "There is one item of equipment about which I have a definite opinion," he said shortly after becoming commandant. "It is the swagger stick. It shall remain an optional item. . . . If you feel the need of it, carry it."[50] Few marines did.

Having marines who could think for themselves and take pride in their appearance were part of Shoup's preoccupation with the Corps's readiness. His initial emphasis on combat readiness rather than defense policy was a response to the Eisenhower administration's hostility toward preparation for conventional warfare and concern about the economy. That concern had a devastating impact on the Marine Corps's budget, which was cut from the modest 942 million dollars for fiscal year 1958 to $902 million for fiscal year 1961. The austere budget and a manpower ceiling of 175,000 for the Corps were severe limitations on Shoup. "Nevertheless," he said, "our most important job is always to think and work hard to get as much fight from our plight as we possibly can."[51] To that end, he planned to remove marines from the logistical and supporting organizations and reactivate to full strength five of the six cadred battalion landing teams.[52]

The situation changed after Kennedy was in office. Kennedy's policy of flexible response benefited the Corps immediately. In the first six months, the administration recommended that the Marine Corps be increased to 190,000 and its budget be increased by 67 million dollars. Supplements proposed for the fiscal year 1962 budget and the administration's request for increased defense spending for fiscal year 1963 benefited the Corps. That largesse was augmented by Secretary of Defense Robert S. McNamara's policy, allocating funds by military function, not by branch of military service.

Ironically, a major difficulty emerged as a result of the new administration's favorable attitude toward the Corps's mission in conventional warfare. It led to an embarrassment of riches. These developments exposed serious weaknesses in the Corps's supply system. Specifically the weakness was in accounting, and stemmed from the lack of a central automated inventory control system. Both Marine Corps Headquarters in Washington, D.C., and the Philadelphia supply depot participated in procurement and storage accounting. Headquarters maintained records on more costly equipment, and the supply depot kept records on materials used in great volume and on replacement parts. The arrangement caused such confusion that the Fleet Marine Force never knew what supplies it had or what supplies it needed.

One of Shoup's solutions to the supply problem was to eliminate the "Supply Duty Only" category of personnel. In his testimony before the Senate Armed Services Committee on 13 July 1961, he defended House Resolution 4328, which reassigned officers designated for supply duty as officers not restricted in the performance of their duties to that one area. Shoup argued that supply matters could not be isolated. Sound fiscal management and logistics planning and operations had become so interrelated with supply that the restrictive designation "Supply Duty Only" was unrealistic and artificial. Shoup argued that the need to do away with the SDO system was hastened in recent years by the Corps's procedure of holding a commander responsible for the management of his command's fiscal affairs. To succeed therefore, the commanding officer had to be competent in both supply and fiscal matters since neither could be handled separately.[53] "There is no better way," Shoup continued, "to learn the requirements of supply in our small organization, which is devoted mostly to combat organization, than to get out and . . . understand what the supply is all about."[54]

Shoup's testimony was followed by a statement from Maj. Gen. William P. T. Hill, then retired, the former quartermaster general of the Marine Corps. Hill objected to the bill because, in his judgment, most of the current SDO personnel would "suffer enormously when considered by later selection boards as best fitted for promotion to the next higher grade."[55] He advised against disturbing the supply arrangement in the Corps, or, as an alternative, turning over all aspects of supply to the Bureau of Supplies and Accounts and allowing present supply officers to transfer to that organization if they wished.[56]

Hill's fears proved to be unfounded. After the bill was enacted, Shoup created a new occupational field in the Corps which included the areas of supply, financial management, and logistical support. Those who served in the new branch were not limited in promotion or restricted in assignments.[57] Nor did former SDO's suffer under the new system. As Shoup subsequently pointed out in a letter to Mrs. Hill: "Since you were so sincere in your belief that former SDO's would suffer in selection for promotion, I thought you might be interested to know that in recent selections, indicated on the attached sheet, the former SDO's made out better than anyone else. Of course this is an indication that they had some mighty fine people in the business."[58] Shoup put an end to the subordination of supply personnel.

Another of Shoup's solutions to the supply problem was his development of an effective inventory management program that applied modern data-processing techniques to supply, disbursement of funds, and the management of deposits.[59] On 1 August 1960, the Data Processing Division was set up at Headquarters to centralize the data processing functions of the Supply Department, the Personnel Department, and the Administrative Division.[60] The data processing officer who directed the division was responsible to the commandant for recommending policies for the program.

But Shoup's administrative successes were not always matched by similar gains on security matters. Soon after the Kennedy administration took over, he was faced with the intrusive activities of the Central Intelligence Agency. Problems began when the agency carried out Kennedy's order to continue its plans for a covert operation against Fidel Castro in Cuba. Kennedy endorsed the operation, originally sponsored by Eisenhower, within the first weeks of his administration. Castro had made insulting remarks about the United States during the presidential campaign, and Kennedy promised to do something about Cuba. After the election, he decided to continue the CIA's plan to "Guatemalize" Cuba. In effect, the CIA planned to duplicate an operation that had succeeded in Guatemala in 1954. That operation involved overthrowing a reputedly Communist-oriented regime with American-trained rebels. Similarly, the CIA was training Cuban refugees to invade Cuba in hopes that other Cubans on the island would join forces with the rebels. About fifteen hundred Cuban refugees were recruited by the CIA and secretly trained in Guatemala by American officers with American equipment.

At first, Shoup knew nothing about the operation. When he was asked by the CIA to supply the agency with an officer, it did not reveal the purpose of the request.[61] Shoup did not object to the agency's clandestine behavior, but later, when he learned they were requisitioning Marine supplies without consulting him, he was infuriated. The CIA, he recalled, "had carte blanche on anything you had. They could take your tanks, your artillery, or your any other thing, and you [had to] put 'em on the dock in accordance with the document they had in their hands."[62]

Shoup learned about the operation after the invasion started. On the night of the attack, the Marine colonel he had assigned to the CIA telephoned Shoup in a desperate attempt to enlist the commandant's help. He asked Shoup to appeal to the president to provide air support for the invading force. Apparently Kennedy had been persuaded by his advisers to reverse his earlier decision to use American air cover. The colonel believed that without air support, the whole operation was doomed. But Shoup did not intervene. No air support was provided, and the rebels were defeated.

After the disaster at the Bay of Pigs, the Joint Chiefs were blamed for the failure of the invasion. Shoup thought the criticism was unfair because the Joint Chiefs were never called upon to assist in the early planning of the operation. They knew that an amphibious operation could not succeed without air cover, but they were not consulted.[63] Surely, Shoup maintained, the Joint Chiefs were not in a position to argue with the president once a decision had been made.[64] In the final analysis, Shoup argued, any blame had to be leveled at the CIA for not consulting with the military when the agency was planning the invasion.[65]

Shoup also failed to resist counterinsurgency warfare strategy, an approach that was favored by the Kennedy administration. In 1962, Kennedy created the Special Group (counterinsurgency), which included representatives from the State Department, AID, the Defense Department, USIA, the JCS, and the Justice Department. The purpose of the group was to unify the U.S. effort in preventing and resisting subversive insurgency and other forms of indirect aggression. Meeting weekly, the group discussed a diverse agenda of items that ranged from reports on operations in places like South Vietnam to developing a national counterinsurgency doctrine.

While most senior generals in the Corps shared Shoup's antipathy toward counterinsurgency, Maj. Gen. Victor H. Krulak was a staunch supporter of that strategy. He shared the administration's belief that the primary targets in Third World countries were not the usual military ones, like seizing territory or destroying communications systems. Rather, it was a form of psychological and ideological warfare, a battle for the loyalty of a people.[66] Krulak believed that "our soldiers were ill-prepared for a war where you weren't going to capture anything; [and] that we needed to re-orient our thinking in terms of how you win a battle which is inside a man's bosom."[67]

Krulak became the Marine Corps expert on counterinsurgency in his capacity as special assistant for counterinsurgency and special activities under the direction of the JCS. In that assignment, he was charged with the preparation of plans, policy, and doctrine in the field of counterinsurgency, psychological and unconventional warfare, and special plans and operations. How he came to be named to that position is unclear. General Krulak himself heard three stories: "My acquaintance with the President went back to World War II when he was a PT boat commander. And I won't go into the adventures which we shared together, but suffice it to say he knew me. When I got to Washington, he told me that he had selected me personally. General Shoup told me that he had selected me . . . [and] an admiral who knew me very well told me that he had suggested my name."[68] In any case, Krulak recalled that "Shoup was not in the least antagonistic to my assignment, and, as a matter of fact, probably was in favor of it."[69]

But they disagreed on the viability of counterinsurgency. Krulak believed that Shoup oversimplified the strategy, comparing it to the earlier Marine combat against guerrillas in Central America. Consequently, Krulak remembered that Shoup only "gave it lip service because the president demanded it. But he was very frank with me to say that he didn't believe in it."[70] Certainly Shoup gave only nominal support to its implementation in the Marine Corps. Aside from increasing formal instruction in counterinsurgency in the Marine Corps Schools and training troops in counterguerrilla warfare, he did nothing to realize the ambitious socioeconomic, psychological, and ideological goals of counterinsurgency preparation.[71]

Shoup's fear that counterinsurgency warfare was a dangerously unrealistic response to political developments in the Third World increased when events in South Vietnam became more ominous in 1962. At the time, the government of South Vietnam was fighting a losing battle against Communist guerrillas. Kennedy responded to South Vietnamese appeals for help by sending military advisers, which included a small Marine contingent, to train South Vietnamese troops. Although the initial involvement of the Corps was very limited, Shoup anticipated the possibility of a much greater commitment in the future. Consequently, he decided to go to Vietnam in 1962. His visit was brief, but he saw enough to be convinced that under no circumstances should the United States become involved in a land war in Southeast Asia.[72] At that juncture, Shoup cooperated with the limited efforts to help the South Vietnamese. Despite some initial reservations, in April 1962, he sent a helicopter squadron and supporting troops to provide South Vietnamese forces with more air mobility.[73]

Operation Shufly, as it was called, coincided with a similar effort on the part of the United States Army to provide helicopter transport to the Vietnamese who were attacking the Viet Cong guerrillas in the Mekong area. The helicopters proved to be vulnerable to ground fire, and when members of Congress learned that they were being knocked down by Vietcong forces, they expressed concern. But Shoup, in testimony before the House Subcommittee on Appropriations, believed that "considering the terrain and the tactics of approaching with general forces, plus an envelopment from overhead, that is the only way they are really going to catch these people."[74] Subsequently, when a more ambitious role for helicopter units was being discussed, Shoup demurred. Using helicopter gunships to provide air support did not appeal to Shoup. When he testified before Congress, in 1963, he argued that "the helicopters, to do this job in an area where the enemy is actually present, makes a poor platform and is not as good as an attack airplane."[75] In any case, Shoup remained skeptical about any greater military involvement in Vietnam.

Later, in the summer of 1963, when Kennedy expanded the advisory role of the United States in South Vietnam, Shoup grew alarmed. He expressed his objections in graphic terms to Col. Edwin H. Simmons, one of his action officers who had been participating in some discreet interservice negotiations. Simmons's efforts led to an informal understanding as to what the Marine Corps's involvement in the advisory effort in Vietnam would be. Simmons thought he won a considerable victory by securing a generous share for the Marines. When Simmons reported his triumph to Shoup, the commandant said, "Simmons, what makes you think that I want to put any more Marines into Vietnam?" Simmons replied that he thought it was in keeping with the on-the-job training program Shoup instituted when he commanded the 3d Marine Division in Okinawa in 1959. "We don't want to piss away our resources in that rat hole," Shoup replied.[76]

Shoup was also concerned about the squandering of U.S. military resources elsewhere. When, for example, the Cuban missile crisis emerged, he counseled restraint and he found himself taking a minority position. Aerial reconnaissance over Cuba in mid-October 1962 revealed that Russian technicians were installing nuclear missiles, which were estimated capable of striking targets as far away as two thousand miles, endangering major cities and industrial centers in the United States. Kennedy responded to the Soviet activity by declaring a "quarantine" on all ships carrying weapons to Cuba. He also issued an ultimatum threatening war to the Soviet Union.

American military forces were placed on alert. The Joint Chiefs convened to discuss various military alternatives, and they calculated what it would cost in men and materials to invade Cuba. For the most part, they were optimistic and predicted that an invasion would not involve large casualties or much loss of equipment. Shoup disagreed. To illustrate his pessimistic assessment, at one session of the JCS, he used an overhead projector. First he placed a map of Cuba on the top of a map of the United States. On the screen, the island appeared to stretch from New York to Chicago, demonstrating that Cuba was not small, but eight hundred miles long.[77] Then Shoup placed a transparency with a red dot on top of the map of Cuba. The dot represented the island of Tarawa, the scene of one of the bloodiest battles of World War II and the place where Shoup won the Medal of Honor. Shoup told the JCS it took three days and eighteen thousand marines to take Tarawa. Imagine, he implied, the cost to take Cuba. Shoup was not opposed to invading Cuba. But he wanted the Joint Chiefs to realize the high price for victory.[78] As events unfolded during the period of the Cuban crisis from 1 October to 15 December 1962, the Fleet Marine Force had to be ready to perform a number of important duties, including evacuating dependents from the naval base at Guantánamo Bay, conducting reconnaissance flights over Cuban territory, preparing to defend Guantánamo from attack, conducting aerial bombing sorties on specified military targets in Cuba, and launching an amphibious assault to seize Cuba.[79] These efforts were of such a magnitude that preparation to carry out the overall mission involved the participation of over forty thousand troops.[80] Fortunately, combat was averted when Kennedy and Soviet premier Nikita Khrushchev resolved the crisis with diplomacy that removed the missiles.

Fear of the spread of communism in the Caribbean kept the Marines active in the area. When it appeared that instability in both Haiti and the Dominican Republic might invite Castroism there, the United States had amphibious forces training near Puerto Rico and the west coast of Hispaniola. In addition to those troops, there was a small detachment, mainly Marines, in Haiti assigned to train their armed forces as well as carrying out the regular functions of a naval mission under the ambassador. The commander of the mission was Col. Robert Heinl, and while he was an effective leader in many ways, he became the center of considerable controversy. He was not only very critical of the dictatorial François "Papa Doc" Duvalier regime, but he was very vocal as well. An accomplished writer, he was approached by *Life* magazine to write an article about conditions in Haiti, which soon immersed him in controversy at home as well as in Haiti. In February 1963, Heinl was declared persona non grata and asked to leave the country. In the 8 March issue of *Life,* an article, "It's Hell to Live in Haiti," appeared.

The publication of the story prompted an investigation. Heinl was called to Washington to stand before an investigation headed by Brig. Gen. Bruno D. Hochmuth, and he was found culpable for not complying with regulations which stipulated that he secure special approval by appropriate authority prior to publishing the article. Shoup concurred with the investigation and "chewed out" Heinl privately.[81] Later, Heinl was passed over for brigadier general.

A year after the missile crisis, Khrushchev startled the world by proposing a nuclear test ban agreement. When Khrushchev made his proposal, Kennedy was amenable to the idea of a ban, but he sought the advice of the Joint Chiefs to ascertain its military implications. When the issue was placed before them, it provoked a heated debate so intense that the chairman, Gen. Lyman Lemnitzer, arranged for each member of the JCS to meet privately with Kennedy. Shoup was excluded, ostensibly because he was not a full-fledged member and his sitting with them was supposed to be limited to those matters that directly affected the Corps. But by that time Shoup had gained the president's confidence and had frequently been called to the White House for private consultations. Consequently, on this occasion too Kennedy sought Shoup's views. When Shoup met with Kennedy, he endorsed the treaty, saying that "the President of the United States, with his responsibility to posterity had to do everything he could to get a test ban treaty." Then Kennedy asked Shoup why he had not come over earlier, along with the other members of the Joint Chiefs. Shoup reminded him, "You know, Mr. President, I'm only a member, or get to participate in the manner of a member, on matters pertaining to the Marine Corps." Kennedy just smiled.[82]

Perhaps he smiled because Kennedy liked Shoup. In 1963, when Shoup's term as commandant was coming to an end, Kennedy asked him to remain. Shoup refused. He told the president that he could not serve because "if I did so I would prevent ten or eleven other general officers with varying years of service from twenty-five to thirty from ever being considered for the job."[83] Kennedy acquiesced though it is likely he would have found some way to keep Shoup close to his administration. After the Cuban missile crisis, President Kennedy's relationship with the Joint Chiefs was strained and, increasingly, he turned to Shoup for advice. In time Shoup became his favorite general, a feeling that was evident in the friendly way he acted toward Shoup. On one occasion, for example, he teasingly challenged Shoup to carry out a directive by President Theodore Roosevelt in 1908 requiring Marine Corps company officers to march fifty miles in twenty-four hours. Kennedy also said he would ask his own staff to do the same. Shoup accepted the challenge and sent out a Marine detachment from Camp Lejeune, North Carolina. The Marines surpassed the 1908 standard, but only one member of the president's staff went the distance. Attorney General Robert Kennedy hiked fifty miles from Washington to Camp David.[84]

A more significant indication of the president's growing trust in Shoup was how Kennedy was moving away from the McNamara-Taylor commitment toward involvement in South Vietnam and embracing Shoup's view that it was not our fight. By September 1963, Kennedy was publicly expressing his view that the South Vietnamese government had to win its own struggle.[85] The following month, on 30 October 1963, Kennedy met Senator Wayne Morse of Oregon and discussed the war in Vietnam. Kennedy told Morse he was planning to withdraw all advisers from Vietnam on 19 March. Kennedy also told his private secretary, Mrs. Evelyn Jones, that after he returned from Dallas, the first one thousand advisers would be withdrawn, followed by others until all of them were home.[86] Kennedy was killed three days later. And the assassin's bullet also ended Shoup's influence on the administration's Vietnam policy.

Shoup retired when his tour as commandant was over in December 1963, but he did not just fade away. Unable to influence the Johnson administration directly, which continued and expanded American involvement in Vietnam, Shoup became a war protester. His public attacks on the administration's Southeast Asian policy started in May 1966, when, in a speech to an audience primarily of college students, he said,

> I believe if we had and would, keep our dirty, bloody, dollar crooked fingers out of the business of those nations, so full of depressed, exploited people, they will arrive at a solution of their own, which they will design and want, that they will fight and work for. And if, unfortunately, their revolution must be of the violent type, because the "haves" refuse to share with the "have nots" by any powerful method, at least what they get will be their own and not the American style which they don't want crammed down their throat by Americans.[87]

He reiterated that view in testimony before Congress in 1968, noting, "I would like to say that I am pretty sure that more people today believe in what I said than they did a year and a half ago."[88] Shoup continued to protest the war in Vietnam, and he broadened his indictment of the United States national security policy. In an article published in the *Atlantic Monthly* in April 1969, he and his collaborator, Col. James Donovan, accused America of becoming a militaristic and aggressive nation, a country ready to "execute military contingency plans and to seek military solutions to problems of political disorder and potential Communist threats in the areas of our interest."[89]

Shoup's outspoken criticism of the Vietnam War upset many in the Corps, including those who had been closest to him. In retrospect, some thought he was slipping mentally;[90] others believed, at the time and later, that his behavior was treasonous.[91] One marine who criticized Shoup's war protesting was the retired-officer-turned-journalist Robert Heinl. In a number of scathing articles for the *Detroit News,* he accused Shoup of going sour on his country and his brother officers.[92] Many agreed, including one of his closest friends and fellow officers, Gen. Rathvon M. C. Tompkins. Tompkins was so incensed by Shoup's war protesting that he refused to speak to Shoup for many years.[93]

Now virtually isolated, Shoup sailed his last cruise in a storm of national controversy over the war in Vietnam. For Shoup, participating in some way in the major events of his day was normal for him. His military career spanned a period of American history disturbed by the Depression, a world war, and the cold war. And he met the vicissitudes of a career caught up in those very troubled times, surmounting each new trial, strengthened by his ordeals, and better prepared to meet the next test. Tempered by his experiences, he was prepared, as commandant, to take the Marine Corps out of the mire of internal and external politicking and bring it to a new high in combat readiness. The methods he used were often unpleasant, even unfortunate, but always a fine officer if not always a refined gentleman, his excesses have been forgiven by those who worked closely with him. In a tribute to Shoup, General Greene acknowledged:

> There can be no doubt that General Shoup was a tough and brutal individual, but his type was needed at this point in Marine Corps history. Like General [Thomas E.] Watson whose chief of staff he had been during the campaigns for Saipan and Tinian, Shoup had an undying faith in the Marine Corps and the ideals and traditions which it represented. A sundowner or a bastard as you may choose to term him, he was worth every ounce of support because of his loyalty to the Corps for which he was quite prepared to die (witness Tarawa). Extremely shrewd, the best poker player of his time (both in cards and the military), a fine judge of men and their motivations and behavior, he came to the commandancy at a time when such a driving force was sorely needed. Truly a great man! Let us remember that.[94]

Shoup died of a heart ailment in Alexandria, Virginia, on 13 January 1983. He was buried in Arlington National Cemetery with full military honors on 17 January, an appropriate recognition for a marine who always had been faithful to his country and the Corps.

23

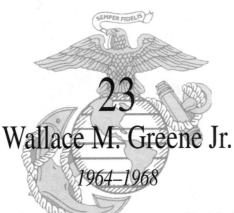

Wallace M. Greene Jr.

1964–1968

COL. ALLAN R. MILLETT, USMCR (RET.)

Wallace M. Greene's first day as commandant of the Marine Corps went according to schedule, following the time-honored rituals of installing a new head of the Marine Corps. At 0900 the secretary of the navy, the urbane Paul H. Nitze, administered the oath of office in Room 4E710 in the Pentagon. After a brief reception for close friends and associates in the secretary's office, the commandant returned to his quarters at Marine Barracks, Washington, the brick compound three blocks from the navy yard. At 1000 the Marine Band serenaded the commandant and Mrs. Greene and then entered the Commandant's House for punch and snacks. The next day, all the ceremony ended. After brief courtesy calls on the members of the Joint Chiefs of Staff, the new commandant flew west for a two-week visit to Marine commands in the western Pacific. With the United States widening its commitment to the war in South Vietnam, the tour seemed the most pressing order of business, for General Greene wanted a personal look at the officers, troops, and equipment that he might soon send into battle. Wallace Greene's tour as commandant began and ended with the war in Vietnam as his central concern.[1]

Born on 27 December 1907 in Waterbury, Vermont, Wallace Greene grew up in the modest, warm household of his father, a prosperous grocer, and mother, a successful milliner. An avid outdoorsman, Greene, a short, sturdy youth, roamed the woods and fields of the Winooski River Valley and the forested slopes of the Green Mountains. He also worked in his father's stores and learned something of poverty in Burlington's working class neighborhood. He excelled in school, and he supplemented his formal schooling with self-improvement projects. Graduating from high school in Burlington, he then attended the University of Vermont for one year. Attracted by the competitive examination and the lure of service life, Greene won an appointment to the U.S. Naval Academy in 1926. As a student of history, he knew the local tales of the "Green Mountain Boys" and the superb performance of Vermont's regiments in the Civil War, in

Gen. Wallace M. Greene Jr., twenty-third commandant.
U.S. Marine Corps Photo.

which his grandfather had served as a corporal. The only marine Greene saw before he entered Annapolis was an aviator on leave in Waterbury, but that marine's dress blue uniform impressed the youth. At the Naval Academy, Greene learned much more about the Marine Corps. Navy officers discouraged promising midshipmen from "wasting" their talents in the Corps, but Greene found the prospects of adventurous service and the chance to develop military skills wider as an officer of marines. Upon his graduation in 1930 (118 in a class of 402), he accepted a commission as a second lieutenant and immediately entered the Basic School, Marine Barracks, Philadelphia, for a year's special training as a junior officer.[2]

Until the United States' entry into World War II, Greene's career followed the normal course of promising young ground officers who pleased their superiors with their attention to duty, discipline, troop leading skills, and general military smartness. Greene's assignments in his first ten years of service showed his growing capacity. After a year's assignment to the Navy Yard, Portsmouth, New Hampshire, he joined the Marine detachment of the battleship *Tennessee* for two years' sea duty. Following a new fascination with naval aviation, Greene reported to Pensacola for flight training but found he lacked the skill to become a first-rate pilot. His appreciation for aviation and aviators, however, did not crash with his ambition to be a pilot. More shore duty in the United States and additional training with the Army in chemical warfare ended with a short assignment to the Marine Barracks on Guam.

Selected for promotion to captain in 1937, Greene left Guam to join the 4th Marines in Shanghai, where he spent two highly educational and satisfying years as a company commander and regimental staff officer amid the Sino-Japanese battles that roared around the borders of the International Settlement. During this service he experimented with dividing his rifle squads into four-man "fire teams" for security duty and street-fighting operations. Returning to the United States, Greene attended the Junior Course at the Marine Corps Schools, then commanded the new 1st Chemical Company of the 1st Marine Brigade during the 1940 Caribbean landing exercises. In an expanding Fleet Marine Force, Greene moved into the operations section of the new 1st Marine Division in April 1941. Six months later, he traveled to embattled Great Britain as a "special naval observer" for three months service with British commando units and attended amphibious warfare and demolition schools. His reports contributed to the development of new landing force techniques. Promoted to major during his trip, he returned to Camp Lejeune in February 1942 to a Marine Corps and nation at war.

A planner with a thirst for detailed information, Greene sailed with the 3d Marine Brigade to Samoa in April 1942 for what appeared to be a new front in the South Pacific, the islands protecting the delicate supply line between the United States and Australia. For a year, however, the war left Greene behind as Samoa changed from a potential Japanese target to a major training base for Marine units bound for the Solomons. As the operations and training officer of the brigade (AC/S, G-3), Greene again proved his ability as an organizer of training, and as a new lieutenant colonel, he joined the headquarters of the V Amphibious Corps in Hawaii in November 1943. Dominated by its perfectionist, impatient commander, Maj. Gen. Holland M. Smith, the V Amphibious Corps staff was no haven for the fainthearted as it studied the lessons of Tarawa and prepared for the assault on the Marshalls. As part of the campaign, Smith formed Tactical Group (TG) 1, an ad hoc Marine-Army brigade formed to exploit the 4th Marine Division and 7th Infantry Division assaults on Roi-Namur and Kwajalein. Green's assignment as G-3, Tactical Group 1 was an obvious choice since Greene was intimately familiar with the 22d Marines, the largest Marine unit assigned to the force. Greene also proved capable of working for Brig. Gen. Thomas E. Watson, the TG 1 commander and one of the ablest (and worst-tempered) Marine senior officers. Greene survived the Eniwetok landing despite the worst "Terrible Tommy" the Japanese could throw at the undermanned TG 1 staff and won his first Legion of Merit for exceptional service.

Moving with General Watson into the command of the 2d Marine Division in March 1944, Greene teamed for the first time with another sturdy driver, Col. David M. Shoup, the division chief of staff and Medal of Honor winner for his command of the Tarawa assault. For the V Amphibious Corps offensive upon the Marianas, a key objective in the Central Pacific war, Wallace Greene served as the 2d Division G-3, which meant that his three immediate superiors were Shoup, Watson, and Holland M. Smith, a trio of vocal, volatile extroverts who demanded prompt, perfect staff work. Wallace Greene again performed with aplomb on Saipan and Tinian and won a second Legion of Merit. He also formed a personal bond with David Shoup, sharing with him the division's periodic crises and an occasional foxhole when the Japanese endangered the division command post with shelling and banzai attacks. Rich in recent operational experience, Greene returned to the United States in October 1944 and finished the war in responsible billets at Headquarters Marine Corps.

As a lieutenant colonel and colonel, Greene fought the battles of readiness, training, roles, missions, and joint actions until his promotion to brigadier general in 1955. In a service not overly endowed with managers, he served in operations and training billets with Troop Training Unit, Amphibious Force Atlantic and the Marine Corps Schools before attending the National War College. Greene then moved to the Joint Staff for two years of highly educational experience (1953–55) as a JCS special assistant and representative on the staff of the National Security Council. He did not serve with the 1st Marine Division in Korea, largely because colonels' billets were few in number and tended to go to the highly decorated combat commanders of World War II who were favorites of Cmdt. Clifton B. Cates and Cmdt. Lemuel C. Shepherd. These favored officers tended to come from the "Guadalcanal gang," the 1st Marine Division veterans who had served with Cates and Shepherd in the 1st, 4th, and 6th Marine Divisions. Veterans of the 2d Marine Division, including Dave Shoup and Wallace Greene, did not receive the same personal attention in seeking the choice combat assignments during the Korean War.

In 1956, however, Shoup and Greene, both junior general officers, faced another challenge together, a challenge with career-destroying risks. The problem was Marine Corps recruit training in general and the public relations damage created by the accidental drowning of six recruits in Ribbon Creek at the Parris Island recruit depot. Cmdt. Randolph McCall Pate, another member of the "Guadalcanal gang," acted on the assumption that the whole Marine Corps, not a single incompetent drill instructor, stood in judgment for the Ribbon Creek tragedy. Promising congressional leaders that he would clear up the problem of recruit abuse before public opinion forced a congressional investigation, Pate made Shoup inspector general of recruit training (a new billet) and Greene commanding general, Recruit Training Command, Parris Island (another instant billet). Greene entered a storm of controversy. He found himself simultaneously responsible for conducting an investigation of the accident, arranging the court-martial of Staff Sgt. Matthew C. McKeon, and ending the rampant abuse by DIs. Although Pate's support proved inconsistent, the commandant wanted Greene to reform recruit training—in the face of hostility from the depot cadre and those active and former marines who believed that hazing and physical abuse made the best recruits. Harried by the press and uncooperative officers and DIs, Greene cracked down on abusers, increased physical training for recruits, tightened DI screening and training, and created a set of positive incentives for high recruit performance. A victim of hazing at Annapolis, Greene saw the difference between demanding physical performance and quixotic harassment. Institutionalizing his reforms, he found he had only one true champion at Headquarters Marine Corps: Dave Shoup. Believing in his cause if not his commandant, Greene pursued his reforms regardless of cost of his personal future. His policies, and demands for highly competent assistants, alienated some senior officers, and he was at first passed over for promotion to major general.[3]

After his Parris Island tour (May 1956–July 1957), Greene served briefly as commanding general at Marine Corps Base, Camp Lejeune, then returned to Washington as assistant chief of staff, G-3, in January 1958. Promoted to major general in August, he became deputy chief of staff (Plans), the commandant's principal liaison with the JCS. Then President Dwight D. Eisenhower, on the advice of Secretary of Defense Thomas S. Gates, surprised the Corps's senior generals by selecting Maj. Gen. David M. Shoup to be the next commandant. Shoup followed by assigning Wallace M. Greene Jr. to be his chief of staff with the rank of lieutenant general. Far different in personality and operating style, Shoup and Greene nevertheless shared an intense desire to reform Headquarters, to focus the Corps's attention on readiness-related administrative and logistical management efficiency, and to stress combat training, not the ceremonial functions and affectations favored by the Pate administration.

As Shoup's chief of staff, Greene spent 1960 adhering to Shoup's personal promise to Secretary of Defense Gates that the Marine Corps would abide by the manpower ceilings imposed by the budget-stabilizing policies of the "second new look." In practical terms this agreement meant not lobbying for 190,000 officers and men rather than the funded 178,000, a figure well below the Corps's peacetime needs. Instead, Shoup concentrated on improving FMF readiness—with his strategic eye on the Mediterranean and the Caribbean—while Greene restructured the Headquarters staff, improved the quality of Marine staff work for the Navy and Joint Staff, and carried on Shoup's reforms in logistical and financial management. Predicting more battles with the Army and the Air Force over tactical aviation roles and missions, Shoup and Greene drew the aviation staff at Headquarters closer to the chief of staff's direct supervision. In the meantime, John F. Kennedy and Fidel Castro combined to create a new era for the Corps, a period of expanding budgets, accelerated modernization, and increased contingency deployments in the Caribbean, where communism rooted in Cuba and instability plagued Haiti and the Dominican Republic.[4]

Although the "New Frontier" seemed to require ready conventional forces like the Corps to help bear any burden in the defense of freedom, the Kennedy administration also brought a new adversary to Washington, Secretary of Defense Robert S. McNamara. Using the 1958 amendments of the National Security Act, which authorized the creation of central defense agencies, and the president's firm support, McNamara brought dismaying activism to defense policy planning and management. He and his civilian subordinates introduced a bewildering array of procedural reforms to the Pentagon: program budgeting, cost effectiveness analysis, and commonality in service procurement. Headquarters Marine Corps enjoyed generally good relations with the White House (largely because of the Kennedy brothers' admiration for rough, iconoclastic Shoup), but Greene bore the burden of working with the harried Joint Staff and the frenetic assistant secretaries in the office of the secretary of defense. Greene organized a series of successful holding actions against OSD efforts to phase out major Marine logistical functions and installations, reduce tactical aviation, and strip administrative authority from the Department of the Navy. In sum, the Kennedy administration gave the Corps a degree of executive branch approval it had not enjoyed since World War II, but exacted a high price in administrative labor at Headquarters for its greater fiscal abundance. McNamara also made it more difficult for the Corps to maintain its traditional ties with Congress by stifling the independence of the chiefs and service secretaries. Wallace M. Greene bore the major responsibility for shaping the Headquarters staff for the explosion of demands for studies, data, quantitative analysis, and detailing programming that followed from OSD.[5]

The battle, however, was worth fighting, since the Kennedy administration and the Marine Corps agreed that the nation's most likely military challenges would be limited military confrontations with Third World Communists and Soviet surrogates. Although the Corps did not embrace one administration fad—counterinsurgency—it proved adaptable to the Kennedy strategy of "flexible response" in recurring Caribbean emergencies, including the 1962 Cuban missile crisis. At Headquarters, Greene established a special command center for crisis actions. He also recognized that the FMF needed major improvements in communications and logistics if it were to perform force-in-readiness missions for the impatient Kennedy administration. He and Shoup also repeated their concern over the decline in the Navy's amphibious capability and naval gunfire support. Greene became especially concerned about the armed forces' need for greater strategic mobility and the application of space age technology to rush troops and supplies to the world's trouble spots.[6]

Greene's services as chief of staff made him a natural choice to succeed Shoup as commandant in 1964—if "natural" means the broad approval of the White House, secretary of defense, secretary of the navy, the JCS, and a substantial portion of the Corps's other generals. Greene's only service drawback was his lack of combat command and field experience. As an effective administrator, astute political leader, and Marine Corps champion in the joint arena, his experience was unmatched at his rank. Although no logistics specialist, he appreciated supply problems and the arcane knowledge required of logistical managers. A tireless worker with no hobbies or vices, Greene demanded thorough staff work and long-range planning. When presented with sloppy briefings and incomplete data, his ire could match Shoup's, although his outbursts were less frequent and his language more restrained. His forte was a grasp of detail and an equal command of complex, large issues. He trusted the dedication and competence of the other Headquarters generals, which made him an attractive man to work for. Although blessed with an extraordinary memory, he kept detailed notes in a succession of pocket notebooks, which soon filled with line upon line in Green's precise, small handwriting. When an issue was in doubt or a position uncertain, Greene could usually find his subordinate's prior commitments and views safely recorded in one of his notebooks, a technique that encouraged his subordinates to take care and precision in stating their views. Articulate in speech and in writing style, Greene enjoyed cordial relations with Congress and his candor and charm commanded the respect of the JCS and OSD.[7]

Despite the pressures of the Eisenhower administration's new look, the Marine Corps held its institutional position that it was the nation's force-in-readiness for crises short of general war, crises that by 1964 seemed a permanent fixture of the cold war and the era of decolonialization. The Corps, of course, had fought more firmly for its roles and missions under David M. Shoup than it had under Randolph McC. Pate. Wallace M. Greene benefited from Shoup's successes and the Defense Department's commitment to flexible response and "a strategy of options" even after those concepts' champion, John F. Kennedy, died in November 1963. Greene foresaw an interminable series of crises abroad for which the Corps should continue to prepare. The Corps needed to perfect its operational readiness, response time, and sustainability in order to serve as the nation's primary strategic reinforcement outside of NATO. As long as the nation joined forward defense with strategic nuclear deterrence, it required a quick reaction force like the Fleet Marine Force. Greene and his planners saw no reason to scrap naval roles and missions or a maritime strategy of forward defense, and they saw both political and operational reasons to stay close to the Navy. But they believed that the Marine Corps should not be "artificially restricted to the maritime environment."[8]

Greene knew what the ready FMF would need in the future, and he formally endorsed a long-range plan for crisis control and alliance assistance operations in nonnuclear military confrontations. He established the highest priority programs for the FMF: the development of a VSTOL light attack aircraft, the accelerated procurement of heavy-lift helicopters, more and better fire support, sea-based logistics, electronic data processing equipment for both tactical and administrative purposes in the field, and an increase in the Navy's amphibious forces. Greene saw no reason to infringe on the Army's new role in counterinsurgency operations; he reflected, in fact, Shoup's position that the counterinsurgency mission did not serve the Corps's long-range needs and might retard its modernization. Greene was more interested in quick responses to international crises—and quick withdrawals. In his first news conference as commandant-select, he made headlines by suggesting that a space-age Marine Corps might ultimately send battalions by suborbital space vehicles to reinforce endangered allies. Greene believed that new technology would make traditional Marine tactical skill and esprit even more awesome.[9]

In part, the FMF's good health depended upon Greene's ability to maintain the Corps's political power within the Navy Department, and in 1964–65 the commandant believed that the Navy (with McNamara's urging) would assist, not impede, the Corps's modernization. Although the secretary made routine planning an arduous process, he had programmed a dramatic improvement in the Navy's amphibious force, which would expand to 143 ships by fiscal year 1972. For fiscal year 1965–69, he authorized 67 new vessels, primarily high-speed landing platform docks (dual surface-air assault amphibious ships) and landing platform helicopters (helo-assault carriers). This force would allow the FMF to deploy two Marine Expeditionary Forces (two division-wing task forces) with three-quarters of the force in twenty-knot assault shipping. In addition, a change in the wording of Navy Department General Orders 5 and 19 clearly gave the commandant control over all Marine Corps shore installations, especially aviation facilities, and made the chief of naval material responsible to the commandant for services provided the Marine Corps by the Navy, again primarily in the area of aviation logistics. Although the commandant remained responsible to the CNO for the readiness of those Marine operating forces assigned to the fleet, he had undeniable access to the secretary of the navy and enjoyed coequal status with the CNO not only for planning and programming but also as a "naval executive assistant" in the execution of plans. In sum, Greene helped enlarge the commandant's power to increase the Navy's support for the Corps's long-range plans and routine management.[10]

Concerned about the concurrent deployment of both Marine ground and air units, Greene insisted that FMF commanders and their Navy operational superiors plan to use only air-ground task forces. Although the Marine Corps had abandoned the concept of all-helo amphibious assaults for both operational and logistical reasons, Greene gave the LPD and LPH building programs the highest priority, for he believed that the FMF's unique tactical capability rested in its combination of ground combat and aviation units, a position he had championed as Shoup's chief of staff. As commandant, he advocated the same concept for FMF deployments that did not involve amphibious assaults. Greene cautioned his generals not to surrender this principle of FMF deployment. He reminded them that the recently established Army–Air Force "Strike Command" posed a possible threat to the Corps's force-in-readiness mission, primarily because McNamara had given "Strike Command" the principal responsibility for quick response missions in the Middle East. Although the FMF would continue to rehearse for Middle East contingencies, it would not conduct such exercises under the operational control of "Strike Command" if the commandant could prevent it. Instead, the Marine Corps would stand by its position that the FMF operated best under a naval task force commander, even if the operations themselves did not involve an amphibious assault.

Greene believed that the Navy would respect the inviolate nature of the Marine air-ground team while the Army and Air Force would not.[11]

During his first two years as commandant, Greene sought to hold the Fleet Marine Force on a steady, prudent path toward readiness and modernization. Benefiting from the early fiscal largesse of the Kennedy administration, Greene held his fiscal year 1965 budget request at $1.46 billion, then actually reduced it to $1.01 billion the following year when Marine procurement programs hit a temporary lull. Marine Corps category budgeting held steady: about 50 percent for personnel and personnel services; 15 percent for operations and maintenance; 15 percent for procurement; and the remaining 20 percent for base operations and research and development. General Greene's major internal concerns upon becoming commandant, in fact, focused on personnel policies: increasing Corps strength from 190,000 to 198,000 to allow fuller manning of the FMF, lobbying with the other service chiefs for a pay increase, extracting better medical care and housing from the Navy Department, and retaining noncommissioned officers with scarce technical skills.[12]

Although McNamara's analysis made periodic forays upon the Corps's aviation plans, in terms of numbers and aircraft types, Greene's initial problems with the air portion of the air-ground team stemmed from changes in Marine air made in Shoup's regime. As chief of staff, Greene approved of the changes, and as commandant he was determined to see the changes brought to fruition. Fundamentally, Marine aviation remained at around 1,100 aircraft, but its fixed-wing component in every aircraft type declined between 1961 and 1965. The fighter-attack squadrons largely switched from the single-seat F-8 Crusader to the dual-seat F-4 Phantom II and fell by 71 aircraft. The light attack force of A-4 Skyhawks improved with each model and added the first squadron of all-weather, dual-seat A-6 Intruders in 1966, but it declined by twenty aircraft. The reconnaissance-electronic warfare and tanker-transport forces also dropped in numbers. On the other hand, the transport and observation-utility helicopter force grew from 261 aircraft in 1961 to almost 400 in 1965.

The change in the aviation structure required a redistribution of Marine Corps aviators. Much to the dismay of fixed-wing pilots, who regarded helo pilots as second-class citizens in the aviation community, Headquarters forced five hundred pilots to shift from high-performance jets to helicopters. With Greene's support, the deputy chief of staff air, Maj. Gen. Norman J. Anderson, selected the pilots for helo transition in order to prevent group and squadron commanders from dumping their cast-offs on the helicopter squadrons. Greene also rejected a proposal, largely sponsored by the fixed-wing community, to create a special class of aviation warrant officers to fly helos, a program then under way in the Army, largely because he did not want to recreate a crop of Marine pilots who could not be assigned to general duties throughout the Corps. Acutely aware of the divisions between air and ground officers in World War II, the commandant wanted to ensure that the air-ground Corps was more than an abstract tactical principle maintained only for its uniqueness. Greene knew that only close collaboration by Marine officers who shared both ground and aviation assignments and who worked together to perfect vertical envelopment assaults would ensure the Corps's future. He also wanted to curb the fixed-wing aviators' bad habit of playing off the commandant against the deputy chief of naval operations (Air) whenever a favorite aviation program seemed endangered.[13]

On another aviation issue, Greene's decision displeased his helo pilots, for he ruled against the adoption of a special armed helicopter for escort and fire suppression missions. Although he allowed the arming of transport helos and the temporary modification of the UH-1 Huey utility helo as a gunship, Greene believed that jets could supply adequate helo support, despite their problems in target acquisition. Marine helo pilots already flying in Vietnam as part of Operation Shufly did not agree since their experience with South Vietnamese Air Force escorts was not happy. The commandant, however, argued that Marine air, including the new twin-prop OV-10A Bronco, a reconnaissance-light attack airplane, could provide close air support for helicopter assaults. In making a temporary concession, that Marine helos in Vietnam could arm, Greene insisted that aviators perfect the air-air team of fixed-wing attack aircraft and transport helicopters. His policy pleased his jet pilots but disappointed the helo community, which continued to argue for a force of gunships of its own.[14]

In addition to his concern about aviation programs, General Greene continued to modernize the Marine Corps logistical management system, largely through the aggressive leadership of his G-4, Maj. Gen. Leonard F. Chapman. Although no logistics expert, Greene knew that the Corps had endangered its credibility with Congress since the late 1950s through its ineptness in supply and fiscal accounting. In 1964, the General Accounting Office conducted major audits of Marine Corps maintenance, procurement, and supply distribution performance and found the Corps wanting. The fundamental difficulty was inventory control and data processing, which had led to chronic problems in locating and distributing equipment the Corps already had at its major supply depots. Without adequate information on its own inventories, the Corps had procured ammunition and equipment items it already had—not a happy development for a service whose logistical austerity had always been a selling point with Congress. Bringing an end to several Headquarters studies of the problem, Greene ordered the introduction in 1965 of the Marine Corps Unified Management System (MUMMS), which depended upon extensive use of electronic data processing equipment and intricate programming. MUMMS linked thirteen logistics subsystems through a primary inventory control point, the supply depot in Philadelphia. Although the shift to MUMMS was complicated by contemporaneous standardization programs imposed by McNamara's management experts, the reform eventually improved depot performance in meeting the orders from the Fleet Marine Force.[15]

The need to improve logistics performance helped dramatize another issue that drew General Greene's personal attention: the increased utilization of Women Marines (WM). In 1964, the commandant ordered a Headquarters board to examine the status and role of women in the Marine Corps and then endorsed its findings that the Corps could expand assignments open to WMs, especially logistics and base operations, in order to free more male technical specialists for service in the Fleet Marine Force. The number of Women Marines could be increased above 1,300, and, in fact, the WM force climbed to 168 officers and 2,158 enlisted persons by 1968. The commandant realized, too, that in order to attract quality women recruits and to retain WMs to the Corps, a bastion of Americanized machismo, it would have to allow WMs to work without sexual harassment and job discrimination while allowing them to maintain their femininity. Conscious that the public image of WMs did not enhance quality recruiting—the legend was that WMs were only anatomical variants of the most gung-ho Marine infantrymen—General Greene established a new training syllabus for WMs at Parris Island that included schooling in feminine grooming and social deportment. Greene considered his attention to improving the lot of WMs one of the most satisfying aspects of his tour as commandant.[16]

The reforms of Greene's Marine Corps increased the effectiveness of the Fleet Marine Force, and in 1964 and 1965 the FMF found several opportunities outside of Southeast Asia to demonstrate its heightened readiness. The major deployments also dramatized the Corps's limitations, largely imposed by the lack of shipping and logistical sustainability. With the Caribbean temporarily quiet, Greene approved FMF Atlantic's plans to expand its NATO-oriented exercises. Instead of limiting Marine amphibious exercises to thc Mediterranean, where Marine units embarked with the Sixth Fleet fell outside the central concerns of SACEUR, FMF Atlantic wanted a greater involvement in NATO exercises outside the Mediterranean. It was particularly interested in the reinforcement role for Norway on NATO's vulnerable northern flank. Although Marine participation in northern flank contingencies existed on paper, the first real training occurred in 1964 when a single rifle company from the 2d Marine Division went to Norway for a short period. The JCS, in the meantime, had approved a 1966 amphibious exercise in Norway by a complete amphibious squadron and embarked Marine Expeditionary Unit (a reinforced infantry battalion and helicopter squadron). Despite SACEUR's reluctance to involve a Navy-Marine air-ground task force into NATO's autumn war games, the JCS was examining plans to send an MEU to the Jutland peninsula for landings.[17]

To run a full test of its ability to reinforce NATO's ground forces, FMF Atlantic and the Second Fleet staged Operation Steel Pike in 1964, the first full test of II MEF's ability to deploy as an integrated air-ground team. Greene and his staff saw the exercise primarily as an opportunity to demonstrate the FMF's strategic mobility, which, in practical terms, meant that Steel Pike was meant to demonstrate the Navy's shipping shortages. When the assault elements of II MEF crossed the beaches of Spain, including the helo lift of an entire Marine regiment, Steel Pike had created an amphibious force of forty-three Navy vessels and seventeen MSTS cargo ships under military charter. In one sense Steel Pike produced impressive statistics, for II MEF embarked 21,642 troops, 5,174 vehicles, and nearly a million cubic feet of cargo. On the other hand, the Navy could not muster the shipping to load out enough vehicles and supplies to equip and sustain a full MEF in operations ashore. An exercise the next year on the California coast, Operation

Silver Lance, revealed the same sort of shipping problem, although I MEF's landing involved only about half the troops, vehicles, and supplies of Steel Pike. As tactical exercises, Steel Pike and Silver Lance pleased Headquarters, for both landings made full use of vertical envelopments and close air support as well as demonstrating the traditional élan and skill of Marine ground-combat units.[18]

In April 1965, FMF Atlantic demonstrated its operational readiness by leading the American military intervention in the civil war in the Dominican Republic. Neither side in the civil war warmed the heart of the Johnson administration and the State Department; on one side were rightist officers and troops associated with the Trujillo dictatorship, on the other were radicals from the Constitutionalist party and elements of the Army and police who supported the return of Juan Bosch, a leftist unacceptable to the Dominican military. Prompted by alarmist reports and political interpretations from the State Department that the civil war was opening the way for a Communist coup on the Cuban model, Lyndon Johnson authorized the Caribbean amphibious ready group (Amphibious Squadron 10 with the 6th MEU embarked) to land at the scene of the fighting, the capital city of Santo Domingo. The MEU's initial assignment was to guard the American embassy and provide an enclave for foreign civilians, including Americans, caught in the fighting.

As the American intervention widened to halt the fighting, the Marine commitment widened until FMF Atlantic had three reinforced battalions and supporting units ashore with an additional battalion and air units offshore in Navy vessels. The 4th Marine Expeditionary Brigade (MEB) could call for fixed-wing aircraft from the squadrons deployed to the naval bases at Guantánamo Bay, Cuba, and Roosevelt Roads, Puerto Rico. As the American diplomatic position tilted toward the rightist junta, the Marines moved east from the positions around the Hotel Embajador into the city in order to create an "International Security Zone," a Marine-held corridor that effectively isolated the rebels in the inner city. The advance brought accelerated sniping and, eventually, open street fighting in which nine marines died and thirty fell wounded before the fighting along the corridor faded away. In the meantime, Johnson ordered fifteen thousand soldiers (primarily from the 82d Airborne Division and the XVIII Airborne Corps) and one thousand airmen to the Dominican Republic to ensure that the leftist military forces did not interfere with the negotiations the president had opened through the Organization of American States.[19]

Assessing FMF Atlantic's performance in the Dominican crisis, and comparing it with Strike Command's, Greene found considerable cause for organizational congratulation. The FMF had again demonstrated its ability to respond quickly to emergency deployments with an afloat MEU, reinforced by additional ship-borne ground and aviation units. From Headquarters' perspective, Strike Command had, on the other hand, shown that Army–Air Force joint operations had not escaped their traditional bureaucratic obstacles and that Strike Command posed no serious threat to the FMF's force-in-readiness mission. Greene had no illusions about the 4th MEB's problems, for it had deployed without adequate civil affairs and service units. He also recognized that the

FMF's material readiness for sustained operations ashore was still short of the levels of supply established by Headquarters. Nevertheless, the commandant firmly believed that the Fleet Marine Force had in 1965 reached the highest peak of peacetime readiness in its history and had proven its effectiveness.[20]

However, the FMF faced its greatest test since World War II in the growing war in Southeast Asia. As Dave Shoup's chief of staff, Wallace Greene watched with dismay the Kennedy administration's gradual commitment of American prestige, wealth, and lives to the war in Vietnam. Unlike Shoup, however, who concluded that the United States had no great stakes in Vietnam, Greene saw the Communist insurgency as a direct challenge to American interests in the Pacific and a critical test of the nation's collective defense against "People's War." When Greene became commandant in 1964, he took Shoup's seat on the JCS and entered the deliberations that committed the Marine Corps to its longest and most trying foreign war. In 1964, there were fewer than a thousand marines in Vietnam, the majority serving either as advisers to the South Vietnamese Marine brigade or conducting helicopter operations with the Vietnamese Army (ARVN) from the airbase at Da Nang. When Greene left the active Corps at the end of 1967, the III Marine Amphibious Force (III MAF), an air-ground corps numbering 81,115 marines and sailors and reinforced by over 20,000 U.S. Army troops, was locked in battle with the guerrilla forces of the National Liberation Front and the regulars of the North Vietnamese Army (NVA). In part, Greene bore the responsibility for the Marines' presence, but he did not approve of the conditions and methods that characterized the ground war intervention.[21]

As the possibility of open American combat intervention mounted in 1964, despite Lyndon Johnson's fervent campaign pledges that he would not send American troops into an Asian land war, Greene carefully examined the Vietnam issue and decided that almost any path was better than the gradual escalation adopted by the Johnson administration. Although he did not believe the administration had defined a vital national interest that required intervention in Vietnam, he thought that American political credibility and military prowess were too committed to allow a withdrawal without victory. He could see no clear advantage to waging a proxy war with Communist China and the Soviet Union in Southeast Asia, and he was even more certain that the American public would not bear the taxes and casualties of a protracted conflict. He was absolutely sure that the war should be fought for a quick victory if it was fought at all, and he urged his military colleagues and civilian superiors to apply American military power, especially air power, as massively as possible. He did not urge the use of nuclear weapons, believing that air and limited ground operations against enemy sanctuaries in Laos and Cambodia and against North Vietnam itself offered the best chance for victory. Greene did not believe that the half-measures of 1964 would turn the tide, and he pressed the JCS and Johnson's OSD and NSC civilian advisers for a clear decision to wage the war as if the United States had the skill and will to win it.[22]

General Greene found the Johnson administration's policy-making practices especially frustrating. He had no great respect for the president himself, whose ignorance of foreign affairs, nervousness in dealing with senior military officers, and bullying all of his advisers made trips to the White House normally unpleasant. Greene knew that Johnson listened principally to Secretary of State Dean Rusk, Secretary McNamara, and Maxwell D. Taylor, chairman of the JCS. Greene had no confidence in the military judgment of any of these men, and Taylor, the former Army chief of staff turned White House flatterer, particularly irritated him for Taylor would not accurately report the positions of the other chiefs. By standing up to Johnson, however, Greene won the president's grudging attention, and LBJ occasionally used Greene's analysis of the war to challenge McNamara's advice. Greene also attempted to expand his influence over policy making by developing a close relationship with Vice President Hubert H. Humphrey, whom Greene personally briefed on the war. The commandant found the Johnson administration's theories of graduated escalation, illusions about negotiated settlements, and naive faith in the psychological impact of limited American operations an insurmountable barrier to rational policy analysis by the principal members of the National Security Council.[23]

When both the United States and North Vietnam escalated the war in early 1965—the first with a bombing campaign against the north, the second with a ground invasion to split South Vietnam through the Central Highlands—Greene and the rest of the JCS reexamined the possibility of American ground forces intervention, a politically impossible option before Johnson's reelection in 1964. The JCS's estimates were not optimistic, for they thought an American expeditionary force would reach almost one million men and require three years to defeat the Communists—if Johnson insisted on limiting the force's operations to South Vietnam. Such a commitment would require a Reserve mobilization, which the chiefs recommended. Johnson again equivocated, but he could not avoid an unpleasant fact: the ARVN could not stop the Communist offensive and protect American bases, particularly the airfields. To provide base security, two reinforced Marine battalions from the 3d Marine Division on Okinawa landed in the Da Nang area in early March 1965. Such a commitment—in fact, deployment of the entire 3d Marine Division—had been an active option for more than a year. The March operation, however, represented another minimal commitment, for Gen. William C. Westmoreland, commander, U.S. Military Assistance Command Vietnam (COMUSMACV), envisioned the Marines as local security forces only. Lt. Gen. Victor H. Krulak, commanding general FMF Pacific, had a larger view: Da Nang could be an enclave to either expand or withdraw an American expeditionary force for operations in the strategic northern provinces of South Vietnam. Clear strategic direction for the Marines, however, awaited further developments in the war.[24]

As the NVA offensive across the Central Highlands and against ARVN positions northwest of Saigon continued, Westmoreland requested that the JCS commit two complete Marine divisions and the 1st Marine Aircraft Wing to Vietnam's five northern provinces (I Corps) in order to secure his right flank from a third invasion. With Greene's support, Marine ground and aviation units from Okinawa, Japan, Hawaii, and California joined the war as part of the III Marine Amphibious Force, commanded by

Maj. Gen. Lewis W. Walt. Greene approved of the rapid ground buildup, just as he urged an unrestricted air war against North Vietnam and the Communists' supply lines.

At that point, however, Greene parted company with COMUSMACV on strategy, for he shared with Krulak and Walt a different vision of how the ground war should be conducted. In the summer of 1965, the troops of III MAF occupied three separate enclaves around Phu Bai, Da Nang, and Chu Lai. All three regions were heavily populated; in the An Hoa basin southwest of Da Nang, the Vietnamese averaged over one thousand people per square mile. Amid this sea of villagers moved the cadres and guerrillas of the NLF, mocking the attempts of the ARVN to root them from their lowland bases. Guided by instinct, some knowledge of British and French counterinsurgency operations, and the imperatives of security patrolling and intelligence gathering, III MAF Marines rapidly developed pacification techniques within the enclaves. These operations emphasized the protection of rice-harvesting villagers, cordon-and-search operations, night ambushes, and the constant movement of small patrols throughout the villages. Greene, Krulak, and Walt concluded that III MAF pacification-and-hold operations in the enclaves, which included effective operational direction of ARVN and all civil affairs programs, offered the best path of ultimate victory since, as Greene argued, "pure military action will not win."[25]

From his own study of the situation in I Corps, General Westmoreland concluded that III MAF did not have enough men or time to make pacification work, and he ordered Walt to stage multibattalion raids against Vietcong (VC) and NVA strongholds beyond the enclaves. Walt had no objection to big unit operations against VC strongholds near the enclaves; at the mildest urging he had ordered the first such attack in August 1965, which resulted in a major Marine victory over the 1st VC Regiment in Operation Starlite. Westmoreland, however, wanted Walt to create a two-three battalion mobile force in each of I Corps's five provinces, a policy that would have effectively ended III MAF's pacification strategy. With Greene and Krulak's support, Walt managed to balance token multibattalion operations with his pacification program. In part, he argued, his precarious logistical situation and limited helo lift prevented a more aggressive approach, and he was not satisfied that the ARVN and the South Vietnamese regional and local paramilitary forces could carry on pacification operations alone.

Greene and Krulak used their own ties with the JCS and CinCPac to blunt Westmoreland's call for more big battles, exercising an influence upon III MAF operations that COMUSMACV regarded as obstructionist at best and disloyal at worst. The argument over strategy reached Secretary McNamara, who sided with Westmoreland despite Krulak's persuasive evidence that small unit pacification operations killed as many Communists (and more important ones) as big unit sweeps—and with fewer American casualties and greater lasting political impact. Greene, also to no avail, urged that land operations focus on population control while air and naval units attacked NVA base camps and infiltration routes in Cambodia, Laos, and lower North Vietnam. The Johnson administration, however, chose to widen the ground war and limit air and naval operations against the Communists.[26]

Throughout 1966, III MAF managed to walk a fine line between large unit operations and pacification, possible largely because of the full commitment of both the 3d and 1st Marine Divisions. Large unit operations, which now encountered NVA regulars, concentrated upon the hill country and coastal regions along Route 1, the "rue sans joie" of Indochina war fame, and Route 9, which led to Laos. Despite awesome supply and maintenance problems, compounded by the monsoon rains and nagging transportation shortages, III MAF took the war to the Communists and expanded its enclaves until it contained eighteen hundred square miles and a million Vietnamese. Its big unit operations and hundreds of thousands of small patrols and ambushes had killed at least ten thousand Communists at a cost of seventeen hundred Marine dead. In fact, III MAF was fulfilling its multiple responsibilities to protect bases, assist the ARVN and GVN, pacify the countryside, and attack main force VC and NVA units when they emerged from their mountain bases. III MAF's emphasis upon pacification had been approved by President Johnson, at least implicitly, when he and his advisers met the South Vietnamese leaders in two 1966 conferences in Honolulu and Manila and pledged to concentrate on the political and economic aspects of national reconstruction. General Greene shared the administration's judgment that the Communists were now losing, that the VC infrastructure had been strained. But he still doubted that limiting the war to South Vietnam would bring it to a quick conclusion. He worried that the chronic instability of the South Vietnamese government and the inconsistent performance of ARVN would prolong the war beyond the point that public opinion would support it.[27]

Already bewildered by the first antiwar protests in the United States, President Johnson asked Greene about the Corps's morale. Greene reassured the president that all the vital signs—extensions of tours in Vietnam and enlistments and reenlistments—indicated that the Marine Corps held fast to its belief that the war was worthwhile and winnable. Greene was more concerned about the baleful influence of McNamara and his civilian associates upon the conduct of the war than he was about the enthusiasm of his marines. True to his conviction that the war, once accepted, had to be won, Greene had no trouble committing the Corps's considerable public relations skill to sustaining public support for the war effort. Accepting the fact that the nation's major newspapers and television networks were cooling toward the war, Headquarters Marine Corps concentrated on speeches, new conferences, television shows, and radio interviews through local media outlets. In 1967 alone, speakers from Headquarters made eleven thousand appearances in forty states; the busiest single speaker was General Walt, brought home from III MAF to serve in the new billet of deputy chief of staff for manpower and principal stump speaker for the Corps's war effort. Despite his growing dismay at the Johnson administration's failure to attack the North Vietnamese with its full military powers, Greene dutifully kept the Marine Corps, for the honor of country and Corps, squarely behind the war effort.[28]

The politburo of the Democratic Republic of Vietnam also remained solidly behind the war, as Ho Chi Minh, Vo Nguyen Giap, Pham Van Dong, Le Duan, Troung Chinh, and their associates had been since December 1946. Buffeted by the American military intervention in the ground war, the North Vietnamese regrouped in their sanctuaries and moved to change the battle for I Corps, which they were losing to III MAF. In the summer of 1966, a full division of the NVA crossed the Demilitarized Zone (DMZ) and moved toward the lightly defended coastal region between Dong Ha and Quang Tri. Marine battalions, lifted by air and sea, struck back in III MAF's bloodiest sustained fighting. The parry and thrust across the DMZ continued into 1967, and III MAF developed a system of combat bases along the DMZ. Their names entered Marine lore: Camp Carroll, the "Rockpile," Con Thien, Cam Lo, Dong Ha, and Khe Sanh.

Wallace Greene shared "Brute" Krulak's analysis of the changing tactical situation: the NVA offensive along the DMZ endangered the pacification campaign and increased Marine casualties without any appreciable gain. Restrained by Johnson's misguided ban on attacks north of the DMZ or into Laos, III MAF surrendered the initiative to the NVA and paid accordingly. There was no doubt about the fact that I Corps had become the ground war's central theater; the Corps's "share" of all battles in South Vietnam climbed from 18 to 45 percent, enemy dead from 13 to 44 percent, and American dead from 20 to 57 percent. Greene asked for more troops. Instead, McNamara and Westmoreland gave him Operation Dyemarker, a plan to create an engineering and electronic barrier across the DMZ. Support for Dyemarker, which Greene doggedly opposed, diverted scarce Marine engineering assets and covering infantry from the desperate battles against the NVA.[29]

From Greene's perspective, the Johnson administration and COMUSMACV had locked the American ground campaign into an endless war of attrition in which the Communists could control the tempo of the battle. Westmoreland, Greene reported to his fellow Marine generals in 1967, had become obsessed with matching the NVA, man for man, loss for loss along the DMZ. McNamara, on the other hand, was losing his influence on Johnson, but the damage had already been done since the president could not abandon his quixotic search for a negotiated peace. Using Westmoreland's own statistics on Communist losses, infiltration rates, and military manpower demographics, Greene proved to his own satisfaction that the Vietnam War could go on forever unless one of the belligerents made some dramatic move. He and his closest confidant on the JCS, chairman and Army general Earle G. Wheeler, pressed the president to widen the war directly against the DRV, but Johnson had lost his nerve. As Greene neared the end of his tour as commandant, he feared that the war for South Vietnam would not be won, despite the admirable performance of III MAF. In the cauldron of combat the Marine air-ground team had proven its effectiveness. The tragedy, not yet entirely clear, was that all the battlefield victories, all the administrative and logistical achievements in I Corps had done nothing to alter the war. Instead, the American commitment had only increased the war's ferocity and duration. Wallace M. Greene approached the end of his watch as the head of a Corps that had become one of the war's casualties.[30]

The expanded operations of the III Marine Amphibious Force brought accumulated strains to the Marine Corps, and by 1967 the commandant and his staff recognized that the Vietnam War had dealt serious blows to the Corps's long-term institutional interest.

General Greene did not accept the Vietnam conflict—and III MAF's protracted commitment to a conventional ground war and pacification campaign—as a model for the Corps's future development. Instead, he held to his vision of a high-technology FMF, poised on Navy amphibious forces, designed for sudden, short-term ascents from the sea against America's enemies, whomever and wherever they might be. Greene also saw the FMF as a fully capable air-ground team. He believed that the Corps's major challenge was to integrate its air and ground operations for maximum effectiveness, a challenge that could only be met by extensive investments in electronics equipment, air and ground mobility programs, logistics improvement, and weapons modernization.[31] The war, however, made it progressively difficult for the Corps to pursue plans not directly related to its current combat operations, and as the war continued, Department of Defense decisions actually shook the very foundations of Marine readiness and professional self-esteem.

Following its portion of Plan 1A, the OSD program for the deployment of ground combat forces to Vietnam, Headquarters in 1965 planned to expand the Corps by 85,000 officers and men by the end of 1966. Before this program was completed, HQMC received approval to add an additional increment of 14,000 men, thus increasing the Corps's programmed strength for 1967 to 92,000. Although the manpower expansion was designed to supply the FMF with sufficient marines to fight the war, HQMC plans had other goals. One program, approved in 1966 by OSD, was to raise the Corps's permanent active strength to 206,000, HQMC's long-sought goal for a three division–three aircraft wing FMF. To replace the 1st Marine Division in strategic reserve, the Marine Corps activated the 5th Marine Division at Camp Pendleton, and, at the same time, created additional units for III MAF. In both strength and unit activations, the Marine Corps met its 1966–67 goals.

Much to Greene's concern, the effects of the rapid expansion, which brought the Corps within 60 percent of its World War II peak strength, were widespread and, in some ways, harmful. Most of the problems flowed from Secretary McNamara's too faithful effort to make LBJ's war less domestically painful. Deprived of a mobilized Reserve, the Corps's level of experience and skill in its officer and NCO ranks declined dramatically. In the grade of sergeant (E-5) and corporal, the average years of service fell by half; the dilution came from rapid promotions caused by the expansion of the NCO ranks and the departure of nearly 5,000 sergeants to become temporary officers or warrant officers. At the lowest enlisted levels, most of the enlistees, encouraged by patriotism and the draft, met expectations, but the Corps had to take 19,000 draftees to reach its goals. It also had to accept 18 percent of the Pentagon's "New Standards" men, who could not meet normal enlistment criteria. The combination of personnel actions meant that by the end of 1966, nearly 150,000 marines had less than a year's service, and some of them had a limited desire to become true marines.

With a third of the Marine Corps in Vietnam, personnel turbulence ruined the rest of the FMF Atlantic Coast units, both air and ground, which had more than 100 percent turnover in 1966 and 1967. Readiness plummeted. With demand for combat marines twice that of the Korean War, the Corps attempted to operate from a troop base only thirty-one thousand marines larger than at its Korean era peak. Although HQMC could find adequate junior officers and enlisted men for combat assignments, largely by increased recruiting and shortened training, it soon faced serious personnel shortages in officers and NCOs in combat service support billets. Almost half of the Corps's MOSs (military occupational specialties) were not adequately manned to supply III MAF without ordering the Vietnam veterans of 1965–66 back to the war in less than two years. HQMC extemporized: retirements in some MOSs were suspended, and reenlistment bonuses increased. Nevertheless, career NCOs chose not to reenlist in increasing numbers in 1967. Aviation specialist officers and other support experts had their retirements denied or their active periods extended; even voluntary resignations were refused until the Vietnam buildup slowed in late 1966. Despite its expansion, the Corps needed even more funding for personnel programs by 1968, for its career officers and NCOs were leaving the Corps and the war at alarming rates. The Department of Defense did not adequately meet Greene's requests.[32]

The officer shortages were most acute among Marine pilots, whose numbers were fully 20 percent below the Corps's conservative estimates. Despite desperate measures that ranged from reassigning helo pilots to fixed-wing squadrons, shortening pilot training periods, and culling aviators from many nonflying billets and schools assignments that they should have filled, HQMC never solved the pilot shortage, thus ensuring multiple Vietnam tours at close intervals for those pilots determined enough to stay in the Corps. General Greene watched air-ground training decline outside Vietnam, and a resurgence of envy and dissatisfaction split the aviators again from the ground portion of the officer corps. The essential problem was that McNamara's programmers would not allow the other services to widen the openings for Marine student-aviators and then pressured Greene and his staff to state that there was no pilot shortage. Headquarters received an assist from Congress, which applied counterpressure to open a few additional slots for new pilots. With OSD's acquiescence the Air Force turned over some unused Luftwaffe slots for fixed-wing training, and the Army agreed to provide the Marine Corps with additional billets in its helicopter pilot training program. The 1967 break in the billet blockade did not prevent a pilot shortage for two more years, but it eventually eased the aviation officer situation.[33]

With Secretary McNamara's planners, taking their cue from the White House, unwilling to request all the funds actually necessary to fight the war, Greene saw his long-range programs extended and underfunded. In 1966, OSD cut Marine construction funds in half. Although OSD increased the Corps's procurement funds, the money went for ammunition, supplies, replacement parts, electronic equipment, and other commodities devoured by the war's increased tempo in I Corps. As ominous were the signs that the Navy's amphibious vessel construction program would fall victim to the Vietnam War as the Navy Department shifted its investment funds to financing combat operations.[34]

With the Vietnam War absorbing virtually all the Corps's attention and distorting the global missions of the Fleet Marine Force, Greene spent much of his last six months as commandant defending the Corps in a series of public and interservice controversies. Like a pack of wounded animals, the Johnson administration, Congress, the armed services, and the Washington press turned upon each other in their collective frustration with the war. One public affairs crisis involved III MAF's change of rifles. Conforming to a high-priority plan negotiated by Westmoreland with OSD, all American forces in Vietnam received the 5.56-mm M-16 rifle, a lightweight, high-velocity weapon especially suited for bush warfare. The first marines drew their M-16s in 1967 during the DMZ fighting, and soon reports began to appear in the press that the rifle was undependable. The specific charge was that it jammed easily, especially when the extractor tore the base off the chambered cartridge. In fact, the weapon did need constant cleaning, and its cyclic rate of fire was too high. The latter condition could be cured (and was) by reducing the recoil buffer system in the butt while minor changes in the ammunition and chamber also reduced jamming. While the Marine Corps tackled its ordnance problem, however, Congress, the press, and unhappy citizens deluged Headquarters with critical comments. Greene and his staff fended off the criticism, but the issue was only too typical of the problems inherent in the hurried Vietnam buildup.[35]

The 1967 controversies that involved Marine aviation kept the commandant at the barricades defending the air-ground team. For COMUSMACV, heliborne operations defined the war, and Army planners had already criticized III MAF for its low numbers of helos. Ignoring the fact that Marine helicopters were especially built for heavy lifts over water in amphibious assaults, Army officers suggested to the press that III MAF had too little air mobility. Against this controversy, III MAF and other Marine commands experienced a dismaying series of twelve air crashes by CH-46 transport helicopters. The Boeing-Vertol Sea Knight did, in fact, have structural problems with its tail pylon, and the crash investigations uncovered other minor defects. More leisurely testing and experimentation might have reduced the crashes, but III MAF needed the CH-46, and it went to Vietnam not fully tested and then received modifications and model changes based on actual combat experience. In any event, General Greene found himself explaining the CH-46 problems, and the Corps's corrective actions, to insistent congressional staffers, OSD investigators, and the skeptical press. Having the CH-46 grounded while its problems were corrected required a reduction of III MAF helo operations and the temporary use of other Marine and Army helo types.[36]

As the CH-46 controversy simmered, program planners in McNamara's office announced that they had decided that the Marine Corps had too many high performance jet aircraft and should surrender sixty-seven jets from its inventory. Their argument was that the Air Force and the Navy should provide all-weather interdiction strikes, airborne reconnaissance and electronic warfare missions, and aerial coordination of close air support strikes. Although Greene saw the OSD report as a broad vindication of Marine aviation force structure, he was appalled by the study group's doctrinal ignorance and lack of research. Since his own planners had already reduced Marine fixed-wing numbers from 639 to 435 aircraft earlier, Greene warned his generals that economy arguments were specious and that the Corps intended to retain aircraft for the full range of missions required for amphibious operations. Only the peculiar circumstances of the Vietnam War made OSD's plan at all rational, and Greene had no intention of ruining Marine aviation with false lessons. Influenced by congressional interest and McNamara's declining taste for bureaucratic battles, the plan disappeared, but the issue remained for Greene's successors to address.[37]

Aviation management in South Vietnam also reached a new crescendo of disagreement in 1967 as Air Force general William W. Momyer, Deputy COMUSMACV (air operations) and commander, Seventh Air Force, demanded that his headquarters in Saigon plan all the fixed-wing missions for the 1st Marine Aircraft Wing. Using the Army's increased demand for close air support for its units in I Corps, which the Air Force was not providing to Army satisfaction, as the immediate "crisis," Momyer's greater concerns were asserting Air Force "single management" doctrine for war zone operations and in sending more Marine strikes against the Ho Chi Minh Trail rather than battlefield targets. When the question of single management reached the JCS, Greene argued against any change in the existing system of air mission tasking. Greene was not so naive that he assumed the issue had disappeared; instead, he warned Marine generals that they should make no concessions in air mission management. The assignment of Marine sorties against targets chosen by the Air Force and Army was already working effectively without single management, which would lengthen response time and reduce the number of sorties flown. Greene's holding action on the JCS, buttressing the aggressive defenses already mounted by Maj. Gen. Keith B. McCutcheon and General Krulak, helped prevent the issue from reaching any dramatic resolution in 1967.[38]

As he neared the end of his four years as commandant, Gen. Wallace M. Greene Jr. saw that the Vietnam War was not working well for either the United States or the Marine Corps. At the eye of the storms of controversy that mounted in 1967 against American policy and the Corps's conduct of operation in I Corps, Greene felt the war's impact in institutional terms. With a son in combat as a Marine infantry officer, he experienced the war, too, in personal terms. He had every reason to be proud of the Corps's performance in the face of mounting North Vietnamese pressure and the self-inflicted difficulties attributable to the political cowardice of the Johnson administration. Although still committed to seeing the war through to victory, Greene recognized that the war had already dealt serious blows to the Corps's modernization programs, morale, public esteem, and political power. The damage was not irreparable. As he left office on 31 December 1967, Greene did not leave the Corps, for in the retirement years ahead he would provide continued leadership in managing Marine affairs in the Washington area. He would lend his wise counsel to the younger generation of officers who bore the responsibility of salvaging the bold programs of 1964–65 from the wreckage of American defense policy, the most important casualty of the Vietnam War. General Greene died on 8 March 2003.

24

Leonard F. Chapman

1968–1971

LT. COL. RONALD H. SPECTOR, USMCR (RET.)

On 1 January 1968, Gen. Leonard F. Chapman was sworn in as the twenty-fourth commandant of the Marine Corps at a brief White House ceremony. The fifty-three-year-old commandant assumed leadership of a Corps which was larger than at any time since the end of World War II, with over 300,000 men on the rolls, 80,000 of whom were serving in one of the twenty-four Marine Corps battalions, headquarters, or supporting units currently deployed in Vietnam. A common observation of the time declared that there were only three types of marines: those in Vietnam, those recently returned from Vietnam, and those on orders to go. Yet the war in Vietnam, which was to grow even more intense and bloody in the months ahead, was to pose only one of the major problems facing the man who, in the next four years, was to lead the Corps through one of its most turbulent and challenging eras.

General Chapman's appointment brought to an end a long period of speculation and rumor concerning the successor to retiring commandant Gen. Wallace M. Greene. The three most likely candidates were reported to be Lt. Gen. Victor H. Krulak, commanding general, Fleet Marine Force Pacific; Lt. Gen. Lewis W. Walt, who had just completed a tour as commanding general, III Marine Amphibious Force, the top Marine command in Vietnam; and Chapman, who since July 1967 had served as chief of staff and later as assistant commandant of the Marine Corps. Krulak was widely regarded as one of the Corps's leading theoreticians, an expert on counterinsurgency, and reputedly the personal choice of Defense Secretary Robert F. McNamara.[1]

General Walt, a much-decorated combat hero, was reported to have considerable support on Capitol Hill. The lobbying for his candidacy there was led by former U.S. senator Paul A. Douglas, a distinguished elder statesman who had served under Walt as an enlisted man in the 1st Marine Division during World War II. The *New York Times* reported that Douglas had even been to the White House to urge President Lyndon Johnson to appoint Walt as the next commandant.[2]

Gen. Leonard F. Chapman Jr., twenty-fourth commandant.
U.S. Marines Corps Photo.

General Chapman lacked the political connections of Walt and Krulak but was reported to have the strong support of Gen. David Shoup, who had served as commandant from 1958 to 1962. He had also favorably impressed some of the civilian managers in the Pentagon with his knowledge of, and interest in introducing, modern automated information and management systems to the Marine Corps.[3] Nevertheless, Chapman was considered something of a dark horse compared to his two more celebrated and charismatic rivals and the announcement of his appointment came as a surprise to the public and even to many marines.

The new commandant was born in Key West, Florida, on 3 November 1913, the son of a Methodist minister. A few years after his birth, his father left the ministry and entered business, becoming proprietor of two Florida newspapers and then of a citrus packing company. He also served in the Florida legislature and as superintendent of the Florida prison system.

Chapman entered the University of Florida at Gainesville in 1931 with the intention of becoming a lawyer. During his senior year, Chapman, who had risen to the rank of cadet colonel in the university's compulsory ROTC course, was offered a regular commission in the Marine Corps. Despite the fact that "the first Marine I ever saw was when I went to take the physical exam at Pensacola Naval Air Station," Chapman readily accepted the appointment and entered the Marine Corps in July 1935.[4] In the depths of the Depression, the security and prospects for advancement offered by a commission seemed attractive indeed.[5]

Chapman completed the Basic School at Philadelphia Navy Yard and joined the 1st Battalion, 10th Marines, an artillery battalion at Quantico, Virginia, in April 1936. After completing the U.S. Army Field Artillery School at Fort Sill, he rejoined the 10th Marines and was promoted to first lieutenant in September 1938. Two years later he was assigned to the cruiser *Astoria* as commanding officer of the Marine detachment. Joining the *Astoria* at Pearl Harbor in June 1940, Chapman served on board her through the early cruiser raids of the Pacific war, the Battle of the Coral Sea, and the Battle of Midway. Ordered back to the United States in the summer of 1942, Chapman served as an instructor at various Marine Corps schools. In June 1944, now a lieutenant colonel, he returned to the Pacific. Joining the 1st Marine Division just after the Cape Gloucester campaign, he served with it on Peleliu and on Okinawa. In both campaigns, he commanded the 4th Battalion, 11th Marines, earning the Legion of Merit and Bronze Star with Combat "V."

Following the war, Chapman held a variety of field and staff assignments. He especially distinguished himself in the difficult assignment of logistics planner on the staff of the Fleet Marine Force Pacific during 1945 and 1946. By 1952 he was a full colonel commanding the 12th Marines in California and Japan. In 1956, he was named commanding officer of Marine Barracks, Washington, and following a successful tour in this highly visible assignment, he was promoted to brigadier general.

Chapman's first assignment as a general officer was commanding general, Force Troops, Fleet Marine Force Atlantic. He soon became know as a demanding CG. A man with an eye for detail, he set consistently high standards and held frequent inspections to ensure they were met. In subsequent tours at Headquarters Marine Corps, first as an assistant chief of staff G-4, and then as chief of staff and assistant commandant, Chapman established his reputation as a brilliant and innovative manager.

Chapman's special interest was in the application of automated data and communications systems to the management of the Marine Corps. "The potential contributions of advances in computer capabilities and communication means," wrote Chapman, "as well as advances in techniques which exploit their use are at this time immeasurable."[6]

Under his leadership, an array of information and support systems ranging from personnel management and pay to supply, combat intelligence, and tactical data were subject to integration and automation through the application of the latest computers and digital transmission media. As chief of staff, Chapman laid the solid foundation for the Marine Corps's management and information systems to advance into the computer age. As commandant, however, his principal problems were to be far removed from automated management.

The one overarching preoccupation of the Marine Corps at the time Chapman took the helm was Vietnam. At the beginning of 1968, it was a war to which the Corps was fully committed, both in terms of personnel and resources and in terms of orientation and psychology. Less than one month after General Chapman assumed office as commandant, the North Vietnamese and Vietcong launched a nationwide assault on South Vietnam's cities, towns, and military installations. The Tet Offensive, so called because it was fought during Tet, the Vietnamese lunar new year, ended in bloody failures for the Communists on the battlefield, but it nevertheless changed the course of the war. The Johnson administration halted the bombing of most of North Vietnam and placed a final cap on the number of ground troops it would commit to the war. Peace talks between the Americans and North Vietnamese and their allies opened in Paris but dragged on inconclusively into 1969, when the newly elected Nixon administration began a gradual withdrawal of American troops from Vietnam. Major responsibilities for fighting the ground war would be turned over to the Vietnamese, a process soon dubbed Vietnamization.

During his first year as commandant, Chapman had remained optimistic about Vietnam. Unfazed by the Tet attacks and the erosion of public support for the war in the United States, he continued to believe that the struggle could be brought to a successful conclusion. "We are winning the war decisively on the battlefield," he told the press following one of his visits to Vietnam in September 1968.[7]

A few months before that visit, Chapman and the other service chiefs had become engaged in a bureaucratic battle over Vietnam which soon rivaled in intensity the battles being waged against the Communists. The battle concerned the command and control of Marine aircraft. The issues were technical and highly complex. They arose out of differences in doctrine between the Air Force and Marine Corps concerning air support for ground operations. Air Force commanders, with the support of Gen. William Westmoreland, the top U.S. commander in Vietnam, called for a "single manager" to coordinate and control all sorties by fixed-wing aircraft within South Vietnam. They claimed that Army units operating in the northernmost provinces of Vietnam were not receiving adequate tactical support by Marine aircraft. In March 1968, Westmoreland established a single manager system under his deputy for air operations, Gen. William W. Momyer.[8] The Marines fought a stubborn rear-guard action against single management and eventually carried their battle into the Joint Chiefs of Staff.

Chapman wisely chose not to fight the battle as an issue of doctrine or roles and mission. Such an argument, he perceived, would be abstract, vague, and unpersuasive.[9]

Rather, the Marines attacked single management on thoroughly practical grounds, arguing that the existing system already provided adequate support to both Marine and Army ground troops in I Corps and the new system was, in practice, far less responsive to the needs of the infantrymen. Under the Marine system, a ground commander could request close air support only a few hours before it was required, whereas under single management, the lead time was up to three days. Few infantry officers could anticipate what sort of support they would require three days hence.

In arguments in "the Tank," Chapman was eventually able to win over both the Navy and the Army to his position. Although the Defense Department continued to support single management, the system was progressively modified so as to permit, by 1970, an arrangement closely resembling the traditional Marine Corps system, which stressed the tactical integrity of air-ground units.[10]

Like many other U.S. military leaders, Chapman was probably surprised and somewhat dismayed by President Nixon's abrupt announcement of the beginning of troop withdrawals from Vietnam in June 1969, but he nevertheless adjusted quickly.[11] As the implications of Vietnamization and troop withdrawals became more apparent, Chapman and his close advisers began a reassessment of the Corps's roles and missions now that the limits of commitment in Vietnam had been reached. "By the summer of 1969 the die was pretty well cast," recalled one of his staff officers. "Once he saw the war in Vietnam wasn't going anywhere, he wanted the Marines out early."[12]

The 3rd Marine Division departed first, in late 1969, enabling the Marine Corps to begin rebuilding a Pacific division-wing team for future contingencies. By the end of 1970, only two reinforced regiments together with an air group remained in Vietnam. By June 1971, the last large Marine ground units had departed, leaving behind only specialized organizations such as advisory teams, embassy security guards, and air units.

Redeployment led to deactivation of many units and changes to many others. Personnel turbulence, NCO and officer grade imbalances, and shortages of housing and equipment at many bases were only a few of the problems as marines gradually left Vietnam and began to sort themselves out in a smaller but still widely scattered corps. Chapman recognized that redeployment from Vietnam would be only one problem, and probably not the hardest problem, the Marine Corps would face in the early 1970s. Congress and the Nixon administration were determined to reduce defense spending, and the president had also announced his commitment to ending the draft and introducing an all-volunteer military force. Although the Marines had traditionally been an "all-volunteer force," the Corps's manpower planners worried about the impact the abolition of the draft would have on the ability of the Corps to meet its needs through recruiting. In recent years, many enlistments, especially in the Reserves, had been motivated largely by the desire of the "volunteers" to choose their branch and time of service.[13] Marines had done well competing in a recruitment arena in which the choice was essentially limited to one of the four services. If the choice were extended to include the option of not serving at all, the recruiter would be in a new ball game. As one officer involved in recruiting observed, "The fact remained that [until now] the Marine recruiter (salesman) operated in an environment wherein his product had already been 'sold' to the market by an act of Congress."[14]

Chapman's approach to the challenge of the postwar manpower environment was direct and forthright. The Marine Corps would be smaller but better. As early as December 1968, he had advised the Nixon White House transition team that in the current political climate, "there is a level above which Defense costs will not be tolerated, even if they can be afforded." Therefore it was "better to have fewer forces, but fully modern and ready," than a larger force which could not be properly manned, trained, and equipped due to budget constraints.[15]

This was certainly the course of action which Chapman adopted for the Marine Corps. The commandant opted for "a much smaller, highly professional" Marine Corps in the post-Vietnam era.[16] Under his leadership, the Corps was gradually reduced from its high of 317,000 men to just over 200,000 by mid-1972. Chapman took advantage of the reduction to weed out incompetents, malcontents, and time-servers. By the end of 1970, more than 11,000 men had been discharged for unsuitability, and another 12,000 had been prematurely retired or transferred to the Reserves.[17] Few lamented their departure, but whether better men—or any men—could be found to replace them remained an open question.

If the early 1970s were not "the greening of America" or the Age of Aquarius as some contemporary observers insisted, it was still an age when the prestige and popularity of the military were at low ebb. This was due partly to the growing disillusionment with the war in Vietnam and partly to the changing lifestyles and values of the youth of the 1970s, who placed a high value on nonconformity, personal freedom (including the freedom to experiment with drugs), and a low value of tradition and the wisdom of authority. Antimilitary and antiwar sentiments were particularly strong on college campuses and many universities, and by 1970, colleges were prohibiting military recruiting on campus. This prohibition caused special difficulty for the Marine Corps, which relied heavily on college procurement as a means of recruiting for its officer training programs. By 1969, the problem had become so acute that the Corps was forced to abolish its requirements for a college degree for a commission and to begin actively seeking candidates at junior colleges.

How to recruit some forty thousand men a year from such a youth population was a problem Chapman approached with both forthrightness and ingenuity. While Army recruiters attempted to assure the new generation that "Today's Army Wants to Join You," Marine Corps recruiting advertisements stressed the Corps's toughness and exclusivity by announcing, "The Marines Are Looking for a Few Good Men." A highly effective recruiting film, *We Never Promised You a Rose Garden,* emphasizing the rigors of training, reinforced the campaign.

There was a method in Chapman's madness beyond dedication to traditional Marine Corps values. Aware that the Corps need appeal to only 6 percent of the military-age population, the commandant and his advisers calculated that an appeal to traditional values would be more effective in attracting this small minority than an attempt to appear "hip" and progressive. To a degree, this approach was successful during the early 1970s. The Corps fully met its recruitment quota. Yet as the last vestiges of the draft faded away and the economy improved, recruitment became more difficult, and as later years were to reveal, standards of quality had had to be lowered far more than any of the generals or manpower planners had imagined.

Nor did the Marine Corps escape the societal and racial problems which, by the end of the 1960s, were proving far more worrisome to the armed services than the conflict in Vietnam had ever been. A 1971 survey of marines serving in the Pacific revealed that one-third had used or were using drugs, and 1,700 marines were separated from the Corps for drug use in 1970 alone. In one division in Vietnam, the number of recorded cases rose from 3 in 1968 to 143 in 1970.[18]

To cope with this rising tide of drug abuse, the Marine Corps could only employ its traditional remedies of troop education on the evils of drugs and stiff penalties for those caught abusing them. Special drug abuse education teams were formed in many larger units to make antidrug presentations to troops throughout the command. Those who failed to heed the warnings and were caught dealing in or using drugs normally faced severe punishment in the form of courts-martial and bad discharges. In February 1970, Chapman authorized local commanders to exercise their discretion concerning the retention or discharge of enlisted men guilty of drug abuse, thus allowing the possibility of a second chance or a later punishment for one-time experimenters with narcotics.[19]

The commandant adamantly refused, however, to sanction experiments with amnesty and treatment programs similar to those established by the Army and Air Force. Under such programs narcotic offenders could turn themselves in under a promise of immunity and be given access to treatment and rehabilitation. Although the Army was operating several such programs in Vietnam and elsewhere by 1970, and a Department of Defense task force on drug abuse had recommended them as a promising approach, General Chapman refused to institute such programs. "The Marine Corps is neither funded nor equipped to carry the burden of non-effective members for the inordinate length of time that civilian institutions are finding necessary to achieve the rehabilitation of addicts," he declared. "Even then the reversion rate is discouragingly high." The smaller and more highly professional Marine Corps in the post-Vietnam era could ill afford to include large numbers of convalescing narcotic addicts.[20]

In the area of race relations, the other major "people problem" area for the Corps, Chapman demonstrated far more flexibility. This was just as well since by the end of the 1960s racial tensions had become a major threat to the Corps's morale and cohesion. Although the Marine Corps and the other armed services were fully integrated institutions by the late 1960s, with standards of equal opportunity and treatment superior to most civilian organizations, they could not escape the wave of racial tension sweeping American society at the end of the 1960s. African Americans comprised about 10 percent of the Corps in 1969, and while older black NCOs might view the condition of blacks in the Corps with a feeling of pride and accomplishment, younger black men entering the service at the end of the 1960s, with a heightened sense of racial pride and sensitivity to discrimination and bias, took a far different view.

By 1969, racial clashes on Marine bases had become common, usually arising out of quarrels in clubs or other recreational facilities. Robberies and assaults also increasingly took on racial overtones. Racial tensions were exacerbated by the high personnel turbulence experienced by the Corps during this period, the presence of many recent Vietnam returnees marking time until the end of their enlistment, and a general shortage of black officers. In Vietnam, "fraggings," homicidal assaults by enlisted men using grenades or firearms against NCOs and officers, had become almost commonplace. The 1st Marine Division experienced fifteen such incidents in the first six months of 1969 alone.[21]

In July 1969, a major riot erupted at the sprawling Marine base at Camp Lejeune, North Carolina. A gang of about thirty blacks and Puerto Ricans roamed the base, attacking fifteen whites, one of whom was fatally beaten.[22] Within a year racial violence had erupted at Marine bases in Vietnam, Hawaii, Okinawa, and California.[23] "There's no question about it; we've got a problem," Chapman told reporters shortly after the Camp Lejeune outbreak.[24]

At the beginning of September 1969, the commandant issued a directive on race relations. The ALMAR reaffirmed the traditional Marine Corps adherence to discipline and strong leadership. Violence between marines would not be tolerated. Commanders must take steps to "eradicate every trace of discrimination" and must ensure that channels of communication between commanders, staff NCOs, and men are open and available. In the ALMAR, Chapman stated, "I cannot improve upon the expression of principles of leadership and the relations between officers and NCOs and men as they are written in the Marine Corps Manual. If these were conscientiously carried out, many of our problems would disappear."[25]

At the same time, however, the commandant's message made a number of realistic concessions to African American sensitivities. "Afro" haircuts were to be permitted "providing that they conform with current Marine Corps regulations." The clenched fist "black power" salute, which had become a popular form of greeting between young blacks, was to be tolerated as "a gesture of recognition and unity" but not in formation, at ceremonies, or when rendering military courtesy.

The commandant's message was widely praised in the media as an example of a tough-minded but enlightened approach to racial issues, but within the Marine Corps reactions were more ambivalent. Some white marines complained that the ALMAR in effect represented the granting of special privileges to one group of marines. The staff judge advocate of the 1st Marine Division, Col. Robert. Luch, believed that the commandant's message was "in need of clarification. . . . Our division sergeant major says NCOs do not know how to enforce it. Often when admonished to get a haircut, Negro Marines will pull out a battered copy of ALMAR and wave it at the NCO involved." Even the III Marine Amphibious Force commander, Gen. Herman Nickerson Jr., reported confusion about "what actually is allowable for an Afro-American haircut."[26]

Many black marines, on the other hand, appreciated the spirit of the message but pointed out that by officially recognizing such symbols as the Afro and the black power salute it had, in some ways, made the situation worse. Few blacks, for example, cared for Headquarters' idea of an Afro haircut. "It ain't an Afro, and everybody knows it, especially us Africans," observed one black marine, "but . . . now the Corps has sent out a picture and . . . now everybody will be very uptight about black Marines' hair."[27] Yet though Chapman's ALMAR on race relations provided no miracle solution, it served the important function of "institutionalizing Headquarters' genuine concern with black aspirations—within Marine Corps's definitions of discipline."[28] In the context of the 1960s, this may have been all that was possible.

While Chapman continued to wrestle with the problems of laying the manpower base for the post-Vietnam Marine Corps, he did not neglect the material side of the Corps's needs. Chapman saw the 1970s and 1980s as a time when the Corps would return to its amphibious roots. The "Nixon doctrine," announced by the president in July 1969, emphasized exclusively air and naval support for U.S. allies outside of Europe and seemed to presage a return for the Marine Corps to a rapidly deployable, maritime force in readiness.[29]

Yet though the mission seemed clear, the means would be difficult to acquire. The Navy's once large fleet of amphibious ships was rapidly aging by the 1960s, and the Nixon administration's economies in defense offered little prospect for a one-for-one replacement. Under these circumstances, Chapman pushed hard for two essential items, a new assault amphibious vehicle, the LVTP-7, and a new large, multipurpose amphibious assault ship, the LHA. As large as a World War II aircraft carrier the LHA combined the features of both an assault helicopter carrier and a well-deck amphibious vessel. The LHA could accommodate a reinforced battalion with its logistical support unit and the necessary helicopters and landing craft to put it ashore.

In addition, Chapman worked to procure a new generation of aircraft for Marine aviation: the AV-8A Harrier, a British-built fighter-bomber which could take off and land vertically. Chapman anticipated that the Harrier would greatly increase the flexibility and responsiveness of Marine air support. With its unique capabilities, it would be able to operate from even the most small and primitive airstrips as well as from many air-capable amphibious ships, eliminating the need for large aircraft carriers or jet-capable airfields in forward combat areas. The Harrier was to prove its value in dramatic fashion during the Falklands conflict in 1982, while the LHA proved the prototype of a new generation of multipurpose assault shipping which was to carry the Marines into the last decade of the twentieth century.[30]

As in matter of manpower, so in weapons and equipment, Chapman set the pattern of "doing more with less." It was an approach which was seldom entirely successful. Probably no program could have been in a 1970s environment of shrinking budgets, hostility or indifference to military service, and social upheaval. But Chapman's approach preserved the Corps's essential identity and tradition and built for the future while navigating the storms of one of the Marines' most difficult eras.

25

Robert Everton Cushman Jr.

1972–1975

COL. JOHN GRIDER MILLER, USMC (RET.)

In 1971, the quadrennial contest for the commandancy was less intense than usual, but not for want of qualified candidates. One of the strongest contenders was Lt. Gen. John R. Chaisson, chief of staff at Headquarters Marine Corps, who was well positioned in the billet held by Wallace M. Greene Jr. and Leonard C. Chapman Jr. before they ascended to the top spot. Another leading candidate was Gen. Raymond G. Davis Jr., awarded the Medal of Honor for heroism during the Chosin breakout twenty-one years earlier and more recently the highly successful commander of the 3d Marine Division, whose innovative tactical concepts had revitalized Marine operations along the Demilitarized Zone in Vietnam. Despite his combat successes and his seniority in the role of assistant commandant of the Marine Corps (which now carried a fourth star), Davis was the underdog. By tradition and practice, the chief of staff usually held the true power seat. The office of assistant commandant had ceased to be a largely ceremonial post, traditionally reserved for the senior aviator of the Corps, but the chief of staff still ran Headquarters and had direct access to the commandant on most matters.

For a while, the third contender, Lt. Gen. Robert E. Cushman Jr., went almost unnoticed. He was a veteran of several Pacific campaigns in World War II and had received the Navy Cross for heroism while commanding an infantry battalion during the recapture of Guam. In Vietnam, he had succeeded Lt. Gen. Lewis W. Walt in command of the III Marine Amphibious Force (MAF) and U.S. forces in Military Region I (I Corps). In 1971, he held his own seat of power as deputy director of the Central Intelligence Agency, placed there by presidential appointment upon his return from Vietnam.

Many senior officials—military, elected, and appointed—influence the selection of the commandant of the Marine Corps, but only one official decides. And in November 1971, President Richard M. Nixon nominated Cushman to become the twenty-fifth commandant of the Marine Corps. On 9 December, the Senate Armed Forces Committee reported the nomination favorably to the full Senate, and swift confirmation followed.[1]

Gen. Robert E. Cushman Jr., twenty-fifth commandant.
U.S. Marines Corps Photo.

In the ensuing wave of press speculation, the story emerged that Cushman, who as a national security assistant had briefed Nixon daily on military affairs during his second term as vice president, might have had his choice between heading either the Marine Corps or the CIA. But there was really no choice. "Any Marine would like to be Commandant," Cushman told an associate at the time.[2] In mid-December, *Time* magazine reported that Gen. William Westmoreland, chief of staff of the Army, and Adm.

Elmo Zumwalt, the CNO, would have preferred Chaisson.[3] Despite the magazine's rhapsodic speculation that a series of Zumwalt-Chaisson exchanges would have raised the quality of debate among the Joint Chiefs of Staff to undreamed-of levels, there were probably other reasons for this rather unusual public display of disaffection. Cushman and Westmoreland had clashed in Vietnam over the defense of Khe Sanh and Seventh Air Force control of Marine aviation, among other things. And Zumwalt may have seen a strong-willed commandant with immense political clout as a somewhat unwelcome prospect.

Robert Everton Cushman Jr. was born on Christmas Eve 1914 in St. Paul, Minnesota. As a youngster, he was captivated by his father's tales of naval service during the Spanish-American War and decided early on to follow suit. He received an appointment to the U.S. Naval Academy while still a semester shy of graduating from St. Paul's Central High School (in May 1973, Central formally recognized him as its most distinguished dropout and awarded him an honorary diploma). He was only sixteen years old in the summer of 1931 when he walked through the Maryland Avenue gate of the academy to confront the terrors of Plebe year. Many, if not most, of his classmates had several years of prior college or military experience. They were already older than he would be on the day he graduated—if he made it through.

But he made it through, in style. He even found time to play varsity lacrosse, a contact sport inherited from the American Indians that matched boxing in its brain-scrambling intensity—enough to gain the lacrosse players the nickname "ham-and-eggers." But Cushman managed to make his mark on the athletic field and still wind up tenth in his graduating class of 442.[4]

During his midshipman days, he switched his preference from his father's beloved Navy to the Marines. The turning point may have come one evening when he returned from "French leave" (an unauthorized nocturnal excursion over the academy's wall into downtown Annapolis) and was apprehended by a Marine sentry near the chapel. Instead of placing Midshipman Cushman on report, the sentry told him about better ways to "French." Cushman, greatly relieved, never forgot that.

Upon graduation from the Naval Academy in 1935, he entered the Marine Corps Basic School for newly commissioned lieutenants, located at the Philadelphia Navy Yard. With more than twenty lieutenants under instruction, it was one of the largest Basic School classes since the beginning of the Depression. Fourteen of Cushman's classmates there, including future commandant Leonard F. Chapman Jr., would eventually attain general officer grade. No other class has equaled that record.

After Basic School, Cushman volunteered for duty with the 4th Marines in China. He found Shanghai's international community fully as exotic as John W. Thomason's classic stories and drawings portrayed it, but as a rifle platoon leader he was unhappy about the limited opportunity for serious field work—until the approach of Japanese troops in August 1937. To protect the international settlement, the 4th Marines prepared positions along Soochow Creek and manned them for several months. The U.S. Marines never were combatants in the Sino-Japanese War, but neither the Chinese nor

Japanese took particular care to keep the Americans out of the line of fire. After dodging his share of stray shots and short rounds, Cushman left China in 1938. He had seen his first combat and was wearing his first campaign ribbon.

After a brief assignment in New York at the Marine Barracks, Brooklyn Navy Yard, he reported for duty at the Norfolk Naval Shipyard, located in Portsmouth, Virginia. After a year in Portsmouth, Cushman was detailed to the New York World's Fair, where he commanded the platoon-sized Marine detachment stationed there for drill and ceremonies. As the detachment paraded in the Corps's distinctive dress blues, the fair's crowds were impressed to the point where Headquarters Marine Corps decided to expand the detachment into a two-company battalion. Cushman, still a lieutenant, remained as one of the company commanders until the fall of 1940, interrupting his tour only for a return trip to Portsmouth and his marriage to Audrey Boyce.

The shining promise of the World's Fair had been clouded by war in Europe and Asia. By the time the fair closed, U.S. involvement in conflict overseas was becoming more likely. Cushman was ordered to Quantico to help establish a training center for the thousands of Marine Corps Reserve officers who soon would fill the Fleet Marine Force. He served as the assistant operations (S-3) officer of the center until the spring of 1941, when he was promoted to captain and received orders to assume command of the Marine detachment in the battleship *Pennsylvania* as a relief for Major Wilburt S. "Big Foot" Brown.

The *Pennsylvania,* one of the mainstays of the Pacific Fleet, had recently relocated from California to the Hawaiian Islands. When Cushman arrived there, Hawaii was gripped by war fever. The Honolulu newspapers were inflamed by the revelation that a Japanese midget submarine had recently been detected in home waters, and saw war as imminent. Later allegations to the contrary, the fleet also was placing a new, grim emphasis on combat readiness, maintaining a high tempo of training exercises and surveillance operations. Nevertheless, the Japanese aerial attack on 7 December 1941 found the *Pennsylvania* in dry dock, with her propellers removed. The Marine detachment, under Cushman's direction, was handling ammunition for the ship's antiaircraft batteries when, at 0830 that Sunday morning, a flight of bombers scored several direct hits on both the battleship and the dock. Roughly one-third of the detachment was killed or wounded in the attack, but Cushman escaped injury. Damage to the *Pennsylvania* was severe but not fatal.

Cushman returned to Camp Pendleton, California, in April 1942, to join the 9th Marines, then being formed by Col. Lemuel C. Shepherd Jr., a future commandant. Early in 1943, Cushman assumed command of the 2d Battalion, 9th Marines, which subsequently sailed for the South Pacific, receiving intensive jungle training on Guadalcanal before embarking for the Bougainville campaign.

Bougainville was rough. Cushman's battalion saw two months of constant patrol activity that resulted in occasional sharp clashes with the Japanese defenders. At Piva Forks, they had a serious skirmish, and acquitted themselves well. Cushman was learning quickly about fighting the tenacious Japanese and overcoming the unending logistical problems generated by the debilitating weather and jungle terrain. The battalion left Bougainville at year's end, worn down but not badly bloodied. After several weeks' rest, some reequipping, and some replacements, it would be in relatively good shape for the stiff fights that lay ahead.

Guam was next. The battalion landed under heavy fire on 20 July 1944 and seized the harbor after stiff action at Piti Point. Cushman next conducted a skillful passage of lines, through a hard-hit battalion of the 21st Marines that was still heavily engaged, to join the vicious fight for Fonte Hill. Upon Cushman's recommendation, one of his rifle company commanders, Capt. Louis H. Wilson, another future commandant, received the Medal of Honor for this action. Cushman was awarded the Navy Cross for his own heroic leadership, which led to the annihilation of one enemy battalion and the routing of another.

The biggest battle still lay ahead. On 23 February 1945 (D-Day plus four), while Associate Press photographer Joe Rosenthal was taking his famous short of the flag raising on the top of Mount Suribachi, the 2d Battalion, 9th Marines went ashore at Iwo Jima. The American toehold on the island was secure, but a deadly task remained: clearing thousands of fanatical defenders from their caves and fortified positions. About three weeks later, the battalion attacked into "Cushman's Pocket" to clear out a final complex of caves and effectively end all resistance in its sector. This time, it had indeed been bloodied. Cushman had landed with 800 marines and had received 150 replacements during the battle, but the battalion suffered 750 casualties during those three weeks.

Another rebuilding period was in order. The 9th Marines went back to the Guam they had helped liberate to prepare for the invasion of Japan. Replacement troops were flooding in, and veterans of two or more years' fighting in the Pacific went home, where their experience could be used to train others heading west for the final campaign. Cushman, one of the most seasoned battalion commanders in the Pacific theater, departed for Quantico.

Within months, the war was over and the nuclear age had dawned. Cushman completed the Senior Course at Marine Corps Schools, then stayed on as an instructor. He began to write field manuals, seeking with his contemporaries to recapture and record the most important lessons of the hard fighting they remembered so vividly. They also had to grapple with new problems associated with the atomic bomb, which posed a new threat to massed amphibious formations. At the same time, the embryonic helicopter showed promise of bringing new tactical mobility to the battlefield and its seaward approaches, making dispersion against the nuclear threat a possibility. Innovative thinking was required, and Cushman threw himself into the effort. After writing and teaching during working hours, he used his off-duty time to become a prolific writer for professional journals. During the 1940s and 1950s, he contributed seventeen articles to the *Marine Corps Gazette* and took first prize in the *Gazette*'s annual essay contest four times. Sometimes, his articles reexamined the past, and at other times, he tried to peer into the future, with articles in the Naval Institute's *Proceedings* and *Infantry Journal* as well as the *Gazette.*

Cushman joined the staff of the newly created Central Intelligence Agency in 1949, after spending a year in the Office of Naval Research. The Corps recalled him from the CIA in 1951, and he promptly asked for combat duty in Korea. But his monitor told him that he "already had a war and a medal," and other officers needed to get their chance at combat leadership. Cushman joined the staff of the commander in chief, U.S. Naval Forces, Eastern Atlantic and Mediterranean Fleet. His two-year tour there, split between London and Naples, involved a great deal of air travel, which became increasingly uncomfortable as a chronic back condition worsened. He returned to the United States in mid-1953 and went directly to the naval hospital at Bethesda, where he was admitted for back surgery. He recovered and returned to full duty by January 1954 and was able to enter one of the six-month classes at the Armed Forces Staff College in Norfolk. The school, sponsored by the JCS, concentrated on joint operations and planning. Cushman remained there for two years after graduation, first as an instructor and later as director of plans and operations.

Next, he took command of the 2d Marines at Camp Lejeune, just in time to mount out with the regiment for the 1956 Suez crisis, which President Dwight Eisenhower managed to defuse before U.S. forces could reach the scene. The 2d Marines returned to Camp Lejeune and a peacetime training routine, but Cushman's command tour was destined to be cut short. In 1957, Cmdt. Randolph McCall Pate directed Cushman to report on one day's notice for an interview with Vice President Richard M. Nixon and potential assignment as his military assistant for national security affairs. Cushman received the nod and began one of the most significant relationships of his life. He provided daily briefings and maintained liaison with Cabinet officials and the National Security Council staff and accompanied Nixon on numerous trips across Europe, Africa, and South America. He was promoted to brigadier general in 1958 and remained in the assignment until early 1961, when he departed for Okinawa.

Cushman was promoted to major general in August 1961 and took command of the 3d Marine Division the following month, serving until July 1962. He returned to Headquarters in the dual role of assistant chief of staff for intelligence (G-2) and plans, operations, and training (G-3). He left for California in June 1964 to serve as the commanding general, Marine Corps Base Camp Pendleton and simultaneously as the commander of the 4th Marine Division Headquarters nucleus. Once the buildup for Vietnam commenced, he formed the 5th Marine Division and served briefly as its commanding general.

Cushman left for Vietnam in April 1967 and was initially assigned as deputy commander, III Marine Amphibious Force. That June, he received his third star and took command of what became the largest combat command ever held by a marine. When General Westmoreland established the Army's XXIV Corps along the Demilitarized Zone in 1968, Cushman's command included major elements of three Marine divisions, a heavy Marine aircraft wing, and three Army divisions, along with supporting units, for a total strength that reached 163,000.

In March 1969, the newly inaugurated President Nixon appointed Cushman deputy director of the CIA. For the next thirty-three months, he represented the agency on the U.S. Intelligence Board and, during the infrequent absences of Director Richard Helms, attended meetings of the National Security Council. Cushman's daily exposure to national security policy making at the highest level probably was unique for an incoming Marine Corps commandant. On the other hand, despite his long and distinguished service in the Corps, his sabbatical in the low-profile CIA appointment had made him a relative unknown, both within the Marines and around Washington. Accordingly, there was a great deal of interest in his opening statements.

Cushman issued his first set of marching orders in a message to all Marine Corps commands on his first day in office, 1 January 1972:

> We will continue
> To take care of our own
> To be squared away
> To perform outstandingly as our country's number-one combat-ready fighting force.[5]

The ALMAR lacked detail, but specific concerns began to emerge at Cushman's first Pentagon press conference. When asked about his biggest single challenge, he said, "I think it will be maintaining the quality of the personnel who are enlisted in a no-draft environment. We'll get the numbers, but getting the quality is going to mean very vigorous recruiting."[6]

Coming eighteen months before the draft was to end, this proved to be a prophetic statement. The signs were becoming clearer each day. Except for a sixty-man advisory unit working with the Vietnamese Marine Corps, the Air-Naval Gunfire Liaison Company (ANGLICO), and the Saigon embassy security guard force, the Marines were essentially out of Vietnam. The prospect of draftees being sent to combat duty had virtually ended (although Nixon would not formally declare such until 29 April), but widespread antiwar sentiment remained, still expressed in antimilitary demonstrations. Within six months, Dartmouth and Brown would shut down their NROTC units, ending affiliations with the Navy and Marine Corps that had lasted more than thirty years. Yale, which had formed its first ROTC unit in 1916, went even further, ending *all* ROTC programs on its campus. The loss in numbers was relatively small; the symbolic loss was significant.

At this point, Marine Corps personnel planners still were comfortable with the notion that more than 90 percent of enlistments were not draft-induced. A cautious optimism prevailed. The other armed services were relaxing their standards of conduct and appearance, perhaps out of desperation, but the Marines would still hold to the hard line. In the same press conference, Cushman announced his intention to pursue the same recruiting themes, "Looking for a Few Good Men" and "We Don't Promise You a Rose Garden," initiated by his predecessor. The J. Walter Thompson advertising agency, which for years had serviced the Marine Corps as a prestige account, reported some marketing research: only 50 percent of draft-age males wanted any part of military service whatsoever, and only 7 percent responded favorably to a hard-line "Rose Garden" recruiting pitch. The Marines needed roughly fifty thousand recruits each year, and if the anticipated 7 percent of draft eligibles were really out there, that would constitute an adequate recruiting base, allowing for a few predictable losses to the Army airborne, Navy SEALs, and other natural competitors for the same hardy souls.

As events unfolded, however, relying heavily on a strong response to the Rose Garden theme would soon become the equivalent of whistling in a graveyard. The tipoff, unrecognized at the time, had come in 1971, when, for a brief period, Selective Service legislation was not on the books. Enlistments suffered in both quantity and quality. Reserve enlistment fell by half. And Officer Candidate School enrollment (traditionally draft-motivated) dropped sharply. All these trends had halted abruptly as soon as the draft was renewed.

Cushman also used the press conference to call for a "close partnership with the Navy" as essential for accomplishing the Marine Corps mission. This theme would develop over the next several months, with spotty results. For the Navy, the notion of partnership carried an overtone of shared responsibility, which was good. It also carried an overtone of more shared dollars for amphibious shipbuilding and aviation programs which, in the Navy's eyes, was *not* necessarily good. As the nature of this unilaterally proclaimed partnership became more sharply defined, Navy resistance would grow.

Less than one month after he was sworn in, Cushman traveled to Capitol Hill to present his first annual posture statement.[7] By tradition, Marine Corps commandants refrain from making waves when they go to the Hill. They ask for the traditional 3 percent or so of the Defense budget in "green" dollars, count on the Navy to bring in its fair share of "blue" dollars (for aviation, amphibious shipping, medical support, etc.), and quietly leave the stage. The fiscal year 1973 testimony followed this pattern. No one at Headquarters wanted to subject a brand-new commandant to the detailed inquisition from the four Hill committees (Senate and House Appropriations and Armed Services) that startling new initiatives would provoke. So the posture statement was crafted into a seamless web, lacking handles for the committee staffers to seize. Nevertheless, Cushman's personal guidance managed to lead the document into new areas.

He began by tying amphibious forces into the recently announced "Nixon doctrine" and Secretary of Defense Melvin Laird's complementary "National Security Strategy of Realistic Deterrence," both of which emphasized forward naval deployments in support of allies who would provide their own forces on the ground. Cushman's emphasis—on peacetime military presence without automatic commitment and peaceful military support for diplomatic undertakings—became the underpinning of later calls to maintain an adequate amphibious capability despite an austere funding environment.

The words were convincing, but the numbers were coming out wrong. Overall amphibious-lift capacity was at its lowest ebb since the Korean War, but the Navy was wrapping up a program that had delivered forty new amphibious ships in four years. The "Gator Navy," in fact, was the most modern mission force in the fleet, but it still couldn't lift all the marines, supplies, and equipment it had transported in the past. This would become a point of contention for the next decade.

The aviation proposals in the posture statement proclaimed "modest modernization," but some major long-term changes were proposed in another assault on "blue" dollars. The Marines would trade in their F-4 Phantoms, workhorses in Vietnam, for the new F-14 Tomcat. They also proposed an all-V/STOL light attack force for the 1980s, based on a second-generation AV-16 Harrier (a straight growth model the Navy would not support because naval aviators were trying to design a supersonic version). These "modest" suggestions constituted a major challenge to naval aviation, and the challenge was not well received—at first, anyway.

Cushman also showed interest in another concept: seabasing, and its supporting seaborne mobile logistics system (SMLS), a natural for the nickname "Smells" awarded by its detractors. Logistic support from the sea made some sense, particularly in light of the Vietnam War experience of having to defend huge shore-based logistic facilities from enemy attack and local thievery. Nevertheless, the notion sent tremors through the ranks of both blue- and green-suiters. The Navy disliked the idea of vulnerability being shifted from land bases to their own ships lingering offshore, a primal fear that went back as far as Guadalcanal and Iron Bottom Sound. Ironically, many marines also focused on the Guadalcanal experience and searing memories of their supporting fleet steaming away from Red Beach with marines and supplies still unloaded. Feelings ran so high at Headquarters, in fact, that a hasty "counter-posture statement" emerged from the Plans and Programs Division, only to be quashed quickly by the chief of staff, Lieutenant General Chaisson.

After the seabasing excursion, Cushman moved to the issue that worried him most: manpower. He cited the sag in enlistments caused by the temporary lapse of Selective Service legislation and zeroed in on a new worry: the drop in officer accessions after OCS procurement had fallen by half. Sensing a long-term trend, he called for increased reliance on (i.e., funding for) the longer-term programs: the U.S. Naval Academy, the NROTC (the Ivy League's surprise announcements were still around the corner), and the Platoon Leader Candidate (PLC) program, for which he sought a basic retainer fee for those enrolled.

In mid-March, Cushman continued to carry his message to the outside world, addressing the District of Columbia council of the Navy League. He began by plugging the Marines into the Navy's primary missions, as stated by Admiral Zumwalt, then shifted gears, citing the distance the Corps had to travel in order to carry out its part of those missions. Vietnam had disrupted a longstanding pattern of Navy-Marine teamwork, and an entire generation of marines had gone without making a wet-net amphibious landing. In order to fill pilot seats in Vietnam, moreover, a generation of Marine Corps aviators had forfeited its chance to attend the Amphibious Warfare School at Quantico.

Cushman went on: "We are pulling our heads out of the jungle and getting back into the amphibious business. . . . We are redirecting our attention seaward and re-emphasizing our partnership with the Navy and our shared concern in the maritime aspects of our strategy. In my view, there is room for concern—especially in the areas of amphibious lift and naval gunfire support capability. We will watch these closely."[8]

Despite these efforts, the Vietnam aberration returned to haunt Cushman. At the end of March, the North Vietnamese Army (NVA) launched its 1972 Easter Offensive, Gen. Vo Ngyuen Giap's two-pronged invasion that drove into South Vietnam's central highlands and down its coastal plain. The NVA had waited until virtually all the U.S. combat units were withdrawn from South Vietnam, but a handful of Marine advisers and ANGLICO were still in-country to support the South Vietnamese marines.

A few weeks later, Cushman spoke at a luncheon in Harrisburg, Pennsylvania. Nearby college students had planned a demonstration to protest U.S. military response to the Easter Offensive (such was the intellectual climate of the time). The demonstrators arrived, with guerrilla-theater clothes and a large banner that read "Blood Is on Your Hands, General Cushman." Central Pennsylvania is not especially strong Marine Corps turf, but it has its full share of patriots. The luncheon crowd began to get restive. As the demonstrators were led away, Cushman turned (and captured) the audience with a brief ad lib: "It's a question of mistaken identity. They should be showing that sign to General Giap." The audience surged to its feet and cheered. From that point on, Cushman could have received a standing ovation for doing no more than reading a set of tide tables. It was a small, sweet victory.[9]

In response to the Easter Offensive, U.S. naval forces returned to Vietnamese waters in strength not seen since mid-1968. Four carrier groups took station and sent aircraft to mine Haiphong and other North Vietnamese ports and rivers. Gunfire support ships answered calls for fire from ANGLICO and the Marine and ARVN advisers along the coastline. The 9th Marine Amphibious Brigade (MAB), with four battalion landing teams and two composite helicopter squadrons embarked in Seventh Fleet amphibious shipping, hovered near the fierce fighting along the DMZ. National policy forbade U.S. ground combat troops from being reintroduced, but the 9th MAB was able to support Vietnamese marine counterattacks with its helicopters and amphibian tractors. At the same time, Marine Aircraft Group (MAG) 15, with three F-4J squadrons, flew into Da Nang and commenced operations in South Vietnam's Military Regions I and II. Several weeks later Marine Aircraft Group 12 moved to the Bien Hoa airfield in Military Region III, and began flying sorties in the southern half of South Vietnam and along the Cambodian border. Also in mid-May, Task Force Delta was established in northern Thailand, to open an airfield at Nam Phong. SeaBees from the 30th Naval Construction Regiment completed a ten-thousand-foot runway that had been begun five years earlier as a standby facility. Marines promptly named the austere airfield the Rose Garden, in double-edged reference to the current recruiting slogan. MAG 15 redeployed from Da Nang and was joined by a squadron of all-weather A-6 Intruders for operations in the north.[10]

In time, Quang Tri City was recaptured and the Easter Offensive fizzled out. A sense of equilibrium was restored. But even as the situation in South Vietnam seemed to stabilize and Cushman refocused his attention on ways to cope with a new set of peacetime problems, significant numbers of marines remained engaged in a hot war. Nevertheless, the peacetime worries were real, and became greater by the minute. Cushman's early sense of foreboding about recruiting difficulties was reinforced by the 28 August announcement by Nixon and Laird that draft calls would end on 30 June 1973.

After the end of the draft was announced, Cushman stepped up the attack. In September, he addressed the Marine Corps Combat Correspondents Association on its thirtieth anniversary.[11] After recalling the comment of the founder, Brig. Gen. Robert Denig, that the best publicity for the Corps was "the naked event," he urged the audience to get the story out. Many then held positions in media and advertising that could indeed help local recruiters. They responded, and before long the recruiting service was calling for help in turning off unsolicited offers of assistance that were overwhelming local recruiters.

Through the fall of 1972, Cushman continued to reiterate his concerns about recruiting, in particular, the thirty-seven hundred–man shortfall in Reserve recruiting. He also gave voice to a Headquarters estimate that "92 [percent] of our enlistees are true volunteers, whose visits to their Marine recruiters were not prompted by unfortunately Selective Service lottery numbers."[12] By this time, some of the nervousness about the advent of the all-volunteer force had worked its way up to the highest echelons of the Department of Defense, which proposed a bonus of fifteen hundred dollars for reenlisting in the combat arms of either the Army or the Marine Corps. Cushman agreed to give it a try. The bonus would introduce inequities into the Corps, but it kept Marine recruiters in the game with Army paratroopers, Navy SEALs, and other recruiters with whom they competed to attract the hardiest and most adventuresome segment of American youth.

The prospective end of the draft keyed directly on the progress of the war in Vietnam. After a late September 1972 show of U.S. naval support had helped bring the moribund North Vietnamese Easter Offensive to a close, peace talks began again in earnest. On 26 October, presidential adviser Henry A. Kissinger announced to a waiting world that "peace is at hand" in Indochina. Amid reports that a final agreement was as close as a single negotiating session away, U.S. bombing of the north above the twentieth parallel, just three degrees above the DMZ, was halted. Twelve days later, President Nixon was elected to a second term in a landslide over Senator George McGovern of South Dakota. By 18 December, the peace talks in Paris were at loggerheads, and the White House announced resumption of full-scale bombing and mining of North Vietnam, warning that the raids would continue until a settlement was reached. The attacks continued for twelve days. On 30 December, President Nixon announced the halt to bombing and naval bombardment north of the twentieth parallel and the resumption of private peace negotiations in Paris.

On 23 January 1973, Henry Kissinger and North Vietnam's chief negotiator, Le Duc Tho, initialed an agreement "to end the war and bring peace with honor in Vietnam and Southeast Asia." Secretary of Defense Laird waited only four days to announce to the service secretaries that "the Armed Forces henceforth will depend exclusively on volunteer soldiers, sailors, airmen, and marines. Use of the draft has ended." The announcement was Laird's swan song. Two days later, the Senate confirmed Elliott L. Richardson as the new secretary.

Cushman's second annual trip to Capitol Hill to testify in support of the Marine Corps's fiscal year 1974 budget requests went relatively unnoticed amid the euphoria surrounding the return of prisoners of war from North Vietnam. But he got in some solid modernization proposals, most of which would become far-reaching. He called for a buy of the new M60A1 main battle tank, to replace those old workhorses, the M-48 and M-103. He continued to purchase the LVTP-7 amphibian tractor, one of the few major end items that still had a lower unit cost than its predecessor, the LVTP-5. He called for future procurement of two infantry missile systems, DRAGON (man-packed, with an effective range of one kilometer) and TOW (vehicle or, later, helicopter-mounted, with an effective range of three kilometers) to help end the chronic problem of antiarmor defense in the early stages of amphibious assault. For once, the Marines appeared to be on the verge of getting state-of-the-art tanks and antitank systems.[13]

In his request for new aviation systems, Cushman proceeded with confidence in calling for the completion of the AV-8A Harrier buy—a total of 114 aircraft to form one training squadron and three operational ones. The "moment of truth" for the Harrier had come the previous year, in a ten-day test ordered by the secretary of defense. The inspectors checked payloads, strike results, downtime for maintenance, and every other conceivable facet of Harrier operations. Then they played the results against an elaborate statistical model to pull out long-range implications. The results: 150 percent of expectations as a light attack aircraft. An added bonus came from the Harrier's ability to maneuver effectively in the air-to-air environment against both supersonic and subsonic opponents. Cushman expressed great faith in their survivability in a sophisticated air war.

The Navy kept refusing to issue the operational requirement document for the straight-growth AV-16 (later to resurface as the AV-8B), but its hopes for a supersonic V/STOL were dimmed by news that Northrop's estimated engine development costs would exceed $1 billion, almost guaranteeing that the project would collapse under its own fiscal weight.

An even more significant breakthrough loomed in Cushman's request to buy into the F-14 Tomcat fighter program, whose chronic financial troubles had driven Grumman to a claimed threshold of bankruptcy. The rationale for the high-tech fighter buy, like seabasing, seemed to have some emotional roots in the Guadalcanal experience. Would the Corps entrust its protection against the most severe air threats to carrier-based Navy aircraft? For the Navy, the issue was more one of driving down unit cost, with a bigger Tomcat buy than they could justify for the Navy alone.

The situation came to a head during the fiscal year 1974 budget hearing before the Senate Appropriations Committee, chaired by the venerable John McClellan of Arkansas. Cushman, who had asked for F-14s earlier and had been rebuffed by Department of Defense analysts, was midway through his testimony, extolling the virtues of the F-4J with a slotted wing as the next step in modernizing Marine aviation, when he was interrupted by the CNO, Admiral Zumwalt. "That was a bad decision," Zumwalt said, then settled back into his seat under Cushman's stare. Cushman had continued reading his prepared statement when Zumwalt interrupted again: "That was a bad decision, and when we go into executive session, I'll tell you why that was a bad decision." The second outburst was too much for McClellan, who adjourned the hearing and told Secretary of the Navy John Warner to return when he had a single Department of the Navy position to present.[14]

In the closed-door session that followed, Cushman agreed to take on the F-14s he had wanted all along, with the promise of added funding to support the buy. At the time, it seemed like a no-lose deal. But in time, the piper would have to be paid.

In the second week of April 1973, Cushman found himself in another unusual head-to-head situation, this time with Secretary of Defense Richardson, during the annual meeting of the Defense Advisory Council on Women in the Service (DACOWITS). It was the Marine Corps's turn to host the conference, which meant that the commandant would be the keynote speaker at the Pentagon. The high-powered members of DACOWITS had direct access to the secretary on matters affecting the health and well-being of women in the services. According to preliminary reports, they had decided that the Marine Corps, whose level of active-duty women had remained at roughly 2 percent of total strength for years, was a prime target for attack.

Secretary Richardson didn't make things easier. Introducing General Cushman, he said that he did not see why the percentage of women in the services could not be doubled within the next five years—and drew an appreciative response. (This appearance of forward-looking, long-haul leadership was to prove somewhat illusory. Three weeks later, Richardson would leave the Department of Defense, after three months' service there, to become the attorney general.) Cushman then had to tell the DACOWITS why this prediction would not be realized in the Marine Corps—because of the large percentage of forward-deployed marines in combat units, among other reasons. But he was able to sweeten the message with announcements of new initiatives worked out in advance with the newly appointed director of Women Marines, Col. Margaret Brewer. These included the opening of new military occupational fields and assignments to command for women.

The DACOWITS seemed won over, and Cushman ended his remarks with a show of faith, recalling the day in 1943 when Cmdt. Thomas Holcomb announced to his dinner guests that he had just signed the Marine Corps order creating the Women's Reserve. According to legend, the portrait of Archibald Henderson, the nineteenth-century commandant for thirty-nine years, crashed to the floor at that very instant. "Well, times have changed," Cushman said. "So when you tour the Commandant's

House, take a good look at Old Archibald. He's not shaky about our one-of-a-kind Women Marines any more. He's hanging in there—and up there—tight."[15]

On 30 June 1973, the draft ended. As Cushman described it later, there was "a collective awakening of draft-age males" that they no longer had to serve. He went on to quote a young prospect's response to a Marine Corps recruiter in Florida: "Look, man—I've got a car and a chick and I make 600 bucks a month. Why should I go to Parris Island?"[16] The notion that fewer than 10 percent of enlistments were draft-motivated quickly vanished as the pool of recent enlistees awaiting shipment to the recruit depots quickly dried up, and few new prospects stepped forward to replenish it. The situation was even worse in the Marine Corps Reserve. Congress managed to compound the crisis six months later when they finally passed the Defense Appropriations Act for fiscal year 1974 and directed the elimination of 234 career-counselor billets. In Section 718 of the act, they imposed a retroactive requirement on the Corps to enlist at least 55 percent high school graduates. This left the Marines in the unhappy position of having to turn down virtually all non–high school graduates in the latter part of the fiscal year, introducing monthly recruiting shortfalls of 30 percent or more. Between the end of March and the end of April 1974, for example, Marine Corps recruiting would plummet from 108 percent to 45 percent of quota.

On his next trip to the Hill, Cushman would seek relief from Section 718, voicing his disbelief in the high school diploma as the best predictor of success on active duty. Preenlistment testing that placed recruits in one of four mental groups was a better indicator of trainability than diplomas, which in fact were possessed by more than half of the mental group IVS, the slowest learners, forced upon the Corps during the Vietnam War. In time, however, the Corps would acknowledge that even a "social" diploma represented a measure of perseverance that made a graduate more likely to complete his first enlistment.[17]

By the fall of 1973, the real war for the Marines had shifted to the recruiting stations and recruit depots, which had to cope with the uncertain quality of enlistees in the all-volunteer force. For the first time in a decade, no marines, anywhere in the world, were in hot combat. But it was a near thing. On 6 October, Syria and Egypt launched simultaneous attacks against Israel on the Golan Heights and Sinai fronts, respectively. The 32d and 34th Marine Amphibious Units linked up in the Eastern Mediterranean to form the 4th Marine Amphibious Brigade, with a strength of about forty-four hundred marines and sailors. This rather small amphibious brigade was large enough to signal direct U.S. interest in the conflict and to serve as a counterweight to the deployment of a Soviet airborne division, then under way. Fortunately for all concerned, the superpowers were able to impose a cease-fire by 23 October, without direct military intervention.

The ferocity of the fighting was such that after several days, more than fifteen hundred hulks of destroyed tanks and armored vehicles littered the desert battleground. Within days of the cease-fire, military observers and analysts from many nations were crawling over the battlefield wreckage, measuring entry and exit holes and calculating angles of fire. It was clear that new hand-held antiair and antitank missiles were creating new lethal conditions for armored, mechanized, heliborne, and close air support forces. They also presented new challenges for long-established Marine Corps tactical concepts, and in coming years critics would urge the Marines to "heavy up" for mechanized war despite declining levels of amphibious lift, needed to carry them to the fight.

Toward the end of 1973, General and Mrs. Cushman took part in the launching of the *Tarawa* (LAH-1), planned as the first of a nine-ship class of amphibious assault vessels from the Ingalls Shipbuilding Company. The program had extensive Marine Corps participation from the earliest stages. Cushman saw the LHA as the potential "backbone of the amphibious forces for the remainder of the 20th century" and warned against those who would use the ship for "other than its intended purpose" (e.g., sea control or flagship) before his wife, the ship's sponsor, sent the *Tarawa* sliding down the ways.[18]

In addition to calling for relief from the provisions of the onerous Section 718, Cushman used his fiscal year 1975 posture statement and subsequent appearances on the Hill early in 1974 to request funding for two prototypes of the CH-53E, designed to lift 93 percent of the supplies and equipment needed by a Marine division, as opposed to the 41 percent that could be lifted by the CH-53D model. With a sixteen-ton lift capacity, the CH-53E would double the capability of its predecessor. Initial deliveries of the new helicopter were projected for 1977. In the posture statement, Cushman also announced plans for a service life extension program for the aging CH-46 medium helicopter, as well as the expected delivery of the first F-14A Tomcat fighter aircraft to the Marine Corps during that fiscal year, predicting an initial operating capability for the first F-14 squadron by 1 January 1976, his own expected retirement date. He also expressed his continuing faith in an all-V/STOL light attack force, predicated on the development of a straight-growth version of the AV-8H Harrier.

In July 1974, Cushman made a ceremonial and inspection visit to the Far East that included a nostalgic stop at Guam for the island's thirtieth Liberation Day ceremonies, where he served as guest of honor and parade marshal. On the return leg, he stopped in San Francisco, where he spoke to the Navy League national convention assembled on the flight deck of the USS *Enterprise.* With obvious relish, he was able to announce that the lifting of the Section 718 recruiting restriction in June had enabled Marine recruiters to bring in 124 percent of quota.[19] An important corner was being turned. But even as he spoke, the nation's attention was riveted on televised Watergate hearings. Nixon's resignation from office on 9 August removed Cushman's strongest political ally, surely a troubling turn of events.

Other changes were taking place in the Joint and Navy hierarchies. Air Force general George S. Brown succeeded Adm. Thomas H. Moorer as chairman of the Joint Chiefs, with Gen. David C. Jones filling in behind Brown as Air Force chief of staff. Adm. James L. Holloway III relieved Admiral Zumwalt as CNO, and Gen. Frederick C. Weyand was named by President Gerald Ford to succeed Army chief of staff Creighton W. Abrams, who had died on 4 September following surgery to remove a cancerous lung. Within three months, Cushman had become the only holdover on the

JCS. (In fact, Cushman was not a permanent member of the Joint Chiefs but by law was to sit in on only meetings pertaining to Marine Corps matters. But in practice during recent years, the commandant of the Marine Corps attended all the meetings.)

This new team continued to deal with a volatile international situation. The balance of power in Vietnam continued to destabilize, as the United States distanced itself from that unhappy nation. By the end of January, Cushman was telling the San Diego Council of the Navy League that "not since World War II have expectations—worldwide—been so unsettled."[20] His uneasiness was soon borne out, as heavy fighting erupted throughout Vietnam on 11 March, signaling another major North Vietnamese offensive. Unlike the situation in 1972, U.S. assistance to the beleaguered South Vietnamese consisted mostly of positioning ships and aircraft for evacuation operations. Early tactical blunders by the defenders led to loss of confidence and within weeks the invasion had become a rout. On 21 April, President Thieu resigned, denouncing the United States as "untrustworthy," and eight days later the evacuation of Saigon began, with the last Marine Corps helicopter lifting off from the roof of the American embassy at 1952 on 29 April 1975.

By this time, speculation about the next changeover of commandants had already begun, even earlier than usual. Cushman queried the Marine Corps generals about their preferences for his successor, and drew criticism for the way the letters had been prepared, although Under Secretary of the Navy David S. Potter later described allegations about "coded" letters as "unprovable."[21] Questioned later about the reason for such an early canvas of the generals, the commandant cited a pending pay-inversion situation that would penalize officers for remaining on active duty beyond October 1975 by making sharp cuts in their retired pay. Early announcement of a new commandant, he reasoned, would enable senior officers to gauge their prospects for advancement under his successor and make early retirement plans that ultimately saved them money.

On 1 May 1975, President Ford announced his nomination of Lt. Gen. Louis H. Wilson, then serving as commanding general, Fleet Marine Force Pacific, to be the twenty-sixth commandant. Within a week, General Cushman and the assistant commandant, Gen. Earl E. Anderson, had submitted their requests for retirement, effective 1 July 1975.[22]

The afternoon of the retirement and change-of-command ceremony at the Marine Barracks was sunny and unusually mild for midsummer Washington. Nostalgia prevailed, as the former commanding officer of the 1st Battalion, 9th Marines passed the baton to one of his former company commanders—the man he had recommended for the Medal of Honor. In presenting his remarks, Secretary of the Navy J. William Middendorf inadvertently referred to III Marine Amphibious Force as the "Hundred-and-Eleventh Marine Amphibious Force," but the spectators pretended not to notice.

26
Louis H. Wilson
1975–1979

COL. DAVID H. WHITE JR., USMCR (RET.)

A forceful leader with a sense of history, Gen. Louis H. Wilson, the twenty-sixth commandant of the Marine Corps from 1975 to 1979, guided the Corps from a shadowy post-Vietnam purgatory into its third century of existence as a fighting force. Awarded the Medal of Honor as a company commander in the battle for Guam, Wilson distinguished himself as a combat infantryman during World War II. He was the last Marine commandant to have fought in the Pacific island-hopping campaign of that war. As commandant, Wilson's military professionalism, his leadership style, his tremendous capacity for involvement with people, and his political finesse combined to create a veritable deus ex machina that would retrieve the Marine Corps from its Vietnam legacy, and permit it to survive its organizational crisis of the 1970s.[1]

Vietnam, both the costly war and the fragmenting historical phenomenon it represented, confronted the Marine Corps with unprecedented criticism of its mission, personnel policies, and force structure, and therefore diminished the prestige of this elite service. With the collapse of a global containment consensus during the Nixon and Ford administrations, the Marine Corps adjusted to a strategy of global flexibility while American defense planners shifted from Southeast Asia to a more Europe-oriented NATO defense posture. Amid lingering polarization between the American people and the armed forces, with inflation gnawing at the defense budget, critics within the American defense establishment and think-tankers without labeled the Corps's amphibious assault mission/capability obsolete and questioned its independent existence as a special force in readiness. Indeed, the challenging half-decade from 1975 to 1979 is a crucial chapter in the continuum of Marine Corps history, a "story of institutional adaptation in both peace and war."[2]

Wilson's selection as twenty-sixth commandant, following a publicized intra-Corps struggle for the post and an attempted purge of senior lieutenant generals, including Wilson, by the incumbent commandant, Gen. Robert E. Cushman, can be attributed

Gen. Louis H. Wilson Jr., twenty-sixth commandant.
U.S. Marine Corps Photo.

largely to the evolution of American national security policy in the wake of the Vietnam War. In the spring of 1975, Cushman recommended the appointment of his assistant commandant, Gen. Earl E. Anderson, but Secretary of the Navy J. William Middendorf II and Secretary of the Defense James R. Schlesinger pressed instead for Wilson to succeed Cushman.[3]

During the interview process, Schlesinger and Middendorf found Wilson, then the commanding general, Fleet Marine Force Pacific, an innovative and responsive officer who favored reorientation of the Marine Corps for worldwide commitments, with attention to Western Europe and NATO. Impressed by Wilson's adaptability and his credentials, Schlesinger obtained President Ford's approval of the nomination by telephone in April with Wilson still sitting in the secretary's Pentagon outer office. In early May, the Senate Armed Services Committee, chaired by Senator John C. Stennis, a staunch supporter of Wilson and fellow Mississippian, unanimously and with dispatch confirmed the appointment.[4]

After a six-week interim stint as special assistant to the commandant, a somewhat distant four wings down from Cushman's office at Headquarters Marine Corps, Wilson was promoted to general and embarked upon his commandancy. At the outset, Wilson demanded organization obedience to bring the Corps's performance up to his standards and to meet Schlesinger's expectations of flexibility. At the change of command ceremony at Marine Barracks in Washington on 30 June 1975, Wilson laid out his job philosophy in a very short sentence: "I call upon all Marines to get in step, and to do it smartly." And two days later, at the Pentagon swearing-in ceremony, Secretary Schlesinger called upon the Marine Corps to retain its special competence in amphibious operations while broadening its capabilities as a "general purpose" force. During the next four years, commandant Wilson aimed to prepare the Marine Corps for global missions and to restore its elitist image.[5]

At first, Wilson faced a barrage of external criticism about the Marine Corps's mission and force structure, all of which led up to a crescendo in January 1976 with publication of the Brookings Institution study on the future of the Corps. Declaring that the end of the age of amphibious warfare had arrived, the authors warned that the Corps had to shift its focus to a more relevant mission, such as the defense of Korea or Central Europe, or be diminished to a costly amphibious anachronism.[6] The passage of time makes the Brookings study appear jaded, especially after the Falklands War, but it did contribute to institutional self-examination which psychohistorians will no doubt one day explain.

When defense and media analysts questioned the survival of his Corps, Wilson struck back with the earnestness of a Scots Presbyterian and the incisiveness of a cobra. While interviewing the commandant for a Marine Corps birthday feature in 1975, CBS newsman Ike Pappas observed that the amphibious assault mission appeared to be out of date. Wilson responded that the "critics had said that before. They were wrong then and just as wrong now." As for searching for a mission, Wilson reported to Congress at the end of that year that as a ready, mobile, general purpose force with amphibious expertise, the Corps had a mission—a global force in readiness.[7] The ability to project combat power over the seas and onto a hostile shore was, in Wilson's mind, a building block of American strategy in the 1970s—a given, much like a geometric postulate. In this sense, Wilson was to the core a traditionalist.

But, after disengagement from Southeast Asia, Wilson broadened his own vision of a Marine Corps poised for development in low or high intensity combat around the globe. While he opposed specialized restructuring for combat in Europe only, he prepared Marine forces as a strategic reserve for deployment in Europe to support a NATO war contingency. Wilson's "best use" northern flank scenario, based on advance notice of an enemy threat, held that the Marine Corps could send one Marine Amphibious Force (MAF) to Denmark and one brigade to Norway to protect the Baltic approaches and to provide air support against an enemy threat to Iceland. Wilson theorized that the Marines could establish a defensive position between the North Sea and the Baltic, along the Kiel Canal, in case of Russian movement across the north German plain, and attack from the flank if Russian forces penetrated West Germany.[8]

Convinced that the Corps should not be typecast as exclusively an amphibious force, Wilson directed a Headquarters Marine Corps staff board, headed by Maj. Gen. Fred Haynes, to analyze the Corps's structure and mission in order to cope with future wars. From the Haynes study grew an emphasis on imaginative task organizing to provide flexibility rather than a radical departure to new technology. On the ground, the M-60 tanks replaced the M-48, the TOW and Dragon missiles increased the infantry's antiarmor capability, and the M-198 155-mm howitzer was selected to become the primary direct support artillery weapon. Basic infantry weapons remained: the M-16 rifle, the M-60 machine gun, and mortars. By 1979 the streamlined Marine division boasted centralized logistics and increased firepower.[9]

Structural refinements and the twin principles of task-organization and intensive training created the traditional foundation upon which Wilson's Marine Corps prepared for future combat. For that purpose, Wilson established the Air-Ground Combat Center at Twentynine Palms, California, to practice combined arms training, desert maneuver warfare, and mechanized/antimechanized operations.[10] Amphibious operations and maneuvers in northern Europe, the Caribbean, the Mediterranean, and in East Asia ensured global training for a Marine Corps with a global mission. Wilson delivered what he promised Schlesinger.

Determined to recapture the public admiration lost during the Nixon-Cushman years, Wilson also attacked the problem of quality in the Marine Corps as a priority military and political imperative. On his first day as commandant, Wilson ordered action on grooming and weight control for all personnel, and he broadcast to the ranks an absolute insistence on quality all the way from the recruiting effort, through the training pipeline, into the operating and support forces. Said Wilson, "The battlefield is no place to find out that our standards should have been higher." But Wilson had more in mind than operational readiness. In striving for the highest moral, mental, and physical standards, he intended to restore in the American people the traditional conviction that the Marines truly represented the epitome of elitism.[11] Wilson's now legendary commitment to quality control began the reconstruction of the popular, hence political, image of the Corps.

Wilson did not shrink from the challenge of maintaining the quality of the Marine Corps in a competitive, all-volunteer environment with manpower costs consuming seventy to eighty cents of every budget dollar. What has been dubbed the "Great Personnel Campaign, 1973–1977" became Wilson's inheritance from the Cushman-Anderson regime. In 1973 and 1974, unacceptably high rates of courts-martial, nonjudicial punishment, confinement, unauthorized absence, and desertion threatened combat readiness. Making matters worse, the Cushman assumption that mental aptitude (IQ) was the best indicator of quality caused the percentage of high school graduate enlistees to drop from 54 percent in 1973 to 51 percent in 1974 despite a congressional order to enlist 55 percent high school graduates in fiscal year 1974.[12]

To combat the recruiting problem, Wilson called upon the expertise of newly promoted and newly appointed Lt. Gen. Robert H. Barrow, deputy chief of staff for manpower at Headquarters. Barrow, who had just arrived from a tour as commanding general, Marine Corps Recruit Depot, Parris Island, South Carolina, held strong convictions about recruiting and recruit training and therefore proved an able adviser to the commandant, who had never himself been stationed at a recruit depot. The Wilson-Barrow reform initiatives in late 1975 grew out of Wilson's willingness to accept a Corps below its budget-authorized strength of 196,000, thus opening the way for an offensive on substandard marines through disciplinary action and an expedited discharge program.

In the recruiting arena, the main enlistment criterion shifted from IQ test scores to high school diploma as the most reliable indicator of quality in terms of retention, trainability, and acceptance of discipline. Wilson also set the new enlistment standard for fiscal year 1976 at 67 percent high school graduates and 75 percent for fiscal year 1977. In the fall of 1975, Headquarters in Washington began to shift responsibility for recruiting from the six Marine Corps district headquarters to the commanding generals of the recruit depots at Parris Island and San Diego in order to give control of recruit selection to the two commanders who were responsible for boot camp production of quality marines.[13]

These key recruiting reforms, along with increased budget outlays for the recruiting service, coincided with Headquarters' comprehensive review of recruit training beginning at the close of 1975. The thrust of policy making was to reduce recruit training stress and eliminate abuse of authority by training personnel, but a gulf existed between policy and drill instructor practice during the winter of 1975–76. When drill instructors increased pressure on recruits of 1975 vintage quality—what the late Col. Robert Heinl described as the effort to make silk purses out of sows' ears—attrition rates and complaints of abuse rose.[14]

Early in 1976, before Wilson could either implement reforms or fine-tune the system, allegations and several notorious cases of recruit abuse prompted ranking leaders in the Senate and House to call for congressional investigations into Marine Corps recruiting and recruit training. The case of Pvt. Harry Hiscock who was shot in the hand by a drill instructor at Parris Island and the death of Pvt. Lynn McClure as a result of head injuries sustained in mock bayonet practice with pugil sticks at San Diego generated critical press reports. Possibly more significantly, it aroused doubts among politicians that the Corps could cope with its manpower problems. The Hiscock and McClure cases also resurrected the ghost of Ribbon Creek, where six recruits drowned during a march into a tidal creek on Parris Island in 1956. As Wilson recalled, "The American public remembrance of Marine training is very long and the Ribbon Creek affair . . . was constantly brought up as if it happened yesterday."[15]

Hearings before the House Armed Services Committee accelerated the pace and broadened the scope of change in recruit training. In their testimony and statements from May to August 1976, Wilson and Barrow outlined specific changes/practices to curb abuses of authority and made four general commitments to Congress:

1. To reduce the level of stress on both recruits and drill instructors by eliminating the "motivation platoons," shortening the training syllabus, and permitting recruits a limited amount of free time daily and on weekends.
2. To strengthen and improve supervision of recruit training at all levels by doubling the number of officers assigned to recruit companies and platoon series and by assigning a brigadier general to each depot to reinforce the supervisory program.
3. To review and improve the processes of screening, selection, and training of drill instructors, including psychiatric evaluation and counseling instruction.
4. To provide the recruits with a protected, confidential channel through which to report abuses (personal interviews with officers).[16]

Wilson expected drill instructors at the depots to rise up en masse against the changes, but senior noncommissioned officers at Parris Island and San Diego rallied to support the commandant's order that training abuses would not be tolerated. But changes at the highly structured depots did produce discontent among drill instructors whose authority was eroded, and Wilson could foresee dissatisfaction among young officers who would rather lead in the Fleet Marine Force (FMF) than supervise at the depots. Nevertheless, Wilson honored the mandate of Congress to implement rigorous reforms and guarantee their enforcement. And when Barrow was selected as twenty-seventh commandant, Wilson was confident that the reforms would remain in place for at least four more years. Even now, the conduct of training is in compliance with the 1976 reforms. Wilson's vigilance preserved the integrity of recruit training and protected its ultimate purpose: to produce marines to fight, survive, and win in any future combat.[17]

Wilson's performance under fire during the 1976 hearings proved a successful test of his ability to represent the Marine Corps before Congress. A critical advantage during his commandancy was Wilson's past experience from 1967 to 1968, when he served as legislative assistant to Cmdt. Wallace M. Greene Jr. and Cmdt. Leonard F. Chapman Jr., both of whom enjoyed the respect of Congress. In that staff assignment, unique among the services, then Brig. Gen. Wilson had developed close working relationships with senators, House members, and congressional staff assistants who would be influential contacts when he became commandant in 1975.[18]

Supporters included senior southern Democrats, conservative Republicans, congressional marines, and defense-oriented congressmen. A longtime friend and political ally was Senator John Stennis (D-Mississippi), chairman of the Senate Armed Services Committee. Other staunch supporters on that committee included John Tower (R-Texas), who provided backing especially on Marine Corps aviation issues; Stuart Symington (D-Missouri), who retired from the Senate but remained a powerful figure in the Democratic party; Dewey F. Bartless (R-Oklahoma), ranking minority member and former lieutenant colonel aviator in the Marines; and Daniel K. Inoue (D-Hawaii), a former member of the committee. On the Senate Appropriations Committee, Wilson depended upon Stennis again and Senator Milton R. Young (R–North Dakota), the ranking minority member. Wilson assiduously courted his friends on the Armed Services Committee and paid courtesy calls on many during his first month in office. Although they were not on the Armed Services Committee, several other senators offered support on major issues: James Eastland (D-Mississippi), chairman of the Judiciary Committee; John Glenn (D-Ohio), the Marine aviator and astronaut who vigorously supported Wilson's efforts to acquire the AV-8B Harrier aircraft; and John Warner (R-Virginia), also a former Marine officer and former secretary of the navy, a "great booster" of the Marine Corps.[19]

On the House side, Wilson's network included many personal and official friends, especially members of the House Armed Services Committee. A primary adviser and Marine Corps Basic School classmate of Wilson's, Maj. Gen. John R. Blandford, had for many years served as chief counsel for the Armed Services Committee under the late chairman Mendel Rivers (D–South Carolina). Blandford had worked closely with Wilson when the latter was legislative assistant to the commandant, and even though Blandford was phasing out as chief counsel in 1975, he continued to be an important point of contract and general adviser. Wilson was a constituent and close personal friend of Congressman G. V. "Sonny" Montgomery (D-Mississippi), who, as a member of the Armed Services Committee, had participated in the 1976 hearings on recruit training. Congressman George H. Mahon (D-Texas), Wilson's golf partner and longtime friend, chaired the House Appropriations Committee.[20]

Because it afforded him opportunities to deal personally with congressmen and thus established his credibility, the legislative assistant job was Wilson's best preparation for the commandancy. The job also taught him the legislative process, since he accompanied Greene and Chapman in all their appearances before the House and Senate Authorization and Appropriation Committees. From Greene, a meticulous organizer of data, Wilson learned and perfected for his own use a flash card system for the annual hearings on the Marine Corps budget. A military assistant would pass to the commandant—"very much like a surgeon is handed his instruments"—a card bearing information requested during the hearings.[21] In this fashion, Wilson could respond flawlessly to any query related to the budget request. Surely, Wilson cherished his relationship with Congress.

Wilson's budgetary knowledge and mastery of the legislative process carried the Corps through three of President Jimmy Carter's defense budgets. With personnel costs skyrocketing due to 10 percent–plus inflation, Carter and Secretary of Defense Harold Brown authorized Wilson to save money through manpower reductions in order to fund operations, maintenance, and procurement. This management flexibility permitted Wilson to plan a reduction of ten thousand marines in the fiscal year 1981 budget ($10,000 marine/year) and thereby save $1 million for procurement and operations and maintenance.[22]

Together with manpower, amphibious shipping and aviation posed serious budget problems throughout the Carter years. The Carter budgets from 1977 to 1979 and the Navy's efforts to maintain a balanced fleet forced a continual reduction in amphibious (MAF) lift capability, thus a reduction in strategic mobility. Wilson and his former National War College classmate, CNO Adm. James L. Holloway III, compromised on a 1.33 MAF lift goal for the 1970s which was overly ambitious. Wilson also hoped for Navy's replacement of the aging Landing Ship, Dock (LSD) 28s on a one-for-one basis by the 1980s with the LSD-41s, which could carry the futuristic LCAC, landing craft air cushion.[23]

The modernization of Marine Corps aviation resulted in nothing short of bureaucratic warfare. In July 1975, Wilson canceled Cushman's earlier plan to purchase the Grumman F-14 despite the objections of senior Marine aviators who wanted the high technology fighter with its Phoenix missile and sophisticated tracking system. Opting for greater versatility, Wilson decided to retain the F-4 Phantoms and await development of the McDonnell-Douglas F-18 with its attack/fighter capability. The Corps pulled four F-14 squadrons from Naval Air Station Miramar in order to transfer those aircraft to the Navy, saving the CNO "blue water" aviation dollars. Wilson's military decision yielded a political benefit because the Navy badly needed the F-14s. Admiral Holloway in return promised Wilson in writing that the Marines would be first to receive the F-18s.[24]

At the same time, Wilson insisted that while waiting for the F-18, the Marine Corps would go forward with plans to acquire the new Harrier (VSTOL, vertical take-off aircraft), the AV-8B, to replace the AV-8A. The commandant demanded both the F-18 and the AV-8B. To be built by McDonnell-Douglas, the AV-8B was considered vital to assure land-based, fixed-wing close air support in amphibious operations without having to rely on existing airfields.

Wilson fought the Defense Department and Navy for the new Harrier. His chief opponent in DOD, Russell Murray, assistant secretary of defense for program analysis and evaluation, had great influence over Secretary Brown. In 1978, DOD blocked continued development and procurement. Wilson then appealed directly to his friends and allies in Congress. Senator Glenn, a strong supporter of the AV-8B and respected by his Senate colleagues for his aviation knowledge, may have been a key player, among others, in the struggle. In any case, Congress in early 1979 authorized $180 million for the AV-8B program for 1980, but in the spring, Wilson faced opposition from the new CNO, Adm. Thomas B. Hayward. Hayward, in the Navy Department Program Objective Memorandum FY 1981–1985 (POM-81), questioned the affordability of the AV-8B. Disappointed and furious over what he perceived as a "carefully woven tapestry of truths, half-truths and innuendoes," Wilson reacted in a blistering confidential letter to Hayward and dismissed "affordability" as a smoke screen for the real issue. He declared that the Navy opposed the AV-8B because it represented a significant threat to the large aircraft carrier. Wilson, refusing to be pressured into a decision unfavorable to Marine interests, outflanked the CNO and mobilized support for the Harrier from Secretary of the Navy W. Graham Claytor and his undersecretary, R. James Woolsey. In the end, Wilson felt confident that Congress, "which has always been our friend in time of need," would appropriate funds in the 1981 budget for the follow-on Harrier. Time would tell that Wilson and his allies had won the bureaucratic battle for the AV-8B.[25]

The crowning achievement of Wilson's stewardship of the Corps came in 1978, when the CMC became for the first time a permanent member of the Joint Chiefs of Staff. Technically limited by law to discussions of Marine Corps interest, the commandant's position had evolved by the 1970s to the point that Wilson participated in practically all JCS decisions. Wilson's strategy all along had been to wait until his fourth year in office to try to get the law changed, to make it clear that he was acting on behalf of the Corps and his successors, not himself. A catalyst that prompted Wilson to press for statutory change was the recent past behavior of Gen. George Brown, USAF, chairman of the JCS. Brown tolerated the commandant's collaboration in JCS decision making as an appeasement of Congress, but by his attitude made Wilson aware that the commandant was not actually a JCS member.[26]

Sensitive on the status issue and caught in an Orwellian position—the other service chiefs more equal than the commandant—Wilson girded himself for a major political drive. He consulted over a dozen close allies on how best to legislate the change, and followed a course of action suggested by Congressman Bob Wilson (R-California), the ranking minority member of the House Armed Services Committee. Congressman Wilson recommended the addition of a clause to the Senate Defense Authorization bill for 1979 to make CMC a full JCS member. Desiring to "have it happen on my watch," Commandant Wilson asked Senator Stennis to intercede on his behalf, to grant a favor. Said Stennis, "I'll do it for you." Tactical assistance came from Senator Bartlett (R-Oklahoma), a member of the Armed Services Committee. The World War II Marine dive-bomber pilot proposed an amendment to the Defense Authorization bill making the commandant a permanent member of JCS. With support of Stennis, Tower, and other loyalists, the resolution passed unanimously, a tribute to the incumbent commandant and Bartlett who was serving his last term in the Senate because of lung cancer. The commandant kept his strategy a well-guarded secret from DOD and JCS members until after the Senate voted, telling only Secretary Clayton what he was doing twenty-four hours in advance of the vote. The next morning Secretary of Defense Brown was reported to be surprised and appalled—and he knew that CMC was behind the strategy.[27]

Ranking members of the House Armed Services Committee held the key to passage in that chamber, and General Wilson lobbied hard and heavy among committee members. The commandant had secured secret pledges of support from Congressmen Melvin Price (D-Illinois), Samuel S. Stratton (D–New York), Bob Wilson, and others if the Senate passed the resolution without controversy, which it had done. Despite ruffled feathers at the Pentagon, no one openly criticized the commandant's full membership on the JCS and no organized opposition materialized to delete the enabling amendment from the authorization bill which breezed through the House Conference

Committee without dissent. After a Carter veto, and revision of the bill to remove a nuclear carrier which the president opposed, Carter finally signed the Appropriations Authorization Act of 1979 and presented Commandant Wilson with a plaque welcoming him as a full member of JCS. Even the reluctant Secretary Brown "congratulated the Marine Corps for the high prestige it has in the Congress which permitted such a potentially controversial bill to [go] through in such a smooth manner."[28]

Wilson had mobilized his political capital and had engineered the triumph to raise the commandant to his rightful place as a full JCS member to benefit future generations of marines. Marines and friends of the Marine Corps alike looked upon the JCS battle as a righteous crusade. Symbolically, it ended the Marines' desperate thirty-five-year-old struggle for survival and recognition as a separate military service. It was now in position to demand fair treatment from the three larger services and an often-hostile defense bureaucracy. Cast in the phraseology of the late Colonel Heinl, the Marine Corps had come to the end of a long march to the top.[29]

The JCS victory marked the high point of Wilson's commandancy and his distinguished Marine Corps career. When he retired to Mississippi in 1979 after thirty-eight years of active duty, Wilson could look to the distant past with individual pride as a Medal of Honor hero during the golden age of amphibious warfare, World War II. As custodian of the Marine Corps as an institution for four years, he could recall the recent past with proud confidence that his Corps had successfully adapted to the American defense evolution which came hard on the heels of the Vietnam War. With a curious blend of egoism and humility, Wilson remarked from retirement: "I leave [it] to future historians to judge my watch in comparison to the many fine commandants who were my predecessors and that long line who will be my successors."[30]

The Wilson era was a test of institutional survival for the Marine Corps and a test of the commandant's force. Wilson proved to be a consummate politician, an accumulator and user of political capital, ideally suited to negotiate the politico-military terrain of Headquarters Marine Corps, the Pentagon, and Congress. The Wilson legacy was a revitalized yet traditionally elite Corps esteemed by the public and Congress, more versatile, and more independent. Those same characteristics apply to Wilson the leader—traditional but adaptable and politically adept. In many ways, the twenty-sixth commandant owed his successful "watch" to the fact that he personified the best institutional characteristics of his Corps.

27
Robert Hilliard Barrow

1979–1983

BRIG. GEN. EDWIN H. SIMMONS, USMC (RET.)

To no one's surprise, Robert Hilliard Barrow was nominated in the spring of 1979 to succeed Louis H. Wilson as commandant of the Marine Corps. The two generals had been closely associated for many years. To a large extent they had been formed in the same mold. Both were products of the Old South: two tall, courtly men whose dignified good manners cloaked firm purpose and iron resolve.

Barrow was born in Baton Rouge, Louisiana, on 5 February 1922. The family plantation, Rosale, in West Feliciana Parish, had diminished in size, impoverished by events as distant as the Civil War and Reconstruction and as recent as the boll weevil. The family's past would exert a strong influence on Bob Barrow throughout his life. The Barrows, of English and Scots-Irish stock, had come to Louisiana from North Carolina by way of Tennessee in the late 1790s. The American settlers broke the weak hold of the Spanish on Baton Rouge and set up the Republic of West Florida, which was annexed to the United States in 1810. Rosale Plantation, six miles from the little town of St. Francisville, came into the Barrow family in 1844. Bob's great grandfather, another Robert Hilliard Barrow, outfitted a company called the Rosale Guards at the beginning of the Civil War and by the time of Shiloh was commanding its parent regiment. Great Uncle Charlie Barrow had enlisted in the Louisiana cavalry at age fifteen and fought for three years in the Civil War.

When Bob was about six, the family moved back to the country. Growing up at Rosale, Bob seldom saw a sizable town or city. Baton Rouge was thirty-five miles downriver and New Orleans a further eighty-five miles to the south. Both were long drives over bad roads. He had two brothers, both considerably older, and he grew up pretty much without their companionship. African American tenant farmers worked much of the place, and most of his playmates were black.

There was not much money, but it was a happy life, a kind of Mark Twain boyhood, though more Tom Sawyer than Huck Finn. He read all of the books he found on

Gen. Robert H. Barrow, twenty-seventh commandant.
U.S. Marines Corps Photo.

the shelves at home and was a prodigious borrower from the public library: Mark Twain, Edgar Allan Poe, Jack London, Rudyard Kipling, Robert Louis Stevenson, and Zane Grey. The house had no electricity, and he read by the light of a kerosene lamp. He often roamed the woods and streams alone. In addition to loving parents, nature and books were the early major influences on his life. He picked up a rudimentary knowledge of folk music and the guitar. Interest in folk music, the blues, and jazz became a lifetime passion.

He graduated from school in St. Francisville in 1939 at seventeen in a class of twenty-two members. He was tall and skinny, played football, and was president of his class and editor of the school paper. When it came to choosing a college, there was really only one option: Louisiana State University in Baton Rouge (tuition was free and boarding costs modest). He borrowed the $150 he needed for the general fee from his Episcopal minister. He served tables at what was called the Boarding Club, a school-run eating establishment, for his meals ($14.50 a month). He met his rent at the cadet barracks (three to a room, $6.50 a month) by working as the janitor for a twelve-room common area.

All physically fit males—there were no females—were required to serve in LSU's Corps of Cadets. In this, Barrow was following in the footsteps of John A. Lejeune, one of the Corps's greatest commandants. Lejeune was born twelve miles from Rosale, but the French-speaking side of the Mississippi was a world away and Barrow did not become aware of Lejeune until he came into the Marine Corps. The cadets wore their Confederate gray uniforms three times a week. Bob's half-formed ambition was to get a U.S. Army commission through the ROTC. He was in his third year at LSU when Pearl Harbor happened and America entered the war. The heroic defense of Wake Island, his first real awareness of the Marine Corps, impressed him enormously, as did a double-page recruiting ad in the *Baton Rouge Morning Advocate.* When a tall, fine-looking, Marine major came to the campus on 17 March 1942, Barrow signed up for the Platoon Leaders Class.

He finished out the school year and worked through the summer of 1942. His enrollment in the PLC program would have kept him in school until graduation, but he was impatient to get into the war. He asked for active duty and in November 1942 was sent to recruit training at San Diego. He never saw an officer. His platoon had two corporal drill instructors who were adequate, but not outstanding. The six-week recruit experience, in his opinion, "was not one that prepared someone to go off and be a fighting member of a fighting organization. . . . Probably the most important thing in boot training was learning . . . how to shoot the rifle . . . and discipline and obedience to orders, to be sure, although most of us were already adherents."[1]

His recruit photo shows him as being a shade under six feet, three inches. His time in the Reserve Officers Training Corps gave him an edge over most of the recruits. He stayed on as a junior drill instructor under the eye of a veteran staff sergeant. The tall Louisiana private "jawboning" as a drill instructor attracted favorable attention. He was ordered to depot headquarters for an interview and then given some tests. "The next thing you know," as he remembers it, "I was told that I was going to Officer Candidate Class."[2]

Barrow joined the 25th Officer Candidate Class at Quantico, Virginia, in March 1943 and finished fifth in a class of 236. He then went through the 28th Reserve Officers Course. He graduated in late July 1943 and was recommended for a regular commission. He had orders to Sea School but was sent instead to Marine Barracks, Naval Ammunition

Depot, New Orleans, where he was assigned as guard officer and mess officer. The CO was a mustang major with thirty-five years service, and the young lieutenant found it "a great learning experience, because he [the major] was so skilled in understanding human nature, and he had heard it all."[3]

Lieutenant Barrow received his regular commission while he was at the ammunition depot. He left in February 1944 with orders to Camp Lejeune, where he joined the 51st Replacement Battalion. He was on liberty in New York when a telephone call from Camp Lejeune reached him: did he want to go to China? Yes, sir, he did, and he dashed back to Camp Lejeune.[4] Sent to Washington, Barrow found that he was being assigned to the Sino-American Cooperation Organization (SACO), specifically to U.S. Naval Unit 2 in central China. During a six-week wait for transportation, Barrow learned that SACO had been formed with the blessing of Chiang Kai-shek and President Roosevelt. The Navy's primary interest was in the weather that originated in the China land mass. The Nationalist Chinese, in return for cooperating in the establishment of weather stations, wanted support for their irregular forces who varied widely in organization, training, and motivation. Navy captain Milton E. "Mary" Miles had gone out to China early in the war and formed a partnership with the extremely powerful Lt. Gen. Tai Li, who, among other things, was the commander of the Loyal Patriotic Army, a loose aggregation of tens of thousands of Chinese irregulars. An agreement signed 15 April 1943 established SACO under the command of Tai Li with Miles as his deputy.

Barrow received no special training but was simply shipped out to China, going on board an Army transport in Norfolk, transiting the Panama Canal, and reaching Bombay in forty-five-days sailing time. A day later, he was headed east to Calcutta on an old British train, a ten-day trip.

After a brief stay in Calcutta, he boarded a DC-3, owned by the China National Aviation Corporation and crewed by Australians, bound for China. His flight took him on a zigzag route over the Himalayas to avoid Japanese fighters and then into Kunming. A few days later he caught a flight to a forward fighter base at Chihkiang (Zhijiang). A rough ride over a primitive track took him from there to a very small mountain village, the new location of Unit Two, relocated as a consequence of the Japanese offensive to seize the six-hundred-mile stretch of railroad from Hankow (Wuhan) to Canton (Guangzhou).

At Camp Two he joined a column led by a Colonel Wong, known as the "Yellow Tiger," and took part in two successful attacks against Japanese garrisons. Wong achieved surprise by night marches and with the help of intense cold and heavy snowfall. The Japanese offensive to the south led to Barrow's reassignment to Nanning, ninety miles from the border with Japanese-controlled French Indochina. He spent most of his time at Nanning recovering from a bad case of dengue fever.

On his return to Camp Two, he was assigned to lead a party of four Americans and about twenty Chinese irregulars to resupply and operate with the Second Column of the Chinese Commando Army which was located to the east of the Japanese corridor. His Americans were all U.S. Navy: two chiefs who were demolitions experts, a radio operator (without radio), and a hospital corpsman. Each day along the way parties of about two hundred coolies would be pressed into service to carry the heavy (eighty to one hundred pounds each) loads of demolitions, ammunition, and limited, but essential, medical supplies.

The railroad was well patrolled by the Japanese, but Barrow's heavily laden foot caravan slipped across on a very dark night. Later he would say it was an accomplishment "which would repeat itself many, many times in the Korean and Vietnam War."[5] Barrow and his team would stay inside of or east of the Japanese corridor until the war ended five months later. In 1948, then–vice admiral Miles would present him with a Bronze Star for directing and coordinating "guerrilla operations in Hunan Province along the Hankow-Kweilin (Guilin) railroad."[6]

In late August 1945, Barrow learned through Chinese rumor that the war was over. In the next ten days, dodging isolated Japanese garrisons, he led about 450 Chinese guerrillas to Yo Yang north of Changsa. Here he was suspiciously received by the Japanese garrison commander who told him that the railroad south of there had been badly cut up by the Chinese—evidence of the good work done by the guerrillas. After nearly a month of waiting, time shared with thousands of Japanese soldiers awaiting surrender, Barrow and his team, still without orders, boarded a box car to Hankow and eventually got to Shanghai. Shanghai was a liberty port for the Seventh Fleet, and Barrow was assigned as officer-in-charge of the Shore Patrol every third day. Being a shore patrol officer in Shanghai, he found, was something like being the marshal in a wide-open western cow town. "It was not America at its best," he remembered.[7]

In March 1946, the Marine Corps reclaimed him and he was transferred to III Amphibious Corps in Tientsin (Tianjin). The III Amphibious Corps, commanded by Maj. Gen. Keller E. Rockey, had moved up from Okinawa to North China at the war's end to oversee the surrender and repatriation of the Japanese army. More important, the Marines were there to hold the ports, coal mines, and railroads, until Chiang Kai-shek's Nationalists could redeploy from South China. The alternative was their loss to Mao Tse-tung's Communist army, reinforced by the Soviet forces coming south from Manchuria. General Rockey wanted to hear of the young lieutenant's experiences in the interior. A few days later Rockey asked him if he would like to be his aide. Routinely Rockey kept his aides for no more than six months. Barrow would be with him for two and a half years.

General Rockey was not known for being a warm or communicative person, but he took a liking, almost paternal, to the tall young lieutenant from Louisiana. When Rockey left China to become briefly the commanding general, Department of the Pacific, in San Francisco, and then the commander of the new Fleet Marine Force, Atlantic, in Norfolk, Virginia, Barrow went with him. As an aide to Rockey, the alert young lieutenant learned much about the machinations of command and the delicacy of relations with the Navy. Barrow remembered, "It gave me a great insight into another level of life in the Marine Corps, at the very top at the time."[8]

Barrow's next assignment was to the Amphibious Warfare School, Junior Course, at Quantico. By then a captain, he checked in at the school in August 1948. All of the students, ranging from first lieutenants to majors, were veterans of World War II with a wide variety of experience. Much of the value of the school, he found, came in practical application, drawing on the knowledge of the class. He lived in bachelor quarters in Harry Lee Hall and had an enjoyable time. On graduating in June 1949, he stood in the middle third of the class academically and top third in practical application.

From Quantico he went to the 2d Marine Division at Camp Lejeune, North Carolina, and was given command of Company A, 1st Battalion, 2d Marines, a rifle company at half-strength. Being one of the few bachelor officers at Camp Lejeune qualified him for many social events as an escort for some senior officer's guest. In this way, he met Patty Pulliam. Her husband, a West Pointer, had been killed in an air crash, leaving her a widow with two small children, Charles and Cathy.

In late June 1950, with the beginning of the Korean War, the 1st Battalion, 2d Marines was sent across country by rail to Camp Pendleton to become the 1st Battalion, 1st Marines, 1st Marine Division. After about ten days, the newly reactivated 1st Marines, filled out to war strength with Reserves and under command of the legendary Col. Lewis B. "Chesty" Puller, sailed from San Diego. They staged through Kobe and then headed for Inchon, landing on 15 September 1950 as one of two assault regiments. The 1st Battalion, 1st Marines was in regimental reserve and landed well after dark and on the wrong beach. All was confusion. For most of the early advance on Seoul the 1st Battalion was the division's right flank unit. Able Company came into its own in the fight for Yongdung-po, the suburb across the Han River from Seoul. Company A was ordered on 19 September to relieve a company of the 5th Marines on Hill 188. Barrow pushed his company hard in the march to the hill. On 21 September, his company swept down the slope, crossed a dry rice paddy and the Kalchon River, and entered Yongdung-po.

After several fire fights his company reached the intersection of the Kimpo-Seoul road with the Inchon-Seoul road. The Kimpo-Seoul road ran along a dike that kept the Han on its course. Barrow, recognizing it as a very defensible piece of ground, dug in for the night in a sausage-shaped position. All radio contact was lost. Five North Korean T-34 tanks, unaccompanied by infantry, led off the attack against his company. His rocket gunners beat them back. North Korean infantry attacks then closed to within fifty yards. It was an all-night fight; 275 enemy dead were counted in the morning.

After the capture of Seoul, the 1st Marine Division reembarked and, after spending an inordinate amount of time at sea because of Soviet mines in Wonsan harbor, landed on 26 October against no resistance on North Korea's east coast. The division fanned out its battalions to the west and south to intercept the retreating North Koreans. The 1st Battalion, 1st Marines was put into railroad coal cars (a sort of semi-armored train) and sent south to occupy the picturesque coastal town of Kojo. Barrow's company was given a low hill mass to occupy west of the railroad. North Korean Army units, some of them still full of fight, were beating their way northward. The dispersed 1st Battalion came under attack. Able Company was sent out to do a reconnaissance-in-force while the rest of the battalion curled together to form a defensive perimeter. Barrow made contact with the enemy and used both close air support and naval gunfire to good effect. The 1st Battalion was then pulled back to Wonsan to be in regimental reserve.

Puller gave Barrow's company the mission of escorting a convoy of trucks loaded with rations and ammunition to Majon-ni, a critical road junction twenty-six miles west of Wonsan. Majon-ni was held by the 3d Battalion, 1st Marines, against a North Korean division and the road link had been cut for some days. Starting out in midafternoon, the convoy had to move along a narrow road that wound its way up through the mountains, the hairpin turns offering the enemy good ambush positions. Meeting heavy opposition and with night approaching, Barrow withdrew to try again the next day. Getting off with an early start he successfully punched his way through to Majon-ni, delivered his load of supplies, and had his trucks reloaded with 619 prisoners. Two days later he was back in Wonsan, having aided a beleaguered Marine rifle company along the way.

The Chosin Reservoir campaign came next. The U.S. 3d Infantry Division landed at Wonsan, having come out from the States, and relieved the 1st Marine Division so it could concentrate in the Hamhung-Hungnam area. The 1st Battalion, 1st Marines went north by motor march and train. With most of the fighting elements of the 1st Marine Division up on the plateau or in the mountains, 1st Battalion had drawn the rearmost position of any of the infantry battalions, that of holding Chinhung-ni at the foot of Funchilin Pass.

It was not a position that promised glory, but when the division recoiled on itself in its withdrawal from the reservoir, it was critical that Funchilin Pass, leading up into the mountains, be held. Tenure was threatened when the Chinese blew up an essential bridge on the winding road that threaded its way down the pass. The 1st Battalion was relieved on 7 December by elements of the 3d Infantry Division so that it could attack north to secure the high ground dominating the pass, and thus cover the withdrawal of the 1st Marine Division.

The critical feature was Hill 1081. Barrow's company was tasked to seize the summit. Approaching Hill 1081 involved a six-mile road march at night and in a snow storm. The snow proved a blessing. Its falling covered the sight and sound of their approach. The fight for the hilltop went on for two days, advancing by day, holding by night, with the extreme cold, twenty-five degrees below zero and worse, more of an enemy than the Chinese. The final assault jumped off on a clear, cold day against an entrenched enemy. Just about half of Barrow's company were casualties, made so either by the Chinese or the weather. But Hill 1081 was taken. Down below them Marine engineers rebuilt the bridge and the 1st Marine Division marched out intact, complete with vehicles, to Hungnam.

By now the tall captain with the Louisiana drawl was attracting considerable attention. His performance at Yongdung-po brought him a Silver Star and, for the taking of Hill 1081, the Navy Cross. Lynn Montross, the Corps's chief historian at the time and principal writer and editor of the Corps's five-volume history of the Marines in Korea, considered him, after due professional thought, the most outstanding Marine company commander of the war.

Barrow, on coming home from Korea, was assigned to Headquarters Marine Corps, where he had a year with the enlisted detail section. He had been corresponding with Patty. She lived in Washington and the romance blossomed.

In 1952, because of his World War II experiences in China, he was picked for a special, highly classified, assignment in the Far East. He made his way to a string of islands over two hundred miles north of Taiwan and very near the Communist Chinese mainland. Barrow remembered dryly, "There were some who believed that a diversion of any kind along the China mainland would be helpful to our efforts in Korea."[9] His activities included agent operations, signal intelligence, raids on Communist held islands, defense of friendly islands, and intercept of Chinese coastal shipping. The intercept "fleet," some captured, grew to twenty-three motorized junks, each with crude armor plate, 20-mm guns, and new engines installed at the "shipyard." During this assignment, the commandant, General Shepherd, sent him a handwritten note of encouragement.

He was now a major. He proposed to Patty by long-distance telephone on his way home and they were married on 29 August 1953. The following year, he and Patty had two more children, twin daughters May and Barbara. He began another tour at Headquarters Marine Corps, this time first with the training section and then with the operations section of G-3. He finished off the requirements for his bachelor's degree, left dangling since World War II, with night classes at the University of Maryland, majoring in military science.

In February 1956, he went again to Camp Lejeune where he was assigned to the 2d Battalion, 6th Marines as the S-3 or operations officer, later becoming the executive officer. The battalion went out to the Mediterranean on a routine deployment. Drawing on his Shanghai experience, Barrow volunteered to be the permanent shore patrol officer. There were accolades for the low rate of unpleasant incidents ashore. In August 1957, he joined the naval ROTC unit at Tulane University in New Orleans for a three-year tour as the Marine officer instructor. His duties allowed him time to take on some graduate work in history. He and Patty had their fifth child, Robert.

He left Tulane in June 1960, with a promotion to lieutenant colonel, and reported in to the Senior Course, Amphibious Warfare School, at Quantico in August. After two weeks he was pulled out of class to join the Publications Branch of the Landing Force Development Center, which was engaged in turning out a new family of field manuals and other doctrinal publications. He worked on the *Landing Force Manual* and an FMFM-21, *Guerrilla and Counter-Guerrilla Operations.* After a wait, he and his family received quarters—old frame houses moved there shortly after World War I—in "Whiskey Gulch" on Snake Hill Road at Quantico. Col. Lou Wilson, then commanding the Basic School, lived two doors down, and they became close friends.[10]

In August 1962, Barrow was reassigned to the Senior Course. He finished in May 1963 and was chafing to get away from the academic world. With orders to the 3d Marine Division in the Western Pacific in hand, he, his wife, five children, and a German shepherd dog made a hot summer trip in an aging station wagon without air conditioning to the family home in Louisiana where Patty and the children would stay. Barrow spent his year on Okinawa with Task Force 79/III Marine Expeditionary Force (III MEF), a small planning staff which as TF 79 interfaced with the Seventh Fleet. Maj. Gen. James Masters was both commanding general, 3d Marine Division, and CG III MEF. Brig. Gen. Raymond A. Davis was the assistant division commander.

"There was unlimited opportunity to do things," said Barrow.[11] He became G-3, a colonel's billet, as a lieutenant colonel. He represented TF 79/III MEF at Seventh Fleet scheduling and planning conferences. Planning for Southeast Asia Treaty Organization (SEATO) exercises took him to Bangkok. Much of the planning had to do with the growing U.S. involvement in South Vietnam. Contingency plans committed the III Marine Expeditionary Force to the northern five provinces of South Vietnam. He visited Da Nang. The Marines had a CH-34 helicopter squadron operating there in support of South Vietnamese forces. When the 9th Marine Expeditionary Brigade, under General Davis, was alerted to mount out for Vietnam, Barrow was assigned as the brigade G-3.

He did a great deal of briefing. His work impressed the new commander of Fleet Marine Force, Pacific, Lt. Gen. Victor H. Krulak. In September 1964, coincidentally just after the Tonkin Gulf crisis, Krulak handpicked him to be the G-3 Plans officer in his headquarters in Hawaii. Between stations, Barrow went home, got Patty and the children, and drove across country in the same 1959 Chevrolet, still without benefit of air conditioning. Serving under "Brute" Krulak, who rewarded him with a Legion of Merit, would be "three hard-working but wonderful years."[12] He made thirty some trips in these years, mostly to Vietnam, and was selected for promotion to colonel.

He recalled, "I have never worked in any job in the Marine Corps that I've thought was more demanding of my time and whatever abilities I had, than my assignment at FMFPac. . . . I thrived on it. . . . The G-3 Plans [officer] at FMFPac, as General Krulak saw it, was a kind of generalist, utility infielder, designated hitter, whatever you choose to call him, called upon to do just about anything."[13]

Barrow's next orders took him to the National War College in Washington in August 1967. He and his family returned to the continental United States in the liner SS *Lurline,* which the restless Bob Barrow found boring. His individual research paper at the National War College was a prophetic "Sea-Based Counterinsurgency: Another Dimension of Sea Power." But Barrow had no great enthusiasm for high-level schools. "Why am I doing this when there's something else I think I can do well and I ought to be doing it?" he asked himself.[14]

That "something else" was command of a regiment in Vietnam. Before leaving Washington, he settled his family in a house he had purchased in the Aurora Hills area close to the Pentagon. His orders were to the 1st Marine Division, where he would have been the G-3. In a stopover at FMFPac headquarters in Hawaii, he paid a call on the new commanding general, Henry W. Buse, who informed him that there was a change of orders: he was going to have command of the 9th Marines in the 3d Marine Division, now under his friend, Maj. Gen. Ray Davis.

He arrived in South Vietnam in July 1968. An intermediate Headquarters, XXIV Corps, commanded by Lt. Gen. Richard G. Stilwell, USA, stood between the 3d Marine Division and the III Marine Amphibious Force, the Corps's senior field command in Vietnam. Both Stilwell and Davis were advocates of high-mobility operations. The 9th Marines command post at that time was collocated with that of the 3d Marine Division at Dong Ha, close to the coast. Barrow's first actions were to get his regimental headquarters out of its bunkers and move it up into "Leatherneck Square," near the Demilitarized Zone.

He next moved his headquarters to Vandegrift Combat Base, the second of fourteen regimental command post displacements. General Davis visited him almost daily. Davis, said Barrow, had a "kind of sixth sense about the enemy." They would sit silently staring at a mapboard until Davis gestured at a point on the map with a comment, "You know, we ought to take a look at that."[15]

During a six-month period, the reinforced 9th Marines conducted a series of highly successful operations south of the western part of the DMZ and in the Khe Sanh and Ba Long Valley areas. Barrow, an excellent map reader with the ability to turn a map into a picture in his mind of the terrain, would pick up what looked like good fire-support base sites, to be confirmed by personal aerial reconnaissance. Working with his supporting artillery battalion commander and combat engineer officer, "we became literally masters at building fire support bases."[16]

The greatest payoff came with Operation Dewey Canyon. On 22 January 1969, Barrow's 9th Marines went into North Vietnamese Base Area 611, where the Da Krong and A Shau Valleys almost meet. Depending entirely upon helicopters for logistic support from bases thirty miles away, the regiment's battalions attacked overland, always within the fan of artillery fires from fire support bases. By 19 March, Base Area 611 was cleaned out. The regiment counted 1,617 enemy dead and had captured 1,461 weapons and hundreds of tons of ammunition and supplies.[17]

After nine months with the 9th Marines, longer than most colonels got to command a regiment, Barrow left in April to spend the last four months of his tour as deputy G-3 of the III Marine Amphibious Force. For his Vietnam service he received yet another award of both the Bronze Star and Legion of Merit plus the Army's Distinguished Service Cross for his prowess in Dewey Canyon. General Stilwell, not a man noted for lavish praise, called Barrow "the finest regimental commander in Vietnam."[18]

Colonel Barrow departed Vietnam in late July 1969 and a month later, as a new brigadier general, was in Okinawa as the commanding general of Marine Corps Bases. His wife and three of his children accompanied him. His headquarters was at Camp Smedley D. Butler, but "Camp Butler" was not a single camp. It was an array of camps. As the base commander, Barrow had cognizance over facilities totaling something like 750 buildings and forty-four thousand acres. His largest tenant command was the 3d Marine Division. Also present were the rear headquarters of the III Marine Amphibious Force and a portion of the 1st Marine Aircraft Wing. Under him was a succession of camp commanders who changed frequently. Black-white racial problems, always endemic on Okinawa, were at their height.

He found himself working closely with Army lieutenant general James B. Lampert, the U.S. high commissioner. Planning was being done for the reversion of Okinawa to Japanese sovereignty. All the services had a large number of Ryukyuan workers and there was a good deal of labor unrest and anti-Americanism. In May 1972, the U.S. flag was lowered and the Japanese flag raised over all previous U.S. facilities. Relations with the Japanese throughout the whole reversion process were strained. For his role in the reversion, Barrow received the Joint Services Commendation Medal from General Lampert.

Barrow had handled his problems as base commander on Okinawa well; he arrived as a "frocked" brigadier general and left three years later as a selected major general. For his tour he received his third Legion of Merit. He would find his Okinawa experience of great use during his remaining twelve years of active service.

His next assignment, as a freshly promoted major general, would be to the Marine Corps Recruit Depot, Parris Island, South Carolina, the fabled "boot camp" for Marines recruited east of the Mississippi. Barrow said years later, "Discipline is achieved by the regimen that these young men are put through and demands placed on them by this unusual personality called a drill instructor."[19] He attended the graduation parade of every class and always found it a moving experience. Most drill instructors were good; a few were not. Barrow set out to eliminate the poor ones and to eradicate any vestige of recruit abuse. He introduced psychiatric screening for prospective drill instructors. Told that he could not "attrit" more than 10 percent of the recruits, he confronted his subordinate commanders and told them, "We are not going to be bound by ten percent. Let water seek its own level. Is that clear to everyone?"[20]

Attrition went up to close to 25 percent. Barrow found statistical proof of what he had long believed: a high school diploma was the best predictor of a recruit's eventual success. "In 1974 we had 49 percent high school graduates, and it didn't seem to bother anyone at Headquarters," he later remembered.[21] Barrow saw many virtues for the high school graduate criterion, among them, "If he finished high school, he has manifested some amenability to discipline, although school discipline can't equate to Marine discipline. . . . More importantly, the high school graduate probably came from a caring family."[22]

The commanding generals of the recruit depots at Parris Island and San Diego had no direct control over the actual recruiting, which was under the district directors. Barrow found the recruiters bent on "making quota." He later declared, "I was frustrated by the quality of people that was being . . . sent to Parris Island, and I am afraid I took it out on the recruiting service."[23]

In his next assignment he would be able to make some fundamental changes. Barrow's longtime friend Lou Wilson became commandant on 1 July 1975 and, in selecting his generals for key positions, brought Barrow up from Parris Island to be his deputy chief of staff for manpower. This billet carried with it a promotion to lieutenant general. With Wilson's backing, Barrow set in motion certain reforms. Too much effort, in his opinion, was going into trying to salvage marginal recruits. He deplored the false assumption "that Parris Island and San Diego, the two recruit depots, could make Marines out of anyone."[24] "We had to reform recruiting," he recalled, "and at the same time we recognized the need to reform recruit training, like getting rid of all this remedial business."[25]

One of the first Wilson-Barrow pronouncements, made within a week of their July arrival in Washington, was that recruiting was going to be brought under the command of the recruit depot commanders: all recruiting east of the Mississippi under the commanding general at Parris Island, all west of the Mississippi under the general at San Diego. Barrow believed that the tests given prospective recruits were badly "normed" and in many cases compromised. He set about to have that corrected. To rid the ranks of unsatisfactory marines, he began something called the Expeditious Discharge Program by which such marines could be swiftly discharged, without prejudice, administratively.

Barrow's recruiting reforms were barely under way when the Marine Corps was staggered by the two most publicized cases of recruit abuse since the Ribbon Creek tragedy of 1956, when a drill instructor had taken his platoon on an unauthorized night march which resulted in six drownings.[26] A recruit died in March 1976 after being struck in the head in December in San Diego by a "pugil stick," a wooden staff padded at both ends and used to train recruits in bayonet fighting. It might have been written off as just an unfortunate training accident, but the recruit's congressman called for a congressional investigation on the grounds that the recruit was mentally retarded and should never have been recruited. A more blatant, if not fatal, case of abuse occurred at Parris Island when a drill instructor accidentally shot a recruit through the hand with an M-16 rifle as a climax to a bout of inappropriate harassment. The two cases brought forth a spate of reports in the media of other abuses.

The House of Representatives' Subcommittee on Military Personnel held special hearings in May and June 1976. Barrow was an impressive and effective witness before this and the several other congressional committees that concerned themselves with defense matters. Criticism of the recruit process subsided.

Barrow's Manpower post brought with it official quarters at the Marine Barracks in Washington. The Barrows entertained often and well in a very southern style. Barrow left Manpower in October 1976, after fifteen months, going to Norfolk to take command of Fleet Marine Force, Atlantic, the same billet held by his patron, Gen. Keller Rockey, nearly thirty years earlier. His operational superior was Adm. Isaac C. ("Ike") Kidd Jr., then commander in chief, Atlantic Fleet as well as commander in chief, Atlantic. The two got along famously. Kidd had him visit such diverse places as Iceland and the Azores. He would give Barrow a second Joint Services Commendation Medal.

Barrow remembered, "This was a time when we were talking about the Panama Canal Treaty, and never knew when it might erupt into something."[27] He applied the lessons he had learned while G-3 Plans officer at FMFPac to his command of FMFLant: "We planned for deployment of Marines from extreme Northern Europe, around through the Mediterranean . . . all the way into Panama and places in between."[28] Barrow was the commanding general, II Marine Amphibious Force, as well as CG FMFLant. There was not more than a brigade's worth of amphibious shipping in the Atlantic. A 4th Marine Amphibious Brigade was created and deployed frequently for NATO exercises in Norway and northern Germany. The winter exercises in Norway led to the prepositioning of a brigade's worth of supplies and equipment in Norway, something that was new for both the Marines and Norway. Cold-weather training was begun at Fort Drum, New York, and Camp Ripley, Minnesota, as well as continued at the longtime Marine Corps cold-weather training camp at Pickel Meadows, California. Other exercises, just as important, were being conducted in the Mediterranean, particularly the Eastern Mediterranean.

One of Barrow's greatest concerns was that he found so many FMF units, whatever their strength might be on paper, badly undermanned. Actual "foxhole strength" was a problem in Korea, again in Vietnam, and it would be a problem he would work on for the rest of his career.

His stay in Norfolk was less than two years. On 1 July 1978, General Wilson brought Barrow back to Washington to be his assistant commandant with a promotion to four stars. The Corps took this as a clear and final signal that Barrow was Wilson's choice to be the next commandant. If so, Barrow did not take it as such. In a 1989 interview, he said that, while he and Wilson were close friends, "I was never made to feel, by anything he said or anything else, that I was the heir apparent."[29] As assistant commandant, Barrow routinely took part in virtually all briefings given the commandant and sat with the Joint Chiefs of Staff in Wilson's absence. It was about this time that Wilson achieved full membership on the JCS. There was a fair amount of acrimony, Barrow found, among the chiefs. "Not ugly, but it was there," he said.[30]

The Barrows again had quarters at the Marine Barracks, this time Quarters 1, immediately next to the Commandant's House. Overall, it was a pleasant year, and, despite his demurral, it was a year in which Barrow understudied Wilson. President Jimmy Carter called Barrow to the White House for an interview. As it ended, the president said, "General Barrow, I would like you to be the next Commandant of the Marine Corps."[31] The public announcement that the president had nominated Barrow for appointment as the twenty-seventh commandant came on 18 April 1979. The first thing Barrow did after the nomination was announced was to gather together all the generals then in Headquarters to expound a bit about his philosophy "which they were probably curious about."[32] Much of what was said had to do with quality.

Confirmation hearings were held on 1 May. Senator John Stennis of Mississippi chaired the Senate Armed Services Committee. It was a friendly, not challenging, committee. Senator Sam Nunn of Georgia was present, and so was Senator Russell Long of Louisiana, who spoke glowingly about Barrow and his family. In his statement to the committee, Barrow stressed that "the Marine Corps was embarked on an era of getting better in areas of people and equipment."[33] As assistant commandant, he had "felt like a fifth wheel . . . not underemployed [but] underinformed."[34] On 14 May, President Carter announced the nomination of Lt. Gen. Kenneth McLennan as assistant commandant effective 1 July. Barrow had chosen McLennan and had decided to combine the billets of assistant commandant and chief of staff.

On Friday evening, 29 June 1979, at the traditional parade at Marine Barracks, Washington, Barrow symbolically took command of the Marine Corps, relieving Wilson. In his remarks he reminded the audience that when Wilson took command in 1975, his first order was to "get in step and do so smartly." Barrow said his first order was to follow Wilson's admonition and "to keep in step."[35]

L. Edgar Prina, a veteran writer on naval affairs, devoted an article in the June 1979 *Sea Power,* the magazine of the Navy League, to the coming commandancy of General Barrow. In it, he said, "Barrow will inherit a Corps that has attained a high degree of combat readiness for peacetime. He will also inherit a number of serious and nagging problems, including this key one: how to ease the impact of inflation on morale and modernization so that the highest quality personnel and material may be obtained?"[36] Barrow, Prina continued, "makes no secret that quality recruiting remains at the top of his list of priorities. . . . Barrow, like Wilson, will not ease his demands for quality first in the individual Marine: in appearance, conduct, and performance. He would rather see the Corps come down some in total numbers than lower its standards."[37]

Barrow had to balance the operations and maintenance of the Marine Corps at the moment against modernization for the future. During his first week as commandant, he announced that he was willing to accept a decrease in end-strength in fiscal year 1980 from 189,000 to 179,000 in order to obtain funds to maintain combat readiness. Barrow meant it, but it came across as a scare tactic. He persisted and received $58 million in reprogrammed dollars. Fiscal year 1980 began on 1 July 1979 with 185,250 marines and ended a year later with 188,469.

In Barrow's opinion the "all-volunteer" recruiting effort, which had replaced the draft, was working, but only marginally. Recruiting of high school graduates was now hovering around 75 percent. "I thought we could go all the way to close to, if not, 100 percent," he stated.[38] And he was willing to go to a smaller Corps to do it: "I let people know that . . . maybe in peacetime the most important thing the Marine Corps could do [was to] recruit well."[39] Ed Prina also said in his *Sea Power* article, "The new Commandant may find himself running into some resistance when and if he pushes for the advanced AV-8B Harrier vertical/short take-off and landing aircraft and a new class of amphibious ships, LSD-41, to replace the aging LSD-28s."[40]

The Navy was loath to spend "blue" dollars for new amphibious ships or special-purpose Marine Corps aircraft. Barrow believed that relations with the Navy could be improved. One of his first acts as commandant was to meet with the CNO, Adm. Thomas B. Hayward. His message was, "We either hang together or we hang separately. Together we make a very positive presentation about the importance of naval forces, but if we let anyone pick away at us individually or we ourselves shoot at the other side, the other part of the partnership, we're doing ourselves a great disservice."[41]

On 5 July, Barrow called a press conference at the Pentagon, speaking at considerable length concerning the Navy–Marine Corps team. He talked about the importance of a maritime strategy built on control of the sea and power projection. He would carry this message to many other audiences.

As he later declared, "One of the things I attempted to do as commandant was to reestablish as much understanding as possible on the part of the public, the Congress, and everyone else, of the utility and usefulness of the Marine Corps. You cannot do that without talking about the Navy or speaking of sea power or maritime strategy or whatever you choose to call it."[42]

In November 1979, as a byproduct of the Islamic revolution that toppled the Shah of Iran, the U.S. Embassy in Tehran was sacked and sixty Americans, including nine marines, were taken hostage. It shook America that the Carter administration was apparently helpless. In the same month, the U.S. Embassy in Islamabad was sacked and burned. A marine security guard was killed.

The requirement for a "rapid deployment" force was an imperative coming out of the debacle in Iran. The question was: how could military force best be projected into the Middle East? The Army had begun to talk of a "rapid deployment force," a 100,000-man strike force that could be air-lifted to any point around the globe. Barrow did not regard this as a threat to the Marine Corps's amphibious mission because he saw limits as to what could be air-lifted.

Barrow found Harold Brown, the secretary of defense, a brilliant man who did not like small talk. He met with him officially, along with the other service chiefs and department secretaries, twice a week. Only rarely did he see him on a one-on-one basis. In one of his few personal interchanges with Barrow, Brown asked the rhetorical question: "Do Marines always have to storm ashore?"[43] Barrow answered that amphibious assaults were just a means to an end and that the Corps did most of its fighting after getting ashore, by whatever means. Brown then advanced the idea of ships being preloaded with necessary supplies and equipment to meet with the Marines at a safe port where they could be unloaded. Barrow told him that marines were "accustomed to having one foot on the beach and one foot in the sea."[44]

Barrow took the concept back to his staff "to come up with a force of some size and structure that could do the kinds of things one might have to do."[45] What evolved was an emphasis on the creation of Marine amphibious brigades that could "marry-up" with prepositioned ships at some safe port close to the projected area of operations. Barrow briefed the JCS in terms of a 16,500-man air-ground brigade with far more combat potential than the Army's recommendation of an armored cavalry regiment.

By now it was public knowledge that Secretary Brown had approved a concept called "Maritime Prepositioning." First step was "Near-Term Prepositioning Ships," an improvisation with readily available commercial cargo ships. There was an immediately perceptible relationship between maritime prepositioning, a Marine amphibious brigade, and the new rapid deployment force. The brigade took shape as the 7th Marine Amphibious Brigade with headquarters at Twentynine Palms, California.

In December 1979, Secretary Brown announced that the new "Rapid Deployment Joint Task Force" would be headed by a Marine general. That appointment and a promotion of lieutenant general went to Paul X. "P.X." Kelley, at least partly because of Barrow, who feared that if the assignment went to an Army general, the rapid deployment force would be regarded as an all-Army show. Somewhat surprisingly, this recommendation received the support of Gen. David C. Jones, the JCS chairman, not known to be a particular friend of the Marine Corps. In the Joint Chiefs' discussion of the appointment, Jones suggested that the top job be rotated between the Army and the Marine Corps, with the first appointment going to the Marine Corps.

On 31 January 1980, Barrow delivered his first "posture" statement as commandant to the House Armed Services Committee. Although there was always a formal, written statement, it was Barrow's style to speak without notes, a practice he would follow for four years. He set a goal of ten thousand women marines. The goal was not reached, but it was Barrow's way of emphasizing that there were more places in the Marine Corps where women could be used. He remained unalterably opposed, however, to the assignment of women to the combat arms.

The Rapid Deployment Joint Task Force (RDJTF) was activated on 1 March 1980 with Lieutenant General Kelley as its first commander and with headquarters at McDill Air Force Base, Tampa, Florida. Key contributions by the Marine Corps would be the training of the 7th Marine Amphibious Brigade in desert operations and the implementation of maritime prepositioning. Barrow visited the loading-out of the Near-Term Prepositioned Ships at Wilmington, North Carolina, with stores drawn from the Marine Corps Logistics Base at Albany, Georgia. Some time later he flew to Australia to see the concept tested with an exercise involving the landing of a Marine amphibious unit near Perth.

The Barrows' style of gracious entertaining was well suited to the historic Commandant's House. Invitations to dinner with the Barrows or to attend the summer parties inside the walled garden, enlivened most often by a jazz combo, followed by the unmatched Evening Parade, were much sought after.

But another tragedy was in the offing. President Carter directed the Joint Chiefs to find a way to get the hostages out of Iran. Gen. David Jones, the chairman, became, in effect, according to Barrow, the action officer, "the one individual that knew all the parts better than anyone else."[46] Barrow himself thought too much was being expected of the Navy helicopters which were to be flown mostly by Marine pilots and said so at the JCS. While he thought the rescue effort was high risk, he did not think it impossible. In April 1980, the United States armed forces experienced the terrible failure of Desert One. Carter's term was nearing an end: "The hostage situation in Teheran was Jimmy Carter's albatross," opined Barrow in 1991. "It preoccupied, I suppose most of his waking hours."[47]

Ronald Reagan's election in November 1980 brought with it a growing optimism among the service chiefs. Not only were the services going to be better funded, but they now would have a commander in chief "with firm convictions about a strong America."[48]

Barrow was in the reviewing stand for the parade following Reagan's inauguration in January 1981, when the new president whimsically asked him if it would be all right if he saluted the passing colors while in civilian clothes. Barrow assured him that it would be. He found the new secretary of defense, Caspar Weinberger, "a hard-driving, determined," and sincere person whom he came to admire greatly. Early on, Barrow had a long, wide-ranging talk with the new secretary of the navy, the much-younger John Lehman, with emphasis on the Marine Corps's contribution to a maritime strategy.[49] That started a dialogue that would continue.

By February 1981 the press was reporting a split among the Joint Chiefs over command arrangements for the Rapid Deployment Force. Barrow favored placing the RDJTF under the Pacific Command. Jones and most of the other chiefs thought it should be under the European Command. The outcome was that the Rapid Deployment Force became a new unified command, the Central Command, the command that would fight the Persian Gulf War.

In August 1981, General Barrow stood before his generals at the opening of the year's General Officers Symposium (which brought in three-quarters of the Marine generals from all parts of the world) and asked them, "Do I look like a Marine Corps general?" All would have answered yes, the epitome of a Marine Corps general, but the question was rhetorical. What he was getting at was the short-sleeved khaki shirt (very popular in Washington's summer heat) he was wearing, going on to compare it with a sport shirt. At that point he announced his "Let's dress up, not down" uniform policy. He decreed that the green service uniform would be the uniform of the day, with the wear of the "woolly-pully" sweater limited to working hours. He stressed the wear of the blue dress uniform by all who had it on all appropriate occasions and encouraged the wear of both the green and blue uniforms off duty. He discouraged the wearing of slacks by women Marines. He smartened up the appearance of gate sentries and military police.[50]

In his appearances before congressional committees, Barrow repeatedly expressed his concern over the shortage of amphibious shipping and the slowness with which obsolescent amphibious shipping was being replaced. The total of sixty-seven amphibious ships then in commission fell far short of the established goal to lift one MAF and one MAB simultaneously. Barrow's efforts to increase amphibious lift meshed nicely with Secretary Lehman's goal of a six-hundred-ship Navy. Barrow would have the satisfaction of going to the keel-laying of the *Whitbey Island,* the first of the new LSD-41 class of "landing ship, dock," at the Lockheed shipyard in Seattle, Washington, on 4 August 1981.

Beyond amphibious shipping, he was also concerned about the adequacy of naval gunfire, medical support, and mine countermeasures, all Navy responsibilities. Having had several discussions on the subject with Lehman, he was delighted when the secretary testified to a Senate subcommittee on the Navy's intentions to bring two battleships, with their 16-inch guns, out of mothballs. (In December 1982, the battleship *New Jersey* would be recommissioned. President Reagan would attend, and Barrow would be in the official party.)

Both Wilson and Barrow had argued for the procurement of the F/A-18 Hornet as the replacement for the aging McDonnell-Douglas F-4 Phantoms of the Vietnam era. The first Marine Corps F/A-18 rolled off the line at the Northrup plant, in Hawthorne, California, on 13 January 1982. "The F/A-18 was a much-welcomed airplane, because it was replacing an ancient one that had served us well, the F-4," said Barrow.[51]

In traveling about the Corps, Barrow encountered a good deal of apathy on the part of the Corps's younger leaders on the subject of drug use. He decided to use the full authority of the commandant's office in a very personalized way. He visited all major commands, addressing audiences of officers and promising to provide the policies and tools to deal with the problem. On 1 February 1982, he issued an "ALMAR" launching a concentrated campaign to eliminate the use of illegal drugs in the Marine Corps. A key provision of the order was that all Marines would be subject to random urinalysis testing: "In the case of staff NCOs and officers, no second chance. Out! Gone! We would encourage probable cause searches, searches at the gate. We got sniffer dogs trained and brought in."[52]

He "energized," to use his term, the leadership. Detected drug use began to go down, not dramatically at first, but it went down. In the years that followed a random test of a sizable unit such as a Marine aircraft group or regiment would reveal only 0.5 to 1.0 percent usage. "That's better than any institution in America. Hands down," said Barrow in 1992, then, on reflection: "Maybe the Girl Scouts can do better."[53]

In his 1982 posture statement, Barrow reported to Congress, "My personal observations of your Marines convince me that they are as tough and ready as United States Marines have ever been."[54] He attributed this toughness and readiness to greatly expanded training opportunities. Exercises were taking Marines to some ninety to a hundred places around the globe each year. In that same posture statement, Barrow said, "The Marine Corps's ability to deploy rapidly and accomplish its mission, however and whenever called, depends on quality individuals who can endure rigorous training, accept firm discipline, respond to sound leadership, and perform with intelligence and capability."[55]

Barrow's sergeant major of the Marine Corps throughout his tenure as commandant was Leland Crawford, a handsome man with a great deal of presence. "He was a master of direct talk," remembered Barrow of the Corps's senior NCO. "He could bring problems to me that perhaps no one else could and . . . I could be confident that he wasn't being superficial."[56]

In April 1982, some ten thousand marines and sailors from the 7th Marine Amphibious Brigade took part in Gallant Eagle '82 at Twentynine Palms, an exercise that involved an additional fifteen thousand members of the other services. The exercise simulated a combat situation in a desert environment. The Gallant Eagle series of exercises continued annually. They would be, as it turned out, a rehearsal for Desert Storm.

The Israeli invasion of Lebanon in June 1982 created a fresh crisis in the Middle East. The 32d MAU, under Col. James M. Mead, landed its ground elements at Beirut in late August. The MAU formed the U.S. element of a multinational force which oversaw the safe and orderly departure by sea of Palestine Liberation Organization forces. Mission accomplished, the 32d MAU withdrew from Lebanon in early September. Barrow visited the unit ashore and at sea on 26 September, presenting it with the Navy Unit Commendation for the success of the evacuation. Three days later, the 32d MAU had to land again because of the increasing disorder ashore. It was the beginning of the lengthy, and eventually tragic, Marine Corps "presence" in Lebanon. A month later, the 24th MAU under Col. Thomas M. Stokes Jr. replaced the 32d MAU at Beirut. Almost immediately the marines ashore assumed a more warlike stance. By the first week of November, they were making jeep patrols out to the "Green Line" which separated the Christian from Moslem sectors of the city.

On 7 December, President Reagan announced the activation of the U.S. Central Command, the expected outgrowth of the Joint Rapid Deployment Force. For political reasons, Israel and Lebanon were not included in the USCENTCOM's geographical area of responsibility. Barrow thought this a mistake.

By the first half of 1983, which would be Barrow's last six months as commandant, the Marine Corps was benefiting in an increasing way from the Reagan administration's investment in new and improved weapons and equipment. Problems in Lebanon, however, were increasing. On 2 February 1983, Marine captain Charles B. Johnson created an international incident by drawing his pistol while blocking an attempt by three Israeli tanks to pass through his checkpoint near the Beirut University Library. Barrow sent him a personal message commending him for standing up to what was obviously a planned provocation. Two weeks after the Johnson incident, on 15 February, the 22d MAU (the renumbered 32d MAU, still under Colonel Mead) replaced the 24th MAU in Beirut. The danger signs in Lebanon grew worse as the U.S. tilted more and more in favor of the Christian side of the dispute.

On 14 March 1983, Barrow wrote a strong letter to Secretary Weinberger demanding "firm and strong action" be taken to stop the Israeli forces in Lebanon from putting the Marines in "life-threatening situations." Weinberger sent the letter to Secretary of State George Shultz, himself a World War II Marine officer. The State Department released it to the press.[57] In Beirut, on 18 April, a large car bomb exploded just outside the U.S. Embassy, causing massive structural damage, killing sixty-one people and wounding at least a hundred more. One of the dead was a marine security guard, and seven of the wounded were marines.

Barrow made his last visit to Beirut on 26 and 27 May. He gave out five Purple Hearts to Marines who had been wounded in the bombing. He also decorated twelve French marines who had assisted after the bombing. He inspected the building that was ultimately blown up in October. To him the reinforced-concrete, thick-walled structure appeared very sturdy and well suited to be the command post. Later he would lament not questioning the number of persons sleeping in the building. Two days later, the 24th

MAU, now commanded by Col. Timothy J. Geraghty, relieved the 32d MAU. The 24th MAU would be in place, and Barrow would no longer be commandant, when on 23 October 1983, a truck bomb was driven under the building, killing 241 American servicemen, 220 of them marines.

In his final weeks as commandant, Barrow made a last swing through the Far East, visiting marines in Okinawa and Japan and the scenes of so much of his service. His term would officially end at midnight on 30 June. The ceremony for the turnover of the commandancy to General Kelley was held Sunday evening, 26 June, at Marine Barracks, Washington. It was a beautiful evening. President Reagan attended. All three—Reagan, Barrow, and Kelley—spoke. In his remarks, Barrow looked back to his days in command at Parris Island and how he would question the graduating marines as to what they had gotten out of their training. The best answer he received, he said, came from a Marine who said, "Sir, the private will always do whatever needs to be done."[58]

On his last day as commandant, 30 June 1983, the strength of the armed forces was 2,223,400, of whom 193,993 were marines. The next day, the first day of his retirement, he and Patty flew down to Louisiana in the commandant's plane. A crowd of people, including the governor, and the 4th Marine Aircraft Wing band from New Orleans, met them at the Baton Rouge airport.

Barrow had acquired in 1950 the family plantation, Rosale, which had shrunk over the years to five hundred acres. He now found a master carpenter to undertake its restoration. A guest house was built first, a place for the Barrows to live while work was done on the big house. Part of the house dated to 1834; the other half had been built in 1893. It was set in rolling hills "about six miles from the Mississippi as the crow flies," with a lake in front of the house and another lake in the back.[59]

He joined several boards of directors, some regional, some local. He was a charter member of the Louisiana Nature Conservancy. He became a vestryman at the Grace Episcopal Church. He received honorary degrees from Louisiana State University, Tulane, and the Citadel. President Reagan appointed him to his Foreign Intelligence Advisory Board. Later Barrow would serve on the Packard Commission, which focused on defense management. He became chairman of the board of the Marine Corps Command and Staff College Foundation. He also served a long stint on the board of the Center for Naval Analysis. With all this, there was still time now for the grandchildren and a vacation home in the mountains of North Carolina.

Summing up his personal credo in a few words, he said, "In any institution or undertaking, the importance of people transcends all else."[60] The Wilson and Barrow commandancies, taken together, had done much to repair the damage done to the Marine Corps by the Vietnam War and a divided American society.

Notes

Abbreviations

ACS	Assistant chief of staff
ADC	Assistant division commander
AEF	American Expeditionary Force
ANJ	*Army-Navy Journal*
ARSN	*Annual Report, Secretary of the Navy*
CG	Commanding general
CinC	Commander in chief
CMC	Commandant Marine Corps
CNO	Chief of Naval Operations
COMUSMACV	Commander U.S. Military Assistance Command, Vietnam
FMF	Fleet Marine Force
FMFPac	Fleet Marine Force Pacific
FRC	Federal Records Center, Suitland, Md.
GB	General Board
GOS	General Officers Symposium
H&MD	History and Museums Division, HQMC
HQMC	Headquarters Marine Corps, Washington, D.C.
JCC	*Journals of the Continental Congress*
LC	Library of Congress
MAF	Marine Amphibious Corps
MCHC	Marine Corps Historical Center, Washington, D.C.
MCO	Marine Corps Order
MCRC	Marine Corps Research Center, Quantico, Va.
MRR	Manuscript Reading Room, LC
NARA	National Archives and Records Administration
NDAR	*Naval Documents of the American Revolution*
ND/QWF	*Naval Documents Related to the Quasi War between the United States and France*
OA	Operational Archives, H&MD
OHC	Oral History Collection, H&MD

OQR	Officer Qualification Record
PPC	Personal Papers Collection, H&MD
SecNav	Secretary of the Navy
USMC	United States Marine Corps
USNIP	United States Naval Institute *Proceedings*

Chapter 1. Samuel Nicholas

1. John Hancock to George Washington, 5 Oct. 1775, and Minutes of the Connecticut Council of Safety, 3 Aug. 1775, in William Bell Clark and William James Morgan, *NDAR,* 10 vols. to date (Washington, D.C.: Naval Historical Center, 1964–), 1:1054, 2:31.

2. Nevertheless, the Marine Corps today celebrates 10 November as its birthday. *JCC,* 9–10 Nov., *NDAR,* 2:957–58, 972.

3. Washington's steps toward establishing the two battalions can be followed in Charles R. Smith, *Marines in the Revolution* (Washington, D.C.: H&MD, 1975), 10–12.

4. *NDAR,* 2:1174–78.

5. Carl Bridenbaugh, *Cities in Revolt: Urban Life in America, 1743–1776* (New York: Oxford University Press, 1965), 178, 365.

6. Naval Committee to Esek Hopkins, 5 Jan. 1776; *NDAR,* 3:637–38; "Marines on Board Commodore Esek Hopkins' Fleet" *NDAR,* 3:302–4; cf. 3:614 and the table compiled in Smith, *Marines in the Revolution,* 45.

7. John Paul Jones (lieutenant on board the *Alfred*) to Joseph Hewes, 14 Apr. 1776, *NDAR,* 3:815–17.

8. Nicholas's description of the entire expedition is included in a letter to an unknown correspondent, 10 Apr. 1776, *NDAR,* 4:748–52.

9. *JCC,* 25 June 1776, *NDAR,* 5:736.

10. These duties are described in Smith, *Marines in the Revolution,* 87–88, and can be followed in various documents in *NDAR,* 6:141, 171, 271, 863.

11. *NDAR,* 5:637. cf. *NDAR,* 7:307, 367.

12. Capt. George Jerry Osborne, USMC, to New Hampshire Committee of Safety, 6 Feb. 1777, *NDAR,* 7:1116.

13. The fourth company was on board the *Randolph,* which was due to sail at any time. Robert Morris to John Hancock, 14 Dec. 1776, *NDAR,* 7:483.

14. Washington to John Cadwalader, 7 Dec. 1776, *NDAR,* 7:404.

15. Smith, *Marines in the Revolution,* 105.

16. *JCC,* 20 Nov. 1776, *NDAR,* 7:223. The frigates were authorized on 13 Dec. 1776 (ibid., *NDAR,* 3:90).

17. For a brief summary of their operations, see James C. Bradford, "The Navies of the American Revolution," in *In Peace and War: Interpretations of American Naval History, 1775–1978,* ed. Kenneth J. Hagan (Westport, Conn.: Greenwood Press, 1978), 14–15, 18–19; William J. Fowler Jr., *Rebels under Sail* (New York: Scribner's, 1976), 234–56.

18. Robert Morris to John Paul Jones, 5 Feb. 1777, *NDAR,* 7:1109–11.

19. Smith, *Marines in the Revolution,* 155–61.

20. Ibid., 204–14.

21. Samuel Eliot Morison, *John Paul Jones: A Sailor's Biography* (Boston: Little, Brown, 1959), 138–59.

22. Most of Jones's Marines on board the *Richard* were French. For accounts of the battles, see Gardner W. Allen, *A Naval History of the American Revolution,* 2 vols. (New York: Houghton, Mifflin, 1913), 2:377–78, 457–70.

23. Reproduced in facsimile in Smith, *Marines in the Revolution,* 215.

24. *JCC* (1779): 667.

25. For a full account of these events, see Smith, *Marines in the Revolution,* 216, 310.

26. *Journals of the Congress of the United States* (New York, 1787), 7:136; Morison, *Jones,* 315.

27. Nicholas to the President of Congress, 10 Aug. 1781, *Papers of the Continental Congress,* vol. 17, no. 78, pp. 301–2; *JCC* (1781): 851.

28. E. James Ferguson et al., eds., *The Papers of Robert Morris,* 9 vols. to date (Pittsburgh: University of Pittsburgh Press, 1973–), 2:223–24.

29. Morris to Francis, and Morris to Nicholas, all 11 Sept. 1781, Morris Diary 3:223; 22 Nov. 1781, in ibid. 3:232.

30. Morris to Nicholas, James Craig, and Nathaniel Falconer, 21 Nov. 1781, Morris Diary 3:223; 22 Nov. 1781, in ibid. 3:232.

31. *JCC* (1781): 885, 942–43, 1131.

32. *JCC* (1782): 735, 747–48; Smith, *Marines in the Revolution,* 460.

33. *JCC* (1782): 735, 747–48.

34. Wallingford's commission, signed by Jones, is reproduced in Smith, *Marines in the Revolution,* 119. While in France, Jones "made (William Nicolson) Captain of Marines in Ariel" but was unable to convince Congress to confirm the appointment and a committee appointed to consider the matter reported to Congress that "Commissions heretofore Granted by the Ministers of these United States at foreign Courts . . . are to be considered as temporary Brevets and not giving rank in the Navy or Marine of these States and that therefore all such Commissions are hereby revoked." Morison, *Jones,* 306; Smith, *Marines in the Revolution,* 241.

35. For a facsimile of the letter, see Smith, *Marines in the Revolution,* 285.

36. Francis Vinton Greene, *The Revolutionary War and the Military Policy of the United States* (New York: Scribner's, 1911), 220.

37. Charles Oscar Paullin, *Paullin's History of Naval Administration, 1775–1911* (Annapolis: Naval Institute Press, 1968), 23–26. The entire chapter (3–53) provides a good summary of the administration of naval forces during the Revolution.

Chapter 2. William Ward Burrows

1. *Journal of the House of Representatives,* 5th Cong., 2d sess., 1797–98, 28 May 1798, in *Journal of the House of Representatives, 1st–14th Congress, Mar./Sept. 1789–Dec. 1816/Mar. 1817,* 14 vols. (Wilmington, Del.: M. Glazier, 1977); Marshal Smelser, *The Congress Founds a Navy, 1787–1798* (South Bend, Ind.: Notre Dame University Press, 1959), 191; G. Terry Sharrer, "In Search for a Naval Policy, 1783–1812," in Hagan, *In Peace and War,* 27–43.

2. Burrows's appointment was reported in the 19 July 1798 issue of *Claypoole's American Daily Advertiser,* Philadelphia; Karl Schuon, *Home of the Commandants* (Quantico, Va.: Marine Corps Association, 1956), 52.

3. Genealogical information is provided by the Burrows-Thompson Bible, discovered in 1971 by Richard Long of the MCHC in the possession of Burrows's descendant, Mrs. Keith Neville. The Bible contains a record of births and deaths in the Burrows family, some written by William Ward Burrows.

4. Edwin N. McClellan, "First Commandant of the Marine Corps, William Ward Burrows," *DAR Magazine* 59 (Mar. 1925): 155–59; Lew Feldman, "William Ward Burrows: First Commandant of the U.S. Marine Corps," *Leatherneck* 11 (Apr. 1928): 6.

5. William Ward Burrows Biographical File, Reference Section, H&MD, contains copies of Stub entries to indents issued in payment of claims growing out of the Revolution, Book Y-Z, p. 105, no. 676, "indicating Burrows was paid for militia duty on foot in 1780 and 1781."

6. Harold Syrett, ed., *The Papers of Alexander Hamilton,* 27 vols. (New York: Columbia University Press, 1961–87), 21:55 n. 10; George Washington to James McHenry, 13 Dec. 1798, ibid. 21:353–54.

7. Jacob Reed to Alexander Hamilton, 16 Jan. 1798, ibid. 21:338.

8. William Ward Burrows to John Rutledge Jr., 16 July 1799, John Rutledge Jr. Papers, Southern Historical Collection, University of North Carolina Library, Chapel Hill, N.C. (hereafter cited as Rutledge Papers). Burrows wrote to Rutledge: "This is the anniversary of my commission for which I hold myself indebted to you." Rutledge was a congressman from South Carolina at the time of Burrows's appointment.

9. Secretary of War James McHenry to Lieutenant of Marines, Frigate Constitution, 19 Mar. 1798, Historical Division, U.S. Navy, *ND/QWF,* 7 vols. (Washington, D.C.: GPO, 1935–38), 1:40–41.

10. J. McHenry to Samuel Sewell, 9 Apr. 1798, *ND/QWF,* 1:52–53.

11. Lt. Daniel Wynkoop to Maj. Cmdt. William Ward Burrows, 5 Aug. 1798; Lt. John Tallman to Maj. Cmdt. William Ward Burrows, 19 Sept. 1798; Lt. John Hall to Maj. Cmdt. William Ward Burrows, 17 Oct. 1798; all in Letters Received, 1798–1817, Records of the United States Marine Corps, RG 127, NARA (hereafter cited as Letters Received, 1798–1817).

12. Maj. Cmdt. William Ward Burrows to Lt. John Hall, 5 Sept. 1798; Maj. Cmdt. William Ward Burrows to Lt. Henry Williams, 10 Sept. 1798; Maj. Cmdt. William Ward Burrows to Lt. James Weaver, 29 Sept. 1798; all in HQMC, Letters Sent, August 1798–June 1801 and March 1804–February 1884, RG 127, NARA (hereafter cited as Letters Sent, 1798–1884).

13. Lt. Jonathan Church to Maj. Cmdt. William Ward Burrows, 7 July 1799, *ND/QWF,* 3:442.

14. Bernard C. Nalty and Lt. Col. Ralph F. Moody, *A Brief History of the U.S. Marine Corps Officer Procurement, 1775–1969,* rev. ed, Marine Corps Historical Reference Pamphlet (Washington, D.C.: H&MD, 1970); Secretary of the Navy Benjamin Stoddert to President John Adams, 3 Aug. 1798, *ND/QWF,* 1:269–70; Thomas Pinckney to Maj. Cmdt. William Ward Burrows, 30 Aug. 1798, *ND/QWF,* 1:335.

15. Maj. Cmdt. William Ward Burrows to Daniel Cotton, 3 Mar. 1800, Letters Sent, 1798–1884. Lt. Reuben Lilly, although an invalid, refused to resign his commission. Burrows urged other officers to persuade him to do so, and, irate at his continued refusal, wrote, "He is a disgrace to the Corps and it is infamous of him to hold his commission. If he does not shortly send it in I will fall upon some plan to publickly [*sic*] disgrace him." Maj. Cmdt. William Ward Burrows to Daniel Cotton, 17 Mar. 1800, Letters Sent, 1798–1884.

16. Maj. Cmdt. William Ward Burrows to Lt. Stephen Geddes, 16 Jan., 21 Feb. 1800, and Maj. Cmdt. William Ward Burrows to B. Stoddert, 3 Apr. 1800, Letters Sent, 1798–1884.

17. Lt. Benjamin Strother to Maj. Cmdt. William Ward Burrows, 24 Feb. 1800, Letters Received, 1798–1817.

18. Capt. Daniel Carmick to Maj. Cmdt. William Ward Burrows, 9 July 1798, *ND/QWF,* 3:480.

19. Allan R. Millett, *Semper Fidelis: The History of the United States Marine Corps* (New York: Macmillan, 1980), 31.

20. Maj. Cmdt. William Ward Burrows to Lt. J. Church, 9 Nov. 1798 and 4 June 1799, Letters Sent, 1798–1884.

21. Lt. Reuben Lilly to Maj. Cmdt. William Ward Burrows, 9 Nov. 1798, Letters Received, 1798–1817; Maj. Cmdt. William Ward Burrows to Lt. Lilly, 15 Dec. 1798, Letters Sent, 1798–1884.

22. B. Stoddert to Maj. Cmdt. William Ward Burrows, 1 Apr. 1799, *ND/QWF,* 3:1.

23. Maj. Cmdt. William Ward Burrows to Lt. S. Geddes, 28 Oct. 1799, Letters Sent, 1798–1884; Lt. Col. Cmdt. William Ward Burrows to [?], 1 Aug. 1800, Letters Sent, 1798–1884.

24. Maj. Cmdt. William Ward Burrows to Lt. J. Weaver, 29 Sept. 1798, Letters Sent, 1798–1884; Maj. E. N. McClellan, "How the Marine Band Started," *USNIP* 49 (Apr. 1923): 581–86; the *Philadelphia Gazette and Daily Advertizer,* 7 July 1800, reported that the Society of the Cincinnati enjoyed the Marine Band's "animating notes of martial music" during their meeting at the City Tavern.

25. Millett, *Semper Fidelis,* 37; Constance M. Green, *Washington—Village and Capital, 1800–1878* (Princeton: Princeton University Press, 1962), 18, 37.

26. Lt. Col. Cmdt. William Ward Burrows to Jonathan Williams, 19 July 1800, Letters Sent, 1798–1884; Schuon, *Home of the Commandants,* 49–50; Paullin, *History of Naval Administration,* 127.

27. Maj. Cmdt. William Ward Burrows to Lt. S. Geddes, 28 Aug. 1798 and 28 Oct. 1799; to Capt. J. Clarke, 30 Oct. 1798; and to Lt. James Middleton, 25 May 1799, Letters Sent, 1798–1884.

28. Lt. Robert Harwood to Maj. Cmdt. William Ward Burrows, 29 Jan. 1799, Letters Received, 1798–1817.

29. Lt. J. Hall to Maj. Cmdt. William Ward Burrows, 2 Nov. 1799, Letters Received, 1798–1817; Maj. Cmdt. William Ward Burrows to Lieutenant Hillar, 1 Aug. 1800, Letters Sent, 1798–1884.

30. Maj. Cmdt. William Ward Burrows to B. Stoddert, 2 Dec. 1799; and to Lt. Bartholomew Clinch, 7 Mar. 1800, Letters Sent, 1798–1884.

31. Lt. B. Strother to Maj. Cmdt. William Ward Burrows, 24 Feb. 1800, Letters Received, 1798–1817; Maj. Cmdt. William Ward Burrows to B. Stoddert, 19 Feb. 1800, to Lt. B. Strother, 8 Mar. 1800, and to Lt. H. Caldwell, 22 Mar. 1800, Letters Sent, 1798–1884.

32. Lt. Col. Cmdt. William Ward Burrows to Lt. H. Caldwell, 22 Sept. 1800, Letters Sent, 1798–1884. See also the essay on Anthony Gale in this volume for a further description of the incident.

33. Lt. Col. Cmdt. William Ward Burrows to B. Stoddert, 31 July, 25 Nov., and 27 Nov. 1800, Letters Sent, 1798–1884; Lt. Col. Cmdt. William Ward Burrows to Lt. B. Clinch, 2 Dec. 1799, Letters Sent, 1798–1884.

34. Lt. Col. Comdt. William Ward Burrows to the Secretary of the Navy, 27 Nov. 1800, Letters Sent, 1798–1884.

35. Capt. Thomas Truxton to Commanding Officer, USMC, Frigate *President,* 28 July 1800, *ND/QWF,* 6:189–90.

36. Maj. Cmdt. William Ward Burrows to J. Williams, 19 July 1800, Letters Sent, 1798–1884; Capt. T. Truxton to Maj. Cmdt. William Ward Burrows, 21 July 1800, Letters Received, 1798–1817.

37. Lt. Col. Cmdt. William Ward Burrows to B. Stoddert, 24 July 1800, Letters Sent, 1798–1884.

38. Capt. T. Truxton to Lt. Col. Cmdt. William Ward Burrows, 12 Apr. 1801, *ND/QWF,* 7:187–89; and to Secretary of the Navy, 15 Apr. 1801, *ND/QWF,* 7:195.

39. Circular to Commanding Officers of U.S. Ships of War concerning general rules of conduct in the U.S. Navy and Marine Corps, 19 Apr. 1801, U.S. Navy, Historical Division, *Naval Documents Related to the United States Wars with the Barbary Powers,* 7 vols. (Washington, D.C.: GPO, 1939–44), 1:556–58 (hereafter cited as *Naval Documents–Barbary Powers*).

40. Lt. Col. Cmdt. William Ward Burrows to J. Williams, 28 Aug. 1800, Letters Sent, 1798–1884.

41. Alfred J. Marini, "The British Corps of Marines, 1746–1771, and the United States Marine Corps, 1798–1818: A Comparative Study" (Ph.D. diss., University of Maine, 1979), 159.

42. Alfred J. Marini, "Political Perceptions of the Marine Forces: Great Britain 1699, 1739 and the United States, 1798–1804," *Military Affairs* 44 (Dec. 1980): 171–76.

43. Mary Bond Burrows died 6 February 1803; *South Carolina Historical and Genealogical Magazine* 28 (Apr. 1917): 89; Secretary of the Navy Robert Smith to Lt. Col. Cmdt. William Ward Burrows, 13 Feb. 1804, Letters Received, 1798–1817.

44. Marini, "Political Perceptions," 174–75.

Chapter 3. Franklin Wharton

1. *Journal of the Executive Proceedings of the Senate of the United States of America* (Washington, D.C.: Duff Green, 1896), 1:281–82, for presidential nomination 25 June 1798 and confirmation 26 June 1798. See also "Franklin Wharton, Lieutenant of Marines . . . vice M'Crea, appointed a captain of Artillery," *Gazette of the United States and Philadelphia Daily Advertiser,* 2 July 1798.

2. See James L. Mooney, ed., *Dictionary of American Naval Fighting Ships,* 8 vols. (Washington, D.C.: Naval History Division, 1959–81), 7:413–15, for early history of the frigate *United States.* See also "Receipt Book of John Harris," Naval Agent at Philadelphia, Entry 377, Naval Records Collection, Office of Naval Records and Library, RG 45, NARA (hereafter cited as Naval Records Collection), showing issues to Lieutenant Wharton beginning 6 July 1798.

3. See "Muster Roll of a Detachment of Marines under the Command of Lieutenant John Darley on board the United States Ship *United States* from the 6th July 1799 the time they were last mustered to the 31st of August 1800." This is the earliest surviving report and recapitulates prior information. Microfiche, Reference Section, H&MD.

4. Edwin W McClellan, "History of the United States Marine Corps," mss, vol. 1, chap. 12, p. 16. Copy in H&MD.

5. Edgar P. Richardson, "The Athens of America," in *Philadelphia: A 300-Year History,* by Russell F. Weigley (New York: Norton, 1982), 208–13.

6. McClellan, "History," vol. 1, chap. 14, p. 6.

7. Anne H. Wharton, *Genealogy of the Wharton Family of Philadelphia, 1664–1880* (Philadelphia: Collins, 1880), 9–10, 101–2.

8. See *Stephens's Philadelphia Directory,* 1796; *Stafford's Philadelphia Directory,* 1797, 1798. *Porcupine's Gazette,* 14 Oct. 1797, listed Wharton as Water Inspector, and the *Aurora,* 19 May 1798, reported Wharton's defeat for election as city commissioner from the Southwark district.

9. Paullin, *History of Naval Administration,* 119–20. Theodore J. Crackel, *Mr. Jefferson's Army: Political and Social Reform of the Military Establishment, 1801–1809* (New York: New York University Press, 1987), 48–51.

10. Burrows to John Rutledge Jr., 2 Mar. 1803, Rutledge Papers.

11. SecNav Robert Smith to the President, 27 Mar. 1804, U.S. Navy, Historical Division, *Naval Documents–Barbary Powers,* 3:534.

12. McClellan, "History," vol. 1, chap. 15, pp. 23–25.

13. Ibid., vol. 1, chap. 17, pp. 3–7. See also "Protection of New Orleans," No. 59, 15 Jan. 1807, *American State Papers, Class 6, Naval Affairs,* 4 vols. (Washington, D.C.: Gales and Seaton, 1834–61) (hereafter cited as *American State Papers, Naval Affairs*), 1:162.

14. Wharton to Carmick, 11 Dec. 1806, Wharton Biographical File, Reference Section, H&MD (hereafter cited as Wharton Biographical File); Carmick to Wharton, 31 Aug. 1812, and Wharton to Carmick, 1 Oct. 1812, in William S. Dudley, ed., *The Naval War of 1812: A Documentary History,* 2 vols. (Washington, D.C.: Naval Historical Center, 1985, 1992), 1:411–16.

15. SecNav to Wharton, 15 Mar. 1805, required him to send detachments of varying strengths to ten gunboats at six locations between Charleston, South Carolina, and Boston. *Naval Documents–Barbary Powers,* 5:415.

16. SecNav to Wharton, 20 Aug. 1804, Wharton Biographical File.

17. Paullin, *History of Naval Administration,* 120–22.

18. SecNav to Wharton, 3 July 1810, Wharton Biographical File.

19. McClellan, "History," vol. 1, chap. 20, pp. 8–12.

20. *National Intelligencer,* 30 June 1809, re: Wharton as founding stockholder of the Bank of Washington; 5 Mar. and 28 Sept. 1811, as a stockholder of Washington's first library. Wharton was also a founding member and vestryman of Christ (Episcopal) Church, a block from his G Street home, attended by many barracks marines and known in later years as "the Commandant's church." See Gail Karesh Kassan, "Residents of the Area Around the Marine Corps Barracks, 1800–1850," ms., Reference Section, H&MD, 15.

21. Crackel, *Mr. Jefferson's Army,* 14.

22. See Capt. Frank E. Evans, "The Corps One Hundred Years Ago," *Marine Corps Gazette* 1 (Mar. 1916): 61–62.

23. McClellan, "History," vol. 1, chap. 19, pp. 6–9.

24. SecNav to Wharton, 19 June 1812 in Dudley, *Naval War of 1812,* 1:138–39, authorized a twenty-dollar enlistment bounty to help offset "Congress having offered extraordinary inducements to Soldiers." See also Millett, *Semper Fidelis,* 46.

25. See Dudley, *Naval War of 1812,* 1:296–302 for SecNav to Chauncey letters, 31 Aug. and 4 Sept. 1812, and 2:433–35 for SecNav to Chauncey, 8 Apr. 1813. While the "Agreement Governing Joint Operations" transmitted by the latter can be interpreted as applying to the Marines as "Naval forces," it is by no means explicit, and the word "Marine" appears nowhere in the document.

26. Wharton to "My Dear Friends," 28 Aug. 1814, Wharton Biographical File, describes how he and Captain Crabb, the paymaster, led the barracks guard to assist with defense of the navy yard, retreating only when it was burned by authority of the president.

27. See John Hall Biographical File, Reference Section, H&MD, for TRS, 8 and 18 Apr. 1817. The first, signed by Brevet Majors Gale, Miller, and Henderson as well as by ten more junior officers, alleges that Hall "did, in a most malovent [*sic*], vindictive and dishonorable manner, attempt to destroy the character & respectability of the Col. Commandant . . . has used, and continues to use, the most disrespectful and unmilitary and dishonorable language against the head of the corps." The second, from SecNav to Hall, informs him that his commission is vacated.

28. *American State Papers, Naval Affairs,* No. 161, "Trial of Franklin Wharton, Lieutenant Colonel of Marines," 503–10.

29. Extensive quotations from *New York Gazette,* 3 Sept. 1818, and *National Intelligencer,* 5 Sept. 1818, are reprinted in Maj. Edwin N. McClellan, "Marine Corps History, 1817 to 1821," *Marine Corps Gazette* 8 (Mar. 1924): 75–76.

Chapter 4. Anthony Gale

I gratefully acknowledge the assistance of Richard A. Long, Special Projects Curator, MCHC, for sharing his extensive material on Gale. An earlier version of this essay appeared as Merrill L. Bartlett, "Court-martial of a Commandant," *USNIP* 111 (June 1985): 69–72.

1. McNight to CMC, 29 Dec. 1799, *ND/QWF,* 4:580. See also Gale's card in the ZB File, Naval Records Collection; Gale's petition for citizenship, 27 Nov. 1801, Eastern District Court of Pennsylvania; and census of 1840, Lincoln County, Ky. Col. Don Wyckoff, USMC (Ret.), research of Gale's lineage at Dublin Castle in 1967 for the MCHC. While the first *Navy Register* lists Gale's date of commission as 2 September 1798, the muster roll of the *Ganges* indicates that he was commissioned on 26 July 1798.

2. Burrows to Henry Caldwell Trumball, 22 Sept. 1800, *ND/QWF,* 6:374 and Burrows to Bartholomew Clinch, 2 Dec. 1799, Entry 4, Letters Sent, 1798–1884. See also the essay on William Ward Burrows in this volume for the commandant's reaction.

3. *ND/QWF,* 8:359.

4. *Claypoole's American Daily Advertiser* (Philadelphia), 18 Jan. 1800. Catherine Swope Gale was probably born in 1772; in 1840, she mentioned her age as sixty-eight in a letter requesting her husband's pension. See Anthony Gale's pension file, Records of the Veterans Administration, 1773–1985, RG 15, NARA; *Register of Commissioned Officers of the U.S. Navy and Marine Corps* (Washington, D.C.: GPO, 1800), 11; and Records of Gloria Dei Church, Philadelphia, 23 Nov. 1801. Gale's surviving children, Anthony and Emily K., can be found in the following census records: Southworth Township, Philadelphia County (1910); 6th Ward, Washington D.C. (1820); and Lincoln County, Ky. (1830).

5. *Register of Officer Personnel: United State Navy and Marine Corps and Ships Data, 1801–1807* (Washington, D.C.: GPO, 1945), 63; *American State Papers: Documents, Legislative and Executive,* 38 vols. (Washington, D.C.: GPO, 1789–1838) (hereafter cited as *American State Papers*), 1:318; Muster Rolls of the *Constitution,* 1803–1824, Entry 90, RG 45, NARA. For details of the formative years of the U.S. Navy, see K. Jack Bauer, "Naval Shipbuilding Programs, 1794–1860," *American Neptune* 29 (Spring 1965): 29–32.

6. CMC to Anthony Gale, 20 Mar., 21 Apr., and 2 May 1804, Entry 4, Letters Sent, 1798–1884; *The Navy Register* (Washington, D.C.: GPO, 1817), 17; and *American State Papers,* 2:350.

7. Court of Inquiry, Philadelphia, Pa., 19 Mar. 1816, General Courts-Martial and Courts of Inquiry 1799–1861, Records of the Judge Advocate General, RG 125, NARA (hereafter cited as Court of Inquiry, followed by date).

8. Court of Inquiry, Washington, D.C., Feb. 1819.

9. Benjamin Homand to James Monroe, 12 Feb. 1818, and Samuel Miller to James Monroe, 13 Sept. 1818, Samuel Miller Papers, PPC; and Richard Smith to Benjamin W. Crowninshield, 2 Sept. 1818, Miller to Crowninshield, 6 Sept. 1818, Smith to Benjamin Homand, 9 Sept. 1818, Gamble to Henderson, 4 Nov. 1818, and Henderson to Smith Thompson, 18 Nov. 1818, Miscellaneous Letters Received by the Secretary of the Navy, RG 45, NARA (hereafter cited as Miscellaneous Letters Received).

10. David F. Long, "The Navy under the Board of Commissioners," in Hagan, *In Peace and War,* 63–78.

11. Archibald Henderson to Smith Thompson, 12 Apr. 1820, Miscellaneous Letters Received.

12. Edwin M. Hall, "Smith Thompson," in *American Secretaries of the Navy,* 2 vols., ed. Paolo E. Coletta (Annapolis: Naval Institute Press, 1980), 1:123–28.

13. Anthony Gale to Smith Thompson, 8 Aug. 1820, Entry 4, Letters Sent, 1798–1884.

14. Samuel Miller to Smith Thompson, 25 Aug. 1820, Miscellaneous Letters Received.

15. Order for a general court-martial, 7 Sept. 1820, Entry 19, Orders Issued and Received, 1800–1820, RG 127, NARA.

16. Record of court-martial, Anthony Gale, 18–26 Sept. 1820, RG 125, NARA.

17. Samuel Miller to Anthony Gale, 19 Oct. 1820, Entry 4, Letters Sent, 1798–1884.

18. Catherine Gale to Smith Thompson, 28 Dec. 1820, RG 45, NARA; Patients alphabetical listing, 1816–1826, Archives of the Pennsylvania Hospital, Philadelphia, Pa.

19. Anthony Gale to President Martin Van Buren, 23 Oct. 1838, Anthony Gale's pension file, RG 15, NARA.

20. Anthony Gale to J. L. Edwards (Commissioner of Pensions), 13 Apr. 1841, Anthony Gale's pension file, RG 15, NARA.

21. Catherine Gale to Edwards, 22 July 1852, Anthony Gale's pension file, RG 15 NARA; 28th Cong., 1st sess., 19 Apr. 1844, S. Doc. 324, and House Committee on Naval Affairs, 33d Cong., 1st sess., 4 Jan. 1854, H. Doc. 19.

Chapter 5. Archibald Henderson

I acknowledge the contributions of historians Col. Allan R. Millett, USMCR, Charles Richard Smith, and the late Ralph W. Donnelly. I also received outstanding professional support in preparing this essay during 1994–95 from Robert Aquilina.

1. Information on the Henderson family gleaned from Ralph W. Donnelly, "Archibald Henderson: Marine," *Virginia Cavalcade* 20 (Winter 1971): 39, and *Prince William: The Story of Its Places and Its People,* compiled by the Virginia Writers' Program of the Works Projects Administration (Richmond, Va.: Whittet & Shepperson, 1941), 93.

2. *Prince William,* 93.

3. W. J. Morgan, Head, Historical Research Branch, Naval Historical Center to Ralph W. Donnelly, 15 Feb. 1971, Reference Section, H&MD.

4. Excerpt from muster roll for USS *Constitution,* 1 Dec. 1807, signed by 1st Lt. Archibald Henderson, USMC; copy contained in Reference Section, H&MD.

5. Ralph W. Donnelly, comp., "Composite Henderson Chronology," Reference Section, H&MD, 1–2.

6. "Charleston, SC—1809," memo, Henderson File, Reference Section, H&MD (hereafter cited as Henderson File).

7. Captain Henderson to Secretary Hamilton, 4 Feb. 1812, summarized in Donnelly, "Composite Henderson Chronology," 2.

8. Captain Henderson to John G. Henderson, 2 May 1813, Donnelly, "Composite Henderson Chronology."

9. Deposition testimony sworn to by Captain Henderson to Thomas Welsh, Justice of the Peace, Boston, 20 July 1815, copy in Henderson File.

10. McClellan, "History," vol. 1, chap. 25, p. 35.

11. For another perspective of Franklin Wharton, see the essay on the Wharton commandancy in this volume.

12. Donnelly, "Composite Henderson Chronology," 4; Henderson to Secretary Thompson, 1 Feb. 1819, Letters from Marines, General Records of the Department of the Navy, RG 80, NARA (hereafter cited as Letters from Marines).

13. Henderson to Lieutenant Colonel Commandant Gale, 8 Nov. 1819, Letters Sent, 1798–1884.

14. Donnelly, "Composite Henderson Chronology," 4.

15. Henderson to Secretary Smith Thompson, 29 Nov. 1819, 27 Mar. and 12 Apr. 1820, Letters from Marines.

16. Henderson to President Monroe, 13 Jan. 1823, Letters Sent, 1798–1884.

17. Millett, *Semper Fidelis*; Col. Robert D. Heinl, *Soldiers of the Sea* (Annapolis: Naval Institute Press, 1962), 31.

18. See, for example, Henderson to Secretary Mahlon Dickerson, 7 Oct. 1834, Letters Sent, RG 127, NARA.

19. Events summarized from Jack Sweetman, *American Naval History* (Annapolis: Naval Institute Press, 1984).

20. Henderson to Secretary William A. Graham, 19 Nov. 1850, Letters Sent, 1798–1884.

21. Henderson to Secretary Isaac Toucey, 20 Nov. 1858, Letters Sent, 1798–1884.

22. Donnelly, "Archibald Henderson," 40.

23. Order of the Lieutenant Colonel Commandant, 29 Mar. 1822, copy in Henderson File.

24. Ralph W. Donnelly, *The History of the Confederate States Marine Corps* (Washington, D.C.: Self-published, 1976), 141.

25. Donnelly, "Composite Henderson Chronology," 6–7; Marguerite duPont Lee [Henderson's granddaughter] to Maj. Edwin N. McClellan, USMC, HQMC, 19 May 1932; copy in Henderson File.

26. Edwin N. McClellan, *Uniforms of the American Marines, 1775–1829* (Washington, D.C.: H&MD, 1974), 69–82.

27. Ibid., 85. General Henderson's own Mameluke sword has been preserved and is on display at MCHC.

28. Henderson to Bvt. Lt. Col. Richard Smith, USMC, 13 Feb. 1826, ibid., 89.

29. Henderson to Secretary Southard, 26 Sept. 1827, Letters Sent, 1798–1884; Col. Robert H. Rankin, USMC (Ret.), *Small Arms of the Sea Services* (New Milford, Conn.: Flayderman, 1972), 165–66, 173–75.

30. Millett, *Semper Fidelis,* 56; Lt. Col. Clyde H. Metcalf, USMC, *A History of the United States Marine Corps* (New York: Putnam, 1939), 105.

31. Stevenson Archer, Committee of Expenditures, Navy Department, report to the House of Representatives, 28 Feb. 1821, *American State Papers,* 1:739–43.

32. Henderson to Secretary Thompson, 7 Feb. 1821, Letters Sent, 1798–1884.

33. Millett, *Semper Fidelis,* 60.

34. Metcalf, *History of the United States Marine Corps,* 105.

35. Amos Kendall to Navy Secretary John Branch [relayed to the House of Representatives], 25 May 1830, "Statement Relative to the Pay and Emoluments of the Officers of the Marine Corps," *American State Papers,* 3:581–88.

36. As quoted in Heinl, *Soldiers of the Sea,* 37.

37. Comments attached to Navy Secretary John Branch to U.S. Senate, 23 Mar. 1830, "On the Expediency of Dispensing with the Marine Corps as Part of the Armed Equipment of a Vessel of War," *American State Papers,* 3:560–69.

38. Henderson to Secretary Woodbury, 16 Oct. 1833, Letters Sent, 1798–1884.

39. Henderson to Lieutenant Colonel Wainwright, 1 June 1836, HQMC, Orders Issued and Received, RG 127, NARA.

40. Metcalf, *History of the United States Marine Corps,* 97–98.

41. Henderson Journal, "Camp Hillsborough, 7 Miles from Tampa," 13 Apr. 1837, A-8, copy in Henderson File.

42. Henderson to "Soldiers," 24 July 1838, HQMC, Orders Issued and Received, RG 127, NARA.

43. See, for example, John G. Reynolds, *A Conclusive Exculpation of the Marine Corps in Mexico* (New York: Stringer and Townsend, 1853), copy in H&MD.

44. Henderson to Navy Secretary John Y. Mason, 12 May 1848, Letters Sent, 1798–1884.

45. Harry A. Ellsworth, *180 Landings of United States Marines, 1800–1934* (Washington, D.C.: HQMC, 1974).

46. Commander Farragut to Brevet Brigadier General Henderson, 28 July 1852, contained in Letters Sent [Henderson's letter to ship captains of 24 July 1852], 1798–1884.

47. Maj. John Harris to Henderson, 23 Dec. 1852, HQMC, Miscellaneous Records of the Adjutant and Inspector, RG 127, NARA.

48. Henderson to Secretary Samuel L. Southard, 18 Nov. 1823; Henderson to Secretary George E. Badger, 11 May 1841; Henderson to Secretary John Y. Mason, 28 Apr. 1848; Henderson to Secretary James C. Dobbin, 17 Nov. 1853, all in Letters Sent, 1798–1884; 1st Lt. Isaac Greene to Henderson, 21 Mar. 1856, copy in Henderson File; Donnelly, "Composite Henderson Chronology," 7; Navy Secretary Isaac Toucey to Col. Cmdt. John Harris, 1 Oct. 1859, Secretary of the Navy, Letters Sent, RG 80, NARA.

49. *Washington Star,* 1 June 1857; Henderson, "Statement of Occurrences on Monday, 1st June 1857," both in Henderson File.

50. Henderson to Secretary Toucey, 20 Nov. 1858, Letters Sent, 1798–1884.

51. Lt. Col. H. B. Tyler to Secretary Toucey, 7 Jan. 1859, Letters Sent, 1798–1884.

52. Isaac Toucey, *Annual Report of the Secretary of the Navy,* 1859, (hereafter cited as *Annual Report,* followed by the date), as quoted in Heinl, *Soldiers of the Sea,* 61.

Chapter 6. John Harris

1. Biographic Summary, Sept. 1949, Harris Biographical File, Reference Section, H&MD (hereafter cited as Harris Biographical File).

2. For details of joint Army–Navy–Marine Corps operations against the Seminoles, see George E. Buker, *Swamp Sailors* (Gainesville: University of Florida Press, 1975).

3. Harris's nearest contenders for that distinction, Maj. William Dulany and Maj. James Edelin, had initial commissioning dates of 19 June 1819 and 18 April 1817, respectively. Source, Mr. Robert Aquilina, Reference Section, H&MD, June 1988.

4. Harris was detached from the USS *Delaware* in March 1836, his last seagoing assignment. His last deployment was command of a battalion at the end of the Mexican War which sailed from New York in March 1848, arrived in Veracruz later that same month, and performed garrison duty in Alvarado after the armistice until redeployment to Washington on 26 July 1848.

5. Metcalf, *History of the United States Marine Corps,* 192.

6. Lieutenant Colonel Reynolds to Secretary Welles, 23 July 1862, vol. 50, Item 134, Letters from Marines.

7. The census of 1860 of the "free citizens of Washington, D.C.," lists the following inhabitants of the commandant's House: John and Mary G. Harris, J. Gamble Harris, listed as a clerk, plus a coachman, waiter, and three domestics, "mostly Irish." J. Gamble Harris may in fact have been J. C. Harris, the commandant's nephew, then a law student, and later a Marine lieutenant who served with distinction under Farragut at New Orleans. With regards to other family members, Harris wrote Secretary Toucey on 5 March 1861, "I have received the distressing intelligence of the death of two of my brothers, one of whom will be buried tomorrow and the other on the following day. I will leave this afternoon for Philadelphia." Harris and his second wife, the former Mary Gilliat Gray, are buried together in Georgetown. Her inscription reflects that she was born in Bermuda on 18 May 1810 and died in Washington, D.C., on 16 July 1883. She was thirty-five years old when she married John Harris; he was then fifty-two.

8. Gideon Welles, *Diary of Gideon Welles,* 3 vols. (Cambridge, Mass.: Houghton Mifflin, Riverside Press, 1911). Welles refers to Col. Harris on only two significant occasions: page 89 of volume 1, entry dated 20 August 1862, with reference to the Reynolds charges and the letters of reproof, and page 31 of volume 2, entry dated 14 May 64, with reference to his funeral and the issue of succession.

9. The Harris Biographical File refers to a letter from Wharton to Commodore John Rodgers of 9 August 1814, apprising him of Harris's assignment to *Guerrière.*

10. Information from Harris Biographical File.

11. Ibid.

12. Major Harris to Brevet Brigadier General Commandant Henderson, 17 May 1847; copy in ibid.

13. Metcalf, *History of the United States Marine Corps,* 166.

14. Major Harris's battalion consisted of 1 major, 1 captain, 3 first lieutenants, 6 second lieutenants, 10 sergeants, 6 corporals, 3 drummers, and 3 fifers, a total of 369 marines. Miscella-

neous Records of the Adjutant, 1798–1880, Records of the Adjutant and Inspector's Department, 1798–1949, Records of the U.S. Marine Corps, RG 127, NARA.

15. Major Tyler to Secretary Toucey, 7 Jan. 1859, vol. 45, Letters from Marines.

16. Monthly report, Jan. 1859, Monthly Reports of Details of Officers of the Marine Corps, Records of the United States Marine Corps, Series 65, RG 127 (hereafter cited as Monthly Reports, followed by date).

17. Major Tyler to Secretary Toucey, 10 Jan. 1859, vol. 45, Letters from Marines.

18. Col. Harris to Secretary Toucey, 17 Jan. 1859, ibid.

19. Millett, *Semper Fidelis,* 68–69 and 93, with notes; plus a general scrutiny of all the correspondence between Colonel Commandant Harris and Secretaries Toucey and Welles, Jan. 1859–May 1864, Letters from Marines.

20. 2d Lt. Henry B. Tyler to Secretary Toucey, 18 Apr. 1860, vol. 46, Letters from Marines.

21. Bernard C. Nalty, *United States Marines at Harpers Ferry and the Civil War* (Washington, D.C.: H&MD, 1983), 2–5.

22. Ibid., 2.

23. Maj. Richard S. Collum, USMC, *History of the United States Marine Corps* (New York: L. R. Hamersly, 1903), 112.

24. Col. Harris to Secretary Toucey, 28 Dec. 1859, vol. 45, Letters from Marines.

25. Col. Harris to Secretary Toucey, 21 Nov. 1859, vol. 45, Letters from Marines.

26. Col. Harris to Secretary Toucey, 26 Apr. 1860 (14 days after Fort Sumter), vol. 45, Letters from Marines.

27. William S. Dudley, *Going South: U.S. Navy Officer Resignations and Dismissals on the Eve of the Civil War* (Washington, D.C.: Naval Historical Foundation, 1981), 53–55. The best source on this subject is Ralph W. Donnelly, *The History of the Confederate States Marine Corps* (Washington, D.C.: published by the author, 1976).

28. Donnelly, *History,* 141.

29. Col. Harris to Major Marston, 8 Nov. 1860, vol. 47, Letters from Marines. Note: Marston's petitions appear throughout volumes 47–49.

30. Major Ward Marston to Secretary Toucey, 5 Dec. 1860, vol. 47, Letters from Marines.

31. This refers to Lieutenant Colonel Marston's alleged mishandling (perhaps a kind description) of his recruits' bounty funds in 1865 while in command of Marine Barracks, Boston; see the essay on Brig. Gen. Jacob Zeilin in this volume.

32. Millett, *Semper Fidelis,* 90. Nearly half of the forty-four years' experience Harris eventually brought to the office of Commandant were influenced by service with the Navy, and only a few months of that long service had anything at all to do with the Army. This was another key difference between Harris and Henderson, one which had significant implications when roles and missions of the Corps were evolving during the Civil War.

33. Capt. Louis E. Fagan, USMC, from USS *Vandalia* in Smyrna, Turkey, to 1st. Lt. Henry Clay Cochrane, USMC, 11 Sept. 1877, Henry Clay Cochrane Papers, PPC (hereafter cited as Cochrane Papers).

34. First Manassas, Fort Sumter, and Fort Fisher are the leading examples. Even a large-scale administrative deployment proved disastrous when Maj. Addison Garland's two Marine companies, sailing on board *Ariel* to establish the new barracks at Mare Island, California, were part of the prize captured by CSS *Alabama* off the coast of Cuba on 7 Dec. 1862.

35. Major Reynolds to Colonel Harris, 21[?] July 1861, vol. 49, Letters from Marines. One of the company commanders was Bvt. Maj. Jacob Zeilin, a volunteer for the campaign, who was wounded and hospitalized.

36. Col. Harris to Secretary Welles, 26 July 1861, vol. 49, Letters from Marines.

37. Russell's wife, Virginia, died in childbirth in February 1860, leaving him with six children under the age of eight to raise. His brother, Alexander Russell, had the corresponding job as paymaster of the Navy. Russell Biographical File, Reference Section, H&MD (hereafter cited as Russell Biographical File).

38. Admiral DuPont to his wife, 23 Mar. 1862: "I found that [Army brigadier general] Sherman had sent a lieutenant colonel and two companies to St Augustine, though he had my note saying I was going to place the [Marine] battalion there the most unhandsome thing he has done. I will send the battalion home now—it is idle to fit it in anywhere and they are a fine body of well-drilled and disciplined troops." John D. Hayes, ed., *Samuel Francis DuPont: A Selection from His Civil War Letters,* 3 vols. (Ithaca: Cornell University Press, 1969), 1:377–86. DuPont's commendatory letter to Reynolds upon the detachment of the Marines, dated 25 March 1862, was entered by Reynolds's defense counsel in the general court-martial of 7–20 May 1862.

39. Major Reynolds to Colonel Harris, n.d. (generally assumed to be 23 Feb. 1862), vol. 50, Letters from Marines.

40. Although Reynolds was unsuccessful in introducing the issue of Russell's alleged drunkenness and Harris's attempt to keep same under cover, the issue soon got out of hand. By early September 1862, Harris could no longer keep his paymaster's frequent absences a secret. He placed Russell on report for extended AWOL, and Secretary Welles issued a letter of reproof. Russell committed suicide in his boardinghouse on I Street in Washington on 31 October 1862. Russell Biographical File.

41. *Proceedings of a Marine General Court-Martial, Convened at Washington City, May 7, 1862 for the Trial of Lieut. Col. John Geo. Reynolds, U.S. Marine Corps* (Washington, D.C.: Henry Polkinhorn, 1862). Copy available at MCHC.

42. Lieutenant Colonel Reynolds to Secretary Welles, 23 July 1862, vol. 50, Letters from Marines.

43. "Sent a letter of reproof to Colonel Harris and also one to Lieutenant Colonel Reynolds of the Marine Corps between whom there is a bitter feud." Gideon Welles, *Diary of Gideon Welles,* 3 vols. (Cambridge: Houghton Mifflin, Riverside Press, 1911), 1:89, 20 Aug. 1862.

44. Heinl, *Soldiers of the Sea,* 75–76.

45. "Annual Report of the Colonel Commandant to the Secretary of the Navy, 1863" (hereafter cited as CMC, "Annual Report," followed by the date), copy in Harris Biographical File.

46. Colonel Harris to Major Garland, 28 Dec. 1863, Item 120, ser. 4, vol. 11, Letters Sent, 1798–1884.

47. Admiral Porter to Colonel Harris, quoted in Heinl, *Soldiers of the Sea,* 86–87. See also Item 194, ser. 4, vol. 11, Letters Sent, 1798–1884. See also Lt. Winfield Scott Schley, USN, to Colonel Harris, 8 Dec. 1863, Harris Biographical File.

48. Colonel Harris to Secretary Welles, 5 May 1864, Item 335, ser. 4, vol. 11, Letters Sent, 1798–1884.

49. 1st Lt. Frank L. Church, USMC, assigned to Admiral Porter's flagship *Cricket* for the Red River campaign, made this diary entry on 18 May 1864: "The dispatch boat came along-

side with mail[.] Got news of Colonel Harris's death." James P. Jones and Edward F. Keuchal, ed., *Civil War Marine: A Diary of the Red River Expedition, 1864* (Washington, D.C.: H&MD, 1975).

Chapter 7. Jacob Zeilin

I would like to acknowledge the assistance rendered by Maj. George C. Solley, USMC, for his earlier research on Jacob Zeilin, and to Robert Aquilina, Reference Section, H&MD for his consistently outstanding support.

1. Welles, *Diary,* 2:31.

2. Monthly Reports, June 1864.

3. Colonel Dulany to Secretary Welles, 17 May 1864, vol. 52, Item 120, Letters from Marines.

4. Millett, *Semper Fidelis,* 80. Colonel Commandant Harris to Secretary Welles, 25 Mar. 1864, Item 291, ser. 4, vol. 11, Letters Sent, 1798–1884. For background information on Lieutenant Colonel Marston, Lieutenant Colonel Reynolds, and Major Garland, refer to the essay on Colonel Harris in this volume.

5. Welles, *Diary,* 2:51. Note that Welles had involuntarily retired nine admirals for "being overage" in 1862.

6. Major Nicholson, Adjutant and Inspector, to the officers indicated, 11 June 1865, Item 379, vol. 11, Letters Sent, 1798–1884. Major Doughty was junior to Zeilin but considered "overage."

7. Heinl, *Soldiers of the Sea,* 598. Generals Holcomb and Shoup were similarly "deep selected" to be commandant in the twentieth century.

8. Colonel Commandant Zeilin to Secretary Welles, 1 July 1864, vol. 11, Letters Sent, 1798–1884.

9. Thomas Fendall, Headmaster, the Washington Academy, Philadelphia, to President Monroe and others, 9 Dec. 1820, copy of microfilm provided by assistant archivist, U.S. Military Academy (USMA) Archives.

10. Kenneth W. Rapp, USMA Archives, to Lt. Col. Merrill L. Bartlett, USMC, 2 Feb. 1982. Zeilin's actual appointment came from Congressman John Sergeant of Philadelphia. The class of 1826 was relatively undistinguished, save for Albert Sidney Johnston, Confederate General killed at Shiloh in 1862.

11. Jacob Zeilin Jr. to Secretary Southard, 27 Mar. 1827, Applications for Commissions in the Marine Corps, 1815–1831, Records of the United States Marine Corps, Series 69, RG 127, NARA.

12. Zeilin to President Jackson, 21 July 1831, in ibid.

13. Information from Zeilin Biographical File, Reference Section, H&MD (hereafter cited as Zeilin Biographical File).

14. Ibid.

15. For an account of the Plug Ugly riot and the role of Archibald Henderson and the Marines, see the essay on Henderson in this volume.

16. Zeilin Biographical File. For details of Zeilin's wounding and subsequent evacuation from Bull Run, see also David M. Sullivan, *The United States Marine Corps in the Civil War: The First Year* (Shippensburg, Pa.: White Mane, 1997), 142.

17. *Proceedings of a Marine General Court-Martial,* 70–71.

18. Colonel Harris to Secretary Welles, 22 July 1863; Major Zeilin telegram to Secretary Welles, 30 July 1863; Colonel Harris to Secretary Welles, 31 July 1863, vol. 51, Items 187, 194, and 195, respectively, Letters from Marines.

19. Heinl, *Soldiers of the Sea,* 79.

20. February 1834 from New York, early 1848 from Mexico, March 1854 from Japan, and September 1863 from Morris Island.

21. Colonel Commandant Harris to Major Zeilin, 2 Dec. 1863, Item 134, ser. 4, vol. 11, Letters Sent, 1798–1884.

22. Entries for June 1864 and for every month thereafter through Nov. 1876, Monthly Reports, RG 127. Of the remaining field grades, Garland died at Mare Island in June 1864, Shuttleworth was promoted directly to colonel, the other four were "retired-on-active-duty."

23. Millett, *Semper Fidelis,* 91–93.

24. Colonel Commandant Zeilin to Lieutenant Colonel Marston, 26 July 1864, Item 415, vol. 11, Letters Sent, 1798–1884.

25. Ibid. See also Items 63, 76, 88, 121, and 166 in vol. 12. Zeilin was issued this directive from Secretary Welles about 22 February 1865: "You will require officers receiving bounty-money belonging to recruits to render to you monthly detailed statements of their receipts and disbursements, and you are also authorized to establish such checks as you may think advisable to guard against any improper use of such funds." Lt. Col. Marston had reputedly invested these funds in the stock market; he was suspended and then dismissed from the service.

26. Lt. George Dewey, USN, quoted in Heinl, *Soldiers of the Sea,* 82.

27. Heinl, *Soldiers of the Sea,* 82–83.

28. DuPont to William Whetten, 19 Jan. 1865, in Hayes, *DuPont,* 3:427–28.

29. Metcalf, *History of the United States Marine Corps,* 220.

30. Colonel Commandant Zeilin to First Lieutenant Cochrane, 27 Mar. 1865, Item 181, vol. 12, Letters Sent, 1798–1884.

31. Heinl, *Soldiers of the Sea,* 86.

32. Ibid., 623.

33. Assistant Secretary Fox to James W. Grimes, 1 June 1865, quoted in Hayes, *DuPont,* 3:372–73.

34. Heinl, *Soldiers of the Sea,* 87.

35. Ibid., 87.

36. Metcalf, *History of the United States Marine Corps,* 244–45.

37. Report, 11 June 1864, from Marine Barracks, Washington, signed by Captain Graham, First Lieutenant Tilton, and Second Lieutenant Nokes, later forwarded to the secretary of the navy, vol. 52, Item 155, Letters from Marines.

38. Rankin, *Small Arms of the Sea Services,* 178–79.

39. Metcalf, *History of the United States Marine Corps,* 250.

40. Capt. McLane Tilton, USMC, to Brigadier General Commandant Zeilin, quoted in Heinl, *Soldiers of the Sea,* 88.

41. Ibid., 90–91.

42. Brigadier General Commandant Zeilin to Captain Collum, 27 Nov. 1870, quoted in Collum, *History,* 199–200.

43. Brigadier General Commandant Zeilin to Secretary Welles, 17 and 22 Nov. 1868, copies contained in Zeilin Biographical File. An M1859 saber adorns the gravestone of Colonel Harris.

44. Brigadier General Commandant Zeilin to Maj. T. Y. Field, 5 Jan. 1872, quoted in Millett, *Semper Fidelis,* 104.

45. Heinl, *Soldiers of the Sea,* 98. Zeilin was permitted to retain his rank of brigadier general.

46. 1st Lt. Henry Clay Cochrane, *The Status of the Marine Corps: A Plan for Its Reorganization* (Annapolis, Md., 1 Oct. 1875), Cochrane Papers.

47. "A Bill to Reduce, Reform and Increase the Efficiency of the Marine Corps included in Minutes, Norfolk, Va., 12 Feb. 1876," Cochrane Papers.

48. Quoted in Jack Shulimson, *The Marine Corps' Search for a Mission, 1880–1898* (Lawrence: University Press of Kansas, 1993), 18–19.

49. Information from Zeilin Biographical File. Funeral services were held in St. John's Church. His body was escorted to the train station for the final trip to Philadelphia by four Marine companies, a battery of United States Artillery, the Washington Light Infantry, and the Marine Band. He was buried in the Laurel Hill Cemetery next to his son.

Chapter 8. Charles G. McCawley

1. Virginia Farragut to John L. Broome, 5 Mar. 1874, Folder 7, Broome Papers, PPC; Lt. Robert Huntington to father, 3 Apr. 1876 and 25 Feb. 1877, Robert W. Huntington Papers, PPC (hereafter cited as Huntington Papers); 2d Lt. C. P. Porter to Lt. Col. Charles McCawley, 17 Jan. 1873, copy, enclosure to Lieutenant Colonel McCawley to CMC to SecNav, 20 Jan. 1873, Marine Officer Supplement, 1870–75, General Records of the Department of the Navy, RG 80, NARA; Cochrane to sister, 6 Aug. 1876, and entry for 18 Oct. 1876, Cochrane Diary, Cochrane Papers; Lt. Col. C. G. McCawley to SecNav, 19 Oct. 1876, Letters Received, Marines, RG 80, NARA (hereafter cited as Letters Received, Marines) and SecNav to McCawley, 1 Nov. 1876, Letters Sent, Marines, RG 80, NARA (hereafter cited as Letters Sent, Marines). Much of the material for this essay is derived from Shulimson, *Marine Corps Search for a Mission.*

2. "Authorized Strength of United States Marine Corps, 1798–1916," 15 May 1916, File 6758, RG 80, NARA; CMC, "Annual Report," 24 Oct. 1874, in SecNav, *Annual Report, 1874;* CMC to SecNav, 4 Jan. 1875, Marine Officers Letter Supplement, 1870–75, RG 80, NARA; *New York Times,* 29 Dec. 1875, p. 5; *Congressional Record,* 44th Cong, 1st sess., 5 Jan. 1876, 260; *Hearings before House Naval Affairs Committee,* 44th Cong., 1st sess., 1876, 38–39, 56–57; *New York Times,* 8 Feb. 1876, p. 1, 6 May 1876, p. 1, 18 May 1876, p. 2, and 24 May 1876, p. 1; *Congressional Record,* 44th Cong., 1st sess., 17 May 1876, p. 3127, 19 May 1876, p. 3202, 20 May 1876, p. 3244, 23 May 1876, 3281–82, and 22 June 1876, p. 4025; Henry Clay Cochrane, "A Resuscitation or a Funeral," 1 Oct. 1875, Cochrane Papers.

3. *Army and Navy Journal,* 4 Sept. 1875, 55, 11 Sept. 1875, 73; clipping from *Washington Chronicle,* 9 Nov. 1875, Scrapbook, 71, Cochrane Papers.

4. Cochrane, "Resuscitation or a Funeral."

5. CMC, "Annual Report," 25 Oct. 1876, in SecNav, *Annual Report, 1876,* 283–84.

6. Lt. Robert Huntington to father, 21 Oct. 1870 and 25 Feb. 1877, Huntington Papers; Porter to McCawley, 17 Jan. 1873; William H. Russell, "The Genesis of Fleet Marine Force Doctrine: 1879–1899," pt. 1, *Marine Corps Gazette,* Apr. 1951, 52–59, 56; Millett, *Semper Fidelis,* 108–9.

7. James Forney, "The Marines," *United Service,* Apr. 1889, 89 and 94–95.

8. Millett, *Semper Fidelis,* 92; "Register of Officers, U.S. Marine Corps, 1798–1903," in Collum, *History,* 430–49; *Navy and Marine Corps Register, 1880;* Lt. Robert W. Huntington to father, 20 Mar. 1864, Huntington Papers; Henry Clay Cochrane, "A Scrap of Marine Corps History," Folder 101, and Henry Clay Cochrane Journal, 1869–, vol. 55, Cochrane Papers; "Examining Board of the Marine Corps," n.p., c. 1866, Clipping File, Cochrane Papers; CMC to Charles G. Petit, 25 Feb. 1874, vol. 20, p. 506, Letters Sent, 1798–1884; D. D. Porter to Rep. B. F. Butler, 9 Feb. 1870, Box 18, D. D. Porter Papers, MRR.

9. "Our Social Marines," clipping from the *Philadelphia Times,* 7 Jan. 1882, Marine Corps Scrapbook, 1880–1898, RG 127, NARA. See also "Our Social Marines," clipping, *Washington Republican,* 9 Jan. 1882, Thomas N. Wood Papers, MRR.

10. "Changes in the Marine Corps, which suggested themselves to father before he became Col. Comd't," presented to HQMC, 17 Oct. 1921, Maj. Gen. Charles L. McCawley Papers, PPC (hereafter cited as McCawley Papers). The original list is not extant. On the copy, Maj. Gen. Charles L. McCawley, USMC, the son of the commandant wrote, "The above memorandum in his own hand writing, was written by my father the late Col. Comd't. C. G. McCawley before his appointment as comd't, probably in 1875 or 1876."

11. Maj. August S. Nicholson to Maj. J. L. Broome, 9 Feb. 1877, vol. 23, p. 333, Letters Sent, 1798–1884; Marine Corps Circular, 2 May 1877 in Navy and Marine Corps Orders, 1877–1903, Rare Book Collection, H&MD.

12. CMC to Capt. L. C. Dawson, 4 Aug. 1877, vol. 24, Letters Sent, 1798–1884, and CMC to SecNav, 2 July 1877, Letters Received, Marines.

13. CMC to SecNav, 28 Mar., 30 Apr. 1877, vol. 23, pp. 392–93, 443, Letters Sent, 1798–1884; SecNav to 2d Lt. J. C. Shailer, vol. 9, Letters Sent, Marines; CMC to SecNav, 8 and 12 May 1877, vol. 23, p. 459, Letters Sent, 1798–1884; CMC to SecNav, 4 and 12 May 1877, and 1st Lt. E. T. Bradford to SecNav, 15 May 1877, Letters Received, Marines, 1876–77 Supplement; Capt. James Forney to CMC, 25 June 1877, Letters Received, Historical Section, RG 127, NARA; 2d Lt. Andrew Stevenson, to SecNav, 20 Aug. 1877, Letters Received, Marines, 1876–77 Supplement; 1st Lt. R. S. Collum to 1st Lt. H. C. Cochrane, 14 Aug. 1877, Folder 22, Cochrane Papers; *Army and Navy Journal,* 24 Nov. 1877, 247.

14. Senator James McPherson to SecNav Thompson, 17 Apr. 1877, Folder 7, Broome Papers, PPC, and Col. M. R. Kintzing to SecNav, 20 Apr. 1877, with endorsement by Navy Department, Letters Received, Marines, 1876–77 Supplement.

15. SecNav to CMC, 17 Aug. 1877, Letters Received, "N," RG 127, NARA (hereafter cited as Letters Received, "N"); USMC General Order No. 1, 21 Aug. 1877, Navy and Marine Corps Orders, 1877–1903, H&MD; CMC, "Annual Report," 16 Nov. 1877, in SecNav, *Annual Report, 1877.* See also Jerry M. Cooper, *The Army and Civil Disorder: Federal Military Intervention in Labor Disputes, 1877–1900* (Westport, Conn.: Greenwood Press, 1980), 43–83, and H. C. Cochrane, "The Naval Brigade and the Marine Battalions in the Labor Strikes of 1877," *United Service,* pt. 1 (Jan. 1879): 115–29, pt. 2 (Oct. 1879): 617–25.

16. CMC to Maj. J. S. Broome, 21 Mar. 1878, vol. 34, p. 269, Letters Sent, 1798–1884. For examples of letters relating to retirements, courts-martial, and resignations, see CMC to SecNav 19 Nov. 1877, Letters Received, Marines, 1876–77 Supplement; CMC to SecNav, 11 Feb. 1878, vol. 24, p. 232, Letters Sent, 1798–1884; 1st Lt. James Breese to CMC, 16 Aug. 1879, Letters

Received, Marines, 1879, RG 80, NARA; SecNav to Mr. Andrews, 25 Apr. 1879, vol. 10, Letters Sent, Marines.

17. SecNav to new second lieutenants, 16 June 1880, vol. 10, Letters Sent, Marines, RG 80, NARA; *Navy and Marine Corps Register, 1880; Military Academy Register, 1876;* George Denny Scrapbook, Rare Book Collection, H&MD; Clipping, "Career of Maj. Waller," n.p., n.d., Entry 46, Clipping Book No. 2, RG 127, NARA.

18. Entry for 31 Dec. 1880, Cochrane Diary, Cochrane Papers; CMC to Capt. W. A. T. Maddox, 3 Jan. 1880, Letters Received, Marines; Capt. Woodhull S. Schenck to SecNav, 10 Mar. 1880, Letters Received, Marines; *New York Times,* 3 Mar. 1880, p. 1; *Army and Navy Journal,* 13 Mar. 1880, 646–47; CMC, "Annual Report," 1880, 529.

19. SecNav to Col. Thomas Y. Field, 8 Dec. 1880, Letters Sent, Marines, RG 80, and SecNav to Col. Thomas Y. Field, 3 Mar. 1881, Letters Received, "N."

20. Peter Karsten, *Naval Aristocracy: The Golden Age of Annapolis and the Emergence of Modern American Navalism* (New York: Free Press, 1972), 122–24; C. C. Todd, "The Personnel of our Ships' Companies," *United Service,* Mar. 1882, 257–63; Cochrane to CMC, 19 Nov. 1881, draft of letter, Folder 26, Cochrane Papers; SecNav to 2d Lt. L. W. T. Waller, 20 Dec. 1881, vol. 11, p. 28, Letters Sent, Marines; Col. Frederic M. Wise and Meigs 0. Frost, *A Marine Tells It to You* (New York: J. H. Sears, 1929), 1.

21. CMC to SecNav, 20 Apr. 1880, vol. 25, pp. 457–58, Letters Sent, 1798–1884; SecNav to CMC, 16 June 1880, Letters Received, "N"; SecNav to CMC, 24 May 1882, vol. 11, Letters Sent, Marines, RG 80; CMC to SecNav, 24 Jan. 1884, vol. 28, pp. 53–54, Letters Sent, 1798–1884.

22. Entries for 19 Oct. 1879 and 25 Feb.–3 Mar. 1881, Cochrane Diary, Cochrane Papers; Charles Mason Remey, "Reminiscences of His Childhood, 1874–1884," mss., 1943 (copy in LC), 108; *Army and Navy Journal,* 12 Mar. 1881, 667; SecNav to CMC, 27 Apr. 1881, Letters Received, "N"; CMC to SecNav, 18 May 1881, vol. 26, p. 274, Letters Sent, 1798–1884.

23. William H. Russell, "Genesis of FMFPac Doctrine," pt. 1, *Marine Corps Gazette,* Apr. 1951, 56; CMC Letters to Col. J. H. Jones, 31 May 1879 and 12 June 1879, vol. 25, pp. 101, 113–14, Letters Sent, 1798–1884; Navy Department, General Order 273, 23 Aug. 1881, Navy Department General Orders, 1863–87, p. 200, RG 80, NARA.

24. CMC to Col. J. H. Jones, 31 May and 12 June 1879, vol. 25, pp. 101 and 113–14, Letters Sent, 1798–1884.

25. C. D. Hebb to CMC and CMC to Hebb, 9 Aug. 1882, Letters Received, "H," RG 127, NARA; CMC to SecNav and CMC to C. D. Hebb, 5 Dec. 1882, vol. 27, pp. 296–97, Letters Sent, 1798–1884.

26. *Congressional Record,* 47th Cong., 1st sess., 1882, p. 6644; SecNav to CMC, 19 Apr. 1880, vol. 10, p. 397, Letters Sent, Marines, 1880, RG 80; CMC to SecNav, 25 Nov. 1881 and 10 Jan. 1882, vol. 26, pp. 516–17, 552–53, Letters Sent, 1798–1884; SecNav to CMC, 12 Jan. 1882, Letters Received, "N."

27. Chandler to Sen. Nelson W. Aldrich, 13 Dec. 1884, vol. 71, p. 2937, Chandler Papers, MRR; Frank L. Denny to Postmaster General Graham, telegram, 25 Aug. 1884, Letters Received, Marines, 1884, and Acting SecNav to 2d Lt. Frank L. Denny, 1 Sept. 1884, vol. 11, p. 288, Letters Sent, Marines, RG 80, NARA.

28. CMC to Staff, 30 Mar. 1878, vol. 24, p. 277; CMC to Maj. W. B. Slack, 12 Feb. 1879, vol. 25, p. 2; CMC to Maj. W. B. Slack, 6 Jan. 1879, vol. 24, pp. 539–40, all in Letters Sent, 1798–1884.

29. CMC to Capt. Schenck, 13, 21 Dec. 1880, vol. 26, pp. 132–33, and 138–39, Letters Sent, 1798–1884; SecNav to CMC, 28 Jan. 1884, with attachments, Letters Received, "N"; CMC to SecNav, 12 Sept. 1884, vol. 1, pp. 72–78, Letters Sent to the Secretary of the Navy, Records of the U.S. Marine Corps, RG 127, NARA (hereafter cited as Letters Sent to the Secretary of the Navy), and SecNav to CMC, 1 Oct. 1884, vol. 11, Letters Sent, Marines, RG 80, NARA.

30. McCawley to Chandler, 12 Mar. 1884, Chandler Papers, MRR.

31. Brig. Gen. Jacob Zeilin to SecNav, 28 Oct. 1873, Letters Received, Marines, and C. G. McCawley to Naval Solicitor, John A. Bolles, 2 Aug. 1877, Letters Received, Historical Section, RG 127, NARA.

32. Marine Corps Circular Order, 4 Aug. 1877, and Marine Corps General Order, 29 Dec. 1877, *Navy and Marine Corps General Orders, 1877–1903,* Rare Book Collection, H&MD; Navy Dept General Order 237, 12 Mar. 1878, Navy Department General Orders, 1863–1887, RG 80, NARA; Marine Corps Order, 10 Dec. 1878, Letters Received, Historical Section, RG 127, NARA; CMC to Commanding Officers, 22 June 1880, vol. 25, p. 536, Letters Sent, 1798–1884. CMC to Maj. J. S. Broome, 23 Dec. 1878, vol. 24, p. 526, Letters Sent, 1798–1884; CMC to SecNav, 6 Sept. 1879, Letters Received, Marines, 1879, RG 80; Capt. James Forney to CMC, 29 Nov. 1880 and 7 Oct. 1881, Letters Received, "F," RG 127, NARA; Maj. George P. Houston to CMC, 30 May 1882, Letters Received, "H," RG 127, NARA. and memo, n.d., copies of Letters Now on File Recommending Sale of Malt Liquors, Letters Received, Historical Section, RG 127, NARA; Millett, *Semper Fidelis,* 103.

33. Jack D. Foner, *The United States Soldier Between Two Wars, 1865–1898* (New York: Humanities Press, 1970), 223; Peter Karsten, ed., *Soldiers and Society: The Effects of Military Service and War on Americans* (Westport, Conn.: Greenwood Press, 1978), 29; Capt. James Forney to CMC, 29 Nov. 1880, Letters Received, "F," RG 127, NARA.

34. CMC to Maj. George Butler, 14 Sept. 1881, Letters Received, Historical Section, RG 127, NARA; *Army and Navy Journal,* 29 Aug. 1885, 77, and 14 Nov. 1885, 297.

35. Cochrane to Col. Cmdt. Heywood, 30 Dec. 1893, draft of letter, Folder 41, Cochrane Papers; entry for 14 Jan. 1881, Cochrane Diary, Cochrane Papers; House Committee on Naval Affairs, *Appointments and Promotions in the Marine Corps,* 46th Cong., 3d sess., Feb. 1881, H. Doc. 314; Senate Naval Affairs Committee, *Appointments and Promotions in the Marine Corps,* 46th Cong., 3d sess., Jan. 1881, S. Rept. 762; *Congressional Record,* 46th Cong., 3d sess., Dec. 1880–Feb. 1881, pp. 11, 16, 257, 710, 904; *Army and Navy Journal,* 30 Apr., 11 June, and 18 June 1881, 817, 938, and 968.

36. *Congressional Record,* 47th Cong., 1st sess., Dec. 1881–Jan. 1882, pp. 3, 166, 398; Senate Naval Affairs Committee, *Appointments and Promotions in the Marine Corps,* 47th Cong., 1st sess., Dec. 1881, S. Rept. 15; *U.S. Statutes at Large,* 47th Cong., 1881–83, vol. 22, chap. 391; *Army and Navy Journal,* 24 Dec. 1881, 450; CMC to SecNav, 9 May 1882, vol. 27, pp. 104–5, Letters Sent, 1798–1884; *Army and Navy Journal,* 20 May 1882, 966; Cochrane to CMC, 16 Aug. 1882, Letters Received, Historical Section, RG 127, NARA.

37. Peter Karsten, "Armed Progressives: The Military Reorganized for the American Century," in *Building the Organizational Society,* ed. Jerry Israel (New York: Free Press, 1972), 197–232, 199–201; Lt. Cdr. Allan D. Brown, "Naval Education," *USNIP* (1879), 305–21; Lt.

Cdr. C. F. Goodrich, "Naval Education," *USNIP* (1879), 323–44; Capt. W. T. Truxton, "Reform in the Navy," *United Service,* July 1879, 378–82; Bowman H. McCalla, "Memoirs of a Naval Career," mss., chap. 12, pp. 15–16, Navy Library, Naval Historical Center; *U.S. Statutes at Large,* 47th Cong., 1881–1883, vol. 22, chap. 391.

38. James G. Courts, Clerk, Committee of Appropriations to SecNav, 15 Jan. 1884 (copy), enclosure to SecNav to CMC, 16 Jan. 1884, Letters Received, "N"; CMC to SecNav, 17 Jan. 1884, and 11 Feb. 1884, vol. 28, pp. 44–45, 71, Letters Sent, 1798–1884; *Congressional Record,* 48th Cong., 1st sess., 12 Feb., 6 Mar. 1884, pp. 1072 and 1666; SecNav to Senator Eugene Hale, 12 Jan. 1885 (Copy), Letters Received, "N"; *Congressional Record,* 48th Cong., 2d sess., 14 Jan. 1885, p. 686, 27 Jan. 1885, p. 1019, and 28 Jan. 1885, p. 1041; *Army and Navy Journal,* 31 Jan. 1885, 523.

39. Jack Shulimson, "U.S. Marines in Panama, 1885," in Lt. Col. Merrill L. Bartlett, USMC (Ret.), ed., *Assault from the Sea: Essays on the History of Amphibious Warfare* (Annapolis: Naval Institute Press, 1983), 107–20. For general accounts of the revolution in Panama see, E. Taylor Parks, *Colombia and the United States, 1765–1934* (Durham, N.C.: Duke University Press, 1935), 202–28; Kenneth J. Hagan, *American Gunboat Diplomacy and the Old Navy* (Westport, Conn.: Greenwood Press, 1973), 158–87; Gerstle Mack, *The Land Divided: A History of the Panama Canal and Other Isthmian Canal Projects* (1944; reprint, New York: Octagon Press, 1974), 350–54; Collum, *History,* 234–53; Clyde Metcalf, "The Naval Expedition to the Isthmus of Panama," mss., Geographic Files, Reference Section, H&MD; Daniel H. Wicks, "Dress Rehearsal: United States Intervention on the Isthmus of Panama, 1885," mss.; Bowman H. McCalla, "The U.S. Naval Brigade on the Isthmus of Panama," in Office of Naval Intelligence, *Papers on Naval Operations during the Year ending July 1885,* Information from Abroad, General Information Series (Washington, D.C., 1885), 4:41–100; Milton Plesur, *America's Outward Thrust, Approaches to Foreign Affairs, 1865–90* (DeKalb: Northern Illinois University Press, 1971), 176–78; David M. Pletcher, *The Awkward Years: American Foreign Relations under Garfield and Arthur* (Columbia: University of Missouri Press, 1962), 232–33, and 347.

40. *Army and Navy Journal,* 6 June 1885, 918, and 13 June 1885, 935; SecNav to CMC, 12 June 1885, Letters Received, "N."

41. McCalla, "U.S. Naval Brigade," 61.

42. CMC to SecNav, 12 July 1885, vol. 1, pp. 193–204, Letters Sent to the Secretary of the Navy.

43. CMC, "Annual Report," 1885–88; CMC to SecNav, 1 Dec. 1887, vol. 1, pp. 492–93, and CMC to SecNav, 21 May 1888, vol. 2, pp. 37–38, both in Letters Sent to the Secretary of the Navy.

44. *Army and Navy Journal,* 29 May 1886, 894, and 20 Aug. 1887, 67.

45. Ibid., 27 Aug. 1887, 80.

46. Ibid., 3 Sept. 1887, 106–7. Cochrane notes in his diary on 28 Aug. 1887 that he wrote the editor of the *Army and Navy Journal* "a reply to Col Commandant's McC's letter 'On Reckless Recruiting.'" Entry for 28 Aug. 1887, Cochrane Diary, Cochrane Papers. CMC, "Annual Report," 1 Oct. 188, in SecNav, *Annual Report, 1888,* 525.

47. CMC to SecNav, 21 Feb. 1887, vol. 1, p. 318, Letters Sent to the Secretary of the Navy; Acting SecNav to CMC, 25 May 1887, vol. 1, Letters Received, "N"; CMC to SecNav 6 June 1887, vol. 1, pp. 419–20, Letters Sent to the Secretary of the Navy; SecNav to CMC, 9 Dec. 1887; J. G. Walker to 1st Lt. O. C. Berryman, 10 Oct. 1887; Dept of Navy, General Court-

Martial Order No. 61, 14 Nov. 1888, attached to JAG to CMC, 12 Dec. 1888, all in Letters Received, "N."

48. CMC to SecNav, 13 July 1886 and 3 Aug. 1887, vol. 1, pp. 307, 448, Letters Sent to the Secretary of the Navy.

49. Entries for 22 Feb., 21 Apr., and 31 May 1888, Cochrane Diary; Cochrane to Capt. Louis E. Fagan, 15 May 1888, and Cochrane to Lt. Lauchheimer, 31 May 1888, draft of letter, Folder 33, all in Cochrane Papers.

50. Cochrane to Fagan, 15 May 1888; Senate Committee on Naval Affairs Committee to Equalize the Grades of Officers of the Marine Corps, 50th Cong., 1st sess., 1888, S. Rept. 931 to Accompany Bill S. 2049.

51. Cochrane to Fagan, 15 May 1888.

52. *Congressional Record,* 50th Cong., 1st sess., 17 May 1888, p. 4313; Cochrane to Fagan, 15 May 1888.

53. SecNav, *Annual Report, 1887,* iii–v, and *Annual Report, 1888,* iii–iv; Mark D. Hirsch, *William C. Whitney, Modern Warwick* (New York: Dodd, Mead, 1948), 263, 255–336, 337–41; Paullin, *History of Naval Administration,* 378–79, 398–99; Ronald Spector, *Professors of War: The Naval War College and the Development of the Naval Profession* (Newport, R.I.: Naval War College Press, 1977), 50–51; Leonard D. White, *The Republican Era: A Study in Administrative History, 1869–1901* (New York: Macmillan, 1958), 162–69; Harold Sprout and Margaret Sprout, *The Rise of American Naval Power, 1776–1918* (Princeton: Princeton University Press, 1946), 189–90; James L. Abrahamson, *America Arms for a New Century, the Making of a Great Military Power* (New York: Free Press, 1981), 37–40, 187; B. Franklin Cooling, *Benjamin Franklin Tracy: Father of the Modern American Navy* (Hamden, Conn.: Archon Books, 1973), 56–58; John D. Alden, *The American Steel Navy* (Annapolis: Naval Institute Press, 1972), 31–32; John D. Long, *The New American Navy,* 2 vols. (New York: Outlook, 1903), 1:40; Donald J. Sexton, "Forging the Sword: Congress and the American Naval Renaissance, 1880–1890" (Ph.D. diss., University of Tennessee, 1976), 193–94; Daniel H. Wicks, "New Navy and New Empire: The Life and Times of John Grimes Walker" (Ph.D. diss., University of California, Berkeley, 1979), 174–75, 180–82; Robert Seager II, *Alfred Thayer Mahan* (Annapolis: Naval Institute Press, 1977), 145–46; Karsten, "Armed Progressives," 197–232, 204–5; Hagan, *American Gunboat Diplomacy,* 34–35.

54. Cooling, *Tracy,* 69–70, 79–87; Walter R. Herrick Jr., *The Naval Revolution* (Baton Rouge: Louisiana State University Press, 1966), 44–49, 56; Wicks, "New Navy and New Empire," 194–96, 208–9, 214–19, 247; Daniel H. Wicks, "The First Cruise of the Squadron of Evolution," *Military Affairs* 44 (Apr. 1980): 64; SecNav, *Annual Report, 1889,* passim; Sprout and Sprout, *Rise of American Naval Power,* 207–8; Millett, *Semper Fidelis,* 122.

55. CMC to SecNav, 1 Oct. 1889, vol. 2, pp. 188–89, Letters Sent to the Secretary of the Navy.

56. Mannix to Cochrane, 14 Sept. 1889, Folder 35, Cochrane Papers. For background of Mannix, see Jack Shulimson, "Daniel Pratt Mannix and the Marine School of Application, 1889–1894," *Journal of Military History* 55 (Oct. 1991): 469–85.

57. Cdr. Henry Glass, memo, 31 Aug. 1889, File 4715, General Correspondence Files, RG 80, NARA; entry for 13 May 1892, Cochrane Diary, Cochrane Papers; Col. C. G. McCawley to S. B. Luce, 18 Dec. 1889, Stephen B. Luce Papers, MRR; Millett, *Semper Fidelis,* 122. Glass may have moved, as Cochrane claims, that the board recommend the removal of marines from Navy warships, but William F. Fullam was certainly the point man on the issue. The Greer board

did not make an overall report but made a series of recommendations varying from signaling lanterns to employment of artillery; for example, President of the Board to SecNav, 5 Nov. 1889, File 5229, 9 Nov. 1889, File 5261, and 10 Dec. 1889, File 5779, all in RG 80, NARA. The only formal reference to the recommendation about marines is an entry that shows the Navy Department received a letter from the Board of Organization on 19 November 1889 relative to their duties. A note states that the letter went to the chief clerk. Briefing Book, 1889, Entry 5412, RG 80, NARA. A search of pertinent records and finding aids failed to locate the actual recommendation or the secretary's action. In all probability, the letter was destroyed.

58. CMC to SecNav, 27 May, 7 July, 28 Aug., and 4 Sept. 1890, and Lieutenant Colonel Heywood to SecNav, 6 Aug. 1890, vol. 2, pp. 256–57, 270–71, 282, 284, 289–90, Letters Sent to the Secretary of the Navy.

Chapter 9. Charles Heywood

1. To permit Colonel McCawley, although in poor health, to remain on active duty until his eligibility for retirement, the secretary of the navy appointed Colonel Hebb, the next senior Marine officer, to serve as acting commandant in his stead. Hebb used the title "Colonel, Commanding" rather then "Colonel Commandant" when he signed the 1890 annual report. See "A Brief of the Facts Pertaining to the Detail of C. N. Hebb as Acting Commandant of the Marine Corps," n.d., Richard A. Long Files, MCHC, and also the essay on McCawley in this volume. Much of the material for this essay like the one on McCawley is derived from Shulimson, *Marine Corps Search for a Mission.*

2. "Commander of the Marines," clipping from *Baltimore Sun,* 8 Oct. 1890, Frank L. Denny Scrapbook, Rare Book Collection, H&MD; *Army and Navy Journal,* 8 Nov. 1890, 173; "To Command the Marines," *New York Times,* 9 Oct. 1890, p. 5; "Col Heywood Promoted," *New York Times,* 31 Jan. 1891, p. 8; "Service Salad," *United Service,* Feb. 1891, 211–12.

3. Lt. William F. Fullam, "The Systems of Naval Training and Discipline Required to Promote Efficiency and Attract Americans," *USNIP* 16 (1890): 473–95; *Army and Navy Journal,* 29 Nov. 1890, 228–29, 6 Dec. 1890, 247, and 10 Jan. 1891, 327; Col. C. D. Hebb to SecNav, 15 Jan. 1891, vol. 2, pp. 342–43, Letters Sent to the Secretary of the Navy.

4. For the details of Captain Mannix and the Greer board, see the essay on Col. Charles G. McCawley in this volume.

5. CMC to Commodore James A. Greer, 18 Oct. 1889, and attached memoranda, Subject File, NF, 1889, Naval Records Collection; CMC, "Annual Report," 1891, 3–5; CMC to Col. James Forney, 23 Mar. 1891, vol. 37, p. 171, Letters Sent, RG 127.

6. CMC to Greer, 18 Oct. 1889 and CMC, "Annual Report," 1891, 4–5.

7. CMC, "Annual Report," in SecNav, *Annual Report, 1890,* 607; Ensign A. P. Niblack, "The Enlistment, Training, and Organization of Crews for Our New Ships," *USNIP* 17 (1891): 3–49; CMC, "Annual Report," in SecNav, *Annual Report, 1889,* 825.

8. *Army and Navy Journal,* 4 Apr. 1891, 547.

9. CMC to SecNav, 13 Apr. 1891, vol. 2, p. 336, Letters Sent to the Secretary of the Navy; Headquarters, Marine Corps, General Order No. 1, 1 May 1891, Marine Corps General and Special Orders, Rare Books Collection, H&MD.

10. Ibid.; Marine Corps Circular to all Shore Commanders, 23 July 1891, Order Book 19, p. 394, RG 127, NARA.

11. Report of Capt. D. P. Mannix, Commanding School of Application, 1 Oct. 1892, as reprinted in Collum, *History,* 288–98; *Army and Navy Journal,* 4 Apr. 1891, 547, and 25 Apr. 1891, 602.

12. CMC, "Annual Report," 1891, 8; Report of Capt. D. P. Mannix, 289; *Army and Navy Journal,* 5 Sept. 1891, 27.

13. CMC to SecNav, 22 July 1891, vol. 2, p. 402, Letters Sent to the Secretary of the Navy; SecNav to CMC, 29 July 1891, Letters Received, "N"; CMC to Maj. P. C. Pope, 31 July 1891, Order Book, 19, p. 437, RG 127, NARA.

14. CMC to SecNav, 17 Oct. 1891, vol. 2, pp. 442–43, Letters Sent to the Secretary of the Navy; Board of Reorganization to CMC, 21 Sept. 1891, reprinted in *Army and Navy Register,* 24 Oct. 1891, 681–82.

15. CMC, "Annual Report," 1891, 3–4.

16. Ibid., 4–5.

17. CMC to SecNav, 18 Nov. 1891, vol. 2, pp. 471–74, Letters Sent to the Secretary of the Navy; CMC to Senators Eugene Hale and J. R. McPherson, 17 Dec. 1891, and CMC to members of the Senate Naval Affairs Committee, 18 Dec. 1891, vol. 38, pp. 368–69, 372, Letters Sent, RG 127; *Army and Navy Journal,* 26 Dec. 1891, 311.

18. CMC Endorsement No. 13, 9 Jan. 1892, Endorsement Book 17, and CMC to SecNav, 21 Jan. 1892, vol. 2, pp. 489–91, Letters Sent to the Secretary of the Navy.

19. *Army and Navy Journal,* 9 Apr. 1892, 575; House, *Promotions in the Marine Corps,* 52d Cong., 2d sess., 27 May 1892, H. Doc. 1502; *Congressional Record,* 52d Cong., 1st sess., 21 July 1892 and 26 July 1892, vol. 23, pp. 6539 and 6743; CMC, "Annual Report," 1892, 4.

20. *Army and Navy Journal,* 20 Aug. 1892, 901, and 3 Sept. 1892, 93; CMC to SecNav, 11 July 1892, vol. 2, p. 585, Letters Sent to the Secretary of the Navy, and copy of SecNav order to Lt. Col. McLane Tilton, 23 Aug. 1892, Letters Received, "N."

21. F. M. Ramsay to SecNav, 1 Nov. 1892, and CMC to Asst. SecNav, 30 Nov. 1892 and Act SecNav endorsement, 14 Dec. 1892, all in Letters Received, "N."

22. "Abolish the Marines," clipping from *New York Herald,* 17 Mar. 1893, vol. 1, HQMC Scrapbook, RG 127, NARA; CMC, "Annual Report," 1892, 5.

23. CMC, "Annual Report," 1893, 3.

24. *Army and Navy Journal,* 13 May 1893, 631; SecNav to 1st Lt. George T. Bates, 23 May 1863, copy, Letters Received, "N"; SecNav, *Annual Report, 1893,* 53; "Report of Board of Visitors of School of Application," 26 Apr. 1893 in CMC, "Annual Report," 1893, 9.

25. "Report of Commander of School of Application," 15 Sept. 1893, in CMC, "Annual Report," 1893, 9.

26. CMC, "Annual Report," 1894, and "Report of Commanding Officer of School of Application," 1 Oct. 1894, in CMC, "Annual Report," 1894, 7.

27. CMC to SecNav, 21 July 1891 and 26 July 1892, vol. 2, p. 400, 604, Letters Sent to the Secretary of the Navy; SecNav to CMC, 28 July 1892, Letters Received, "N"; CMC to SecNav, 26 Apr. 1894, vol. 3, p. 409, Letters Sent to the Secretary of the Navy.

28. CMC to SecNav, 20 Apr. 1894, vol. 3, p. 386, Letters Sent to the Secretary of the Navy. See also clipping from *Washington Evening Star,* 4 May 1894, vol. 1, HQMC Scrapbook, RG 127, NARA.

29. For Goodloe's ambitions for the commandancy, see entries for 10, 13, and 18 Jan. 1891, Cochrane Diary, Cochrane Papers; SecNav to CMC, 15 Nov. 1892, enclosure letter of reprimand to Maj. G. C. Goodloe, Letters Received, "N."

30. F. M. Ramsay to CMC, 20 Oct. 1892, Letters Received, "N," and CMC to SecNav, 2 Feb. 1897, vol. 6, pp. 398–406, Letters Sent to the Secretary of the Navy.

31. CMC, "Annual Report," 1893, 4; Cochrane to CMC, 30 Dec. 1893, draft of letter, Folder 41, Cochrane Papers; "Small Chance for Promotion," *New York Times,* 4 Jan. 1894, p. 10. Clipping from *Boston Daily Advertiser,* 16 Jan. 1894, vol. 9, Clipping Book, microfilm, Reel 2, Hilary A. Herbert Papers, Southern Historical Collection, University of North Carolina Library, Chapel Hill; Paullin, *History of Naval Administration,* 420; Senate, *Report of a Board . . . to Report upon Stagnation,* 53d Cong., 2d sess., Sept. 1894, S. Misc. Rept. 98.

32. Unidentified clipping, n.d., n.p. vol. 1, HQMC Scrapbook, RG 127, NARA; CMC to SecNav, 16 Feb. 1894, File 2205/1894, General Records of the Department of the Navy, RG 80, NARA.

33. Heywood's testimony before the Committee is quoted in *Congressional Record,* 53d Cong., 3d sess., 20 Feb. 1895, 27:2459.

34. 1st Lt. Littleton W. T. Waller to CMC, with enclosures, 17 July 1894, Letters Received, "W," RG 127, NARA, and CMC to SecNav, 20 July 1894, vol. 4, pp. 13–15, Letters Sent to the Secretary of the Navy.

35. For reprints of the secretary's circular letter of 31 July 1894, see *Army and Navy Journal,* 4 Aug. 1894, 863 and various clippings in vol. 1, HQMC Scrapbook, RG 127, NARA. For references to Herbert's evaluation of the Marine Corps, see SecNav, "Annual Report," 1895, xxxvii–xxxviii, and "Annual Report," 1896, 34–35. For Major Reid's influence, see Herbert to President, 2 June 1903, vol. 7, p. 1202, William H. Moody Papers, Manuscript Division, LC (hereafter cited as Moody Papers).

36. CMC to SecNav, 1 Oct. 1894, vol. 4, pp. 96–97, Letters Sent to the Secretary of the Navy.

37. Ibid.; SecNav to CMC, 26 Oct. 1894, Letters Received, "N"; CMC, "Annual Report," 1894, 3.

38. *Congressional Record,* 53d Cong., 2d sess., 24 Aug. 1894, 26, p. 8648; "A Marine Artillery Corps," *New York Times,* 26 Aug. 1894, p. 1; CMC to SecNav, 20 Dec. 1894, vol. 4, pp. 226–28, Letters Sent to the Secretary of the Navy; *Army and Navy Journal,* 22 Dec. 1894, 274.

39. House Naval Affairs Committee, *Personnel of the Navy,* 53d Cong., 3d sess., 12 Jan. 1895, H. Doc. 1573; *Congressional Record,* 53d Cong., 3d sess., 12 Jan. 1895, 27, p. 910; Karsten, "Armed Progressives," 197–232, 211–14.

40. SecNav to Capt. Robley D. Evans, 1 Nov. 1895, Letters Received, Historical Section, RG 127, NARA; *Army and Navy Journal,* 2 Nov. 1895, 135.

41. CMC to SecNav, 31 Oct. 1895, vol. 5, pp. 170–75, Letters Sent to the Secretary of the Navy; *Army and Navy Journal,* 2 Nov. 1895, 135.

42. SecNav to Capt. Robley D. Evans, 1 Nov. 1895.

43. SecNav, *Annual Report, 1895,* xxxvii–viii; CMC to SecNav, 18 Dec. 1895, vol. 5, p. 235, Letters Sent to the Secretary of the Navy.

44. Lt. William F. Fullam, "The Organization, Training, and Discipline of the Navy Personnel as Viewed from the Ship," *USNIP* 22 (1896): 83–116.

45. CMC to SecNav, 14 Apr. 1896, vol. 5, pp. 375–76, Letters Sent to the Secretary of the Navy. See also copy of letter in William F. Fullam Papers, Manuscript Division, LC (hereafter cited as Fullam Papers). On his copy of the letter, Fullam wrote, "This must not be published; but it is perfectly proper to give publication to the fact that such a report was made against me by the Col. Comdt. in an attempt to stop discussion."

46. SecNav to CMC, 20 Apr. 1896, Letters Received, Historical Section, RG 127, NARA.

47. CMC, *Annual Report, 1895,* 4–5; CMC to SecNav, 14 Jan. 1896, and SecNav to C. A. Boutelle, 20 Feb. 1896 (copy), vol. 5, p. 271, Letters Sent to the Secretary of the Navy.

48. House Committee on Naval Affairs, *Appropriations for the Naval Service,* 54th Cong., 1st sess., 24 Mar. 1896, H. Doc. 904; *Congressional Record,* 54th Cong., 1st sess., 25 Mar. 1896, 28, p. 3194.

49. Senate Committee on Appropriations, *Appropriation Report,* 54th Cong., 1st sess., 9 Apr. 1896, S. Rept. 652; Buss Buckingham to Fullam, 20 Apr. 1896, and Richard Wainwright to Fullam, 11 Apr. 1896, Fullam Papers.

50. *Congressional Record,* 54th Cong., 1st sess., 2 May 1896, 28, pp. 4728–29.

51. CMC, "Annual Report," 1896, 3, 5–6.

52. "Report of School of Application," 8 July 1897, CMC, "Annual Report," 1897, 7; CMC, "Annual Report," 1896, 6; CMC to SecNav, 26 Sept. 1896, vol. 6, pp. 148–49, Letters Sent to the Secretary of the Navy.

53. Major Reid, Acting CMC to SecNav, 21 Aug. 1896; CMC to SecNav, 9 and 12 Oct. 1896, vol. 6, pp. 86–87, 184–88, 194–95, Letters Sent to the Secretary of the Navy. On the copy of Major Reid's letter, the clerk wrote, "Letter canceled: Personally attended to by Major Reid."

54. SecNav to CMC, 10 Oct. 1896, Letters Received, "N"; CMC to SecNav, 12 Oct. 1896, vol. 6, pp. 184–88, Letters Sent to the Secretary of the Navy.

55. Acting SecNav McAdoo to CMC, 4 Dec. 1896, Letters Received, "N," and CMC to SecNav, ts. of annual report, 9 Oct. 1896, vol. 6, pp. 194–95, Letters Sent to the Secretary of the Navy. The annual report typescript contains the following statement: "The following paragraphs have been omitted by secretary's directions." Although there is no documentary evidence, it is not too farfetched to believe that Commodore Ramsay of the Bureau of Navigation may have been behind the department's decision to veto the experiment with the Marine guard at Newport. The fact that the Newport facility came under his jurisdiction gives some credibility to this supposition. In that he had tried to deny the assignment of the Marines to the secondary battery gives additional strength to this conjecture. The guard of the *Brooklyn* actually trained at Newport, not departing until 30 November 1896. See Cochrane to CMC, 1 Dec. 1896, Letters Received, "N."

56. For the 1896 revision of Navy Regulations, see "Changes in Naval Rules," *New York Times,* 9 July 1896, p. 11; Acting SecNav (McAdoo) to Capt. James H. Sands, 4 Feb. 1897, Letters Received, "N"; CMC, "Annual Report," 1897, 8.

57. "Col. Higbee Had to March," HQMC Clipping Book, vol. 2, RG 127, NARA.

58. JAG to CMC, 17 Oct. 1895, and SecNav to Lowry (copy), Letters Received, "N"; CMC to SecNav, 14 Nov. 1896, CMC to SecNav, 30 Jan. 1897, and CMC to SecNav, 2 Feb. 1897, vol. 6, pp. 254, 338–39, 398–406, Letters Sent to the Secretary of the Navy; Acting SecNav to CMC, 17 Feb. 1897, Letters Received, "N"; *Army and Navy Journal,* 23 Jan. 1897, 371.

59. CMC, "Annual Report," 1897, 9; Acting SecNav to Maj. Horatio B. Lowry, 18 June 1897 and to Maj. Richard S. Collum, 26 June 1897, Letters Received, "N"; JAG to CMC, 21, 30 June, 23 July 1897, Letters Received, "N."

60. Roosevelt to Richard Olney, 9 June 1897, in Elting E. Morison, ed., *The Letters of Theodore Roosevelt,* 8 vols. (Cambridge: Harvard University Press, 1951–54), 1:623; entry for 21 Aug. 1897, Cochrane Diary, Cochrane Papers.

61. CMC to SecNav, 12 June 1897, vol. 6, pp. 670–71, Letters Sent to the Secretary of the Navy; Asst. SecNav to CMC, 15 June 1897, Letters Received, "N"; "Favor the Engineer Corps," *New York Times,* 1 Feb. 1897, p. 7.

62. Copy of SecNav (CHL) to Capt. John R. Read, 24 May 1897, Letters Received, Historical Section, RG 127, NARA, and *Army and Navy Register,* 12 June 1897, 384–85; CMC, "Annual Report," 1897, 7–8.

63. Cochrane to CMC, 16 July 1896, Letters Received, "N." The Army established its post exchange system in 1895. See Russell F. Weigley, *History of the United States Army* (New York: Macmillan, 1967), 270.

64. Entries for 4, 7, and 18 Aug. 1897, Cochrane Diary, Cochrane Papers; Acting SecNav to CMC, 6 Aug. 1897, and SecNav to CMC, 17 Oct. 1901, Decision in Regard to Status of the Post Exchange in the Marine Corps, with attachments, Letters Received, "N." See also *New York Times,* 18 Aug. 1897, p. 3.

65. SecNav, *Annual Report, 1897,* 29–30.

66. CMC to SecNav, 29 May 1896, vol. 5, pp. 451–52, Letters Sent to the Secretary of the Navy; SecNav to CMC, with enclosures, 15 June 1896, Letters Received, "N"; Navy Department General Order No. 478, 4 Sept. 1897, Entry 45, Scrapbook of Navy Dept Issuances, 1885–1900, RG 127, NARA.

67. *Army and Navy Register,* 13 Nov. 1897, 318; Asst. SecNav to Erwin Stewart, Paymaster General, 9 Nov. 1897, File 5288/3; Asst. SecNav to CMC, 9 Nov. 1897, File 5288/4, RG 80, NARA.

68. Heywood to Lt. Col. J. H. Higbee, 10 Nov. 1897, attached to Higbee to Stephen B. Luce, 13 Nov. 1897, Stephen B. Luce Papers, Manuscript Division, LC; CMC to President of the Board of Reorganization of Naval Personnel, 22 Nov. 1897, vol. 7, pp. 1–14, Letters Sent to the Secretary of the Navy; *Army and Navy Register,* 20 Nov. 1897, 334.

69. 1st Lt. George Barnett to CMC, 16 Nov. 1897, Letters Received, Historical Section, RG 127, NARA. For other samples of Marine officers' replies, see 1st Lt. Dion Williams to CMC, 27 Nov. 1897; 1st. Lt. Charles L. Lauchheimer to CMC, 19 Nov. 1897; 1st Lt. B. S. Neumann to CMC, 13 Nov. 1897; Maj. Robert L. Meade to CMC, 13 Nov. 1897; Capt. Charles L. McCawley to CMC, 16 Nov. 1897; Capt. W. S. Muse to CMC, 15 Nov. 1897; Capt. F. H. Harrington to CMC, 13 Nov. 1897; Capt. William F. Spicer to CMC, 13 Nov. 1897; Capt. O. C. Berryman to CMC, 26 Nov. 1897; Capt. J. M. T. Young to CMC, 18 Dec. 1897; and Lt. Col. Robert W. Huntington to CMC, 15 Nov. 1897; all in Letters Received, Historical Section, RG 127, NARA.

70. CMC to President of the Board of Reorganization of Naval Personnel, 22 Nov. 1897, vol. 7, pp. 1–14, Letters Sent to the Secretary of the Navy.

71. *New York Times,* 28 Nov. 1897, p. 24; House, *Reorganization of Naval Personnel,* H. Doc. 10403, with Accompanying Report, H. Doc. 1375, 55th Cong., 2d sess, 1898.

72. David F. Trask, *The War with Spain in 1898,* Macmillan Wars of the United States Series (New York: Macmillan, 1981), 83–90; Long, *New American Navy,* 1:165–66.

73. In 1892, the Army adopted for the infantry and cavalry the .30-caliber five-shot, magazine-fed, Krag-Jorgenson rifle to replace the .45-caliber, single-shot, breech-loading Springfield rifle, model 1873. The Navy Department which had also used the Springfield as its standard rifle refused to go along with the selection of the "Krag." Instead, the Navy chose the Lee "Straight-pull" 6-mm, five-shot, magazine-fed rifle for the Marine Corps and Navy. Navy small-arms

experts argued that the smaller-caliber and lighter Lee because of its faster muzzle velocity could cause as much if not more damage than the heavier and larger-caliber Krag. The Corps began partial distribution of the new Lee rifles in 1897. Weigley, *History,* 268–96; Graham A. Cosmas, *An Army for Empire: The United States Army in the Spanish-American War* (Columbia: University of Missouri Press, 1971), 87–89. See also Trask, *War with Spain,* 8; SecNav, *Annual Report, 1895,* xiv–v; CMC, "Annual Report," 1897, 4–5.

74. SecNav to CMC, 10 Mar., 6 and 11 Apr. 1898, Letters Received, "N"; CMC to SecNav, 13 and 15 Mar. and 6 and 9 Apr. 1898, vol. 7, pp. 187, 194–95, 245–46, 252, Letters Sent to the Secretary of the Navy; CMC, "Annual Report," 1898, 6.

75. SecNav to CMC and copy of letter to C. A. Boutelle, 10 Mar. 1898, Letters Received, "N"; CMC to SecNav, 11–12 Mar. 1898, vol. 7, pp. 184, 188–89, Letters Sent to the Secretary of the Navy.

76. SecNav to Boutelle, 12 Mar. 1898; *Army and Navy Journal,* 12 Mar. 1898, 515; Lt. Cdr. Richard Wainwright, "Our Naval Power," *USNIP* 24 (Mar. 1898): 39–87, 48.

77. Lt. Col. R. W. Huntington to CMC, 15 Feb. 1898, Letters Received, "N."

78. CMC to SecNav, 18 and 23 Apr. 1898, vol. 7, pp. 250–52, 266, Letters Sent to the Secretary of the Navy; Acting CMC to SecNav, 19 Apr. 1898, Letters Received, "N"; entries for 17–22 Apr. 1898 and Battalion Orders 1–3, 19–20 Apr. 1898 in Journal of the Marine Battalion under Lt. Col. Robert W. Huntington, Apr.–Sept. 1898, RG 127, NARA; CMC, "Annual Report," 1898, 7 and 10; "Report of the Adjutant and Inspector of the USMC," 20 Sept. 1898, CMC, "Annual Report," 1898, 50 and 56; Charles L. McCawley, "The Marines at Guantanamo," undated mss., 2–4, McCawley Papers; "Marine Battalion at Guantanamo," reprinted in *Appendix to the Report of the Chief of the Bureau of Navigation,* in SecNav, *Annual Report, 1898,* 2:440–41 (hereafter cited as *Appendix to the Report*). Graham A. Cosmas observed that the "Marine mobilization coincides in time with the order for concentration of most of the Regular Army at Chickamauga Park, New Orleans, Mobile, and Tampa, which went out on 15 April [1898]." Graham A. Cosmas comments as quoted in Shulimson, *Marine Corps Search for a Mission,* 248 n. 12.

79. Maj. George C. Reid to Pendleton, 19 Apr. 1898, Maj. Gen. Joseph H. Pendleton Papers, PPC; Long to Sampson, 21 Apr. 1898, reprinted in *Appendix to the Report,* 174–75; Long, *New American Navy,* 2:5; Cochrane to Betsy, 1 June 1898, Folder 51, Cochrane Papers.

80. CMC, "Annual Report," 1898, 7; "Marine Battalion at Guantanamo," reprinted in *Appendix to the Report,* 440–41; Surgeon General to CMC, 5 May 1898, Letters Received, "N."

81. Ch. Bu of Ordnance to CMC, 9 Apr. 1898; Commander, Northern Patrol Squadron to CMC, 29 and 30 Apr. 1898; SecNav to CMC, 7 May 1898; all in Letters Received, "N"; House, *Estimates of Appropriation,* 55th Cong., 2d sess, 1898, H. Doc. 478.

82. *New York Times,* 25 Mar. 1898, p. 3.

83. CMC to SecNav, 28 Mar. 1898, with enclosures, vol. 7, pp. 210–27, Letters Sent to the Secretary of the Navy; House, *Reorganization of Naval Personnel,* H. Doc. 10403, with *Accompanying Report,* H. Doc. 1375, 55th Cong., 2d sess, 1898, pp. 12–13.

84. *Congressional Record,* 55th Cong., 2d sess., 29 Apr. 1898, 31, p. 4422; CMC, "Annual Report," 1898, 11.

85. *Congressional Record,* 55th Cong., 2d sess., 19 May 1898, 31, pp. 5058–59; CMC, "Annual Report," 1898, 16–17; SecNav, *Annual Report, 1898,* 54–57; Cochrane to wife, 12 and 28 May 1898, Folder 51, and entry for 4 June 1898, Cochrane Diary, Cochrane Papers.

86. The sources for this and the following paragraph are CMC to SecNav, 5, 9, 13–16, 17, 18, 20, 21, 25 May and 6 June 1898, vol. 7, pp. 305, 308–14, 329–45, 353, 370–74, Letters Sent to the Secretary of the Navy; Asst. SecNav to CMC, 3–4 May 1898, Letters Received, "N."

87. Additional source for this paragraph is CMC, "Annual Report," 1898, 11. The records do not indicate why a fourth NCO was not commissioned. Sgt. Henry Good, the sergeant major of the Marine battalion under Huntington, was nominated. One can surmise that his untimely death at Guantánamo prevented his appointment and that the war ended before another choice could be made.

88. CMC to SecNav, 18 June 1898, vol. 7, p. 415, Letters Sent to the Secretary of the Navy.

89. Capt. F. H. Harrington, School of Application to CMC, 18 Apr. 1898, Letters Received, Historical Section, RG 127, NARA; CMC, "Annual Report," 1898, 11 and 15. See also Hans Schmidt, *Maverick Marine: General Smedley D. Butler and the Contradictions of American Military History* (Lexington: University of Kentucky Press, 1987), 7.

90. CMC to SecNav, 12 Dec. 1898, vol. 7, pp. 84–45, Letters Sent to the Secretary of the Navy.

91. Cochrane to Betsy, 22 Aug. 1898, Cochrane Papers; Chief, BuNav to CMC, 8 Aug. 1898, Letters Received, Historical Section, RG 127, NARA, and CMC to SecNav, 10 Sept. 1898, vol. 7, pp. 567–68, Letters Sent to the Secretary of the Navy; Ira Nelson Hollis, "The Navy in the War with Spain," *Atlantic,* Nov. 1898, 605–16, Printed Matter Folder, Henry C. Taylor Papers, Manuscript Division, LC (hereafter cited as Taylor Papers); *Army and Navy Journal,* 17 Sept. 1898, 68. Malaria and yellow fever played havoc with the Army's V Corps before Santiago. On 27 July 1898, more than four thousand soldiers in V Corps were in the hospital, and a few days later the death rate reached fifteen per day. Cosmas, *Army for Empire,* 251–52. Although Marine sanitary practices in part accounted for their low sickness rate, the Marines were fortunate that the Guantánamo sector remained dry and bred few of the mosquitoes that spread the yellow fever and malaria among the Army troops.

92. *Army and Navy Journal,* 24 Sept. 1898, 95; Reid, Acting CMC to SecNav, 20 Oct. 1898, vol. 7, p. 702, Letters Sent to the Secretary of the Navy.

93. CMC, "Annual Report," 1898, 14, and *Army and Navy Journal,* 27 Aug. 1898, 1088.

94. Capt. Littleton W. T. Waller to Col. Comdt., USMC, 1 Sept. 1898 in CMC, "Annual Report," 1898, 44–45; H. C. Taylor to SecNav, 18 Sept. 1898, Correspondence Folder, July–Sept. 1898, Taylor Papers; Capt. R. D. Evans to Lt. Col. R. L. Meade, 31 Aug. 1898, Letters Received, Historical Section, RG 127, NARA; Millett, *Semper Fidelis,* 130–31; Trask, *War with Spain,* 104, 265–66; French E. Chadwick, *The Relations of the United States and Spain, The Spanish-American War,* 2 vols. (New York: Russell & Russell, 1968), 2:177; Lt. John Ellicott, USN, *Effect of the Gun Fire of the United States Vessels in the Battle of Manila Bay,* 1 May 1898, Office of Naval Intelligence, War Note V, Information from Abroad (Washington, 1899).

95. Ellicott, *Effect of the Gun Fire;* Commander J., German Navy, *Sketches from the Spanish-American War,* Office of Naval Intelligence, War, Notes III and IV, Information from Abroad (Washington, 1899); CMC, "Annual Report," 1898; "Record of the Marines," *New York Times,* 23 Oct. 1898, p. 13.

96. CMC to SecNav, 9 Nov. 1898, vol. 7, pp. 757–60, Letters Sent to the Secretary of the Navy; SecNav, *Annual Report, 1898,* 19.

97. CMC to SecNav, 12 Dec. 1898, enclosing "A Bill to Increase the Efficiency of the Marine Corps," vol. 7, pp. 843–63, Letters Sent to the Secretary of the Navy.

98. *Army and Navy Journal,* 27 Aug. 1898, 1088; SecNav to CMC, 1 Oct. and 22 Dec. 1898, 19 Jan. and 6 Feb. 1899, Letters Received, "N"; CMC to SecNav, 17 Jan. 1899, vol. 7, pp. 951–52, Letters Sent to the Secretary of the Navy.

99. *Congressional Record,* 55th Cong., 3d sess., 17 Jan. 1899, 32, pp. 720–25; "The Navy Personnel Bill," *New York Times,* 18 Jan. 1899, p. 5; *Army and Navy Journal,* 21 Jan. 1899, 494–95.

100. *Congressional Record,* 55th Cong., 3d sess., 17 Feb., 1 Mar. 1899, 32, pp. 1978, 2663, 2698. For the provisions of the law as they affected the Marine Corps, see Navy Department General Order 510, 6 Mar. 1899, Entry 45, Scrapbook of Navy Department Issuances, 1885–1900, RG 127, NARA.

101. CMC to SecNav, 3 Mar., 7 June 1899, vol. 8, pp. 50, 434, Letters Sent to the Secretary of the Navy, and SecNav to CMC, 17, 20 Mar. 1899, Letters Received, "N"; *Navy Registers*, 1899–1900; "Register of Officers, U.S. Marine Corps," in Collum, *History,* 30–49; *Army and Navy Journal,* 11 Mar. and 17 June 1899, 699 and 994.

102. CMC to SecNav, 4 Mar. 1899, vol. 8, pp. 54–59, Letters Sent to the Secretary of the Navy, and Navy Department, "Circular for the Information of Persons Desiring to Enter the U.S. Marine Corps," n.d., Letters Received, Historical Section, RG 127, NARA.

103. HQMC, "Memorandum relative to the amendment to the Naval Appropriation Bill . . . ," n.d. [May 1900], vol. 9, pp. 387–95, Letters Sent to the Secretary of the Navy; SecNav to CMC, 25 Oct., 12 and 17 Nov. 1900, Letters Received, "N," and CMC to SecNav, 7 Nov. 1900, vol. 10, pp. 167–75, Letters Sent to the Secretary of the Navy; Correspondence relative case of Ward K. Wortman, July–Sept. 1902, Letters Received, Historical Section, RG 127, NARA.

104. Capt. C. H. Stockton Letters to CMC, 21 and 30 Apr. and 24 May 1900, Letters Received, "N"; Lt. Col. B. R. Russell to CMC, 23 Sept. 1901, Letters Received, Historical Section, RG 127, NARA; CMC, "Annual Report," 1900, 11–12, "Annual Report," 1901, 28–30, and "Annual Report," 1902, 31–33.

105. CMC to SecNav, 18 Oct. and 7 Nov. 1901, vol. 11, p. 342, Letters Sent to the Secretary of the Navy; CMC, "Annual Report," 1902, 8, "Annual Report," 1903, 9–10, 19–20.

106. Navy Dept, endorsement, 11 Mar. 1899, File 4541 (4), General Correspondence, 1897–1915, RG 80, NARA; "Marines for Cavite," *New York Times,* 14 Mar. 1899, p. 1; CMC, "Annual Report," 1899, 13–17, and "Annual Report," 1900, 17–28.

107. Millett, *Semper Fidelis,* 152–55; Brian McCallister Linn, "'We Will Go Heavily Armed': The Marines' Small War on Samar, 1901–1902," in *New Interpretations in Naval History, Selected Papers from the Ninth Naval History Symposium Held at the United States Naval Academy, 18–20 October 1989,* ed. William R. Roberts and Jack Sweetman (Annapolis: Naval Institute Press, 1991), 273–92; CMC to SecNav, 2d Endorsement, 18 Feb. 1902, vol. 11, p. 692, Letters Sent to the Secretary of the Navy; CMC, "Annual Report," 1902, 17–27; Heywood to Waller, 19 June 1902, copy, vol. 2, Moody Papers. See also Vernon L. Williams, "Littleton W. T. Waller: The Politics of Command," in *New Interpretations in Naval History, Selected Papers from the Tenth Naval History Symposium Held at the United States Naval Academy, 11–13 September 1991,* ed. Jack Sweetman et al. (Annapolis: Naval Institute Press, 1993), 169–80.

108. CMC to SecNav, 12 Dec. 1898, vol. 7, pp. 843–55, Letters Sent to the Secretary of the Navy; "Memorandum in Relation to the United States Marine Corps" attached to CMC to Rep. George E. Foss, 26 Feb. 1900, reprinted in House Committee on Naval Affairs, *Hearings on Appropriation Bill Subjects, 1900,* 56th Cong., 1st sess., 1900.

109. Navy General Board, 29 May 1915, memo, Subj: "Review of the Naval Advanced Base," General Board File (hereafter GB File) 408; Proceedings of the General Board, 17 Apr., 27 and 29 June, and 31 Aug. 1900, vol. 1, Proceedings of the General Board, 1900–1904, General Records of the Department of the Navy, RG 80, NARA; Admiral Dewey, President of the General Board to SecNav, 6 Oct. 1900, and CMC to Dewey, 22 Nov. 1900, GB File 408-2, Records of the General Board, RG 80, NARA (hereafter cited as Records of the General Board).

110. Millett, *Semper Fidelis,* 152–55, 269; House Committee on Naval Affairs, *Testimony of Col. George C. Reid,* 57th Cong., 2d sess., 9 Dec. 1902, H. Doc. 10.

111. CMC, "Annual Report," 1900, 43–44; Capt. Charles C. Long to CinC Naval Force, 20 July 1901 in attached correspondence from Newport, Torpedo School, 12 Mar. 1901, Letters Received, "N."

112. General Board October Meeting (1901), General Board, 1900–01, George Dewey Papers, Manuscript Division, LC (hereafter cited as Dewey Papers); General Board, meeting of 1 Nov. 1901, Proceedings of General Board, vol. 1, Records of the General Board; HQMC, 2d Endorsement, 16 Nov. 1901, to General Board, No. 221, 1 Nov. 1901, GB File 432, Records of the General Board. See also CMC to SecNav, 16 Nov. 1901, vol. 11, pp. 415–17, Letters Sent to the Secretary of the Navy.

113. General Board Meeting of 25 Nov. 1901, vol. 1, Proceedings of General Board, Records of the General Board; Crowninshield, Snr Member Present, 4th Endorsement, on General Board letter No. 221, 27 Nov. 1901, Letters Received, "N"; CMC to SecNav, 17 Dec. 1901, Confidential Press Letter Book, 30–36, Entry 53, RG 127, NARA.

114. Dewey to Rear Adm. Francis J. Higginson, CinC U.S. Naval Force North Atlantic Station, 11 Oct. 1901, General Board, 1900–01, Dewey Papers; General Board Meeting of 25 Nov. 1901, vol. 1, Proceedings of General Board, Records of the General Board; Correspondence on Marines at Culebra, Nov. 1901–Feb. 1902, Letters Received, "N"; CMC, "Annual Report," 1902, 27–31.

115. CMC, "Annual Report," 1902, 27–31; Capt. George C. Thorpe to Maj. H. C. Haines, 25 Apr. 1902, Letters Received, Historical Section, RG 127, NARA; Maj. H. C. Haines to President, General Board, 25 July 1902, GB File 408, Records of the General Board.

116. For information about General Board reaction to the Venezuela situation and intelligence gathering and contingency planning, see General Board, 1st Endorsement, Lt. C. B. Brown, 3 Dec. 1901, Letterpress Book; Meetings of 23 Apr. 1902, 27 May 1902, and 16–17 June 1902, Proceedings of the General Board, vol. 1, 1900–July 1904; SecNav to Senior Officer Present, U.S. Naval Force, Venezuelan Waters, 9 July 1902, GB 231, Letter Press Book, vol. 2, Records of the General Board. See also Cdr. John E. Pillsbury to Adm. H. C. Taylor, 16 Jan. 1902, attached to Taylor to Adm. George Dewey, 31 Jan. 1902, General Correspondence, Jan. 1902, Dewey Papers. For Dewey assuming command of the exercise, see Roosevelt to Dewey, 14 June 1902, General Correspondence, Dewey Papers. For request for additional appropriations, see House Committee on Naval Affairs, *SecNav to Rep. George Foss,* 57th Cong., 1st sess., 29 Jan. 1902, H. Doc. 70. For report on the maneuvers, see H. C. Taylor, Report of Maneuvers, *CinC Journal,* Dec. 1902–Jan. 1903, 15 Jan. 1903, Dewey Papers. For some of the discussion of the influence of Roosevelt's threat and the maneuvers, see Frederick W. Marks III, *Velvet on Iron: The Diplomacy of Theodore Roosevelt* (Lincoln: University of Nebraska Press, 1979), 38–54; Ronald Spector, *Admiral of the New Navy: The Life and Career of George Dewey* (Baton Rouge: Louisiana State University Press, 1974), 139–47; Howard K. Beale, *Theodore Roosevelt*

and the Rise of America to World Power (Baltimore: Johns Hopkins Press, 1956), 398–431. Dewey is quoted by Admiral Taylor in Taylor to William Henry Moody, 14 Dec. 1902, vol. 5, pp. 764–65, Moody Papers.

117. CMC, "Annual Report," 1902, 43–44; General Board Meeting, 26 Aug. 1902, General Board Folder, Dewey Papers; *Army and Navy Register,* 30 Aug. 1902, 2.

118. Panama Landings, Subj. File, Panama, Reference Section, H&MD; Lt. Col. Russell, Commanding, Marine Battalion, to CinC, U.S. Naval Force, North Atlantic Station, 16 Nov. 1902, and Lt. Col. B. R. Russell, Report to CMC, 15 Dec. 1902, Panama, 1902–04, Entry 43, RG 127, NARA; CMC, "Annual Report," 1902, 16, 44–45; CMC, "Annual Report," 1903, 24–26; *Army and Navy Register,* 27 Sept. 1902, 6 and 11 Oct. 1902, 4.

119. Lt. Col. B. R. Russell to CMC, report, 15 Dec. 1902, Panama, 1902–04, Entry 43, RG 127, NARA.

120. CMC, "Annual Report," 1903, 26–28; Taylor, Report of Maneuvers, Jan. 1903; entries for 3–4 Jan. 1903, *CinC Journal,* 1 Dec. 1902–Jan. 1903, Dewey Papers.

121. Taylor to Wm. H. Moody, 28 Dec. 1902, Moody Papers; Adm. Dewey to Rear Adm. G. J. Higginson, CinC U.S. Naval Force, North Atlantic Station, 3 Jan. 1903, and Adm. Dewey to Rear Adm. J. B. Coghlan, Culebra Maneuver, Letterbox No. 1, Dewey Papers; CMC, "Annual Report," 1903, 27–28.

122. Maj. H. C. Haines to CMC, 10 Feb. 1903, Letters Received, Historical Section, RG 127, NARA.

123. Maj. H. C. Haines to captain of *Panther,* 27 Feb. 1903, and Cdr. Wilson to SecNav, 5 Mar. 1903, File 432, Records of the General Board.

124. Rear Adm. Coghlan to SecNav, 20 Mar. 1903; GB, 2d Endorsement, 21 May 1903; CinC Natl Sta.; 4th Endorsement, 23 May 1903; Rear Adm. Coghlan, 1st Endorsement, 29 July 1903, all in File 432, Records of the General Board.

125. CMC, "Annual Report," 1903, 28.

126. Col. F. L. Denny to CMC, 3 Sept. 1903, reprinted in CMC, "Annual Report," 1903, 49–51.

127. CMC, "Annual Report," 1902, 45–47, 51, and "Annual Report," 1903, 34–35. Quotation is from *Army and Navy Register,* 30 Aug. 1902, 2.

128. For Heywood's illness and Reid's efforts to succeed him, see Cochrane to Betsy, 22 Mar. 1901, Cochrane Papers. For Reid's influence, see Hilary A. Herbert to President, 2 June 1903, vol. 7, p. 1202, and Mark A. Hanna to President, 22 Sept. 1903, vol. 9, p. 1530, Moody Papers; Proceedings of the General Board, 1900–1904, Records of the General Board; Maj. Gen. John A. Lejeune, USMC (Ret.), "Memorandum Concerning the Appointment of Several Commandants of the U.S. Marine Corps," 1935, John A. Lejeune Papers, Manuscript Division, LC (hereafter cited as Lejeune Papers).

129. For the failure of Reid to receive the commandancy because of his staff status, see, for example, Lejeune, "Memorandum Concerning the Appointment of Several Commandants," Lejeune Papers. On events leading to court-martial of Colonel Meade and Heywood's testimony, see CMC to SecNav, 18 July 1901, vol. 10, pp. 973–76, Letters Sent to the Secretary of the Navy, and *Army and Navy Register,* 30 Nov. 1901. For Heywood's differences with the General Board relative to the advanced base structure, see his letters to SecNav, 16 Nov. 1901, vol. 11, pp. 415–17, Letters Sent to the Secretary of the Navy, and 17 Dec. 1901, Confidential Press Letter Book, 30–36, Entry 53, RG 127, NARA.

130. Hilary A. Herbert to President, 2 June 1903, vol. 7, p. 1202, and Mark A. Hanna to President, 22 Sept. 1903, vol. 9, p. 1530, Moody Papers; Bureau of Medicine and Surgery, Department of the Navy, Report of Death, Charles Heywood, 1 Mar. 1915, Charles Heywood Personnel Jacket, RG 127, NARA.

131. CMC, "Annual Report," 1903, 37–38.

132. CMC, "Annual Report," 1897–1903.

133. *Army and Navy Illustrated Supplement* to the *Army and Navy Register,* 4 Apr. 1903, 25 and 27.

Chapter 10. George Frank Elliott

1. George Frank Elliott Service Record Book, "Military History," HQMC (hereafter cited as "Military History"). Unless otherwise specified, all pertinent dates for tours of duty during Elliott's career are derived from this source. Elliott's boyhood move to New Hampshire, together with his unspecified Civil War service, is derived from his obituary that appeared in the *New York Times,* 5 Nov. 1931, p. 27. Information on Elliott's brief career at West Point is contained in the Military Academy's Archives. All information on the types and movements of the ships to which Elliott was assigned during his career is derived from the source folders on the various vessels in the files of the Ships' Histories Branch, Naval Historical Center. For biographies of the secretaries of the navy during Elliott's time as commandant, see Paul T. Heffron, "William H. Moody," Paul Morton, "Charles J. Bonaparte," "Victor H. Metcalf," and Paulo E. Coletta, "George von Lengerke Meyer," in *American Secretaries of the Navy,* 2 vols., ed. Paolo E. Coletta (Annapolis: Naval Institute Press, 1980), 1:461–522.

2. Gardner Elliott to Col. Cmdt. Jacob Zeilin, 26 Apr. 1872, Letters Received, "E," RG 127, NARA. Young was ordnance officer at the time; a biography of Young is contained in Lewis R. Hamersly, *The Records of the Living Officers of the U.S. Navy and Marine Corps* (Philadelphia: J. B. Lippincott, 1878), 110–11.

3. Commander Wadleigh's reports are contained in SecNav, *Annual Report, 1881,* 767–74. Elliott's own account of the voyage is contained in Harold C. Reisinger, "The Cruise of the U.S.S. Alliance in the Arctic—1881," *Marine Corps Gazette,* Sept. 1928, 178–86. Of his only time in the polar regions, Elliott told Reisinger, "The tropics are more to my liking. The Arctic is a cold, inhospitable place, and the elements are against the intrusion of man. I am well pleased never to have seen it since the *Alliance* cruise."

4. Harold C. Reisinger, "On the Isthmus—1885," *Marine Corps Gazette,* Dec. 1928, 230–39; Capt. Bowman S. McCalla to Secretary of the Navy W. C. Whitney, reprinted in Collum, *History,* 252.

5. Background for sending the *Baltimore*'s marines to Seoul is contained in *Foreign Relations of the United States, 1894* (Washington, GPO: 1895), 19ff; Elliott's own account of his service with the *Baltimore*'s guard is contained in Harold C. Reisinger, "The March from Chemulpo to Seoul, Korea," *Marine Corps Gazette,* June 1929, 70–80, and "Port Arthur, November 22, 1894," *Marine Corps Gazette,* Sept. 1929, 159–69; see also Jeffrey M. Dorwart, "The Independent Minister: John M. B. Sill and the Struggle against Japanese Expansion in Korea, 1894–1897," *Pacific Historical Review,* Nov. 1975, 485–502. Ironically, the experience of *Baltimore*'s Marine guard later figured in the attempts to have Marine guards removed from ships, as Lt. William H. Halsey (father of the future fleet admiral) commented on the lack of discipline

exhibited by the Marines when they were encamped at Seoul in the "Discussion" section, *USNIP* 22 (Jan. 1896): 133–36. The muster roll of the *Baltimore*'s Marine guard (microfilm copy in Reference Section, H&MD) confirms Halsey's recollection of one marine being returned to the ship as undesirable.

6. Verbatim accounts of the Cuzco Well expedition can be found in Collum, *History,* 340–54 (which contains reprints of Huntington's, McCalla's, and Elliott's original reports); see also Bowman H. McCalla, "Memoirs of a Naval Career," 3–8; also the *Appendix to the Report;* Howbart Dillman, "Marines at Cusco [*sic*] Hill," in *The Chicago Record's War Stories by Staff Correspondents in the Field, 1898,* 46–50. Accompanying Elliott as a volunteer adjutant was journalist Stephen Crane, who recounted the experience in "Marines Signaling Under Fire at Guantanamo," *McClure's,* copy in Huntington Papers.

7. Of Elliott's being in command of the expedition to destroy Cuzco Well, Reisinger recounts, "The General [Elliott] always considered himself as an exceedingly lucky man to have had command of the Marines in the Cuzco Well fight. As he puts it, 'It was only the fact that Huntington was sick that morning gave command of this detachment to me. It was a mighty lucky incident in my life and had much bearing on my later career.'" Harold C. Reisinger, "A Home Builder: The Battle of Novaleta and Service in Cavite, P.I., 1899–1900," *Marine Corps Gazette,* Dec. 1929, 273–84.

8. *Army and Navy Register,* 29 June 1899, 1.

9. Reports concerning Novaleta are reprinted, verbatim, in Collum, *History,* 366–77; see also Reisinger, "Home Builder," and Lowell Thomas, *Old Gimlet Eye: The Adventures of Smedley D. Butler* (New York: Farrar and Rinehart, 1993), 31–41.

10. Reports of medical survey, 21 Mar., 1 May 1900, "Military History."

11. *Army and Navy Journal,* 10 Oct. 1903, 134. See also the essay on General Heywood in this volume for further discussion of the bureaucratic maneuvering in the selection of Elliott as Commandant.

12. *Army and Navy Journal,* 24 Oct. 1903, 187.

13. Elliott's testimony of 10 Jan. 1905 in *Hearings before the Committee on Naval Affairs on Appropriation Bill for 1906 Subjects* (Washington, D.C.: GPO, 1905), 302.

14. Ibid., 305.

15. *Annual Reports of the Navy Department for the Year 1905* (Washington, D.C.: GPO, 1906), 1235–45.

16. "Report of the Secretary of the Navy," in *Annual Reports of the Navy Department for the Year 1905,* 14–15.

17. Elliott's testimony of 2 Feb. 1906 in *Hearings Before the Committee on Naval Affairs of the House of Representatives on Estimates Submitted by the Secretary of the Navy, 1907* (Washington, D.C.: GPO, 1907), 681 and 701.

18. Ibid., 723.

19. Ibid., 724.

20. "Report of the Secretary of the Navy," in *Annual Reports of the Navy Department for the Year 1906* (Washington, D.C.: GPO, 1907), 16.

21. None would be until Congress authorized the *Henderson* (Transport No. 1) on 4 March 1913.

22. Elliott's 13 February 1908 testimony is contained in *Hearings Before the Committee on Naval Affairs of the House of Representatives on Estimates Submitted by the Secretary of the Navy, 1908–1909* (Washington, D.C.: GPO, 1908), 581.

23. Jack Shulimson and Graham A. Cosmas, "Teddy Roosevelt and the Corps' Sea-Going Mission," *Marine Corps Gazette,* Nov. 1981, 54–62. Jack Shulimson kindly provided me a draft copy of that article, which listed the sources consulted by the authors in their study. See also John G. Miller, "William Freeland Fullam's War with the Corps," *USNIP,* Nov. 1975, 38–45.

24. Fullam to William S. Sims, Box 59, William S. Sims Papers, Manuscript Division, LC (hereafter cited as Sims Papers).

25. Fullam to Sims, 11 Sept. 1908, Box 59, Sims Papers. Interestingly, while Fullam complained of the Corps's using "influence" to retain its mission (and its existence), he was not above using "influence" to attempt to eliminate that mission.

26. One of those senior officers was, however, Capt. Charles J. Badger, Elliott's brother-in-law.

27. Sims to Theodore Roosevelt, memo, 16 Sept. 1908, Box 97, Sims Papers.

28. Fullam to Sims, 3 Nov. 1908, Box 8, Sims Papers.

29. Headquarters, Marine Corps to Secretary of the Navy, memo, 6 Nov. 1908, quoted in Shulimson and Cosmas, "Teddy Roosevelt."

30. "Statement of Maj. Gen. George F. Elliott, Commandant, United States Marine Corps," in *Hearings Before the Subcommittee on Naval Academy and Marine Corps Committee on Naval Affairs, House of Representatives, on the Status of the U.S. Marine Corps* (Washington, D.C.: GPO, 1909), 217 (hereafter cited as *Status of the U.S. Marine Corps*).

31. Text of the executive order appears in *Status of the U.S. Marine Corps,* 218–19.

32. Predictably, Fullam, who overzealously compared Executive Order 969 with the Emancipation Proclamation, and other naval officers, rejoiced openly. Sailors at the Newport Naval Training Station collectively telegraphed their thanks to President Roosevelt. Fullam's permitting them to do so, however, drew a reprimand from the department as well as criticism from the press. The *Army and Navy Register,* 21 Nov. 1908, for example, considered the telegram a "discourtesy to the commandant and officers and enlisted men of the Marine Corps which should be rebuked from the White House. An example of such insubordination," the *Register* declared, "ought not to pass without official notice."

33. *Army and Navy Register,* 21 Nov. 1908, 6, and *Army and Navy Journal,* 28 Nov. 1908, 339.

34. Roosevelt's comments to Butt are quoted in Shulimson and Cosmas, "Teddy Roosevelt." Ironically, Roosevelt had particularly praised the Corps's "indispensable service" in Cuba in 1906.

35. C. L. McCawley and F. L. Denny to Leonard Wood, 24 Nov. 1908, enclosure to letter, Wood to Theodore Roosevelt, 26 Nov. 1908, Reel 86, Theodore Roosevelt Papers, LC (hereafter cited as Theodore Roosevelt Papers).

36. George F. Elliott to Leonard Wood, 24 Nov. 1908, Reel 86, Theodore Roosevelt Papers.

37. Theodore Roosevelt to Leonard Wood, 28 Nov. 1908, in Morison, *Letters of Theodore Roosevelt,* 6:1389.

38. Elliott testimony in *Status of the U.S. Marine Corps,* 220.

39. *Hearings Before the Committee on Naval Affairs of the House of Representatives on Estimates Submitted by the Secretary of the Navy, 1909* (Washington, D.C.: GPO, 1909), 329–30; *Army and Navy Journal,* 26 Dec. 1908, 455.

40. Fullam testimony in *Status of the U.S. Marine Corps,* 169.

41. Wayne A. Wiegand, "The Lauchheimer Controversy: A Case of Group Political Pressure During the Taft Administration," *Military Affairs,* Apr. 1976, 54–59. Robert Heinl quotes former commandant Thomas Holcomb as recalling that "the old boy [Elliott] had the worst temper

I've ever known." Heinl, *Soldiers of the Sea,* 147. Lowell Thomas records Smedley Butler as recalling that Elliott was "one of the kindest men in the world but when anything upset him, he flew into a hurrican[e] of violence." Thomas, *Old Gimlet Eye,* 37.

42. Unless otherwise specified, all pertinent information on the Board of Inquiry into the Elliott-Lauchheimer controversy are found in a copy of the report, 15 July 1910, "Military History."

43. Major General Commandant to the Secretary of the Navy, 18 Apr. 1910, in Kenneth J. Clifford, *Progress and Purpose: A Developmental History of the United States Marine Corps, 1900–1970* (Washington, D.C.: H&MD, 1970), 13.

44. "Military History." Lauchheimer was detached from Washington duty and sent to the Philippines but ultimately returned to Washington, where he again resumed his duties as adjutant and inspector. Attaining the rank of brigadier general in 1916, he died on active duty on 14 January 1920. Some question had been raised whether anti-Semitism was involved in the dispute, but the evidence indicates that the differences between Elliott and Lauchheimer were based largely on personality.

45. "Report of the Secretary of the Navy," in *Annual Reports of the Department of the Navy for the Fiscal Year 1910* (Washington, D.C.: GPO, 1910), 51.

46. "Report of the Commandant of [the] United States Marine Corps," in *Annual Reports of the Navy Department for the Fiscal Year 1910,* 797–813.

47. Undated mss. in "Military History."

Chapter 11. William Phillips Biddle

I would like to express my appreciation to the John M. Olin Foundation, Yale University's International Security Program, and the Military Studies Institute of Texas A&M University for providing funding to make the research and writing of this article possible.

1. During Biddle's tenure, military nomenclature made no distinction between "advanced base" and "advance base." For purposes of convenience, the currently accepted term of "advanced base" will be used except in citations.

2. Schmidt, *Maverick Marine,* 36–37; J. Robert Moskin, *The U.S. Marine Corps Story* (New York: McGraw Hill, 1977), 398; Heinl, *Soldiers of the Sea,* 165. Biographic material on Biddle is from the William P. Biddle File, Reference Section, H&MD.

3. Wise and Frost, *Marine Tells It to You,* 42.

4. Biddle's fitness reports are located in the William P. Biddle File, Box 82, Entry 62, Records of the Office of the Judge Advocate General (Navy), RG 125, Records of the Washington National Records Center, Suitland, Md. I am indebted to Timothy Nenninger for bringing these records to my attention.

5. Wiegand, "Lauchheimer Controversy," 54–59.

6. *Annual Report of the Major General Commandant, 1909* (Washington, D.C.: GPO, 1909), 4.

7. See the previous essay in this volume on George F. Elliott for further discussion about the controversy over the Marine guards in 1908–9 and the March 1910 court of inquiry.

8. General Board 408, 31 Jan. 1910, General Board Correspondence, vol. 6, General Records of the Navy Department, 1798–1947, RG 80, NARA; Ralph Earle to Chief Bureau Ordnance, 28 Feb. 1910, File 10190-3, Entry 17, Records of the United States Marine Corps, RG

127, NARA; George F. Elliott to Assistant Secretary of the Navy, 18 Aug. 1910, File 10190, Entry 17, RG 127, NARA; Dion Williams, "The Defense of Our New Naval Stations," *USNIP* 28 (June 1902): 181–94. For background on the advanced base mission, see Millett, *Semper Fidelis,* 267–86; Graham A. Cosmas and Jack Shulimson, "The Culebra Maneuver and the Formation of the U.S. Marine Corps' Advance Base Force, 1913–1914," in *Changing Interpretations and New Sources in Naval History: Papers from the Third U.S. Naval Academy History Symposium,* ed. Robert W. Love (New York: Garland, 1980), 293–99. See also the essay on Charles Heywood in this volume concerning the initiatives taken during his commandancy relative to the Advanced Base mission.

9. Alexander S. Williams to Post Commander, Olongapo, 29 Aug. 1911, File 10190-2, Entry 17, RG 127, NARA.

10. Eli K. Cole to Officer in Charge, Advance Base School, 18 Nov. 1911; M. J. Shaw to Commandant, 29 July 1910; William P. Biddle to Assistant Secretary of the Navy, 20 Jan. 1911, all in File 12110, Entry 17, RG 127, NARA; Officers and Men who have been detailed to the Advance Base School, 1 Apr. 1913, Box 239, Entry 18, RG 127, NARA.

11. Biddle to Josephus Daniels, 24 Feb. 1913, File 408-1913, Box 33, General Board, RG 80, NARA; L. Karmany to Daniels, Subj: Duties performed by Marines, 1 Aug. 1913, Box 3, Fullam Papers.

12. John R. Edwards to Daniels, Subj: Report of Inspection of Navy Yard, Philadelphia, 19 Apr. 1913, File 10190-6, Entry 17, RG 127.

13. Fullam to Daniels, Subj: Comments of Maj. Gen. Commandant on Memorandum from Aid for Inspections Concerning the Subject of the Advanced base, 23 June 1913; Fullam to Daniels, Subj: Readiness of the Marine Corps and its efficiency in handling the fixed defense part of the Advanced Base Outfit, 27 June 1913, both in Box 3, Fullam Papers; Fullam to Daniels, Subj: Establishment of Advanced Base Outfit, 1 May 1913, File 408-1913, Box 33, General Board, RG 80, NARA.

14. Biddle to Daniels, Subj: Navy Yard, Philadelphia, 17 May 1913, Box 239, Entry 18, RG 127; Biddle to Daniels, Subj: Establishment of advance base outfit, 7 June 1913, File 5103-150, General Correspondence 1897–1915, RG 80, NARA.

15. Comment of Colonel Cole, Hearings before the General Board Relative to Marines and the Advanced Base Situation, 29 Sept. 1913, General Board 408, File 408-13, Box 33, General Board, RG 80, NARA.

16. Henry C. Davis to W. W. Phelps, 9 Aug. 1913, Box 83, Fullam Papers; Millett, *Semper Fidelis,* 278–79.

17. General Board 432, 21 July 1913, Subj: Duties of marines and their connection with advance base outfits; Josephus Daniels to General Board, 23 June 1913, File 10190-5, Entry 17, RG 127; George Dewey to Daniels, Subj: Detail[ed] plans for advanced base operations next winter, 15 Oct. 1913, File 16721-61, General Correspondence 1897–1915, RG 80, NARA.

18. Fullam to Daniels, 22 Sept. 1913, Box 3, Fullam Papers.

19. Dion Williams, "Report on Men, Material and Drills Required for Establishment of a Naval Advance Base," 2 Nov. 1909, File 10190-3; "Table showing various recommendations in the record to [*sic*] guns for an advance naval base," n.d. [1913], File 10190-5; Biddle to Daniels, Subj: Information regarding material for advance base outfit, 5 Aug. 1912, File 10190-4, all in Entry 17, RG 127, NARA.

20. Biddle to Daniels, Subj: Duties of the Marines and their connection with advanced base outfits, 16 Sept. and 18 Dec. 1913; Daniels to Biddle, Subj: Duties of Marines and their connection with advanced base outfits, 30 Jan. 1914, all in Box 239, Entry 18, RG 127, NARA.

21. General Board 408, Subj: Recommendation concerning advance base outfits and their location, 5 Feb. 1913, File 408-1913, Box 33, General Board, RG 80, NARA.

22. Cosmas and Shulimson, "Culebra Maneuver," 305; Biddle to Daniels, 24 Feb., 10 Apr. 1913, File 408-1913, Box 33, General Board, RG 80, NARA; General Board 432, 3 Mar. 1913, Subj: Drill of expeditionary force of Marines with advance base outfit in West Indies, File 10190-5, Entry 17, RG 127.

23. Biddle to Daniels, 24 Feb. 1913, File 408-1913, Box 33, General Board, RG 80, NARA.

24. R. Dickens to Biddle, Subj: Report on arrangement of buildings for the establishment of a Marine Corps post at the Navy Yard, 13 May 1911, File 23398-21; Biddle to Daniels, Subj: Advance base material at Olongapo, 11 Mar. 1913, File 16721-59, both in General Correspondence 1877–1915, RG 80, NARA; Biddle to Daniels, Subj: Duties of the Marines and their connection with advanced base outfits, 16 Sept. and 18 Dec. 1913, Box 239, Entry 18, RG 127.

25. Biddle to Daniels, Subj: Duties of the Marines and their connection with the advance base outfits, 16 Sept. 1913, Box 239, Entry 18, RG 127. Biddle's recommendations can be found in *Annual Reports of the Major General Commandant, 1911–1913.*

26. Biddle to Daniels, Subj: Recommendations affecting the betterment of the condition of the Marine Corps, 24 Feb. 1914, File 7128-11, General Correspondence 1897–1915, RG 80, NARA.

27. Millett, *Semper Fidelis,* 276.

28. Heinl, *Soldiers of the Sea,* 165.

Chapter 12. George Barnett

1. From a recollection of a conversation between Biddle and John A. Lejeune, Lejeune to John H. Russell, 1935, Reel 6, Lejeune Papers; see also Wayne A. Wiegand, "Patrician in the Progressive Era: A Biography of George von Lengerke Meyer" (Ph.D. diss., Southern Illinois University, 1975), 110–15; and Wiegand, "Lauchheimer Controversy," 54–59. See also the essay on William F. Biddle in this volume concerning his appointment as commandant.

2. Lejeune to John H. Russell, n.d. [1935], Reel 6, Lejeune Papers; *Register of the Commissioned and Warrant Officers of the United States Navy and Marine Corps* (Washington, D.C.: GPO, 1913); E. David Cronin, ed., *The Cabinet Diaries of Josephus Daniels, 1913–1921* (Lincoln: University of Nebraska Press, 1962), 83; Josephus Daniels, *The Wilson Era: Years of Peace, 1910–1917* (Chapel Hill: University of North Carolina Press, 1944), 322–23; George Barnett, "Soldier and Sailor Too," chap. 23, unpublished autobiography, George Barnett Papers, PPC (hereafter cited as Barnett Papers). A comparison of fitness reports of the major contenders for the commandancy in 1913–14 show that Barnett had the most superior record. See Entry 62, Marine Corps Examination Boards, Records of the Judge Advocate General of the Navy, RG 125, FRC.

3. *Boscobel Dial,* 5 June 1877, p. 3. According to a Barnett relative, his father once served as the mayor of the small town and managed the local hotel. James Barnett, according to this recollection, was known for "his genial nature and rugged integrity." J. Evans Barnett to the author, 3 Oct. 1980.

4. *Annual Register of the United States Naval Academy, 1880–1881* (Washington, D.C.: GPO, 1881), 16–19 (hereafter cited as *Annual Register,* followed by the date); Monthly Reports of Relative Class Standing, Marks, and Demerits, 1855–1907, Entry 96, Records of the U.S. Naval Academy, RG 405, NARA (maintained in the archives, Nimitz Library, U.S. Naval Academy); *Annual Register,* 1878–79, 21–23, 26–27; Register of Grades Received on Examinations for Admission by Applicants for Cadet appointments, 1873–86, Entry 70, RG 405, NARA; and George Barnett, "Soldier and Sailor Too" 1:10; for samples of naval cadet life during the era, see Cyrus T. Brady, *Under Tops'ls and Tents* (New York: Scribner's, 1901); Park Benjamin, *The United States Naval Academy* (New York: Putnam, 1900); and Barnett, "Soldier and Sailor Too," chaps. 1–5.

5. Walter R. Herrick, "William E. Chandler," in *American Secretaries of the Navy,* 2 vols., ed. Paolo E. Coletta (Annapolis: Naval Institute Press, 1980), 1:401; Peter Karsten, "Armed Progressives," in *The Military in America: From the Colonial Era to the Present,* ed. Peter Karsten (New York: Macmillan, 1980), 230–46; Barnett, "Soldier and Sailor Too," chap. 4; Log of the *Essex* (1881–1883), Naval Records Collection.

6. Benjamin, *United States Naval Academy,* 314; Naval Personnel Act of 5 Aug. 1882, *Statutes at Large* 22 (Washington, D.C.: GPO, 1883), 285; John E. Greenwood, "The Corps' 'Old School' Tie," *USNIP* 101 (Nov. 1975): 47–53; and Merrill L. Bartlett, "Annapolis Marines," *USNIP* 118 (Apr. 1992): 90–95. For further discussion of providing Marine officers from the Naval Academy, see the McCawley article in this volume and Shulimson, *Marine Corps Search for a Mission,* 49–53.

7. Journal of the Academic Board, 28 June 1883, Entry 201, RG 405, NARA; Barnett, "Soldier and Sailor Too," chap. 1.

8. Karsten, *Naval Aristocracy,* 1–19, 385–95; "Class of 1881, Fifth Report" (n.p., 1887), and "Class of 1881, Sixth Report" (n.p., 1890) (copies of both class reports are in the Annapolis Room, Nimitz Library, U.S. Naval Academy). One hundred twenty-five cadets began with the class of 1881, and twenty-four failed to graduate; twenty-four accepted commissions as assistant engineers. Of the remaining seventy-two, three were Japanese, three were commissioned as naval constructors, eight were commissioned as ensigns of the line, eleven were commissioned in the Marine Corps, and the remainder received discharges and severance pay ($950). Number twenty-two in the class, Horace B. Andrews, failed his pre-commissioning physical because of secondary syphilis. For disparities in statistics, see *Register of Alumni* (Annapolis: Naval Academy Alumni Association, 1976), 22–23; SecNav, *Annual Report, 1883,* 29, 369; *Annual Register, 1877; Annual Register, 1883.* Barnett's hometown newspaper waxed euphoric over a native son's accomplishment: "He has graduated with honors to himself, his family, and his friends. During his four years of study, he has never received a demerit or a set back." *Boscobel Dial,* 17 June 1881, p. 3.

9. Log of the *Iroquois,* RG 45, NARA; William A. Gilmer, "The Cruise of the USS *Iroquois,* One Hundred and Ten Days from Honolulu to Puget Sound Bound for Samoa, 1889–1890" (n.p., 1937); Routine Movement of Ships, 1871–1910, Box Gal-Ley, RG 45, NARA; and Merrill L. Bartlett, "Cruise of the Iroquois, 1889–1890: Lost at Sea for Eighty Days," *USNIP* 107 (Nov. 1981): 128–29.

10. George Barnett to the Class of 1881, 23 Feb. 1900, "Report of the Class of 1881" (n.p., 1900), Annapolis Room, Nimitz Library, U.S. Naval Academy; see also GB, "Soldier and Sailor Too," chaps. 6–8; and Logs of the *San Francisco, New Orleans,* and *Chicago,* RG 45, NARA.

11. Lelia Montague Barnett, "Command Performances," unpublished memoir, Barnett Papers; Barnett, "Soldier and Sailor Too," chaps. 17–22; Mrs. Albert Lucas (née Lelia Gordon, Mrs. Barnett's daughter), interview with author, Wakefield Manor, Huntly, Va., 8 June 1979.

12. See also the essay on Biddle in this volume concerning the initial planning of the Culebra maneuver.

13. Cosmas and Shulimson, "Culebra Maneuver," 293–308.

14. Quoted in Paolo E. Coletta, "Josephus Daniels," in *American Secretaries of the Navy,* 2 vols., ed. Paolo E. Coletta (Annapolis: Naval Institute Press, 1980), 1:525; see also Merrill L. Bartlett, "Josephus Daniels and the Marine Corps," in *New Interpretations in Naval History: Selected Papers from the Eighth Naval History Symposium,* ed. William B. Cogar (Annapolis: Naval Institute Press, 1989), 190–208.

15. The Diary of Theodore Roosevelt Jr., 6 Dec. 1921, Theodore Roosevelt Jr. Papers, LC.

16. Josephus Daniels to Woodrow Wilson, 5 Apr. 1913, Marine Corps General File, 1899–1913; and William F. Fullam to Daniels, 5 Dec. 1913, Marine Corps General File, September–December 1913 File, both files in Container 531, Josephus Daniels Papers, Manuscript Division, LC (hereafter cited as Daniels Papers). In the same memo, Fullam argued to keep the size of the Marine Corps below ten thousand men suggesting that it had become an unnecessary small army.

17. Josephus Daniels to George Barnett, 12 Apr. 1914, Barnett's officer qualification record, HQMC (hereafter cited as OQR); and Daniels to Barnett, 28 June 1915, Barnett 1914–1917 File, Container 64, Daniels Papers.

18. For the most complete discussion of Marine Corps personnel matters during the World War I era, see Jack Shulimson, "First to Fight: Marine Corps Expansion, 1914–1919," *Prologue* 8 (Spring 1976): 5–16.

19. Marine Corps Personnel Board to the Secretary of the Navy, 3 Feb. 1916, File 9236, Entry 18, General Correspondence, Records of the U.S. Marine Corps, RG 127, NARA.

20. George Barnett's testimony, 28–29 Feb. 1916, in House Committee on Naval Affairs, *Hearings on Estimates by the Secretary of the Navy, 1916,* 64th Cong., 1st sess.

21. Smedley D. Butler to Mrs. Thomas S. Butler, 21 Feb. 1916, Butler Papers, Newtown Square, Pa. (privately held) (hereafter cited as Butler Papers–Pa.).

22. Barnett to William S. Benson, 17 Mar. 1917, Container 3, Benson Papers, LC; and House Naval Affairs Committee, *Hearings on Estimates Submitted by the Secretary of the Navy, 1917,* 65th Cong., 1st sess., 1917.

23. Josephus Daniels, *The Wilson Years: Years of War and After* (Chapel Hill: University of North Carolina Press, 1946), 150. See also Barnett, "Soldier and Sailor Too," chap. 25, Barnett Papers; and Secretary of War to the Secretary of the Navy, 16 May 1917, Table of Organization Subject File, Reference Section, H&MD.

24. John J. Pershing to the Adjutant General, Department of War, 31 Aug. 1917; and Adjutant General to Pershing, 17 Sept. 1917, Entry 6, Correspondence of the Commander-in-Chief, Records of the American Expeditionary Forces, RG 120, NARA.

25. *Second Division: Summary of Operations in the World War* (Washington, D.C.: GPO, 1944), 23; Robert B. Asprey, *Belleau Wood* (New York: Putnam's Sons, 1965), passim; Frederick G. Wheeler to Lejeune, 29 Mar. 1919, Reel 3, Lejeune Papers; Floyd Gibbons, "The Hottest Four Hours I Ever Went Through," *American Magazine* 87 (Mar. 1919): 34–35, 143–48; Newton D. Baker to Daniels, 19 May 1917, and Daniels to Baker, n.d., Container 60, Reel 39, Daniels Papers.

26. Pershing to the Secretary of War, AEF 1331-S, 18 June 1918 and War Department to Pershing, 1561-R, 20 June 1918, Entry 269, RG 120, NARA.

27. Cronin, *Cabinet Diaries,* 295.

28. Frederick G. Wheeler to Lejeune, 29 Mar. 1919, Reel 3, Lejeune Papers; and Paul D. Malone to James G. Harbord, 13 June 1919, 13 June 1919, Entry 15, File 21678-A-592, Files of the Chief of Staff, RG 120, NARA.

29. James G. Harbord, *The American Army in France, 1917–1919* (Boston: Houghton Mifflin, 1936), 290–91; see also Paul D. Malone to Harbord, 13 June 1919, Entry 15, File 21678-A-592, Files of the Chief of Staff, RG 120, NARA; and Frederick Palmer, *Newton D. Baker at War,* 2 vols. (New York: Dodd, Mead, 1931), 2:222.

30. Daniels to Franklin D. Roosevelt, 26 Dec. 1934, Container 95, Reel 59, Daniels Papers; Barnett's version is in "Soldier and Sailor Too," chap. 29. See also Daniels, *Wilson Years,* 155.

31. Lelia Montague Barnett, "Command Performances," and "Washington Dinner Disasters," unpublished memoirs, Barnett Papers; Brig. Gen. Lester Dessez, interview with author, 11 July 1979.

32. Barnett to Arthur I. Caperton, 26 Aug. 1919, Barnett June–December 1919 File, Container 64, Daniels Papers; see also Mrs. Caperton to Lejeune, n.d., and Daniels to Lejeune, 28 Aug. 1919, Lejeune 1920–1924 File, Container 88, Daniels Papers.

33. Thomas S. Butler to Franklin D. Roosevelt, 27 Apr. 1918, Container 88, Roosevelt Papers, Franklin D. Roosevelt Presidential Library, Hyde Park, N.Y. (hereafter cited as FDR Papers).

34. *Congressional Record,* 65th Cong., 2d sess., 27 June 1918, p. 8374; Arthur Sears Henning, "House Jumps U.S. Navy to 131,485 Men; Refuses Promotion to Gen. Barnett, Marines Chief," *Chicago Tribune,* 19 June 1918, Barnett Biographical File, H&MD. See also Congressman A. W. Gregg to George Barnett, 23 May 1918, Barnett's OQR; Barnett to Daniels, 28 June 1918, GB January–June 1918 File, Container 64, Daniels Papers; Leigh C. Palmer, Chief of the Bureau of Navigation, to William S. Sims, 29 May 1918, Sims Papers; Daniels's diary entries, 23 May, 3 June, and 26 June 1918, Daniels Papers.

35. Lejeune's version of the ouster is found in Lejeune to CMC, n.d. [1935], Reel 6, Lejeune Papers.

36. Butler to his mother, 16 Aug. 1915, Butler Papers–Pa.

37. Littleton W. T. Waller to Lejeune, 31 Aug. 1916, Reel 3, Lejeune Papers.

38. Littleton W. T. Waller to Lejeune, 12 Jan., 12 Apr., 28 July, and 20 Aug. 1916, Reel 3, Lejeune Papers.

39. Jonathan Daniels to his parents, 23 Feb. 1919, Container 23, Daniels Papers; see also Butler to his parents, 5, 30 Oct. 1918, Butler Papers–Pa.

40. Butler to his father, 20 Mar. 1919, Butler Papers–Pa.

41. A handwritten copy of the letter of dismissal is in the Barnett 1920 File, Container 64, Daniels Papers; and a typed copy appears in the Edwin H. Denby Papers, Burton Collection, Detroit Public Library (hereafter cited as Denby Papers). The typed order, dated 20 June 1920 with Daniels's signature, is in Barnett's OQR.

42. Barnett, "Soldier and Sailor Too," chap. 30; and Lelia Montague Barnett, "Command Performances."

43. Thomas S. Butler to Lejeune, 6 July 1920, Reel 13, Lejeune Papers.

44. See transcripts of Oral History with Gen. Clifton B. Cates, 1967 (hereafter cited as Cates Oral History); Maj. Gen. Ray A. Robinson, 1968; and Maj. Gen. William A. Worton, 1967, OHC.

45. Barnett's death certificate, Barnett's OQR.

46. Daniels to Franklin D. Roosevelt, 26 Dec. 1934, Container 95, Reel 59, Daniels Papers (original not in the FDR Papers).

Chapter 13. John A. Lejeune

1. John A. Lejeune, *The Reminiscences of a Marine* (Philadelphia: Dorrance, 1930), 15–33; Joe Simon, "Lieutenant General John A. Lejeune: The Greatest Leatherneck of Them All" (master's thesis, Louisiana State University, 1966), 2–12.

2. Records of Lejeune's era at the Naval Academy are found in Records of the U.S. Naval Academy, RG 405, NARA, and in the Naval Academy's *Annual Reports* for 1884–90. For his impressions of life as a naval cadet, see Lejeune to Augustine Lejeune, June 1884–June 1888, Reel 1, Lejeune Papers. For a useful study of the Navy's officer personnel problem, see Peter Karsten, "The Military Reorganizes for the American Century," in *The Military in America,* ed. Peter Karsten (New York: Free Press, 1980), 230–35.

3. SecNav, *Annual Report, 1883,* 1:372; "Shrewd Annapolis Men," *New York Times,* 8 Sept. 1890, p. 8; Senator Randall L. Gibson to Lejeune, 22 June 1890, Reel 3, Lejeune Papers; and Edward L. Beach, "From Annapolis to Scapa Flow," unpublished memoir, 54–57.

4. Logs of the *Bennington, Cincinnati,* and *Massachusetts,* Naval Records Collection. Lejeune apparently fell afoul of his commanding officer in the *Bennington,* the unpopular and widely disliked Cdr. Royal Bradford, who reported Lejeune's alleged shortcomings to the colonel commandant of the Marine Corps. By return mail, Lejeune received a scathing letter of admonition. CMC to Lejeune, 8 June 1891, Entry 1, Letters Sent, Records of the U.S. Marine Corps, RG 127, NARA.

5. Lejeune to Augustine Lejeune, 2 Jan. 1907, Reel 1, Lejeune Papers. Lejeune remained a devoted husband and father, dreading duties that resulted in family separation. During the year before his assignment to the Philippines, he wrote, "The children are well and happy, and are the greatest joy of our lives. I feel sad to think of my next absence from home." Lejeune to Augustine Lejeune, 26 Feb. 1906, Reel 1, Lejeune Papers.

6. Maj. Gen. William A. Wotherspoon to the Secretary of the Navy, 7 Nov. 1910, File 1578591, Records of the Adjutant General's Office, 1780s–1917 [U.S. Army], RG 94, NARA. Lejeune's class papers are kept by the U.S. Army Military History Institute, Carlisle Barracks, Pa. For details of the class of 1909–20, see George P. Ahern, "A Chronicle of the Army War College" (Washington, D.C.: Army War College, 1919), 97–98, and Harry P. Ball, *Of Responsible Command* (Carlisle Barracks, Pa.: Army War College, 1984), 109–17.

7. Lejeune, *Reminiscences of a Marine,* 219–48.

8. James G. Harbord, diary entry for 4 Sept. 1918, Harbord Papers, Manuscript Division, LC; and John J. Pershing, diary entry for 26–27 July 1918, John J. Pershing Papers, Manuscript Division, LC (hereafter cited as Pershing Papers). See also Lejeune to Augustine Lejeune, 2 Apr. 1918, Reel 2, Lejeune Papers; and Josephus Daniels to Lejeune, 12 Sept. 1918, Container 88, Reel 56, Daniels Papers.

9. Quoted in Hunter Liggett, *Ten Years Ago in France* (New York: Dodd, Mead, 1928), 155.

10. Quoted in Ernest Otto, "The Battle at Mont Blanc," *USNIP* 56 (Jan. 1930): 9. The author commanded a German infantry battalion during the assault. See also John W. Thomason, "Marines at Mont Blanc," *Scribner's,* Sept. 1925, 227–42.

11. American Expeditionary Forces secret letter, 10 Nov. 1918, Central File 201.6e.e., Box 1953, Records of the American Expeditionary Forces, RG 120, NARA.

12. Robert E. Lee Bullard, *Fighting Generals: Illustrated Biographical Sketches of Seven Major Generals in World War I* (Ann Arbor, Mich.: Edwards, 1944), 190. For a contrasting view of Lejeune's combat leadership, see Harbord to Lejeune, 14 Nov. 1918, Reel 3, Lejeune Papers.

13. Lejeune to George Barnett, 1 Feb. 1919, Container 64, Daniels Papers; and Lejeune to Lt. Gen. Thomas Holcomb, 22 Oct. 1940, Lejeune's officer qualification record, HQMC. Operational summaries for the Second Division in the St. Mihiel, Mont Blanc, and Meuse-Argonne campaigns are in *Record of the Second Division,* 6 vols. (Washington, D.C.: Second Division Association, 1930–32), vol. 6, passim.

14. See the essay on Barnett in this volume for further discussion of the controversy over his relief as commandant.

15. Kenneth W. Condit, John H. Johnstone, and Ella W. Nargele, *A Brief History of Headquarters Marine Corps Staff Organization,* rev. ed. (Washington, D.C.: HQMC, 1971), 1–16.

16. John H. Reber, "Pete Ellis: Amphibious Warfare Prophet," *USNIP* 103 (Nov. 1977): 53–64; David W. Wagner, "The Destiny of Pete Ellis," *Marine Corps Gazette* 60 (June 1976): 50–51; Mark Selfrin, "The Story of Pete Ellis," *Mankind* 2 (1970): 70–76; Dirk A. Ballendorf, "The Micronesian Ellis Mystery," *Guam Recorder* 5 (May 1975): 35–40.

17. Edwin H. Denby to Marine Corps mail guards, 11 Nov. 1921, Green Box (1918–1921), Denby Papers.

18. John A. Lejeune, "Preparation," *Marine Corps Gazette* 7 (Mar. 1922): 53.

19. Maj. Gen. Wendell C. Neville to Lejeune, 16 Sept. 1931, Entry 18, General Correspondence, File 12110-110, Records of the U.S. Marine Corps, RG 127, NARA.

20. Brig. Gen. Robert H. Williams, USMC (Ret.), "Those Pesky Boards," *Marine Corps Gazette* 66 (Nov. 1982): 92.

21. SecNav, *Annual Report, 1923,* 949–50.

22. "The Promotion Bill Before Congress," *Marine Corps Gazette* 7 (Dec. 1922): 365.

23. Roger K. Heller, "Curtis Dwight Wilbur," in *American Secretaries of the Navy,* 2 vols., ed. Paolo E. Coletta (Annapolis: Naval Institute Press, 1980), 2:605; Beach, "From Annapolis to Scapa Flow," 28; Lejeune, *Reminiscences of a Marine,* 16.

24. Mayor W. Freeland Kendrick to President Calvin Coolidge, n. d. [1923], Reel 23 (18D), Calvin Coolidge Papers, Manuscript Division, LC (hereafter cited as Coolidge Papers).

25. Thomas S. Butler to Curtis Wilbur, 18 Dec. 1924, Reel 3, Lejeune Papers.

26. Smedley D. Butler to Lejeune, 26 Jan. 1925, and Lejeune to Butler, 28 Jan. 1925, Reel 3, Lejeune Papers.

27. Lejeune to Curtis Wilbur, 27 Dec. 1926, Reel 23 (1BE), Coolidge Papers.

28. Senate Naval Affairs Committee, *Hearings,* 71st Cong., 2d sess., 20 Jan. 1927.

29. "Fleet," *Cincinnati Inquirer,* 28 Oct. 1924, n.p., Lejeune Biographical File, Reference Section, H&MD.

30. Theodore Roosevelt Jr., entry for 24 Feb. 1922, diary, Theodore Roosevelt Jr. Papers, Manuscript Division, LC.

31. SecNav, *Annual Report,* 1925, 1215–16.

32. Dion Williams, "Coordination in Army and Navy Training," *USNIP* 48 (Apr. 1922): 593–620; "The Fall Exercises of 1924," *Marine Corps Gazette* 10 (June 1925): 30–35; "Blue

Marine Corps Expeditionary Force," *Marine Corps Gazette* 10 (Sept. 1925): 76–88; and John J. Breckinridge, "Why Quantico?" *USNIP* 54 (Nov. 1928): 969–75.

33. Adm. E. W. Eberle, Senior Member, Joint Army-Navy Board, to the Secretary of the Navy, 14 Nov. 1926, serial 325/279, Records of the Department of the Navy, RG 80, NARA. See also Files 308 and 350, Records of the Joint Army-Navy Board and Committees, RG 225, NARA.

34. Thomas S. Butler to Curtis Wilbur, 27 Apr. 1928, and Wilbur to Butler, 21 May 1928, Files of the House Naval Affairs Committee, LC.

35. John A. Lejeune, "The U.S. Marine Corps, Present and Future," *USNIP* 54 (Oct. 1928): 859–61.

36. Josephus Daniels to Franklin D. Roosevelt, 26 Dec. 1934, Container 95, Reel 59, Daniels Papers; John R. M. Wilson, "Herbert Hoover and the Armed Forces" (Ph.D. diss., University of Illinois, 1971), chap. 3. The original of Daniels's letter to Roosevelt cannot be located in the FDR Papers.

37. William Couper, *One Hundred Years at VMI,* 4 vols. (Richmond, Va.: Garrett and Massie, 1939), 4:268–71.

38. Smedley D. Butler to Lejeune, 18 Feb. 1935, Reel 5, Lejeune Papers.

39. Ben H. Fuller to Lejeune, 29 Jan. 1931; and Lejeune to Fuller, 29 Jan. 1931, Lejeune's officer's qualification record (OQR), HQMC; and Lejeune to Smedley D. Butler, 18 Sept. 1931, Reel 5, Lejeune Papers. For more on this incident, see the Fuller essay in this volume and Merrill L. Bartlett, "Old Gimlet Eye," *USNIP* 112 (Nov. 1986): 65–72.

40. Lt. Gen. Thomas Holcomb to Lejeune, 17 Feb. 1939, Reel 7, Lejeune Papers; Midshipman Edward L. Beach to Lejeune, 13 Oct. 1937, Reel 7, Lejeune Papers, LC; and Rear Adm. Wilson Brown to Lejeune, 11 May 1939, Reel 7, Lejeune Papers.

41. John J. Pershing to Ellie Murdaugh Lejeune, 21 Nov. 1942, Box 116, Pershing Papers. Lejeune's death certificate is in his OQR.

Chapter 14. Wendell C. Neville

1. Census, 1888, Portsmouth, Va., vol. 22, ED 80, sheet 1, line 1; death certificate, Willis H. Neville, Commonwealth of Virginia; John P. Vest, *The Ancestry of the Children of John Vest and Frances Neville* (Centreville, Md.: Queen Anne's Printing and Publishing, 1972), passim.

2. Entry 62, Records of the U.S. Naval Academy, RG 405, NARA; *Register of Alumni* (Annapolis: Naval Academy Alumni Association, 1982), 185–86; Logs of the *Kearsage* and *Newark,* Records of the Bureau of Naval Personnel, RG 24, NARA; transcript of Oral History with Frances N. Vest, 8 July 1983, 4, OHC (hereafter cited as Vest Oral History).

3. See the essays on McCawley and Heywood in this volume.

4. CMC to Neville, 30 Oct. 1893, Letters Sent, Records of the U.S. Marine Corps, RG 127, NARA; Shulimson, *Marine Corps' Search for a Mission,* 115, 123, 134; Shulimson, "Daniel Pratt Mannix and the School of Application, 1889–1894" (paper presented at the Annual Meeting of the American Military Institute, Lexington, Va., 15 Apr. 1889); and Jack Shulimson, "The Transitional Commandancy: Colonel Charles G. McCawley and Uneven Reform, 1876–1891," *Marine Corps Gazette* 72 (Oct. 1988): 70–77.

5. Logs of the *Cincinnati, Raleigh,* and *Texas,* RG 24, NARA; Col. Wendell N. Vest, USMC (Ret.) to the author, 20 Mar. 1989; and Vest Oral History.

6. Carolyn A. Tyson, ed., *The Journal of Frank Keeler, 1898* (Quantico, Va.: Marine Corps Museum, n.d.); Bernard C. Nalty, *The United States in the War with Spain* (Washington, D.C.: HQMC, 1967), 7–11; and Trask, *War with Spain,* 139–40.

7. John A. Lejeune to CMC, 1935, Reel 6, Lejeune Papers.

8. *Medal of Honor Recipients, 1863–1963* (Washington, D.C.: GPO, 1964), 765–66. For a comment on the numerous awards of the Medal of Honor presented at Veracruz, see Col. Don Wyckoff to the editor, *Marine Corps Gazette* 67 (Apr. 1983): 14.

9. Records of Marine Corps Examining Boards, Entry 62, Records of the Judge Advocate General of the Navy, RG 125, FRC; Neville to Lejeune, 27 Jan. 1914, File 1975-80-20, General Correspondence, Entry 18, RG 127, NARA.

10. Neville's fitness report, 28 July–30 Sept. 1918, Entry 62, RG 125, FRC.

11. Maj. Gen. Hunter Liggett to the Secretary of the Navy, 5 July 1919, File 26521/356 and John A. Lejeune to the Chief of Naval Operations, 16 Aug. 1920, File 11112/1644, General Correspondence of the Secretary of the Navy, General Records of the Department of the Navy, RG 80, NARA.

12. Smedley D. Butler to John A. Lejeune, 18 Dec. 1928, Butler Papers, PPC, quoted in Schmidt, *Maverick Marine,* 200. This correspondence begs scrutiny: the original of the letter cannot be found in the Lejeune Papers, the file copy cannot be located in the Butler Papers, and the subject of the correspondence suggests that although Lejeune's decision to step down from the commandancy was not made public until February 1929, he apparently discussed his intentions with Butler two months earlier. But on 27 December 1927, Butler informed Lejeune, "It is my intention to retire as soon as this Chinese show is over and, at the latest, when you hand over the reigns." Butler to Lejeune, 27 Dec. 1927, Butler Papers, PPC.

13. Josephus Daniels to Franklin D. Roosevelt, 26 Dec. 1934, Container 95, Daniels Papers; however, the original copy of this correspondence cannot be located in the FDR Papers. See also Commandant of the Marine Corps File, 1929, Container 36, Herbert C. Hoover Papers, Hoover Presidential Library, West Branch, Iowa (hereafter cited as Hoover Papers); "Lejeune to Retire as Head of Marines," *New York Times,* 7 Feb. 1929, p. 19; "Neville Named to Head Marines," *New York Times,* 8 Feb. 1929, p. 7; Wendell C. Neville to James G. Harbord, 24 Aug. 1928, Correspondence File, "N," Harbord Papers, New York Historical Society; and "Gen. Cole Dies," *ANJ* 66 (13 July 1929): 947.

14. "C. S. Radford Asks for Retirement," *New York Times,* 29 Sept. 1929, sec. 2, p. 2.

15. "S. D. Butler to Maj. Gen.," *New York Times,* 14 July 1929, p. 1; Charles F. Adams to Herbert C. Hoover, 4 Sept. 1929, Container 35, Hoover Papers.

16. Quoted in Schmidt, *Maverick Marine,* 205. See also "General Butler to Get Assignment Soon," *ANJ* 66 (23 Feb. 1929): 505; "New Post for General Butler," *New York Times,* 5 Apr. 1929, p. 7; SecNav, *Annual Report, 1930,* 1248.

17. "Maj. Gen. Butler Forbids Marines to Patronize Quantico, Virginia, Merchants Unless Town Gets Rid of Bootleggers," *New York Times,* 20 Sept. 1929, p. 34.

18. "Praises Marines for Service Abroad," *New York Times,* 14 Dec. 1929, p. 4.

19. Hans Schmidt, *The United States Occupation of Haiti, 1915–1934* (New Brunswick, N.J.: Rutgers University Press, 1971), 189–206; and Robert D. Heinl Jr. and Nancy G. Heinl, *Written in Blood: The Story of the Haitian People* (Boston: Houghton Mifflin, 1978), 494–97.

20. Quoted in Schmidt, *Maverick Marine,* 207.

21. Neville, "The U.S. Marine Corps," *USNIP* 55 (Oct. 1929): 865; see also John Richard Meredith Wilson, "Herbert Hoover and the Armed Forces: A Study of Presidential Attitudes and Policy" (Ph.D. diss., Northwestern University, 1971), 44–66; Gerald E. Wheeler, "Charles Francis Adams," in *American Secretaries of the Navy,* 2 vols., ed. Paolo E. Coletta (Annapolis: Naval Institute Press, 1980), 2:633–53; House Naval Affairs Committee, *Hearings on Naval Appropriations for FY 1930,* 70th Cong., 2d sess., 23 Jan. 1929.

22. Senate Naval Affairs Committee, 70th Cong., 2d sess., 19 Jan. and 16 May 1929; House Naval Affairs Committee, 71st Cong., 2d sess., 19 Dec. 1929; House Naval Affairs Committee, 71st Cong., 2d sess., 7 May 1930; "Navy-USMC Bills to Be Reported Soon," *ANJ* 66 (26 Jan. 1929): 421, 426.

23. SecNav, *Annual Report, 1929,* 1171, and *Annual Report, 1930,* 1241.

24. Neville to Lejeune, 12 Apr. 1930, Reel 4, Lejeune Papers; see also Lejeune to Ben H. Fuller, 2 Apr. 1930, and Lejeune to Augustine Lejeune, 1 July 1930, Reel 4, Lejeune Papers; "Gen. Neville Has Stroke," *New York Times,* 28 Mar. 1930, p. 25. Detailed medical information on Neville's illness may be found in his officer's qualification record, HQMC.

25. "Gen. Neville Dead; Leader of Marines," *New York Times,* 9 July 1930, p. 1; "Full Military Honors for General Neville," *New York Times,* 10 July 1930, p. 25; "Gen. Neville Interred," *ANJ* 67 (12 July 1930): 1075. Neville's death certificate is in his officer's qualification record at HQMC.

26. "Death Ends Career of Maj. Gen. Neville," *Washington Post,* 9 July 1930, p. 1; see also Philip N. Pierce, "The Whispering Commandant," *Leatherneck* 67 (Apr. 1984): 36–51.

Chapter 15. Ben H. Fuller

1. Smedley D. Butler to Samuel Butler, 28 July 1930, Butler Papers–Pa.; see also "Four Are Mentioned to Head Corps," *New York Times,* 13 July 1930, sec. 2, p. 6. Apparently, Neville never considered Butler as his successor, a conclusion he shared with his daughter; see Vest Oral History.

2. Charles R. Train to Herbert Hoover, 21 July 1930, Candidates for Commandant File, Container 36, Hoover Presidential Library, West Branch, Iowa; letters to and from Logan Feland, Correspondence Files, Harbord Papers, New York Historical Society. For a complete study of the controversy, see Merrill L. Bartlett, "The 'Admirals Without Ships' Win," *Naval History,* forthcoming. The news that General Douglas MacArthur would be the next chief of staff of the Army obscured the announcement of Fuller's appointment; see "Gen. MacArthur to Be Next Chief of Staff; Command of Marines Goes to Gen. H. B. [*sic*] Fuller," *ANJ* 67 (9 Aug. 1930): 1153, and "MacArthur Named Chief of Army Staff; Fuller to Head Marines," *New York Times,* 6 Aug. 1930, p. 21.

3. Census, 1880, Big Rapids, Michigan, vol. 17, ED 180, sheet 59; Register of candidates for admission, Entry 62, Records of the U.S. Naval Academy, RG 405, NARA; *Register of Alumni, 1845–1882* (Annapolis: Naval Academy Alumni Association, 1982), 185; Gilmer, "Cruise of the USS *Iroquois*"; Bartlett, "Cruise of the Iroquois," 128–29.

4. Shulimson, *Marine Corps' Search for a Mission,* 103–4; Ben F. Fordney to the author, 16 Nov. 1988.

5. Letters and Telegrams sent to Officers Conveying Orders, June 1882–Oct. 1898, Entry 24; Record of Military Service of Marine Corps Officers, Entry 67; Press Copies of Military His-

tories and Statements of Service of Marine Corps Officers, Entry 68; Register of Officers' Sea Duty, Entry 72; Records of the U.S. Marine Corps, RG 127, NARA; logs of the *Atlanta* and *Columbia,* Records of the Bureau of Naval Personnel, RG 24, NARA.

6. "Butler's Brawl," "Salesmanship," "Let There Be Light," and "The Little Major," Fuller Papers, PPC; George F. Elliott to CMC, 12 Oct. 1899, in SecNav, *Annual Report, 1899,* 1105–6; Department of the Navy General Order No. 55, 19 July 1901, Entry 67, RG 127, NARA; Fuller's fitness reports as a junior officer, Records of Boards of Examinations, Entry 62, Records of the Judge Advocate General of the Navy, RG 125, FRC.

7. Stephen M. Fuller and Graham A. Cosmas, *Marines in the Dominican Republic, 1916–1924* (Washington, D.C.: H&MD, 1974), 29; fitness report submitted for 1–25 Oct. 1920, Entry 62, RG 125, FRC; Josephus Daniels to Josephus Daniels Jr., 1 Aug. 1919, Container 23, Daniels Papers.

8. Joseph W. Fordney to Edwin H. Denby, 31 Dec. 1921, 17 and 21 Nov. 1922, to John A. Lejeune, 22 Nov. 1922, and Lejeune to Fordney, 23 Nov. 1922, Fuller's Officers Qualification Record, HQMC; President Calvin Coolidge to Denby, 30 Jan. 1924, Denby Papers. Fuller's examining board met on 9 February 1924 and consisted of Charles L. McCawley, Rufus H. Lane, and Logan Feland; the results are in Entry 62, RG 125, FRC. In 1922 Feland sought Lejeune's approval for Fuller to assume command at Quantico, but the assignment never took place. Although in 1930, Feland denigrated Fuller, a decade before he described him as "an officer of executive ability, poise, and sound judgment." Logan Feland to Lejeune, 28 Jan. 1922, Fuller's OQR.

9. Fuller to Lejeune, 18 Sept. 1930, Reel 4, Lejeune Papers.

10. House, *Hearings Before the House Naval Affairs Committee on Appropriations for FY 32,* 71st Cong., 3d sess., 9 Feb. 1931; [Fuller to Adams?], 20 May 1931, Container 36, Hoover Papers; Fuller to the Secretary of the Navy, 17 Jan. 1931 in General Board Study 432, RG 80, NARA; "Will Destroy Marine Corps," *ANJ* 71 (14 Jan. 1932): 1; "Navy Estimates Cut, Sent to White House," *ANJ* 69 (17 Oct. 1931): 145; "Marine Cut to Stay," *ANJ* 69 (12 Sept. 1931): 30; "Oppose Marine Cut," *New York Times,* 17 Dec. 1932, p. 14; "House Fights Cuts in Marine Corps," *New York Times,* 12 Jan. 1933, p. 2; "No New Cut in Marines," *New York Times,* 17 Aug. 1931; "Economy Plans Cut Naval Air Program," *New York Times,* 12 June 1931, p. 42; "Marine Corps Stops Enlisting in Effort to Save $1,000,000; May Cut Force to 16,000," *New York Times,* 11 June 1931, p. 1; "Marine Corps Economy," *New York Times,* 15 June 1931, p. 18. For a scholarly overview of the Department of the Navy during the Hoover administration, see John Richard Meredith Wilson, "Herbert Hoover and the Armed Forces: A Study of Presidential Attitudes and Policy" (Ph.D. diss., Northwestern University, 1971), chaps. 2–3.

11. Bartlett, "Old Gimlet Eye," 65–72.

12. House Naval Affairs Committee, *USMC Commissioned Officer Distribution, Promotion, and Retirement 25 Provisions,* 72d Cong., 2d sess., 2 Feb. 1932; J. Clawson Roop, Director, Bureau of the Budget, to Hoover, 13 Oct. 1931, Container 36, Hoover Papers. See also Lejeune to Burton C. French, 19 May 1932; Lejeune to Rufus H. Lane, 19 May 1932; Lejeune to Frederick D. Hale, 20 May 1932; and Lane to Lejeune, 24 May 1932, Reel 5, Lejeune Papers; "President Approves USMC Personnel Bill," *ANJ* 69 (10 Oct. 1931): 121; and "Promotion Bill Fails," *ANJ* 69 (Dec. 1931): 319.

13. George S. Simonds, "Amalgamation of the Marine Corps with the Army," 8 May 1931, Folder M (Correspondence, 1929–1931), Simonds Papers, Manuscript Division, LC; George Van Horn Moseley, "One Soldier's Journey," 159–62, Moseley Papers, Manuscript Division,

LC. William Veazie Pratt's diary is silent on the affair, but his biographer notes that many senior officers considered the Chief of Naval Operations somewhat of an unprotesting agent of the Hoover Administration. See Craig L. Symonds, "William Veazie Pratt as CNO," *Naval War College Review* 30 (Mar.–Apr. 1980): 17–38. Douglas MacArthur's papers are also silent on the proposal, but see Pratt to MacArthur, 18 Jan. 1952, RG 10, MacArthur Papers, Norfolk, Va., in which Pratt compares MacArthur to Churchill.

14. *ARSN 1932,* 1141–63; "USMC Aviation Unites Placed on Carriers," *ANJ* 69 (26 Sept. 1931).

15. Smedley D. Butler to Franklin D. Roosevelt, 17 July 1933, File 18E, FDR Papers; see also "Major Generals Appointed," *ANJ* 71 (9 Sept. 1933): 21, 39; Fuller to Adams, 7 June 1933, File 18E, Roosevelt Papers; Ernest L. Jahnke to Walter H. Newton, 15 and 20 Oct. 1931, Jahnke to Herbert Hoover, 5 Sept. 1931, Container 36, Hoover Papers.

16. Director, War Plans Division, to the General Board, 10 Aug. 1931, File KA-KV (secret), RG 80, NARA; see also CNO to CMC, 20 Apr. 1931, in the same file.

17. General Board Study 432, 28 Aug. 1931, RG 80, NARA; Director, War Plans Division, to the General Board, 10 Aug. 1931, File OP 12F-CD, and CMC to CNO, 3 Nov. 1932, SecNav/CNO Secret Files, both in RG 80, NARA. See also CMC to Director, Division of Operations and Training, HQMC; Commandant, Marine Corps Schools, Quantico, Va.; Director, War Plans Division, General Board of the Navy, 29 Nov. 1932, SecNav Confidential Files, RG 80, NARA.

18. CMC to CNO, 3 Nov. 1932, File KA-KV (secret); CMC to Division of Operations and Training, War Plans Section, Quantico, Va., 24 Nov. 1932, File KG-KW (confidential), RG 80, NARA.

19. CNO to SecNav, with CMC's comments, 2 Mar. 1933, CMC to SecNav, 11 Apr. 1933, Adm. J. V. Chase, Chairman, General Board, to SecNav, 10 Aug. 1932, and Adm. William Veazie Pratt to SecNav, 2 Mar. 1933, File 1240-30, Entry 18, General Correspondence, RG 127, NARA.

20. Ben H. Fuller to Commandant, Marine Corps Schools, Quantico, Va., 28 Oct. 1933, File 1520-30-120, Entry 18, General Correspondence, RG 127, NARA. John Russell, however, lays claim to initiating this change; see Russell, "The Birth of the Fleet Marine Force," *USNIP* 72 (Jan. 1946): 49–51.

21. *ARSN 1934,* 9–10; for commentary on the birth of the Fleet Marine Force, see "Marine Force Put Under Fleet Head," *New York Times,* 15 Dec. 1933, p. 1; "New Marine Force Will Operate as Fleet Unit," *ANJ* 71 (16 Dec. 1933): 305; "The Marine Corps Girds the Globe," *New York Times,* 24 Dec. 1933, pp. 10, 28.

22. Death Certificate, Fuller's Officers Qualification Record; "Gen. Ben Fuller Dies; Former Marine Leader," *Washington Post,* 9 June 1937, p. 1. Materials on the death of Ted Fuller are in Folders 17 and 18, Fuller Papers, PPC; see especially Holland M. Smith to Ben H. Fuller, 13 June 1918, Folder 18, in that collection.

23. Lejeune to Harbord, 6 Aug. 1930, and Feland to Harbord, 22 Aug. 1930, Correspondence Files, Harbord Papers, New York Historical Society; Harbord to Lejeune, 25 Aug. 1930, Reel 4, Lejeune Papers.

Chapter 16. John H. Russell

1. Heinl, *Soldiers of the Sea,* 299.
2. *New York Times,* 22 Feb. 1934; *Time,* 5 Mar. 1934, 9.

3. One of Russell's aides later described him: "Gentlemanly, composed, thorough, far sighted, astute, and introspective" (Lt. Gen. George Good to author, 3 Oct. 1984).

4. Brooke Astor (née Russell), *Patchwork Child: Early Memoirs by Brooke Astor* (New York: Harper & Row, 1962), 13. This and a second memoir, *Footprints: An Autobiography* (New York: Doubleday, 1980), provide background on the family. The press described Russell's meeting with Cleveland upon his appointment as commandant and in obituaries in 1947; reports agreed on the general theme, but specific details varied.

5. Both father and son are listed in *Register of Alumni: Graduate, and Former Naval Cadets and Midshipmen, 1845–1983* (Annapolis: Naval Academy Alumni Association, 1983), 135 and 156. "U.S. Naval Academy, Record of Naval Cadets, 1888–1892, No.11," Inventory 86, Box 30, Records of the U.S. Naval Academy, RG 405, NARA. Russell's academic, discipline, and medical records can be found on 355–61. The *Annual Registers* for 1888–89 to 1894–95 contain data on Order of Merit lists, cruises, cadet billet assignments, and discipline infractions.

6. *Evening Bulletin,* 13 Sept. 1893, the *Times,* 14 Sept. 1893, and the *ANJ,* 16 Sept. 1893. However, these list Russell as serving in USS *New York.* Box 1, Folder 1, Russell Papers, PPC (hereafter cited as Russell Papers).

7. Commanding Officer, USS *Massachusetts* to Secretary of the Navy, 5 Sept. 1898; Brigadier General Commandant of the Marine Corps to Secretary of the Navy, 7 Nov. 1898. Russell Biographical File.

8. Guam had a terrible reputation and Russell's illness was not unusual. In 1899, there were five Marine officers there and their fates were one death, one evacuation due to mental illness, one serious injury (lost eye), and Russell's dysentery. Only the commanding officer, an "old man," served a full tour. Maj. Gen. John H. Russell to Anthony Marshall, 14 June 1945, as recounted in Anthony Marshall to author, 15 Mar. 1989. Col. Frederic Wise described Guam as "the hell of the United States Marines" and "one of the world's lost spots," while Colonel Heinl simply noted that Guam was "reviled for the next 40 years as the hellhole of the Corps." Wise and Frost, *Marine Tells It to You,* 11–12; Heinl, *Soldiers of the Sea,* 118. For a minority view, see transcript of Oral History with Gen. Oliver P. Smith, U.S. Marine Corps (Ret.), 1973, 8, OHC (hereafter cited as O. P. Smith Oral History), and U.S. Naval Hospital, Yokohama, Report of Medical Survey, 10 Apr. 1900, Case of Captain John H. Russell, Russell Biographical File.

9. *Army and Navy Journal,* 8 Aug. 1908, and Astor, *Patchwork Child,* 28–37.

10. Inquiry: School of Application. n.d., Text in Russell's handwriting, Russell Biographical File.

11. Astor, *Patchwork Child,* 48, 60–63, and 98.

12. The Veracruz operation is covered in Jack Sweetman, *The Landing at Vera Cruz: 1914—The First Complete Chronicle of a Strange Encounter in April 1914, When the United States Navy Captured and Occupied the City of Vera Cruz, Mexico* (Annapolis: Naval Institute Press, 1968), and, more briefly, in Lester Langley, *The Banana Wars: An Inner History of American Empire, 1900–1934* (Lexington: University of Kentucky Press, 1983), 91–100. Neither mention Russell. For details from the Russell family perspective, see Astor, *Footprints,* 186–94.

13. Russell repeatedly requested service in France during World War I. But as the commander of the 4th Regiment in the Dominican Republic commented in his endorsement of 13 June 1917, on Russell's request of 2 June 1917: "All officers of this brigade ardently desire such a detail, and in approving this request, I do not desire to designate Lieutenant Colonel Russell above others who have not made application for such detail." Russell Biographical File. Russell's

daughter later wrote, "Still he [Russell] never quite got over not being able to take his regiment to France. He felt it a stain on his career." Astor, *Footprints,* 89.

14. For a discussion of these incidents and the resulting investigation, see Brig. Gen. Robert H. Williams, USMC, "Those Controversial Boards," *Marine Corps Gazette* 66 (Nov. 1982): 91–99.

15. There are many accounts of the Marine experience in Haiti. See especially Schmidt, *Occupation of Haiti,* and Heinl and Heinl, *Written in Blood.* For an overview, see Millett, *Semper Fidelis,* 178–211.

16. For a discussion of the Forbes commission, see Schmidt, *Occupation of Haiti,* chap. 11, and Heinl and Heinl, *Written in Blood,* 497–505. Russell wrote an unpublished essay titled "A Marine Looks Back on Haiti," n.d., Box 3, Folder 6, Russell Papers.

17. Chairman, the Presidential Commission for the Study of Conditions in the Republic of Haiti to the Secretary of the Navy, 8 May 1930, and reply of 13 May 1930, File 00-Russell, John H., Box 3746, General Records of the Department of the Navy, RG 80, NARA. The commission also supported him to appointment as commandant of the Marine Corps!

18. Secretary of State to Secretary of the Navy, 24 Oct. 1928 and 19 July 1929, and the Secretary of the Navy replies of 30 Oct. 1928 and 24 July 1929, in ibid. In 1931, the State Department supported Russell for promotion to major general if Smedley Butler retired; see Secretary of State to President Hoover, memo, 3 July 1931, Cabinet Officers, "Marine Corps" Presidential Papers, Herbert Hoover Presidential Library.

19. Gen. Merrill B. Twining, USMC to author, 28 Dec. 1982. Twining described two pre–World War I factions: the "Navy-haters (Butlerites)" or "traditionalists" and "reformists" (who "believed in a more logical and acceptable relationship with the Navy." After the War, two more emerged: "Independents" (those influenced by World War I/U.S. Army experience or who did not know where the future lay), and a fourth who believed all the Corps needs was to "maintain trained troops in readiness for the day they were needed."

20. Maj. Gen. John H. Russell, USMC. "A Fragment of Naval War College History," *USNIP* 58 (Aug. 1932): 1164–65. Russell linked study of general staff procedures and application problems. In 1944 he wrote: "If you remember I introduced it [the general staff system] at the Naval War College, or rather I was responsible for the studying of problems and the introductory of the applicatory system." Maj. Gen. John H. Russell to Anthony Marshall, 16 May 1944, as quoted in Anthony Marshall to author, 15 Mar. 1989.

21. The four papers of Russell are: "An Outline Study of the Defense of Advanced Naval Bases," 30 Sept. 1909; "General Principles Governing the Selection and Establishment of Advanced Naval Bases and the Composition of an Advanced Base Outfit," 9 Dec. 1909; "Additional Notes of Field Work Construction for Advanced Base Guns," Dec. 1909; and "Lecture: The Preparation of War Plans for the Establishment and Defense of Naval Advanced Base," 23 May 1910, all in File XBAA, Box 79, RG B, U.S. Naval War College Archives. The subsequent studies of Maj. Robert Dunlap (1911), Maj. Dion Williams (1912), and Capt. Earl Ellis (1913) are also in the Naval War College Archives.

22. Jeffrey Dorwart, *The Office of Naval Intelligence: The Birth of American's First Intelligence Agency, 1865–1918* (Annapolis: Naval Institute Press, 1979), 94–103.

23. Maj. John H. Russell, USMC "A Plea for a Mission and Doctrine," *Marine Corps Gazette* 1 (June 1916): 109–22, quote on 111.

24. Maj. Earl Ellis, USMC, "Continued Discussion on a Plea for a Mission and Doctrine," *Marine Corps Gazette* 1 (Dec. 1916): 403–4.

25. Russell "Plea for a Mission," 122; Ellis, "Continued Discussion on a Plea," 403–4.

26. C. R. Train to President, memo, 21 July 1930, Presidential Papers, Cabinet Offices, Marine, Herbert Hoover Presidential Library.

27. His date of rank as commandant was 1 March 1934. Russell was promoted to brigadier general on 1 January 1922, and then to temporary major general on 1 September 1933. He was serving in that grade when appointed major general commandant. Why Russell? Officers serving at the time have commented on his appointment as follows: General Twining wrote that Russell, upon his return from Haiti, had "favorable recognition in Congress, [the] White House, and the State Department. For the first time since Lejeune, we had a 'man of party' in Washington. His appointment was a foregone conclusion" (Twining to author, 28 Dec. 1982); General Williams remembered that there was "no real opposition to General Russell as Commandant. . . . No real opposition or other candidate for the office before it became vacant" (Brig. Gen. Williams to author, 27 Dec. 1982); and General Hogaboom succinctly noted that Russell was "considered the best general officer available at the time" (Maj. Gen. Hogaboom to author, 16 Feb. 1983). These officers and others queried about other candidates such as Generals Harry Lee or James Breckinridge, generally state that there were no other serious contenders but do not say why they believe this.

28. Chief of Naval Operations (Admiral Standley) to Capt. Walter Venon, USN, Naval Aide to the President, 1 Sept. 1933, RG OF 18e, Box 28, FDR Papers. There was no further correspondence pertaining to Fuller's successor in the FDR Papers, nor in the Standley Papers at the University of Southern California or Secretary of the Navy Claude Swanson Papers at the University of Virginia.

29. CMC, "Annual Report for Fiscal Year 1934," 23 Aug. 1934; CMC, *Final Report,* 2 Sept. 1936; SecNav, *Annual Report for Fiscal Year 1937.* Fifteen capital ships were under construction and would increase the diversion of manpower. In the text and citations, references made to either secretary of the navy or major general commandant annual reports for various fiscal years are all in H&MD.

30. For overviews of the evolutionary events leading to the creation of Russell's Fleet Marine Force, see Millett, *Semper Fidelis,* 274–86; Jeter A. Isely and Philip A. Crowl, *U.S. Marines and Amphibious War: Its Theory and Its Practice in the Pacific* (Princeton: Princeton University Press, 1951), 21–29; and Clifford, *Progress and Purpose,* 45.

31. Maj. Gen. John H. Russell, USMC (Ret.), "The Birth of the FMF," *USNIP* 72 (Jan. 1946): 49–51. On this piece, Russell commented to his grandson: "I wrote it purely to keep the record straight for there has been so much misinformation published on the subject that I felt someone should tell the facts and I knew no one better qualified than I was as I started the business." Maj. Gen. John H. Russell to Anthony Marshall, 22 Mar. 1945, as quoted in Anthony Marshall to author, 15 Mar. 1989.

32. Lt. Gen. Pedro del Valle, USMC, *Semper Fidelis: An Autobiography* (Hawthorne, Calif.: Christian Book Club of America, 1976), 67 and 71; for another example, see 20–21.

33. Brig. Gen. John H. Russell, USMC, "A New Naval Policy," *Marine Corps Gazette* 18 (Aug. 1933): 13–16.

34. Major General Commandant to Chief of Naval Operations, 17 Aug. 1933, Folder 2, Box 3, Russell Papers. The Russell Papers contain copies of this correspondence and the subsequent staffing through the naval chain of command, followed by the implementing instructions. Marine Corps correspondence was signed by General Russell.

35. The complete text of Navy Department General Order 241 of 7 December 1933 can be found in Heinl, *Soldiers of the Sea,* 302.

36. *New York Times,* 15 Dec. 1933, p. 1.

37. "What the Fleet Marine Force Means to the Marine Corps," *Quantico Sentry,* 23 Feb., 24 Nov., and 13 Mar. 1936.

38. Maj. Gen. John H. Russell, USMC, "The Fleet Marine Force," *USNIP* 62 (Oct. 1936): 1409–10.

39. Ibid., 1408; Major General Commandant of the Marine Corps, *Report for Fiscal Year 1936,* 31 Aug. 1936; Major General Commandant of the Marine Corps, *Final Report,* 2 Sept. 1936.

40. Col. Paul Drake, USMC, to author, 25 Apr. 1984. Transcript of Oral History with Lt. Gen. Julian Smith, USMC, 1973, 160–61, OHC (hereafter cited as J. Smith Oral History).

41. Lt. Gen. H. M. Smith, USMC, "The Development of Amphibious Tactics in the U.S. Navy," pt. 1, *Marine Corps Gazette* 30 (June 1946): 14–15.

42. Commandant, Marine Corps Schools, to Major General Commandant, 5 Oct. 1931. Historical Amphibious File 8, Archives, Marine Corps University, MCRC. For discussions of this, see Kenneth J. Clifford, *Amphibious Warfare Developments in Britain and America from 1920–1940* (Laurens, N.Y.: Edgewood, 1983), 96–99, and del Valle, *Semper Fidelis,* 56–57.

43. For a study of the curriculum and history of the Field Officers Course, see Lt. Col. Donald F. Bittner, USMCR, *Curriculum Evolution: Marine Corps Command and Staff College, 1920–1988* (Washington, D.C.: H&MD, 1989), 8–30.

44. Col. E. B. Miller to Commandant, Marine Corps Schools, 15 Aug. 1932, with Major General Breckinridge's forwarding endorsement of 18 Aug. 1932, Historical Amphibious File, Archives, MCRC. For a summary of this lengthy proposal, see Bittner, *Curriculum Evolution,* 18–22.

45. Prof. W. H. Russell (no relation to John H. Russell) to author, 7 Dec. 1983. This account is based upon Russell's interviews with Rear Adm. Walter Ansel. He also wrote: "In answer to my specific question, Ansel thought that letter might have been written in October 1933." In a subsequent letter, Russell commented that "my current recollection places the Ansel-McLean conversation in 1933, fairly close to McLean's October letter." Ansel also recounted the following to Russell: later when he visited Barrett in Washington or Quantico, "Barrett et al. braced him for 'dropping the roof on them'" and commented Barrett "said in Ansel's presence, 'Walter's initiative finally got Headquarters moving' (or words to that effect)" (Russell to author, Labor Day, Sept. 1984). Russell was a retired professor of history, U.S. Naval Academy. John H. Russell and McLean were Naval Academy classmates, Russell class of 1892 and McLean, 1894. See *Register of Alumni: Graduates, Former Naval Cadets, and Midshipmen, 1845–1979* (Annapolis: Naval Academy Alumni Association, 1980), 178.

46. Millett, *Semper Fidelis,* 33; and Clifford, *Amphibious Warfare,* 100–103. See also Isely and Crowl, *U.S. Marines and Amphibious War,* 35–36, and Heinl, *Soldiers of the Sea,* 299–301.

47. *Final Report of the Major General Commandant,* 2 Sept. 1936. Russell also noted that the Schools had published a "Tentative Manual for Defense of Advanced Bases" and "The Manual of Small Wars." Transcript of Oral History with Lt. Gen. George F. Good, USMC, 1970, 82–83, OHC; Lt. Gen. Good to author, 9 Apr. 1984.

48. Lejeune, *Reminiscences of a Marine,* 228–29, 473–74. Maj. Gen. Lejeune to Maj. Gen. Russell, 20 Feb. 1935, Folder 1, Box 1, Russell Papers. Lt. Gen. Edward Craig to author, 11 Sept. 1984.

49. Senate Committee on Naval Affairs, *Selection, Promotion, and Retirement of Commissioned Officers of the Marine Corps, Hearing on S. 3058,* 73d Cong., 20 Apr. 1934. Forty-nine years later, Gen. James Berkeley illustrated Russell's point: "Promotion was slow, in 1927 in Nicaragua two company commanders were over 60." Lt. Gen. James Berkeley, interview with author, 2 May 1983. For a general analysis of the proposed legislation, see "Legislation: Personnel Situation," *Marine Corps Gazette* 19 (Feb. 1934): 16–27. Russell gave similar testimony before the House Naval Affairs Committee on 5 April 1934.

50. Maj. J. C. Fegan to Presidential Secretary, 25 Apr. 1934, "Marine Corps and Women's Reserve, 1933–45," RG OF 18e, Box 29, FDR Papers.

51. *New York Times,* 15 Jan. 1934; transcript of Oral History with Lt. Gen. Robert B. Luckey, 1973, 8, OHC; Heinl, *Soldiers of the Sea,* 316. For examples of the problems in the existing system, see Brig. Gen. John S. Letcher, USMC, *One Marine's Story* (Verona, Va.: McClure Press, 1970), 57, 104–8, and 113–14; del Valle, *Semper Fidelis,* 27; and J. Smith Oral History, 62–63.

52. Roger Willock, *Lone State Marine: A Biography of the Late Colonel John W. Thomason, Jr., USMC* (Princeton: Privately published, 1961), 3 and 15; Brig. Gen. Robert Devereux, interview with author, 17 Nov. 1982; Gen. Jerry Thomas to author, 23 Dec. 1982; Roger Willock, *Unaccustomed to Fear: A Biography of the Late General Roy S. Geiger, USMC* (Princeton: Haskins Press, 1968), 168; Norman Cooper, "The Military Career of General Holland M. Smith, USMC" (Ph.D. diss., University of Alabama, 1974), 101, 104; O. P. Smith Oral History, 12–13.

53. *Major General Commandant Final Report,* 2 Sept. 1936.

54. SecNav, *Annual Report for Fiscal Year 1934.* (Note: the wording is extracted from General Russell's *Annual Report for Fiscal Year 1934.*)

55. CMC, "Annual Report for Fiscal Year 1934"; Letcher, *One Marine's Story,* 108; Gen. Twining to author, 28 Dec. 1982.

56. Major General of the Marine Corps to Secretary of the Navy, "Report of Proceedings of a Senior Selection Board," convened at Headquarters, Marine Corps, 25 June 1934; Senior Promotion Board Reports, 7 Jan. and 2 Dec. 1935, File 1965-75-35-10, Box 133, Records of the U.S. Marine Corps, RG 127, NARA. Heinl later wrote that capable officers "found themselves promoted with bewildering speed after years of stagnation." Heinl, *Soldiers of the Sea,* 298.

57. Junior Selection Board Report, 25 June 1934, File 1965-75-35-10, Box 133, RG 127, NARA; Drake to author, 25 Apr. 1984.

58. Headquarters, Marine Corps Circular Letter 153, 27 Sept. 1934, and Circular Letter 149, 14 June 1934. For material pertaining to promotion examinations, see Headquarters, Marine Corps Bulletins 115, 119, 122, 126, and 134 of 15 Apr., 15 Aug., 15 Nov. 1935, and 15 Mar., 15 Nov. 1936. Specifics on examinations can be found in transcript of Oral History with Lt. Gen. Merwyn Silverthorn, USMC, 1969, 101–3, OHC, and Letcher, *One Marine's Story,* 47–48. Transcript of Oral History with Maj. Gen. Omar T. Pfeiffer, USMC, 1968, 130–31, OHC (hereafter cited as Pfeiffer Oral History), discussed promotion board operating procedures and noted the Butler comments on fitness reports.

59. For a detailed account of this controversy, see Dr. Donald F. Bittner, "Conflict under the Dome: Senator Hugo Black, Major General Smedley Butler, and the Challenged Promotion of Major General John H. Russell, United States Marine Corps," unpublished manuscript, copies at MCHC and MCRC.

60. Major General Commandant of the Marine Corps to Secretary of the Navy, 30 Aug. 1934, File 1965-75-20, Box 131, RG 127, NARA.

61. Much of the correspondence from officers nonselected for promotion can be found in the "Investigation of the Marine Corps, 1935." Box 226, Senator Hugo Black Papers, Manuscript Division, LC (hereafter cited as Black Papers).

62. *Congressional Record,* 74th Cong., 1st sess., Senate, 5 Mar. 1935, 2930–33.

63. Ibid., 2930–31.

64. Maj. Gen. John A. Lejeune to Senator Park Trammell, 14 Feb. 1935. This letter is published in ibid., 2862–63, and Senate Committee on Naval Affairs, *Marine Corps Nominations, Report of Proceedings,* 18 Feb. 1935. A copy is also in Box 226 of the Black Papers, LC.

65. *Quantico Sentry,* 25 Oct. 1935.

66. Senator Hugo Black to Jim Smith, 13 Mar. 1935, Box 226, Black Papers, LC. He also stated this publicly; see the *New York Times,* 5 Mar. 1935. Butler's specific motives are unclear. For the status on legislation, see CMC, "Annual Report for Fiscal Year 1935" and "Annual Report for Fiscal Year 1936," 28–30 and 38–40, respectively.

67. Maj. Gen. John H. Russell to Maj. Gen. John A. Lejeune, 18 Feb. 1935. Folder 4, Box 1, Russell Papers. The bitterness in his family remained; see Astor, *Footprints,* 85–89, 173, 187–93. If Russell remained silent, his opponents did not; see *New York Times,* 1, 3, 5, and 6 Mar. 1935.

68. Transcript of Oral History with Gen. Lemuel Shepherd, USMC (Ret.), 1967, 362 and 366, OHC (hereafter cited as Shepherd Oral History). For a view of duty at the barracks during the Russell and Holcomb commandancies, see Brig. Gen. Robert H. Williams, USMC, *The Old Corps: A Portrait of the U.S. Marine Corps between the Wars* (Annapolis: Naval Institute Press, 1982), chaps. 7–10.

69. CMC, "Annual Report for Fiscal Year 1936."

70. Headquarters Bulletin 129 of 15 June 1936.

71. CMC, "Annual Report" (for fiscal years 1934, 1935, and 1936) and *Final Report of 2 September 1936.*

72. J. Smith Oral History, 208. Smith gives a detailed account of what happened: the contenders, how the announcement was made, and the atmosphere that night (204–8). For the Quantico view, see *Quantico Sentry,* 13 Nov. 1936.

73. Public comments on his service can be found in the *New York Times,* 26 Nov., 4 Dec. 1936, and *Quantico Sentry,* 18 Dec. 1936.

74. Astor, *Footprints,* 194–96. Copies of all Russell articles for the *San Diego Union* can be found in Box 3, Russell Papers.

75. An account of Russell's death is contained in Astor, *Footprints,* 224–26.

76. Maj. John Thomason to Maj. Gen. J. C. Breckinridge, 24 May 1936, J. C. Breckinridge Papers, Archives, MCRC.

Chapter 17. Thomas Holcomb

1. I gratefully acknowledge the research assistance of the Citadel Development Foundation, the Military History Institute, U.S. Army War College, and the National Endowment for the Humanities. In addition, I wish particularly to express my appreciation for the invaluable support rendered by the following institutions: the Marine Corps Historical Center (especially Brig. Gen. E. H. Simmons and Evelyn Englander), Washington Navy Yard; the Breckinridge Library, Education Center, Marine Corps Development and Education Command, Quantico, Va.; the George C. Marshall Research Library, Lexington, Va.; and the National Archives of the

United States and the Library of Congress, Washington, D.C. For a listing of commandants and their ranks and tours, see Department of the Navy, *United States Marine Corps Ranks and Grades, 1798–1962,* Marine Corps Historical Reference Series, Number 11 (Washington, D.C.: Historical Branch, G-3, HQMC, 1962), App. A, 41–42.

2. For strengths, see Samuel E. Morison, *History of United States Naval Operations in World War II,* 15 vols. (Boston: Atlantic Little Brown, 1947–62), vol. 15, Supplement and General Index, table 16, p. 116, quoting SecNav, *Annual Report,* 10 Jan. 1946.

3. Holcomb to Vandegrift, 23 Nov. 1943, Box 81, Thomas Holcomb Papers, PPC (hereafter cited as Holcomb Papers). This collection has been superbly ordered and catalogued by Gibson B. Smith.

4. Quoted in Theodore Ropp, *War in the Modern World* (Toronto: Collier Books, 1969), 306.

5. Prime Minister Winston Churchill to Field Marshal Wilson, 30 Mar. 1945, quoted in Forrest C. Pogue, *George C. Marshall: Organizer of Victory, 1943–1945* (New York: Viking, 1973), 585; Forrest C. Pogue, interview with author, Washington, D.C., 29 June 1977.

6. Service Record of Thomas Holcomb, Sheet No. 1 and Military History of Lieutenant General Thomas Holcomb, USMC, 0436-1/AHC-303-mls, Holcomb Papers; Military Record/Record of Data in Thomas Holcomb 17th CMC, Holcomb Biographical File, Reference Section, H&MD (hereafter cited as HBF).

7. News clipping, marked *Journal–Every Evening,* Wilmington, Del., 1943, HBF.

8. News clipping, marked *Journal–Every Evening,* Wilmington, Del., 13 Mar. 1942, HBF; Report of Physical Examination, 27 Dec. 1943 and Service Record of Thomas Holcomb, Sheet No. 1, Holcomb Papers.

9. Service Record, Sheet No. 1, Holcomb Papers. The Corps adopted the U.S. rifle, caliber .30, or Krag-Jorgenson, in 1900. Metcalf, *History of the United States Marine Corps,* 250–51.

10. Service Record, Sheet Nos. 1–3, and Military History of Lieutenant General Thomas Holcomb, 3, Holcomb Papers. For a detailed account of these matches, see Robert E. Barde, *The History of Marine Corps Competitive Marksmanship* (Washington, D.C.: Marksmanship Branch, G-3, HQMC, 1961), 9–47 and App. L, 437–45.

11. Service Record, Sheet Nos. 2–4; Naval Attaché Tokyo to Secretary of the Navy, 21 May 1914; and CMC to Capt. Thomas Holcomb, 26 June 1914 (all in Holcomb Papers). On Stilwell, see Barbara M. Tuchman, *Stilwell and the American Experience in China, 1911–1945* (New York: Macmillan, 1971), 25–41.

12. Military History of Lieutenant General Thomas Holcomb, 3, Holcomb Papers. For the Corps's response to the move, see Millett, *Semper Fidelis,* 137–44.

13. President Theodore Roosevelt to Franklin Delano Roosevelt, 18 Mar. 1913, in Morison, *Letters of Theodore Roosevelt,* 7:714 and fn., "Places held by both Roosevelts." For FDR in those years, see Kenneth S. Davis, *FDR: The Beckoning of Destiny, 1882–1928: A History* (New York: G. P. Putnam's Sons, 1972), 208–10, 213; James M. Burns, *Roosevelt: The Lion and the Fox* (New York: Harcourt, Brace, 1956).

14. News clipping marked the "*Arizona [Star?]:* An Independent Newspaper, Tucson, Arizona, 121 (Jan. 30, 1962)," lodged in HBF; Barde, *Competitive Marksmanship,* 45–48; Service Record, Sheet No. 4, Holcomb Papers; and *Time* 36 (11 Nov. 1940), portrait (cover) and 21–24.

15. Service Record, Sheet No. 5, and Military History of Lieutenant General Thomas Holcomb, 4–5, Holcomb Papers; John W. Thomason Jr., *Fix Bayonets!* (New York: Scribner's 1926), x–xiii. Woodrow Wilson quoted in Heinl, *Soldiers of the Sea,* 219.

16. For Holcomb's views of serving with U.S. Army units in the Second Division, see Holcomb to Lt. Gen. Robert L. Bullard, USA (Ret.), 15 Feb. 1937, Box 1, Holcomb Papers; for the role of his first brigade commander, see Harbord, *American Army in France,* 274–300; Department of the Army, *United States Army in the World War, 1917–1919* (Washington, D.C.: Historical Division, Department of the Army, 1948), 328–29; and Weigley, *History,* 355–94.

17. Service Record, Sheet Nos. 6–7, and Military History of Lieutenant General Thomas Holcomb, 5, Holcomb Papers; German Army Military Intelligence Summary, quoted in *Leatherneck Magazine,* Nov. 1957, 82; Harbord, *American Army in France,* 355.

18. Frederick Palmer, *Newton D. Baker: America at War,* 2 vols. (New York: Dodd, Mead, 1931), 2:222; Report by Commanding General, V Corps, AEF, 2 Nov. 1918, quoted in Heinl, *Soldiers of the Sea,* 218; and Military History of Lt. Gen. Thomas Holcomb, 5, Holcomb Papers.

19. U.S. Department of the Navy, *Register of Retired Commissioned and Warrant Officers, Regular and Reserve, of the United States Navy and Marine Corps* (Washington, D.C.: GPO, 1964), 446; and *New York Times,* 15 May 1965, HBF.

20. John A. Lejeune to Thomas Holcomb, 22 Nov. 1937, Box 1, Folder No. 10, Holcomb Papers.

21. Harold Sprout and Margaret Sprout, *Toward a New Order of Sea Power: American Naval Policy and the World Scene, 1918–1922* (Princeton: Princeton University Press, 1946), 3–160; Clark G. Reynolds, *The Fast Carriers: The Forging of an Air Navy* (New York: McGraw-Hill, 1968), 1–21; Raymond G. O'Connor, "The U.S. Marines in the 20th Century: Amphibious Warfare and Doctrinal Debates," *Military Affairs* 38 (Oct. 1974): 97–103.

22. The standard account is Isely and Crowl, *U.S. Marines and Amphibious War,* esp. 3–44; Clifford, *Progress and Purpose,* 25–39.

23. Department of the Army, *Army War College Directory: Present Staff and Faculty, Former Staff and Faculty, President Resident Class, and Graduates (Resident and Nonresident), 1905–1976* (Carlisle Barracks, Pa.: Army War College, 1976), 160–61; Heinl, *Soldiers of the Sea,* 207; Dion Williams, "The Education of a Marine Officer," *Marine Corps Gazette* 18 (Nov. 1934): 24–32; Service Record, Sheet Nos. 9–12, Holcomb Papers.

24. Record of Educational Qualifications, Thomas Holcomb, 19 Nov. 1924, and Lt. Col. J. G. Pillow to Holcomb, 19 June 1925, Holcomb Papers; Editors, Army Times, *The Challenge and The Triumph: The Story of General Dwight D. Eisenhower* (New York: G. P. Putnam's Sons, 1966), 36–39; and Service Record, Sheet No. 9, Holcomb Papers.

25. For the Naval War College, see Spector, *Professors of War,* esp. 144–51; Service Record, n.p.; NWC Senior Class of 1931, Department of Operations, Operations Problem I; Discussion and Critique of Operations Problem IV—1931, Strategical Phase, dated 6-31; Operations Problem III—1931, 5 Jan. 1931; certificate of graduation (copy to major general commandant) for Col. Thomas Holcomb, U.S. Marine Corps, 27 May 1931, all in Holcomb Papers.

26. Department of the Army, *Army War College Directory,* 160–61.

27. For the Army War College (AWC), see George S. Pappas, *Prudens Futuri: The U.S. Army War College, 1901–1967* (Carlisle Barracks, Pa.: Alumni Association of the U.S. Army War College, 1967), 123–37; Card Catalogue Index of AWC Student Theses, AWC; Rudyard Kipling, "Soldier An' Sailor Too," in *Collected Verse,* by Rudyard Kipling (New York: Doubleday, 1946), 305–7.

28. See Ellis B. Miller, "The Marine Corps in Support of the Fleet," revised from lectures delivered by Col. E. B. Miller at the Naval War College and Marine Corps Schools (Quantico,

Va.: Marine Corps Schools, 1933); General Order No. 241, 7 Dec. 1933, quoted in Clifford, *Progress and Purpose,* 45; Service Record, n.p., Holcomb Papers; Military History of Lieutenant General Thomas Holcomb, 7, Holcomb Papers; Military History and Interview, Author and Cadet Joseph Britt with Gen. Edwin A. Pollock, 5 Nov. 1977, Charleston, S.C. Included in the membership of the "Tentative Manual" study group were 1st Lts. William O. Brice and Edwin A. Pollock, from the Citadel's classes of 1921 and 1922, respectively, both future general officers. Clifford, *Progress and Purpose,* 45–48, traces the advent of the "Tentative Manual."

29. Charles A. Fleming, R. L. Austin, and C. A. Braley III, *Quantico: Crossroads of the Marine Corps* (Washington, D.C.: H&MD, 1978), 65–68; Nalty and Moody, *Marine Corps Officer Procurement, 1775–1969,* 8–14; Department of the Navy, *The Marine Corps Reserve: A History* (Washington, D.C.: Division of Reserve, HQMC, 1966), 45, 64–70.

30. Service Record, Sheet Nos. 11–12, and Military History of Lieutenant General Thomas Holcomb, 7, Holcomb Papers; and Metcalf, *History of the United States Marine Corps,* 540–46.

31. Lyman to Colonel Drum, 7 Dec. 1936; Lyman to Hon. G. A. Davidson, 15 Jan. 1937; Lyman to Maj. Carleton Penn, 18 Nov. 1936; Lyman to Col. Holland Smith, 13 Nov. 1936; all in Extracts from Personal Correspondence of General Lyman: The Appointment of General Holcomb as Major General Commandant, marked "20 Feb. 1937?"

32. Service Record, Sheet No. 12, Holcomb Papers; *Time* 36 (11 Nov. 1940): 24.

33. See Chairman, Navy General Board to Secretary of the Navy, memo, 31 Aug. 1939, quoted in Millett, *Semper Fidelis,* 342; Tables of Organization (Peace Strength) U.S. Marine Corps, Approved 6 February 1935; George C. Dyer, *On the Treadmill to Pearl Harbor: The Memoirs of Admiral James O. Richardson* (Washington, D.C.: Naval History Division, 1974), 31–64.

34. Extracts from CMC, "Annual Report for the Fiscal Year 1935," press release of 15 Dec. 1935, 5, copy in Army War College Library; Metcalf, *History of the United States Marine Corp,* 545–46; Nalty and Moody, *Marine Corps Officer Procurement,* 6–9; and Lewis Metzger, "The Basic School—1939," *Marine Corps Gazette* 65 (Nov. 1981): 22–24.

35. MGC letter, Holcomb to Brig. Gen. F. L. Bradman, 23 Feb. 1937, Folder 3, Box 1, Holcomb Papers.

36. Holcomb to Gen. George C. Marshall, 5 Nov. 1940, and COS Marshall to Holcomb, 6 Nov. 1940, both in Box 4, Holcomb Papers. For the development of landing craft, see George C. Dyer, *The Amphibians Came to Conquer: The Story of Admiral Richmond Kelly Turner,* 2 vols. (Washington, D.C.: GPO, 1969) 1:202–6; Clifford, *Progress and Purpose,* 44–57.

37. Clifford, *Progress and Purpose,* 48–57.

38. Geoffrey Perret, *There's a War to Be Won: The United States Army in World War II* (New York: Ballantine Books, 1997), 181.

39. For Army efforts, see ibid., 181–83, and Weigley, *History,* 478–80.

40. See MGC Holcomb to Lt. Col. James Roosevelt, 23 Nov., 7 Dec. 1937, and 1, 3, 27 Feb. and 22 Mar. 1939; James Roosevelt to Holcomb, 23 Jan., 2 Feb., and 1 Mar. 1939, Boxes 1–3, Holcomb Papers.

41. Martha Anne Turner, "Legend and Legacy of John W. Thomason," *Marine Corps Gazette* 63 (Nov. 1979): 59–72; Holcomb to Lt. Col. John W. Thomason, 21 Feb. and 23 Mar. 1939, and Holcomb to Harry Warner of Warner Brothers Pictures, 27 Jan. 1944, Boxes 1–3 and 8, Holcomb Papers. For the movies, see John B. Moran, *Creating a Legend: The Complete Record of Writing About the United States Marine Corps* (Chicago: Moran/Andrews, 1973), 633–45.

42. Ronald H. Spector, *Eagle Against the Sun* (New York: Free Press, 1985), 54–71, for U.S. plans.

43. Weigley, *History,* 444, 448; and Perret, *There's a War to Be Won,* 127–44, 311.

44. Weigley, *History,* 424–75; Perret, *There's a War to Be Won,* 311.

45. Isely and Crowl, *U.S. Marines and Amphibious War,* 61–67; O'Connor, "U.S. Marines in the 20th Century," 101; Weigley, *History,* 451–82; Gen. Mark W. Clark, interview with John W. Gordon, Charleston, S.C., 3 May 1981.

46. Perret, *There's a War to Be Won,* 311; and Clifford, *Amphibious Warfare,* 144–59.

47. Clark, interview with Gordon; Millett, *Semper Fidelis,* 350–51.

48. Holcomb to Lt. Gen. George S. Patton Jr., 14 Aug. 1943, Box 3; Patton to Mrs. Thomas Holcomb, 25 Feb. 1939, Box 3; and Holcomb to Carl Vinson, 9 Jan. 1941, Box 4, all in Holcomb Papers.

49. Holcomb to Samuel W. Meek, 17 Jan. 1944, Holcomb Papers; *Time* 36 (11 Nov. 1940): 22.

50. Department of the Navy, *Marine Corps Reserve,* 59; and Robert Sherrod, *History of Marine Corps Aviation in World War II* (Washington, D.C.: Combat Forces Press, 1952), 130, Appendix 7, 435.

51. *Time* 36 (11 Nov. 1940): cover and 21–24; *New York Times,* 25 May 1965, p. 41.

52. Great Britain, War Office, *Combined Operations: The Official Story of the Commandos* (New York: Macmillan, 1943); U.S. War Department, *Organization and Training of British Commandos* (Washington, D.C.: Military Intelligence Service, 1942), 11–17; Evelyn Waugh, "Commando Raid on Bardia," *Life,* 17 Nov. 1941, 63–74; "Raid on Rommel," *Newsweek,* 12 Jan. 1942, 18; and "British Commandos Raid Hitler's Europe," *Life,* 26 Jan. 1942, 17–21.

53. John W. Gordon, "The U.S. Marine Corps and an Experiment in Military Elitism: A Reassessment of the Special Warfare Impetus, 1937–1943" (paper presented at the Third Naval History Symposium, U.S. Naval Academy, Annapolis, Md., Oct. 1977), published in Robert W. Love, ed., *Changing Interpretations and New Sources in Naval History* (New York: Garland, 1980).

54. Ibid.; John A. White, "Parachute Troops," *Marine Corps Gazette* 24 (June 1940): 11–14; Sherrod, *History of Marine Corps Aviation,* 129; and Charles L. Updegraph, *Special Marine Corps Units of World War II* (Washington, D.C.: H&MD, 1972), 36–53. See "Broadcast by Lieutenant General Thomas Holcomb, Commandant of USMC, on March of Time Program, Thursday, August 13, 1942," HBF.

55. Lt. Col. R. D. Heinl to General Selden, memo, Information received from General Holcomb relative to original status of CMC vis-à-vis the Joint Chiefs of Staff, 18 Apr. 1949, AG-1319-fkf; Service Record, Sheet No. 13; all in Holcomb Papers.

56. See Frank O. Hough, V. E. Ludwig, and Henry I. Shaw Jr., *Pearl Harbor to Guadalcanal* (Washington, D.C.: Historical Branch, HQMC, 1958); Robert Leckie, *Strong Men Armed: The United States Marines Against Japan* (New York: Random House, 1962); and George McMillan, *The Old Breed: A History of the First Marine Division of World War II* (Washington, D.C.: Infantry Journal Press, 1949), as the standard accounts.

57. Herbert C. Merillat, *Guadalcanal Remembered* (New York: Dodd, Mead, 1982), 22–29.

58. "Broadcast by Lieutenant General Thomas Holcomb, March of Time Program Thursday, August 13, 1942," HBF; James M. Burns, *Roosevelt: The Soldier of Freedom* (New York: Harcourt Brace Jovanovich, 1920), 284; *Washington Times-Herald,* 28 Oct. 1942, HBF.

59. News clipping, unknown newspaper, 27 Nov. 1942, and the *Washington, D.C. News,* 7 Nov. 1942, both in HBF.

60. See Gen. A. A. Vandegrift with Robert Asprey, *Once a Marine: The Memoirs of General A. A. Vandegrift, United States Marine Corps* (New York: Norton, 1964) and John L. Zimmerman, *The Guadalcanal Campaign* (Washington, D.C.: Historical Division, HQMC, 1949), v.

61. John Winton, *Ultra in the Pacific: How Breaking Japanese Codes and Ciphers Affected Naval Operations Against Japan, 1941–45* (Annapolis: Naval Institute Press, 1993), 66–114; and Herbert C. Merillat, "The 'Ultra Weapon' at Guadalcanal," *Marine Corps Gazette* 66 (Sept. 1982): 44–49.

62. Pfeiffer Oral History, 197–99; transcript of Oral History with Lt. Gen. Alan Shapley, 1971, 73–82, OHC; James Roosevelt's Copies of Opns Orders for Makin Island Raid, 7 Aug. 42/PC 112; 1st Raider Bn-Rep of Oper-7–9 Oct. 42-Guadalcanal/A38-1; 2d Raider Bn-Observations on, at Aola, Guadalcanal, 3 Nov.–4 Dec. 42/A39.5-1; 2d Raider Bn-Misc Reports, all in OA; Gordon, "Experiment in Military Elitism," 362–73.

63. Dyer, *Amphibians Came to Conquer,* 448–52; Pfeiffer Oral History, 213; Updegraph, *Special Marine Corps Units,* quoting CinCPac to CMC, 24 Sept. 42, 15–16, 22–25.

64. Updegraph, *Special Marine Corps Units,* 34, quoting Asst., PacSec, War Plans Div., CNO to ACS, memo, 24 Dec. 1943.

65. Millett, *Semper Fidelis,* 371–73. See also Louis Morton, *Pacific Command: A Study in Interservice Relations,* Harmon Memorial Lectures in Military History 3 (Colorado Springs, Colo.: USAFA, 1961), 1–29.

66. Sherrod, *History of Marine Corps Aviation,* 111, 132–69, 171, 219, 255–56.

67. Kenneth W. Condit, Gerald Diamond, and Edwin T. Turnbladh, *Marine Corps Ground Training in World War II* (Washington, D.C.: Historical Branch, G-3, HQMC, 1956), 165–66, 288.

68. Morison, *History of United States Naval Operations,* vol. 15, table 16, p. 116.

69. Department of the Navy, *Marine Corps Reserve,* 27–82.

70. Forrest C. Pogue, *George C. Marshall: The Education of a General, 1880–1939* (New York: Viking, 1963), 260; Pogue interview, 29 June 1977; Morris Janowitz, *The Professional Soldier: A Social and Political Portrait* (Glencoe, Ill.: Free Press, 1960), 100.

71. Henry I. Shaw Jr. and Ralph W. Donnelly, *Blacks in the Marine Corps* (Washington, D.C.: H&MD, 1975), 1, quoting Executive Order No. 8802, 25 June 1941, and Morris J. MacGregor, *Integration of the Armed Forces, 1940–1965* (Washington, D.C.: Center of Military History, U.S. Army, 1981), 3–5.

72. Shaw and Donnelly, *Blacks in the Marine Corps,* 1; and MacGregor, *Integration of the Armed Forces,* 100, quoting Navy General Board, "Plan for the Expansion of the USMC," 18 Apr. 1941 (No. 139).

73. MacGregor, *Integration of the Armed Forces,* quoting idem to Sen. Arthur Copper, 1 Aug. 1940; memo, Rear Adm. W. R. Sexton to Capt. Morton L. Deyo, 17 Sept. 1940; and Shaw and Donnelly, *Blacks in the Marine Corps,* 2–27.

74. Isely and Crowl, *U.S. Marines and Amphibious War,* 192–213.

75. CMC Holcomb to Maj. Gen. Julian C. Smith, 25 Nov. 1943, Holcomb Papers; CMC Holcomb to Lt. Gen. A. A. Vandegrift, 23 Nov. 1943, Holcomb Papers; Robert Sherrod, "Marines' Show: Report in Tarawa," *Time,* 6 Dec. 1943, 24–25. The standard account is Robert Sherrod, *Tarawa* (New York: Duell, Sloan, and Pearce, 1944).

76. Isely and Crowl, *U.S. Marines and Amphibious War,* 248–52, 220–23, and Dyer, *Amphibians Came to Conquer,* 702–16, 659–82.

77. Heinl to Selden, memo, 18 Apr. 1949; CMC letter, Holcomb to Secretary of the Navy Frank Knox, 30 Nov. 1943, Box 7; SecNav letter, Knox to Holcomb, 1 Dec. 1943, all in Holcomb Papers.

78. Service Record, Sheet Nos. 14–15, Holcomb Papers.

79. "The Commandants: Alexander A. Vandegrift," *Marine Corps Gazette* 59 (Nov. 1975); Holland M. Smith and Percy Finch, *Coral and Brass* (New York: Scribner's, 1949), 164, 213; and Heinl, *Soldiers of the Sea,* 296.

80. J. Smith Oral History, 1968, 164; Millett, *Semper Fidelis,* 405.

81. Knox to Holcomb, 1 Jan. 1944, Holcomb Papers, and Press Release, "Lieutenant General Thomas Holcomb, USMC, Will Become General," 31 Dec. 1943, HBF.

82. Service Record, Sheet Nos. 14–15 and Press Release, "General Holcomb, USMC, Decorated with Distinguished Service Medal," 12 Apr. 1944, HBF; Holcomb to Edward R. Stettinius, 17 Jan. 1944, Holcomb Papers.

83. J. Smith Oral History, 180, and the *Washington Post,* 26 May 1965.

84. Leonard Snider to Holcomb, 26 Jan. 1955; Holcomb to Snider, 28 Jan. 1944, both in Holcomb Papers; *Washington Post,* 15 Aug. 1962, p. B7, and Service Information Release, HQMC, 14 Nov. 1962/RWA-180-62, HBF.

85. Press Release, AP 158, 24 Apr. 1964; clipping, Navy Times (22 Apr. 1964), HBF; Service Record, Sheet Nos. 1–15; Holcomb to Samuel W. Meek, 17 Jan. 1944, Report of Physical Examination, 27 Dec. 1943, all in Holcomb Papers; Daniel E. Mengedoht, M.D., and William Tate, M.D., interviews with author, 11 Jan. 1982, Charleston, S.C.; *New York Times,* 25 May 1965, p. 41; *Time* 85 (4 June 1965): 86; *Marine Corps Gazette* 49 (July 1965): 1; and Service Information Release, n.d., BAM-154-65, HBF. *Washington Post,* 26 May 1965, HBF; *Time* 85 (4 June 1965): 86; *New York Times,* 25 May 1965, p. 41; and BAM-165-65 HBF.

86. J. Smith Oral History, 178, and Pfeiffer Oral History, 233–37; Robert W. Love, "Ernest Joseph King," in *The Chiefs of Naval Operations,* ed. Robert W. Love (Annapolis: Naval Institute Press, 1980), 160–62; Maj. Gen. Charles H. Lyman to Holcomb, 12 July 1938, Box 2, Holcomb Papers.

87. Paolo E. Coletta, ed., *American Secretaries of the Navy,* 2 vols. (Annapolis: Naval Institute Press, 1980), 2:655–727; Pfeiffer Oral History, 237, 240; and John Major, "William Daniel Leahy," in Love, *Chiefs of Naval Operations,* 115–16.

88. A. J. Barker, *British and American Infantry Weapons of World War II* (New York: ARCO, 1969), 28.

89. See "The United States Marine Corps" in SecNav, *Annual Report for Fiscal Year 1943,* 84–87.

90. Condit et al., *Marine Corps Ground Training,* 57–99, 165–66; Metzger, "Basic School," 22–24; Samuel Hynes, *Flights of Passage: Reflections of a World War II Aviator* (New York and Annapolis: Frederic C. Beil and Naval Institute Press, 1988), 148–50.

91. Millett, *Semper Fidelis,* 499–501; and J. D. Nicholas and William O. Spears, *The Joint and Combined Staff Officers Manual* (Harrisburg, Pa.: Stockpile, 1959), 22; see Weigley, *History,* 422–23; Love, *Chiefs of Naval Operations,* xiii–xxii; Condit, Johnstone, and Nargele, *Brief History,* 17–22.

Chapter 18. Alexander A. Vandegrift

1. Dale Carnegie, "Little Known Facts," 19 Feb. 1943, Box 2, Alexander A. Vandegrift Papers, PPC (hereafter cited as AAV Papers); transcripts of Oral History with Brig. Gen. Robert C. Kilmartin, 1979, 197, and Gen. Gerald C. Thomas, 1966, 2–3, OHC (hereafter cited as Kilmartin Oral History or Thomas Oral History).

2. Robert B. Asprey to Kurt Hellmer, 9 Apr. 1962, Box 11, AAV Papers.

3. MGC to Vandegrift, 10 Nov. 1915, Box 1; Harold Wood to Vandegrift, 30 May 1943, Box 2, AAV Papers.

4. Gen. Merrill B. Twining Appreciation, June 1987, copy provided courtesy of Ben Frank (hereafter cited as Twining Appreciation).

5. Transcript of Oral History with Lt. Gen. William J. Van Ryzin, 1976, 51, OHC (hereafter Van Ryzin Oral History); Thomas Oral History, 116.

6. Vandegrift to Charles H. Lyman, 14 Jan. 1936, Box 1, AAV Papers.

7. Transcript of Oral History with Brig. Gen. Robert H. Williams, 1983, 269, OHC (hereafter cited as Williams Oral History).

8. Col. Joseph Rossell to Vandegrift, 16 Feb. 1940, Box 1, AAV Papers.

9. Maj. Gen. Thomas Holcomb to Capt. Fielding Robinson, 10 Jan. 1940, Box 7, Holcomb Papers.

10. Memo to FDR, 13 Jan. 1941, Box 18-E, FDR Papers; Brig. Gen. Holland M. Smith to Vandegrift, 19 Dec. 1940, Box 1, AAV Papers.

11. Vandegrift to Brig. Gen. Charles F. B. Price, 8 July 1941, Box 2, AAV Papers.

12. Vandegrift to Brig. Gen. John Marston, 29 June 1940, Box 1, AAV Papers.

13. Vandegrift to Maj. Gen. William P. Upshur, 16 Aug. 1941, Box 2, AAV Papers.

14. Thomas Oral History, 608; Williams Oral History, 272; Vandegrift to Ruth Jeffcott, 7 Nov. 1939, Alexander A. Vandegrift Biographical File, Reference Section, H&MD (hereafter cited as AAV Biographical File).

15. H. M. Smith to Vandegrift, 4 Feb. 1940; Vandegrift to Col. Allen H. Turnage, 19 Feb. 1940, Box 1, AAV Papers.

16. Vandegrift to Marston, 22 July 1940, Box 1, AAV Papers.

17. Holcomb to Brig. Gen. Philip H. Torrey, 4 Oct. 1941, Box 8, Holcomb Papers.

18. Vandegrift to Col. Leroy P. Hunt, 22 Oct. 1941; Twining to ADC, 26 Nov. 1941, Box 2, AAV Papers; Twining Appreciation.

19. Twining Appreciation.

20. Transcript of Oral History with Gen. Graves B. Erskine, 1975, 290, OHC; Kilmartin Oral History, 234; del Valle Oral History, 129–31, Allan R. Millett, *In Many a Strife* (Annapolis: Naval Institute Press, 1993), 156.

21. See Millett, *In Many a Strife;* Gen. Merrill B. Twining, *No Bended Knee* (Novato, Calif.: Presidio Press, 1996); Jon T. Hoffman, *Once a Legend: 'Red Mike' Edson of the Marine Raiders* (Novato, Calif.: Presidio Press, 1994).

22. Vandegrift to Brig. Gen. Arch F. Howard, 7 Nov. 1942, Box 2, AAV Papers; Thomas Oral History, 371.

23. Twining Appreciation; Vandegrift, *Once a Marine,* 119–20.

24. Twining, *No Bended Knee,* 114; Rear Adm. Richmond K. Turner to Vandegrift, 28 Sept. 1942, Box 9, AAV Papers.

25. Thomas Oral History, 398; Pfeiffer Oral History, 199–204.

26. Vandegrift to Howard, 7 Nov. 1942; Holcomb to Vandegrift, 17 Nov. 1942, Box 2, AAV Papers.

27. Thomas Oral History, 374–75.

28. Press Release, 29 Aug. 1942, AAV Biographical File.

29. Twining Appreciation.

30. Holcomb to Vandegrift, 15 Sept. 1942, Box 9, Holcomb Papers; Holcomb to Vandegrift, 14 Aug. 1942, Box 2, AAV Papers.

31. Holcomb to Maj. Gen. Douglas C. McDougal, 14 Aug. 1942, Box 9, Holcomb Papers; *Time,* 2 Nov. 1942.

32. Holcomb to Vandegrift, 15 Sept. 1942, Box 9, Holcomb Papers; Holcomb to Vandegrift, 29 Sept. 1942, Box 2, AAV Papers.

33. Holcomb to Vandegrift, 29 Sept. and 13 Dec. 1942, Box 2, AAV Papers.

34. Holcomb to Vandegrift, 13 and 15 Dec. 1942, Box 2, AAV Papers PPC.

35. Holcomb to Vandegrift, 14 Aug. and 29 Sept. 1942, Box 2, AAV Papers.

36. Holcomb to Vandegrift, 15 Dec. 1942, Box 2, AAV Papers.

37. Vandegrift to Adm. William F. Halsey and Vandegrift to Holcomb, 1 Jan. 1943; Vandegrift to Maj. Gen. Clayton B. Vogel, 20 Dec. 1943, Box 9, AAV Papers.

38. Dale Carnegie, "Little Known Facts," 19 Feb. 1943, Box 2, AAV Papers.

39. Holcomb to Adm. Chester A. Nimitz, 3 Feb. 1943, Box 10, Holcomb Papers.

40. Vandegrift, memo for Colonel Riley, 5 Feb. 1943, Box 9, AAV Papers.

41. Holcomb to James V. Forrestal, 28 June 1943, Box 2, AAV Papers.

42. Vandegrift to Holcomb, 10, 16 July, and 6 Oct. 1943; Holcomb to Vandegrift, 29 June 1943, Box 9; Holcomb to Adm. Ernest J. King, 7 July 1943, Box 2, AAV Papers; transcript of Oral History with Brig. Gen. F. P. Henderson, 1974–76, 336, OHC.

43. Vandegrift to Holcomb, 16 July 43, Box 9, AAV Papers.

44. Holcomb to Vandegrift, 14 July 1943, Box 9; 17 July 1843, Box 2, AAV Papers.

45. Holcomb to Vandegrift, 11 and 13 Aug. 1943, Box 9; Vandegrift to Holcomb, 23 Aug. 1943, Box 2, AAV Papers; transcript of Oral History with Gen. Merrill B. Twining, 1967, 238 (hereafter cited as Twining Oral History).

46. Holcomb to Vandegrift, 15 July 1943; Vandegrift to Holcomb, 28 Aug. 1943, Box 10, Holcomb Papers; Vandegrift to Maj. Gen. William H. Rupertus, 27, 31 July 1943; Holcomb to H. M. Smith, 22 Oct. 1943, Box 9, AAV Papers.

47. Vandegrift to Holcomb, 14 Oct. 1943, Box 9, AAV Papers.

48. Rear Adm. Theodore S. Wilkinson to Halsey, 14 Oct. 1943, Box 9, AAV Papers.

49. Vandegrift to Holcomb, 4 Nov. 1943, Box 9, AAV Papers.

50. Holcomb to Vandegrift, 19 Nov. 1943, Box 2, AAV Papers.

51. Mrs. Allan G. Armstrong to Vandegrift, 30 Nov. 1943, Box 2, AAV Papers. For more on the reaction to the Tarawa operation, see the Holcomb essay in this volume.

52. Vandegrift, "Legion Address," 14 Dec. 1943, Box 2, AAV Papers; Vandegrift, *Once a Marine,* 235; Jon T. Hoffman, "Red Mike Fights On," *Naval History* (Nov./Dec. 1993): 17.

53. Vandegrift, *Once a Marine,* 238; Holcomb to Vandegrift, 23 Nov. 1943, Box 2, AAV Papers.

54. Holcomb to Vandegrift, 6 Aug. 1943, Box 9, AAV Papers.

55. Lt. Col. E. R. Hagenah to Vandegrift, 20 June 1943, Box 9, AAV Papers.

56. Vandegrift to Holcomb, 6 and 14 Oct. 1943; Holcomb to Vandegrift, 6 Apr., 6 Aug. 1943, Box 9, AAV Papers; Thomas to Brig. Gen. Merritt A. Edson, 14 Oct. 1944, Box 6, Merritt A. Edson Papers, Manuscript Division, LC (hereafter cited as Edson Papers). For a somewhat different perspective on the role of Holcomb and the Marine Corps relative to the acceptance of the specialized units such as the Raider and Parachute battalions, see the essay on Holcomb in this volume.

57. Holcomb to Vandegrift, 23 Nov. 1943, Box 2, AAV Papers; Pfeiffer memo, 24 Dec. 1943, and CNO to CMC, 25 Dec. 1943, Parachute Subject File, Reference Section, H&MD; Updegraph, *Special Marine Corps Units,* 53, 60, 75.

58. Edson to Thomas, 6 Oct. and 25 Nov. 1944; Thomas to Edson, 9 Nov. 1944, Box 6, Edson Papers; Vandegrift to Holcomb, 7 Apr. 1945, Box 9; Vandegrift to Maj. Gen. Thomas E. Watson, 18 Sept. 1944; Vandegrift to Maj. Gen. Harry Schmidt, 19 Oct. 1944; Vandegrift to H. M. Smith, 9 July 1945, Box 3, AAV Papers; Henry I. Shaw Jr., Bernard C. Nalty, and Edwin T. Turnbladh, *History of U.S. Marine Corps Operations in World War II: Central Pacific Drive* (Washington, D.C.: USMC, 1966), 240, 636; Benis M. Frank and Henry I. Shaw Jr., *History of U.S. Marine Corps Operations in World War II: Victory and Occupation* (Washington, D.C.: USMC, 1967), 691–702, 840; Millett, *In Many a Strife,* 234–35.

59. Vandegrift to Maj. Gen. Ross E. Rowell, 3 Apr. 1945, Box 3; Vandegrift to Holcomb, 7 Apr. 1945; Vandegrift to Price, 25 May 1945, Box 9, AAV Papers.

60. Vandegrift to Edson, 3 Feb. 1945; Maj. Gen. Clifton B. Cates to Edson, 12 June 1945; del Valle to Edson, 10 May 1945; Thomas to Edson, 26 Feb. 1945, Box 6, Edson Papers; J. Smith to Vandegrift, 13 Dec. 1943; Vandegrift to Holcomb, 7 Nov. 1943; Vandegrift to H. M. Smith, 9 Feb. 1945, Box 9, AAV Papers; Turner to Holcomb, 13 Oct. 1943, Box 10, Holcomb Papers; Vandegrift, *Once a Marine,* 240.

61. Smith to Vandegrift, 7 Dec. 1943; Vandegrift to Holcomb, 7 Nov. 1943; Nimitz to Vandegrift, 3 Feb. 1944; Vandegrift to Holcomb, 6 June 1944, Box 9; Holcomb to Vandegrift, 19 Oct. 1943, Box 2, AAV Papers.

62. Vandegrift to Holcomb, 7 Apr. 1945, Box 9; Vandegrift to Maj. Gen. Joseph C. Fegan, 14 Mar. 1945, Box 3, AAV Papers; Turner to Holcomb, 13 Oct. 1943, Box 10, Holcomb Papers.

63. H. M. Smith to Nimitz, 27 Oct. 1943; Holcomb to Vandegrift, 4 Nov. 1943, Box 9, AAV Papers.

64. Edson to Thomas, 20 May 1945, Box 6, Edson Papers; Vandegrift to Holcomb, 6, 14, and 16 Oct. 1943; Holcomb to Vandegrift, 4 Nov. 1943; H. M. Smith to Vandegrift, 7 Dec. 1943, Box 9, AAV Papers.

65. Hoffman, *Once a Legend,* 302.

66. Holcomb to Vandegrift, 19 Oct. 1943, Box 2; Vandegrift to Holcomb, 16 Oct. 1943; Holcomb to Vandegrift, 4 Nov. 1943, Box 9, AAV Papers; Thomas to Edson, 19 Mar, 29 May, and 14 July 1945; Edson to Thomas, 19 June, 1 and 11 July 1945, Box 6; "The Growth and Development of the Service Command," Box 5, Edson Papers.

67. Thomas to Edson, 20 Oct. 1944; Vandegrift to Brig. Gen. Frank Whitehead, 30 July 1945; CG FMFPac to CMC re: Supply Service, c. Apr. 1945, Box 6, Edson Papers; Vandegrift to H. M. Smith, 12 June 1945, Box 9; "Comments on Termination of the European War," c. May 1945, Box 3, AAV Papers.

68. Price to Vandegrift, 28 Sept. 1944; Constituent to Congressman Richard J. Welch, 24 Aug. 1944; Draft Speech, c. July 1944, Box 3; Vandegrift to Holcomb, 24 Nov. 1944; H. M.

Smith to Vandegrift, 2 Nov. 1944, Box 9; Vandegrift to H. M. Smith, 5 and 15 Jan. 1944, Box 10, AAV Papers; Vandegrift to Holcomb, 13 July 1944, Box 1, Holcomb Papers; *Time,* 12 Mar. 1945.

69. Vandegrift to Holcomb, 5 Sept. and 24 Nov. 1944, Box 9; Vandegrift Statement, 11 May 1944, Box 11, AAV Papers.

70. J. Smith to Vandegrift, 27 May 1944; Vandegrift to J. Smith, 14 June 1944; Vandegrift to Price, 4 May 1944, Box 2; Holcomb to Vandegrift, 29 June 1943; Holcomb to H. M. Smith, 22 Oct. 1943, Box 9; Vandegrift to H. M. Smith, 27 June 1944, Box 10; Vandegrift Statement, 11 May 1944, Box 11, AAV Papers; Thomas Oral History, 545.

71. Rowell to Vandegrift, 14 and 27 May 1944, Box 2; Vandegrift to H. M. Smith, 26 Apr. 1944; Vandegrift to Rowell, 6 June 1944; Vandegrift to Holcomb, 7 Apr. and 6 June 1944, Box 9, AAV Papers; *Time,* 12 June and 23 Oct. 1944; *New York Times,* 28 July 1944.

72. Sherrod, *History of Marine Corps Aviation,* 329–33, 342.

73. Vandegrift to H. M. Smith, 26 Mar. 1945, Box 10; Vandegrift to H. M. Smith, 18 May 1945; Vandegrift to Holcomb, 6 June 1944; Maj. Gen. John H. Russell to Vandegrift, 19 Nov. 1944; Holcomb to Vandegrift, 2 Nov. 1944, Box 9; all in AAV Papers; Thomas to Edson, 14 Oct. 1944, Box 6, Edson Papers.

74. Vandegrift to Price, 13 June 1944, Box 9, and Vandegrift to H. M. Smith, 9 July 1945, Box 3, AAV Papers.

75. Vandegrift to Maj. Gen. Henry L. Larsen, 15 Jan. 1944; Col. Ruth Cheney Streeter to Vandegrift, 14 Feb. 1944; speech at Pennsylvania Military College, 28 Jan. 1944, Box 2, and Vandegrift to Erskine, 9 Oct. 1944, Box 3, AAV Papers; transcript of Oral History with Maj. Gen. John H. Masters, 1971, 68, OHC.

76. Vandegrift to H. M. Smith, 17 Aug. and 25 Sept. 1945; Vandegrift to Holcomb, 25 Oct. 1945, Box 3; Vandegrift to H. M. Smith, 4 Feb. 1946, Box 9; "Annual Report for Fiscal Year 1946," Box 10, AAV Papers.

77. Vandegrift to Lt. Gen. Roy S. Geiger, 5 Nov. 1945; Vandegrift to H. M. Smith, 29 Dec. 1945, Box 3; Vandegrift to Maj. Gen. Keller E. Rockey, 11 Jan. 1946; Geiger to Vandegrift, 11 Jan. 1946, Box 4, AAV Papers; Vandegrift to Geiger, 18 Oct. 1945, Box 4, Edson Papers; transcript of Oral History with Brig. Gen. Fred D. Beans, 1971, 111, OHC.

78. Vandegrift to Col. Melvin J. Maas, 9 Aug. 1945; Vandegrift to Holcomb, 25 Oct. 1945, Box 3; Vandegrift to Holcomb, 22 Apr. 1946, Box 9; "Annual Report for Fiscal Year 1946," Box 10, AAV Papers; PL 305, 21 Feb. 1946.

79. Vandegrift to H. M. Smith, 30 Nov. 1945; Vandegrift to Schmidt, 24 Oct. 1945, Box 3; Vandegrift to Rockey, 31 Oct. 1945, Box 9, AAV Papers. For detailed accounts of the 1946–47 unification struggle, see Hoffman, *Once a Legend,* 333–81; Millett, *In Many a Strife,* 245–59; Lt. Gen. Victor Krulak, *First to Fight: An Inside View of the U.S. Marine Corps* (Annapolis: Naval Institute Press, 1984); Col. Gordon W. Keiser, *The U.S. Marine Corps and Defense Unification: 1944–47* (Washington, D.C.: National Defense University Press, 1982).

80. Vandegrift to Marston, 26 Dec. 1945, Box 3; testimony to Senate Military Affairs Committee, 24 Oct. 1945, AAV Papers; entry for 2 Jan. 1946, 1946 Diary, Box 56, Edson Papers; Pfeiffer Oral History, 283.

81. "Statement of General Alexander A. Vandegrift, USMC, before the Senate Naval Affairs Committee at Hearings on S. 2044," AAV Papers.

82. Vandegrift to Geiger, 3 and 10 June 1946; Vandegrift to Maj. Gen. A. H. Noble, 11 and 24 June 1946; Vandegrift to Turnage, 30 Dec. 1946, Box 4; Vandegrift to Schmidt, 21 Aug. 1946; Vandegrift to Nimitz, 28 Aug. 1946; Vandegrift to Turnage, 12 Feb. 1947, Box 9; all in AAV Papers; Thomas Oral History, 681; Special Board, Marine Corps Schools, "Summary of Findings and Recommendations Respecting Future Amphibious Operations," 16 Dec. 1946, CMC-CNO Correspondence, Records of the U.S. Marine Corps, RG 127, NARA.

83. Millett, *In Many a Strife,* 243; Millett, *Semper Fidelis,* 447.

84. Vandegrift to H. M. Smith, 4 Feb. 1946, Box 9, AAV Papers; Millett, *In Many a Strife,* 230–34.

85. Vandegrift to Holcomb, 5 Nov. 1946, Box 9; Memo of Vandegrift presentation to Truman, 10 Dec. 1946, Box 11, AAV Papers; ALNAV 21, 18 Jan. 1947, Box 14, Edson Papers.

86. Vandegrift to Col. Melvin L. Krulewitch, 1 Apr. 1947; Vandegrift to Schmidt, 14 Apr. 1947; Vandegrift to Maj. Gen. E. P. Moses, 14 May 1947, Box 4; Vandegrift to Turnage, 12 Feb. 1947, Box 9, AAV Papers; Edson Diary, Apr.–May 1947, Box 56, Edson Papers; Twining Appreciation.

87. Vandegrift to Watson, 16 Apr. 1947; Vandegrift to Turnage, 9 June 1947; Vandegrift to Adm. Louis E. Denfield, 7 July 1947, Box 4; Vandegrift to Schmidt, 22 May 1947, Box 9; Vandegrift to Brig. Gen. Robert Kilmartin, 14 Dec. 1962, Box 11, AAV Papers; Van Ryzin Oral History, 106–16; Thomas Oral History, 715; transcript of Oral History with Lt. Gen. Louis E. Woods, 1968, 339, OHC; Twining Oral History, 294; Division of Aviation to CMC, 3 June 1947, File 1240, Records of the U.S. Marine Corps, RG 127, NARA.

88. Vandegrift to Turnage, 30 July 1947, and Vandegrift to Schmidt, 5 Aug. 1947, Box 4, AAV Papers.

89. Vandegrift to Thomas, 25 Nov. 1947, and Vandegrift to Maj. Gen. Lemuel C. Shepherd, 31 Dec. 1947, Box 4, AAV Papers; A. A. Vandegrift, "The Marine Corps in 1948," *USNIP* (Feb. 1948): 135–43; *New York Times,* 3 Jan. 1948; Vandegrift, *Once a Marine,* 327.

Chapter 19. Clifton Bledsoe Cates

1. Cates Oral History, 3–4.
2. *Time,* 5 July 1954.
3. Sgt. Harry Polete, "The New Commandant [Cates]," *Leatherneck* 31 (Mar. 1948): 24.
4. See Clifton B. Cates, "Battle of the Tenaru," *Marine Corps Gazette* 27 (Oct. 1943): 5; Vandegrift, *Once a Marine,* 99–204.
5. Polete, "New Commandant [Cates]," 27. See also Clifton B. Cates, "Iwo Jima," *Marine Corps Gazette* 49 (Feb. 1965): 28–31; Vandegrift, *Once a Marine,* 280–85.
6. Secretary of the Navy to Cates, late 1947, and Truman to Cates, 20 Dec. 1947, Clifton B. Cates Papers, PPC (hereafter cited as Cates Papers); Cates Oral History, 208; Vandegrift, *Once a Marine,* 327.
7. Polete, "New Commandant [Cates]," 23.
8. Cates Oral History, 208–9.
9. Ibid., 220–21.
10. Ibid., 222–23.
11. Ibid.

12. Ibid., 223–24; Smith and Finch, *Coral and Brass,* 168–80; H. M. Smith, "My Troubles with the Army on Saipan," *Saturday Evening Post* 231 (13 Nov. 1948): 32. See also thirteen pertinent documents on the controversy in "The Saipan Incident," *Army and Navy Register* 69 (27 Nov. 1948): 20.

13. Moskin, *Marine Corps Story,* 664; "Equality in Military Establishment," *Army and Navy Register* 69 (31 July 1948): 6.

14. Transcript of Oral History with Lt. Gen. Victor H. Krulak, U.S. Marine Corps (Ret.), 1964, 128–30, OHC (hereafter cited as Krulak Oral History).

15. O. P. Smith Oral History, 294.

16. Lynn Montross, Hubard K. Kuokka, and Norman W. Hicks, *U.S. Marine Operations in Korea, 1950–1953: The East Central Front,* 5 vols. (Washington, D.C.: HQMC, 1962), 4:187.

17. Edwin H. Simmons, *The United States Marines, 1775–1975* (New York: Viking, 1976), 230–31.

18. Krulak Oral History, 114–18; Vandegrift, *Once a Marine,* 319–20; Moskin, *Marine Corps Story,* 431.

19. Cates Oral History, 213–14. See also transcript of Oral History with Lt. Gen. William J. Wallace, USMC (Ret.), 1967, 120–21, OHC.

20. Heinl, *Soldiers of the Sea,* 563; "Presidential Visit," *Marine Corps Gazette* 34 (Aug. 1950): 29. See also 1st Lt. Roy L. Anderson, "The Marine Corps and the Helicopter," *Marine Corps Gazette* 33 (Aug. 1949): 13–19; 1st Lt. Nicholas Canzona, "The Atomic Bomb in Tactical Warfare," *Marine Corps Gazette* 34 (Sept. 1950): 34–37; Lt. Col. J. D. Hittle, "The Transport Helicopter: New Tool of Sea Power," *Marine Corps Gazette* 34 (Mar. 1950): 14–21; Capt. Robert A. Strieby, "Employment of the Small Helicopter," *Marine Corps Gazette* 34 (June 1950): 14–21; Lt. Col. Robert E. Cushman Jr., USMC, "Amphibious Warfare: Naval Weapon of the Future," *USNIP* 74 (Mar. 1948): 301–78. Photographs of the "Flying Banana" and of Truman are found in Fleming, Austin, and Braley, *Quantico,* 85–87.

21. Thomas Oral History, 715.

22. Steven L. Rearden, *History of the Office of the Secretary of Defense: The Formative Years, 1947–1950,* 2 vols. to date (Washington, D.C.: Office of the Secretary of Defense, 1984), 1:19–24.

23. Cates Oral History, 228; Krulak, *First to Fight,* 60–61.

24. Thomas Oral History, 917.

25. Ibid., 785.

26. Krulak Oral History, 119.

27. Transcript of Oral History with Gen. Vernon E. Megee, USMC (Ret.), 2 vols., 1973, 2:92, OHC (hereafter cited as Megee Oral History).

28. Cates Oral History, 217–18; Thomas Oral History, 788–90; Vandegrift, *Once a Marine,* 324–25. See also Shulimson, "First to Fight," 5–16, and Dennis E. Showalter, "The Evolution of the U.S. Marine Corps as a Military Elite," *Marine Corps Gazette* 63 (Nov. 1979): 44–58. According to Robert D. Heinl Jr., "The Marine Corps: Here to Stay," *USNIP* 76 (Oct. 1950): 1085, the British Marines were "a few ceremonial troops entrusted with very minor combat missions and with a multitude of odd jobs which range anywhere from acting as ships' butchers, bandsmen, and printers to manning landing craft to put the British army ashore."

29. Polete, "New Commandant [Cates]," 26.

30. Hamilton M. Hoyler, "Legal Status of the Marine Corps," *Marine Corps Gazette* 34 (Nov. 1950): 124–34.

31. Heinl, *Soldiers of the Sea,* 524–25.

32. Cates Oral History, 235. See also Robert D. Heinl Jr., "The Cat with More than Nine Lives," *USNIP* 80 (June 1954): 658–71.

33. Heinl in Thomas Oral History, 832.

34. Matthews to Tydings, 18 Apr. 1950, Cates Papers.

35. Undated report of conversation with Secretary Johnson by Jim Lucas (hereafter cited as Lucas and Johnson conversation); Johnson to Secretary of the Navy, 5 Apr. 1949, Cates Papers; Krulak, *First to Fight,* 129.

36. Thomas Oral History, 715.

37. Heinl passed to General Selden on 2 May 1949 information that on 29 April the newspaperman Robert Sherrod had seen on Johnson's desk "the entire plan for transfer of Marine Corps aviation to the Air Force." On 19 October 1949, Cates's director of public information, Brig. Gen. C. Jerome, informed Cates that at a banquet at the Waldorf Astoria Hotel in New York Johnson had said that "there were too many Air Forces" and he was "therefore taking steps to do away with Marine Corps aviation." Cates Papers. The annual cost of a Marine and an Army man is from Richard Tregaskis, "The Marine Corps Fights for Its Life," *Saturday Evening Post,* 5 Feb. 1949, 20.

38. Heinl, *Soldiers of the Sea,* 526.

39. Rearden, *History,* 51.

40. Krulak, *First to Fight,* 130.

41. Heinl, *Soldiers of the Sea,* 526–27.

42. Ibid., 527 n. 36.

43. House Committee on Armed Services, *National Defense Program: Unification and Strategy,* 81st Cong., 1st sess., 1949, 394 (hereafter cited as *Unification Hearings*); O. P. Smith Oral History, 181, 184, 191; Thomas Oral History, 712; Paolo E. Coletta, *The United States Navy and Defense Unification, 1947–1953* (Newark, Del.: University of Delaware Press, 1981), 169–203; Rearden, *History,* 101; Clifton B. Cates, "Marine Corps Fights for Life," *U.S. News and World Report* 29 (15 Sept. 1950): 20–21; "Complete Text of Statement in Defense Dispute," ibid. 27 (28 Oct. 1949): 53–57; "Summary of the Marine Corps Position," *Marine Corps Gazette* 33 (Dec. 1949): 17–19.

44. Megee Oral History, 215–16.

45. *Unification Hearings,* 567.

46. Transcript of Cates' opening remarks for conference held 29 Nov.–1 Dec. 1949, Cates Papers.

47. Heinl, *Soldiers of the Sea,* 530.

48. Ibid. According to another source, that after accompanying the commandant on several trips, Secretary Johnson confided that "Cates' attitude has improved 3000 percent since Denfield went out" and that the secretary found him "fine company and an able gent." Lucas and Johnson conversation.

49. Cates, "Opening Remarks at . . . Conference," 29 Nov.–1 Dec. 1949, Cates Papers.

50. Heinl, *Soldiers of the Sea,* 531.

51. Ibid., 532; Heinl in Thomas Oral History, 840–45.

52. Cates Oral History, 160.

53. Vandegrift, *Once a Marine,* 89.

54. O. P. Smith Oral History, 185.

55. Cates Oral History, 214.

56. Moskin, *Marine Corps Story,* 445.

57. Krulak, *First to Fight,* 131.

58. Ibid., 132; Cates Oral History, 230.

59. Cates Oral History, 235.

60. O. P. Smith Oral History, 120; transcript of Oral History with Lt. Gen. Merwyn H. Silverthorn, USMC (Ret.), 1969, 449, OHC (hereafter cited as Silverthorn Transcript).

61. Krulak, *First to Fight,* 131.

62. Ibid., 131.

63. Ibid., 62–64; Cates, "Annual Report," included in the annual report of the Secretary of the Navy, which in turn is included in *Semiannual Report of the Secretary of Defense, July 1–December 31, 1951* (Washington, D.C.: GPO, 1951), 3, 151; Krulak Oral History, 140, 148–49; Silverthorn Transcript, 450–51; O. P. Smith Oral History, 195–97. On 25 June 1950, there were twenty-seven thousand men in the FMF. In fifty-three days, the entire organized Marine Reserve and part of the Air Reserve had been mobilized, and on 15 September, Inchon Day, there were thirty-one thousand marines in Korea. Clifton B. Cates, "The Challenge of 1950: Address to the American Ordnance Association, December 6, 1950," copy in Cates Papers; clipping, *Charleston (S.C.) State,* 30 June 1954, in ibid. A copy of Truman's letter to McDonough remains in Cates Papers.

64. Years later Cates commented that Truman had been right about the Marines having a propaganda machine almost equal to Stalin's: "There wasn't any questions about that. We did everything in the world to get our friends behind us. And the former Marines and friends that had served with the Marine Corps—correspondents and things—they poured it on Congress and on the White House—letters and telegrams." Cates Oral History, 225–26.

65. Cates Oral History, 235–36.

66. Ibid., 236; Krulak Oral History, 149–50. Krulak was on the *Mount McKinley* with Almond during the Inchon landing. While Marines were transferring from LSTs to LVTs, Krulak said, "You know that LVT is a really wonderful machine." Almond responded, "Yes, can those things float?" Krulak Oral History, 151–52.

67. Cates Oral History, 236.

68. This conclusion is amplified in Thomas Oral History, 728, 730, 847–50, and in Heinl, "Here to Stay," 1085–93. The legislative history of the bill is found in Department of the Navy, *Marine Corps Reserve,* 156–59.

69. O. P. Smith Oral History, 207; Thomas Oral History, 751, 767.

70. Cates Oral History, 236–37.

71. Thomas Oral History, 911.

72. Ibid., 280.

73. Megee Oral History, 2:235.

74. Cates Oral History, 245–52.

75. I wish to express my heartfelt appreciation to Capt. Clifton Cates Jr., USN (Ret.), who carefully read this essay, corrected errors, and added material on personal and family matters. In addition, he supplied a history of the regiment with which his father served in World War I and proffered the names of others from whom information about his father might be obtained.

Chapter 20. Lemuel Cornick Shepherd Jr.

1. Family background from Shepherd Oral History.
2. Ibid.
3. Ibid.
4. Lemuel C. Shepherd Jr., interview with author, 8 Oct. 1986.
5. Shepherd Oral History.
6. USMC, *Manual for Drummers and Trumpeters* (U.S. Marine Corps, 1935).
7. Bevan G. Cass, ed., *History of the Sixth Marine Division* (Washington, D.C.: Infantry Journal Press, 1948).
8. Shepherd, interview with author, 20 Dec. 1986.
9. Shepherd, interview with author, 1 Feb. 1987.
10. Author's diary.
11. Ibid.
12. Remarks at change of command ceremony.
13. Shepherd Oral History.
14. Shepherd, interview with author, 16 Aug. 1987.
15. Shepherd Oral History.
16. Joint Chiefs of Staff message 300662, June 1950.
17. Author's diary.
18. Ibid.
19. Shepherd, interview with author, 24 Feb. 1987.
20. Ibid.
21. Shepherd Oral History.
22. Shepherd, interview with author, 27 Feb. 1987.
23. Author's diary.
24. Shepherd, interview with author, 7 Mar. 1987.
25. Thomas Oral History.
26. Remarks to Staff, 2 Jan. 1952, in Condit, Johnstone, and Nargele, *Brief History.*
27. Shepherd, interview with author, 14 June 1986.
28. Shepherd, interview with author, 19 June 1986.
29. Ibid.
30. Ibid.
31. Author's dairy.
32. Ibid.
33. SecNav Notice 5420, 14 Oct. 1953.
34. Author's diary; Shepherd, interview with author, 18 July 1987; Thomas Oral History.
35. Report of the Committee in Organization of the Department of the Navy, 16 Apr. 1954.
36. Shepherd, interview with author, 18 July 1987.
37. Ibid.
38. SecNav Notice 5430, 24 Nov. 1954.
39. CMC, "Annual Report for Fiscal Year 1954."
40. "Memorandum of Agreement Pertaining to Use of Marine Corps Personnel in the Foreign Service, Departments of State and Defense," 18 Dec. 1948. The Corps began by committing three hundred officers and men to the project.

41. Carlisle H. Humelsine, Deputy Secretary of State to CMC, 18 May 1984.
42. Shepherd, interview with author, 15 Sept. 1987.

Chapter 21. Randolph McCall Pate

1. Gen. Randolph McCall Pate Biographical File, Reference Section, H&MD (hereafter cited as Pate Biographical File).

2. The official biographical sketch issued by HQMC upon Pate's nomination as commandant, a document almost surely approved by General Pate, contains this story. See also "Gen. Pate Goes to ACMC Post," *First Word* 1 (14 May 1954): 1, copy in Pate Biographical File (*First Word* was the newspaper published by the 1st Marine Division in Korea after the armistice that ended the fighting).

3. Pate Biographical File; Millett, *Semper Fidelis,* 527–28.

4. "Marines Who Know Him Recall Exploits of Next Commandant," *Marine Recruiting Notes* 10 (Nov. 1955): 1.

5. "Human Interest Notes on General Randolph McC. Pate, USMC, Commandant of the Marine Corps," issued by HQMC, Feb. 1956; copy in Pate Biographical File.

6. Transcript of Oral History with Brig. Gen. Samuel R. Shaw, 1970, 292, OHC (hereafter cited as Shaw Oral History).

7. Pate Biographical File.

8. Millett, *Semper Fidelis,* 528.

9. "Pate Renamed Marine Chief," *Washington Post,* 28 Sept. 1957.

10. The Marine Corps usage of the organizational term "wing" differs from that of the U.S. Air Force. In the latter, a wing is composed of two or more squadrons under the command of a colonel. The corresponding Marine unit is the aircraft group. A Marine aircraft wing consists of several aircraft groups and logistic support units. It normally is commanded by a major general.

11. Millett, *Semper Fidelis,* 520–28.

12. Brig. Gen. William B. McKean, *Ribbon Creek* (New York: Dial Press, 1958); Record of Proceedings, Court of Inquiry, Marine Corps Recruit Depot, Parris Island, South Carolina, with endorsements, 20 Apr. 1956, Subject Files, Reference Section, H&MD (hereafter cited as Inquiry Report); Albion C. Hailey, "Marines Fear Ease-Up in Boot Training," *Washington Post,* 15 Apr. 1956; Associated Press, "Marine Court Hears Details of Tragedy," *Washington Post,* 12 Apr. 1956; Clay Blair Jr., "The Tragedy of Platoon 71 Puts Marine Training Under Fire," *Life,* 23 Apr. 1956, 52–54.

13. Bem Price (former AP senior reporter), interview with author, 17 Jan. 1983.

14. Lt. Gen. Wallace M. Greene Jr. to Col. Robert D. Heinl Jr., 19 Nov. 1960, copy in Box 43, Folder 8, Wallace M. Greene Papers, PPC (hereafter cited as Greene Papers). This was about the time Colonel Heinl was writing his history of the Marine Corps, *Soldiers of the Sea.*

15. Shaw Oral History, 293; transcript of Oral History with Lt. Gen. Joseph C. Burger, 1969, 291, OHC (hereafter cited as Burger Oral History).

16. Department of Defense news release, 8:00 p.m., 9 Apr. 1956; Capt. Ralph C. Wood, "Summary of Events, 9–10 April 1956"; and transcript of press interview with General Pate, 10 Apr. 1956 (all in "Ribbon Creek" file, Reference Section, H&MD); see also Burger Oral History, 291, and McKean, *Ribbon Creek,* 113.

17. Transcript of Oral History with Brig. Gen. James D. Hittle, 321, OHC (hereafter cited as Hittle Oral History).

18. Shaw Oral History, 293–94.

19. Twining Oral History, 353 (used by special permission of General Twining); Gen. Merrill B. Twining to author, 8 Apr. 1984; Brig. Gen. Samuel R. Shaw, telephone comments to author, 20 Apr. 1984; Shaw Oral History, 295.

20. Hittle Oral History, 324–26; Twining Oral History, 353; Shaw Oral History, 295; "House Delays Marine Quiz," *New York Daily News,* 13 Apr. 1956; Albion B. Hailey, "Marines Fear Ease-Up on Boot Training," *Washington Post,* 15 Apr. 1956. See also Victor K. Fleming Jr., "The Marine Corps in Crisis: The Institutional Response to the Ribbon Creek Incident" (Ph.D. diss., Ohio State University, 1984), 109–40.

21. Joe McCarthy, "The Man Who Helped the Sergeant," *Life,* 13 Aug. 1956, 52–59; Linda Charlton, "Emile Zola Berman, 78, Dead; Defense Attorney for Sirhan," *New York Times,* 5 July 1981; Hittle Oral History, 329; Shaw Oral History, 201.

22. Bem Price, "Marine Boss Says He Would 'Bust' McKeon and Give Him Transfer," *Birmingham News,* 1 Aug. 1956, copy in Price Papers, PPC; transcript of Oral History with Bem Price, 1983, OHC (hereafter cited as Price Oral History).

23. Shaw Oral History, 302–3; Secretary of the Navy, Court-Martial Order 1–56, 5 Oct. 1956, quoted in McKean, *Ribbon Creek,* 527–31.

24. Many in the Corps realized that getting troops somewhere quickly was not the same as having them arrive ready for sustained combat. Even today, ships, with their enormous cargo capacity, can transport a division and all its equipment and supplies to a combat zone more quickly than jet transport aircraft. The latter can do the job, but require a huge number of flights. In 1956, the issue was, in reality, political.

25. Millett, *Semper Fidelis,* 524–28.

26. Ibid., comments on draft essay by Lt. Gen. Victor H. Krulak, USMC (Ret.), 23 June 1988.

27. Shaw Oral History, 290–91.

28. Don MacLean, "Top Leatherneck Has Special Livery Service," *Washington Daily News,* 15 May 1957; "Marine Corps Explains Pate Chauffeurs' Livery," *Washington Evening Star,* 15 May 1957.

29. "Marine Corps Explains."

30. Price Oral History.

31. Jim Lucas, "Marines Have Atom Arms in Mediterranean," *New York World Telegram,* 3 Jan. 1957.

32. Tom Lambert, "Atom Story Puts Pate on Carpet," *New York Herald-Tribune,* 4 Jan. 1957.

33. "Pate Renamed Marine Chief," *Washington Post,* 28 Sept. 1957.

34. Pate Biographical File.

35. These irritations did not disappear until the post–Vietnam War years when the Army gave up its major base area and housing on Okinawa to the Marines.

36. Don A. Stance, "Return of the Old Breed," *Esquire,* Jan. 1961, 118. Copy in Shoup Biographical File, Reference Section, H&MD (hereafter cited as Shoup Biographical File).

37. Gen. Wallace M. Greene Jr., interview with author, 31 Aug. 1983.

38. Fleming, "Ribbon Creek Incident," 232. See also Shoup Biographical File and Greene Biographical File, Reference Section, H&MD (hereafter cited as Greene Biographical File).

39. Fleming, "Ribbon Creek Incident," 232. See also Stance, "Return of the Old Breed," 118, and the Pate, Shoup, and Greene Biographical Files.

40. Advertisement, Classified Section, *Army–Navy–Air Force Register* and *Defense Times,* 5 Nov. 1960, 45.

41. Press Release No. PNP-80-61, 1 Aug. 1961, HQMC; "Gen. Pate Dies at 63: 21st CMC," *Barstow (Calif.) Prospector,* 11 Aug. 1961; copies of both in Pate Biographical File.

42. Current law permits a retired member of the armed services to take a reduced annuity in a program which would permit a surviving spouse to continue receiving a monthly income.

43. Gen. Wallace M. Greene Jr. to author, 22 May 1982; copy in Greene Papers.

Chapter 22. David Monroe Shoup

1. Transcript of Oral History with Gen. David M. Shoup, Eisenhower Administration, 29 Aug. 1972, 11, Oral History Research Office, Columbia University, copy in OHC (hereafter cited as Shoup Oral History, Columbia University).

2. Ibid., 12–13.

3. Ibid., 15.

4. Gen. Wallace M. Greene Jr., interview with author, 23 Feb. 1981.

5. Shepherd Oral History.

6. Thomas Oral History, 920–21.

7. Transcript of Oral History with Lt. Gen. Frederick L. Wieseman, 1971, 228, OHC.

8. Ibid., 229.

9. Maj. Gen. D. M. Shoup to Brig. Gen. W. M. Greene, 14 Aug. 1956, David M. Shoup Papers, Hoover Institution on War, Peace, and Revolution, Palo Alto, Calif. (hereafter cited as Shoup Papers); Greene, interview with author, 23 Feb. 1981. See also the essay on General Pate in this volume on the Ribbon Creek incident and its impact on the Marine Corps.

10. The background material for this essay is based upon the excellent account in Allan R. Millett and Peter Maslowski, *For the Common Defense: A Military History of the United States of America* (New York: Free Press, 1984), chap. 16.

11. Ibid., 532. See also Alain C. Enthoven and K. Wayne Smith, *How Much Is Enough?* (New York: Harper and Row, 1971), chap. 2.

12. Millett and Maslowski, *For the Common Defense,* 530.

13. Ibid., 536.

14. Thomas Gates, interview with author, 26 May 1982.

15. Megee Oral History; transcript of Oral History with Lt. Gen. Robert E. Hogaboom, 1972, OHC (hereafter cited as Hogaboom Oral History).

16. Gates, interview with author, 26 May 1982.

17. Krulak, *First to Fight,* 24.

18. Ibid., 28–29. See also Enthoven and Smith, *How Much Is Enough?* chap. 2.

19. Greene, interview with author, 23 Feb. 1981.

20. Frederick L. Wieseman to David M. Shoup, 8 Aug. 1959, Shoup Papers. Reference is also made to those who supported Pollock and Shoup in the letter. It is also possible, as General Megee recalls, that the selection of Shoup was a compromise appointment to avoid choosing among the frontrunners. Megee Oral History, 227. It is more likely, however, that Gates wanted

an independent leader who "was free of any alliances or any cluttering up of people. He didn't bring any boys along with him. . . . He was a free agent and a man with a tremendous record and we thought that image would be the kind of image the Marine Corps ought to return to." Gates, interview with author, 26 May 1982.

21. Also see Gen. Lewis W. Walt's adverse comments about the Twining campaign and his support for Shoup. Lewis W. Walt to David M. Shoup, 27 June 1959, Shoup Papers. General Walt made a number of astute observations. Before the announcement of Shoup's appointment, he predicted: "I believe General T. will lose because of Navy opposition to him. I don't believe he has Mr. Gates' support. . . . Mr. Gates, I believe, appreciates the political situation in the M.C. and doesn't want another team member as CMC. You have been built up as a non-team combat marine in every quarter we can spread the word." Ibid.

22. See Megee Oral History, 229. Lt. Gen. Robert E. Hogaboom believed he was encouraged to leave. See Hogaboom Oral History, 342, 343, 346. All five lieutenant generals retired: Megee, Pollock, Twining, Hogaboom (all effective 1 Nov. 1959), McCall effective 1 January 1960; Major General Gullick retired effective 1 January 1960; Brigadier General Strickney retired effective 1 January 1960.

23. Shoup consulted with others before making his selections for the important billets. Victor H. Krulak to David M. Shoup, 20 Aug. 1959; Frederick L. Wieseman to David M. Shoup, 20 Aug. 1959; T. A. Wornham to David M. Shoup, 22 Aug. 1959; and Robert Hogaboom to David M. Shoup, 24 Aug. 1959, all in Shoup Papers.

24. Pate to David M. Shoup, 14 Aug. 1959, Shoup Papers.

25. David M. Shoup to Pate, memo, 8 Sept. 1959, Shoup Papers; Hogaboom Oral History, 342–46. In the Hogaboom case, Shoup may have viewed his retention as a liability because of his close association with Twining. Both generals were targets for the Secretary of the Navy's office.

26. David M. Shoup to Pate, memo, 16 Oct. 1959, Shoup Papers.

27. Gates claimed Eisenhower went along with his recommendations. Gates, interview with author, 26 May 1982.

28. Dwight D. Eisenhower, *The White House Years: Waging Peace, 1959–1961* (Garden City, N.Y.: Doubleday, 1965); Shoup Oral History, Columbia University.

29. Shoup Oral History, 18–19.

30. Ibid., 9–23.

31. Victor H. Krulak to David M. Shoup, 20 Aug. 1959, Shoup Papers.

32. Gen. David M. Shoup address, "Remarks by Commandant of the Marine Corps to Staff," 4 Jan. 1960, 1, Shoup Biographical File.

33. Ibid., 2.

34. Ibid., 5.

35. Ibid., 2.

36. Ibid., 6.

37. Ibid.

38. Ibid., 7.

39. Ibid., 8.

40. Ibid., 9.

41. Shoup Oral History, Columbia University, 33.

42. Millett, *Semper Fidelis,* 547.

43. Frederick L. Wieseman and Edwin H. Simmons, interview with author, 22 May 1980 (hereafter cited as Wieseman-Simmons interview).

44. Ibid.

45. Gen. John H. Masters, interview with author, 17 Aug. 1980.

46. Edwin H. Simmons, interview with author, 27 Feb. 1980.

47. Zola Shoup, interview with author, 28 Feb. 1980.

48. Simmons, interview with author, 27 Feb. 1980.

49. Greene, interview with author, 23 Feb. 1981.

50. *New York World Telegram and Sun,* 8 Jan. 1969, p. 12; David M. Shoup to Stanley Novak, 13 Jan. 1960, Shoup Papers. Shoup wrote, "The effect on your business and other firms engaged in the manufacture of the swagger sticks is regrettable. . . . I recognize that my view in this matter has had a definite effect. I sincerely trust that from the business standpoint, you will be able to adequately counter any difficulties that may confront you."

51. Shoup, "Remarks to Staff, 1960," 5.

52. Millett, *Semper Fidelis,* 544.

53. Senate, *Hearing before the Committee on Armed Services on HR4328, "Reassigning U.S. Marine Corps Supply-Duty-Only Officers,"* 87th Cong., 1st sess. (Washington, D.C.: GPO, 1961), 5.

54. Ibid., 6.

55. Ibid., 19.

56. General W. P. T. Hill to David M. Shoup, 17 July 1961, Shoup Papers. Hill wrote, "My only fear, and that was expressed at the hearing should the bill be enacted that the S.D.O. people would be discriminated against. Hope they won't."

57. Gen. David M. Shoup, "Remarks by the Commandant of the Marine Corps to Staff," 4 Jan. 1961, 6, Shoup Biographical File.

58. David M. Shoup to Edith Hill, 11 Oct. 1963, Shoup Papers.

59. Shoup, "Remarks to Staff," Jan. 1961, 11; Millett, *Semper Fidelis,* 547.

60. HQ Order 5430.3, 3 Aug. 1960, Subject: Data Processing Division, Headquarters, U.S. Marine Corps, Establishment of; Project to expand the central data processing installation at Camp Lejeune. House, *Hearings before Subcommittee on Appropriations,* 87th Cong., 2d sess. (Washington, D.C.: GPO 1962), 360–61.

61. Shoup Oral History, Columbia University, 13.

62. Ibid., 15.

63. Ibid., 19.

64. Ibid., 21.

65. Ibid., 20.

66. Krulak Oral History, 49.

67. Ibid.

68. Victor Krulak, interview with author, 1 Jan. 1987.

69. Ibid.

70. Ibid.

71. Millett, *Semper Fidelis,* 548. House, *Hearings before Subcommittee of the Committee on Appropriations,* 87th Cong., 1st sess. (Washington, D.C.: GPO, 1963), 573.

72. Transcript of Oral History with David M. Shoup, John F. Kennedy Library, 6 Apr. 1967, 35, copy in OHC (hereafter Shoup Oral History, Kennedy Library).

73. Shoup was initially concerned about the possibility that the squadron sent from Okinawa might have to be replaced thereby uprooting long-range deployment schedules. See Robert H. Whitlow, *U.S. Marines in Vietnam: The Advisory and Combat Assistance Era, 1954–1964* (Washington, D.C.: H&MD, 1977), 59.

74. House, *Hearings before Subcommittee of the Committee on Appropriations,* 87th Cong., 2d sess. (Washington, D.C.: GPO, 1962), 421.

75. House, *Hearings before Subcommittee of Committee on Appropriations,* 88th Cong., 1st sess. (Washington, D.C.: GPO, 1963), 381.

76. Simmons, interview with author, 27 Feb. 1980.

77. David Halberstam, *The Best and the Brightest* (New York: Random House, 1969), 66.

78. Ibid., 154.

79. Wieseman-Simmons interview.

80. CinCLant Historical Account O, Cuban Crisis, 1963, 153.

81. See Edwin H. Simmons, "Director's Page," *Fortitudine* 9 (Summer 1979): 7; House, *Hearings, Appropriations Fall, 1964, before Subcommittee of Committee on Appropriations,* 88th Cong., 1st sess. (Washington, D.C.: GPO, 1963), 364–66.

82. Shoup Oral History, Kennedy Library, 37–41, passim.

83. Ibid.

84. Evelyn Jones (Kennedy's personal secretary) to author, 4 Apr. 1986.

85. Ibid.

86. Ibid.

87. *Congressional Record,* 13 Mar. 1968, 84.

88. Ibid.

89. David M. Shoup, "The New American Militarism," *Atlantic Monthly* 223 (Apr. 1969): 51.

90. Wallace M. Greene and Frederick L. Wieseman, interviews with author.

91. Maj. Gen. Rathvon McC. Tompkins, interview with author, 17 Aug. 1980.

92. *Detroit News,* 28 Mar. 1969, p. 8A. See also "Guest Editorial" in ibid., 12 Apr. 1969 and 23 Apr. 1970, p. 30.

93. Tompkins, interview with author, 17 Aug. 1980.

94. *Marine Corps Gazette* 67 (Mar. 1968): 14.

Chapter 23. Wallace M. Greene Jr.

1. Entry for 1 Jan. 1964, Daily Journal, CMC, Greene Papers.

2. "General Wallace M. Greene, Jr., USMC (Retired)," Greene Biographical File; speech, Rutland, Vt., 21 Mar. 1964, Speech Files, Greene Papers; Greene to author, 17 May 1982.

3. Wallace M. Greene, interview with author, 22 Feb. 1982; W. M. Greene to Dr. E. Alvarez, 13 Jan. 1982, Greene Papers; W. M. Greene to the author, 28 Jan. 1982; House Committee on Armed Services Hearings, *Report of the Commandant on Parris Island Incident,* 84th Cong., 2d sess., 1956; Maj. Gen. D. M. Shoup to Brig. W. M. Greene, 14 Aug. 1956, Shoup Papers. See also the essays on Generals Pate and Shoup in this volume for the effect of the Ribbon Creek incident upon the Marine Corps.

4. For a summary of the 1960–64 period of Marine Corps history, see Millett, *Semper Fidelis,* 543–58; statements of CMC and principal staff officers, HQMC before the Subcommittee

(Defense Appropriations) of the Committee on Appropriations, House of Representatives, during hearings, Department of Defense appropriations for FY 1960–64, 86th–88th Congresses; *Marine Corps Posture Brochure, 1963,* attached to House Committee on Armed Services, *Hearings on Military Posture,* 88th Cong., 1st sess.

5. Report, Headquarters Marine Corps Reorganization Board, 31 July 1961, OA; Condit, Johnstone, and Nargele, *Brief History,* 30–34; Policy Analysis Division, HQMC, "A History of Marine Corps Roles and Missions, 1775–1970," 1970, "Roles and Missions" File, Reference Section, H&MD; Paul R. Schratz, "John B. Connally," "Fred Korth," and "Paul Henry Nitze," in *American Secretaries of the Navy,* 2 vols., ed. Paolo E. Coletta (Annapolis: Naval Institute Press, 1980), 2:910–59.

6. CMC letter A03B15, "Policy on the Deployment and Employment of Marine Corps Forces," 25 Sept. 1963, copy in Keith B. McCutcheon Papers, PPC (hereafter cited as McCutcheon Papers); Lt. Gen. W. M. Greene to Brig. Gen. J. G. Bouker, 5 Sept. 1962, Greene Papers.

7. Transcripts of oral history interviews with Maj. Gen. William F. Battell (1971) (272–302), Lt. Gen. Lewis J. Fields (1971) (241–45), Gen. Raymond G. Davis (1977) (231–35), and Lt. Gen. Charles H. Hayes (1970) (214–38), OHC.

8. "Marine Corps Long Range Study," Proceedings, General Officers Symposium (GOS), 1964, OA; "A Long Range Marine Corps Concept," Greene letter 8-65, 3 May 1965, McCutcheon Papers. Greene formally endorsed the latter document for research and development and long-range planning for the 1970s and 1980s.

9. MCO 003410.1B, "Marine Corps Cold War Plan—1965," 10 June 1964, McCutcheon Papers; Krulak Oral History, 188–89; *Washington Post,* 24 Sept. 1963.

10. "Chief of Staff's Remarks" and "Logistics," *Proceedings,* GOS, 1964, OA; "Relationships Resulting from General Orders No. 5 and 19," *Proceedings,* GOS, 1965, OA.

11. MCO 3340.3, "Employment of Marine Air-Ground Task Forces in Amphibious Operations," 20 Apr. 1962, and CMC to Distribution List, "Tentative Draft-Concept of Employment of Marine Corps Forces in Joint Operations Other than Amphibious," 9 June 1964, both in McCutcheon Papers; opening remarks, CMC, *Proceedings,* GOS, 1964, Speech Files, Greene Papers.

12. CMC to Distribution List, "USMC Positions within Department of Defense, of the Navy, Department of Defense, and before Committees of 89th Congress," Greene letter 20-64, 4 Nov. 1964, Greene Papers; Senate Subcommittee (Defense Appropriations) of the Committee on Appropriations and the Committee on Armed Forces, Statements of Gen. Wallace M. Greene Jr., Commandant of the Marine Corps, *Hearings: Department of Defense Appropriations, 1965, and 1966,* 88th Cong., 2d sess., and 89th Cong., 1st sess.

13. Gen. W. M. Greene to the author, 16 Dec. 1981; Lt. Col. William R. Fails, *Marines and Helicopters, 1962–1973* (Washington, D.C.: H&MD, 1978), 63–78. The aviation figures are taken from the *Journal of the Armed Forces,* 7 Apr. 1966.

14. CMC to Distribution List, "Air Support and Protection of Assault Transport Helicopters," 30 Dec. 1964, Greene letter, Greene Papers; Fails, *Marines and Helicopters,* 79–91.

15. CMC, "Annual Report" (for fiscal years 1964 and 1965), copies in H&MD; Van Ryzin Oral History, 188–95; "Fiscal Highlights," *Proceedings,* GOS, 1963, Greene Papers.

16. Report of the Commandant of the Marine Corps to the Secretary of the Navy, 1966, copy, H&MD; Greene, interview with author, 22 Feb. 1982; Col. Margaret A. Brewer, "Men and Women Working Together," *Marine Corps Gazette* 60 (Apr. 1976): 18–25.

17. Remarks, Commanding General, Fleet Marine Force Atlantic, *Proceedings,* GOS, 1964, OA; Greene, interview with author, 22 Feb. 1982.

18. Lt. Col. James B. Soper, "Observations: STEEL, PIKE and SILVER LANCE," *USNIP* 91 (Nov. 1965): 46–58.

19. Maj. Jack K. Ringler and Henry I. Shaw Jr., *U.S. Marine Corps Operations in the Dominican Republic, April–June, 1965* (Washington, D.C.: H&MD, 1970); Maj. Gen. R. McC. Tompkins, "Ubique," *Marine Corps Gazette* 49 (Sept. 1965): 32–39.

20. "Chief of Staff's Overview," *Proceedings,* GOS, 1965, OA; Green, interview with author, 22 Feb. 1982. "Our Posture Is the Most Favorable in the History of Our Corps," *Armed Forces Management* 12 (Nov. 1965): 56–58.

21. For the early phase of Marine Corps participation in the Vietnam war, see Whitlow, *Marines in Vietnam.* For operational analyses and summaries, see the "Marine Operations in Vietnam" (1965–72) series by Brig. Gen. Edwin H. Simmons, which appeared originally in the annual "Naval Review" issue of the U.S. Naval Institute *Proceedings* and was then reprinted in H&MD, *The Marines in Vietnam, 1954–1973: An Anthology and Annotated Bibliography* (Washington, D.C.: H&MD, 1974).

22. CMC, opening remarks, GOS, 7 July 1964, Speech Files, Greene Papers; CMC remarks to joint assembly, National War College and Industrial College of the Armed Forces, 1 Dec. 1964, Speech Files, Greene Papers; notes on CMC interview with Chairman, JCS, Dec. 1964, Speech Files, Greene Papers. On the role of the Joint Chiefs of Staff in crisis decision making, see especially Richard K. Betts, *Soldiers, Statesmen, and Cold War Crises* (Cambridge: Harvard University Press, 1977) and Leslie H. Gelb with Richard K. Betts, *The Irony of Vietnam: The System Worked* (Washington, D.C.: Brookings Institution, 1979).

23. CMC, opening remarks, GOS, 7 July 1964, Speech Files, Greene Papers; Greene to the author, 16 Dec. 1961 and 27 Jan. 1982; Greene, interview with author, 22 Feb. 1982. See also Herbert Y. Schandler, *The Unmaking of a President: Lyndon Johnson and Vietnam* (Princeton: Princeton University Press, 1977) and Halberstam, *Best and the Brightest.*

24. SecNav to SecDef, memo, 16 July 1964; see 003A19864, "Movement Capabilities of Marine Forces in the Western Pacific," Greene Papers; CG FMFPac to CinCPac, "Contingencies in Vietnam," 24 Sept. 1964, Victor H. Krulak Papers, PPC (hereafter cited as Krulak Papers). For the authoritative account of Marine operations in Vietnam in 1965, see Jack Shulimson and Maj. Charles M. Johnson, *U.S. Marines in Vietnam: The Landing and Buildup 1965* (Washington, D.C.: H&MD, 1978). Marine operations in 1966 and 1967 are covered in the succeeding two volumes: Jack Shulimson, *U.S. Marines in Vietnam: An Expanding War, 1966* (Washington, D.C.: H&MD, 1982) and Maj. Gary L. Telfer, Lt. Col. Lane Rogers, and V. Keith Fleming Jr., *U.S. Marines in Vietnam: Fighting the North Vietnamese, 1967* (Washington, D.C.: H&MD, 1984).

25. CMC remarks to flag/general officer selectees, USN and USMC, 10 Aug. 1965, Speech Files, Greene Papers; Lt. Gen. V. H. Krulak, "A Strategic Concept of the Republic of Vietnam," memo, June 1965, Krulak Papers; Maj. Gen. Lewis W. Walt, *Strange War, Strange Strategy* (New York: Funk and Wagnalls, 1970).

26. Brig. Gen. W. E. DePuy, USA, J-3 MACV to Gen. W. C. Westmoreland, "Situation in I Corps," 15 Nov. 1965, and COMUSMACV to CG III MAF, "Operations in I Corps," 15 Nov. 1965, both in Gen. W. E. DePuy Papers, U.S. Army Military History Institute, Carlisle Barracks; Gen. William C. Westmoreland, *A Soldier Reports* (Garden City, N.Y.: Doubleday, 1976), 164–67; Lt. Gen. V. H. Krulak to SecDef R. S. McNamara, 9 May 1966, and interview with Lt.

Gen. V. H. Krulak, 22 June 1970, both in Krulak Papers; "CMC After-Trip Report," memo, 17 Jan. 1966, Greene Papers.

27. "General Greene Tells the Story of Vietnam War," *U.S. News and World Report* 61 (5 Sept. 1966): 34–40.

28. Gen. W. M. Greene to W. D. Moyers, 19 July 1966, and S. Markman to W. M. Watson, 7 Feb. 1968, both ExFG 125-5, White House Central Files, Lyndon B. Johnson Papers, Johnson Library, University of Texas at Austin; Greene, interview with author, 22 Feb. 1982.

29. Report, CG FMFPac, "Fleet Marine Force, Pacific Operations," GOS, 1967, and Lt. Gen. V. H. Krulak to Gen. W. M. Greene, 8 Sept. 1967, both in Krulak Papers.

30. "CMC Remarks," GOS, 1967, Greene Papers; Greene, interview with author, 22 Feb. 1982.

31. "Statement of General Wallace M. Greene, Jr., U.S. Marine Corps before the Joint Session of the Senate Armed Services Committee and the DOD Subcommittee of the Senate Appropriations Committee Concerning FY 68 Marine Corps Posture," 1 Feb. 1967, Greene File, Reference Section, H&MD; CMC remarks, Ground Warfare Panel, President's Scientific Advisory Committee, 22 Feb. 1967, Greene Papers; CMC remarks, Navy Warfare Panel, President's Scientific Advisory Committee, 19 July 1967, Greene Papers.

32. CMC to Distribution List, "Summary of Current Year SecDef Programming Decisions on Marine Corps Structure," 13 Dec. 1966, Greene letter 24-66, Greene Papers; Report of the Commandant to the Secretary of the Navy, 1967, copy in H&MD; Lt. Gen. L. F. Chapman, testimony, Special Committee on National Defense Posture, House Committee on Armed Forces, 12 Oct. 1967 (hereafter cited as Chapman testimony); Greene letter 15-67, Greene Papers; "Chief of Staff's Overview," "Personnel," "G-1 Briefing," "Deprived MOS," "Report of CG FMF LANT," and "Report CMCS," all in *Proceedings,* GOS, 1967, OA; *Journal of the Armed Forces,* 16 Oct. 1966, and 11, 25 Feb. 1967, and 2 Mar. 1968; Senate, *Report by Preparedness Investigating Subcommittee of the Committee on Armed Forces, "Investigation of the Preparedness Program: U.S. Navy and U.S. Marine Corps in Southeast Asia,"* 90th Cong., 1st sess.

33. Chapman testimony; "Aviation," *Proceedings,* GOS, 1967; *Journal of the Armed Forces,* 1 July 1967; Fails, *Marines and Helicopters,* 129–48.

34. "Logistics," "Research and Development," and "Material Readiness," *Proceedings,* GOS, 1967. See also House Subcommittees of the Committee on Appropriations, statements of the Commandant of the Marine Corps, *Department of Defense Appropriations for 1967* and *Department of Defense Appropriations for 1968,* 89th Cong., 2d sess., and 90th Cong., 1st sess., copies in Greene Papers.

35. Appropriations Subcommittee, *Defense Appropriations FY 1968 Hearings,* 90th Cong., 1st sess., testimony of Gen. W. M. Greene Jr., Maj. Gen. R. G. Davis, and Brig. Gen. E. E. Anderson, 1967.

36. Fails, *Marines and Helicopters,* 99–108, 121–25.

37. CMC to Distribution List, "News Article 'Loss of Jet Aircraft Threatens Marines,'" 20 July 1967, Greene letter 11-67, Greene Papers.

38. Lt. Col. Gary W. Parker, "The Single Management Issue," mss., 1979, H&MD; Warren A. Treat, "Single Manager for Air in SVN," mss., July 1968, CHECO No. 64, Office of the Chief of Air Force History; Lt. Gen. K. B. McCutcheon to Maj. Gen. H. S. Hill, 22 Aug. 1970, "Single Management" Reference File, OA.

Chapter 24. Leonard F. Chapman

1. John W. Finney, "The Pentagon: Some Politicians in Uniform Make the Pros Gasp," *New York Times,* 3 Dec. 1967, p. 4.

2. John W. Finney, "White House Enmeshed in Fight Over Choice of a New Marine Chief," *New York Times,* 28 Sept. 1967, p. 1.

3. Ibid.

4. Transcript of Oral History with Gen. Leonard F. Chapman, 7 Jan. 1981, pt. 3, p. 1, OHC (hereafter cited as Chapman Oral History).

5. Ibid., 18.

6. Lt. Gen. L. F. Chapman Jr., "Marine Corps Command and Management Systems Development: An Overview," *Marine Corps Gazette,* Sept. 1967, 22.

7. *Marine Corps Gazette,* Sept. 1968, 1.

8. Westmoreland, *Soldier Reports,* 342–45; William W. Momyer, *Air Power in Three Wars* (Washington, D.C.: Office of Air Force History, 1978), 65–110; Lt. Col. Gary W. Parker, USMC, "The Single Management Issue," unpublished manuscript, H&MD. For a Marine Corps historical perspective on the single manager issue, see Jack Shulimson, Leonard A. Blasiol, Charles R. Smith, and David Dawson, *U.S. Marines in Vietnam: The Defining Year, 1968* (Washington, D.C.: H&MD, 1997), 487–515.

9. Chapman Oral History, 70–72.

10. Millett, *Semper Fidelis,* 589–90.

11. Col. John Miller, interview with author, 16 Feb. 1987.

12. Brig. Gen. Edwin Simmons, interview with author, 24 Jan. 1987.

13. Maj. P. P. Dugan, "The All-Volunteer Force and Its Impact on the Marine Corps," *Marine Corps Gazette,* June 1970, 21.

14. Maj. Robert L. Walsh, "Manpower: The Problem Element," *Marine Corps Gazette,* June 1970, 24–25.

15. Chapman, memo on problems of defense facing the new President, attachment to memo, Franklin B. Lincoln to President-elect, 3 Dec. 1968, White House Central Files, Subject Files, FG-13, 69–70, Nixon Presidential Materials, NARA.

16. Chapman Oral History, 94.

17. UPI news story, 17 Feb. 1972, copy in DivInfo Files, H&MD; Mel Jones, "Can the Marines Be a Band of Spartans in the Age of Aquarius," *Family,* 3 Nov. 1971.

18. Graham A. Cosmas and Terrence P. Murray, *U.S. Marines in Vietnam: Vietnamization and Redeployment, 1970–1971* (Washington, D.C.: H&MD, 1986), 359–60.

19. CMC message, ALMAR, 9 Feb. 1970, copy in H&MD.

20. Cosmas and Murray, *Vietnamization and Redeployment,* 361.

21. Thomas A. Johnson, "Marine Chief Vows to End Racial Rift," *New York Times,* 16 Aug. 1969, p. 1.

22. Cosmas and Murray, *Vietnamization and Redeployment,* 354.

23. Johnson, "Marine Chief Vows."

24. Message, CMC to ALMAR, "Race Relations and Instances of Racial Violence within the Marine Corps," 2 Sept. 1969, H&MD.

25. Lt. Col. Gary D. Solis, *Marines and Military Law in Vietnam: Trial by Fire* (Washington, D.C.: H&MD, 1989), 129.

26. James T. Wooten, "Marines Divided by Order Allowing Afro Hairstyles," *New York Times,* 15 Sept. 1969, p. 4.

27. Ibid.

28. Millett, *Semper Fidelis,* 600.

29. Leonard F. Chapman, "State of the Marine Corps," *Marine Corps Gazette,* Sept. 1970, 20.

30. "Statement of General Leonard F. Chapman, Jr., USMC, Before the Committee on Appropriations, Subcommittee on Defense, House of Representatives, concerning FY72 Marine Corps Posture," 10, copy in H&MD.

Chapter 25. Robert Everton Cushman Jr.

1. "SASC Approved Cushman," *Washington Post,* 10 Dec. 1971, p. 13.

2. "Commandant Cushman," *Newsweek,* 13 Dec. 1971, 37.

3. "A New Top Leatherneck," *Time,* 13 Dec. 1971, 13–14.

4. *Register of Alumni: 1845–1987* (Annapolis: Naval Academy Alumni Association, 1986), 223.

5. ALMAR-1, 1 Jan. 1972.

6. CMC Press Conference, Pentagon, Washington, D.C., 4 Jan. 1972.

7. CMC Statement concerning FY 1973 Marine Corps Posture.

8. CMC Remarks to Navy League of the United States (Washington, D.C., Council), Washington, D.C., 14 Mar. 1972.

9. CMC Remarks to Armed Forces Day luncheon, Harrisburg, Pennsylvania, 11 May 1972.

10. Edwin H. Simmons, "U.S. Marines in Vietnam, 1972," *USNIP* (May 1973): 221–22.

11. CMC Remarks to Marine Corps Combat Correspondents Association, 23 Sept. 1972.

12. CMC Remarks to Navy League of the United States (New Orleans Council), 13 Oct. 1972.

13. CMC Statement concerning FY 1974 Marine Corps Posture.

14. Reuters, *New York Daily News,* 20 Sept. 1973.

15. CMC Remarks to Defense Advisory Council on Women in the Service (DACOWITS), Washington, D.C., 9 Apr. 1973. It should be noted that there was some residual objection to the connotation of "up tight" (or "uptight") in then-current parlance, although CMC's argument clearly had carried the day.

16. CMC Remarks to Naval Academy Alumni Assembly, Annapolis, Md., 13 Oct. 1973.

17. CMC Statement concerning FY 1975 Marine Corps Posture.

18. CMC Remarks at launching of the USS *Tarawa* (LAH-1), Pascagoula, Mississippi, 1 Dec. 1973.

19. CMC Remarks to Navy League of the United States (San Francisco Council), 31 July 1974.

20. CMC Remarks to Navy League of the United States (San Diego Council), 23 Jan. 1975.

21. *Navy Times,* 23 Apr. 1975, 1.

22. *Washington Post,* 6 May 1975, p. 1.

Chapter 26. Louis H. Wilson

1. Millett, *Semper Fidelis,* 560; Millett, "The United States Marine Corps: Adaptation in the Post-Vietnam Era," *Armed Forces and Society* (Spring 1983): 363–92.

2. Millett, *Semper Fidelis,* xiv.

3. Transcript of Oral History with Gen. Robert E. Cushman, 1984, 405–520, OHC (hereafter cited as Cushman Oral History); see also news clippings from the *Washington Post,* 27 Apr. 1975, p. A4, 6 May 1975, p. A14, and 1 July 1975, p. A3, Wilson Biographical File, Reference Section, H&MD (hereafter cited as Wilson Biographical File).

4. Transcript of Oral History with Gen. Louis H. Wilson, 1984, 5, OHC (hereafter cited as Wilson Oral History); Wilson to Middendorf, 8 Apr. 1975, and news clipping from *St. Louis Post Dispatch,* 30 June 1975, p. A5, Wilson Biographical File; Senate, *Hearings Before the Committee on Armed Services on Nomination of Lt. Gen. Louis H. Wilson to Become Commandant of the Marine Corps,* 94th Cong., 1st sess., 6 May 1975, 3.

5. Wilson Oral History, 23 and 38; news clipping from the *Washington Post,* 1 July 1975, p. A5, and remarks by Secretary of Defense James R. Schlesinger at swearing-in ceremony, Pentagon, 2 July 1975, Wilson Biographical File; Millett, "United States Marine Corps," 389.

6. Martin Binkin and Jeffrey Record, *Where Does the Marine Corps Go from Here?* (Washington, D.C.: Brookings Institution, 1976), 88.

7. Memo, 24 Oct. 1975, and Wilson to Sen. Sam Nunn, 31 Dec. 1975, Wilson Biographical File.

8. Wilson Oral History, 205–6.

9. HQMC news release, 24 Oct. 1975, Wilson Biographical File; Wilson Oral History, 405; Millett, *Semper Fidelis,* 615–17.

10. Millett, "United States Marine Corps," 386.

11. Wilson Oral History, 43 and 57; quoted in "A Message from the Commandant," *Leatherneck,* July 1975, 16.

12. Notes, Plans and Operations Department, HQMC, Oct.–Nov. 1975, Wilson Biographical File; Cushman Oral History, 424–25; Millett, *Semper Fidelis,* 619–20.

13. Wilson, "Spirit of '76," *Marine Corps Gazette,* Mar. 1976, 16; Wilson Oral History, 43.

14. Excerpt from Robert D. Heinl, "The DI Mystique: Sows' Ears and a Delicate Imponderable," *Sea Power,* June 1976, Wilson Biographical File; Millett, *Semper Fidelis,* 621.

15. Wilson Oral History, 177.

16. House Committee on Armed Services, Subcommittee on Military Personnel, *Hearings on Marine Corps Recruit Training and Recruiting Programs,* 94th Cong., 24–26 May, 2–29 June, and 9 Aug. 1976 (Washington, D.C.: GPO, 1976), 126–30, 161–76, 192, and 215–16.

17. Wilson Oral History, 176–77.

18. Ibid., 139 and 583.

19. Ibid., 21 22, 49, and 74.

20. Ibid., 112, 16, and 20–21.

21. Ibid., 582–83.

22. Ibid., 164.

23. Ibid., 47.

24. Millett, *Semper Fidelis,* 612; Wilson Oral History, 68–69.

25. Wilson Oral History, 22, 69, 277, and 281; Millett, *Semper Fidelis,* 612; Wilson to Chief of Naval Operations, memo, 18 May 1979, Wilson Biographical File; Millett, "United States Marine Corps," 384.

26. Wilson Oral History, 50 and 473.

27. Ibid., 474–76.

28. CMC White Letter, "CMC Status as a Member of the Joint Chiefs of Staff," No. 12-78, 24 Oct. 1978, Wilson Biographical File; Wilson Oral History, 476–80.

29. Wilson Oral History, 480; Heinl, "Marine Corps Comes to End of a Long March to the Top," copy of news release, 4 Aug. 1978, Wilson Biographical File.

30. Wilson Oral History, 609.

Chapter 27. Robert Hilliard Barrow

1. Transcript of Oral History with Gen. Robert H. Barrow by Brig. Gen. Edwin H. Simmons, Session 1, 27 Jan. 1986, OHC (hereafter cited as Barrow Oral History, followed by session number and date), 44–45; Barrow comments, 4 Mar. 1997.

2. Barrow Oral History, 50.

3. Ibid., 62. Barrow comments, 4 Mar. 97. The major's name was Herbert S. Keimling. The writer of this essay was Barrow's map-reading instructor in Officer Candidate Class.

4. Ibid.

5. Barrow comments, 4 Mar. 1997.

6. Ibid.

7. Barrow Oral History, Session 2, 28 Jan. 1986, 108.

8. Ibid., 122. Adm. Marc Mitscher was commander in chief, Atlantic, and Commodore Arleigh Burke his chief of staff. Admiral W. H. T. Blandy was commander in chief, Atlantic Fleet. All, according to Barrow, got along well.

9. Barrow Oral History, Session 5, 3 June 1986, 314–15.

10. The writer of this essay was the senior editor of the Publications Group.

11. Barrow Oral History, Session 6, 10 June 1986, 409.

12. Ibid., 423–29.

13. Barrow Oral History, Session 7, 30 Jan. 1987, 460–61. There is much in this session concerning Lt. Gen. Victor H. Krulak as CG FMFPac and his role in the Vietnam War, which is very valuable but beyond the purview of this essay.

14. Barrow Oral History, Session 8, 30 Jan. 1987, 538.

15. Ibid., 500.

16. Ibid., 506. Barrow comments, 4 Mar. 1997.

17. Ibid., 512–36, passim. For a detailed account of the Laos incursion, see Charles R. Smith, *U.S. Marines in Vietnam: 1969, High Mobility and Standdown* (Washington, D.C.: H&MD, 1988), 41–51.

18. General Stilwell repeated this compliment on a number of occasions. He reaffirmed it in conversation with the writer shortly before his death.

19. Barrow Oral History, Session 10, 26 Jan. 1989, 610.

20. Ibid., 624.

21. Barrow Oral History, Session 11, 13 Dec. 1989, 9.

22. Ibid., 10. Barrow comments, 4 Mar. 1997.

23. Barrow Oral History, Session 10, 26 Jan. 1989, 616. During the Vietnam War, the pressure of the draft kept the Marine Corps ranks filled, but in 1973 the Marine Corps once again became an all-volunteer force.

24. Barrow Oral History, Session 11, 13 Dec. 1889, 10.

25. Ibid., 11.

26. For discussion of the Ribbon Creek incident, see the essay on General Pate in this volume.

27. Barrow Oral History, Session 12, 13 Dec. 1889, 58.

28. Ibid., 60.

29. Chronological Record, Barrow Oral History, Session 13, 13 Dec. 1889. (The pages of the transcript for this session are unnumbered.) General Wilson, in his own oral history interview, says, "I was delighted to see him [Barrow] made Commandant. There are, of course, many capable officers [in the Corps] and I don't think the President could have gone wrong in selecting any of them." Wilson Oral History, 37.

30. Barrow Oral History, Session 13, 13 Dec. 1889.

31. Ibid., Session 14, 17 Dec. 1991, 5–6.

32. Ibid., 19–20.

33. CMC (Designate) Confirmation Statement, 17 May 1979, USMC news release DS-116-79, "New Commandant Confirmed by Senate," in Gen. Robert H. Barrow, PC 957, Box 95, PPC.

34. Barrow Oral History, Session 14, 17 Dec. 1991, 36.

35. Ibid., 37–38. Barrow actually became the twenty-seventh commandant on 1 July 1979.

36. L. Edgar Prina, "Wilson's Legacy, Barrow's Inheritance: A Combat Ready Corps," *Sea Power,* June 1979.

37. Ibid.

38. "Marine Leader Says Recruits Lack Discipline," UPI, *Raleigh (N.C.) News and Observer,* 3 Sept. 1979; Barrow Oral History, Session 14, 17 Dec. 1991, 43.

39. Barrow Oral History, Session 14, 17 Dec. 1991, 25.

40. Prina, "Wilson's Legacy."

41. Barrow Oral History, Session 14, 17 Dec. 1991, 20–21.

42. Ibid., Session 15, 20 Dec. 1991, 2.

43. Ibid., Session 14, 17 Dec. 1991, 41–42, quotation on 69.

44. Ibid., 70.

45. Ibid., 72.

46. Ibid., Session 15, 20 Dec. 1991, 30–32.

47. Ibid., 24–27.

48. Ibid., 46–47.

49. Ibid., Session 16, 27 Jan. 1992, 4–8.

50. Brig. Gen. Edwin H. Simmons, "Uniform Matters," General Officers Symposium, 27 Sept. 1983. Copy in blue notebook 7.12, Simmons Uniform Board Papers, Museums Branch, H&MD. However, against the pressures of an increasingly casual society, Barrow's uniform reforms would not last much beyond his tenure as Commandant.

51. Barrow Oral History, Session 18, 6 June 1994, 14.

52. Ibid., Session 17, 20 Mar. 1992, 8–9.

53. Ibid.

54. Ibid., 16–17.

55. Ibid., 17, 21.

56. Ibid., 13–14.

57. Barrow Oral History, Session 18, 6 June 1994, 21–22.

58. Ibid., 11.

59. Ibid., Session 1, 27 Jan. 1986, 13, and Session 19, 6–7 June 1994, 84–89.

60. Barrow to Simmons, 4 Mar. 1997.

Bibliography

Abrahamson, James L. *America Arms for a New Century: The Making of a Great Military Power.* New York: Free Press, 1981.

Allen, Gardner W. *A Naval History of the American Revolution.* 2 vols. New York: Houghton, Mifflin, 1913.

American State Papers, Class 6, Naval Affairs. 4 vols. Washington, D.C.: Gales and Seaton, 1834–61.

American State Papers: Documents, Legislative and Executive. 38 vols. Washington, D.C.: GPO, 1789–1838.

Astor, Brooke. *Footprints: An Autobiography.* New York: Doubleday, 1980.

———. *Patchwork Child: Early Memoirs by Brooke Astor.* New York: Harper & Row, 1962.

Ball, Harry P. *Of Responsible Command.* Carlisle Barracks, Pa.: Army War College, 1984.

Barde, Robert E. *The History of Marine Corps Competitive Marksmanship.* Washington, D.C.: Marksmanship Branch, G-3, HQMC, 1961.

Barker, A. J. *British and American Infantry Weapons of World War II.* New York: ARCO, 1969.

Bartlett, Lt. Col. Merrill L., USMC (Ret.), ed. *Assault from the Sea: Essays on the History of Amphibious Warfare.* Annapolis: Naval Institute Press, 1983.

———. *Lejeune: A Marine's Life, 1867–1942.* Columbia: University of South Carolina Press, 1991.

Beale, Howard K. *Theodore Roosevelt and the Rise of America to World Power.* Baltimore: Johns Hopkins Press, 1956.

Benjamin, Park. *The United States Naval Academy.* New York: Putnam, 1900.

Binkin, Martin, and Jeffrey Record. *Where Does the Marine Corps Go from Here?* Washington, D.C.: Brookings Institution, 1976.

Bittner, Lt. Col. Donald F., USMCR. *Curriculum Evolution: Marine Corps Command and Staff College, 1920–1988.* Washington, D.C: H&MD, 1989.

Buker, George E. *Swamp Sailors.* Gainesville: University of Florida Press, 1975.

Bullard, Robert E. Lee. *Fighting Generals: Illustrated Biographical Sketches of Seven Major Generals in World War I.* Ann Arbor, Mich.: Edwards, 1944.

Burns, James M. *Roosevelt: The Lion and the Fox.* New York: Harcourt, Brace, 1956.

Cass, Bevan G., ed., *History of the Sixth Marine Division.* Washington, D.C.: Infantry Journal Press, 1948.

Chadwick, French E. *The Relations of the United States and Spain, The Spanish-American War.* 2 vols. New York: Russell & Russell, 1968.

Clifford, Kenneth J. *Amphibious Warfare Developments in Britain and America from 1920–1940.* Laurens, N.Y.: Edgewood, 1983.

———. *Progress and Purpose: A Developmental History of the United States Marine Corps, 1900–1970.* Washington, D.C.: H&MD, 1970.

Coletta, Paolo E., ed. *American Secretaries of the Navy.* 2 vols. Annapolis: Naval Institute Press, 1980.

———. *The United States Navy and Defense Unification, 1947–1953.* Newark, Del.: University of Delaware Press, 1981.

Collum, Maj. Richard S., USMC. *History of the United States Marine Corps.* New York: L. R. Hamersly, 1903.

Condit, Kenneth W., Gerald Diamond, and Edwin T. Turnbladh. *Marine Corps Ground Training in World War II.* Washington, D.C.: Historical Branch, G-3, HQMC, 1956.

Condit, Kenneth W., John H. Johnstone, and Ella W. Nargele. *A Brief History of Headquarters Marine Corps Staff Organization.* Rev. ed. Washington, D.C.: HQMC, 1971.

Cooling, B. Franklin. *Benjamin Franklin Tracy: Father of the Modern American Navy.* Hamden, Conn.: Archon Books, 1973.

Cosmas, Graham A. *An Army for Empire: The United States Army in the Spanish-American War.* Columbia: University of Missouri Press, 1971.

Cosmas, Graham A., and Terrence P. Murray. *U.S. Marines in Vietnam: Vietnamization and Redeployment, 1970–1971.* Washington, D.C.: H&MD, 1986.

Cronin, E. David, ed. *The Cabinet Diaries of Josephus Daniels, 1913–1921.* Lincoln: University of Nebraska Press, 1962.

Daniels, Josephus. *The Wilson Era: Years of Peace, 1910–1917.* Chapel Hill: University of North Carolina Press, 1944.

Davis, Kenneth S. *FDR: The Beckoning of Destiny, 1882–1928: A History.* New York: G. P. Putnam's Sons, 1972.

Del Valle, Lt. Gen. Pedro. *Semper Fidelis: An Autobiography.* Hawthorne, Calif.: Christian Book Club of America, 1976.

Department of the Army. *Army War College Directory: Present Staff and Faculty, Former Staff and Faculty, President Resident Class, and Graduates (Resident and Nonresident), 1905–1976.* Carlisle Barracks, Pa.: Army War College, 1976.

———. *United States Army in the World War, 1917–1919.* Washington, D.C.: Historical Division, Department of the Army, 1948.

Department of the Navy. *The Marine Corps Reserve: A History.* Washington, D.C.: Division of Reserve, HQMC, 1966.

Donnelly, Ralph W. *The History of the Confederate States Marine Corps.* Washington, D.C.: published by the author, 1976.

Dorwart, Jeffrey. *The Office of Naval Intelligence: The Birth of American's First Intelligence Agency, 1865–1918.* Annapolis: Naval Institute Press, 1979.

Dudley, William S., ed. *The Naval War of 1812: A Documentary History.* 2 vols. Washington, D.C.: Naval Historical Center, 1985, 1992.

Dyer, George C. *The Amphibians Came to Conquer: The Story of Admiral Richmond Kelly Turner.* 2 vols. Washington, D.C.: GPO, 1969.

———. *On the Treadmill to Pearl Harbor: The Memoirs of Admiral James O. Richardson.* Washington, D.C.: Naval History Division, 1974.

Eisenhower, Dwight D. *The White House Years: Waging Peace, 1959–1961.* Garden City, N.Y.: Doubleday, 1965.

Ellsworth, Harry A. *180 Landings of United States Marines, 1800–1934.* Washington, D.C.: HQMC, 1974.

Enthoven, Alain C., and K. Wayne Smith. *How Much Is Enough?* New York: Harper and Row, 1971.

Fails, Lt. Col. William R. *Marines and Helicopters, 1962–1973.* Washington, D.C.: H&MD, 1978.

Fleming, Charles A., R. L. Austin, and C. A. Braley III. *Quantico: Crossroads of the Marine Corps.* Washington, D.C.: H&MD, 1978.

Fleming, Keith. *The U.S. Marines Corps in Crisis: Ribbon Creek and Recruit Training.* Columbia: University of South Carolina Press, 1990.

Fowler, William J., Jr. *Rebels under Sail.* New York: Scribner's, 1976.

Frank, Benis M., and Henry I. Shaw Jr. *History of U.S. Marine Corps Operations in World War II: Victory and Occupation.* Washington, D.C.: USMC, 1967.

Fuller, Stephen M., and Graham A. Cosmas. *Marines in the Dominican Republic, 1916–1924.* Washington, D.C.: H&MD, 1974.

Gelb, Leslie H., with Richard K. Betts. *The Irony of Vietnam: The System Worked.* Washington, D.C.: Brookings Institution, 1979.

Greene, Francis Vinton. *The Revolutionary War and the Military Policy of the United States.* New York: Scribner's, 1911.

Hagan, Kenneth J. *American Gunboat Diplomacy and the Old Navy.* Westport, Conn.: Greenwood Press, 1973.

———, ed. *In Peace and War: Interpretations of American Naval History, 1775–1978.* Westport, Conn.: Greenwood Press, 1978.

Halberstam, David. *The Best and the Brightest.* New York: Random House, 1969.

Hamersly, Lewis R. *The Records of the Living Officers of the U.S. Navy and Marine Corps.* Philadelphia: J. B. Lippincott, 1878.

Harbord, James G. *The American Army in France, 1917–1919.* Boston: Houghton Mifflin, 1936.

Heinl, Col. Robert D. *Soldiers of the Sea.* Annapolis: Naval Institute Press, 1962.

Heinl, Robert D., and Nancy G. Heinl. *Written in Blood: The Story of the Haitian People.* Boston: Houghton Mifflin, 1978.

Herrick, Walter R., Jr. *The Naval Revolution.* Baton Rouge: Louisiana State University Press, 1966.

Hirsch, Mark D. *William C. Whitney, Modern Warwick.* New York: Dodd, Mead, 1948.

History and Museums Division. *The Marines in Vietnam, 1954–1973: An Anthology and Annotated Bibliography.* Washington, D.C.: H&MD, 1974.

Hoffman, Jon T. *Once a Legend: 'Red Mike' Edson of the Marine Raiders.* Novato, Calif.: Presidio Press, 1994.

Hough, Frank O., V. E. Ludwig, and Henry I. Shaw. *Pearl Harbor to Guadalcanal.* Washington, D.C.: Historical Branch, HQMC, 1958.

Hynes, Samuel. *Flights of Passage: Reflections of a World War II Aviator.* New York and Annapolis: Frederic C. Beil and Naval Institute Press, 1988.

Isely, Jeter A., and Philip A. Crowl. *U.S. Marines and Amphibious War: Its Theory and Its Practice in the Pacific.* Princeton: Princeton University Press, 1951.

Janowitz, Morris. *The Professional Soldier: A Social and Political Portrait.* Glencoe, Ill.: Free Press, 1960.

Karsten, Peter. *Naval Aristocracy: The Golden Age of Annapolis and the Emergence of Modern American Navalism.* New York: Free Press, 1972.

———, ed. *The Military in America: From the Colonial Era to the Present.* New York: Macmillan, 1980.

Keiser, Col. Gordon W. *The U.S. Marine Corps and Defense Unification: 1944–47.* Washington, D.C.: National Defense University Press, 1982.

Krulak, Lt. Gen. Victor. *First to Fight: An Inside View of the U.S. Marine Corps.* Annapolis: Naval Institute Press, 1984.

Langley, Lester. *The Banana Wars: An Inner History of American Empire, 1900–1934.* Lexington: University of Kentucky Press, 1983.

Leckie, Robert. *Strong Men Armed: The United States Marines Against Japan.* New York: Random House, 1962.

Lejeune, John A. *The Reminiscences of a Marine.* Philadelphia: Dorrance, 1930.

Letcher, Brig. Gen. John S. *One Marine's Story.* Verona, Va.: McClure Press, 1970.

Long, John D. *The New American Navy.* 2 vols. New York: Outlook, 1903.

Love, Robert W., ed. *Changing Interpretations and New Sources in Naval History.* New York: Garland, 1980.

MacGregor, Morris J. *Integration of the Armed Forces, 1940–1965.* Washington, D.C.: Center of Military History, U.S. Army, 1981.

Marks, Frederick W., III. *Velvet on Iron: The Diplomacy of Theodore Roosevelt.* Lincoln: University of Nebraska Press, 1979.

McKean, Brig. Gen. William B. *Ribbon Creek.* New York: Dial Press, 1958.

McMillan, George. *The Old Breed: A History of the First Marine Division of World War II.* Washington, D.C.: Infantry Journal Press, 1949.

Medal of Honor Recipients, 1863–1963. Washington, D.C.: GPO, 1964.

Merillat, Herbert C. *Guadalcanal Remembered.* New York: Dodd, Mead, 1982.

Metcalf, Lt. Col. Clyde H. *A History of the United States Marine Corps.* New York: Putnam, 1939.

Millett, Allan R. *In Many a Strife.* Annapolis: Naval Institute Press, 1993.

———. *Semper Fidelis: The History of the United States Marine Corps.* New York: Macmillan, 1980.

Millett, Allan R., and Peter Maslowski. *For the Common Defense: A Military History of the United States of America.* New York: Free Press, 1984.

Momyer, William W. *Air Power in Three Wars.* Washington, D.C.: Office of Air Force History, 1978.

Montross, Lynn, Hubard K. Kuokka, and Norman W. Hicks. *U.S. Marine Operations in Korea, 1950–1953: The East Central Front.* 5 vols. Washington, D.C.: HQMC, 1962.

Moran, John B. *Creating a Legend: The Complete Record of Writing About the United States Marine Corps.* Chicago: Moran/Andrews, 1973.

Morison, Elting E., ed. *The Letters of Theodore Roosevelt.* 8 vols. Cambridge: Harvard University Press, 1951–54.

Morison, Samuel E. *History of United States Naval Operations in World War II.* 15 vols. Boston: Atlantic Little Brown, 1947–62.

———. *John Paul Jones: A Sailor's Biography.* Boston: Little, Brown, 1959.

Morton, Louis. *Pacific Command: A Study in Interservice Relations.* Harmon Memorial Lectures in Military History 3. Colorado Springs, Colo.: USAFA, 1961.

Moskin, J. Robert. *The U.S. Marine Corps Story.* New York: McGraw Hill, 1977.

Nalty, Bernard C., and Lt. Col. Ralph F. Moody. *A Brief History of the U.S. Marine Corps Officer Procurement, 1775–1969.* Rev. ed. Marine Corps Historical Reference Pamphlet. Washington, D.C.: H&MD, 1970.

Naval Documents of the American Revolution. Edited by William Bell Clark and William James Morgan. 10 vols. to date. Washington, D.C.: Naval Historical Center, 1964– .

Nicholas, J. D., and William O. Spears. *The Joint and Combined Staff Officers Manual.* Harrisburg, Pa.: Stockpile, 1959.

Palmer, Frederick. *Newton D. Baker: America at War.* 2 vols. New York: Dodd, Mead, 1931.

Paullin, Charles Oscar. *Paullin's History of Naval Administration, 1775–1911.* Annapolis: Naval Institute Press, 1968.

Perret, Geoffrey. *There's a War to Be Won: The United States Army in World War II.* New York: Ballantine Books, 1997.

Pogue, Forrest C. *George C. Marshall: The Education of a General, 1880–1939.* New York: Viking, 1963.

———. *George C. Marshall: Organizer of Victory, 1943–1945.* New York: Viking, 1973.

Rearden, Steven L. *History of the Office of the Secretary of Defense: The Formative Years, 1947–1950.* 2 vols. to date. Washington, D.C.: Office of the Secretary of Defense, 1984.

Register of Alumni: 1845–1987. Annapolis: Naval Academy Alumni Association, 1986.

Register of Officer Personnel: United State Navy and Marine Corps and Ships Data, 1801–1807. Washington, D.C.: GPO, 1945.

Reynolds, Clark G. *The Fast Carriers: The Forging of an Air Navy.* New York: McGraw-Hill, 1968.

Ringler, Maj. Jack K., and Henry I. Shaw Jr. *U.S. Marine Corps Operations in the Dominican Republic, April–June, 1965.* Washington, D.C.: H&MD, 1970.

Roberts, William R., and Jack Sweetman, eds. *New Interpretations in Naval History, Selected Papers from the Ninth Naval History Symposium Held at the United States Naval Academy, 18–20 October 1989.* Annapolis: Naval Institute Press, 1991.

Ropp, Theodore. *War in the Modern World.* Toronto: Collier Books, 1969.

Schandler, Herbert Y. *The Unmaking of a President: Lyndon Johnson and Vietnam.* Princeton: Princeton University Press, 1977.

Schmidt, Hans. *Maverick Marine: General Smedley D. Butler and the Contradictions of American Military History.* Lexington: University of Kentucky Press, 1987.

———. *The United States Occupation of Haiti, 1915–1934.* New Brunswick, N.J.: Rutgers University Press, 1971.

Schuon, Karl. *Home of the Commandants.* Quantico, Va.: Marine Corps Association, 1956.

Seager, Robert, II. *Alfred Thayer Mahan.* Annapolis: Naval Institute Press, 1977.

Shaw, Henry I., Jr., and Ralph W. Donnelly. *Blacks in the Marine Corps.* Washington, D.C.: H&MD, 1975.

Shaw, Henry I., Jr., Bernard C. Nalty, and Edwin T. Turnbladh. *History of U.S. Marine Corps Operations in World War II: Central Pacific Drive.* Washington, D.C.: USMC, 1966.

Sherrod, Robert. *History of Marine Corps Aviation in World War II.* Washington, D.C.: Combat Forces Press, 1952.

Shulimson, Jack. *The Marine Corps' Search for a Mission, 1880–1898.* Lawrence: University Press of Kansas, 1993.

———. *U.S. Marines in Vietnam: An Expanding War, 1966.* Washington, D.C.: H&MD, 1982.

Shulimson, Jack, Leonard A. Blasiol, Charles R. Smith, and David Dawson. *U.S. Marines in Vietnam: The Defining Year, 1968.* Washington, D.C.: H&MD, 1997.

Shulimson, Jack, and Maj. Charles M. Johnson. *U.S. Marines in Vietnam: The Landing and Buildup 1965.* Washington, D.C.: H&MD, 1978.

Simmons, Edwin H. *The United States Marines, 1775–1975.* New York: Viking, 1976.

Smelser, Marshal. *The Congress Founds a Navy, 1787–1798.* South Bend, Ind.: Notre Dame University Press, 1959.

Smith, Charles R. *Marines in the Revolution.* Washington, D.C.: H&MD, 1975.

———. *U.S. Marines in Vietnam: 1969, High Mobility and Standdown.* Washington, D.C.: H&MD, 1988.

Solis, Lt. Col. Gary D. *Marines and Military Law in Vietnam: Trial by Fire.* Washington, D.C.: H&MD, 1989.

Spector, Ronald. *Admiral of the New Navy: The Life and Career of George Dewey.* Baton Rouge: Louisiana State University Press, 1974.

———. *Eagle Against the Sun.* New York: Free Press, 1985.

———. *Professors of War: The Naval War College and the Development of the Naval Profession.* Newport, R.I.: Naval War College Press, 1977.

Sprout, Harold, and Margaret Sprout. *The Rise of American Naval Power, 1776–1918.* Princeton: Princeton University Press, 1946.

———. *Toward a New Order of Sea Power: American Naval Policy and the World Scene, 1918–1922.* Princeton: Princeton University Press, 1946.

Sullivan, David M. *The United States Marine Corps in the Civil War: The First Year.* Shippensburg, Pa.: White Mane, 1997.

Sweetman, Jack. *American Naval History.* Annapolis: Naval Institute Press, 1984.

———. *The Landing at Vera Cruz: 1914—The First Complete Chronicle of a Strange Encounter in April 1914, When the United States Navy Captured and Occupied the City of Vera Cruz, Mexico.* Annapolis: Naval Institute Press, 1968.

Sweetman, Jack, et al., eds. *New Interpretations in Naval History, Selected Papers from the Tenth Naval History Symposium Held at the United States Naval Academy, 11–13 September 1991.* Annapolis: Naval Institute Press, 1993.

Telfer, Maj. Gary L., Lt. Col. Lane Rogers, and V. Keith Fleming Jr. *U.S. Marines in Vietnam: Fighting the North Vietnamese, 1967.* Washington, D.C.: H&MD, 1984.

Thomason, John W., Jr. *Fix Bayonets!* New York: Scribner's 1926.

Trask, David F. *The War with Spain in 1898.* Macmillan Wars of the United States Series. New York: Macmillan, 1981.

Tuchman, Barbara M. *Stilwell and the American Experience in China, 1911–1945.* New York: Macmillan, 1971.

Twining, Gen. Merrill B. *No Bended Knee.* Novato, Calif.: Presidio Press, 1996.

Tyson, Carolyn A., ed. *The Journal of Frank Keeler, 1898.* Quantico, Va.: Marine Corps Museum, n.d.

Updegraph, Charles L. *Special Marine Corps Units of World War II.* Washington, D.C.: H&MD, 1972.

U.S. Navy. Historical Division. *Naval Documents Related to the United States Wars with the Barbary Powers.* 7 vols. Washington, D.C.: GPO, 1939–44.

Vandegrift, Gen. A. A., with Robert Asprey. *Once a Marine: The Memoirs of General A. A. Vandegrift, United States Marine Corps.* New York: Norton, 1964.

Vest, John P. *The Ancestry of the Children of John Vest and Frances Neville.* Centreville, Md.: Queen Anne's Printing and Publishing, 1972.

Walt, Maj. Gen. Lewis W. *Strange War, Strange Strategy.* New York: Funk and Wagnalls, 1970.

Weigley, Russell F. *History of the United States Army.* New York: Macmillan, 1967.

Westmoreland, Gen. William C. *A Soldier Reports.* Garden City, N.Y.: Doubleday, 1976.

Whitlow, Robert H. *U.S. Marines in Vietnam: The Advisory and Combat Assistance Era, 1954–1964.* Washington, D.C.: H&MD, 1977.

Williams, Brig. Gen. Robert H. *The Old Corps: A Portrait of the U.S. Marine Corps between the Wars.* Annapolis: Naval Institute Press, 1982.

Willock, Roger. *Lone State Marine: A Biography of the Late Colonel John W. Thomason, Jr., USMC.* Princeton: Privately published, 1961.

———. *Unaccustomed to Fear: A Biography of the Late General Roy S. Geiger, USMC.* Princeton, N.J.: Haskins Press, 1968.

Winton, John. *Ultra in the Pacific: How Breaking Japanese Codes and Ciphers Affected Naval Operations Against Japan, 1941–45.* Annapolis: Naval Institute Press, 1993.

Wise, Col. Frederic M., and Meigs 0. Frost. *A Marine Tells It to You.* New York: J. H. Sears, 1929.

Zimmerman, John L. *The Guadalcanal Campaign.* Washington, D.C.: Historical Division, HQMC, 1949.

Contributors

Col. Joseph H. Alexander, USMC (Ret.), is the author of several chapters in this volume. He holds a master's degree in history and has written extensively on Marine Corps history. He was a recipient of the Marine Corps Heritage Foundation General Wallace M. Greene Jr. Award in 1996 for his book on the Tarawa Campaign, *Utmost Savagery.*

Lt. Col. Merrill L. Bartlett, USMC (Ret.), is a former member of the U.S. Naval Academy History Department. He is the author of several books on Marine Corps subjects, including a biography of John A. Lejeune. Bartlett originated the idea of this volume and wrote several of the chapters.

Lt. Col. Donald F. Bittner, USMCR (Ret.), is a longtime faculty member of the Marine Corps University at Quantico, Virginia, and has written extensively about both the Marine Corps and the British Royal Marines.

James C. Bradford is a professor of History at Texas A&M. He is the editor of the *John Paul Jones Papers* and has several publications to his credit in both military and naval history.

Paolo E. Coletta is a former professor of history at the U.S. Naval Academy and has published several works on naval history, including the two-volume *American Secretaries of the Navy,* which he edited.

Robert J. Cressman is a former historian with the Reference Section of the Marine Corps Historical Center and is at present a historian with the Naval Historical Division. He has published extensively on Marine Corps and Navy history subjects.

V. Keith Fleming Jr. is a former member of the Marine Corps Historical Center and a former administrative education adviser for the Marine Corps University. He based his chapter on Gen. Randolph McCall Pate on his dissertation and later book about the Ribbon Creek training tragedy at the Marine Corps recruiting base at Parris Island, South Carolina.

Col. John W. Gordon, USMCR (Ret.), is a retired member of the history faculty of the Citadel College in Charleston, South Carolina.

Col. Jon T. Hoffman, USMCR, is deputy director of the Marine Corps History and Museums Division. He holds both a master's degree in history and a law degree and has recently published a biography of Brig. Gen. Lewis "Chesty" Puller.

Howard Jablon is a member of the history faculty of the North Central Campus of Purdue University at Westerville, Indiana. He has extensively researched the career of the twenty-second commandant of the Marine Corps, David M. Shoup.

Lt. Gen. Victor H. Krulak, USMC (Ret.), ended his career as commanding general, Fleet Marine Force, Pacific and was considered a contender for the commandancy. After his retirement, he wrote *First to Fight,* a well-received "insider" account of the twentieth-century Marine Corps.

Brian McAllister Linn of Texas A&M University is an award-winning author of three books on the American military experience in the Philippines.

Col. John G. Miller, USMC (Ret.), retired in August 2000 as managing editor of U.S. Naval Institute *Proceedings.* During his Marine Corps career, he served as speech writer for Generals Chapman and Cushman, and he retired from the Marine Corps in the position of deputy director of the Marine Corps History and Museums Division.

Col. Allan R. Millett, USMCR (Ret.), is a faculty member at Ohio State University and coeditor of this volume. He is the author of the standard history of the Marine Corps, *Semper Fidelis: The History of the United States Marine Corps.*

Maj. Brendan P. Ryan, USMC (Ret.), was a former member of the history faculty of the U.S. Naval Academy. He is deceased.

Jack Shulimson is coeditor of this volume and the author of two of its chapters. He was, until his retirement from the Marine Corps History and Museums Division, head of the history writing section, author or coauthor of three of the official volumes in the U.S. Marines in Vietnam series, and author of the prize-winning history *The Marine Corps' Search for a Mission, 1880-1898.*

Brig. Gen. Edwin H. Simmons, USMC (Ret.), is a former director of the Marine Corps History and Museums Division and now holds the title of director emeritus of that institution.

Lt. Col. Ronald H. Spector, USMCR (Ret.), is chairman of George Washington University's History Department and author of several works, including a volume on the war in the Pacific in World War II and one of the outstanding books on the war in Vietnam, *After Tet.* He served as a sergeant in the Marine Corps during the Vietnam War.

Col. Gerald C. Thomas, USMC (Ret.), was a retired U.S. Marine Corps colonel with advance degrees in history. He has written extensively on Marine Corps subjects. He died in 2003.

Col. David H. White Jr., USMCR (Ret.), is a faculty member of the history department at the Citadel.

Index

The Naval Institute Press is the book-publishing arm of the U.S. Naval Institute, a private, nonprofit, membership society for sea service professionals and others who share an interest in naval and maritime affairs. Established in 1873 at the U.S. Naval Academy in Annapolis, Maryland, where its offices remain today, the Naval Institute has members worldwide.

Members of the Naval Institute support the education programs of the society and receive the influential monthly magazine *Proceedings* and discounts on fine nautical prints and on ship and aircraft photos. They also have access to the transcripts of the Institute's Oral History Program and get discounted admission to any of the Institute-sponsored seminars offered around the country.

The Naval Institute also publishes *Naval History* magazine. This colorful bimonthly is filled with entertaining and thought-provoking articles, first-person reminiscences, and dramatic art and photography. Members receive a discount on *Naval History* subscriptions.

The Naval Institute's book-publishing program, begun in 1898 with basic guides to naval practices, has broadened its scope to include books of more general interest. Now the Naval Institute Press publishes about one hundred titles each year, ranging from how-to books on boating and navigation to battle histories, biographies, ship and aircraft guides, and novels. Institute members receive significant discounts on the Press's more than eight hundred books in print.

Full-time students are eligible for special half-price membership rates. Life memberships are also available.

For a free catalog describing Naval Institute Press books currently available, and for further information about subscribing to *Naval History* magazine or about joining the U.S. Naval Institute, please write to:

Membership Department
U.S. Naval Institute
291 Wood Road
Annapolis, MD 21402-5034
Telephone: (800) 233-8764
Fax: (410) 269-7940
Web address: www.navalinstitute.org